Beyond Occupation

# BEYOND OCCUPATION

Apartheid, Colonialism and International Law
in the Occupied Palestinian Territories

Edited by Virginia Tilley

**PlutoPress**
www.plutobooks.com

First published 2012 by Pluto Press
345 Archway Road, London N6 5AA

www.plutobooks.com

Distributed in the United States of America exclusively by
Palgrave Macmillan, a division of St. Martin's Press LLC,
175 Fifth Avenue, New York, NY 10010

Copyright © Virginia Tilley 2012

The right of Virginia Tilley and the individual contributors to be identified as the authors of this work has been asserted by them in accordance with the Copyright, Designs and Patents Act 1988.

British Library Cataloguing in Publication Data
A catalogue record for this book is available from the British Library

ISBN  978 0 7453 3236 9   Hardback
ISBN  978 0 7453 3235 2   Paperback
ISBN  978 1 8496 4743 4   PDF eBook
ISBN  978 1 8496 4745 8   Kindle eBook
ISBN  978 1 8496 4744 1   EPUB eBook

Library of Congress Cataloging in Publication Data applied for

This book is printed on paper suitable for recycling and made from fully managed and sustained forest sources. Logging, pulping and manufacturing processes are expected to conform to the environmental standards of the country of origin.

10  9  8  7  6  5  4  3  2  1

Designed and produced for Pluto Press by Chase Publishing Services Ltd
Typeset from disk by Stanford DTP Services, Northampton, England
Simultaneously printed digitally by CPI Antony Rowe, Chippenham, UK and
Edwards Bros in the United States of America

# Contents

*Preface*     xi

## 1 Sources of Law and Key Concepts

EXPLORING COLONIALISM AND APARTHEID AS MATTERS OF
INTERNATIONAL LAW     1

SCOPE OF THE STUDY     3
    State versus individual responsibility     3
    Scope of empirical evidence     4

INTERNATIONAL LAW IN OCCUPIED TERRITORY     6
    International humanitarian law     6
       Defining 'belligerent occupation'     7
       General provisions of the Fourth Geneva Convention     8
    Human rights law     9
    Prohibition of colonialism in international law     14
       The right to self-determination in international law     15
       The Declaration on Colonialism     17
    The prohibition of apartheid in international law     21
    The legal authority of an ICJ advisory opinion     24

CONCLUSION     24

## 2 The Legal Context in the Occupied Palestinian Territories

INTRODUCTION     26

THE PALESTINIAN PEOPLE'S RIGHT TO SELF-DETERMINATION     26
    The question of Palestinian statehood     26
    The right of the Palestinian people to self-determination     28
       The legal status of the Palestinians as a people     29
       The territorial substance of Palestinian self-determination     33

LEGAL STATUS OF THE OPT     36
    The 'missing reversioner' argument     36
    East Jerusalem: status as occupied territory     37
    Legal implications of the Oslo Accords     39
       The Oslo Accords and Palestinian governance     39
       The PA and PLO as 'authorities of the occupied territories'     41
    Continuing occupation of the Gaza Strip     45

|   |   |
|---|---|
| Israeli settlements in the OPT | 52 |
| Status of settlements under international humanitarian law | 52 |
| Legal status of the settlers | 54 |
| The jurisprudence of Israel's Supreme Court regarding settlements | 55 |
| Prolonged occupation | 60 |
| APPLICATION OF ISRAELI LAW IN THE OPT | 64 |
| Israeli laws governing settlements and settlers | 65 |
| Discriminatory application of Israeli civil legislation to Israeli settlers | 66 |
| Discrimination in the adjudication of rights | 69 |
| Application of military legislation to Palestinians | 72 |
| Military legislation applying to Palestinians | 72 |
| Enforcement by military courts | 74 |
| Inadmissibility of discrimination based on citizenship | 76 |
| CONCLUSION | 77 |

## 3 Review of Israeli Practices Relative to the Prohibition of Colonialism

|   |   |
|---|---|
| INTRODUCTION | 79 |
| REVIEW OF ISRAEL'S PRACTICES IN THE OPT RELATIVE TO COLONIALISM | 80 |
| Violations of territorial integrity | 80 |
| Supplanting institutions of governance | 82 |
| Altering the laws in place in the occupied territory | 82 |
| Extraterritorial application of Israeli civil law to Jews in the OPT | 83 |
| Subjecting the local population to foreign administration | 85 |
| Preventing the local population from exercising political authority | 86 |
| Economic integration | 88 |
| Israeli practices breaching the prohibition on economic integration | 89 |
| Examples of integration: value-added tax and electricity grids | 92 |
| Violation of permanent sovereignty over natural resources | 94 |
| The right to water | 95 |
| Water rights and allocations in the OPT | 97 |
| Impact of the Oslo Accords on water allocation and control | 98 |
| Impact of the Wall on Palestinian access to water | 100 |
| Suppression of Palestinian culture | 101 |
| THE PRINCIPLE OF GOOD FAITH AND THE DUTY NOT TO FRUSTRATE | 102 |
| CONCLUSION | 104 |

## 4 Review of Israeli Practices Relative to the Prohibition of Apartheid

| | |
|---|---|
| INTRODUCTION: DEFINING APARTHEID IN INTERNATIONAL LAW | 107 |

### Part I: Applicability of the Definition to this Case

| | |
|---|---|
| RACE AND RACIAL DISCRIMINATION IN INTERNATIONAL LAW | 109 |
|    The politics of racial terminology in South Africa | 111 |
|    Interpreting identity: the International Criminal Tribunals | 113 |
|    Race and identity in the OPT | 115 |
|       Jewish identity | 115 |
|       Jewish national identity: Israel as a Jewish state | 117 |
|       Palestinian identity under the terms of ICERD | 120 |
|       Inadmissibility of discrimination based on citizenship | 122 |
|    Domination as the purpose of policy | 123 |
| APPLICATION OF THE APARTHEID CONVENTION OUTSIDE SOUTHERN AFRICA | 124 |
| APARTHEID IN SOUTH AFRICA: LEGISLATIVE FOUNDATIONS | 125 |

### Part II: Review of Israeli Practices in the OPT

| | |
|---|---|
| INTRODUCTION | 129 |
| ARTICLE 2(a)(i) – DENIAL OF RIGHT TO LIFE BY MURDER OF MEMBERS OF A RACIAL GROUP | 129 |
|    Interpretation | 129 |
|    Practices in apartheid South Africa | 130 |
|    Israeli practices in the OPT | 131 |
| ARTICLE 2(a)(ii) – DENIAL OF RIGHT TO LIFE AND LIBERTY OF PERSON BY SUBJECTION TO TORTURE OR TO CRUEL, INHUMAN OR DEGRADING TREATMENT OR PUNISHMENT | 133 |
|    Interpretation | 133 |
|    Practices in apartheid South Africa | 134 |
|    Israeli practices in the OPT | 134 |
| ARTICLE 2(a)(iii) – DENIAL OF RIGHT TO LIBERTY OF PERSON BY ARBITRARY ARREST AND ILLEGAL IMPRISONMENT OF MEMBERS OF A RACIAL GROUP | 137 |
|    Interpretation | 137 |
|    Practices in apartheid South Africa | 138 |
|    Israeli practices in the OPT | 140 |
|       Administrative detention in the OPT | 141 |
|       Incompatibility of Israel's practice with international law | 142 |
|       Israel's discriminatory use of administrative detention | 143 |

ARTICLE 2(b) – IMPOSITION ON A RACIAL GROUP OF LIVING CONDITIONS CALCULATED TO CAUSE ITS PHYSICAL DESTRUCTION IN WHOLE OR IN PART — 144

ARTICLE 2(c) – ANY LEGISLATIVE MEASURES AND OTHER MEASURES CALCULATED TO PREVENT A RACIAL GROUP OR GROUPS FROM PARTICIPATION IN THE POLITICAL, SOCIAL, ECONOMIC AND CULTURAL LIFE OF THE COUNTRY AND THE DELIBERATE CREATION OF CONDITIONS PREVENTING THE FULL DEVELOPMENT OF SUCH A GROUP OR GROUPS, IN PARTICULAR BY DENYING TO MEMBERS OF A RACIAL GROUP OR GROUPS BASIC HUMAN RIGHTS AND FREEDOMS, ... — 146

- Article 2(c)(1) – Denial of the right to freedom of movement — 147
  - Interpretation — 147
  - Practices in apartheid South Africa — 147
  - Israeli practices in the OPT — 148
    - Visible infrastructure: checkpoints, the Wall and separate roads — 148
    - The permit regime — 151
    - Case study of an apartheid policy: the Seam Zone — 152
    - Access to Jerusalem and the closure of the Gaza Strip — 154
- Denial of the right to freedom of residence — 155
  - Interpretation — 155
  - Practices in apartheid South Africa — 155
  - Israeli practices in the OPT — 156
    - Family unification — 158
- Denial of the right to leave and to return to one's country — 161
  - Interpretation — 161
  - Practices in apartheid South Africa — 162
  - Israeli practices in the OPT — 162
- Denial of the right to a nationality — 163
  - Interpretation — 163
  - Practices in apartheid South Africa — 165
  - Israeli practices in the OPT — 165
- Denial of the right to work — 167
  - Interpretation — 167
  - Practices in apartheid South Africa — 167
  - Israeli practices in the OPT — 167
    - Labour and the economy in the OPT — 167
    - Impact of movement restrictions on Palestinian labour — 169
    - Restrictions on access to jobs in East Jerusalem and Israel — 170
    - Restriction of imports and exports — 170
- Denial of the right to form recognised trade unions — 172
  - Interpretation — 172
  - Practices in apartheid South Africa — 173
  - Israeli practices in the OPT — 174

Denial of the right to education 177
  Interpretation 177
  Practices in apartheid South Africa 177
  Israeli practices in the OPT 177
    School closures and attacks 178
    Restrictions on movement 180
    Prevention of Palestinian students from studying abroad 182
    Discrimination in East Jerusalem 182
Denial of the right to freedom of opinion and expression 184
  Interpretation 184
  Practices in apartheid South Africa 185
  Israeli practices in the OPT 185
    Censorship 185
    Restrictions on freedom of movement 186
  Intimidation, harassment, and targeting of media installations and journalists 187
Denial of the right to freedom of peaceful assembly and association 188
  Interpretation 188
  Practices in apartheid South Africa 189
  Israeli practices in the OPT 189
Case study: impact of combined practices in the Gaza Strip 190
Overview 191
Initial phase of the siege, June 2007–08 191
Aftermath of 'Operation Cast Lead' 194

ARTICLE 2(d) – MEASURES DESIGNED TO DIVIDE THE POPULATION ALONG RACIAL LINES BY THE CREATION OF SEPARATE RESERVES AND GHETTOS FOR THE MEMBERS OF A RACIAL GROUP OR GROUPS, THE PROHIBITION OF MIXED MARRIAGES AMONG MEMBERS OF VARIOUS RACIAL GROUPS, THE EXPROPRIATION OF LANDED PROPERTY BELONGING TO A RACIAL GROUP OR GROUPS OR TO MEMBERS THEREOF 196

Creation of separate reserves and ghettos 196
  Interpretation 196
  Practices in apartheid South Africa 197
  Israeli practices in the OPT 202
Prohibition of mixed marriages 203
  Practices in apartheid South Africa 203
  Israeli practices in the OPT 204
Expropriation of landed property 205
  Interpretation 205
  Practices in apartheid South Africa 205
  Israeli practices in the OPT 205

| | |
|---|---:|
| ARTICLE 2(e) – EXPLOITATION OF THE LABOUR OF THE MEMBERS OF A RACIAL GROUP | 210 |
| Interpretation | 210 |
| Practices in apartheid South Africa | 210 |
| Israeli practices in the OPT | 211 |
| ARTICLE 2(f) – PERSECUTION OF ORGANISATIONS AND PERSONS, BY DEPRIVING THEM OF FUNDAMENTAL RIGHTS AND FREEDOMS, BECAUSE THEY OPPOSE APARTHEID | 212 |
| Interpretation | 212 |
| Practices in apartheid South Africa | 213 |
| Israeli practices in the OPT | 214 |
| CONCLUSION | 215 |

## 5 Conclusion – Legal Implications

| | |
|---|---:|
| SUMMARY FINDINGS | 222 |
| CRIMINAL RESPONSIBILITY OF INDIVIDUALS AND STATES | 223 |
| RESPONSIBILITY OF THIRD-PARTY STATES | 224 |
| RESPONSIBILITY OF INTERNATIONAL ORGANISATIONS | 227 |
| CONCLUSION | 228 |
| *Notes* | 230 |
| *Index* | 312 |

# Preface

Some readers, picking up this book and finding it to be an analysis of the Israeli-Palestinian conflict from the perspective of international law, might well be tempted to put it back down. A jaded view would be understandable. No conflict over the last century has proved itself more impervious to the norms and rules of international law – particularly international humanitarian law, the law of war and occupation. The conflict's history is littered with the detritus of failed legal efforts, including a multitude of United Nations (UN) resolutions (ignored or vetoed), analyses by foreign ministries, forgotten academic studies, and thousands of human rights reports by non-governmental organisations reporting the same violations of law noted in earlier reports and demanding action that is never forthcoming. Even an advisory opinion by the International Court of Justice, the highest authority on the interpretation of international law, has not impacted events on the ground. In light of this dismal history, it was not surprising that the findings of this study, when first presented to the public in London and Cape Town in 2009, were met in both cities by audience members who first rose to ask, 'Fine, but why should we care?'

Nonetheless, this study must be recognised as essential, precisely because it responds to the past futility of international law and, more generally, the world's failure to resolve this tortuous conflict. The scale of that failure is sobering. As this book goes to press, Israel's occupation of the West Bank, East Jerusalem and the Gaza Strip has not only lasted forty-five years but shows every sign of having entrenched irrevocably. The driving condition of the conflict – Israel's formation in part of Mandate Palestine, while the rest of the territory and millions of its native people remain stateless – has endured for sixty-four years and appears similarly intractable. Although alarmed, the world's community of states has mostly slumped toward ennui and fatalism regarding a problem that has plagued the UN since its inception. But continuing international paralysis has become untenable. The conflict between Israel and the Palestinians has its own drama, pathos, and human suffering, which have compelled the sympathy and concern of many, but it has also created toxic spin-offs for international security globally. Now the mass revolutions of the Arab Spring have raised the ante, while debunking some of the conflict's ideological gloss in the West of a Manichaean battle between western liberal democracy and revanchist Arab and Islamic terror. At this volatile and sensitive juncture, as Middle East regimes are violently transformed, any proposal that the Israeli-Palestinian conflict should remain subjected to the shallow pageantry of the 'peace process' is clearly unsustainable. It has become imperative to examine past efforts frankly in order to determine why all have failed so badly – to look at the entire conflict with fresh and critical eyes.

That effort, made in this book, finds that the conflict now faces a paradigm shift. For decades, international lawyers have understood the Israeli-Palestinian conflict as a case of belligerent occupation – which is, indeed, incontestably the situation in the West Bank, East Jerusalem and the Gaza Strip, a legal fact that this study takes as its point of departure. Thus scholars have assumed that the relevant international law is international humanitarian law, particularly the Fourth Geneva Convention, which establishes the rights of the population under occupation and related responsibilities of the Occupying Power. This approach has generated the decades of (mostly fruitless) scholarship mentioned earlier, including cycles of unproductive argument about whether humanitarian law truly applies and exhaustive documentation of Israel's violations of this or that provision of it. But concentrating narrowly on humanitarian law, while technically correct, has introduced a debilitating analytical error by obscuring recognition that Israel's occupation also involves a crime against humanity. This discovery is no mere technicality. Recognising that Israel is perpetrating illegal regimes in the Occupied Palestinian Territories (OPT) illuminates different motives, logics and constraints driving the Israeli-Palestinian conflict and so sheds new light on prospects for its resolution.

Since the late 1940s, international efforts to resolve the Israeli-Palestinian conflict have generally adopted the interpretation that it involves 'two peoples in one land'. This was the paradigm that guided the United Nations General Assembly Resolution 181 of 1947, which proposed partition of Mandate Palestine into a 'Jewish state' and an 'Arab state'. As discussed in these pages, this paradigm was in fact not universally held in the 1940s and arguably did not reflect international 'consensus' as we would understand it today. Yet the model has concretised over time, such that, by the 1990s, the solution to Israel's belligerent occupation was universally understood as Israel's withdrawal from the OPT to allow partition of Mandate Palestine into two states.

Thus the world's absorption with coaxing Israel into making this essential step, which appears – to international stakeholders as well as Israel's allies and many Israeli citizens – so obviously necessary to Israel's survival as a Jewish state, as well as a stable peace. And thus collective bafflement at the stark failure of the Oslo process to achieve this outcome. Even the most diligent efforts by the Palestinian Authority (PA) to satisfy Israel's terms for withdrawal – repressing all open Palestinian resistance to Israel's occupation, through measures admitted by Israel to be generally successful – have not even slowed down the growth of Israeli civilian settlements in East Jerusalem and the West Bank. Vast, elaborate and immensely expensive development projects, the Jewish settlements are clearly designed to be permanent, especially as they are linked into Israel through equally elaborate and expensive grids of civil infrastructure. That such a major project must reflect a geostrategic imperative of the State is demonstrated by the obvious paradox that the settlements actually increase insecurity to Jewish civilians, by positioning them in such close proximity to people made only more hostile to their presence by the land invasions and annexations that settlement construction entails. So stark are the contradictions of the settlement policy with a stable two-state solution that even the PA, otherwise pliable to Israeli demands, has declared the 'peace process' meaningless as long as settlement growth is allowed to continue.

Hence the mystery: why a goal presumably shared by all – a viable two-state solution – is being undermined so deliberately. Since the government of the State of Israel is run by people of incontestably high capabilities and talent who presumably see these implications as well as anyone else, the only reasonable conclusion is that the State's true purpose and logic have not been correctly understood.

The scholars of international law who were invited to contribute to this study were accordingly asked to examine Israel's occupation afresh. Their task was not to displace the fact of belligerent occupation but to review the whole body of Israel's practices to see whether, if filtered through the lenses of different legal instruments, new patterns would emerge to reveal a different whole. Establishing the theoretical framework for this project proved more complicated than expected and consumed months: especially, how to apply international humanitarian and human rights law within one setting. But once the framework was established, the empirical review flowed readily and the conclusions gelled swiftly: Israel's many discrete violations of international *humanitarian* law, when considered holistically in light of *human rights* law, were found to constitute two distinct and comprehensive regimes which are both considered inimical to international peace and security: namely, colonialism and apartheid. It has been the collective failure of the international community to recognise and address Israel's imposition of these regimes that has stalled all progress toward ending the conflict. And if this neglect continues – if the doctrines and agendas driving Israel's strategic objectives are not recognised, and the specific offences they entail do not draw the international action stipulated by related law – then the conflict will most certainly remain immune to all efforts to resolve it.

Finding that Israel is practising apartheid and colonialism indeed explains why mediation and negotiations to date have proved so unproductive. For at least thirty years, the liberal model of conflict resolution has uncritically adopted the Israeli government's claims that its main concern is fear of Arab attack. Hence peace talks have focused on improving Israel's security – or at least, the government's sense of it – and addressing what are assumed to be mutual 'hatreds'. This approach has inspired a ream of projects to forge Israeli-Palestinian agreements on matters such as border controls, as well as encourage 'dialogue' at various levels, from summit meetings among heads of state to summer camps for Jewish and Palestinian youth. The general goal of all these measures was to build mutual 'confidence' and 'understanding'. And yet, despite ephemeral flashes of seeming accomplishment, none has had long-term benefits or even deflected Israel's policies in the occupied territories to any meaningful extent.

This book reveals why this is so: because all have missed the real point. Colonialism is not driven by 'hatred'. It is a foreign grab for land and resources (here including symbolic resources, such as sacred sites) enabled by superior military power. Thus a colonial conflict is not resolved by getting people to 'see each other as human beings' but by addressing the basic injustice of foreign domination and restoring the people's capacity to exercise their right to self-determination. Similarly, an apartheid regime is not created out of 'misunderstanding', but to serve a group's survival agenda by physically excluding other groups – a policy that has little to do with the nature of others except that they are, by definition, others. A group that believes it cannot survive and flourish with others, and so must absolutely dominate others to preserve a life-world essential to its own cultural or physical survival, will remain concerned to maintain that domination no matter what others do or say or any underlying justice of their demands.

As domination is inherent to both colonialism and apartheid, it inevitably triggers resistance, sometimes armed, by the dominated group. Unfortunately, resistance is then seen by the dominator as confirming the necessity for domination and even legitimising its intensification, which inevitably offends people more deeply and generates more resistance. Resolving this vicious cycle too often focuses on the violence of the resistance. Yet the wellspring of violence is the logic and project of domination, not the resistance it inspires. International law recognises this fact in denouncing colonialism and apartheid, holding that conflict is inherent to both regimes and will continue until they are ended – that is, when the root logics, values and practices of domination are identified, discredited and defeated.

When we consider that Israel's occupation has assumed the character of colonial and apartheid regimes, which by definition have domination as their central purpose, the apparent mysteries of the failed 'peace process' fall away. We can at last recognise that Israel's first concern is not with Palestinian or Arab (or Iranian, or other) attack, Israel's first concern is with maintaining absolute domination (demographic, political, cultural, juridical) by Jewish people over non-Jewish people in territory under Israel's sway. This domination is indeed treated as non-negotiable, as an overwhelming Jewish majority is deemed essential to enabling Israel's existence as a 'Jewish state'. This tenet draws ideologically from centuries of past cruelties and atrocities committed against Jews, but it is not simply defensive. In Zionist thought, sustaining an overwhelming Jewish majority is the essential condition for an ennobling project of cultural, religious and political construction undertaken collectively by the entire Jewish people. This proactive vision is indeed essential to giving Zionism its romantic gloss of Jewish-national liberation. But a logic of demographic engineering, when deployed in a modern territorial state, stumbles into a fatal moral flaw regarding outsiders: it requires dominating them.

This essential moral flaw in the Jewish-state project has been overlooked by too many outsiders, especially sympathetic westerners whose knowledge of anti-Semitism is intimate and whose Christian majorities are prone to view the whole Zionist project in biblical soft-focus. Nonetheless, that moral flaw must be faced now, dispassionately, for pragmatic reasons. It is a matter of historical record that the Zionist project to establish and maintain an overwhelming Jewish majority in Mandate Palestine has driven every event shaping the present conflict: to take just a few highlights, the early purchases of land by the Jewish Agency in the 1920s, coupled with the systematic exclusion of Palestinian labour, which triggered mass Arab unrest and rebellion; the forced transfer of hundreds of thousands of Arabs and razing of hundreds of Palestinian villages by Zionist forces in 1948, generating the Palestinian refugee problem; and Israel's dividing the West Bank into exclusive ethnic enclaves today, entrapping five million Palestinians in a permanent condition of statelessness and therefore unending resistance. The same doctrine drives Israel's systematic political marginalisation of over a million Palestinian citizens of Israel and its refusal to allow the return of Palestinian refugees who have property, ancestral ties and rights in the country.

Recognising that Israel's logic of territorial-demographic domination has shaped the entire conflict also illuminates why a stable peace has so far proved impossible: because a doctrine of domination creates its own insecurity. The apartheid regime in South Africa found it could not stabilise apartheid within the country's own borders because its agenda to maintain white-racial supremacy generated a permanent security dilemma that inevitably spilled across South Africa's borders. Perceiving a 'total onslaught' against apartheid, the regime felt compelled to raise a 'total response' of military and covert action against its opponents, including by bombings and assassinations. Israel faces the same intrinsic dilemma: it cannot maintain ethnic domination domestically without destabilising its borders on all fronts. This inherent instability then generates Israeli perceptions of a generic campaign of 'terror' against Israel, comprised not only of actual terrorist acts but any kind of resistance to Israel's policies – even the moral 'delegitimation' of the international divestment, boycott and sanctions campaign. Perception of this (genuinely 'terrifying') existential threat then legitimises – even glorifies – Israel's 'total response' in ruthless military terms: that is, ongoing military rule in the OPT; the shocking assault on Gaza in 'Operation Cast Lead'; periodic military invasions of Lebanon; proxy invasions and occupations (by its United States ally) of Iraq and Afghanistan; perilous brinksmanship with Iran; subversion in Syria, and alliances with Arab dictatorships and monarchies that have found their own advantages in helping Israel resist the 'demographic threat' posed to Jewish statehood by the Palestinians.

How best to address and unravel Israel's commitment to domination in Palestine, which cannot help but generate these dangers for international security? This question is well beyond the scope of international law, which provides only that states have general obligations to end colonialism and apartheid. Nonetheless, international human rights law does provide one crucial key to moving forward, in providing a vital new insight: territorial partition will not help. Colonialism might be ended simply by a foreign power's withdrawal, if the people's self-determination is truly enabled by this, but apartheid is not ended by moving a border. South Africa's withdrawal from Namibia (then South West Africa) hardly signified that the white government was absolved of the crime of apartheid inside South Africa, and the conflict within South Africa retained all its force and violence after that withdrawal. The conflict in South Africa reflected not the incongruence of borders with legitimate white rule, but the logic of domination, which flowed from the belief that white domination was essential to preserving white culture, democracy and civilisation. This belief then appeared to justify systematically repressing black South Africans solely because their very existence, in their disenfranchised millions, threatened white society in its racially exclusive form. Similarly, Palestinians are repressed because they threaten Jewish statehood, through their mere existence as 'non-Jews', in their millions and in their deep attachment to their native land.

The gist of the findings presented in this book builds from this premise: apartheid within any country – whether the dominant group is a minority or a majority – is truly ended only by eliminating the doctrine of domination that steers the State to authorise its officials to commit what the Apartheid Convention calls 'inhuman acts'. Thus the findings here clarify that the Israeli-Palestinian conflict will not be resolved by final status talks that establish various 'security guarantees' or fine-tune the 1949 Armistice line. It will be resolved only when the logic of ethno-racial domination is defeated.

How to do this? Discarding a doctrine of ethnic or racial domination whole cloth is never easy for any group. It requires not only prodigious leaps of faith – typically undertaken by both sides only when faced as absolutely necessary – but collectively re-imagining the nature of the conflict itself, which involves dismantling some deeply held beliefs. Here the limitations of international law again become obvious, for it cannot advise or even describe such a process. Law is helpless to address even some concepts shaping its own principles: not least, as discussed in this book, what is a 'race'; under what conditions a given group is legally a 'racial group'; what makes a group a 'people'; or the periodic social reconstruction of a 'people' or 'nation' to serve different political goals. Thus the principle often cited here, 'every people has the right to self-determination', which all states are obliged to respect and uphold, falters before arguments about whether a given group truly has standing as a 'people'.

These arguments are typically heated, because they have existential implications for the states in which they live. Mandate Palestine is hardly unique in suffering from them. Hundreds of indigenous peoples around the world, despite decades of fraught negotiations, will bitterly attest that their state governments absolutely deny their claims to standing as 'peoples' in this crucial legal sense. Rivalries to define such identities – and, effectively, the nature of their conflicts – can therefore become the centre of disputes because, for those involved, they are matters of national survival. Just such an argument characterised the anti-apartheid struggle in South Africa, where African political philosophers and activists rejected the apartheid regime's discursive division of South Africa's population into distinct 'peoples' – white,

Indian, and the black 'peoples' of the Zulu, Xhosa, Twana, and so forth – by insisting that South Africa was really one nation, wrongfully divided by a racist doctrine, and that the country 'belongs to all who live in it'.

Such meta-conflicts are conducted by people at the coal-face of conflicts, who realise the need for them, and while they draw on international law, they are essentially matters of social and political construction. This study of international law can therefore only suggest that a reconstruction of the conflict in Israel-Palestine is warranted and could illuminate hitherto unimagined routes toward its resolution. Thoughtful readers will recognise that this potential shift in direction is precisely the deeper paradigm shift suggested by this book: not just that different international law might be applicable, but that the conflict's very nature may be rethought. Occupation may arguably end when a foreign power's withdrawal allows the people control over their affairs. But colonialism is not ended by a withdrawal that still denies the people the full expression of their right to self-determination, nor is apartheid ended by moving a border. Both are truly ended only when the doctrine of domination that drives them is finally identified, opposed and ended.

\* \* \*

Concluding that Israel is practising apartheid and colonialism was not done here either easily or lightly. The rigour of the scholarship in this book – which may sometimes tire non-specialists – reflects keen appreciation of its editor and all its contributors that the highest scholarly standard is due to matters of such gravity. It should therefore be made clear from the start that this study does not spring from polemics on the conflict. The term 'apartheid' has been slung about for years among activist circles, particularly regarding Israel's monolithic Wall ('security barrier'), but this polemical usage has not been illuminating. Many ethnic conflicts involve barriers, checkpoints, discrimination, even ethnic cantons. Determining whether Israel's practices truly accord with apartheid or colonialism, as suggested originally by UN Special Rapporteur John Dugard, required reopening the law books and carefully scrutinising their definitions, related commentary and theory. The tortuous scholarly project that emerged included contributions by many people, mostly scholars of international law but also sociologists and political scientists (including the editor).

This book began its life as a report to the Department of Foreign Affairs (DFA, now the Department of International Relations and Cooperation) of the Republic of South Africa. It was conducted as part of the Middle East Project, an independent two-year project based at the Human Sciences Research Council of South Africa (HSRC) which was established to conduct analysis of Middle East politics relevant to South African foreign policy. That project, led by the editor of this book, was wholly funded by the DFA, and a report on whether Israel's policies were truly consistent with colonialism and apartheid was requested by the Deputy Minister. However, the resulting report and the present book do not represent or suggest any views held by the Government of South Africa, nor does it constitute an official position of the HSRC.

Originally planned as a four-month study, the primary research on this project extended to nearly two years and the report went through several complete drafts, followed by a thorough revision in 2011 for Pluto Press. The scholars who were invited to contribute to the study's conceptual development, theory-building, data-gathering and drafting were involved to varying degrees at different stages over several years. Consequently, no chapter, section or even subsection of this book is entirely solo-authored and no one can claim full 'ownership' of any of it. Still, special credit can be extended, particularly to a core group of people who developed the study's theoretical framework and authored draft sections of the original report, which the editor then had the formidable task of reordering and editing for logical flow, empirical consistency, citations and style.

The first thanks must be to the tremendous contribution by Iain Scobbie, Sir Joseph Hotung Research Professor in Law, Human Rights and Peace Building in the Middle East, in the School of Law at SOAS. Much of the material in Chapter 2 traces to his ground-breaking scholarship for this study and he was principally responsible for the analysis of colonialism in Chapter 3, as well as a myriad of insights, corrections, shorter drafted sections and general intellectual oversight. His wisdom as a senior scholar of international law provided intellectual leadership throughout several meetings of the contributors on successive drafts. Formidable and brilliant human rights lawyers Hassan Jabareen and Rina Rosenberg, respectively founding Director and International Advocacy Director of the Adalah Legal Centre for Arab Minority Rights in Israel (Haifa), were invaluable in consulting on the study's theory and method and providing much of the legal documentation by arranging access to Adalah's archives of human rights reports and legal cases. Sections on Israel's Supreme Court decisions, among many others, trace principally to their work. Also contributing vital theoretical insight and fine collegial support, as well as most of the material on South African apartheid law, was Max du Plessis, Professor of Law at the University of KwaZulu-Natal (Durban). John Reynolds, initially from his position at al-Haq, was involved consistently throughout the study and assembled much of the enormous volume of empirical material in Chapter 4 – work that brings further thanks to al-Haq Director Shawan Jabareen, who authorised John's time and generous access to al-Haq's archives. Throughout the project and especially in the early organisational stages, Victor Kattan was a bastion, and significant contributions to early editorial meetings and draft sections were made by Shane Darcy and Michael Kearney. Special gratitude is extended to Iain, Rina and John for helping the revision for Pluto Press in 2011.

Other advisors in early stages of the original report included lawyer Michael Sfard (Tel Aviv), whose staff contributed some draft material to Chapter 2; Gilbert Marcus, Senior Counsel and Constitutional Lawyer (Johannesburg); and Professor Daphna Golan, Director of the Minerva Centre for Human

Rights in the Faculty of Law at the Hebrew University (Jerusalem). Professor John Dugard, who provided the original inspiration for this study (through his capacity as Special Rapporteur on human rights in the OPT, as noted in Chapter 1), was not involved directly in the study due to his UN role, but generously provided doses of good sense and scholarly insight whenever requested.

Archival research, which provided the empirical meat and potatoes of this study, was conducted by many people: at Adalah, these included Fatmeh el-Ajou, Rana Asali, Katie Hesketh, and Belkis Wille; at al-Haq, Michelle Burgis, Gareth Gleed, Lisa Monaghan, Fadi Quran, and Mays Warrad; and in South Africa, Godfrey Musila, then at the South African Institute for Advanced Constitutional, Public, Human Rights and International Law (Johannesburg). Stephanie Khoury provided valuable comments on some early draft sections. Thanks are also warmly due to outside readers, whose comments were immensely valuable to the final version: here this book owes a particular debt of gratitude to professors Christine Chinkin, Omar Dajani, George Bisharat and Orna Ben-Naftali, as well as John Quigley. The study also received comments from Jody Kollapen when he was serving as CEO of the South African Commission on Human Rights (Pretoria).

Respectful gratitude is also expressed to those who made the original project possible in 2007–2009. First among these is Aziz Pahad, then Deputy Minister of Foreign Affairs in the Republic of South Africa, who supervised the HSRC's Middle East Project. Thanks are due also, and especially, to Ronnie Kasrils, former Minister of Intelligence Services for the Republic of South Africa. At the HSRC, Professor Adam Habib helped to launch the Middle East Project, in his capacity as Director of the Democracy and Governance Programme, while Director Adrian Hadland provided oversight and MEP assistant Tania Fraser assisted wonderfully in organising the report's printing and release in Cape Town. Sarah Hibbin and other staff at the Sir Joseph Hotung Project did valiant work in organising the public release of the unedited study in May 2009 at SOAS. At the DFA, Douw Vermaak, at the Middle East Desk, served most helpfully as liaison and Pieter A. Stemmet assisted with coordination, in an observer capacity, as DFA Advocate and Senior State Law Advisor.

Beyond this, thanks are due, but inexpressible, to those who deserve it most: the world's community of principled scholars and activists who promote human rights even when the effort runs contrary to what is easy or convenient. Through their courage and fortitude, the edifice of international human rights has been building brick by brick, and so has come to provide the firm foundation of theory, commentary and principle on which this study is able to stand. This book is therefore dedicated to those thousands of visionaries who have struggled and sacrificed for human rights and dignity in Israel-Palestine, especially when this required going courageously against the tide. The conflict in Israel-Palestine seems all too often to trigger and showcase the worst impulses in humanity, but it also regularly inspires the very best.

Virginia Tilley<br>
March 2012

# 1
# Sources of Law and Key Concepts

EXPLORING COLONIALISM AND APARTHEID AS MATTERS
OF INTERNATIONAL LAW

In January 2007, the United Nations (UN) General Assembly received an unprecedented report from the Special Rapporteur on the human rights situation in the Occupied Palestinian Territories (OPT). Drawing from his long experience with human rights law in apartheid South Africa, John Dugard had been struck by the similarities of practices he was witnessing in the OPT. Now he posed a question for international law:

> The international community has identified three regimes as inimical to human rights – colonialism, apartheid and foreign occupation. Israel is clearly in military occupation of the OPT. *At the same time, elements of the occupation constitute forms of colonialism and of apartheid, which are contrary to international law.* What are the legal consequences of a regime of prolonged occupation with features of colonialism and apartheid for the occupied people, the occupying Power and third States? It is suggested that this question might appropriately be put to the International Court of Justice for a further advisory opinion.[1]

Dugard's formal assertion that the conflict had 'elements' or 'features' of colonialism and apartheid, to the extent that serious consideration was warranted by the International Court of Justice (ICJ), was both startling and provocative. The terms 'colonial' and 'apartheid' are often used in polemics regarding the Israeli-Palestinian conflict, but he did not use them lightly or as a heuristic allusion. A sober, cautious and highly respected South African legal scholar, author of the magisterial *Human Rights and the South African Legal Order* and other classic tomes on South African apartheid policy, Dugard's observation that elements of Israel's policies constitute colonialism and apartheid carried the weight of an acknowledged world expert on both matters and elevated questions about whether they were operating in Israel-Palestine to a new and more serious level.

An advisory opinion by the ICJ on the legality of an occupation would not be unprecedented. The Court issued such an opinion in 1971, regarding South Africa's occupation of South West Africa (now Namibia). After the First World War, South Africa had assumed authority over the territory under a League of Nations mandate, after the defeat and withdrawal of Germany, its former coloniser. After the Second World War, when the people of South West Africa sought full independence, South Africa not only refused to withdraw but insisted on sustaining its own apartheid policies there, drawing increasing condemnation by the international community. In 1970, the UN Security Council declared South Africa's continuing presence in South West Africa illegal, partly on grounds of its violations of the civilian population's right to self-determination and human and civil rights (especially, through arbitrary detentions and arrests). In 1971, in the last of four advisory opinions on the question,[2] the ICJ was asked to rule on the controversy and considered South Africa's defence of these policies – that 'separate development' (apartheid) actually reflected the true rights and needs of all peoples in the territory. Rejecting this argument, the Court held that a policy of 'complete physical separation of racial and ethnic groups' entailed a 'denial of human rights' that was in 'flagrant violation of the purposes and principles of the Charter'.[3] The Court concluded that South Africa's argument for 'separate development' only reinforced the illegitimacy of its governance there, and held that

> the continued presence of South Africa in Namibia being illegal, South Africa is under obligation to withdraw its administration from Namibia immediately and thus put an end to its occupation of the Territory.[4]

The ICJ has never ruled on the legality of Israel's occupation of the OPT. It has dealt only with some aspects of Israel's practices as an Occupying Power, in its 2004 advisory opinion, *Legal consequences of the construction of a wall in Occupied Palestinian Territory*.[5] In that case, the Court was asked to rule on a particular practice by the Occupying Power, not the nature or legality of the occupation itself. Should the General Assembly follow Dugard's recommendation and request the ICJ to consider whether Israel's policies in the OPT breach the international legal prohibitions on colonialism and apartheid, the Court would then be considering whether Israel's occupation is illegal on these grounds.

Such an opinion would be a historic step in the history of the Israeli-Palestinian conflict. Contrary to many assumptions, belligerent occupation is not, in itself, an unlawful situation: it is accepted as a possible consequence of armed conflict. International law regarding such situations presupposes, however, that occupation is a temporary state of affairs that will naturally draw to a close after the cessation of hostilities – or, at the latest, upon the conclusion of a peace agreement. Any other outcome is precluded by the norms of international law which prohibit the acquisition of territory through the use of force. A belligerent occupation that has lasted over four decades therefore suggests that the Occupying Power's intentions should come under review, to assess whether it reflects a policy of annexation (partial or total) that equates with colonialism. If the Occupying Power has also implanted its own population as settlers in the occupied territory, and ensured that the settler population has preferential rights in respect to the population under occupation on grounds of ethnic or racial identity – especially, rights of movement and residence – then this review must also consider whether the occupation regime equates with apartheid.

Such a review must move beyond what some Israeli legal scholars have already criticised as a 'habitual focus on specific actions ... as distinct from the nature of the occupation as a normative regime'.[6] The latter approach entails a comprehensive review of the Occupying Power's doctrines, laws and practices. Such a study must obviously draw from law relevant to occupation: that is, international humanitarian law. But it must also turn to international human rights law – especially, prohibitions of colonialism and apartheid – and other relevant international law and theory to consider whether Israel's belligerent occupation of the OPT since June 1967 is violating those prohibitions and therefore is illegal on those grounds.[7] This study undertakes that comprehensive project.

## SCOPE OF THE STUDY

The scope of this book was intentionally limited in three ways. First, it does not address individual criminal responsibility for practices of apartheid (now considered a crime against humanity). Second, evidence is confined, with few exceptions, to Israeli practices within the OPT and to the period after the 1967 war during which those territories came under military occupation. Finally, the study is confined to whether the occupation is illegal on grounds of colonialism or apartheid; it does not consider whether Israel's occupation may be unlawful on other grounds. Since all three of these limitations might draw controversy, they are explained here with some care.

### State versus individual responsibility

Establishing that an international law – such as the prohibition of apartheid or colonialism – has been breached is different from establishing that individuals have committed an international crime. The latter question requires demonstrating not only that a criminal offence has taken place (the *actus reus*) but also, crucially, that the accused person acted with the requisite awareness, intention or mental state (the *mens rea*) which renders that conduct criminal.[8] (For example, if forced population transfer results in mass deaths, it is not considered a crime of genocide if officials who organised the transfer are found not to have intended this outcome.) Moreover, *mens rea* must be proved in relation to every separate criminal act by each individual. Such an undertaking regarding criminality by individuals was well beyond the scope of this study.

This book focuses instead on State practices and policies that are identified by international law as constituting colonialism or apartheid. Such a finding would give rise to State responsibility. This responsibility would involve neither criminal nor civil law as these are conceived in domestic legal systems, but would signify that a State has breached a general international law that binds all States. If practices of the State of Israel are found to amount to apartheid, then questions of individual criminal responsibility would then arise. For example, the South African Truth and Reconciliation Commission adopted this approach when it convened in 1995 to assess criminal responsibility by individuals for acts of apartheid, based on the long-established premise that an apartheid regime was operating in the country between 1948 and 1993. Colonialism, on the other hand, is considered an internationally wrongful act but not a crime attracting individual criminal responsibility under international law.

State responsibility regarding practices of colonialism or apartheid is a grave matter in itself because prohibitions of both are seen to have *peremptory* status under international law. A peremptory norm (or *jus cogens* rule) is a rule 'accepted and recognised by the international community of States as a whole as a norm from which no derogation is permitted'.[9] Peremptory norms include, for example, prohibitions on slavery and genocide, which are not accepted as legitimate under any circumstances and are seen to affect the vital interests of the international community as a whole. A serious breach of a peremptory norm therefore imposes on all States serious remedial duties that do not arise in relation to other internationally wrongful acts. The International Law Commission,[10] which is responsible for codifying the rules of State responsibility,[11] has clarified that 'racial discrimination and apartheid' are among those practices that are 'prohibited in widely ratified international treaties and conventions admitting of no exception'. At the 1993 World Conference on Human Rights (usually called the Vienna Conference), representatives of States who were attending generally agreed that prohibitions of racial discrimination and apartheid are peremptory norms.

This status makes colonial and apartheid regimes matters of grave concern for all States: all States are responsible for acting appropriately to help end them. A State that is found to be practising colonialism or apartheid carries the primary responsibility: it must terminate related laws and practices immediately, make assurances and guarantees not to return or repeat the policy, give satisfaction for any injuries; and provide full reparations for any material and moral damage its practices have caused.[12] But third-party States also have special responsibilities, which are considered more fully in Chapter 5.

### Scope of empirical evidence

Empirical evidence for this study was assembled from documents assembled by UN organs, human rights organisations and other reputable authorities that have tracked and analysed Israeli practices and policies in the OPT from the perspective of human rights law and international humanitarian law. Reflecting this study's central question – the legality of Israel's occupation – this evidence was confined in two significant (and, to some, controversial) ways.

First, evidence was limited geographically to Israeli law and practices in the Gaza Strip, East Jerusalem and the West Bank – that is, the territories in Mandate Palestine that Israel occupied in June 1967 and that lie beyond the ceasefire lines delineated in Israel's 1949 Armistice Agreements with Egypt and Jordan. (The Golan Heights, although also occupied by Israel in 1967, was excluded from this study only because it was not a part of Mandate Palestine and so fell outside the scope of the Special Rapporteur's 2007 report to which this study responds.) Israeli State law and practices inside the 1949 ceasefire lines were also excluded (with a few exceptions) because the concern here is with the legality of Israel's occupation and accordingly with Israel's practices in territories that are internationally recognised as being held under belligerent occupation.

This decision to confine the study's scope to the OPT was not uncontroversial among the study's contributors. One argument was that Israel's practices inside its 1949 borders are so interdependent with policies in the OPT that they cannot be separated sensibly. Another was that Israel cannot be considered an 'apartheid state' unless its policies throughout the territory under its control are consistent with apartheid as it was practised in South Africa, raising the objection that Palestinian citizens of Israel have the right to vote. These points were considered important by the contributors to larger questions of Israel's comprehensive regime in the entire territory under its control, but not directly relevant to the question of whether Israel's occupation of the West Bank, East Jerusalem and the Gaza Strip is illegal on grounds of colonialism or apartheid. Consensus was finally achieved to focus in this study on the legality of the occupation and hope that others will build on the study's findings by adopting a broader geographic ambit.

In practice, this attempt at geographic limitations did not operate neatly. For one thing, Israeli policy is to extend Israeli Basic Law and other domestic civil law to Jewish settlers in the OPT. This practice required considering how these domestic laws function to construct and privilege Jews relative to Palestinians in ways relevant to a finding of apartheid. For another, the Supreme Court of the State of Israel hears cases from Palestinians living in the OPT, blurring the separation of Israeli and occupied territory in ways especially significant to a finding of colonialism. Trade, tax and customs policies also bridge the boundary, fusing the two economies in ways consistent with colonialism. Therefore, Israeli domestic institutions, law and policy, as well as Supreme Court decisions, were necessarily considered in this book where they become relevant.

Finally, evidence is confined to the period after Israel's occupation began in June 1967, on grounds that matters pertaining to this period are sufficient to test for regimes of colonialism and apartheid. References to earlier history are introduced only where necessary to clarify certain legal questions. This approach (which also drew internal debate) is not meant to imply that events and policy statements prior to 1967 are not relevant to tests of colonialism and apartheid: particularly, to the 'purpose clause' in the definition of apartheid in the Apartheid Convention. Rather, this limitation reflected only the contributors' concern that historiographic controversies not distract from a legal review of Israeli contemporary practices under relevant international human rights law and humanitarian law. Again, it is hoped that subsequent studies will explore whether historical events before 1967 further illuminate the nature of Israel's regime in the OPT. Certainly the findings of this study support the relevance of such a study.

## INTERNATIONAL LAW IN OCCUPIED TERRITORY

This study took as its basic framework, and point of departure, international law that applies to situations of belligerent occupation. In its broadest sense, this law includes laws on the use of force, international humanitarian law, international human rights law and international criminal law, as well as commentary and case law. *International humanitarian law* (known also as the laws of armed conflict or the laws of war) includes, especially, the 1907 Hague Convention IV Respecting the Laws and Customs of War on Land (henceforth, 'the Hague Regulations') and the Fourth Geneva Convention of 1949 relative to the Protection of Civilian Persons in Time of War (henceforth, 'Fourth Geneva Convention'). *International human rights law* concerns the prohibitions of colonialism and apartheid. The prohibition of colonialism is expressed most explicitly in the United Nations' Declaration on the Granting of Independence to Colonial Countries and Peoples of 1960 (hereafter, the 'Declaration on Colonialism'). The prohibition of apartheid was first introduced in the International Convention on the Elimination of All Forms of Racial Discrimination of 1963 (ICERD) and affirmed in 1973 by the Convention on the Suppression and Punishment of the Crime of Apartheid (hereafter, the 'Apartheid Convention').

While all these legal instruments are discussed in subsequent chapters, their general applicability to Israel's policies in the OPT is summarised here to clarify how they comprise the study's theoretical framework. Later sections consider the meaning of 'belligerent occupation' and the significance of an ICJ opinion regarding the prohibitions of colonialism or apartheid.

### International humanitarian law

International humanitarian law is concerned with the relations between an Occupying Power and the civilian population under its authority. Especially important, for the purposes of this study, are those provisions regulating the powers and responsibilities of an Occupying Power (here, Israel) regarding 'protected persons' under its authority (here, Palestinians). The essential provisions of this law are contained in the 1907 Hague Regulations and the Fourth Geneva Convention of 1949.[13]

This study assumes that Israel is bound by both these instruments. Israel is not a formal party to the 1907 Hague Convention,[14] to which the Hague Regulations are annexed, but the Regulations are now recognised as customary international law and so are considered binding on all States, including Israel. Israel's own Supreme Court has agreed that the Hague Regulations of 1907 form part of customary international law and are therefore enforceable in the domestic courts of Israel.[15] Israel did become a party to the Fourth Geneva Convention on 6 July 1951 and so is legally bound by its provisions. The Israeli government has consistently argued on several grounds that the Fourth Geneva Convention is not applicable as a matter of law to the OPT, but these arguments are considered, and found inadequate, in Chapter 2.

Israel is not a party to Protocol I Additional to the Geneva Conventions (1977), which codifies a number of principles governing the conduct of hostilities in ways applicable to Israel's obligations as an Occupying Power. Still, the UN Security Council, the UN General Assembly, the High Contracting Parties to the Convention and the ICJ have all affirmed that Protocol I applies in the OPT and so this is assumed here.[16] In any case, Israel is bound by the provisions of Protocol I that have the status of customary international law: this too has been recognised and applied by Israel's Supreme Court, as discussed later.

*Defining 'belligerent occupation'*

Defining 'belligerent occupation' is important to clarifying when and how international humanitarian law becomes applicable. This is important to addressing Israel's claims that the Fourth Geneva Convention does not apply to the OPT on grounds that its regime of control in the OPT is not technically an 'occupation' (Israeli representatives have argued instead for terms like 'administered territories'). Brief attention to defining 'occupation' is therefore important to the analysis here, which assumes a situation of belligerent occupation and draws extensively on related international law.

Belligerent occupation has been described as 'a transitional period following invasion and preceding the cessation of hostilities'. Such a situation 'imposes more onerous duties on an Occupying Power than on a party to an international armed conflict'[17] because of the complexity and moral responsibility of administering a civilian population and its assets, economy, natural resources, law and order, and so forth. Determining the start of a belligerent occupation can therefore be distinguished from a military invasion, which arguably may not involve such responsibilities.[18] In one summation:

> Invasion is the marching or riding of troops – or the flying of military aircraft – into enemy country. Occupation is invasion plus taking possession of enemy country for the purpose of holding it, at any rate temporarily. The difference between mere invasion and occupation becomes apparent from the fact that an occupant sets up some kind of administration, whereas the mere invader does not.[19]

This distinction flows from Articles in the Hague Regulations, upon which the Fourth Geneva Convention relies:

> 42. Territory is considered occupied when it is actually placed under the authority of the hostile army. The occupation extends only to the territory where such authority has been established and can be exercised.[20]
> 43. The authority of the legitimate power having in fact passed into the hands of the occupant, the latter shall take all the measures in his power to restore, and ensure, as far as possible, public order and safety, while respecting, unless absolutely prevented, the laws in force in the country.

Thus, in 1949, the US Military Tribunal at Nuremberg ruled that

> an occupation indicates the exercise of governmental authority to the exclusion of the established government. This presupposes the destruction of organised resistance and the establishment of an administration to preserve law and order. To the extent that the occupant's control is maintained and that of the civil government eliminated, the area will be said to be occupied.[21]

In any case, this distinction between occupation and invasion is not necessarily relevant to applying the Fourth Geneva Convention in the OPT, for Article 6 of the Convention provides that it applies 'from the outset of any conflict or occupation mentioned in Article 2'. In its authoritative commentary on the Convention, the International Committee of the Red Cross/Red Crescent (ICRC, which is charged with interpreting and defending the Convention) explains that this Article was employed to indicate that the Convention

> became applicable as soon as the first acts of violence were committed ... Mere frontier incidents may make the Convention applicable, for they may be the beginning of a more widespread conflict. The Convention should be applied as soon as troops are in foreign territory and in contact with the civilian population.[22]

Accordingly, the term 'occupation' in Article 6 of the Fourth Geneva Convention bears a wider meaning than in Article 42 of the Hague Regulations:

> So far as individuals are concerned, the application of the Fourth Geneva Convention does not depend upon the existence of a state of occupation within the meaning of Article 42 ... The relations between the civilian population of a territory and troops advancing into that territory, whether fighting or not, are governed by the present Convention. There is no intermediate period between what might be termed the invasion phase and the inauguration of a stable regime of occupation. Even a patrol which penetrates into enemy territory without any intention of staying there must respect the Convention in its dealings with the civilians it meets.[23]

### *General provisions of the Fourth Geneva Convention*

The Fourth Geneva Convention is oriented toward ensuring the protection of civilians under occupation.[24] Human rights law applies without discrimination to all people in a territory, but humanitarian law – the provisions of the Hague Regulations and the Fourth Geneva Convention – apply only to those individuals who qualify as 'protected persons'. Protected persons are civilians 'who, at a given moment and in any manner whatsoever, find themselves, in the case of a conflict or occupation, in the hands of a Party to the conflict or Occupying Power of which they are not nationals' (Article 6). Thus the category of 'protected persons' excludes nationals of the Occupying Power;

it also excludes nationals of neutral third States and of States allied with the Occupying Power. Hence, in the present case, Jewish settlers in the OPT are not 'protected persons' in this legal sense.

This study does not comprehensively review Israel's practices under the Fourth Geneva Convention, but some of its provisions are important to note briefly because the scale of their violation by Israel suggests that the Occupying Power is applying different normative regimes in the OPT. In this respect, several protections in the Fourth Geneva Convention have particular relevance to this study. For example, Article 49(6) is especially relevant because it prohibits the transfer of the occupied power's population into occupied territory: hence the universal international assessment that Jewish settlers and settlements in the West Bank are illegal derives from this Article.[25] Article 53 prohibits destruction by the Occupying Power of real or personal property: 'Any destruction by the Occupying Power of real or personal property belonging individually or collectively to private persons, or to the State, or to other public authorities, or to social or co-operative organizations, is prohibited, except where such destruction is rendered absolutely necessary by military operations.'[26] Demolitions of Palestinians homes would fall under this category.

Other Articles, and their violations by Israel, are discussed in later chapters where relevant and only mentioned here to convey the tenor of the Convention. Article 27 presupposes a general right of free movement for the civilian population, subject only to restrictions made necessary by circumstances of war.[27] Article 27 also ensures a range of rights regarding culture and family: 'Protected persons are entitled, in all circumstances, to respect for their persons, their honour, their family rights, their religious convictions and practices, and their manners and customs.' Article 27 prohibits racial and religious discrimination, stipulating that 'all protected persons shall be treated with the same consideration by the Party to the conflict in whose power they are, without any adverse distinction based, in particular, on race, religion or political opinion'. The same Article provides guarantees for humane treatment and protection against acts or threats of violence, including torture. Article 33 prohibits collective punishments and all measures of intimidation. Other Articles – such as Articles 55, 56, 59 and 60 – require the Occupying Power to ensure adequate food and water to protected persons and access to health care, including allowing in relief supplies. Articles 65–68 and Articles 71–78 provide for due process, penal standards and protections in cases of house arrest or internment.

For experienced observers of the Israeli-Palestinian conflict, these provisions regarding responsibilities and duties of an Occupying Power immediately recall decades of complaints and controversies regarding Israeli practices in the OPT. Whether Israel is abiding by these provisions is not the central focus here but is discussed later in relevant sections.

### Human rights law

Relations of the Occupying Power with the inhabitants of occupied territory are regulated by international humanitarian law, but an Occupying Power must also protect the human rights of the population in territories under its control. International human rights law is therefore cited extensively in this study, particularly the Declaration on Colonialism and the Apartheid Convention. This approach may raise questions, as it suggests that a belligerent occupation, involving international relations (and assuming the remedy of the Occupying Power's eventual withdrawal), may simultaneously be a regime associated domestic policy and a different remedy (territorial reunification and full democratisation). Moreover, successive Israeli governments have rejected the application of human rights law to the OPT, although Israel's Supreme Court has sometimes acknowledged it[28] (and just as Israel rejects the applicability of international humanitarian law). The approach here, which is to apply both spheres of law to a study of policies in the OPT, therefore calls for review in more depth, although the subtler dimensions of the discussion in this section are of concern primarily to specialists.

Some States, such as the United States and Israel, still adhere to the traditional view that human rights law and international humanitarian law are mutually exclusive, because of the different spheres of protection they afford.[29] Put simply, the traditional argument was that human rights law applies during peace time but international humanitarian law applies once a state of armed conflict exists. Human rights law was also seen as applying only within the national territory of a given State, comprising obligations that citizens could claim from their government. International humanitarian law was seen as applying extraterritorially, as it regulated what States could do outside their own territory in wartime in their treatment of non-nationals. The Government of Israel drew on this traditional view as late as 1998, in arguing that:

> Humanitarian law in armed conflicts had to be distinguished from human rights law. Under human rights regimes, the purpose was to protect the individual from loss of life and liberty and from cruel treatment or oppression by the State, inflicted on him either as a citizen or as a person temporally subject to the jurisdiction of the State in question. Humanitarian law in armed conflicts, on the other hand, was designed to balance the needs of humanity against the nature of warfare. His Government believed that the latter situation was much more pertinent to the case of the occupied territories.[30]

In recent decades, however, this traditional (bifurcated) view has been seen increasingly as both inaccurate and inadequate. Even by the late 1960s, UN bodies had affirmed that some human rights law remained relevant during an international armed conflict.[31] In June 1967, in a resolution on the situation in the Middle East, the Security Council noted that 'essential and inalienable human rights should be respected even during the vicissitudes of war'.[32] In 1970, the General Assembly affirmed that 'Fundamental human rights, as accepted in international law and laid down in international instruments, continue to apply fully in situations of armed conflict.'[33]

Other boundaries between the two spheres of law have also softened. For instance, human rights are now recognised to be owed by a State not only to its citizens but to all non-nationals within its territory or subject to its jurisdiction. Regulation of different types of conflict has also converged: many customary rules considered to apply in international armed conflicts are now considered equally applicable in domestic conflicts.[34] In other words, international humanitarian law is now considered to be neither autonomous from human rights law nor comprehensive: human rights law is considered essential to filling out the regime of rights that apply to people living under occupation.[35]

Still, by the mid 1990s, the doctrine that both international human rights law and humanitarian law apply to *international* armed conflict was not yet formalised.[36] The first authoritative ruling on this question came in 1996, when the ICJ considered whether the International Covenant on Civil and Political Rights was applicable during an international armed conflict. In the *Legality of the threat or use of nuclear weapons* advisory opinion, the Court ruled:

> the protection of the International Covenant on Civil and Political Rights does not cease in times of war, except by operation of Article 4 of the Covenant whereby certain provisions may be derogated from in a time of national emergency. Respect for the right to life is not, however, such a provision. In principle, the right not arbitrarily to be deprived of one's life applies also in hostilities. The test of what is an arbitrary deprivation of life, however, then falls to be determined by the applicable *lex specialis*, namely, the law applicable in armed conflict which is designed to regulate the conduct of hostilities.[37]

This opinion affirmed a normative relationship between international humanitarian and human rights law in international armed conflict.[38] It did not provide a completely candid or transparent account of that relationship, but it did finally set aside the traditional idea that these two branches of law are mutually exclusive. In the *Legal consequences of the construction of a wall in the occupied Palestinian territory*, the ICJ reaffirmed this view:

> the Court considers that the protection offered by human rights conventions does not cease in case of armed conflict, save through the effect of provisions for derogation of the kind to be found in Article 4 of the International Covenant on Civil and Political Rights. As regards the relationship between international humanitarian law and human rights law, there are three possible situations: some rights may be exclusively matters of international humanitarian law; others may be exclusively matters of human rights law; yet others may be matters of both these branches of international law. In order to answer the question put to it, the Court will have to take into consideration both these branches of international law, namely human rights law and, as *lex specialis*, international humanitarian law.[39]

In the same case, the Court considered whether some human rights instruments to which Israel is a party – namely, the International Covenant on Civil and Political Rights (ICCPR), the International Covenant on Economic, Social and Cultural Rights (ICESCR), and the Convention on the Rights of the Child[40] – apply extraterritorially to the OPT. The Court followed the view of the UN Human Rights Committee that they do apply, partly on grounds that the Universal Covenant on Human Rights provides for the general rights they embrace:

> Each State party to the present Covenant undertakes to respect and to ensure to all individuals within its territory and subject to its jurisdiction the rights recognised in the present Covenant, without distinction of any kind, such as race, colour, sex, language, religion, political or other opinion, national or social origin, property, birth or other status.[41]

In this ruling, the ICJ noted but rejected Israel's consistent claim made before the Human Rights Committee that it is under no legal obligation to apply the ICCPR or the ICESCR in the OPT.[42] The Court reaffirmed this approach in asserting that Uganda, as the Occupying Power in Ituri, was under an obligation 'to secure respect for the applicable rules of international human rights law and international humanitarian law'.[43] The Court stated that the following instruments were therefore applicable:

- Regulations Respecting the Laws and Customs of War on Land annexed to the Fourth Hague Convention (18 October 1907). (Neither the DRC nor Uganda are parties to the Convention but the Court reiterates that 'the provisions of the Hague Regulations have become part of customary law'[44] and as such are binding on both Parties.)
- Fourth Geneva Convention relative to the Protection of Civilian Persons in Time of War (12 August 1949).
- International Covenant on Civil and Political Rights (19 December 1966).
- Protocol Additional to the Geneva Conventions (12 August 1949) and relating to the Protection of Victims of International Armed Conflicts (Protocol I) (8 June 1977).
- African Charter on Human and Peoples' Rights (27 June 1981).
- Convention on the Rights of the Child (20 November 1989).
- Optional Protocol to the Convention on the Rights of the Child on the Involvement of Children in Armed Conflict (25 May 2000).[45]

Similarly, in the case of *Loizidou* v. *Turkey* (which addressed the scope of Turkey's extraterritorial responsibility to implement and respect the European Convention on Human Rights in Northern Cyprus), the European Court of Human Rights held that the responsibility of Contracting States can be involved by acts and omissions of their authorities which produce effects outside their own territory. Of particular significance to the present case the Court held, in conformity with the relevant principles of international law governing State responsibility, that the responsibility of a Contracting Party could also arise when as a consequence of military action – whether lawful or unlawful – it exercises effective control of an area outside its national territory. The obligation to secure, in such an area, the rights and freedoms set out in the Convention, derives from the fact of such control whether it be exercised directly, through its armed forces, or through a subordinate local administration.[46]

Clearly, therefore, international courts have conclusively negated Israel's argument that it is under no obligation to apply human rights treaties in the OPT.[47] The question is not whether Israel has obligations under the Covenants, but rather the extent of its obligations. At the very least, it is safe to assume that Israel is bound by prohibitions on racial discrimination and apartheid by virtue of their status as *jus cogens* norms. Hence Israel's practices in the OPT can be reviewed in light of international standards prohibiting racial discrimination, colonialism and apartheid.

To conclude, Israel cannot claim that human rights law, including the prohibition of apartheid, is irrelevant to its occupation of Palestinian territories. International humanitarian law does provide the primary legal framework to assess the legality of the conduct of that occupation, but this does not preclude the application of human rights law. On the contrary, international humanitarian law itself mandates that its application must consider relevant norms in other areas of international law, including the prohibitions on apartheid and colonialism.[48]

Hence this study considers that international human rights law and humanitarian law both apply in situations of belligerent occupation. The following instruments are therefore applicable (not to exclude others) and shall be referred to throughout the study:

- International Covenant on Civil and Political Rights
- International Covenant on Economic, Social and Cultural Rights
- Convention on the Prevention and Punishment of the Crime of Genocide (1948)[49]
- Declaration on the Granting of Independence to Colonial Countries and Peoples (1960)
- Convention on the Elimination of All Forms of Racial Discrimination (1965)[50]
- Convention on the Elimination of All Forms of Discrimination Against Women (1979)[51]
- Convention Against Torture and Other Cruel, Inhuman or Degrading Treatment or Punishment (1984)[52]
- Convention on the Rights of the Child (1989)[53]

- Convention on the Suppression and Punishment of the Crime of Apartheid (1973)
- Rome Statute of the International Criminal Court (1998)

Prohibition of colonialism in international law

Whether Israel's belligerent occupation of the West Bank and Gaza constitutes a colonial project has attracted relatively little attention by international law scholars. This neglect may stem from several causes. Some scholars may consider colonialism to be a practice restricted to domination by white European powers over non-white, non-European territories and thus not as obviously applicable in the Israeli-Palestinian context as it was to, say, French and British rule in Africa.[54] Others may simply assume that colonialism, at least as a codified form of foreign governance, has become an obsolete concern for international law since the formal decolonisation of African and Asian States in the 1960s and 1970s.[55] Others may even accept that Israel's establishment in 1948 resulted from a struggle for Jewish self-determination against the British colonial power, a narrative that casts Israel as a decolonised State and precludes consideration of modern Israel as an agent of colonialism (as discussed later).[56]

Nevertheless, as UN Special Rapporteur John Dugard noted, some elements of Israel's occupation *prima facie* replicate practices associated with colonialism: for example, the unlawful mass transfer of settlers into occupied territory; discriminatory policies applied on the basis of ethnicity and religion; appropriation by the Occupying Power of the territory's natural resources; 'de-development' of the Palestinian economy and mergence with the Israeli economy; and, especially and fundamentally, denial of the Palestinian people's right to self-determination. The study thus seeks to appraise whether Israel's policies and practices in the OPT constitute a substantive practice of colonialism by conducting their closer review according to relevant international legal instruments.

It is true that the term 'colonialism' has usually been used in reference to European domination of non-European peoples in the sixteenth through early twentieth centuries.[57] In this period, colonialism was expressed in de facto and de jure seizure of land, denial of indigenous self-governance, and the domination, subjugation and exploitation of such lands and their peoples for the enrichment and greater hegemony of the colonising State. European powers characteristically acquired territory through conquest, treaties of cession, and 'protection' or occupation of lands deemed or claimed to be terra nullius (empty land, or land that is empty of government, as so open to seizure and annexation).[58] Colonial rule then emerged from the coloniser's claim to be the territory's legitimate sovereign or at least to hold exclusive trade rights relative to other European powers. Policies of colonial powers sometimes included formal policies to settle their own population in the colonised territory, but in most cases they merely implanted smaller populations of administrators to serve colonial bureaucracies.[59]

Prohibitions on colonialism emerged gradually, while much of the world was still under European domination in the nineteenth and early twentieth centuries. In the mid twentieth century, however, facing a scale of indigenous resistance that exhausted European energies and funds for sustaining colonial empires, European powers sought to escape chronic rivalries for influence over foreign markets by affirming sweeping prohibition against conquest and foreign domination through the endorsement of the right of all peoples to self-determination.[60]

*The right to self-determination in international law*

The ICJ has declared that self-determination is 'one of the essential principles of contemporary international law'.[61] In the *Wall* advisory opinion,[62] the ICJ affirmed that self-determination is a right *erga omnes*, whose realisation all UN member States, as well as all States parties to the international covenants on human rights, have the duty to promote.[63] The International Law Commission has concluded that self-determination also has *jus cogens* status and is peremptory – States cannot derogate from its exigencies in their international relations.[64]

Self-determination first emerged in the lexicon of international relations in the aftermath of the First World War.[65] Article 22 of the League of Nations Charter (which established the mandate system) did not use the term 'self-determination', but it described the mandate system as providing 'tutelage' to peoples considered deserving of, but unprepared for, independent statehood.[66] The Charter calls the duty to provide such tutelage 'a sacred trust of civilization':

> To those colonies and territories which as a consequence of the late War have ceased to be under the sovereignty of the States which formerly governed them and which are inhabited by peoples not yet able to stand by themselves under the strenuous conditions of the modern world, there should be applied the principle that the well-being and development of such peoples form a sacred trust of civilisation and that securities for the performance of this trust should be embodied in this Covenant.[67]

In its 1971 *Namibia* advisory opinion, the ICJ ruled that the 'sacred trust' was to facilitate self-determination:[68]

> 52. ... the subsequent development of international law in regard to non-self-governing territories, as enshrined in the Charter of the United Nations, made the principle of self-determination applicable to all of them. The concept of the sacred trust was confirmed and expanded to all 'territories whose peoples have not yet attained a full measure of self-government' (Art. 73) ... Obviously the sacred trust continued to apply to League of Nations mandated territories on which an international status had been conferred earlier ...

> 53. ... These developments leave little doubt that the ultimate objective of the sacred trust was the self-determination and independence of the peoples concerned.[69]

Like many legal concepts, the right to self-determination designates a core content and an associated, yet integral, bundle of rights and duties. The core content is clear: it entitles peoples to 'determine their political status and freely pursue their economic, social and cultural development'.[70] Otherwise, a people exercising its right to self-determination may select among several outcomes, as observed in the General Assembly's *Declaration on Principles* (1970):[71]

> The establishment of a sovereign and independent State, the free association or integration with an independent State or the emergence into any other political status freely determined by a people constitute modes of implementing the right of self-determination by that people.

The classic formulation of the right to self-determination reflects these possible outcomes by emphasising *process*: that is, the right of a people to determine freely its political status – for example, full independent statehood, free association with another state, or complete absorption into and annexation by another state. Drew has pointed out, however, that to have true meaning, determining such a choice must also have true *substance*:

> [T]he following can be deduced as a non-exhaustive list of the substantive entitlements conferred on a people by virtue of the law of self-determination ... : (a) the right to exist – demographically and territorially – as a people; (b) the right to territorial integrity; (c) the right to permanent sovereignty over natural resources; (d) the right to cultural integrity and development; and (e) the right to economic and social development.[72]

The most important substance for exercising the right to self-determination is the *territory* in which a people may establish and exercise sovereignty. As Drew underlines:

> Despite its text book characterization as part of human rights law, the law of self-determination has always been bound up more with notions of sovereignty and title to territory than what we traditionally consider to be 'human rights'.[73]

In the *East Timor* case[74] proceedings, Portugal emphasised that the territory that forms the basis of a people's right to self-determination, being legally distinct from any other territory, forms a single unit which must not be dismembered,[75] particularly by a belligerent occupant:

> If an occupant controlled only part of a state and that part was not considered to be a distinct unit entitled to self-determination, the occupant

would not be entitled to effect the secession of the occupied area (as in Northern Cyprus). Similar considerations imply that the occupant would not be entitled to establish a new government in such a region even if its inhabitants supported such an act.[76]

Further,

> ... un territoire qui constitue l'assise du droit d'un peuple á disposer de lui même ... ne peut changer de statut juridique que par un acte d'autodétermination de ce peuple. La Résolution 1541 du 17 décembre 1960 de l'Assemblée générale précise bien cette norme.[77]

Hence territorial integrity comprises a core concern of the *Declaration on Colonialism*, as discussed later. Yet the precise contours of such territory, and other substantive content of self-determination such as precise culture factors and economic needs, are not fixed; it is understood that they may change over time. This principle, sometimes called the 'inter-temporal rule', has arisen particularly in relation to conflicts tracing to former League of Nations mandates.[78]

*The Declaration on Colonialism*

Although self-determination first emerged in the lexicon of international relations in the aftermath of the First World War,[79] it did not mature as a legal norm in customary international law until decolonisation and a sweeping normative rejection of 'alien subjugation, domination and exploitation'. In 1960, norms regarding self-determination were codified in the UN General Assembly's *Declaration on the Granting of Independence to Colonial Countries and Peoples*[80] (henceforth, the Declaration on Colonialism), which comprises the primary basis for discussion in Chapter 3.[81] Although the Declaration is not binding per se, it has acquired the status of a customary rule of international law over time.[82] It has also been described as making 'a significant contribution to developing the concept of the right of self-determination, representing as it does the most definitive statement of condemnation of colonialism by the international community'.[83]

The Declaration does not offer a formal definition of colonialism, but it suggests a definition through its language. It opens with statements affirming the 'passionate yearning for freedom of all dependent peoples'. It then affirms that colonialism 'prevents the development of international economic co-operation, [and] impedes the social, cultural and economic development of dependent peoples'. Article 1 holds that

> The subjection of peoples to alien subjugation, domination and exploitation constitutes a denial of fundamental human rights, is contrary to the Charter of the United Nations and is an impediment to the promotion of world peace and co-operation.

Article 4 calls for an end to armed repression of colonised peoples and Article 5 calls for granting complete independence to such peoples:

> Immediate steps shall be taken, in Trust and Non-Self-Governing Territories *or all other territories which have not yet attained independence*, to transfer all powers to the peoples of those territories, without any conditions or reservations, in accordance with their freely expressed will and desire, without any distinction as to race, creed or colour, in order to enable them to enjoy complete independence and freedom.[84]

Article 5, in referring to 'all other territories which have not yet attained independence', then ensures that the Declaration's provisions apply not only to Trust and Non-Self-Governing Territories but also to any other territory that has 'not yet attained independence'. This would include territories previously placed under a League of Nations mandate,[85] such as Palestine. In 1965, the representative of the United States clarified the goal of the Declaration as applying to all such territories irrespective of their geographic location or legal status:

> The Charter [of the United Nations] declares in effect that on every nation in possession of *foreign territories*, there rests the responsibility to assist the peoples of these areas 'in the progressive development of their free political institutions' so that ultimately they can validly choose for themselves their permanent political status.[86]

In its advisory opinion on *Namibia*, the ICJ also declared that

> the subsequent development of international law in regard to non self-governing territories, as enshrined in the Charter of the United Nations, made the principle of self-determination applicable to all of them ... Thus it clearly embraced territories under a colonial regime ... A further important stage in this development was the Declaration on the Granting of Independence to Colonial Countries and Peoples (General Assembly resolution 1514 (XV) of 14 December 1960), which embraces all peoples and territories which 'have not yet attained independence'.[87]

Colonialism can sometimes be distinguished from other forms of foreign domination (such as prolonged belligerent occupation) by the dominant power's open claim to sovereignty. In broader usage, however, the term 'colonialism' may describe foreign influence that effectively allows the people of a territory only nominal sovereignty. In such cases, a policy of colonialism is indicated by the people's loss of control over their own natural resources, labour, and markets.

The Declaration stresses several times the link between human rights, self-determination and territorial integrity. The Preamble to the Declaration expresses a special concern with territorial integrity and Article 6 emphasises that 'any attempt aimed at the partial or total disruption of the national unity and the territorial integrity of a country is incompatible with the purposes and principles of the Charter of the United Nations'. A finding of colonialism could thus be made for any territory where practices of the colonial power extend beyond the appropriation of land and natural resources to fragmentation of a territory in ways that ultimately preclude a people from effectively exercising its right to self-determination through formation of an independent state.[88]

As the Declaration condemns 'colonialism in all its forms and manifestations', it would appear to prohibit the transfer of civilians into occupied territory if such transfer ultimately compromises the capacity of the local population to exercise its right to self-determination. Hence the concern for mass population transfer in Article 49(6) of the Fourth Geneva Convention, which prohibits an Occupying Power from transferring its own population into the territory it occupies precisely 'to prevent a practice adopted during the Second World War by certain Powers, which transferred portions of their own population to occupied territory for political and racial reasons *or in order to, as they claimed, to colonize those territories*'.[89] The Israeli Foreign Ministry has argued that Article 49(6) is not violated by Jewish settlement in the OPT because demographic growth of the Jewish settler society reflects a voluntary population movement rather than forced transfer.[90] The Article does not specify that the transfer must be 'forced', but it is nonetheless relevant to consider whether the term 'transfer' in Article 49(6) applies to cases where a civilian population moves into a territory spontaneously: for example, due to social pressures such as poverty or land shortages or religious pilgrimage. Hence it is relevant to a finding of colonialism here to establish whether, or in what circumstances, spontaneous mass civilian settlement should be understood legally to constitute a type of colonialism.

That such mass movement does constitute a type of colonialism is suggested by debates within the African National Congress (ANC) and South African Communist Party during the apartheid era in South Africa, which examined this question under the rubric, 'colonialism of a special type'. Sometimes called 'settler colonialism' by social scientists,[91] this 'special type' of colonialism was understood by ANC strategists to raise unique difficulties for decolonisation, for several reasons. First, the settler society has effectively indigenised: it has severed its ideological ties to the home country and identified its collective origins and interests solely in the territory it has seized, such that it perceives itself as having nowhere else to go. Second, settler independence movements in South Africa and North America assumed for themselves the moral mantles of decolonisation struggles (for example, Afrikaner and US-settler rebellions against British rule), claiming the right as now-distinct peoples to self-determination. This discursive manoeuvre positioned them as rivals with the native peoples for self-determination in the same territory rather than foreign rulers suppressing native attempts at self-determination. A third distinguishing feature is the security dilemma that is typically generated by mass civilian settlement of native territories, which is commonly resolved by continual territorial advance.[92] In South Africa (as in North America), Aboriginal title was extinguished not through one comprehensive conquest but through incremental advances of civilian settlement, generating cycles of conflicts that were periodically stabilised through new treaties establishing ever-advancing borders. This historical process progressively reduced native sovereignty, once uncontested over vast regions, to abject political and economic dependency within ascribed enclaves.[93] This inherent 'frontier dilemma' generated by settler colonialism, which generated intractable conflicts between apartheid South Africa with its 'front-line' states, recalls the Declaration's concern for the impact of colonialism on 'world peace and co-operation'.

Hence this study found that mass Jewish-Israeli settlement in the OPT does represent a type of colonialism, and so, even if it is seen as spontaneous, fits the concerns of the Declaration which condemns 'colonialism in all its forms and manifestations'. As Chapter 4 details, however, the movement of Jewish settlers in the OPT reflects a deliberate State strategy, which largely obviates concern for the distinction between spontaneous civilian movement and a State-sponsored mass population transfer.

Where settler colonialism has reached a critical mass, the bid for settler self-determination has been successful and settler colonies have been recognised as independent States. Partly because many influential modern States trace to such origins (for example, the United States, Canada, Australia and New Zealand) and are therefore sensitive to accusations that their colonial pasts have left any meaningful legacy of obligations to native peoples, the Declaration on Colonialism does not consider that a State may be practising colonialism within its own borders.[94] As Israel has been admitted to the United Nations as an independent State, tacitly although not explicitly within its 1949 ceasefire lines, for the purposes of this study it is assumed that the Declaration is not legally applicable within those lines.

One might argue that the Declaration is not applicable to Israeli practices in occupied territory, either, on other grounds. First, the term 'colonialism' might be considered inapplicable to territory contiguous with the dominating State, being associated only with overseas or otherwise distant lands.[95] This point has no substance, as the Declaration makes no reference to geographic distance.[96] One might also argue that the conflict in Israel-Palestine does not replicate the unequal relations associated with colonialism because it is fundamentally a conflict between 'two peoples in one land'. This view may be dismissed on the ground that the conflict is fundamentally characterised, in terms of international law, by a denial of the Palestinian peoples' right to self-determination. UN General Assembly Resolution 2649 condemned 'those Governments that deny the right to self-determination of peoples recognized as being entitled to it, especially of the peoples of southern Africa and Palestine'.[97] Given this coupling of the Palestinian cause with calls for decolonisation (reiterated in numerous other resolutions), Alain Pellet argues that 'there is no doubt that the Palestinian people can claim the benefits of a very comprehensive legal regime applicable to colonial peoples'.[98]

In conclusion, the Declaration and related instruments indicate that an Occupying Power can become a colonial power if it practises policies associated with colonialism: that is,

- if the Occupying Power attempts to annex the territory that it is occupying or administers it in a way that denies the territory's people the right of self-determination;
- if it assumes permanent sovereignty over natural resources; and
- if it transfers its own population into the territory it occupies with apparent intent to colonise it, or systematically and knowingly provides protective conditions for mass civilian settlement that effectively deny the native people their right to self-determination.

If an Occupying Power does these things, the occupation itself could become unlawful on grounds of colonialism, with the attendant consequences under international law.[99] Notably, however, prolonged occupation does not *ipso facto* equate with colonialism. For instance, when South Africa refused to withdraw from South West Africa (today Namibia) after decades of occupation, the UN Security Council declared its presence there 'illegal' but not on grounds of colonialism.[100] Rather, a prolonged belligerent occupation must acquire the characteristics of colonialism – an open claim to sovereignty or through practices that have the effect of permanently denying the people's right to self-determination – in order to be unlawful on that basis.

Concluding that an occupation has acquired the attributes of colonialism has important legal consequences. First, an Occupying Power found to be practising colonialism is required to withdraw its administration from the territory it is holding under colonial rule. Operative paragraph 5 of the Declaration provides that

> immediate steps shall be taken in ... all other territories that have not yet attained independence, to transfer all powers to the peoples of those territories, without any conditions or reservations, in accordance with their freely expressed will and desire, without any distinction as to race, creed or colour, in order to enable them to enjoy complete independence and freedom.

Given the Declaration's concern with territorial integrity, the Occupying Power is also obliged not to fragment, divide or dismember the occupied territory prior to its withdrawal from that territory.

Second, a finding that an occupied population is also under colonial domination would support a claim that this population has a right to resist it.[101] This resistance must be exercised in accordance with the established rules and principles of international humanitarian and human rights law, and the people pursuing self-determination is 'entitled to seek and to receive support in accordance with the purposes and principles of the [UN] Charter'.[102]

### The prohibition of apartheid in international law

The first international instrument expressly to prohibit apartheid was the International Convention for the Elimination of All Forms of Racial Discrimination (ICERD), adopted in 1965.[103] ICERD is a multilateral human rights treaty that seeks, as its chapeau states, to 'build an international community free from all forms of racial segregation and racial discrimination'. Its Preamble cites a general concern with 'racial discrimination still in evidence in some areas of the world' and 'governmental policies based on racial superiority or hatred, *such as policies of apartheid,* segregation or separation'.[104] Article 3 then specifies the obligation of States parties to the Convention to oppose apartheid: 'States Parties particularly condemn racial segregation *and apartheid* and undertake to prevent, prohibit and eradicate all practices of this nature in territories under their jurisdiction.' Including a prohibition of apartheid in ICERD was an exception to the practice of the drafters not to refer to specific forms of discrimination in the treaty. The exception was made because apartheid was considered qualitatively different from other forms of racial discrimination 'in that it was the official policy of a State Member of the United Nations'.[105]

The Apartheid Convention – the International Convention on the Suppression and Punishment of the Crime of Apartheid – was adopted shortly after ICERD, in 1973, to provide a universal instrument that would make 'it possible to take more effective measures at the international and national levels with a view to the suppression and punishment of the crime of apartheid'.[106] The Apartheid Convention further declares that apartheid is a crime against humanity and provides a definition of that crime in Article 2. It also makes the offence an international crime subject to universal jurisdiction, which obliges all States that are parties to the Convention to adopt legislative measures to suppress, discourage and punish its violation.[107]

The Apartheid Convention provides a detailed definition of the crime of apartheid that guides the exhaustive review presented in Chapter 4. It gives several examples of 'inhuman acts' that are considered to amount to apartheid when committed 'for the purpose of establishing and maintaining domination by one racial group of persons over any other racial group of persons and systematically oppressing them'.[108] The formulation used in the Apartheid Convention is similar to that of the Rome Statute of the International Criminal Court, which defines the crime of apartheid as inhumane acts 'committed in the context of an institutionalised regime of systematic oppression and domination by one racial group over any other racial group and committed with the intention of maintaining that regime' (Article 7(2)(h)). Both instruments emphasise the systematic, institutionalised, and oppressive character of the discrimination involved in apartheid. The analysis in Chapter 4 of this study draws primarily on the formulation in the Apartheid Convention, informed also by the codification in the Rome Statute, and by reference to the apartheid practices of South Africa, which provide some indication as to what the international community has sought to prohibit.

Although apartheid is seen as a particularly pernicious manifestation of racial discrimination, the customary status of its prohibition is indicated by its configuration within UN instruments which aim at the eradication of racial discrimination more generally. Article 55 of the UN Charter lays the foundation, by requiring member States to promote 'universal respect for, and observance of, human rights and fundamental freedoms for all without distinction as to race, sex, language, or religion'.[109] Equally important is Article 2 of the Universal Declaration of Human Rights (1948), which states that 'Everyone is entitled to all the rights and freedoms set forth in this Declaration, without distinction of any kind, such as race, colour, sex, language, religion, political or other opinion, national or social origin, property, birth or other status'.[110] The subsequent adoption of ICERD was a more concerted effort to address racial discrimination, including the particular practice of apartheid. State parties to the Convention on the Elimination of Discrimination Against Women affirm that 'the eradication of apartheid, all forms of racism, racial discrimination, colonialism, neo-colonialism, aggression, foreign occupation and domination and interference in the internal affairs of States is essential to the full enjoyment of the rights of men and women'.[111] At the time of writing, there are 175 States parties to ICERD[112] and 185 States parties to the Convention on the Elimination of Discrimination Against Women,[113] demonstrating near-universal support and legal commitment to the elimination of racial discrimination and the prohibition of apartheid.

Although this study is not concerned with individual criminal responsibility for the crime of apartheid, noting that apartheid is in fact considered a crime against humanity clarifies the seriousness with which it is viewed under international law. The UN General Assembly first referred to apartheid as a crime against humanity in 1966.[114] In 1968, the same point was reiterated in the Proclamation of Tehran by the International Conference on Human Rights.[115] Its formulation as a crime by the Apartheid Convention of 1973 was followed in 1977 by inclusion of the crime of apartheid in Additional Protocol I to the 1949 Geneva Conventions[116] and in 1998 by the Rome Statute of the International Criminal Court.[117]

Although the majority of today's States (175) are parties to ICERD and so accept the prohibition of apartheid that it includes, fewer States (107) have ratified the Apartheid Convention.[118] This smaller number reflected, at an early juncture, the heightened political controversies when the Apartheid Convention was created, as well as later impressions that it was obsolete. Some States representatives expressed concern that the Convention was seeking to 'extend international criminal jurisdiction in a broad and ill-defined manner'.[119] A majority of States (168) have ratified Additional Protocol I to the Geneva Conventions of 1949,[120] however, and an ever-increasing number of States, currently standing at 108, have become parties to the Rome Statute of the International Criminal Court, which gives the Court jurisdiction over the crime of apartheid.[121] On the other hand, there is no demonstrable hostility to the apartheid provisions in these treaties by non-States parties and several non-parties to the Apartheid Convention have ratified the latter instruments (for example, the United Kingdom and South Africa).

Hence the prohibition of apartheid is considered a rule of customary law[122] and can be considered a norm of *jus cogens* which creates obligations *erga omnes* – that is, obligations owed by all States towards the community of States as a whole.[123] The Court has stated that such obligations would arise 'from the principles and rules concerning the basic rights of the human person, including protection from slavery and from racial discrimination'.¹²⁴ If the prohibition of racial discrimination is to be considered a rule of *jus cogens*,¹²⁵ then the prohibition of apartheid, which addresses a particularly severe form of racial discrimination, is even more so a rule of *jus cogens* entailing obligations *erga omnes*. The International Law Commission also views the prohibition of apartheid as a peremptory norm and contends that the practise of apartheid would amount to 'a serious breach on a widespread scale of an international obligation of essential importance for safeguarding the human being'.¹²⁶ The Commission has further observed that States generally agree about the peremptory character of the prohibition on apartheid and that apartheid has been prohibited by a treaty admitting of no exception.¹²⁷

### The legal authority of an ICJ advisory opinion

The function of an advisory opinion by the ICJ is to provide legal advice to international organisations. Individual States cannot request an advisory opinion: this power is reserved to UN organs and bodies which have been authorised to do so under Article 96 of the UN Charter.¹²⁸ Formally, advisory opinions of the International Court are not binding, but they have normative force as they constitute an authoritative statement of international law about the question posed.¹²⁹

Earlier ICJ advisory opinions regarding South West Africa (now Namibia) suggest the legal authority of an ICJ advisory opinion. In 1956, Judge Lauterpacht noted that the advisory opinion on the *International status of South West Africa* (1950)¹³⁰ had been accepted and approved by the General Assembly. Consequently:

> [w]hatever may be its binding force as part of international law – a question upon which the Court need not express a view – it is the law recognized by the United Nations. It continues to be so although the Government of South Africa has declined to accept it as binding upon it and although it has acted in disregard of the international obligations as declared by the Court in that Opinion.¹³¹

Similarly, on 2 August 2004 when the General Assembly formally acknowledged its receipt of the *Wall* advisory opinion, it demanded that 'Israel, the occupying Power, comply with its legal obligations as mentioned in the advisory opinion'.¹³² Thus determinations of the ICJ regarding the obligations incumbent upon Israel can be understood as authoritative international law applicable to Israel.¹³³ And the findings of the Court can be relied upon – despite the fact that Israel, like apartheid South Africa in its day, has chosen not to act in conformity with the Court's previous rulings.

### CONCLUSION

This chapter has introduced the fundamental legal concepts that structure this study and determine its principal themes. If the OPT remain in a situation of belligerent occupation by Israel – a question examined in some detail in Chapter 2 – then they are territories over which Israel does not possess sovereignty but only a temporary right of administration. Corollary to this right are legal obligations that international law imposes on Israel regarding the conduct of that administration. Primarily, Israel must abide by the law of armed conflict – especially relevant provisions of the Hague Regulations and the Fourth Geneva Convention – in its administration of the territories. These provisions of international humanitarian law regarding belligerent occupation are supplemented by international human rights law, which also applies in occupied territory.

On this basis, this study tests for the two regimes identified by John Dugard in his January 2007 report as Special Rapporteur: colonialism and apartheid. These regimes have been established in this chapter as egregious violations of human rights and the right to self-determination. Colonialism denies the right to self-determination because it prevents, and aims to prevent, a people from exercising freely its right to determine its own future through its own political institutions. Apartheid is an aggravated form of racial discrimination, manifesting as an institutionalised system of oppression and domination by one racial group over other racial groups. The rules of international law regarding both regimes are peremptory: the duty not to practise them is an obligation owed by all States to the international community as a whole. All States have an interest in ensuring that these rules are respected. Faced with their violation, all have the duty to cooperate to end their violation; all have the duty not to recognise the illegal situation arising from their violation; and all have the duty not to render aid or assistance to the delinquent State which might contribute to maintaining that illegal situation.

Chapter 2 applies this relatively abstract framework to the OPT. In particular, it examines whether the Palestinian people possess the right to self-determination, the international legal status of the OPT, and the application of Israeli law in the OPT. Whether Israel is practising colonialism is then explored in Chapter 3, and whether Israel's practices constitute apartheid is reviewed in Chapter 4.

# 2
# The Legal Context in the Occupied Palestinian Territories

INTRODUCTION

Assessing whether Israel's practices in the Occupied Palestinian Territories (OPT) constitute regimes of apartheid or colonialism first requires establishing the 'entire legal system' that forms the context for these questions.[1] In the OPT, this system includes not only how Israeli civil and military laws operate generally but also some basic legal facts: especially, the legal status of the Palestinians and their territories, and Israel's consequent legal obligations and authority under international law.

The legal status of the Palestinians includes their status as 'protected persons' under the law of occupation and their right to self-determination in the OPT (a legal principle discussed generally in Chapter 1). The latter question further involves establishing the status of the OPT, in which they are presently seeking to express this right. Addressing this issue requires considering Israel's arguments about their status – for example, the 'missing reversioner' argument, the status of East Jerusalem and the status of the Gaza Strip after Israel's 'disengagement' in 2005, and whether the Oslo Accords have altered Israel's obligations as the Occupying Power. It also involves considering whether the prolonged nature of this occupation – having endured over 40 years – has loosened the restrictions and responsibilities placed on Israel by the Fourth Geneva Convention. A general review of how Israeli laws operate in the OPT can then focus on matters of special concern here: how Israeli civil and military law are employed strategically to accord different treatment to Jewish settlers and Palestinians living in the OPT.

Taken together, all these considerations inform and guide the tests for underlying regimes of colonialism and apartheid in Chapters 3 and 4.

THE PALESTINIAN PEOPLE'S RIGHT TO SELF-DETERMINATION

The question of Palestinian statehood

In 2011, whether Palestine is, or should be recognised as, a fully independent State is a controversial and politically charged question that, as this book goes to press, is under consideration by the United Nations (UN) Security Council. For purposes here, however, the contributors did not consider it necessary to adopt a position on this question. A study that considers the application of human rights and humanitarian law in the OPT need only establish that the international legal status of the OPT is that of territories under belligerent occupation and that the Palestinian people have the right to self-determination within these territories. To do this, however, we must review the historical legal history of the territory in which Palestinian self-determination and independent statehood is being proposed, and this touches tangentially on questions of statehood as it involves the changing normative territorial basis for Palestinian self-determination. A short review is therefore engaged here.

The League of Nations Covenant provided that Palestine should be considered an 'independent nation' as early as 1919. Article 22 of the Covenant, which established the mandate system, even indicated that Palestine should be 'provisionally recognised' as an independent state:

> Certain communities formerly belonging to the Turkish Empire have reached a stage of development where their existence as independent nations can be provisionally recognized subject to the rendering of administrative advice and assistance by a Mandatory until such time as they are able to stand alone.

In 1937, the British Colonial Secretary affirmed that the mandate for Palestine was intended to ensure the self-determination of the territory's people. Palestine 'should be developed, not as a British colony permanently under British rule, but as a self-governing State or States with the right of autonomous evolution'.[2]

The 1945 Pact of the League of Arab States cited this legal history to support its own view in accepting Palestine as a 'member state':

> At the end of the last Great War, Palestine, together with the other Arab States, was separated from the Ottoman Empire. She became independent, not belonging to any other State ... Even though Palestine was not able to control her own destiny, it was on the basis of the recognition of her independence that the Covenant of the League of Nations determined a system of government for her. Her existence and her independence among the nations can, therefore, no more be questioned de jure than the independence of any of the other Arab States.[3]

Within three years, however, UN proposals for partition and open war had thrown the status and ultimate disposition of the Mandate Palestinian territory into doubt. In 1949, Israel was recognised as an independent State in part of the mandate territory and admitted to the United Nations, thus effectively partitioning the territory (although not on the terms the UN had proposed, as discussed later). The rest of Mandate Palestine remained in legal limbo.

Forty years later, the right of the 'Palestinian people' (as discussed later) to self-determination and independent statehood had mostly devolved – in international diplomacy, politics and law – to the OPT. In November 1988, the Palestine National Council declared the existence of the State of Palestine, implying that its borders were those of the OPT,[4] and the Palestine Liberation Organisation (PLO) has used the language of statehood in its own diplomacy ever since. The General Assembly then acknowledged that it was 'aware' of this declaration and affirmed 'the need to enable the Palestinian people to exercise their sovereignty over their territory occupied since 1967'.[5] In the same resolution, the General Assembly decided to re-designate the UN observer mission of the PLO simply as 'Palestine' – without, however, changing its non-state status. On the basis of the 1988 Algiers Declaration, approximately 100 States recognised Palestine as a State and the PLO's membership in the Arab League was transferred to the 'State of Palestine'. In January 2009, the Palestinian Authority (PA)[6] spoke in the name of the 'Government of Palestine' in recognising the jurisdiction of the International Criminal Court (ICC) regarding 'acts committed on the territory of Palestine since 1 July 2002'.[7]

Nonetheless, UN Security Council Resolutions 1397 (2002) and 1515 (2003) have referred to an independent 'Palestine' only as a 'vision' for the future. In the *Wall* advisory opinion, the International Court of Justice (ICJ) also treated Palestine's statehood as not yet established, urging 'as soon as possible, on the basis of international law, a negotiated solution to the outstanding problems *and the establishment of a Palestinian State*, existing side by side with Israel and its other neighbours, with peace and security for all in the region'.[8] The PA's diplomatic drive in 2011 for admission of 'Palestine' to the UN as a member State – and Israel's strong opposition of this move – indicate that both parties recognise the importance of UN membership to realising Palestine's full diplomatic and normative standing as a State. Thus international legal practice and doctrine has remained divided about whether Palestine already fulfils the requirements of statehood.[9]

Examination of this question remains tangential to this study, however, because assessing whether Israel's occupation is illegal on grounds of colonialism or apartheid requires establishing just three legal facts: (1) that Palestinians have the right to self-determination in the territory of Mandate Palestine; (2) that the OPT comprise territory in which this right can be expressed; and (3) that the OPT are being held under belligerent occupation. If these three criteria hold, then they establish the foundation for determining whether Israel's practices amount to colonialism, in denying the Palestinian people their right to self-determination, or apartheid, in establishing a discriminatory regime in territory where Israel holds ultimate and effective administrative control.

### The right of the Palestinian people to self-determination

The existence of a 'Palestinian people' is firmly established in international law and diplomacy, including by Israel and the ICJ.[10] As the ICJ observed, in its *Wall* advisory opinion:

> As regards the principle of the right of peoples to self-determination, the Court observes that the existence of a 'Palestinian people' is no longer in issue. Such existence has moreover been recognized by Israel in the exchange of letters of 9 September 1993 between Mr. Yasser Arafat, President of the Palestine Liberation Organization (PLO) and Mr. Yitzhak Rabin, Israeli

Prime Minister. In that correspondence, the President of the PLO recognized 'the right of the State of Israel to exist in peace and security' and made various other commitments. In reply, the Israeli Prime Minister informed him that, in the light of those commitments, 'the Government of Israel has decided to recognize the PLO as the representative of the Palestinian people'. The Israeli-Palestinian Interim Agreement on the West Bank and the Gaza Strip of 28 September 1995 also refers a number of times to the Palestinian people and its 'legitimate rights' ... The Court considers that those rights include the right to self-determination, as the General Assembly has moreover recognized on a number of occasions ...[11]

The question then is to identify the substance of this right. As explained in Chapter 1, the substance of a right to self-determination may change over time, regarding both the character of the people that holds the right to self-determination and the territory in which that people can express its right. The internal character of what is now understood as the 'Palestinian people' has changed since the Mandate era, as the conflict has split the original designation of the territory's population from one people holding the right to self-determination into two. Territorial and other conditions have also changed since the principle of self-determination was vested in the populations of Palestine as a whole, when the British Mandate was created in 1922.[12]

*The legal status of the Palestinians as a people*

It is a point often elided in international law (which is, indeed, ill-equipped to handle it) that 'peoples', while established as having the crucial right to self-determination, are empirically often not unchanging social units. Rather, a 'people' is a collective identity developed through social experience and political experience, and thus constructed both internally and in relation to other peoples, much as other group identities are constructed. Like other terms for group identities (such as 'race', discussed in Chapter 4), before the Second World War diplomatic and legal language used the term 'peoples' more loosely to refer sometimes to national groups but also to what today we would call 'ethnic groups' or possibly 'nationalities': hence it was not inconsistent for the British Mandate to use the terms 'Arab people' and 'Jewish people' for parts of the whole population of Palestine while simultaneously conceiving of that population as one national unit being prepared for independent statehood. The UN Charter, by establishing that 'peoples' have the right to self-determination, ramped up political tensions regarding the term by implying that status as a 'people' conveyed a potential right of secession (as demonstrated in the extreme sensitivities by UN member States during drafting of the Declaration on the Rights of Indigenous Peoples).

Since the Second World War, therefore, to make a claim to self-determination is to affirm an identity as a 'people' in this specifically political, nationalist mode. As this step involves conveying specific political rights to group members, it also requires establishing the terms and boundaries for group membership more precisely. Claiming the right to self-determination further involves affirming an ancestral or other compelling moral bond with the geographic territory in which that right is being claimed. As the political context for such claims may evolve, the precise territorial boundaries and even the composition of the 'people' seeking self-determination may also evolve.

The original terms for self-determination established by the League of Nations for the British Mandate for Palestine clearly held that the entire population of Palestine – including Muslims, Christians, Jews and all other residents – was to become one unified and independent nation-state. Yet over subsequent decades, the term 'Palestinian people' came by stages to mean the Arab population only and to exclude Jewish residents of the territory, as these members were co-opted into the Zionist movement's political construction of the 'Jewish people'. A factor essential to reconstructing the 'Palestinian people' in this sense was indeed the late-nineteenth-century Zionist movement's affirmation that Jews everywhere constitute one people and therefore have the right to self-determination in Palestine. Thus the internal meaning of the 'Palestinian people' was forcibly reconstructed in a dialectic with Zionist affirmations about the 'Jewish people'. (A later example of this Zionist dialectic, on the opposite tack, was Golda Meir's often-misinterpreted denial that the Palestinian 'people', in this unitary political sense, has ever existed as such.)

The modern construction of the 'Palestinian people' thus traces to the terms of the Mandate for Palestine. Palestine was a Class A Mandate, defined by Article 22 of the League of Nations Covenant to include territories that had 'reached a stage of development where their *existence as independent nations* can be provisionally recognised ... until such time as they are able to stand alone'. The Mandate itself, reflecting British and French agreements, distinguished 'Palestine' from other territories in Greater Syria and so established the territorial jurisdiction for Palestinian statehood, implying that the territory's territorially defined (non-sectarian) 'people' had the right to self-determination.

The League of Nation's language in establishing the Palestine Mandate confused this purely territorial premise for self-determination, however. In the Balfour Declaration of 1917,[13] the British Government had authorised a 'national home for the Jewish people' in Palestine, with the qualifier, 'it being clearly understood that nothing shall be done which might prejudice the civil and religious rights of existing non-Jewish *communities* in Palestine' (emphasis added). In 1922, the Mandate for Palestine provided for establishing a Jewish 'national home' with the same qualifier. By recognising the existence of a 'Jewish *people*' that had unspecified legal and political unity with Jewish 'communities' in Palestine, the Mandate thus distinguished between Jewish and non-Jewish 'communities' and 'other sectors of the population'. Reflecting the legal muddiness of the term 'people' at this juncture, the terms of the Mandate made no explicit reference to the 'non-Jewish population' being a distinct 'people' yet indicated that other 'peoples' existed by referring (in Article 9) to 'various peoples and communities' in the territory. The Palestine Mandate provided that the Zionist Organisation would function as the 'Jewish agency', which would cooperate with the Mandate authorities to facilitate Jewish immigration, naturalisation, and development of the country.[14] (The Mandate also made English, Arabic and Hebrew the official languages.[15])

Yet the Mandate also specified, in Article 15, that 'No discrimination of any kind shall be made between the inhabitants of Palestine on the ground of race, religion or language', thus suggesting that creation of a Jewish national home was not meant to entail any physical division of Palestine or its people. This non-discrimination clause did not fully clarify what was intended, however.[16] The Zionist Organisation sometimes denied that its goal of establishing a 'Jewish national home' in Palestine meant the eventual formation of a separate Jewish state:[17] for example, the 1921 resolution of the Zionist Congress affirmed that 'The determination of the Jewish people is to live with the Arab people on terms of concord and mutual respect, and together with them to make the common home into a flourishing community.'[18] The Jewish Agency and Zionist programme was, however, directed toward establishing a Jewish state both in word and deed, by purchasing and reserving land for exclusively Jewish use, organising mass Jewish immigration and setting up a proto-government for the Jewish *yishuv* (settlement community). Resulting tensions triggered not only Palestinian Arab rebellion and violent clashes with Zionist and British forces but also legal controversies about the terms of the Mandate. By now, the term 'people' had crystallised to describe both the Jewish and Arab populations. For example, in May 1939, the British Government issued a White Paper clarifying its vision that an independent Palestine should be established as a 'state in which the *two peoples in Palestine*, Arabs and Jews, share authority in such a way that the eventual interests of each are secured'.[19] The next day, the Zionist movement issued a proclamation denouncing the White Paper and vowing that 'the Jewish *population* will fight it to the uttermost',[20] but other Zionist documents of the period clarified that this 'population' was considered the local part of 'the Jewish people'.

Nonetheless, the British vision of a unitary nation-state in Palestine was sustained in the recommendations of the 1946 Anglo-American Committee of Enquiry and the 1948 draft UN Trusteeship Agreement. In 1947, the Second Subcommittee of the General Assembly on the question of Palestine (composed of all the Arab States members and Colombia) argued that the terms of the Mandate legally precluded partition and recommended a unitary state in which discrimination on the basis of ethnicity would be prohibited.[21] By contrast, the 1937 Peel Partition Plan[22] and what came to be known as the UN Partition Plan, formulated in General Assembly Resolution 181 of 1947,[23] recommended partition of Palestine into a 'Jewish state' and an 'Arab state'. Thus Resolution 181 altered the original terms of the Mandate (and reversed the British position as clarified in 1939) by proposing Palestine's geographic division into two self-determination units serving two distinct 'peoples' who were separately understood to have the right to self-determination. The gerrymandered map proposed in Resolution 181 was overtaken by events, however, as Zionist forces swept across the proposed boundaries of the Jewish state during the war of 1947–48. The final ceasefire lines in 1949 established the de facto borders of Israel as comprising 78 per cent of Mandate Palestine, including the entire Galilee and the stretch of Mediterranean coast that had been designated for the Arab state, except for the small coastal belt that became the Gaza Strip.

In the aftermath of the war, the Palestinian Arab population's right of self-determination was left without expression and was soon effectively submerged as a concern for international law and diplomacy, displaced by concerns for the return of 'Arab refugees'.[24] In 1964, the Arab League formed the PLO to work toward the 'liberation' and reunification of the territory. In 1968, the PLO was taken over by a new generation of Palestinian liberation parties dominated by Fatah under the leadership of Yasir Arafat. In a revised PLO Charter, this new PLO explicitly committed the organisation to 'the total liberation of Palestine' on behalf of the 'Arab Palestinian people'.[25] The PLO Charter defined the organisation's purpose as 'national struggle for the liberation of Palestine' from 'forces of Zionism and of imperialism', and explicitly linked the liberation movement to pan-Arab nationalism and decolonisation in Africa and southeast Asia. In Article 6, the Charter specified that 'The Jews who had normally resided in Palestine until the beginning of the Zionist invasion' (a date not specified, but roughly associated with the major rise in Jewish immigration beginning in the 1910s) would be considered 'Palestinian'. As significant portions of Palestine's pre-Zionist Jewish population had been religious scholars of European origin, this left their conceptual fit into the 'Arab Palestinian people' unclear.

All subsequent language in international law indicated that the 'people of Palestine' was now distinguished from the entire population of Mandate Palestine, in clearly excluding residents of the State of Israel, which had been admitted as a member State and whose Jewish citizens did not face problems with self-determination.[26] Thus, in 1969, the UN General Assembly responded to the PLO's 1968 political initiative by recognising the 'inalienable rights' of 'the people of Palestine', meaning the Arab population. In November 1970, the General Assembly passed a resolution affirming 'the legitimacy of the struggle of peoples under colonial and alien domination recognized as being entitled to the right of self-determination'[27] and condemning 'those Governments that deny the right to self-determination of peoples recognized as being entitled to it, especially of the peoples of southern Africa and Palestine'.[28] A week later, the General Assembly passed another resolution recognising that 'the people of Palestine are entitled to equal rights and self-determination, in accordance with the Charter of the United Nations'.[29] In 1973, the General Assembly declared that both the Palestinian people and the peoples of southern Africa had a right to engage in armed struggle in pursuit of their right of self-determination.[30]

Thus, since 1967, the term 'Palestinian people' has come to mean that portion of the Arab population of Mandate Palestine that has remained stateless (although this has, notoriously, left the status of Palestinian citizens of Israel both ambiguous and controversial). In 1975, the General Assembly expressed its grave concern that no progress had been made toward 'the exercise by the Palestinian people of its inalienable rights in Palestine, including the right to self-determination without external interference and the right to national independence and sovereignty'.[31] It also expressed concern that the Palestinians had not been able 'to return to their homes and property from which they have been displaced and uprooted'.[32] It then established a Committee on the Exercise of the Inalienable Rights of the Palestinian People to assist them in exercising their right of self-determination.[33] Since then, the General Assembly has repeatedly reaffirmed the right of the Palestinian people to 'self-determination, national independence, territorial integrity, and national unity and sovereignty without external interference'.[34] The only question was precisely where that right should (or could) be expressed.

*The territorial substance of Palestinian self-determination*
Like the evolving meaning of 'Palestinian people', the territorial basis for Palestinian self-determination has also altered, initially in its early separation from lands that would become the state of Jordan. As ratified by the League of Nations in July 1922, the Mandate for Palestine included within its territorial scope land east of the River Jordan. As the Balfour Declaration had also authorised a 'Jewish national home' in Palestine, these wider boundaries complicated British plans to grant part of Palestine to Arab allies from the First World War (in practice, this would be King Abdullah, a son of Sherif Hussein of Mecca). In September 1922, the British Government therefore excluded the east side of river from all the provisions dealing with Jewish settlement.[35] Although, technically, only one Mandate existed, Britain thus adopted separate regimes for the two territories, administering territory west of the river as 'Palestine' and territory east of the river as 'Transjordan'. Transfer of authority proceeded incrementally and culminated in the independence of Transjordan as a separate state under Hashemite rule.[36]

This history explains why, although representatives of the State of Israel and others sometimes argue that Jordan is the Palestinian national home, this argument has no substance in international law. It was already obsolete in 1945, when the Supreme Court of Palestine ruled:

> Trans-Jordan has a government entirely independent of Palestine – the laws of Palestine are not applicable in Trans-Jordan nor are their laws applicable here. Moreover, although the High Commissioner of Palestine is also High Commissioner for Trans-Jordan, Trans-Jordan has an entirely independent government under the rule of an Amir and apart from certain reserved matters the High Commissioner cannot interfere with the government of Trans-Jordan – at the most he can advise from time to time. His Britannic Majesty has entered into agreements with His Highness the Amir of Trans-Jordan in which the existence of an independent government in Trans-Jordan under the rule of the Amir has been specifically recognised (see Agreement dated 20.2.28). It is clear there from that Trans-Jordan exercises its powers of legislation and administration through its own constitutional government which is entirely separate and independent from that of Palestine.[37]

As a result of this early administrative separation of Palestine and Transjordan, the *uti possidetis* rule[38] excludes any consideration that the territory to the east of the River Jordan is relevant to the question of the self-determination of the Palestinian Arab population. As James Crawford has observed, issues of self-determination regarding 'Palestine properly so called, that is the area west of the 1922 line' must be considered on their own.[39] This same view was adopted by the International Court in the *Wall* advisory opinion.[40]

Some have nonetheless argued that the ultimate sovereign of the West Bank is properly the Hashemite Kingdom of Jordan, because Jordan administered the West Bank (including East Jerusalem) from 1948 until 1967.[41] In this view, self-determination for Palestinians in the West Bank should be expressed by their adopting Jordanian citizenship and West Bank land (or portions of it) should be transferred to Jordanian sovereignty. A former legal advisor to the Israeli Foreign Ministry has emphasised Jordan's potential role:

> Since Israel seized the West Bank from the Kingdom of Jordan in the 1967 Six-Day War, this territory has essentially been disputed land with the claimants being Israel, Jordan, and the Palestinians. Its ultimate status and boundaries will require negotiation between the parties, according to Security Council Resolutions 242 and 338.[42]

After the 1948 war ended, Jordan did adopt a policy to incorporate the West Bank. On 24 April 1950, the Jordanian House of Assembly passed a resolution which provided, in part, that '[a]pproval is granted to complete unity between the two banks of the Jordan, the Eastern and the Western, and their amalgamation in one single State ... [although] this unity shall in no way be connected with the final settlement of Palestine's just case within the limits of national hopes, Arab cooperation and international justice'. After the Six-Day War in 1967, the United States suggested to King Hussein of Jordan that it was prepared to support the accession of the West Bank to Jordan 'with minor boundary rectifications'.[43] Reflecting this so-called 'Jordan option', Israel's stance between 1967 and 1988 was to ignore calls by Palestinians in the West Bank for a separate state, preferring instead to deal with Jordan.[44]

By contrast, the Arab League declared that Jordan's 1950 annexation of the West Bank violated the League's resolution of 12 April 1950, which had prohibited the annexation of any part of Palestine. A compromise was reached between the League and Jordan, and on 31 May 1950 Jordan affirmed again that the annexation was without prejudice to the final settlement of the Palestine issue.[45] Only the United Kingdom and Pakistan formally recognised Jordan's annexation of the West Bank (not including Jerusalem).[46] Jordan formally renounced its claim to sovereignty over the West Bank in 1988.[47] In the Israel-Jordan Peace Treaty of 1994, the boundary employed was the Mandate boundary (as amended in 1922). Article 3 of the Treaty provided, in part, that 'the boundary definition under the Mandate' would be considered 'the permanent, secure and recognized international boundary between Jordan and Israel, without prejudice to the status of any territories that came under Israeli military government control in 1967'.[48]

With the 'Jordan option' regarding the West Bank set aside, the territory considered in most international law to constitute the Palestinian people's self-determination unit has become the portion of Mandate Palestine occupied by Israel during the 1967 war: that is, the West Bank (including East Jerusalem) and the Gaza Strip. In the Oslo Accords, Israel and the PLO agreed that the West Bank and Gaza Strip form 'a single territorial unit' whose integrity is to be preserved pending the conclusion of permanent status negotiations.[49] Israel's Supreme Court, also relying on the Israeli-Palestinian Interim Agreement, has affirmed Israel's recognition of the unity of the West Bank and Gaza as a single territorial unit.[50] The Wye River Memorandum and the Sharm el-Sheikh Memorandum prohibited 'any step that will change the status of the West Bank and the Gaza Strip in accordance with the Interim Agreement'.[51] In its written submissions to the ICJ during the *Wall* advisory opinion process, the PLO referred to these territories as 'the territorial sphere over which the Palestinian people are entitled to exercise their right of self-determination'.[52] The ICJ's conclusion that the Interim Agreement affirmed the Palestinian people's right to self-determination[53] could be read as confirming the OPT to be the territorial self-determination unit upon which the Palestinian people is entitled to exercise the right to self-determination. The UN General Assembly, in a 2007 pronouncement concerning the territorial dismemberment of the West Bank by the construction of the Wall, also stressed 'the need for respect for and preservation of the territorial unity, contiguity and integrity of all of the OPT, including East Jerusalem'.[54] UN Security Council, after Israel's 'Operation Cast Lead' in the Gaza Strip in December 2008–January 2009, stressed that 'the Gaza Strip constitutes an integral part of the territory occupied in 1967 and will be a part of the Palestinian state'.[55]

None of this signifies that the territorial substance of Palestinian self-determination, having changed since 1922, is now frozen and will never change again. Having the right to self-determination, Palestinians may elect to redefine the territory in which to express that right through, for example, mutually negotiated adjustments to the 1967 Green Line, further capitulations to territorial advances in Israeli settlement, or even by reclaiming the right to self-determination in all of Mandate Palestine, as proposed and conceived by the League of Nations and the British Mandate. They may even reject the Zionist doctrine that Mandate Palestine's population consists of 'two peoples in one land' by affirming that the entire population of Palestine is properly one nation and therefore one 'people' that has been wrongfully divided (thus emulating the African National Congress's position that South Africa was rightly one nation belonging 'to all the people who live in it').

Such speculations need not be considered here, however, as the legal principle essential to this study has been established: that the OPT comprise territory in which the Palestinian people now has the right to self-determination. Thus Israel's system of governance in those territories, which has deprived the Palestinians of the capacity to express that right, can be examined for constituting regimes that are considered infamous for doing so – colonialism and apartheid.

## LEGAL STATUS OF THE OPT

The Government of Israel and its defenders have rejected the common assumption that the Palestinian territories are under belligerent occupation, referring to them as 'administered' or 'disputed'. Within Israel, the matter is often elided entirely by referring to the West Bank as 'Judea and Samaria', and Israeli legal scholarship often employs this term.[56] A former legal advisor to the Israeli Foreign Ministry has explained this view:

> Since Israel seized the West Bank from the Kingdom of Jordan in the 1967 Six-Day War, this territory has essentially been disputed land with the claimants being Israel, Jordan, and the Palestinians. Its ultimate status and boundaries will require negotiation between the parties, according to Security Council Resolutions 242 and 338.[57]

Several justifications for this view have been proffered. One is that the West Bank and Gaza Strip lacked legitimate sovereigns when Israel seized them during the 1967 war – the 'missing reversioner' argument – and thus the law of occupation does not apply. Israel has further claimed to annex East Jerusalem and thus remove it permanently from the regime of occupation. Other arguments tacitly accept that the Palestinian territories were under belligerent occupation until the Oslo Accords but that their status has now changed as the PA has assumed authority. Finally, Israel's unilateral 'disengagement' and withdrawal of settlements from the Gaza Strip in 2005 is frequently argued to have terminated Israel's status as Occupying Power there. Although the international community has rejected all these arguments, they nonetheless require attention and are considered here.

### The 'missing reversioner' argument

Immediately after the 1967 war, Israeli legal advisors accepted that the West Bank and Gaza were occupied territories and that the Fourth Geneva Convention was therefore the governing law in the OPT.[58] This position was soon reversed, however, and the 'missing reversioner' argument gained currency in Israeli legal and political circles.[59] Briefly, this argument holds that Israel is not a belligerent occupant in the OPT because neither Jordan nor Egypt, which had been holding the West Bank and Gaza Strip respectively, were true and legitimate sovereigns there. (Notably, this argument contradicts other Israeli arguments about the 'Jordan option', discussed in the previous section.)

According to this argument, Jordan and Egypt invaded Mandate Palestine in 1948 in order to eradicate Israel and so used force unlawfully in contravention of Article 2(4) of the United Nations Charter.[60] This means they acquired control over the West Bank and Gaza Strip unlawfully, and so were entitled, at most, to claim the status of belligerent occupants of these territories.[61]

Hence they have no rights to regain these territories and no legitimate interest or authority to intervene in Israel's administration of them. In the event of Israel's withdrawal, control over the OPT does not automatically 'revert' to them, should Israel withdraw, as it would if they had been legal sovereigns. Hence Israel has no obligation to consider their rights as 'reversioners' in terms of Article 43 of the Hague Regulations. In this argument, Israel is in lawful control of the territories because no other State can show better title. (Blum even contends that Israel's possession of the territories is 'virtually indistinguishable from an absolute title ... valid *erga omnes*'.[62]) Consequently, only those rules of international humanitarian law that are narrowly intended to safeguard the humanitarian rights of the civilian population can be considered to apply.[63]

Those who have rejected the 'missing reversioner' argument have, ironically, included a legal advisor to the Israeli Foreign Ministry, Theodor Meron, who in September 1967 wrote a legal opinion holding that the Fourth Geneva Convention did apply and noting that the international community had rejected Israel's claim to the contrary.[64] Forty years later, in its advisory opinion regarding the *Wall*, the ICJ ruled unanimously that the Fourth Geneva Convention applied to any armed conflict between High Contracting Parties and it was therefore irrelevant whether territory occupied during that conflict was under their juridical sovereignty.[65] The ICJ based this interpretation largely on the drafting history of the Fourth Geneva Convention, the practice of parties to the Convention, and the views of the International Committee of the Red Cross/Red Crescent (ICRC), General Assembly and Security Council as well as Israel's Supreme Court.[66]

Further, Israel had contradicted its own argument in practice by not contesting the lawfulness of Jordan's control of the West Bank prior to 1967 or for years later.[67] On the contrary, Israel had sought to conclude a peace treaty after the Six-Day War which would have returned the West Bank to Jordan, albeit with modified borders. Jordan's repossession of the West Bank was indeed the premise of the diplomatic negotiations and exchanges which preceded the adoption of Security Council Resolution 242. Israel's implicit recognition that Jordan possessed title and rights to the West Bank thus negates the 'missing reversioner' argument and the rationale for claiming that the Fourth Geneva Convention is inapplicable.

### East Jerusalem: status as occupied territory

The State of Israel claims that East Jerusalem – the eastern part of the city, held under Jordanian rule between 1948 and 1967 – has been annexed permanently to Israel and is no longer occupied territory. This claim was made immediately after the 1967 war, when the Knesset passed legislation affirming that 'law, jurisdiction and administration' of the State of Israel shall extend to any area of Israel designated by order of the government.[68] The following day, the Israeli government used this amendment to place East Jerusalem under Israeli judicial and administrative control and extended the boundaries of the Jerusalem Municipality over that same area. The East Jerusalem Municipality was ordered to cease operations on 29 June 1967 and Israel completed its annexation by integrating the city's services into one municipal authority. In 1980, Israel confirmed Jerusalem's status as the capital of Israel in its Basic Law.[69]

Thus, much as France did in Algeria,[70] Israel absorbed East Jerusalem into its own territory and has proceeded to exercise sovereign rights there. That this consolidation is intended to be permanent is indicated by Israel's construction of a vast urban complex of integrated Jewish 'neighbourhoods' (housing and commercial complexes) surrounding the entire city and a transportation network that seamlessly connects Jewish urban growth (settlements) in occupied East Jerusalem to Jewish neighbourhoods in West Jerusalem.[71] It is also indicated by Israel's repeated diplomatic insistence that Jerusalem should never again be 'divided'.

Israel's claim to sovereignty over the territory of East Jerusalem has not been recognised as lawful by the international community, however, and is considered null and void on several counts.[72] First, UN General Assembly Resolution 181 recommended that Jerusalem, as the administrative seat of Mandate Palestine and considered holy by three major faiths, should be administered as a *corpus separatum* in which both the Jewish State and the Arab State, possibly with the assistance of the United Nations, would have some authority. This precept has endured in the diplomatic premise that final arrangements for governance of Jerusalem not be pre-empted by one party to the conflict. Second, Israel gained control over East Jerusalem through military conquest, which is inadmissible as a way for any state to gain territory.[73] According to Article 2(4) of the UN Charter, as well as UN Security Council Resolution 242, the prohibition on acquiring territory by force is indeed a peremptory norm of *jus cogens*.[74] Third, Israel's annexation of Jerusalem dismembers the West Bank by dividing East Jerusalem from the rest of Palestinian occupied territory. As discussed in Chapter 1, international law regarding decolonisation as well as friendly relations among states prohibits the violation of territorial integrity that is under foreign domination.[75]

Fourth, and most obviously in this case, international humanitarian law proscribes any alteration in the status of an occupied territory by the Occupying Power, in which sovereignty can never vest. For example, Article 47 of the Fourth Geneva Convention explicitly prohibits an Occupying Power from 'any annexation ... of the whole or part of the occupied territory'. The ICRC's authoritative commentary on the Fourth Geneva Convention confirms that 'occupation as a result of war, while representing actual possession to all appearances, cannot imply any right whatsoever to dispose of territory'.[76]

In conclusion, Israel's annexation of East Jerusalem is unlawful, does not affect that territory's status under international law, and does not impinge on the application of the law of armed conflict to protect the local population. The UN Security Council has supported this view through several resolutions, reiterating its early declaration in Resolution 252 of 1968 that 'all legislative and administrative measures and actions taken by Israel which purport to alter the status of Jerusalem ... are invalid and cannot change that status'.[77]

## Legal implications of the Oslo Accords

It could be argued that the Oslo Accords have altered the legal framework for analysing Israeli practices in the OPT by extinguishing Israel's responsibility for their governance. Several arguments drawing from international law could support this premise. First, the Accords could be held to have ended the condition of belligerent occupation by transferring governance of the OPT to the 'Palestinian Interim Self-Government Authority' (PA) and so terminating, or at least greatly reducing, Israel's obligations as Occupying Power regarding the civilian Palestinian population.[78] Second, the Fourth Geneva Convention provides that 'special agreements' can legitimately be concluded between the Occupying Power and 'the authorities of the occupied territories' if they constitute 'more favourable measures' regarding conditions for protected persons. Upon review, however, these argument are also found here to fail.

### *The Oslo Accords and Palestinian governance*

The term 'Oslo Accords' refers here to those formal agreements signed by the Israeli government and the PLO, which, among other measures, established the PA and authorised it to assume limited responsibilities for governance within the OPT.[79] These agreements were first formalised as the Declaration of Principles on Interim Self-Government Arrangements (1993), sometimes called Oslo I, and later were elaborated as the Interim Agreement on the West Bank and Gaza Strip (1995), usually called Oslo II.[80]

The Accords stipulated that the West Bank be administered in three territorial categories, or jurisdictional zones, known as Areas A, B and C (excluding East Jerusalem, whose future was deferred to 'permanent status' negotiations). By the terms of Oslo II, in Area A – which amounted to approximately 2 per cent of the West Bank and encompassed six major Palestinian cities – the PA was vested with exclusive authority over the internal affairs of the Palestinian population: for example, health, education, policing, and other municipal services. The PA was also made responsible for security, although Israel retained pre-eminent authority over its own citizens and all Jewish settlers, thus maintaining plenary power and overall territorial jurisdiction.[81]

Within Area B, which encompassed many Palestinian villages and towns and approximately 26 per cent of the West Bank, the PA was vested with the same functional authorities regarding Palestinians,[82] but Israel retained overriding responsibility for security as well as complete jurisdiction regarding Jewish settlers and other Israelis.[83] In Area C, comprising approximately 72 per cent of the West Bank[84] and composed of Israeli settlements, major road networks, military installations and largely unpopulated areas (such as parts of the Jordan Valley), Israel retained full authority and responsibility.[85] A similar formula was used in the Gaza Strip and Jericho. The PA became responsible for the Palestinian population within the Gaza Strip and Jericho while Israel retained authority over Jewish settlements and military installations and all jurisdiction for internal and external security and public order in the settlements.[86]

The Accords stipulated that, over time, Israel was to transfer to the PA jurisdiction over Area B and eventually most of Area C, except for Jewish-Israeli settlements and military areas. Meanwhile, throughout the OPT, Israel retained overriding authority to 'exercise its powers and responsibilities with regard to internal security and public order, as well as with regard to other powers and responsibilities not transferred'.[87] The PLO and PA were prohibited from entering into agreements that amounted to foreign relations for the territories.[88]

Although Israel thus retained key powers and ultimate military authority under the Oslo Accords, it could be argued that these were purely formal. Eyal Benvenisti, for example, argues that 'the myth of continuity of the Israeli military administration' through the agency of the PA is 'a myth both parties, each for its own reasons, sought to maintain'.[89] He claims that, under the 1994 Gaza-Jericho Agreement, control over the civilian population in the Gaza and Jericho areas was entrusted to the PA and therefore Israel was no longer responsible for maintaining public order and civil life. Accordingly, the Israeli occupation had ended in those areas, because 'the test for effective control is not the military strength of the foreign army which is situated outside the borders ... What matters is the extent of that power's effective control of civilian life *within* the occupied area.'[90] Similarly, Dinstein has claimed that, to the extent that Israel relinquished to the PA 'territorial jurisdiction with the functions of government', Israel's occupation of that territory had effectively terminated.[91]

These arguments are not compelling, for several reasons. For one thing, all the 'final status' issues – disposition of Jewish settlements in the OPT, the status of Jerusalem, the fate of Palestinian refugees, final borders, and water management – were postponed and so were explicitly excluded from Palestinian jurisdiction.[92] For another, the Accords provided that, even after the final transfer of authority over Area C to the PA, the PA would remain obliged to cooperate with, provide data on, or secure Israeli permission regarding a myriad of matters, such as changes to the Palestinian population registry,[93] the issuing of travel documents,[94] land registration,[95] transportation or exploration of fuel,[96] water,[97] telecommunications, use of the electromagnetic sphere and electrical infrastructural development,[98] nature reserves,[99] and archaeology.[100] In the Accords, these and other core matters of governance were supposed to be decided by Joint Committees. But the Accords provided that both parties held a veto over any changes, so Israel was able to maintain the status quo.[101] Israel also retained an overriding veto of legislation passed by the PA.[102]

Indeed, although they appeared to alter the governance of the OPT in profound ways, in practice the Oslo Accords sustained (and conveyed putative legality to) legal and administrative arrangements that Israel had established over the preceding 24 years, many of which violated the laws of occupation.[103] For example, retaining jurisdiction in Area C enabled Israel to perpetuate settlement expansion, including by land expropriation in violation of the Hague Regulations; destruction of private Palestinian property in violation of Article 53 of the Fourth Geneva Convention; and the continued transfer of its population, in violation of Article 49(6). The Interim Agreement explicitly recognised the land rights of Israeli companies and settlers within the occupied territory.[104] Similarly, retaining overriding responsibility for security allowed Israel to continue to violate Palestinians' rights to life, freedom from arbitrary detention, freedom of movement, and so forth (as detailed in Chapter 4). The Accords' provisions on water allocation also reaffirmed discriminatory allotments in favour of Israeli settlers and settlements (as discussed further in Chapter 3).[105]

Thus the Oslo Accords did not actually transfer meaningful authority over the OPT from Israel to the PLO.[106] Rather, they created a temporary regime – a Palestinian Interim Self-Government Authority, called the 'Council' in the Agreement – pending the outcome of the final-status negotiations. In effect, the PA's competence and jurisdiction extended only to governing the Palestinian population in the territory, not the territory itself.[107] Palestinians living in the OPT ultimately remained under Israeli military control – a fact they confronted daily in Israel's continuing control over their movement between towns and districts.[108] Indeed, a former legal advisor to the Israeli Ministry of Foreign Affairs stated openly that, throughout the 'interim period' established by the Accords (which in practice has proved indefinite), 'the Palestinian Council will not be independent or sovereign in nature'. Rather, 'the military government will continue to be the source of authority for the Palestinian Council and the powers and responsibilities exercised by it in the West Bank and Gaza Strip'.[109]

This view, coupled with the very absence of clarity, indicates that no real change had occurred and Israel continues to hold its obligations under international law, as belligerent occupier. As Bruderlein notes regarding the Gaza Strip,

> The Oslo Agreements were never intended to determine the ultimate legal responsibilities of Israel towards the Palestinian population in the [OPT]. They remained silent on this issue, leaving the question for the negotiation of the final status agreement. As a result, if the transfer of administrative responsibilities to the Palestinian Authority narrowed the scope of duties of Israel as the Occupying Power, it did not extinguish Israel's responsibilities towards the Palestinian people.[110]

*The PA and PLO as 'authorities of the occupied territories'*

In light of the previous discussion, the PA may best be understood as an institution to which the Occupying Power has devolved limited administrative competence. The drafters of the Fourth Geneva Convention envisaged that this could occur during a prolonged occupation without terminating that occupation.[111] From such a situation, however, a special concern arises that authorities under occupation not be brought to compromise the rights of their own people.

As the drafters recognised, an Occupying Power and the population under its control are in a highly asymmetrical relationship. During the Second World War, local authorities had sometimes been coerced, through immense pressure, into concluding agreements to the detriment of their own prisoners of war or civilian population.[112] These agreements were often 'represented to those concerned as an advantage, but in the majority of cases involved drawbacks which were sometimes very serious',[113] such as banning the provision of humanitarian assistance or allowing the deportation or forced enlistment of protected persons.[114]

To ensure that people under occupation could not be threatened or leveraged into forfeiting their rights under the Fourth Geneva Convention, the drafters provided in Article 8 that such rights could not be forfeited:

> protected persons may in no circumstances renounce in part or in entirety the rights secured to them by the present Convention and by the special agreements referred to in the foregoing Article, if such there be.

The drafters also wished to ensure that an Occupying Power not take 'refuge behind the will of the protected persons' to justify its violations of the Convention.[115] No individual member of the protected population, they recognised, should have the power to renounce rights accorded by the Convention so as to 'open a breach which others in much greater numbers might have cause of regret'.[116] Hence they drafted Article 47 to state:

> Protected persons who are in occupied territory shall not be deprived, in any case or in any manner whatsoever, of the benefits of the present Convention by any change introduced, as the result of the occupation of a territory, into the institutions or government of the said territory, nor by any agreement concluded between the authorities of the occupied territories and the Occupying Power, nor by any annexation by the latter of the whole or part of the occupied territory.[117]

Thus Articles 8 and 47 ensured that people normally recognised as authorities among the protected population could not renounce or sign away the protections of international humanitarian law. If they attempted to do so, it would have no legal effect.

At the same time, the drafters had recognised that 'special agreements' may sometimes be required to serve the population or suit the exigencies of war. In the Fourth Geneva Convention, this provision is detailed in Article 7:

> ... the High Contracting Parties may conclude other special agreements for all matters concerning which they may deem suitable to make separate provision. No special agreement shall adversely affect the situation of

protected persons, as defined by the present Convention, nor restri
rights which it confers upon them.

In the same Article, the drafters provided that the Convention's protections might be supplanted by 'more favourable measures' if these truly improve the status and conditions of protected persons.

Protected persons shall continue to have the benefit of such agreements as long as the Convention is applicable to them, except where express provisions to the contrary are contained in the aforesaid or in subsequent agreements, or where more favourable measures have been taken in regard to them by one or other of the Parties to the conflict.

The Oslo Accords might be considered 'special agreements', signed by the PLO and the State of Israel. If so, relevant here is whether these agreements have lifted Israel's responsibility for the human rights of the Palestinian population under occupation, thereby obviating any inquiry into alleged policies of colonialism or apartheid. This question comes down to whether the Accords changed Israel's status as belligerent occupier, by transferring primary responsibility for the welfare of the Palestinian population to the PA. Was the PLO legally authorised, by Article 47 of the Convention, to make such an agreement? Could it legitimately do so, functioning in the capacity of a High Contracting Party, if arranging for 'more favourable measures' regarding protected persons?

The authority of the PLO to make 'special agreements' with the Occupier is uncertain. On the one hand, the PLO would seem to have that authority because its leadership, at least in signing the first Accord in 1993, was not living under occupation (being permitted to reside in the OPT only after July 1994). Consequently, the PLO was not within the definition of 'protected persons' or unequivocally within the definition of 'authorities of the occupied territory' as this was understood in Article 47. Thus the PLO could arguably sign the first Accord as a legitimate 'special agreement'. The PLO leadership is also recognised internationally as the 'sole legitimate representative of the Palestinian people'. Although its top leadership was in exile until 1994, the PLO represented Palestinians residing both outside and inside occupied territory and was considered to be the national authority for negotiations with Israel.[118]

On the other hand, the PLO's attempt to accede to the Geneva Conventions in 1989 in the name of the 'State of Palestine' had been declined by Switzerland, on grounds that Palestine's status as a state remained unsettled.[119] Thus the PLO could not sign the Oslo Accords in the capacity of a High Contracting Party to the Geneva Conventions – the status required to sign a 'special agreement'. Moreover, the PLO continued to negotiate and sign agreements on issues affecting Palestinian protected persons and the occupied territory after its leadership assumed residence in the OPT and so came under Israeli military rule (a vulnerability graphically demonstrated by Israel's eventual bombardment and siege of PA offices in Ramallah).[120] Thus the PLO leadership, morphing into the PA leadership, became the 'authority in the occupied territories' for purposes of Articles 7 and 47.[121] In this status, according to the Fourth Geneva Convention, neither the PA nor the PLO had the authority to make any 'special agreement' that effectively stripped the civilian Palestinian population of protections under the Convention or removed Israel's ultimate responsibility for administering the territory and its civilian population in all ways consistent with human rights and humanitarian law.

The only exception to this rule is if the 'special agreements' constitute 'more favourable measures' for protected persons. This would clearly be the case if such measures led ultimately to ending the occupation: for example, by establishing a Palestinian state, in the context of a two-state solution. Establishing a fully independent and sovereign Palestinian state in the West Bank, East Jerusalem and the Gaza Strip would end Israel's occupation by definition, and so not just modify but terminate application of the Fourth Geneva Convention.

Evaluating whether such 'more favourable' measures are indeed operating must be made not simply by noting the letter of related agreements but also by examining whether they are having the proposed outcomes. Otherwise, 'special agreements' could slip into the risk precluded by the Convention, noted earlier, in which they 'open a breach which others in much greater numbers might have cause of regret'.[122] In applying this test, this study found two fatal shortcomings. First, in 2011 (and arguably long before), progress toward establishing a fully independent Palestinian state in the OPT had infamously stalled: talks collapsed in 2010 and were not held at all in 2011. The PLO's approach to the UN Security Council in September was made on the explicit argument that peace talks based on the Oslo Accords have made no progress and that the objective conditions for Palestinian statehood – especially the territorial integrity of the OPT – had instead greatly deteriorated. Thus the Oslo Accords had not, to date, provided for 'more favourable measures'.

Second, if the intended outcome of Palestinian statehood is eventually achieved by reinvigorating the terms of the Oslo Accords through, say, a General Assembly recognition of a Palestinian state, this would still constitute 'more favourable measures' only if it genuinely allowed the Palestinians to exercise their right to self-determination by *entirely* ending Israel's occupation of the OPT. Otherwise, a nominal Palestinian state – with only partial sovereignty, still under Israel's ultimate territorial control, unable to administer its borders and precluded from establishing meaningfully independent foreign relations – would replicate a policy for which apartheid South Africa was notorious: the Black Homelands (Bantustans) policy. The South African Bantustans were represented by the white government as satisfying the political rights of black South Africans by allowing them to exercise their right to self-determination (in territorial 'Homelands' demarcated by the white government). Yet the international community determined that the Bantustans were only more elaborate figments of apartheid's doctrine of forced racial separation and condemned their creation on this basis. As such an outcome in Palestine would also permanently deny Palestinians the exercise of their right to self-determination, agreements to this end cannot be held to constitute 'more favourable measures' relative to belligerent occupation.

This second observation clarifies a sensitive but essential legal point: that determining when Israel's occupation has truly ended cannot rely solely on claims either by the Israeli government or even by the PLO/PA in its capacity as 'authority of the occupied territory'. Recalling the legal fictions and coercive environment of apartheid South Africa, whether statehood truly fulfils the right of the Palestinian people to self-determination must be determined empirically. In other words, to conform to protections provided by the Fourth Geneva Convention regarding agreements made by authorities under occupation, Palestinian statehood must be confirmed not merely to be perpetuating Israel's occupation under another guise.

Finally, any argument that the Oslo Accords ended the occupation is contradicted by the Accords themselves, which expressly established terms for an 'interim' period that was intended to culminate in an agreement leading to a permanent settlement.[123] This approach reflected and clarified the common assumption by all parties that Israel's military occupation would continue, even during a staged withdrawal of Israel's military forces, until 'final status' talks were completed. Nor did the US-sponsored 'Roadmap' alter that status.[124] As approved by Security Council Resolution 1515 (2003), the Preamble to the Roadmap explicitly acknowledges that the territory is occupied in stating its goal to be a settlement that 'will resolve the Israel-Palestinian conflict, *and end the occupation* that began in 1967'.[125] The Roadmap was held by the ICJ in its *Wall* advisory opinion to represent only 'the most recent of efforts to initiate negotiations' to bring the conflict to an end.[126]

In conclusion, this study finds that the Oslo Accords did not change the status of the OPT as occupied territory. Certainly any argument that the PA has assumed genuinely autonomous or sovereign powers in the OPT is empirically baseless, and any 'special agreements' that purport to transfer ultimate responsibility for governance to authorities under occupation are not legitimate. Nor can the Accords be held to constitute exceptions, provided by the Fourth Geneva Convention regarding 'more favourable measures', because more favourable outcomes expected from them have not emerged. Hence this study can proceed on the firm basis that Israel remains the belligerent occupier of the OPT and so is ultimately responsible for their administration and for the human rights of the Palestinian population, as well as their rights under international humanitarian law.

### Continuing occupation of the Gaza Strip

The situation in the Gaza Strip differs from the West Bank by involving the physical withdrawal of Israel military land forces. Arguably, this step ended Israel's occupation by definition. Assessing this claim engages two questions: when an occupation is considered truly to have ended, a question of international law that has been affected partly by evolving technologies of war, and actual conditions regarding Israel's continuing control over the Gaza Strip.

In August–September 2005, Israel evacuated its settlements and withdrew its land forces in accordance with its Revised Disengagement Plan of 6 June 2004.[127] This plan was intended to ensure that '[i]n any future permanent status arrangement, there will be no Israeli towns and villages in the Gaza Strip'.[128] Israel then claimed that it no longer held responsibility for security in the territory.[129] As an Israel Defence Forces (IDF) spokesperson put it,

> From this point on, the full responsibility for events occurring in the Gaza Strip and for thwarting terror attacks against Israeli targets will be in the hands of the Palestinian Authority and its apparatuses.[130]

On 12 September 2005, the IDF's Chief of Southern Command, Major General Dan Harel, issued a decree ending military rule in Gaza.[131] Two years later, in September 2007, the Israeli Security Cabinet reinforced this claim by declaring that the Gaza Strip was 'hostile territory' and subsequently launching a major military attack against it ('Operation Cast Lead'). The following January, Israel's Supreme Court supported the Government of Israel's assertion that it no longer held the Gaza Strip under occupation and was absolved of any obligations to the civilian population under international humanitarian law:

> … since September 2005, Israel no longer has effective control over the events in the Gaza Strip. The military government that had applied to that area was annulled in a government decision, and Israeli soldiers are not in the area on a permanent basis, nor are they managing affairs there. In such circumstances, the State of Israel does not have a general duty to look after the welfare of the residents of the Strip or to maintain public order within the Gaza Strip pursuant to the entirety of the Law of Belligerent Occupation in International Law. Nor does Israel have effective capability, in its present status, to enforce order and manage civilian life in the Gaza Strip.[132]

Similarly, some commentators have contrasted the degree of physical control exercised by Israel and by the PA (or Hamas) within the territorial confines of the Gaza Strip to conclude that Israel is no longer the occupant.[133] This view is rooted in the traditional law of land warfare and essentially asserts that:

> some form of military presence on land remains a necessary condition for an occupation, i.e., a military occupation cannot be solely imposed by the control of the national airspace by a foreign air force … or of the national seashore by a foreign navy. The law of occupation belongs historically to the law of land warfare which requires, at its core, a land-based security presence.[134]

Because the Gaza Strip is territory in which the Palestinian people hold the right to self-determination, it must be questioned whether a unilateral assertion about its changed status by one party to the conflict is sufficient. An impartial determination of actual conditions would seem necessary – especially as observing the right of peoples to self-determination is an obligation owed to, and by, the international community as a whole. In fact, the answer is more complicated than simply when military forces physically withdraw. As has been frequently noted in this study, 'an international instrument has to be interpreted and applied within the overall framework of the entire legal system prevailing at the time of the interpretation'.[135] Hence Israel's assertion that belligerent occupation ended in Gaza must be assessed in light of the larger legal context. This includes legal debate not only about the Gaza Strip but also evolving legal theory about when military occupations generally can be held to have ended.

Before the implementation of the Revised Disengagement Plan, the Gaza Strip manifestly was territory occupied by Israel. Anticipating Israel's implementation of the Revised Disengagement Plan, the Canadian Government's International Development Research Centre commissioned a report – which became known as the Aronson Report[136] – to examine the implications of disengagement. The Aronson Report noted that when then-Prime Minister Sharon initially announced the unilateral withdrawal plan in April 2004, one declared objective was to end Israel's role and responsibility as the Occupying Power in Gaza. In particular, the original plan provided that, once Israeli civilians and military forced had been withdrawn, there would 'be no basis for the claim that the Gaza Strip is occupied territory'.[137] This express reference to Gaza as 'occupied territory' was deleted in the 6 June 2004 Revised Disengagement Plan, which was approved by the Cabinet. The Revised Disengagement Plan provides only that, 'The completion of the plan will serve to dispel the claims regarding Israel's responsibility for the Palestinians within the Gaza Strip.'

The revised plan is intentionally ambiguous: it refers to the termination of Israel's responsibility for the population of the Gaza Strip, but says nothing about the status of the territory itself. The Aronson Report argues that one reason for this deletion was that the Israeli Cabinet had received legal advice that any claim regarding the end of occupation could not be maintained while Israel remained in control of the Philadelphi corridor (the Salah al Din border road), essentially a buffer zone along the Egypt/Gaza border, and arguably also the Strip's ports and airports. Retaining control of these areas was seen as giving Israel de facto control over the territory and thus maintaining the occupation.[138] In the event, Israel reached an agreement with Egypt, which took over security functions in the Philadelphi Corridor.[139] But Israel retains control of Gaza's airspace and maritime zones.[140] Israel's comprehensive control over the Gaza Strip therefore was sustained:

> despite the withdrawal of its troops and citizens from Gaza and the formal abrogation of military rule, Israel continues to exercise considerable influence over life in the Gaza Strip: the IDF controls the airspace and territorial waters of Gaza; it governs the passage of persons and goods

into Gaza from Israel (and the West Bank) and indirectly monitors passage in the Rafah crossing between Gaza and Egypt. In addition, Israel has not yet surrendered to the Palestinian Authority the Strip's population registration records and has not yet agreed to the opening of Gaza's seaport and airport.[141]

In December 2004, Shavit Matias, deputy to Israel's Attorney-General for international law, argued that this continuing control over land, sea and air ports still did not constitute occupation:

> When we quit Philadelphi, even if the Palestinians don't yet have a port or airport, the responsibility will no longer be ours. The area will not be considered occupied territory. When the Palestinians have a crossing to Egypt and additional options for transferring merchandise, even if there is no port yet, we have no responsibility.[142]

Commentators are divided on the accuracy of claims like this. Some, such as Aronson, argue that because Israel retains a 'security envelope' around the Gaza Strip, controlling who and what goes in and out of the territory, disengagement did not terminate occupation.[143] Israel controls and monitors what goods are allowed into and out of Gaza and collects duties and value-added tax (VAT), based on Israel's rates, on behalf of the Palestinian Authority.[144] Passage through the Rafah crossing between the Gaza Strip and Egypt is regulated by an agreement concluded between Israel and the PA, subject to an annexed statement of principles, and under the supervision of the European Union (EU) Border Assistance Mission.[145] In contrast stand the views of, for example, Bruderlein, Shany, and Israel's Supreme Court, which emphasise the nature of effective control, as derived from the traditional law of land warfare.[146]

This latter view is rather formalistic. The issue is not one of creating an occupation, which as a practical matter would appear to require the use of ground forces to create and maintain control,[147] but rather of determining whether an existing occupation has been terminated. Termination of occupation could well involve considerations other than the physical withdrawal of an Occupying Power from a territory, whether voluntarily or by force of arms. As Roberts counsels: 'the withdrawal of occupying forces is not the sole criterion of the ending of an occupation; and the occupant has not necessarily withdrawn at the end of all occupations'.[148]

The criteria for determining when an occupation has ended have not been as fully fleshed out as those determining when an occupation has been established.[149] Traditionally, the test for an occupation's termination was seen as a simple question of fact: 'Occupation comes to an end when an occupant withdraws from a territory, or is driven out of it.'[150] As one account, written in 1952, expressed it:

the moment the invader voluntarily evacuates [occupied] territory, or is driven away by a levée en masse, or by troops of the other belligerent, or of his ally, the former condition of things ipso facto revives. The territory and individuals affected are at once, so far as International Law is concerned, considered again to be under the sway of their legitimate sovereign. For all events of international importance taking place on such territory the legitimate sovereign is again responsible towards third States, whereas during the period of occupation the occupant was responsible.[151]

This test has, over the past half-century, become anachronistic. For one thing, it does not account for termination of an occupation under the auspices of the Security Council, as occurred in Iraq.[152] For another, it reflects a century-old view of the nature of warfare set out in the 1907 Hague Regulations, when the occupation of territory depended on the physical presence of troops on the ground. Apart from dropping bombs from balloons,[153] aerial warfare did not then exist, nor did remote-surveillance technology. In contemporary conditions, the importance of air power was stressed by, among other sources, Major General Amos Yadlin, an Israeli air force officer, in 2004 after he became head of Israeli military intelligence. He stated:

> Our vision of air control zeroes in on the notion of control. We're looking at how you control a city or a territory from the air when it's no longer legitimate to hold or occupy that territory on the ground.[154]

In the circumstances of Gaza, to consider only Israel's withdrawal of ground troops is to ignore the wider context of such 'control'. This control includes the territory's vulnerability to the re-entry of ground troops, due to its lack of control and authority over its own borders, air space, ports and seas.

Eyal Benvenisti points out that the Hague Regulations are ambiguous as to what test of control should be used to determine whether an occupation has ended, based on the actual or potential control of the territory concerned.[155] Similarly, Bruderlein cites the *Tsemel* case, heard before Israel's Supreme Court, which held that occupation forces do not need to be in actual control of all the territory and population, but simply have the potential capability to do so.[156] This ruling accords with the decision in the post-Second World War *List* case and jurisprudence of the International Criminal Tribunal for the Former Yugoslavia (ICTY). In the *List* case, the US Military Tribunal at Nuremberg, when considering the legal effect of resistance to Nazi occupation, ruled that Germany remained responsible:

> While it is true that the partisans were able to control sections of these countries [Greece, Yugoslavia and Norway] at various times, it is established that the Germans could at any time they desired assume physical control of any part of the country. The control of the resistance forces was temporary only and did not deprive the German Armed Forces of its status of an occupant.[157]

The view that belligerent occupation consists of the capacity to assert control at will was also affirmed by the ICTY, in ruling that one of the guidelines to determine whether an occupation was established was whether 'the occupying power has a sufficient force present, or the capacity to send troops within a reasonable time to make the authority of the occupying power felt'.[158]

Although Benvenisti concludes that, even employing the more stringent potential control test, the Gaza Strip is no longer occupied,[159] other factors must cast doubt on this. Israeli land forces have re-entered Gaza on numerous occasions since 'disengagement': for example, in June 2006 in 'Operation Summer Rain' and in December 2008–January 2009 during 'Operation Cast Lead'. To use the *List* formula, Israel has demonstrated that it 'could at any time [it] desired assume physical control of any part of the country'. These factors indicate that Israel did not relinquish control of Gaza in August 2005, but simply withdrew, or redeployed, the most visible aspect of its control (ground troops within Gaza). Moreover, airspace and the territorial sea form part of a State's territory and, as envisaged in the Disengagement Plan, Israel has manifestly retained authority over Gaza in these areas. Taking into account how this authority has enabled Israel to maintain its control over Gaza – in relation, for example, to the import and export of goods, levying duties and VAT, and controlling its fuel and electricity supply – Israel's withdrawal of land forces clearly did not terminate the occupation. These measures deny the Strip's people the economic aspects of self-determination, by preventing them from exercising 'the right freely to determine, without external interference, their political status and to pursue their economic, social and cultural development'.[160]

The Fourth Geneva Convention, in Article 6, provides that the Convention shall cease to apply in occupied territory one year after 'the general close of military operations', although even at that stage some Articles continue to bind the Occupying Power. In the *Wall* advisory opinion, the ICJ ruled that as 'the military operations leading to the occupation of the West Bank in 1967 ended a long time ago', Article 6 was due to be applied.[161] It appears, however, that the Court misinterpreted the phrase 'the general close of military operations' as referring to the military operations *leading to the occupation*. According to the preparatory Conference of the Fourth Geneva Convention, 'the general conclusion of military operations" means when the last shot has been fired'.[162] This is clearly not the case in the OPT, where the armed conflict and military operations continue.

Accordingly, the ICJ's ruling has been criticised partly because it does not correspond to official Israeli policy regarding the existence of an armed conflict in the OPT.[163] In the *Targeted Killings* case,[164] President Emeritus Barak presumed that 'between Israel and the various terrorist organizations active in Judea, Samaria, and the Gaza Strip ... a continuous situation of armed conflict has existed since the first *intifada*'.[165] Relying on the views of Professor Antonio Cassese, he held that the situation amounted to an international armed conflict,[166] arguing that 'the fact that the terrorist organizations and their members do not act in the name of a state does not turn the struggle against them into a purely internal state conflict'.[167] Barak thus emphatically rejected the respondents' plea that it was difficult to classify the nature of the conflict, ruling:

> for years the starting point of the Supreme Court – and also of the State's counsel before the Supreme Court – is that the armed conflict is of an international character. In this judgment we continue to rule on the basis of that view.[168]

Consequently, it appears that the ICJ erred when it ruled that Article 6 of the Fourth Geneva Convention should be applied in the OPT.

Finally, the ultimate test regarding the end of an occupation is whether the international status of the territory has changed. The Gaza Strip has not changed its status in the only way legally meaningful in the OPT, which is the full expression of self-determination by the Palestinian people. Israel and the PLO have agreed that the West Bank and Gaza Strip form 'a single territorial unit' whose integrity is to be preserved pending the conclusion of permanent status negotiations.[169] Relying on the Interim Agreement, Israel's Supreme Court has affirmed Israel's recognition of the unity of the West Bank and Gaza as a single territorial unit.[170] Therefore, Gaza alone cannot exercise a right of self-determination because that right presently belongs to the Palestinian population of the territorial self-determination unit as a whole, which comprises the West Bank (including East Jerusalem) as well as the Gaza Strip.

The drafters of the Geneva Conventions indeed recognised that, in prolonged occupations, a staged or partial transfer of powers to the administrative departments of the occupied power could happen without altering the fact of occupation.[171] The ICRC, in its commentary on Article 6 of the Fourth Geneva Convention, has clarified this point by stating clearly that de facto withdrawal of armed forces does not terminate an occupation unless it is accompanied by a clear political act clarifying a formal transfer of authority:

> The Convention could only cease to apply as the result of a political act, such as the annexation of the territory or its incorporation in a federation, and then only if the political act in question had been recognized and accepted by the community of States; if it were not so recognized and accepted, the provisions of the Convention must continue to be applied.[172]

As noted, if Israel's unilateral attempt to change the international status of the Gaza Strip actually functions to deny the Palestinian people the right to self-determination, then other States have a duty not to recognise that outcome, by rejecting Israel's claim that the occupation has ended.[173] This clarification by the ICRC, which is charged with interpreting and enforcing the Geneva Conventions, means that non-recognition of Israel's efforts to change the status of the Gaza Strip is doubly mandated.

### Israeli settlements in the OPT

It is a well-established and indeed a much-belaboured observation that Israel's settlements in the OPT[174] violate the Fourth Geneva Convention. Article 49(6) declares flatly that '[t]he Occupying Power shall not deport or transfer parts of its own civilian population into the territory it occupies'.[175] The commentary to the Convention affirms that this clause was intended

> to prevent a practice adopted during the Second World War by certain Powers, which transferred portions of their own population to occupied territory for political and racial reasons or in order, as they claimed, to colonize those territories. Such transfers worsened the economic situation of the native population and endangered their separate existence as a race.[176]

In 1998, this prohibition was confirmed as an international crime by its inclusion in the Rome Statute, which cited as a war crime any policy of direct or indirect transfer 'by the Occupying Power of parts of its own civilian population into the territory it occupies, or the deportation or transfer of all or parts of the population of the occupied territory within or outside this territory'.[177]

Nonetheless, Israel has regularly denied that the settlements are illegal and related arguments must come under review here.

#### Status of settlements under international humanitarian law

The first Jewish-Israeli settlements in the OPT were established immediately after the 1967 war.[178] The plan to use settlements as an annexation strategy was not published until 1978, however, when it was declared a formal programme by the World Zionist Organisation's (WZO's) Department for Rural Settlement as a 'Master Plan for the Development of Settlement in Judea and Samaria 1979–1983'. As the WZO was (and remains) the 'authorised agency' of the State of Israel on such matters,[179] the Master Plan clarified that the State of Israel's purpose in authorising and building settlements was to ensure that the West Bank would be permanently annexed to Israel:

> There must not be the slightest doubt regarding our intention to hold the areas of Judea and Samaria forever … The best and most effective way to remove any shred of doubt regarding our intention to hold Judea and Samaria forever is a rapid settlement drive in these areas.[180]

The Master Plan laid out a pragmatic programme of land appropriation:

> State and uncultivated land should be seized immediately for the purpose of settlement in the areas located among and around the population centres with the aim of preventing as much as possible the establishment of another Arab state in these territories. It will be difficult for the [Arab] minority to form a regional connection and political unity when split by Jewish colonies

... everything will be decided on the basis of the facts that we create in these Territories.[181]

The violations of Palestinian rights inherent in this open policy of annexation are obvious.[182] A fundamental tenet of the international law of belligerent occupation is that the Occupying Power is prohibited from altering the status of an occupied territory. Israel's explicit aim in establishing Jewish settlements in the OPT is to create facts that will predetermine the outcome of any political negotiations by making Israeli withdrawal from the settled parts of the territories unfeasible and even, for practical purposes, unimaginable.[183] Thus Israel's policy would seem incontestably to violate the Fourth Geneva Convention.

As discussed earlier, although Israel is party to the Geneva Conventions, it disputes the applicability of the Fourth Geneva Convention in the OPT. However, Israel further argues that, even if the Convention did apply, its settlement policy does not breach of Article 49(6), on several grounds. For example, the Israeli government has argued that Article 49(6) only prohibits *forcible* transfer of the population of the Occupying Power into occupied territory, and consequently does not prohibit *voluntary* or induced migration.[184] Hence Jewish-Israeli settlements in the OPT are not illegal because their Jewish residents moved into them voluntarily.

The trouble with this argument is that nowhere does the Convention restrict the scope of Article 49(6) to forced population movement. Indeed, the Article specifically uses the unqualified term 'transfer', in contrast to 'forcible transfer' mentioned in Article 49(1) (which prohibits the forcible transfer of protected persons *from* occupied territory). The ICJ has confirmed that Article 49(6) 'prohibits not only deportations or forced transfers of population ... but also any measures taken by an occupying Power in order to organize or encourage transfers of parts of its own population into the occupied territory'.[185] Accordingly, the ICJ resolutely concluded that 'the Israeli settlements in the OPT (including East Jerusalem) have been established in breach of international law'.[186]

Similar conclusions have been reached by the UN Security Council,[187] the UN General Assembly,[188] the High Contracting Parties to the Geneva Conventions,[189] and the authoritative ICRC study on customary international humanitarian law,[190] as well as the majority of legal scholars.[191] To take just one instance, in Resolution 465 the UN Security Council stated that 'Israel's policy and practices of settling parts of its population and new immigrants in [the occupied] territories constitute a flagrant violation of the Fourth Geneva Convention'.[192] In the same Resolution it deplored the 'continuation and persistence of Israel in pursuing those policies and practices and calls upon the Government and people of Israel to rescind those measures, to dismantle the existing settlements and in particular to cease, on an urgent basis, the establishment, construction and planning of settlements in the Arab territories occupied since 1967, including Jerusalem'.[193] It further called upon 'all States not to provide Israel with any assistance to be used specifically in connection with settlements in the occupied territories'.[194]

Even scholars sympathetic to Israel's views have sometimes concurred with this view. On 18 September 1967, Theodor Meron, then legal advisor to Israel's Foreign Ministry, concluded that: '... civilian settlement in the administered territories contravenes explicit provisions of the Fourth Geneva Convention'.[195] On 21 April 1978, the US State Department's legal advisor Herbert J. Hansell concluded that '... the establishment of the civilian settlements in [the occupied] territories is inconsistent with international law'.[196]

In the larger context, international law prohibits a foreign power from dismembering a territory in which a people's self-determination is to be expressed. As discussed earlier, some provisions of the Oslo Accords provide that the West Bank and Gaza Strip form 'a single territorial unit' whose integrity is to be preserved pending the conclusion of permanent status negotiations.[197] The EU has consistently opposed Israel's settlement policy on grounds that it is violating this integrity, and its member states have voted in favour of several UN Security Council Resolutions critical of Israeli settlements.[198] In 1980, the European Nine (as it was then called) issued its Venice Declaration, which considered that 'settlements, as well as modifications in population and property in the occupied Arab territories, are illegal under international law'.[199] In this study, accordingly, that Israel's settlements' in the OPT are illegal is not considered questionable.

*Legal status of the settlers*

Some provisions of international humanitarian law apply to all individuals in occupied territories without distinction, but others differ regarding the rights of 'protected persons' and others who are not protected. Palestinians fall into the category of 'protected persons' under the terms of the Fourth Geneva Convention because they are residents of occupied territory 'in the hands of a Party to the conflict or Occupying Power of which they are not nationals'.[200] Israeli settlers are not 'protected persons' in this sense, because they are nationals of the Occupying Power. It would therefore be incompatible with the object and purpose of international humanitarian law[201] to infringe on the rights of protected persons in favour of the Occupying Power's nationals.[202]

Yet the trend of Israel's Supreme Court has been precisely this, in according preferential rights to Jewish settlers in the OPT.[203] The Court does this partly by disregarding that the very existence of the settlers in the OPT impedes public order and civil life and breaches the laws of occupation: not least, through land management policies associated with constructing the settlements that deprive Palestinians of land, water, and freedom of movement.[204] Indeed, the Supreme Court has avoided the entire question of whether the settlers are present illegally in the OPT, holding that such an issue is political and therefore a matter for the executive to decide. On the contrary, the Court has held that the Israeli military commander in the OPT is responsible for the security of the settlers, thus authorising the occupation forces to ensure their 'public order and safety':

Indeed, in exercising his authority pursuant to the law of belligerent occupation, the military commander must 'ensure the public order and safety.' In this framework, he must consider, on the one hand, considerations of state security, security of the army, and the personal security of all who are present in the area. On the other hand, he must consider the human rights of the local Arab population.[205]

The question raised by this approach is how the contradictory interests of Palestinians and Jewish settlers can possibly be balanced. According to the objects and purposes of the laws of occupation, the Occupying Power must act in the best interest of the local population except where prevented from doing so by military necessity. Thus, settlers cannot be awarded status equal to that afforded to protected persons under international humanitarian law where rights conflict, such as access to land and a right to maintain their property. Settlers enjoy, at most, the protection accorded to aliens in occupied territories (section II of the Fourth Geneva Convention). Certainly, the rights of settlers are limited by obligations imposed on the Occupying Power by humanitarian law not to change the nature of the occupied territory through the creation of permanent 'facts on the ground' – that is, settlements.[206] Yet, in confirming that Israel's Military Commander may interpret 'public order and safety' to include defence of settlements that are prohibited by the laws of occupation, the Supreme Court effectively legitimised the military commander's deviation from this duty toward protected persons. The Court has further held that the rights of protected persons in the OPT are not absolute, but relative: 'They can be restricted ... Some of the limitations stem from the need to take rights of other people into account. Some of the limitations stem from the public interest ...'[207]

This strikingly divergent take by Israel's Supreme Court regarding international humanitarian law impels closer scrutiny of the Court's jurisprudence regarding settlements and the occupation generally. As this matter significantly shapes the legal context for which Israel's administration of the OPT, it is explored next in some detail.

### The jurisprudence of Israel's Supreme Court regarding settlements

Long before the occupation of the West Bank and Gaza Strip began, Israeli courts had adopted the *dualist* approach to enforcing international law in domestic courts.[208] In this approach, customary international law is regarded as part of domestic law and is applied in domestic courts unless it contradicts an act of parliament, while rules contained in treaties must be explicitly incorporated into domestic law by an act of parliament in order to be applied by domestic courts. The laws of occupation prohibiting the establishment of civilian settlements in occupied territory, having acquired customary law status, are thus theoretically enforceable in Israeli courts.

Israel's Supreme Court has considered petitions submitted by Palestinians regarding the legality of Israeli actions in the OPT,[209] but has avoided dealing with the lawfulness of the settlements, ruling that general arguments relating to the legality of settlements are not justiciable.[210] Moreover, the Supreme Court has refused to regard the Fourth Geneva Convention as part of customary international law[211] and thus has exempted itself from expressing its opinion regarding the application of Article 49(6). While the Supreme Court has thereby refrained from providing the state with explicit legitimisation for the settlement policy and from confirming its compatibility with the Fourth Geneva Convention,[212] its decisions have effectively supported the settlement project on various grounds.

The principles that have guided the Supreme Court in this direction were first established in 1972 in the *Helou* case[213] regarding Rafah, in an area separating the Gaza Strip from the Egyptian Sinai. In this case, the Supreme Court ruled that it was necessary for the purposes of security to evict the Bedouin inhabitants from their places of residence, even though the same land on which they were living was designated for Jewish settlement. In the decision, Judge Witkon stated:

> Clearly the fact that these same lands are in part or in full designated for Jewish settlement does not deny the security nature of the entire operation. The stated security considerations as reviewed and detailed in my honourable colleague's opinion, were not refuted, or imaginary, nor meant to camouflage other considerations. General Tal stated himself that the entire area (or part of it) is designated to be settled by Jews, which in this case constitutes a security measure.[214]

This opinion paved the way for the establishment of settlements under the guise of military or security needs. In 1978, in the *Beit El* case,[215] private land was requisitioned from Palestinian landowners on the pretext of military necessity and then consigned to civilian Jewish settlement in accordance with the Israeli military's strategic regional defence plan.[216] In this case, the Supreme Court rejected the distinction between the needs of the occupying army and general security interests:

> … in our opinion, these distinctions hold no merit. As I have just stated, the current state is a state of combat, and the occupying power is responsible for ensuring public order in the occupied territory. It must also address the dangers presented from within the territory to itself and to the [occupying] state. The fighting nowadays has taken the form of sabotage actions, and even those who consider these actions (which affect innocent civilians), a form of guerrilla war-fare, admit that the occupying power is authorized, and even obligated to take all necessary measures to prevent them. The military aspect and the security aspect are therefore one and the same.[217]

These two decisions provided the Israeli authorities with the legal basis for including political and other state interests in military considerations. Benvenisti has pointed out that this broad view of security imperatives paved the way for a policy of implanting settlements in ways incompatible with the

Occupying Power's fundamental duty not to use the occupation as a means of acquiring territory by force.[218]

In 1979, however, in the *Elon Moreh* case,[219] the Supreme Court deviated from the *Beit El* decision by confining 'military needs' to needs based on a rational, military-strategic analysis of the dangers faced by the state, and the measures needed to counter them, rather than ideological goals or outlook: 'the military needs in that article cannot include, according to any reasonable interpretation, the national security needs in their wide meaning'.[220] The factual record revealed that, under pressure from the militant Gush Emunim settlers' movement, the government, rather than the military authorities, had initiated establishment of the settlement. The Supreme Court was convinced that, even if the military supported the decision for military reasons, the dominant consideration had been political. Therefore, the Supreme Court held that the requisition order was invalid since the military cannot take such action on political grounds and, under international customary law, land in occupied territory can be requisitioned only for military needs.[221]

The Supreme Court added:

> The decision to establish a permanent settlement which is designed to stand forever – even longer than the period of the military government which was established in Judea and Samaria – faces a legal obstacle which it cannot defeat. Since the military government cannot create in its territory facts for its military needs that are designed to exist even after the military regime ceases in that territory, when it is still impossible to know the fate of the territory after the end of the military regime, it is a prima facie contradiction, also shown by the evidence in this case, that the determining consideration that motivated the political echelon in deciding to establish the settlement was not a military consideration.[222]

On one hand, this decision rejected the claim that the military requisition of private land for the establishment of permanent settlements could be lawful. On the other, the Supreme Court did not address the illegality of the settlements themselves under international law and so enabled the continuation of the settlement activity on land not considered or acknowledged as private. Indeed, following this case the Israeli authorities pursued an intensive policy aimed at defining and gaining control over 'state lands' on which civilian settlements were subsequently built.[223] Following the *Elon Moreh* decision, the Israeli Cabinet decided that all uncultivated rural land in the OPT would be declared 'state land'.[224] According to the Drobles Plan of 1978, which formed the basis for the settlement policy developed by the then Likud Government:

> state land and uncultivated land must be seized immediately in order to settle the areas between the concentrations of minority population and around them, with the object of reducing to the minimum the possibility for the development of another Arab state in these regions.[225]

Two later Supreme Court decisions dealt with the steps taken to declare land as state land and other aspects of the settlement policy, such as planning decisions, the building of roads, and the expropriation of land for that purpose. In the *Al-Naazer* case in 1981,[226] the Supreme Court held that 'local residents have no special rights in public property and the occupying power has a duty to protect such property against intrusion'. Moreover, the Supreme Court held that, when doubt arises whether property is public or private, the presumption shall be that the property is public until ownership has been established.[227] In the *Ayreib* case,[228] the Supreme Court held that the petitioner, who claimed rights in land that had been declared state land and who argued that the use of that land to build a new Jewish settlement was incompatible with the duty of an Occupying Power to administer public property as a usufructuary, lacked the standing or right to question the use of public land. The Supreme Court also found it unnecessary to consider the fate of the land after the end of the occupation.

In both of these decisions, the Supreme Court did not consider the actual intentions of the authorities as a factor in determining the legality of their acts, as it did in the *Elon Moreh* case. As Kretzmer points out, 'the most glaring feature of these decisions is their total detachment from the context of the government's land-use policy on the West Bank. Public lands are not regarded as land reserves that are first and foremost available for use of the local population; they are regarded as land reserves that serve Israeli interests (as perceived by those in power).'[229] Kretzmer concludes that 'article 55 is cited to legitimize this system of gaining control over state lands; it is ignored when the argument is made that the very same article limits the use that may be made of such lands'.[230]

The planning and building of roads and highways in the occupied territories is intimately connected with settlement policy, having the purpose of integrating the West Bank settlements into Israel and enhancing accessibility between the two.[231] In the *Tabeeb* case,[232] the Supreme Court dealt with expropriation of land for a highway. The expropriation was carried out under a Jordanian law that remained in force in 1967 regarding the acquisition of land for public purposes. The Supreme Court assumed that the military authorities would not have gone to the trouble and expense of planning the highways if there was no military interest in them and so concluded, with no solid basis, that military considerations were the dominant factor in planning the roads network. This decision is contrary to the *Elon Moreh* judgment, in which the onus was set on the military authorities to prove that taking of private property was required for military needs.

In the *Jami'at Ascan* case,[233] land in the Atarot area that had been purchased by a Palestinian cooperative (for the construction of a housing estate for teachers) was expropriated for the Atarot highway interchange.[234] The petitioners argued that the highway network had been planned in the interests of Israel and not in the interests of the residents of the West Bank, and that this expropriation was therefore an unlawful use of power by a belligerent occupant. The petitioners added that Israel, as a belligerent occupant whose rule is by its very nature temporary, may not plan and construct projects that have long-term effects. In reply, the authorities argued that the highway system was being built for the benefit of West Bank residents. They argued that the position that existed at the beginning of the occupation could not be frozen and that it was the duty of the military government to further the interests of the local population in all walks of life, including transportation. In this decision, Justice Barak set the formula for military actions:

> The Hague Regulations revolve around two main axes: one – ensuring the legitimate security interests of the occupier in territory held under belligerent occupation; the other – ensuring the needs of the civilian population in the territory held under belligerent occupation.[235]

In this case, too, the Supreme Court was convinced that the planning was for the good of the local population:

> As we have seen, military rule must perform as a proper government authority, [it is] obligated to attend the needs of the local population and public life, and therefore it is granted ruling authority. While executing this authority, consideration must be given to the fact that we are dealing with prolonged military rule and with major population changes. Under these circumstances the Military Commander is authorised to make basic investments and to undertake long-term planning for the benefit of the local population … Therefore it is clear that there is no wrongdoing in the preparation of the national highway system plan: the transportation needs of the local population have increased; the condition of the roads cannot be frozen. The Military Commander was thus authorised to prepare a road plan that accounts for current and future developments. Indeed, the roads will remain even following the end of military rule, but this is irrelevant. Drawing up these plans does not constitute a blurring between military rule and ordinary government. Furthermore the fact that the plan was drawn up in cooperation with Israel does not disqualify it, provided it was [drawn up] for the benefit of the local population.[236]

In sum, the Supreme Court's jurisprudence on settlements is framed by four key points: it has avoided ruling on the legality of the settlements; rejected arguments based on the prohibition of population transfer as customary law; held that general petitions against the settlement policy are non-justiciable; and accepted that civilian settlement by Israel's own nationals can serve military goals.

The Supreme Court has thus provided a framework of legality, within Israeli law, for Israel's settlement activity. Consequently, two legal classes of people now live in the West Bank: Jewish settlers, who are not protected persons for the purposes of the Fourth Geneva Convention but who enjoy privileges on the basis of their identity as Jews; and Palestinians, who are protected persons but who are often deprived of basic rights in spite of that status.

## Prolonged occupation

Under the law of occupation, the Occupying Power is prohibited from annexing the occupied territory or even from taking actions that effectively annex it.[237] The Hague Regulations and the Fourth Geneva Convention both prohibit measures that effectively annex occupied territory and both regulate Israel's activities in the OPT by virtue of their customary status.[238] Yet, as the previous section indicates, Israel's Supreme Court has sometimes held that special conditions obtain in cases of 'prolonged military government'.[239] The law of armed conflict does not address 'prolonged occupation' and the notion has not been much discussed in commentaries.[240] Roberts even cautions that attempting to define the notion of prolonged occupation 'is likely to be a pointless quest'[241] and cautions against treating them as a special category. To do so might suggest that the law of occupation ceases to apply with its full vigour through the passage of time.[242] Nonetheless, Israel's judicial approach, and the long duration of Israel's occupation, force attention to the prolonged character of the occupation in two ways: first, whether prolonged occupation softens or eliminates legal restrictions on the Occupying Power in making legislative changes in occupied territory; and second, whether Israel has exercised its legislative competence over the OPT such that it has effectively annexed territory, either de jure or de facto. If so, its regime of occupation may be categorised as colonialism.

Drafters of both the Hague Regulations and the Fourth Geneva Convention envisaged that an occupation would be of short duration.[243] They did not conceive that one could last for decades, and their provisions are arguably inadequate to regulate such a prolonged occupation.[244] In a very long occupation, the law of war may even, paradoxically, damage the interests of the very civilians it is supposed to protect – especially if the Occupying Power is prevented from setting up political institutions to allow protected persons some political representation. As Roberts notes, this could

> have the effect of leaving a whole population in legal and political limbo: neither entitled to citizenship in the occupying state, nor able to exercise any other political rights except of the most rudimentary character. If there is any risk at all that the law on occupations might prove, paradoxically, the basis for a kind of discrimination that might bear comparison with apartheid, the causes of that risk need to be identified and possible solutions explored.[245]

Identifying whether this is precisely what has happened in Israel's conduct of its prolonged occupation is, of course, one project of this study. But what responsibilities, powers and flexibility does the Occupying Power legally hold in administering territory over long periods of time, so as to avoid such an outcome?

It is accepted that, over time, a belligerent occupation may face changing conditions, such that changes should be made in the laws and administration of occupied territory in the interests of its population.[246] This principle raises obvious risks: as Dinstein warns, it is 'imperative to guard the inhabitants from the bear's hug of the occupant',[247] especially as the need for change may arise as a result of the occupant's own policies.[248] The Hague Regulations accordingly provide (in Article 43[249]) that changes to laws in territory under occupation should be made only where absolutely necessary:

> The authority of the legitimate power having in fact passed into the hands of the occupant, the latter shall take all the measures in his power to restore, and ensure, as far as possible, public order and safety, while respecting, unless absolutely prevented, the laws in force in the country.[250]

The Fourth Geneva Convention, in Article 64,[251] expands on this provision:

> The penal laws of the occupied territory shall remain in force, with the exception that they may be repealed or suspended by the Occupying Power in cases where they constitute a threat to its security or an obstacle to the application of the present Convention. Subject to the latter consideration and to the necessity for ensuring the effective administration of justice, the tribunals of the occupied territory shall continue to function in respect of all offences covered by the said laws.
>
> The Occupying Power may, however, subject the population of the occupied territory to provisions which are essential to enable the Occupying Power to fulfil its obligations under the present Convention, to maintain the orderly government of the territory, and to ensure the security of the Occupying Power, of the members and property of the occupying forces or administration, and likewise of the establishments and lines of communication used by them.

Where Article 43 of the Hague Regulations restricts legislative changes by an Occupying Power to measures protecting public order and civil life, Article 64 of the Fourth Geneva Convention clarifies that any new measures must be 'necessary' to enable the occupant to fulfil its obligations under the Convention and 'must not in any circumstances serve as a means of oppressing the population'.[252] On the contrary, changes must be 'essential' to fulfilling obligations under the Convention.[253] In other words, an Occupying Power does not have a general authority to change the laws 'unless they are required for the legitimate needs of the occupation'.[254] Private law is generally 'immune from interference on the part of the occupant'. Laws that concern 'family life, inheritance, property, debts and contracts, commercial and business activities, and so forth' are normally not suspended or altered by an occupant.[255]

In practice, determining what legislative changes are truly necessary and permitted is not a simple matter. Even if following the letter of Article 43, the Occupying Power must weigh the duty to 'restore and ensure ... public order and civil life' against the duty to respect 'unless absolutely prevented, the laws in force in the country'. As even Article 64 'sets more of a guideline than a clear rule',[256] this onus involves weighing 'the circumstances of the particular case'.[257] A further limitation is that the Occupying Power is legally only in temporary control of the territory, even if the occupation is prolonged: it does not possess sovereign rights over the territory. Changes that it may legitimately introduce must therefore be commensurate with this transitional and temporary role.[258] The Occupying Power must have some flexibility in administering the territory, and what is necessary for 'public order' may well be wider than military necessity, but arguments by an Occupying Power that it is acting for the benefit of the population cannot be allowed to mask an underlying belligerent agenda. Each change in law must be examined individually for its real motive and not be allowed to become a general pattern.[259] Otherwise, a free hand regarding legislation would 'effectively grant the occupant almost all the powers a modern sovereign government would wield'.[260]

One test of whether a change is genuinely meant to benefit the population under occupation could arguably be whether the Occupying Power has passed the same legislation regarding its own population. Should this not be the case, Dinstein argues, then the occupant's professed concern for the welfare of the occupied territory 'deserves to be disbelieved'.[261] This test, which makes intuitive sense and was expressly adopted by Israel's Supreme Court in the *Abu Aita* case,[262] is actually inadequate and even dangerous. For one thing, an Occupying Power may not amend the law of occupied territory 'merely to make it accord with [its] own legal conceptions'.[263] Since the population under occupation is not able freely to conduct normal processes of government whereby changes of legislation represent the collective will, such measures imposed by the Occupying Power would equate with imperialism. For another, extending laws of the home country into occupied territory, for the express purpose of making legal systems congruent, carries an obvious risk of colonialism:

> In practice the standard implicit in the test may be abused by an occupant interested in a gradual extension of its laws to the occupied territory under a strategy of creeping annexation ... It may not introduce changes simply on the ground that it is 'upgrading' the local institutions to the level obtaining in the occupant's own country and that it is in the interest of the local population.[264]

Finally, an Occupying Power cannot adopt any measure that breaches international law.[265] Although some have argued the Occupying Power cannot be held to the narrow letter of international law, Kretzmer more persuasively contends, relying expressly on Article 43, that such 'flexibility' is prohibited: 'It is self-evident that an occupant may not purport to use its legitimate powers conferred by the regime of occupation to pursue an end that is unlawful.'[266]

Contradicting this view, Israel has asserted that a prolonged occupation modifies the obligations imposed by Article 43 of the Hague Regulations.[267] Israel's Supreme Court has repeatedly relied on the claim that where an occupation is prolonged, the Occupying Power is empowered to employ measures that would not be permissible during a short-term occupation.²⁶⁸ This view was expounded in detail by Acting President Shamgar in *Abu Aita*, on the basis that:

> The needs of any area, whether under military government or otherwise, will naturally change over the course of time, along with attendant economic developments ... The length of time that a military government continues may affect the nature of the needs involved, and the urgency to effect adjustment and reorganization may increase as more and more time elapses. The argument ... that there is no foundation for the idea that the duration of military government affects the character of the duties and the extent of the powers of military government [is] irreconcilable with the character of the duties and powers vested in it by Article 43. It is true that this article contains no rules as to adjustment or reclassification bound up with, or conditional upon the time element, but the effect of the time dimension is implicit in the wording, according to which there is a duty to ensure, as far as possible, order and public life, which patently means order and life at all times, and not only on a single occasion. The element of time is also decisively involved in the question of whether it is absolutely impossible to continue acting in accordance with existing law, or whether it is essential to adapt that law to new realities ... It follows that the time element is a factor affecting the scope of the powers, whether we regard military needs, or whether we regard the needs of the territory, or maintain equilibrium between them.²⁶⁹

Shamgar claimed that the Hague Regulations were too inadequate and fragmentary to guide the occupant and implied that, during a prolonged occupation, the occupant assumes sovereign powers of legislation:²⁷⁰

> a lengthy military occupation, which would be required to find solutions for a wide range of day-to-day problems, similar to those an ordinary government would encounter, is likely not to find answers to its questions in the provisions of the Regulations.²⁷¹

Further, in his interpretation of the phrase 'as far as possible', Shamgar flatly asserted that 'there is no logic in applying the same criterion to a newly established military government and to a military government that has administered a territory with all the problems of civil administration, for ten years or more'.²⁷²

To depart from the terms of Article 43 to such an extent – effectively eliminating the limits it places on the occupant's legislative competence – conflicts with the view expressed by the United States Military Tribunal at Nuremberg in the *IG Farben* case. Although the Nuremburg Tribunal recognised that uncertainties pervade the law of armed conflict, it held that these did not arise in relation to the basic principles of the law of occupation contained in the Hague Regulations: 'We cannot read obliterating uncertainty into these provisions and phrases of international law having to do with the conduct of the military occupant towards inhabitants of occupied territory.'[273]

Yet Israel's Supreme Court has done precisely this, by employing the doctrine of prolonged occupation to buttress an interpretation of the Hague Regulations that obliterated the restraints placed upon the State of Israel. In the *Na'ale* case, two settlements in the West Bank (paradoxically) lodged an objection to a permit allowing the opening of a quarry. The petitioners argued that this would breach Article 55 of the Hague Regulations, which provides that an occupant is only the 'administrator and usufructuary' of publicly owned buildings and estates located in occupied territory. This places on the occupant the duty to 'safeguard the capital of these properties, and administer them in accordance with the rules of usufruct'.[274] The petitioners argued that quarrying consumed the property and thus breached the duty of usufruct. The Supreme Court rejected this plea, ruling, 'even if quarrying cannot be considered as usufructing, no prohibition of such a kind of use applies in cases where an activity is done for the benefit of the local population or local needs'.[275] Yet this ruling is manifestly incorrect: in clearly breaching Article 43, the measure clearly violates international law.

In conclusion, while legitimate deviations might be made from the 'normal' rules of occupation during a prolonged occupation, the law of war requires that legislative changes be limited to the welfare of protected persons.[276] Claims by Israel's Supreme Court that, where an occupation is prolonged, the occupant may introduce measures which would otherwise not be allowed, therefore not only breach international law, they also conflict with the decision of the US Military Tribunal at Nuremberg in *IG Farben*[277] and have been rejected by commentators.[278] In looking at Israel's changes of law in the OPT in greater detail, this study finds that they have been employed to implement a policy of colonialism, partly by effacing the legally mandated separation of the Israeli and Palestinian economies, as discussed in Chapter 3.

## APPLICATION OF ISRAELI LAW IN THE OPT

The previous section established that an Occupying Power must uphold the existing law in occupied territory as far as possible. When Israel occupied the West Bank (including East Jerusalem) and the Gaza Strip, the Israeli Military Commander assumed all legislative powers. In East Jerusalem, the law in force until 1967 was annulled and Israeli civil law imposed, but the Military Commander has retained legislative powers in the rest of the West Bank and the Gaza Strip.[279] As the situation in the Gaza Strip is treated elsewhere in this study, this section will focus on questions of law in the West Bank by way of illustration.

As discussed in the previous section, Israel has given a very wide interpretation to the limited exception in Article 43 of the Hague Regulations that permits the Occupying Power to alter local legislation.[280] Law in the West Bank reflects rules, norms and laws developed over centuries or even millennia by the various empires and governments that have held suzerainty, each of which maintained some laws in force before its arrival and annulled, amended and added others. As a consequence, when the occupation began in 1967, law in the West Bank was already a legal patchwork, codified in Ottoman, British and Jordanian. Over four decades of occupation, Israeli military decrees have further annulled, amended, and supplemented West Bank laws, through military proclamations, regulations, orders, and decrees, resulting in a pastiche of great complexity.

In theory, all the legal systems contributing to the law of the West Bank apply to a geographic area.[281] The law in force in the West Bank is different from the law in Israel. The same law applies to Israelis in the West Bank as applies to Palestinians and foreigners. Thus the law applying to Jewish settlers in the OPT is different from the law applying to Israeli citizens residing within Israel's recognised borders (and in East Jerusalem and the Golan Heights).

In reality, Israeli military and Knesset legislation has created legal segregation in many legal fields, such that a different body of law is applied to Israelis and Palestinians living in the same territory. This finding emerges from recognising how laws operate in the West Bank, in three ways:

- Israeli civil legislation as it applies to settlements and their surrounding restricted areas;
- Israeli civil legislation, including Basic Law, as it applies extraterritorially to Israeli settlers in the OPT;
- Israeli military legislation as it applies to Palestinians in the OPT.

The outcome of all these methods, separately and in combination, is the same: one legal system applies to Palestinians in the West Bank and another to Jewish settlers.

### Israeli laws governing settlements and settlers

The first method by which Israel applies laws differently to Israelis and Palestinians living in the West Bank is by incorporating Israeli civil legislation into military orders dealing with the settlements and settlers. This can be termed 'channelling', whereby the Military Commander channels Israeli domestic legislation into the OPT through the authority of his office and the decrees he issues. Channelling allows a number of Israeli laws to apply to the settlements and their annexed zones of territory, with necessary modifications that are mainly procedural and institutional.

Most Israeli laws channelled into the West Bank law regulate the status and authority of Israeli governmental institutions operating within the settlements. For example, such channelling enables the Israeli Ministry of Environmental Protection to exercise its powers with respect to factory pollution in the settlements; grants the Israeli Ministry of Education authority over schools within the boundaries of the settlements; grants the Israeli Ministry of Health authority over medical facilities, and so forth. Thus channelling creates de facto Israeli enclaves within the boundaries of the West Bank (and previously also within the Gaza Strip).

Two military orders in particular have authorised the Military Commander to regulate the management of municipal local councils[282] and regional (Jewish) councils[283] in the West Bank. Regulations of local councils provide that dozens of Israeli laws are applied within the boundaries of the settlements.[284] Israeli rabbinical tribunals and local affairs courts have also been established within the boundaries of the settlements to deal exclusively with litigation between Jewish settlers. For political reasons, the occupying authorities have refrained from applying Israeli law in its entirety to the local councils; hence channelling has resulted in a partial rather than comprehensive application of Israeli law to the settlements.[285] Nonetheless, this system creates legal 'enclaves' or 'islands' within the West Bank where laws apply that differ from those applying in the rest of the West Bank.[286] This violates the principle of equality before the law, which constitutes the foundation of any modern legal system and is relevant to a review under the international legal prohibition on apartheid.[287] Moreover, by conflating law in the settlements with law in Israel, channelling has the effect of creating a Jewish-Israeli society that is integrated legally, socially and economically across the Green Line in ways consistent with colonialism.[288]

*Discriminatory application of Israeli civil legislation to Israeli settlers*

The second technique by which different laws are applied to Israelis and Palestinians in the West Bank is the application of primary legislation enacted by the Knesset extraterritorially to individual Israelis residing or located in the West Bank. This category includes legislation authorising the Israeli executive to promulgate secondary legislation in the form of regulations and decrees that also apply to Israeli individuals in the West Bank. As noted earlier, this practice contradicts the norm that law should apply equally to all individuals within a territory.

The most important law in this regard is the Extension of Emergency Regulations Law 1977,[289] which authorises Israeli criminal courts to judge Israelis suspected of committing criminal offences in the West Bank according to the penal code and criminal procedure of the State of Israel. Section 2 provides:

> a. In addition to the provisions of any law, the court in Israel shall have authority to deliberate, according to the law in force in Israel, a person located in Israel for his act or omission occurring in the Area [the West Bank] and also an Israeli for his act or omission occurring in the territory of the Palestinian Council, all in case the act or omission would have been offences had they occurred within the jurisdiction of the courts in Israel.
> 
> ...
> 
> c. This Regulation does not apply to a person who at the time of the act or the omission was a resident of the Area or a resident of the territories of the Palestinian Council, who is not an Israeli.[290]

This law therefore applies Israeli criminal law extraterritorially on a personal basis to Israelis in the West Bank, and to tourists and non-residents, with respect to offences they are alleged to have committed in the West Bank, except for the territories designated by the Oslo Accords for jurisdiction by the PA ('Area A').

In addition, the Extension of Emergency Regulations Law applies a long list of Israeli laws to Israelis residing in the West Bank. Section 6(b) to the 1884 Addendum to the Law extends the application of the laws detailed in the Regulations also to residents of the West Bank who are not Israeli citizens but who are entitled to immigrate to Israel by virtue of the 1950 Law of Return;[291] that is, to Jews. Thus law is applied differently to Palestinians not only in respect to Israeli citizens in the West Bank but also to Jews who are not citizens and who are located in the occupied territory. Although the criminal prosecution of Israelis under military law (which applies to Palestinians) is theoretically possible, the express policy of the Attorney-General is not to do so.[292]

This legal duality creates striking disparities of treatment. For example, a Palestinian arrested in the West Bank on suspicion of manslaughter may be detained for up to eight days before being brought before a military judge in a military court, where the pre-charge detention may be extended indefinitely. Being subject to military criminal legislation, such a prisoner can face a maximum penalty of a life sentence.[293] By contrast, an Israeli settler arrested on the same grounds must be brought, within 24 hours, before a civilian judge in a civilian court for charges and faces a penalty of up to 20 years' imprisonment.[294]

Since 1967, the Knesset has enacted other laws that apply extraterritorially on an individual basis to Israeli citizens residing in the West Bank (and before disengagement, to settlers in the Gaza Strip). These include provisions regarding taxation, oversight of products and services, and the census. The rationale for this personal application was the special link created between the state and its citizens located in territory under its control. This reasoning is also the foundation for applying Israeli Basic Law to Israelis residing in unlawful settlements in the occupied territories. In the *Gaza Coast* case in 2005, the Supreme Court reasoned as follows:

> We are of the opinion that the Basic Laws grant rights to every Israeli settler in the vacated area. This application is personal. It derives from the control of the State of Israel over the vacated area. It is the outcome of the concept that the State's Basic Laws regarding human rights apply to Israelis located outside of the State but in an area under its control by way of belligerent occupation.[295]

The outcome of the extraterritorial application of Israeli legislation on a personal basis, combined with the enclave law as described above, is that a settler lives within the framework of the West Bank law only in a very partial way:

> A resident of Ma'ale Adumim, for instance, is supposedly subject to the Military Government and to the local Jordanian law, but in fact he lives

according to the laws of Israel both with respect to his personal law and with respect to the local municipality wherein he lives. The Military Government is nothing more than a symbol, through which Israeli law and governance operate.[296]

Israel's Supreme Court has indeed confirmed the legality of this arrangement, in applying the Basic Law only to a specific population in the OPT and so conferring superior rights to settlers. On the one hand, in affirming that Basic Law embraces Israeli settlers as individuals, the Court endorses the settler's protections of property and residence even though these are held illegally under the terms of the Fourth Geneva Convention (whose applicability the Court itself implicitly affirms in the *Gaza Coast* case by recognising the condition of belligerent occupation). Yet, on the other hand, the Court has avoided ruling on whether those same protections cover everyone in the OPT, thus leaving a lacuna that permits a dual legal system (and thus, ironically, negating some principles of equality and non-discrimination affirmed by Israel's Basic Law). For example, also in the *Gaza Coast* case, the Court rejected any proposal that the constitutional rights of Israeli settlers necessarily imply any rights of Palestinians:[297]

> In light of this conclusion, there is no need to take a stand on the territorial applicability of the Basic Laws and there is no need to examine the question if they grant rights to non-Israelis in occupied territories or to Israelis who are not in territories held by Israel. This question raise problems that we do not have to deal with; and we will leave them open for further consideration.[298]

However, as the Supreme Court cannot legally strike down any law unless it is incompatible with the Basic Law,[299] in the *No Compensation Law* case[300] the petitioners argued explicitly that a law affecting Palestinians (an amendment to the torts law denying Palestinians in the OPT the right to legal remedies for injury sustained due to the actions of Israeli occupying forces) was unconstitutional because it was incompatible with the Basic Law: Human Dignity and Liberty – which, they argued, does apply to the Palestinians in the occupied territories. The petitioners argued first, that while the Basic Law: Freedom of Occupation applies to every Israeli citizen and resident, the Basic Law: Human Dignity and Liberty applies to every person. When the applicability of a Basic Law was intended to be limited, the limitation was explicit (for example, Article 6(b) of the law regarding the right of a citizen to enter Israel).

They argued secondly that the Basic Law expressly applies to every governmental authority and requires them to respect the rights set forth in Article 11 of the law.[301] According to this Article, every soldier carries in his kit bag not only the principles of Israeli administrative law, but also the Basic Law, and is required to respect the rights enshrined therein. Therefore, the Basic Law applies any time that a governmental authority infringes the fundamental right of any person. At a minimum, the Basic Law applies in every area under Israeli control. Any other conclusion, the petitioners argued, would lead to a constitutional apartheid regime, whereby an Israeli in the OPT is entitled to the protection of his fundamental rights while a Palestinian is denied such protection.

However, in the *No Compensation Law* case the Court circumvented the question of the applicability of the Basic Law to OPT Palestinians by stating that the rights that were infringed were granted by Israeli law that is not applicable extraterritorially.[302] The same issue came before the Supreme Court in relation to a petition challenging the constitutionality of the 2003 Citizenship and Entry Into Israel Law (the *Family Unification* case). This law prohibits the granting of residency or citizenship status to Palestinians from the West Bank and Gaza Strip who are married to Israeli citizens, who are, in the overwhelming majority of such instances, Palestinian citizens of Israel. Thus, the law bans family unification in Israel. In this case, the Court similarly refused to apply the protection of the Basic Law to the Palestinians. President Barak's minority opinion focused on the constitutional rights of the Israeli citizen to equality and family life and not on the rights of the 'foreigner' (that is, the OPT Palestinian) spouse.[303]

To sum up the Supreme Court's position on this issue: in the occupied territories where Israel exercises effective control, Israeli settlers are granted the protection of the Basic Law while the Palestinians are not, despite the provision of Article 11 of the Basic Law: Human Dignity and Liberty. In relation to the Palestinians, former Supreme Court President Aharon Barak stated: 'Judea, Samaria, and the Gaza Region are not a state and are not democratic. Israeli control over them is by belligerent occupation. Israeli control did not arise from the choice of the local residents, but as the result of combat actions'.[304]

*Discrimination in the adjudication of rights*

The refusal of the Supreme Court to rule on the legality of the settlements (discussed above, pp. 55–59), combined with its rulings that Palestinians do not enjoy legal protections accorded to Israeli settlers, has led it to render judgments that cumulatively have dissolved the special protection accorded to the protected persons and thus the distinction between rights of Palestinians under occupation and rights of settlers. In effect, this approach has turned the tables to protect the interests of settlers over those of the local population. The most illustrative decision is the *Hess* case, in which the Supreme Court authorised the Israeli army to seize Palestinian land and destroy structures in Hebron owned by Palestinians for the purpose of allowing Jewish settlers safe access to the Cave of the Patriarchs (Machpela Cave). Justice Procaccia wrote:

> Alongside the area commander's responsibility for safeguarding the safety of the military force under his command, he must ensure the well being, safety and welfare of the residents of the area. This duty of his applies to all residents, without distinction by identity – Jew, Arab, or foreigner. The question of the legality of various populations' settlement activity in the area is not the issue put forth for our decision in this case. From the very fact that

they have settled in the area is derived the area commander's duty to preserve their lives and their human rights. This sits well with the humanitarian aspect of the military force's responsibility in belligerent occupation.³⁰⁵

The Supreme Court added:

> ... the worshippers who wish to go to the Machpela Cave by foot on Sabbaths and festivals wish to realize a constitutional right of freedom of worship in a holy place. This right is of special importance and weight on the scale of constitutional rights.³⁰⁶

It further determined:

> In the framework of his responsibility for the well being of the residents of the area, the commander must also work diligently to provide proper defence to the constitutional human rights of the local residents, subject to the limitations posed by the conditions and factual circumstances on the ground ... included in these protected constitutional rights are freedom of movement, religion, and worship, and property rights. The commander of the area must use his authority to preserve the public safety and order in the area, while protecting human rights.³⁰⁷

In its rhetoric, the Supreme Court regarded the Palestinians' rights as equal to Jewish settlers' rights, requiring that opposing interests be balanced.³⁰⁸ The Supreme Court then permitted, in principle and in practice, a violation of Palestinian rights for the benefit of the settlers.

Another example is the case of *Rachel's Tomb*,³⁰⁹ in which the petitioners challenged the legality of a military order requisitioning land near Bethlehem to construct a bypass road and protective wall for Jewish worshippers wishing to go from Jerusalem to the site of Rachel's Tomb. The petitioners argued that the order did not properly balance the rights of the worshippers with the property rights of the occupied population and the Palestinian right to freedom of movement within Bethlehem, both of which were violated by the order. In addition, the petitioners argued that the State of Israel was motivated by improper considerations in making the order, whose purpose, they argued, was not to ensure the rights and security of the worshippers but effectively to annex Rachel's Tomb to Jerusalem. The petitioners did not deny the rights of Israeli worshippers to have access to Rachel's Tomb. Therefore, the Supreme Court's deliberations were restricted to whether the order provided a proper balance between the worshippers' freedom of worship on the one hand and the petitioners' freedom of movement and property rights on the other.

The Supreme Court concluded that the dispute was between constitutional rights of equal standing and importance and that the required balance is horizontal, allowing coexistence of all of these rights. In its deliberation, the Supreme Court did not distinguish between the rights of the Palestinians and the rights of the Jewish worshippers³¹⁰ or draw any distinction between the different sources of the rights and special protections given to the petitioners under international humanitarian law. As in the *Hess* case, Israeli 'security' imperatives were recognised by the Supreme Court without question as justifying the infringement of Palestinians' fundamental rights.

In the *Mara'abe* case, Palestinian petitioners challenged the legality of the route of the Wall surrounding the Alfei Menashe settlement, which created a sealed enclave of Palestinian villages. The state claimed that the specific route was chosen for security reasons, to protect the life and safety of the settlers. The Supreme Court accepted this argument, relying on its interpretation of Article 43 of the Hague Regulations. It concluded that, even if the Military Commander

> acted in a manner that conflicted the law of belligerent occupation at the time he agreed to the establishment of this or that settlement – and that issue is not before us, and we shall express no opinion on it – that does not release him from his duty according to the law of belligerent occupation itself, to preserve the lives, safety, and dignity of every one of the Israeli settlers. The ensuring of the safety of Israelis present in the area is cast upon the shoulders of the military commander.[311]

This specific petition was accepted and the route of the Wall in the area in question was found to be disproportionate, leading the Court to order its re-routing. However, in its conclusion the Court again balanced security needs against the rights of the Palestinians while refusing to rule directly on the legality of the settlements. Ultimately, claims regarding protection of settlers were transformed into a judicial determination that a barrier constructed to incorporate the settlements into Israel is legal.

> We have reached the conclusion that the considerations behind the determined route are security considerations. It is not a political consideration which lies behind the fence route at the Alfei Menashe enclave, rather the need to protect the well being and security of the Israelis (those in Israel and those living in Alfei Menashe, as well as those wishing to travel from Alfei Menashe to Israel and those wishing to travel from Israel to Alfei Menashe).

The Supreme Court's interpretation of Article 43 as allowing protection of the settlers through defence of the settlements disturbs and distorts the delicate balance between military concerns and humanitarian concerns that is basic to Article 43 of the Hague Regulations. In this sense, the *Mara'abe* judgment follows the *Hess* precedent[312] in which the fundamental distinction between protected persons in the OPT and nationals of the Occupying Power was conspicuously missing. Although the *Hess* judgment included a comprehensive analysis of the conflicting considerations and rights, the Supreme Court's balancing approach disregarded the condition of occupation and treated the situation as if it were a democratic society in which all individuals, Palestinians and Israeli settlers, have the same rights and duties.

This fiction shapes the legal situation in the occupied territories. The 'basic structure remains in place: the freedom of Jewish settlers to live in the OPT safely and travel freely is apparently hardly ever challenged, resulting in a regime that regulates people and their movements on the basis of ethnicity'.[313] The result is that 'the Palestinians have been denied most of the rights accorded to people under occupation'[314] while settlers are protected in assuming authority over Palestinian land. As the settler population has reached almost half a million, this trend has created systematic segregation and discrimination throughout the West Bank (as it did formerly in the Gaza Strip).

The Supreme Court's latest stamp of legality for practices contrary to international law was extended to bypass roads for Palestinians. Road 443 is a main artery in the West Bank, built on Palestinian land as part of the Atarot interchange.[315] Until the beginning of the second *intifada*, it was used by tens of thousands of Palestinian villagers to connect them to their neighbouring villages and to the city of Ramallah. Since the end of 2000, the army has prevented Palestinians from using it, limiting its use exclusively to Israelis. To meet Palestinian transportation needs, the Minister of Defence ordered the creation of an alternative road network, known as 'Fabric of Life' roads, built on Palestinian land confiscated for this purpose. The case is pending, but the Supreme Court has asked the Defence Ministry for information on progress in constructing the 'Fabric of Life' roads rather than stop or query their construction.[316] This approach effectively endorses, if passively, the military authorities' decision to build them.

In routinely ignoring the facts, the rule of the law, and its own role in checking the actions of the military authorities, the Supreme Court has effectively approved discriminatory practices in its adjudication of rights.

### Application of military legislation to Palestinians

In reviewing Israel's laws in relation to the international legal prohibitions on colonialism and apartheid, this study refers, where relevant, to military legislation introduced by Israel in the OPT, in the form of military orders. Such orders, particularly those detailing criminal offences and periods of detention, are directed at Palestinians and are enforced by military courts established by Israel in the OPT.

### *Military legislation applying to Palestinians*

In the first three months of Israel's occupation, over 100 pieces of military legislation were enacted in the West Bank. On the first full day of the occupation, Military Proclamation No. 2[317] vested all legislative, executive and judicial powers in the Israeli Military Commander. To date, the military authorities have issued over 2,500 military orders altering pre-existing laws, the majority of which are directed at Palestinians. This matrix of military legislation regulates and controls everything from alcohol taxes[318] to control of natural resources[319] to which fruits and vegetables can be grown by Palestinians.[320] Even where they do not formally discriminate between Palestinians and Jewish settlers, they do in practice, effect and, apparently, intent.[321]

The most significant military orders that relate to 'security' are Military Order No. 378,[322] concerning criminal offences and detention, and Military Order No. 1229,[323] which allows for 'administrative' detention without charge or trial for protracted periods. Military Order No. 378 details a wide variety of 'security'-related offences and contains draconian detention and sentencing provisions. Article 78, for example, allows the Israeli military to detain Palestinians for up to eight days before being brought before a military judge, for up to 188 days before being charged with an offence, and for up to two years between being charged and brought to trial. The supervisor of an interrogation may also prohibit a Palestinian from seeing a lawyer for 15 days upon being detained.[324] This period may be extended by the military judicial authorities to up to 90 days if deemed necessary for security or for 'the good of the interrogation'.[325]

Other military legislation deals with specific contexts as they arise. Military Order No. 1500,[326] for example, was issued in April 2002 to provide for mass detention of Palestinians during military incursions in the West Bank. This order gave every Israeli soldier in the territory the authority to arrest Palestinians without providing a reason and without authorisation of a superior officer. It also allowed the occupying army to detain Palestinians for 18 days without bringing them before a judge.

A recent example of military legislation applying personally to Palestinians is the 'Seam Zone permit regime' (described in more detail in Chapter 4, pp. 152–154), which establishes a special bureaucracy for processing applications for entry permits to the 'closed' Seam Zone. The system exempts Israelis from the prohibition to enter the Seam Zone and from the need to acquire a permit, and thus applies only to Palestinians residing in the West Bank and not to Jewish settlers.

Furthermore, routinely and ostensibly to tackle existing or expected disruptions of public order, the Military Commander issues orders declaring a certain area to be a 'closed military zone,' or 'closed area'. Varying degrees of restrictions are imposed on such areas: for example, complete closure and limiting access to Israeli military forces only; entry only by Jewish-Israelis and other Jews granted the privileges of Jewish-Israelis; or entry permitted to Palestinians but only with a permit from the Israeli authorities.[327] Discriminatory implementation of closed area orders that are ostensibly non-discriminatory is also commonplace. For example, Military Order No. 146[328] declared the Latroun/Ayalon area of the West Bank to be a closed area in 1967. This military order has not been amended or cancelled and the Israeli military authorities recently confirmed that it still applies.[329] Palestinian residents, who were forcibly transferred from this zone and whose villages there were destroyed, continue to be denied access to the area and to their land, yet Israelis are free to enter the area, in violation of the military order, to visit Canada Park, a recreational park that has since been established in the closed area by the Jewish National Fund.

The military legislation described above pertains to the West Bank. The military legislative system in the West Bank was mirrored by a similar system in the Gaza Strip from 1967 until Israel's 'disengagement' from the territory in 2005, with identical versions of most important and non-area-specific military orders being issued by the military commander in the Gaza Strip concomitant to those of his counterpart in the West Bank. Although the military orders for the Gaza Strip have been repealed since 2005, Israel retains authority over matters relating to administration of justice in Gaza through different tools, such as the extension of Israeli civil and criminal law over Palestinians in Gaza.[330]

*Enforcement by military courts*

Military laws are enforced through a military court system that has become 'an institutional centrepiece of the Israeli state's apparatus of control over Palestinians in the West Bank and Gaza'.[331] The military courts were established even before the Six-Day War ended, by Military Proclamation No. 3, *Concerning Security Provisions*, in the West Bank and an equivalent proclamation in the Gaza Strip. Both proclamations outlined the jurisdiction of the military courts and details of procedure. These proclamations were replaced in 1970 by Military Order No. 378, *Order Concerning Security Provisions*, in the West Bank, and a parallel order for the Gaza Strip, Military Order No. 300, which expanded the jurisdiction of the military courts to cover a very broad range of security charges. Since 2005, military law has no longer applied in Gaza and the Israeli military court system remains in place only in the West Bank (excluding East Jerusalem), where Military Order No. 378 continues to be the primary piece of legislation regulating most of the military court process.

The military court system in the OPT is represented by Israel as necessary for prosecuting security-related offences. In reality, the system extends to govern regular criminal offenses and distinctly non-security related offences such as traffic violations. As Jewish settlers in the OPT fall under the personal and extraterritorial jurisdiction of Israeli civil law and civil courts, the military court system is also defined by its discriminatory application to Palestinian civilians.

Article 64 of the Fourth Geneva Convention permits an Occupying Power to establish military courts in the territory it occupies, but such courts must adhere to several standards. They must be 'set up in accordance with the recognised principles governing the administration of justice';[332] they may only be used to enforce penal provisions legally promulgated by the Occupying Power under Article 64; and they must not be used 'as an instrument of political or racial persecution'.[333] A brief discussion can address features of the Israeli military court system in the OPT in relation to these three standards.

Regarding the first standard, Israel's military court system in the OPT does not comply with international standards regarding due process and the administration of justice. For example, regarding a defendant's right to be notified of the charges against him promptly and in a language he understands,[334] a Palestinian defendant and his lawyer will be informed of the charges being brought only at the first hearing, after the indictment has already been filed with the military court. They are required to respond immediately, with no time to study evidence. Indictments, like all documents in the military courts, are written and presented to the courts only in Hebrew, a language the defendant and his counsel often do not understand. The Israeli military court system also allows lengthy detention periods before and between trial sessions and restricts the families of defendants and detainees from attending court hearings. Decisions of the military courts are not published.[335]

Israel's military court system also makes no presumption of innocence: the system has no established procedures to ensure that the burden of proof lies with the prosecution to prove guilt, thus shifting the burden to the defence. The independence and impartiality of the military courts is also questionable. All of the judges are serving Israeli army officers, of whom many are without legal qualifications or any judicial background.[336]

The result has been mass incarceration, with over half a million Palestinians detained by Israel between 1967 and 2005,[337] and more than 150,000 Palestinians prosecuted in the military courts since 1990 alone.[338] Only in 0.29 per cent of the 9,123 cases concluded in the military courts in 2006 was the defendant found not guilty.[339] Only 1.42 per cent of those cases went through a full evidentiary stage, consisting of the presentation of evidence and interrogation of witnesses.[340]

Indeed, of those convicted by the Israeli military courts, approximately 95–97 per cent were convicted as the result of plea bargains.[341] This figure may reflect several factors. The high rate of plea bargains suggests that Palestinian defendants and their lawyers lack trust in the military judicial system. Evidence of torture during interrogation, reviewed in Chapter 4 of this volume, supports claims that prosecutions are often based on confessions or incriminating statements, which are procured through threats or physical measures during interrogation. Moreover, failure to plea bargain usually brings a more severe penalty. Whatever the factors contributing to these plea bargains, the rate of convictions indicate that due process is not functioning: detention hearings last on average three minutes and four seconds.[342]

On the second standard, Article 64 of the Fourth Geneva Convention allows military courts to prosecute only those infringements of penal laws that are enacted as essential to the welfare and rights of the local civilian population or to the absolute military needs or security of the Occupying Power. The Israeli military court system exceeds these limitations in two ways. First, military law extends to issues unrelated to the rights of the Palestinians or the security of the Occupying Power: for example, tax evasion, unauthorised building, traffic violations, and other minor offences.[343]

Second, military orders issued by Israel have changed existing laws in the OPT to an extent that greatly exceeds the legislative competence of the Occupying Power (as described above). Disregard for restricting changes to the local laws was indeed formalised in 1967, when Military Order No. 130, *Concerning Interpretations*, provided that Israeli military orders 'supersede any law [that is, any law effective in the territory on the eve of the occupation], even if the former does not explicitly nullify the latter'.[344] Thus, the military courts system's 'ever-increasing jurisdiction has allowed it to try Palestinians for a range of offences, quite unrelated to national security questions; these include tax evasion, unauthorised building, and other minor offences'.[345] As noted above, administrative offences (such as traffic violations) are also prosecuted by the military courts. From 2002 to 2006, the Military Prosecution filed more than 43,000 indictments to the courts, only a third of which were for offences defined as 'security-related' and only 1 per cent of which involved defendants charged with intentionally causing death.[346] In prosecuting such a broad range of offences, the Israeli military courts in the OPT contravene the rules of international humanitarian law.

Most significantly for the purposes of this study, the primary *raison d'être* of the military court system is to buttress Israeli domination over the institutions and local population of the occupied territory. If established in an occupied territory, military courts should apply equally to all civilians in that territory. In practice, there is no evidence of Jewish civilians[347] in the OPT being tried in military courts under military legislation. Instead, when Israeli settlers are prosecuted for offences committed in the OPT, this is done under Israeli civil law, in a civil court in Israel. As a result, a Palestinian and a Jewish settler who commit the same offence in the same territory will be tried in a different court, under different penal laws,[348] with different procedures,[349] and will invariably receive different sentences.[350]

Further discriminatory attributes of the military court system relate to children and to 'administrative detention'.[351] The Israeli military has not established in the OPT any special juvenile court (as exists for minors in Israel); accordingly, Palestinian minors (under 18) are tried in the regular military courts, under the same procedure as adults. Regarding administrative detention, the military courts function as a tool to legitimise arbitrary arrest and detention without charge, with Palestinians often interned for periods of years. The discriminatory ways in which this practice is applied in the OPT is examined further in Chapter 4.

Finally, the scope of military law and the jurisdiction of the military courts are sufficiently broad to allow prosecution of Palestinians for political and cultural expression and association, movement to certain areas, various forms of non-violent protest, and failure to carry appropriate identification papers.[352] Thus Israel can use the military courts in the OPT to suppress dissent and persecute Palestinians for political activity, rendering its military courts precisely the 'instrument of political or racial persecution' that the parameters of international humanitarian law seek to prevent.

*Inadmissibility of discrimination based on citizenship*

It may be argued that Israel's use of military courts and generally differential treatment of Palestinians arises from their not being Israeli citizens. Regarding racial discrimination, the International Convention on the Elimination of All Forms of Racial Discrimination (ICERD) provides explicitly that 'this Convention shall not apply to distinctions, exclusions, restrictions or preferences made by a State Party to this Convention between citizens and non-citizens'.[353] *Ex facie*, Israel could possibly rely on this exclusion to justify 'distinctions, exclusions, restrictions or preferences' it makes in favour of its own citizens in the OPT.

Such a justification would arguably breach Israel's duty to apply ICERD in good faith.[354] According to the Committee on the Elimination of Racial Discrimination (CERD), the rule in Article 1(2) must be construed 'so as to avoid undermining the basic prohibition of discrimination'.[355]

> Under the Convention, differential treatment based on citizenship or immigration status will constitute discrimination if the criteria for such differentiation, judged in the light of the objectives and purposes of the Convention, are not applied pursuant to a legitimate aim, and are not proportional to the achievement of this aim.[356]

As Keane has observed, '[s]uch distinctions cannot, however, be made on the grounds of race, colour, descent, or national or ethnic origin'.[357]

Whether an Occupying Power may legitimately discriminate against non-citizens within occupied territory must accordingly be determined by reference to the law of belligerent occupation.[358] Only by virtue of being a belligerent occupant is Israel entitled to exercise jurisdiction in the OPT at all; but, by virtue of that same jurisdiction (as clarified in Chapter 1), Israel is also bound to apply human rights law, including ICERD. As Gasser notes, the Occupying Power should not observe provisions of the law in force in occupied territory that are incompatible with international humanitarian law, including 'openly discriminatory measures'.[359] If an Occupying Power should not *apply* existing laws of this nature then, it follows, it should not *introduce* them. This requirement precludes Israel's introducing measures that differentiate between its citizens present in occupied territory (those who are not members of its military forces or the administration of the occupation) and civilians who are not its citizens (and therefore protected persons), to the benefit of the former.

Further, Israel cannot justify discriminating in favour of its citizens who are present in the OPT illegally, in breach of Article 49(6) of the Fourth Geneva Convention.[360] Acting to consolidate the presence of settlers in the OPT is, indeed, not simply the pursuit of an improper purpose: it is the pursuit of an illegal purpose, one pursued knowingly from the start of the settlement process. Thus any attempt to justify discrimination on grounds that settlers are Israeli citizens, drawing on the exclusion provided by Article 1(2) of ICERD, would only be an abuse of right.[361]

CONCLUSION

This chapter has established the framework of international and Israeli law operating in the OPT, in light of which the applicability of international instruments regarding colonialism and apartheid must be considered. Three principle framing facts have been determined. First, the Palestinian people have the right to self-determination and the principles and instruments of international law relevant to self-determination are therefore applicable. Second, the Palestinian population in the West Bank, including East Jerusalem, and the Gaza Strip are protected persons under the terms of the Fourth Geneva Convention, as these territories remain under belligerent occupation. Third, the Fourth Geneva Convention and the Hague Regulations apply generally to Israel's obligations as an Occupying Power and these obligations are not altered by the prolonged nature of Israel's occupation.

Given these three factors, Israel's laws in the OPT manifest as violations of international humanitarian law, both in violating prohibitions not to alter the laws in force and by enforcing a dual and discriminatory legal regime on Jewish and Palestinian residents of the OPT. Israeli policy is to grant to Jewish settlers the protections of Israeli civil law and Basic Law, under the jurisdiction of Israeli civil courts, while administering Palestinians living in the same territory under military law and military courts whose procedures violate international standards for the administration of justice. As a consequence of this system, Jewish residents of the OPT enjoy freedom of movement, civil protections, and services that Palestinians are denied, while Palestinians are deprived of the protections accorded to protected persons by international humanitarian law. Administered and enforced by the state's military and having gained the imprimatur of Israel's Supreme Court, this dual system appears to reflect a policy by the State of Israel to sustain two parallel societies in the OPT, one Jewish-Israeli and the other Palestinian, and to accord these two groups very different rights and protections in the same territory.

The question here is whether this these laws and practices are best understood as entailing discrete violations of international human rights and humanitarian law, properly analysed as individual issues, or whether they operate on such a comprehensive scale as to suggest comprehensive and illegitimate regimes, notably colonialism and apartheid. The next two chapters address this question, first regarding colonialism and then regarding apartheid. Each chapter begins by identifying specific criteria by which regimes of colonialism or apartheid can be identified and then reviews of Israeli policies and practices according to those criteria to establish whether Israel's belligerent occupation of the OPT has obtained their character.

# 3
# Review of Israeli Practices Relative to the Prohibition of Colonialism

INTRODUCTION

This chapter considers whether Israel is not merely occupying but also, in terms of international law, colonising the Occupied Palestinian Territories (OPT). As discussed in Chapter 1, the prohibition of colonialism draws on several principles of international law, which must be considered together to assess whether belligerent occupation has obtained the qualities and character of colonialism. The primary instrument in international law dealing with the prohibition of colonialism is the 1960 *Declaration on the Granting of Independence to Colonial Peoples and Territories*.[1] The Declaration does not provide a definition of colonialism in as direct a manner as the Apartheid Convention defines apartheid, but suggests a definition through its language.

One of the Declaration's primary concerns is development: 'the social, cultural and economic development of dependent peoples' who, it affirms, have the right to 'freely pursue their economic, social and cultural development' and 'freely dispose of their natural wealth and resources'. The Declaration also expresses a special concern for 'territorial integrity', and stresses that 'inadequacy of political, economic, social or educational preparedness should never serve as a pretext for delaying independence'.[2] It rejects 'all forms' of colonial domination on grounds that all violate fundamental norms of human rights and threaten international peace and security, mentioning the damaging effects of colonialism on 'international economic co-operation'.

All these concerns reflect corollary rights and entitlements associated with self-determination, as summarised earlier:

(a) the right to exist – demographically and territorially – as a people; (b) the right to territorial integrity; (c) the right to permanent sovereignty over natural resources; (d) the right to cultural integrity and development; and (e) the right to economic and social development.[3]

To prevent these rights from being violated under the guise of belligerent occupation, the drafters of the Fourth Geneva Convention adopted Article 49(6), which prohibits the deportation or transfer by the Occupying Power of parts of its own civilian population into the territory it occupies, in order to

> prevent a practice adopted during the Second World War by certain Powers, which transferred portions of their own population to occupied territory

for political or racial reasons or in order, as they claimed, to *colonize* those territories.⁴

Taken together, therefore, the Declaration, the Fourth Geneva Convention and other international law indicate that the following practices have the character of a colonial regime:

1. violating the territorial integrity of occupied territory;
2. depriving the people of an occupied territory of the capacity for self-governance, by replacing their legal and political mechanisms;
3. integrating the economy of the occupied territory into that of the occupant to an extent that inhibits the autonomy of the occupied territory;
4. depriving the population under occupation of permanent sovereignty over its natural resources; and
5. cultural domination, which further threatens the identity of the people of an occupied territory and thus its capacity to express its right to self-determination.

Some of these same practices come under review in the next chapter, which considers how they relate to the prohibition of apartheid. Repeating the empirical evidence in both chapters in full detail would be redundant, so discussion here highlights only the main points and readers are referred to Chapter 4 for greater detail.

## REVIEW OF ISRAEL'S PRACTICES IN THE OPT RELATIVE TO COLONIALISM

### Violations of territorial integrity

The Declaration on Colonialism stresses the importance of 'territorial integrity' because a people seeking to express its right to self-determination as an independent state requires, minimally, a national territory in which to do so. The Declaration therefore affirms 'that all peoples have an inalienable right to complete freedom, the exercise of their sovereignty *and the integrity of their national territory*'. Article 4 then directs that *'the integrity of [all peoples'] national territory shall be respected'*. Article 6 emphasises that 'Any attempt aimed at the partial or total disruption of the national unity *and the territorial integrity* of a country is incompatible with the purposes and principles of the Charter of the United Nations.'⁵

As established in Chapter 2, Israeli policy has fragmented Palestinian territory by dividing areas of Jerusalem and the West Bank into separate Palestinian enclaves. According to the United Nations (UN) Office for the Coordination of Humanitarian Affairs, more than 38 per cent of the West Bank has been reserved for Israeli settlements and outposts, nature reserves, and military zones that are off-limits to Palestinian use. More than one-fifth of the West Bank has been declared a closed military zone. Approximately 10,122 hectares of agricultural land has been annexed to the settlements and

Palestinians are banned from using or entering this land.[6] Since Israel signed the Oslo Accords in 1995, Jewish settlements in the West Bank (not including East Jerusalem) have more than doubled in population to 270,000, according to a survey commissioned by the Israeli Defence Ministry.[7] According to Israel's Central Bureau of Statistics, the settler population in East Jerusalem at the end of 2008 had increased by 193,700, while the overall growth rate of the settlement population (excluding East Jerusalem) was at 4.7 per cent compared to 1.6 per cent for the Israeli population in general. This rate of growth supports statements of Israeli government leaders to the effect that Israel intends the majority of these settlements to be annexed permanently to Israel.

Policies related to this fragmentation stifle Palestinian economic and social development. Although the Oslo Accords granted planning powers to the Palestinian Authority (PA) in most of the Gaza Strip and in Areas A and B in the West Bank, Israel retained full formal control over planning in Area C, which constitutes about 60 per cent of the West Bank.[8] Area B (26 per cent of the West Bank) is partitioned by Israeli settlement blocs, over which Palestinians have no planning authority and which preclude the territorial contiguity necessary to building rational transportation and communications grids, agricultural management, water management and other urgent regional development issues.[9] Israel's policy of denying construction permits in the West Bank and its policies of home demolition and razing of agriculture stifle Palestinian land use and planning in favour of settlement expansion and bypass road construction.[10]

A further measure undermining the territorial integrity of the OPT is Israel's construction of major highways integrating Israeli towns and cities with settlement blocs in the West Bank, which has profoundly altered the social and political geography. Israeli State planning of the current highway grid is indicated in the *Settlement Master Plan for 1983–1986*, which proposed a need for special roads to service planned Jewish settlements and 'bypass the Arab population centres'.[11] Prior to 1967, principal roads in the West Bank ran north–south along the spine of the highlands, linking the principal cities of Jenin, Nablus, Ramallah, Jerusalem, Bethlehem and Hebron, while access roads ran laterally east and west to smaller towns and villages and to the Mediterranean coast.[12] In 1984, Israel's *Road Plan Number 50* shifted the West Bank's main highways to an east–west approach in order to integrate it into the Israeli road system for the benefit of Jewish settlers in the West Bank. An attempt at a judicial challenge was unsuccessful[13] and the new road network in the West Bank, primarily if not always exclusively for settler use, continued to expand. By 1993, 400 kilometres of such roads had been built.[14] With the Oslo agreements, plans for a further 650 kilometres of roads were swiftly formulated[15] and Israel spent US$600 million on bypass roads in 1995 alone.[16] By July 2008, Palestinian travel was restricted on 430 kilometres of West Bank roads and banned entirely on 137 kilometres.[17]

Thus Israel's publicly funded settlement policy goes beyond isolated infractions of Israel's obligations under the Fourth Geneva Convention to suggest a State strategy to annex significant portions of West Bank territory permanently to Israel, precluding the establishment of a contiguous and viable independent Palestinian State. This policy of durably obstructing the Palestinian people's ability to exercise the right to self-determination therefore directly violates this provision in the Declaration on Colonialism.

Supplanting institutions of governance

Historically, colonial powers have used law as a principal method of control, supplanting local pre-existing legal systems with their own laws or special laws designed to secure their domination over colonised territory.[18] For this reason, international humanitarian law bars an Occupying Power from 'extending its own legislation over the occupied territory or from acting as a sovereign legislator',[19] except where absolutely prevented. Being only in temporary control, 'the occupier is not the territorial sovereign. He cannot legislate for the occupied people as he does within his own frontiers'.[20] Article 43 of the Hague Regulations provides that the Occupying Power 'shall take all the measures in his power to restore, and ensure, as far as possible, public order and safety, *while respecting, unless absolutely prevented, the laws in force in the country*'.[21]

Article 64 of the Fourth Geneva Convention indicates that the Occupying Power is allowed to take legislative measures only if these are essential to the welfare and rights of the local civilian population or to the absolute bona fide military needs or security of the Occupying Power. These two exceptions have been held to be of a 'strictly limitative nature'.[22] The Occupying Power is precluded from abrogating or suspending the laws of the occupied territory for any other reason, and particularly not to make it accord with their own legal conceptions.

*Altering the laws in place in the occupied territory*

Israel's changes to the legal system in the OPT since 1967 have gone far beyond these permissible boundaries under the law of occupation. In the West Bank, as detailed further in Chapter 4, pre-existing local laws and standards have been widely changed, modified and overridden through the imposition of thousands of military orders by the Occupying Power. As discussed earlier, these modifications extend to controlling everything from alcohol taxes[23] to control of natural resources[24] to which fruit and vegetables may be grown by Palestinians.[25] Thus neither the design nor the impact of such wide-ranging legislation is convincingly explained by military necessity.

Military legislation in the West Bank was mirrored by a similar system in the Gaza Strip until Israel's 'disengagement' from the latter territory in 2005. While the Gaza Strip remains under belligerent occupation, as discussed in Chapter 2, the Palestinian authorities now have autonomous authority over domestic security and civil law within the limits imposed by Israel. Israel presented the unilateral disengagement as serving to 'dispel claims regarding Israel's responsibility for the Palestinians in the Gaza Strip'[26] and the jurisdiction of Israeli military orders in Gaza was repealed. Nonetheless, the 2006 Criminal Procedure Law[27] allows Israel to incarcerate Palestinians from the Gaza Strip suspected of criminal offences in detention facilities in Israel and to prosecute them in Israeli civil courts.

East Jerusalem was effectively absorbed into Israel within a number of weeks of the start of the occupation[28] and as such is subject to the Israeli legal system in its entirety. The entire fabric of laws applicable in East Jerusalem has thus been transformed, as discussed in more detail in Chapter 4.

*Extraterritorial application of Israeli civil law to Jews in the OPT*

Among the most striking examples of legal change is that Israel applies its domestic law to Jewish settlers in the OPT, rather than the local law that was in force prior to the occupation. This practice cannot be considered comparable to earlier practices of capitulations, such as European privileges in the Ottoman Empire,[29] because the OPT have no sovereign government that can grant such privileges. Therefore, this practice violates Article 43 of the Hague Regulations.

As detailed in Chapter 2, jurisdiction over offences and civil matters in relation to Jewish settlers rests with Israeli civil courts inside Israel, in contravention of Article 64(2) of the Fourth Geneva Convention. For example, Israel's Supreme Court has extended its jurisdiction over the actions of the Israeli occupying forces and authorities in the OPT, sitting in such cases as the 'High Court of Justice' (a practice stemming from a policy decision in 1967 by Meir Shamgar, then Israeli Attorney-General). The Supreme Court ruled in 1972[30] that it 'had the power to judicially review any military activity taken beyond the borders of the Israeli democracy'.[31]

An Occupying Power is permitted under Article 66 of Fourth Geneva Convention to establish military courts in an occupied territory, but such courts must be 'set up in accordance with the recognised principles governing the administration of justice'.[32] They must not be used 'as an instrument of political or racial persecution' and may be used only to enforce penal provisions legally promulgated by the Occupying Power under Article 64(2). When Israel created local authorities for its settlements in the West Bank, however, it did not use existing Jordanian law to do so but rather established regional and local councils (through Military Orders No. 783 and 892).

As detailed in Chapter 2, that Israel's military court system in the OPT is incompatible with fundamental international standards regarding due process and the administration of justice is well documented.[33] Fair-trial deficiencies are apparent regarding the right to prepare an effective defence,[34] the right to a presumption of innocence,[35] the right to examine witnesses,[36] and the right to prompt notice of criminal charges.[37] The military courts apply military legislation imposed in violation of international humanitarian law as described above, and are used as an apparatus of domination by the occupation to persecute Palestinians for 'political' activity.

Councils for Jewish settlements have assumed powers and functions significantly different to Palestinian municipal councils in the West Bank but almost identical to the local and regional councils inside Israel.[38] The scope of application of several Israeli laws includes all Jewish settlers in the OPT, whether they are Israeli citizens or not. A 1984 extension to the Emergency Legislation clarified that,

> For the purposes of the enactments enumerated in the Schedule, the expression 'resident in Israel' or any other expression occurring in those enactments denoting residence, living or having one's abode in Israel shall be regarded as including also a person who lives in a zone and is an Israeli national *or is entitled to immigrate to Israel under the Law of Return*, 5710-1950, and who would come within the scope of such expression if he lived in Israel.

As only Jews (and the immediate family members of Jews, even if not Jewish) are entitled to immigrate to Israel under the Law of Return, this law was openly discriminatory in conveying Israel's civil law to Jewish settlers on grounds of their Jewish identity or Jewish family relations. Laws covered by this provision include laws relating to military service, the Income Tax Ordinance, the Election Law,[39] the Population Registry, and the National Insurance Law.[40]

Particularly significant to the question of colonialism is Israeli legislation that formalises direct Israeli government responsibility for encouraging growth of Jewish settlements in the OPT. For example, in 1988 Israel extended the provisions of the Development Towns and Areas Law[41] to settlements in the OPT, thus conveying a broad range of special State benefits to settlers. Benefits under this law include:

- special grants and concessions to investment in the settlement;
- permanent exemption from real estate taxes and employers' taxes;
- a grant to cover costs of moving into the settlement;
- loans for purchasing apartments and for rent and utilities, which convert into a grant after three years' residence in the settlement;
- free education from kindergarten through university;
- scholarships for technical education and a special budget for children's extracurricular activities; and
- preferential allocations of professional training through the Ministry of Labour and Welfare.

These benefits are provided and administered by an appropriate government ministry, under the oversight of the Finance Ministry and the Economics and Planning Ministry. Administration is monitored and directed by a 'Ministers Committee' which includes the Ministers of Finance, Economics and Planning, Energy and Infrastructure, Defence, Building and Housing, Health, Education and Culture, Agriculture, Labour and Welfare, Interior, and Industry and Trade. Thus the government of Israel is comprehensively and formally responsible for annexing and reserving land and developing social services in the OPT for exclusive use by Jewish settlements, constituting a State-directed project of colonisation.

## Subjecting the local population to foreign administration

Article 43 of the Hague Regulations requires that an Occupying Power sustain the local institutions administering public order and safety in the occupied territory (assuming they are operating in accordance with local law) 'unless absolutely prevented'.[42] The Occupying Power's prerogative to change local arrangements 'does not extend to the reconstruction of the fundamental institutions of the occupied area'.[43] This phrasing is construed to prevent an Occupying Power from imposing its own preferred model of governance to an extent that would equate with de facto annexation and colonialism.[44]

As discussed earlier, Israel has extended the 'jurisdiction and administration' of the State of Israel to East Jerusalem, while establishing and charging a military government with the administration of security and civil matters in the rest of the OPT. This administrative separation of East Jerusalem from the rest of the OPT raises two principal questions: may the Occupying Power create different geographical units of administration? And is it lawful for the Occupying Power to integrate the administration of all or part of the occupied territory with the administration of its own State? Both answers must be negative.

That Israel's detaching East Jerusalem from the OPT is illegal is indicated by the international response to legislative measures taken by Germany during the First World War to divide occupied Belgium into two separate administrative districts (one Flemish and the other French-speaking), which 'were unanimously considered to be illegal'.[45] The illegality of partition is compounded in Israel's case by the norm preventing any acquisition of sovereignty through occupation or the use of force. Even Israel's Supreme Court, albeit in relation to the administration of the rest of the West Bank, has acknowledged that an Occupying Power is required to administer occupied territory as a distinct entity, detached from its own territory.[46]

Regarding the rest of the OPT, Israel has replaced the Jordanian and Egyptian institutions of governance, which operated prior to 1967, with military administrations. In the West Bank, occupied by Israeli forces on 6 June 1967, an order was issued by the West Bank Area Commander before the Six-Day War had even ended, stating that:

> All powers of government, legislation, appointment, and administration in relation to the area or its inhabitants shall henceforth be vested in me alone and shall only be exercised by me or by persons appointed by me for that purpose or acting on my behalf.[47]

Israel claimed that it had to transfer administrative powers to a military government because the West Bank had only a local administration and lacked a central government. However, Israel imposed a similar system in the Gaza Strip, which already had its own centralised legislative, executive and judicial branches, which were autonomous from the Egyptian government. The military governments of the two territories were both administered by a military arm, which was entrusted with ensuring security, and a civilian arm, which exercised administrative powers. These arms had little autonomy to make decisions separately on matters relating to their respective mandates, and were largely fused together. Further, the interdependence between the military governments for the West Bank and Gaza Strip and the government of Israel itself cannot be overstated: the OPT, excluding East Jerusalem (which had been juridically incorporated into Israel), effectively fell under the administration of Israel's Ministry of Defence.

In 1981, the military commander of the Israeli forces in the West Bank declared the creation of a Civil Administration in the West Bank.[48] This step institutionalised the separation of military and civil functions in the military government and elevated a large number of military orders from the status of temporary security enactments to one of permanent laws.[49] It also enabled the Civil Administration to regulate and control daily social and economic life of all civilians in the West Bank. It was therefore seen as a unilateral constitutional change, effectively altering the legal status of the West Bank. The Civil Administration continues to function as an arm of the military government dealing with civil affairs in the West Bank, under the ultimate control of the Ministry of Defence.[50]

Thus Israel has profoundly altered the systems of administrative governance in the OPT, and has done so in a manner that is effectively preventing the Palestinians from sustaining or developing their own political institutions with any genuine authority, thereby preventing their exercise of self-determination. Here the law of war may paradoxically aggravate the problem by precluding an Occupying Power from changing the political institutions in occupied territory. As Roberts observed in 1990, in his seminal article on prolonged occupation:

> A further concern is that the law of occupation has provided the basis for denying the inhabitants of the OPT normal political activity, keeping them in effect permanently under Israeli control, but as second-class citizens or worse. From this perspective, the longer the occupation lasts, the more akin to colonialism it seems.'[51]

*Preventing the local population from exercising political authority*

Decisions concerning the OPT are ostensibly made by the military government but, as noted above, are best understood as being 'in the hands of Israeli cabinet ministers and government sub-committees'[52] who are also charged with building the settlements and managing related issues of land and resources. Palestinians have no say in these decisions.

Even at the local level, the Palestinians are not assisted in developing free political institutions, but are actively obstructed from doing so. Between 1967 and 1980, for instance, municipal elections in the OPT were cancelled by the Occupying Power several times.[53] In 1976, the Israeli government allowed elections but found that PLO candidates had swept the mayoralties and took severe measures to limit their powers (two mayors were later deported, two others maimed in bomb attacks). In 1982, the Civil Administration dismissed the majority of the West Bank's elected local councils and mayors and transferred authority over West Bank municipalities to Palestinian 'village leagues', whose assigned role was to enforce Palestinian cooperation with Israeli authorities rather than develop Palestinian political institutions.[54]

The Oslo Accords in the mid 1990s and the creation of the Palestinian National Authority ostensibly granted a degree of autonomy to Palestinians in the OPT, excluding East Jerusalem. But since Israel never relinquished its administrative and security control over the OPT, the Oslo Accords failed to provide an effective Palestinian government. Local decision-making remains impeded through several methods, including legal and administrative barriers to planning and development, restrictions on external trade, freedom of movement, and the detention and imprisonment of Palestinian policy-makers (as detailed in Chapter 4). Although it was agreed in the initial Declaration of Principles that 'the Civil Administration will be dissolved, and the Israeli military government will be withdrawn',[55] this did not happen, and thus led to the provision in the subsequent Interim Agreement that 'Israel shall continue to exercise powers and responsibilities'[56] not transferred to the Palestinian National Authority.

By contrast, Jewish settlers in the OPT have been allowed to participate in high-level decision-making bodies, such as the Higher Planning Council, which determines land-use planning in the West Bank. Jewish-Israeli settlers also enjoy the democratic privilege of voting for representatives in the Knesset who can represent their concerns to the State of Israel, whose ministries administer the settlements, agriculture, industry, natural resources and infrastructure in the OPT. Palestinians living in the OPT have no representation in the Knesset.

The Occupying Power's military and administrative system therefore remains supreme in the OPT, and many of the pre-Oslo military orders remain in force. Indeed, the Oslo Accords did not repeal or revoke any Israeli military orders but merely provided that they be reviewed jointly by both sides,[57] which itself did not happen in practice. Thus, the unlawful Israeli-imposed amendments to the pre-existing local laws were retained and cannot be changed without Israeli approval. As a result, between 1967 and 1993, Palestinians were forbidden 'to conduct a protest march or meeting (grouping of ten or more where the subject concerns or is related to politics) without permission from the Military Commander'. They were also 'forbidden to raise flags or other symbols, to distribute or publish a political article and pictures with political connotations'.[58]

The Oslo Accords loosened or eliminated some of these restrictions on symbolic expression but tightened Israel's control in substantive policy areas. Of particular significance is that, through a consensus provision in the joint committee system, Israel holds an effective veto over any law enacted by the Palestinian Legislative Council (PLC).[59] Moreover, the Accords did not eliminate Israel's capacity or willingness to undermine Palestinian self-governance through military means. For example, after the elections in January

2006, the Israeli air force bombed the Palestinian Interior Ministry, Foreign Ministry and Finance Ministry. Arrests of numerous ministers and parliamentarians, and revocation of others' government identification cards, then prevented them from carrying out their governmental duties as set out in Palestinian Basic Law. In 2008, 50 elected members of the PLC, more than one-third of the total membership, were being detained by Israel.[60] These arrests have paralysed the PLC's ability to meet quorums and therefore to convene or function in its constitutional capacity.

More than 25 years ago, Palestinian legal scholars asserted that Israel was acting as a 'sovereign government exercising complete legislative, administrative, and judicial authority over the [West Bank] and its inhabitants and instituting major changes in the West Bank economy, demography, and institutions'.[61] Although the Oslo Accords transferred some authority to the PA,[62] power was transferred in areas of Israel's choosing. The degree of autonomy transferred to Palestinians cannot challenge Israel's overall demographic, economic, cultural and, perhaps most significantly, territorial domination. In effect, Israel relieved itself of the responsibility for administration and governance of certain Palestinian populations while retaining effective sovereignty over the settlement areas and general control over the OPT as a whole, in a manner which clearly contravenes provisions in the Declaration on Colonialism.

## Economic integration

With the development in international law of an explicit prohibition of colonialism, States holding foreign territory in trust, such as under a League of Nations mandate, were strictly obliged to maintain and keep that territory separate from its own.[63] This prohibition aimed both to forestall attempts by the administering State to annex the dependent territory and to ensure that the territory retained its integrity as the geographic basis for the people's self-determination. Since self-determination also has an economic component, States holding a territory in trust must ensure its economic integrity by maintaining its distinct economic features and structure. Similar obligations are imposed on States holding territory under belligerent occupation, to ensure that such territories sustain their separate political and economic character.[64] As noted earlier, an Occupying Power does not acquire sovereignty over the territory it occupies and is prohibited from annexing it. In keeping with this principle, the Occupying Power is merely a 'de facto administrator'[65] and does not have the authority to extend its domestic legislation to the occupied territory.[66] Its authority to make changes to the laws in force is limited to legitimate security concerns and to maintaining the public life of the local population.[67] Moreover, the Occupying Power is under an obligation to create an administration within occupied territory that is separate and distinct from that of its own territory.

The imperative of preserving the economic integrity of occupied territory extends to the use of property.[68] Article 55 of the 1907 Hague Regulations provides:

The occupying state shall be regarded only as an administrator and usufructuary of public buildings, real estate, forests, agricultural estates belonging to the hostile state and situation in occupied territory. It must safeguard the capital of these properties and administer them in accordance with the rules of usufruct.

The rules of usufruct allow an Occupying Power to sell or lease agricultural land to others, but not to alter its fundamental character or destroy it.[69] The Occupying Power may not exploit immovable property 'beyond normal use' – for example, by cutting more timber than was cut prior to occupation[70] – and must respect the 'substance or capital of publicly owned immovable property', such as office buildings and public infrastructure.[71] The Occupying Power does not gain title to public immovable property and thus cannot dispose of it at will, and cannot confiscate private property whether movable or immovable.[72] Private property can be requisitioned and used temporarily by the Occupying Power, but cannot be sold, even if the proceeds of the sale are given to the rightful owner at the end of the war.[73]

Hence the 1907 Hague Regulations provide for varying treatment of different types of property – public and private, movable and immovable – as the Regulations have been interpreted in litigation arising principally out of the First and Second World Wars. The governing principle is that 'under the rules of war, the economy of an occupied country can only be required to bear the expenses of the occupation, and these should not be greater than the economy of the country can reasonably be expected to bear'.[74] Thus an Occupying Power is allowed to seize or appropriate only property required to fulfil the needs of the occupying army or to defray the costs of administering the occupation of the local population.[75] It is prohibited from taking property for its own commercial or public purposes.[76] It is also forbidden to remove from the occupied territory any private or public property and to merge that property into its domestic economy.[77] The economy of the occupied territory is to be kept intact, except for the carefully defined permissions afforded the Occupying Power.[78] Otherwise, as Eyal Benvenisti has pointed out, economic integration may simply act as an incentive for the occupation to continue.[79]

*Israeli practices breaching the prohibition on economic integration*

Simultaneously with establishing settlements in the OPT, Israel undertook a policy to integrate the economies of the West Bank and Gaza Strip into the State of Israel.[80] This policy included a range of measures designed to appropriate natural resources, redirect Palestinian labour to foster economic dependence on Israel, and integrate the capital markets.[81]

The Israeli government has designated many West Bank settlement blocs as National Priority Areas, authorised to receive financial incentives – tax breaks, grants, and reduced fees – administered through Israeli government ministries.[82] Israel has historically allocated larger proportions of financial resources to the Israeli local settlements authorities situated in the OPT than those situated in Israel.[83] The economic and civil integration of settlements into Israel was achieved by extending Israeli customs and policing services to areas of the West Bank, as if they were in Israel.[84] In 1967, Israel issued Military Order No. 31, which designated the West Bank as a distinct customs zone, but later that year Military Order No. 103 eliminated all tariffs and customs duties on goods entering the West Bank from Israel.[85]

In his opinion in the *Christian Society for the Holy Places* judgment, Deputy President Sussman relied upon the prolonged nature of the occupation to rule that the occupant has a duty to adapt the law to respond to changing needs in economic and social matters. He concluded that the occupant has the duty to legislate for the welfare of the local population, a view that Kretzmer terms the 'benevolent occupant' approach:[86]

> In inquiring whether the legislative measures of an Occupying Power are at one with the provisions of Article 43, considerable importance attaches to the question of the motives of the legislator. Has he legislated in order to advance his own interests or out of a desire to care for the well-being of the civil population, 'la vie publique' of which Article 43 speaks? All agree that any legislative measure not concerned with the welfare of the inhabitants is invalid and goes beyond the authority of the Occupant.[87]

The distinction that Sussman drew between interests of the occupant and of the local population reflects again the fundamental principle of the law of occupation: that the occupant is only in temporary administrative control of the territory and is not its sovereign. The territories involved – the occupied territory and the occupant's home territory – are to be treated as separate entities. While this onus of separation is implicit in prohibitions against annexing occupied territory, it is also expressed in rules governing regulation of the economy of occupied territory

In judgments hinging on its doctrine of prolonged occupation, Israel's Supreme Court has upheld measures that systematically efface the principle of the separateness of the Occupied Palestinian Territories. As discussed earlier, by including settlers within the category of inhabitants whose welfare the occupant must promote, the Supreme Court endorsed an obliteration of the distinction between lawful and unlawful inhabitants. In *Electricity Company No. 1*, the Court simply asserted that 'the residents of Kiryat Arba must be regarded as having been added to the local population and they are also entitled to a regular supply of electricity'.[88] Similarly, in *Economic Corporation for Jerusalem*, the Court held that in assessing changes during a prolonged occupation for the purpose of applying Article 43, a relevant 'new reality' was the existence of settlements.[89] In doing so, the Court thus conferred apparent legitimacy upon the economic integration of Jewish settlements into Palestinian areas.

The Court has also endorsed the permanent economic integration of the OPT into Israel by upholding changes made within the OPT which will subsist after the end of occupation, such as the construction of road systems linking the West Bank, and settlements, to metropolitan Israel,[90] and the integration of Palestinian electricity infrastructure to that of Israel.[91] Water supplies have also been made dependent upon Mekorot, Israel's national water company. Although in the *Elon Moreh* case, Justice Landau ruled that an occupant could not create facts (in this case a settlement) for its military purposes that were intended from the outset to last beyond the termination of military rule,[92] this test was soon reformulated by Justice Cahan in *Electricity Company No. 2* to provide:

> generally, in the absence of special circumstances, the Commander of the region should not introduce in an occupied area modifications which, even if they do not alter the existing law, would have a far-reaching and prolonged impact on it, far beyond the period when the military administration will be terminated one way or another, save for actions undertaken for the benefit of the inhabitants of the area.[93]

While in that case Justice Cahan held that there was insufficient reason to divest the Jerusalem District Electricity Company of its concession to supply electricity within the West Bank in favour of the Israel Electricity Corporation, this had occurred in relation to the supply of electricity to Hebron by virtue of the *Electricity Company No. 1* case.

In *Cooperative Society*, Justice Barak affirmed Sussman's views regarding the changing needs of the population of occupied territory expressed in *Christian Society for the Holy Places*, but found that the occupant's authority extended 'to taking all measures necessary to ensure growth, change and development'.[94] The Court considered objections to a plan to build highways connecting towns in the West Bank with Jerusalem. During the proceedings the respondents had conceded that the roads would benefit residents of Israel and ease travel between Israel and the West Bank, but also argued that many West Bank residents travelled to work in Israel.[95] Affirming the Court's rulings in the *Electricity Company* cases on the legitimacy of the creation of permanent changes in occupied territory, Barak formulated the governing rule as:

> Long-term fundamental investments in an occupied area bringing about permanent changes that may last beyond the period of the military administration are permitted if required for the benefit of the local population – provided there is nothing in these investments that might introduce an essential modification in the basic institutions of the area.[96]

Further, in order to carry out 'fundamental investments and long-range projects for the benefit of the local population ... the military administration is entitled to cooperate with the Occupying State'.[97] Kretzmer commented on this approach thus:

> The notion of 'public benefit' is intimately connected to political objectives and interests. The model applied by Justice Barak is reminiscent of a colonial model of governors who know what is best for the natives. Development is assumed beneficial and large highways must be for the public good, as must

improved connections between the Occupied Territories and Israel itself. There is, however, nothing inherently good about development the adverse consequences of which may override benefits. It is quite true that people may opt for development despite its adverse consequences, but should a temporary regime make this irrevocable decision? Moreover, is improving connections between the West Bank and Israel necessarily for the good of the West Bank residents, on the not unreasonable assumption that many of these residents would prefer to break those connections?[98]

*Examples of integration: value-added tax and electricity grids*

The integration of the OPT's economy into that of Israel is revealed in measures taken in specific economic sectors. One is illustrated in *Bassil Abu Aita et al v. The Regional Commander of Judea and Samaria and Staff Officer in charge of matters of customs and excise*.[99] The immediate cause was the introduction of value-added tax (VAT) into the Occupied Palestinian Territories. Notably, Feilchenfeld rejects the claim that an occupant may create a customs union between its territory and occupied territory because 'this almost invariably would be an intrinsic measure of complete annexation which a mere occupant has no right to effect'.[100] In essence, the economy of occupied territory must be kept separate from that of the occupant as 'the economic substance of the belligerently occupied territory must not be taken over by the occupant or put to the service of his war effort':

> The economy of the belligerently occupied territory is to be kept intact, except for carefully defined permissions given to the occupying authority – permissions which all refer to the army of occupation. Just as the inhabitants of the occupied territory must not be forced to help the enemy in waging the war against their own country or their country's allies, so must the economic assets of the occupied territory not be used in such a manner.[101]

The post-Second World War tribunals may have been influenced to some degree in their strictures against economic convergence by the *Austro-German customs union* advisory opinion.[102] In this opinion, the Permanent Court of International Justice ruled that Austria's independence would be compromised if it lost its 'sole right of decision in all matters economic, political, financial or other'.[103] Axiomatically, if an occupant were to merge the economy of occupied territory with its own, then the latter would lose its independence. It would no longer be sovereign but effectively be annexed, contrary to the fundamental purpose of the law of occupation.

In his opinion in *Abu Aita*, Justice Shamgar started from the proposition that the removal or continued maintenance of customs barriers between an occupant's territory and the territories it occupies was a matter to be decided by the military government of the occupied territories. Its decision could not be contested provided its action caused no significant damage to the economy of the occupied territories.[104] It had been decided at the start of the occupation that 'the two economies would not be separated' because the economy of the occupied territories was 'umbilically tied to the economy of Israel'.[105] This integration was effected by the removal of the customs barriers between the occupied territories and Israel and the introduction of uniform rates of indirect taxes.[106]

Invoking the prolonged occupation argument, that changing circumstances in occupied territory justify the introduction of new measures by the occupant in order that it may fulfil its obligation under Article 43 of the Hague Regulations to ensure civil life, Shamgar asserted that freezing the tax regime as it existed at the start of the occupation could, through time, be detrimental to the economy of occupied territory by preventing its development and adjustment to changes in the world and regional economy, as well as to changes in the economy of the occupant.[107] He ruled that the proposed legislative change did adequately balance the welfare of the population of the occupied territories and Israel's security:

> military government has a clear and direct interest in avoiding any disruptions in the regional economy and *inter alia* it will do all it possibly can to prevent as far as possible reduction in trade or increase in unemployment. To cut off existing markets, especially those created during the period of military government, has a direct effect on incomes and therefore upon the standard of living; unemployment is a fermenting and unsettling factor from the standpoint of security and both these phenomena are among those the military government tries to avoid in so far as possible; at least a military government that aspires to the good of the public in the territory, and the good of the security interests of the occupier in so far as possible and practicable.[108]

In addition, Shamgar employed the parallel application argument, that because VAT had been introduced in Israel as well as in the occupied territories, this was a reasonable use of the powers granted to Israel by Article 43 of the Hague Regulations.[109]

As Kretzmer has observed, there is generally a strong connection between steps taken by the military authorities in the occupied territories and the political agenda of the Israeli government.[110] Israel's association agreement with the European Economic Community (EEC) had made its introduction of VAT vital as a consequence of the removal of customs barriers between Israel and EEC member States, and this has 'had direct repercussions in the territories':

> Economic integration – as a compelling motive for introducing the tax – was obviously a dominant factor in all decisions having implications on the economic relations between Israel and the territories.[111]

Shamgar viewed the only alternative as being to separate the economies of the occupied territories and Israel, but to this he claimed, would breach Israel's duties under Article 43 as it 'would impede the possibility of a return to orderly life and prevent the effective observance of the duty regarding the assurance of "la vie publique"'. Having accepted that a value-added tax must be introduced in Israel, 'the wheel could not have been turned back without affecting the proper fulfilment of the duties deriving from Article 43'. Shamgar concluded that the integration of the economies required that strict attention be paid to parallel fiscal and economic developments: 'The method of tackling economic problems in Israel cannot, it seems, stop at the old pre-1967 borders which today are open for passage of people and trade.'[112]

Although Shamgar paid lip service to the autonomy of the military authorities in economic matters, this is difficult to reconcile with the fact that the introduction of VAT was driven by Israel's own economic policy. The military authorities simply 'served as proxies for the implementation of economic policies decided upon by the Israeli body-politic'.[113] It seems impossible to justify this by reference to the test that innovation within occupied territory should be determined by the interests of its population and not those of the occupant, all the more so when the rationale for its necessity was the earlier unlawful act of the integration of the economies. This was simply a case of compounding illegality under the guise of benevolence.

When one also takes into account the creation of water and electricity dependence – whose consequences gave rise to events leading to *Jaber al Bassouini Ahmed et al* v. *The Prime Minister and Minister of Defence*[114] – and the weight given to the interests of settlers unconnected with the administration of the occupied territories in determining policy, it seems clear that the interests of the Palestinian population of the OPT have been systematically subordinated to Israel's domestic concerns. This rejects the rationale of the law of occupation, as it amounts to a de facto annexation, denying Palestinian interests their proper weight in the formulation of policy and certainly blocking Palestinian participation in policy-making. Although this situation has developed and persisted under the mantle of occupation, it is pointedly akin to colonialist behaviour as prohibited under international law.

### Violation of permanent sovereignty over natural resources

The right and need of peoples to control the natural resources in their territory are among the most sensitive matters in colonial and non-self-governing territories. Disputes about the use of natural resources have accordingly been the trigger for bitter and violent conflict in many colonies and a major grievance driving decolonisation. Reflecting this sensitivity, the Declaration on Colonialism affirms the right of peoples to 'freely dispose of their natural wealth and resources'. The right to self-determination (which is denied by colonialism) assumes 'the right of a State or a people to dispose freely of its natural resources and wealth within the limits of national jurisdiction',[115] and the General Assembly has declared that this right applies to trusteeship territories.[116] The International Covenant on Civil and Political Rights and the International Covenant on Economic, Social and Cultural Rights both include the same provision on this point (listed in both instruments as Article 1(2)):

All peoples may, for their own ends, freely dispose of their natural wealth and resources without prejudice to any obligations arising out of international economic co-operation, based upon the principle of mutual benefit, and international law. In no case may a people be deprived of its own means of subsistence.

The right of a people to control its natural resources is indeed a principle of customary international law (binding on all States).[117] Such control includes the right to prospect, explore, develop, and market them; use them to promote national development; conserve and manage them pursuant to national environmental policies; regulate foreign investment in their development; and have an equitable share in transboundary resources.[118] Hence exploitation or plundering of a non-self-governing territory's marine, riverine, mineral, timber and agricultural resources by foreign States (or private economic interests backed by foreign powers) violates this substantive right,[119] as does preventing a people from exploiting and developing natural resources for its own benefit in its own territory. Consideration of how Israel is managing natural resources in the OPT is therefore central to assessing whether its practices constitute a form of colonialism.

*The right to water*

Water is essential to human life and, accordingly, a special concern of human rights and international humanitarian law. Scholarly consensus is that an individual right to water does not exist in customary international law,[120] but it is considered a collective right – and integral to the exercise of self-determination – because water is essential to a people's economic development.[121] Water is indeed implicitly included in the international bill of rights because it is essential to the enjoyment of other rights that are expressly enumerated.[122] The right of peoples and populations to water has therefore drawn increasing concern and attention by scholars, organisations and States.

The Committee on Economic, Social and Cultural Rights has clarified its view that the right to water is a human right.[123] Noting that Covenant affirms that all people have the right to an adequate standard of living, it observed that several additional rights are implied because they are essential to this goal:

> The right to water clearly falls within the category of guarantees essential for securing an adequate standard of living, particularly since it is one of the most fundamental conditions for survival ... The right to water is also inextricably related to the right to the highest attainable standard of health ... and the rights to adequate housing and adequate food ... The right should also be seen in conjunction with other rights enshrined in the International Bill of Human Rights, foremost amongst them the right to life and human dignity.[124]

The Committee observed that the right to water (and to other essentials for human life) imposes certain obligations on States, including the obligation to ensure that the right to water is exercised without discrimination of any kind.[125] Such obligations are non-derogable: no justification may be made for non-compliance.[126]

Beyond this, the Committee identified three types of obligation incumbent upon States parties: the obligations to *respect, protect* and *fulfil*.[127]

> The obligation to *respect* requires that States parties refrain from interfering directly or indirectly with the enjoyment of the right to water. The obligation includes, inter alia, refraining from engaging in any practice or activity that denies or limits equal access to adequate water; arbitrarily interfering with customary or traditional arrangements for water allocation; unlawfully diminishing or polluting water, for example through waste from State-owned facilities or through use and testing of weapons; and limiting access to, or destroying, water services and infrastructure as a punitive measure, for example, during armed conflicts in violation of international humanitarian law.[128]

A State's obligation to *protect* requires it to prevent third parties from interfering 'in any way' with the enjoyment of the right to water.[129] States parties to the Covenant 'should refrain at all times' from imposing embargoes or other measures that prevent the supply of water or of goods and services essential to secure the right to water. Certainly, '[w]ater should never be used as an instrument of political and economic pressure'.[130] The prohibition of discrimination regarding water allocation is consistent with the broader doctrine of reasonable and equitable use of shared water resources derived from customary international water law.[131]

Israel is not a party to the 1997 Convention. Nevertheless, in adopting the draft of the 1997 Convention which it presented to the General Assembly, the International Law Commission simultaneously adopted a *Resolution on Confined Transboundary Groundwater*, operative paragraph 2 of which provided:

> *Commends* States to be guided by the principles contained in the draft articles on the law of the non-navigational uses of international watercourses, where appropriate, in regulating transboundary groundwater.[132]

In August 2008, the Commission adopted draft Articles on the law of transboundary aquifers. Article 4, in part, provides that, 'Aquifer States shall utilize a transboundary aquifer or aquifer system according to the principle of equitable and reasonable utilization.'[133] In its comments on an earlier draft of these Articles, Israel stated that this principle had 'gained the recognition of States'.[134] Accordingly, whether surface or groundwater, international watercourses such as those shared by Israel and the Palestinians must be divided fairly and reasonably between the two parties.[135]

Thus, as the Occupying Power, Israel has obligations relating to water in the OPT under the principles of public international law which prohibits discrimination regarding its use. Also, although international humanitarian law does not address how water resources should be shared between parties to a conflict,[136] under the Hague Regulations the permissible use of an occupied territory's natural resources by the Occupying Power are limited to the needs of the occupying army, and may not exceed past usage levels. It is therefore unlawful, for example, for Israel to use water resources in the OPT to supply the Israeli settler population (unlawfully present in occupied territory) or the civilian population of Israel. Even if it does so, then it still remains obliged to abide by principles of non-discrimination and equity under human rights and international water law in order to avoid compounding an already existing illegality.

*Water rights and allocations in the OPT*

Mandate Palestine is a relatively arid region where water sources are scarce and increasingly costly to develop. Hence it is a matter of elevated concern in this study that Israel appears to have violated the principle of permanent sovereignty over natural resources in relation to water resources in the OPT.

The territory of Mandate Palestine has three main sources of natural fresh water. The Mountain Aquifer extends under both sides of the Green Line, including most of the West Bank and much of central Israel.[137] It is divided into Northern, Eastern and Western Aquifers radiating from the 'spine' of the West Bank highlands. The Jordan River Basin is a surface-water system shared with Jordan, Syria and Lebanon. The Golan Heights comprises a major watershed that feeds this system and is the principal source feeding Lake Tiberius, the single largest source for Israel's National Water Carrier. Along the coastal plain, the Coastal Aquifer is a smaller source and the only natural source for the Gaza Strip.[138]

Upon the start of the occupation, Israel issued several military orders that integrated the water system of the OPT into the Israeli system denying Palestinian control over this resource. First, Military Order No. 92 (15 August 1967) vested all authority over water in the OPT in the Israeli military authorities and prohibited any individual from establishing, owning or administering a water institution (wells, or processing plants) without a new permit, which could be denied without explanation.[139] Second, Israel declared the lower Jordan River a closed military zone, denying Palestinians direct access to it, while existing Palestinian pumps and irrigation ditches tapping the Jordan were destroyed.[140] Third, Israel established new regulations for other districts that consistently curbed Palestinian access to water and, in some cases, vested the military commander with the power to appoint local water authority members or change the composition of the local water authority.[141] Israel has also reduced water supply to the Coastal Aquifer by diverting water run-off from reaching its natural destination, reducing access by Palestinians in Gaza.[142]

In 1982, Israel placed the water supply system of the West Bank and Gaza under the control of the Israel's national water company, Mekorot, thereby fully integrating Palestinian water into the Israeli system and situating it under

Israeli control.[143] Mekorot still supplies an estimated 54 per cent of all water to Palestinians in the West Bank,[144] although it reduces Palestinian supply by 15–25 per cent during the summer in order to meet consumption needs in Israel and the settlements.[145] The Palestinian Water Authority must purchase water from Mekorot, which is delivered through 25 connection points; this control enables Israel to cut water supplies to Palestinians, as was threatened in 2006 in the Bethlehem area.[146]

These policies reveal a pattern of discrimination in which Palestinians are systematically disadvantaged. In the West Bank, some 215,000 Palestinians now live in over 200 communities that are not connected to a running water network.[147] As a result, they are forced to rely on harvesting rainwater and water purchased from expensive, privately owned water tankers. The Bertini Report notes that such water tankers 'are subject to extensive restrictions on movement imposed by checkpoints and roadblocks throughout the West Bank. In some cases, water tankers are not permitted access to villages for several days.'[148] By contrast, all 149 Jewish-Israeli settlements established in the OPT with the approval and support of the Israeli government are connected to a running water network. Israel's superior pumping capacity also enables it to exercise control of water resources emanating from across the Western Aquifer Basis, which runs under both Israel and the West Bank. This helps to maintain the 'skewed' water distribution with an average of 363 mcm (million cubic metres) for Israel and 22 mcm for Palestinians.[149]

*Impact of the Oslo Accords on water allocation and control*

Under the 1995 Israeli-PLO interim agreement, partial responsibility for water allocation passed to the Palestinian Water Authority.[150] Although the Oslo Accords included measures that would supposedly make access to water more equitable, in effect they consolidated Israeli control over water in the OPT, through several measures.

First, Oslo II ensured that Israel would continue to regulate the water supply.[151] Shares would remain unchanged: the Israeli population would continue to consume 87 per cent of the two underground water aquifers of the West Bank while Palestinians would continue to consume 13 per cent.[152] Palestinians remained purchasers of water and confronted discriminatory pricing which favoured Israeli settlers, who benefit from highly subsidised rates.[153]

The following table shows the division of water from the three sub-aquifers comprising the Mountain Aquifer as provided for in the Interim Agreement and in effect as of 2000.[154]

| Division/Aquifer | Israel (incl. settlements) | | Palestinian Authority | |
| --- | --- | --- | --- | --- |
| | $m^3$ | Proportion | $m^3$ | Proportion |
| West | 350 | 94% | 22 | 6% |
| North | 105 | 70% | 45 | 30% |
| East | 40 | 37% | 67 | 63% |
| Total | 495 | 79% | 134 | 21% |

Second, the Interim Agreement established a Joint Water Committee (JWC), composed of equal numbers of Israeli and Palestinians, whose decisions were to be made by consensus.[155] Supposedly a positive reform for Palestinians, the consensus provision enables either side to veto any proposal, including any alterations to the status quo ante.[156] In this role, Israel has agreed only to those proposed Palestinian water projects that draw from the small Eastern Aquifer, while vetoing projects which would draw from the major Western Aquifer and approving Palestinian development projects from the Eastern Aquifer only if the Palestinians agree to Israeli demands to construct new and enlarged water supplies systems for its settlements.[157] Concomitantly, Israel conducts water projects that serve the settlements even when the Palestinian side, exercising its right of veto through the JWC, votes against such proposals.[158] As a result, water allocations continue disproportionately to favour Jewish settlers and to serve the growth and consolidation of settlements while stunting Palestinian agriculture.

Third, although the Palestinian Water Authority has technical authority over West Bank wells, regulatory authority and ultimate control over supply and allocations reside with Israel. Decisions about allocation to Israeli settlers or Palestinian villages are still made by the Israeli Civil Administration.[159] Military orders (enacted prior to Oslo) allow the Israeli military authorities to veto even those water projects approved by the JWC. Palestinian permits for digging wells for agricultural use are routinely denied,[160] although permits are sometimes given for expanding existing wells for domestic use.[161] In some parts of the West Bank, such as the southern Hebron Hills, permits are denied even for building cisterns.[162]

In the Gaza Strip, water demand still far outweighs the recharge rate of the Gaza Aquifer. Over-extraction by the Occupying Power has caused a deterioration of water quality, including high levels of salination from sea water intrusion. The partial natural replenishment of the Gaza Aquifer by the Wadi Gaza (flowing from the Hebron Hills in the West Bank) has been halted by Israel's construction of an earthen verge in between, diverting the natural run-off and further entrenching separation of the Gaza Strip from the West Bank. By January 2008, 40 per cent of the houses in the Gaza Strip had no running water.[163]

Israel's general blockage of supplies is also preventing Palestinians from accessing and managing what water they have. In 2008, the Coastal Municipal Water Authority, the authority responsible for the water wells and infrastructure, was struggling to maintain wells and sewage pumping stations due to lack of supplies and fuel necessary to operating the system.[164] Water infrastructure projects, funded by the international community, have been put on hold for lack of spare parts, valves and waste-water pumps.[165]

Far from meeting Palestinian needs, Israel's water policy in the OPT is causing 'de-development' in the OPT. A UN study found that daily Palestinian consumption per capita in the West Bank and Gaza Strip in the late 1980s was 139 litres and 172 litres respectively.[166] In 2006, the total per capita daily water consumption for domestic, urban and industrial use by Palestinians in the West Bank and Gaza Strip was 60.5 litres[167] and 88 litres[168] respectively. By comparison, per capita consumption by Israeli settlers in the West Bank is 274 litres; in the Gaza Strip, prior to their removal, it was 584 litres.[169]

Discrimination in water consumption is not limited to domestic, urban and industrial use. While up to 14 per cent of the OPT's GDP is derived from agriculture, 90 per cent of Palestinian farms are forced to rely on rain-fed methods due to their lack of access to water. In the 1990s, areas irrigated by Israeli settlers were, per capita, 13 times larger than the areas Palestinians were able to irrigate in the West Bank.[170] Israeli settlements in the Jordan Valley are particularly dependent on intensive irrigation for agriculture. When they had a settler population of approximately 5,000, these settlements were found to 'consume an equivalent of 75 percent of the water that the entire West Bank Palestinian population of approximately two million consumes for domestic and urban uses'.[171] In the Gaza Strip, prior to Israel's 'disengagement', unlawful exploitation, unequal extraction and discriminatory distribution of water resources in favour of settlers were similarly salient features. At one point Palestinians in Gaza were paying up to 20 times more for water than Israeli settlers.[172]

*Impact of the Wall on Palestinian access to water*

Because 70 per cent of the Western Aquifer recharge area is located in the 'Seam Zone' between the Wall and the Green Line,[173] Israel's construction of the Wall suggests Israel's intent to annex Palestinian water sources permanently. The impact on Palestinian access to water has already been immense:

> The construction of the barrier has closed off the access of Palestinians to 95 per cent of their own water resources (630 million m³ of 670 million m³ annually) by destroying 403 wells and 1,327 cisterns. It has cut off access of owners to 136 wells providing 44.1 million m³ of water annually. The barrier has closed 46 springs (23 million m³/year) and 906 dunums of underground water (99 per cent of underground West Bank water). Consequently, over 7,000 Palestinian agriculture-dependent families have lost their livelihood in a region where water resources are scarce and increasingly costly to develop. The latest barrier route will isolate another 62 springs and 134 wells in the 'seam zone'.[174]

That the Wall indeed is designed to capture water resources is suggested by its route. This route is very similar to former Israeli water commissioner Menachem Cator's 'red line', drawn at the request of the Israeli government in 1977 to delineate those areas of the West Bank from which Israel could withdraw without having to relinquish its control over key water sources used to supply Israel and the settlements.[175]

Further, the Wall will help annex to Israel settlements in the OPT that are strategically located over key water resources in the West Bank. The major settlements of Ariel and Emmanuel in the northern West Bank, for example, sit directly over the Western Aquifer and the Israeli government has indicated that these settlements will be annexed permanently to Israel. Permanent acquisition of the land and water resources of these areas would constitute annexation and thus a practice of colonialism.

In conclusion, the measures taken by Israel regarding the division, distribution and accessibility to water in the OPT demonstrate a deliberate policy to deny Palestinian human rights by exploiting water resources for the benefit of the Occupying Power. Israel's water policies discriminate acutely in favour of Israeli settlers. They also violate a plethora of other rights including the rights to health, to an adequate standard of living, and – most significantly for this section of the study – to permanent sovereignty by the Palestinian people over natural resources in their territory.

## Suppression of Palestinian culture

A collective experience of cultural destruction and loss is, for colonised peoples, one hallmark of the colonial experience. 'Culture' eludes simple definition and is not easily codified, however, as its most valued elements may be experienced by people as intangible. Most international law relating to culture are therefore either vague – the Declaration mentions 'cultural rights' but does not specify what they are – or relate to very specific practices like language and material culture such as art and religious sites.[176] As a comprehensive discussion of this complicated field is beyond the scope of this study, this section will only touch on these concerns where they appear to correlate to a colonial project in the OPT.

Under the Hague Regulations and customary international law, cultural property is singled out for protection during military occupation, such that its destruction, damage or threat is outlawed save under conditions of military necessity.[177] Similarly, an Occupying Power is expected 'to respect and safeguard cultural properties within the territory under occupation and prevent any misappropriation, theft, or vandalism directed against such properties'.[178]

Israel's military manuals include a ban on using cultural buildings of various kinds for military operations and place strict limitations on the use of places of cultural significance where their damage or destruction are likely as a result. Nonetheless, Israeli practice in the OPT displays a consistent lack of regard for cultural property. In particular, the protection and upkeep of religious buildings such as mosques,[179] churches and cemeteries have fallen under the complex web of Israeli military orders relating to land and its ownership. For example, the maintenance and construction of buildings in East Jerusalem and Area C of the West Bank requires a valid permit issued by an Israeli official acting as the registrar of lands, and where the complicated and opaque procedures are not complied with, structures are often destroyed by the Israeli army or requisitioned for 'military purposes'.[180]

In an ironic use of provisions for respecting cultural heritage, amendments to the Jordanian Antiquities Law have enabled Israeli officials to categorise large tracts of land in the OPT as 'archaeological' in nature and to prohibit landholders from building on lands without a special permit.[181] No proof or documentary evidence is required for such decisions. As this land is often turned over to Jewish settlers,[182] the declaration of heritage sites manifests as being less for their historical preservation than for their transfer to Jewish authority. Moreover, such sites are valued and protected by Israel primarily for their Jewish and Hebrew history, rather than their Islamic, Christian, Palestinian and Arabic history.

Israeli has also engaged in the renaming of towns, cities and regions in the OPT in a project to redesign and Hebraize the cognitive map of the region.[183] Discriminatory linguistic policies were first applied extensively within the Green Line after Israel's establishment and were carried over into the OPT after 1967.[184]

Shortly after the West Bank was occupied in 1967, all printing, publishing and distribution of any material was brought under the purview of a designated person under the Military Commander. Military Order No. 50 requires a permit not only in relation to material produced within the OPT, but any materials brought from outside.[185] Further, under Military Order No. 107, the military issued a list of banned publications, including works on Arabic grammar, and histories of the Crusades and Arab nationalism.[186] Education that provides knowledge and training in cultural expression is also routinely impeded by various administrative and military measures of the Occupying Power.[187] These practices damage the Palestinian knowledge base for new generations hoping to participate in Palestinian political, economic and cultural life.

Palestinian cultural associations, often of a charitable nature, have also been closed down through vague references to 'terrorism' or 'public safety'.[188] Such closures hasten the erosion of the cultural life of the Palestinian people.

## THE PRINCIPLE OF GOOD FAITH AND THE DUTY NOT TO FRUSTRATE

The Oslo agreements accorded Israel jurisdiction over the OPT in many ways, including exclusive authority over the Jewish settlements and their connecting roads. Nevertheless, Israel is obliged to exercise its jurisdiction in the OPT in good faith, and especially in such a manner as not to frustrate the object and purpose of negotiations on the permanent status of the OPT by pre-empting the outcome. A review of Israel's continuing activities in the OPT, particularly in relation to its control over the land, economy, and natural resources, finds that Israel has breached this duty. Israel's activities instead demonstrate an intention to consolidate Israel's permanent hold on the occupied Palestinian territories, in a manner which constitutes colonialism.

This is clearly the case with Israel's annexation of East Jerusalem. Annexation breaches not only the law of occupation, which prohibits it, but also the general prohibition on acquiring territory through the use of force, which has peremptory status. In this case, annexation has denied East Jerusalem's indigenous population the free expression of its right to self-determination by denying the opportunity to decide its political status and freely pursue its economic, social and cultural development. Thus it is a flagrant breach of the prohibition of colonialism.

A broader expression of Israel's colonial intent is its settlement policy in the West Bank. In the Revised Disengagement Plan of 6 June 2004, Israel claimed that, although implementation of this Plan would divest Israel of any continued responsibility for Gaza, in contrast:

> it is clear that in the West Bank, there are areas *which will be part of the State of Israel*, including major Israeli population centers, cities, towns and villages, security areas and other places of special interest to Israel.[189]

Israel's self-proclaimed intention to annex areas of the West Bank could not be clearer and is manifestly analogous to the concern of the Fourth Geneva Convention regarding the 'practice adopted during the Second World War by certain Powers, which transferred portions of their own population to occupied territory for political or racial reasons or in order, as they claimed, to colonize those territories'.[190]

The colonial nature of Israel's settlement enterprise is evidenced not merely by the physical fact of settlement but also by the associated legal regime, which extends Israeli civil law and Basic Law extraterritorially to West Bank settlers on a personal basis, rather than subjecting settlers to the local law. As noted above, instituting separate legal regimes to govern settlers and the indigenous population is one characteristic of colonialism.

Furthermore, the fact of prolonged occupation has been employed to justify legislative action that surpasses the limits of Israel's authority as prescribed by Article 43 of the Hague Regulations. On occasion, this authority has been used to effect changes that should be expected to endure beyond the end of occupation, such as the construction of infrastructure integrating Israel and the occupied territories: for example, the highway, electricity and water grids. Justice Barak stated the rule governing the legitimacy of these measures in the following terms:

> Long-term fundamental investments in an occupied area bringing about permanent changes that may last beyond the period of the military administration are permitted if required for the benefit of the local population – provided there is nothing in these investments that might introduce an essential modification in the basic institutions of the area.[191]

In response, Professor Kretzmer has commented that this 'public benefit' approach was 'intimately connected to political objectives and interests. The model applied by Justice Barak is reminiscent of a colonial model of governors who know what is best for the natives.'[192]

On other occasions, Israel has argued that the prolonged nature of the occupation supports changes in the legal system of the occupied territories that essentially fuse it with Israeli domestic law. The most far-reaching change was the integration of the two economies through the assimilation of tax regimes and the eradication of customs barriers between Israel and the occupied territories. As Feilchenfeld observes, an occupant may not create a customs union between its territory and occupied territory because 'this almost invariably would be an intrinsic measure of complete annexation which a mere occupant has no right to effect'.[193] Imposing an economic policy that serves the interests of the occupying State yet denies the population under occupation the exercise of the right to determine and pursue, without external interference, its own economic development is in itself, under contemporary international law, a denial of self-determination, and constitutes colonialism. As Benvenisti observes, economic integration may provide an additional incentive for the occupation to continue.[194]

On the other hand, as President Shamgar observed in *Abu Aita*, 'Economic integration – as a compelling motive for introducing the tax – was obviously a dominant factor in all decisions having implications on the economic relations between Israel and the territories.'[195]

Moreover, integration was not undertaken for the benefit of the occupied territories but were determined by Israel's own economic interests: namely, its association agreement with the EEC.

> Israel's association with the Common Market made its introduction especially important as a side effect of the removal of customs barriers between the members of the EEC and Israel, a matter which understandably had direct repercussions in the territories. The integration of Israel into the EEC and the reduction of customs duties that followed in its steps automatically obligated, the existing political and economic situation, the imposition of the tax, which was present in all the countries of the Market, and the changing of customs duties.[196]

Only if Israel intends to continue to consolidate its control of the OPT would the economic benefits arising under the association agreement need to be secured in this manner. Hence Israel's policy of integrating the two economies breaches the requirement that an Occupying Power keep separate its own economy from that of territory it occupies and indicates an intention to annex the territory as part of a policy of colonialism.

As the dominant power, Israel has the political and military force to determine the outcome of the permanent status negotiations and thus the eventual political status of the occupied Palestinian territories. Its efforts to maintain control over territory and natural resources for its own benefit evince a disinclination to fulfil its good faith obligation not to frustrate or pre-empt the outcome of these negotiations. It thus fails in its duty to promote the realisation of the Palestinian people's right to self-determination: on the contrary, its practices impede this process.

## CONCLUSION

Although international law provides no single decisive definition of colonialism, for the purposes of this study it is understood that a situation may be classified as colonial when acts of a State, particularly in the special areas of concern highlighted in the Declaration on Colonialism, have the cumulative outcome of denying the indigenous population the exercise of its right to self-determination. This chapter has reviewed five dimensions of Israeli practices that, taken together, make evident Israel's colonial domination of the OPT.

1. *Violating the territorial integrity of occupied territory.* Israel has profoundly violated the territorial integrity of the OPT through a systematic programme of settlement and partition. Israel's annexation of East Jerusalem is manifestly an act of colonial intent. The same may also be said of Israel's extensive acquisition of territory for Jewish settlement in the West Bank and East Jerusalem, which, strategically linked to construction of the Wall and a road network whose use is denied to Palestinians in the West Bank, has fragmented Palestinian land into disarticulated cantons.
2. *Depriving the people of an occupied territory of the capacity for self-governance.* Israel's physical control of the OPT is complemented by its system of administration, which prevents the protected population from freely exercising their political authority over their own territory. This determination is unaffected by the conclusion of the Oslo Accords and the creation of the Palestinian National Authority and Legislative Council. The devolution of power to these institutions has only been partial, and Israel retains ultimate control. By preventing the free expression of the Palestinian population's political will, Israel has violated that population's right to self-determination.
3. *Integrating the economy of the occupied territory into that of the occupant.* A State administering a non-self-governing territory is required to keep that territory separate from its own, in order to prevent its annexation. Similarly, the State is also required to keep the two economies separate. Israel has consciously integrated the economies of the OPT within its own, in breach of its obligations under international law. In particular, the creation of the customs union between Israel and the OPT is a measure of prohibited annexation.
4. *Depriving the population of sovereignty over its natural resources.* The Declaration and law regarding self-determination are especially concerned with the right of peoples to permanent sovereignty over their natural resources: that is, to dispose of natural wealth and resources in their territories as they wish. Israel's settlement policy and the construction of the road network and the Wall have deprived the Palestinian population of the control and development of approximately 40 per cent of West Bank land. Israel has also implemented a water management and allocation system that has deprived Palestinians of their accustomed access to water. Israeli water policy is also discriminatory and inequitable in favouring settlers to the detriment of Palestinians, regarding both agricultural and personal use. The route of the Wall suggests that Israel intends permanently to acquire exclusive access to key water resources in the West Bank.

5. *Depriving the population of its accustomed cultural practices and expression.* Self-determination has a cultural component: a people entitled to exercise the right of self-determination has the right freely to determine its cultural development. Israeli practices privilege the language of the occupier, while hampering the educational and cultural development of the Palestinian population. This last issue makes Israel's denial of the right to self-determination in the OPT comprehensive.

In his January 2007 report on the human rights situation in the Occupied Palestinian Territories, Professor Dugard suggested that elements of the occupation constitute a form of colonialism. This review of Israeli practices has demonstrated that Israel's colonial practices have not been implemented piecemeal but are systematic and comprehensive. As in combination they have frustrated the exercise of the Palestinian population's right to self-determination in all of its principal modes of expression, this study concludes that Israel is indeed violating the prohibition of colonialism.

# 4
# Review of Israeli Practices Relative to the Prohibition of Apartheid

INTRODUCTION: DEFINING APARTHEID IN INTERNATIONAL LAW

Whether the State of Israel is practising apartheid in the Occupied Palestinian Territories (OPT) is explored here as a matter of international law. This approach requires scrupulous attention to the formal definition of apartheid as it has been developed in international law, which is contained in the Apartheid Convention – the International Convention on the Suppression and Punishment of the Crime of Apartheid.[1] Although the Convention's definition itself suggests that other practices might be relevant to such a study, the sensitivity of the subject here suggests that a conservative approach is advisable. Discussion here is accordingly structured to follow literally and narrowly the terms provided by the Convention's definition, with reference also to the Rome Statute and commentaries that drew from it.

Chapter 1 of this volume reviewed the Convention's history and its relationship to other human rights law, such as ICERD (International Convention on the Elimination of All Forms of Racial Discrimination) and the Rome Statute. This review confirmed that the Apartheid Convention is applicable to Israel's practices in the OPT, in two ways: first, because Israel, having ratified ICERD, is obliged under its Article 3 to 'prevent, prohibit and eradicate' racial segregation and apartheid in territories under its jurisdiction; and second, because the prohibition of apartheid is a customary norm creating obligations *erga omnes* – that is, all States are obliged to act to end apartheid wherever it may arise.

On this basis, whether Israel's system of control in the OPT constitutes an apartheid regime is examined here in two parts. Part I considers the main paragraph of the definition, which specifies the general framing conditions in which various 'inhuman acts' are considered to constitute the crime of apartheid. Questions here focus on whether the conflict involves 'racial groups', in the sense intended by international law, in a relation of domination and oppression involving segregation and discrimination. This part of the study was steered also by four objections that might be raised *a priori* to applying the Convention's definition of apartheid to Israeli practices:

- Jews and Palestinians are not racial groups and so their relations cannot be understood within the ambit of apartheid;
- Israeli domination of Palestinians is not on the basis of race but rather citizenship;

- Israeli's practices are not 'committed for the purpose of establishing and maintaining domination' over Palestinians but are calculated only to defend Israel from a security threat;
- The Apartheid Convention was composed to address practices by the South African government and is not applicable outside of southern Africa.

Finding that none of these arguments holds up in light of related legal commentary, the first stage then entailed a brief review of apartheid practices in southern Africa, as it was imposed on black South Africans by the government. This overview provides the context for detailed comparisons between Israeli and South African practices regarding specific practices.

Part II considers whether Israel's practices match the six categories of 'inhuman acts' listed as crimes of apartheid in the Convention. Review of

---

International Convention on the Suppression and Punishment of the Crime of Apartheid (1973)

... *Article 2:*
For the purpose of the present Convention, the term 'the crime of apartheid', which shall include similar policies and practices of racial segregation and discrimination as practised in southern Africa, shall apply to the following inhuman acts committed for the purpose of establishing and maintaining domination by one racial group of persons over any other racial group of persons and systematically oppressing them:

(a) Denial to a member or members of a racial group or groups of the right to life and liberty of person:

(i) By murder of members of a racial group or groups;
(ii) By the infliction upon the members of a racial group or groups of serious bodily or mental harm, by the infringement of their freedom or dignity, or by subjecting them to torture or to cruel, inhuman or degrading treatment or punishment;
(iii) By arbitrary arrest and illegal imprisonment of the members of a racial group or groups;

(b) Deliberate imposition on a racial group or groups of living conditions calculated to cause its or their physical destruction in whole or in part;
(c) Any legislative measures and other measures calculated to prevent a racial group or groups from participation in the political, social, economic and cultural life of the country and the deliberate creation of conditions preventing the full development of such a group or groups, in particular by denying to members of a racial group or groups basic human rights and freedoms, including the right to work, the right to form recognized trade unions, the right to education, the right to leave and to return to their country, the right to a nationality, the right to freedom of movement and residence, the right to freedom of opinion and expression, and the right to freedom of peaceful assembly and association;
(d) Any measures including legislative measures, designed to divide the population along racial lines by the creation of separate reserves and ghettos for the members of a racial group or groups, the prohibition of mixed marriages among members of various racial groups, the expropriation of landed property belonging to a racial group or groups or to members thereof;
(e) Exploitation of the labour of the members of a racial group or groups, in particular by submitting them to forced labour;
(f) Persecution of organizations and persons, by depriving them of fundamental rights and freedoms, because they oppose apartheid.

each element involves a short review of relevant international law, a brief summary of practices in apartheid South Africa for illustration, and then an empirical review of relevant Israel state practices.

## PART I: APPLICABILITY OF THE DEFINITION TO THIS CASE

### RACE AND RACIAL DISCRIMINATION IN INTERNATIONAL LAW

Several arguments may be made that the Apartheid Convention is not applicable to the Israeli-Palestinian conflict, making it pointless even to consider whether Israel's specific practices constitute apartheid in terms of the Convention. One such argument is that, since apartheid involves racial groups and Jews and Palestinians are not considered races, their conflict simply does not fit the definition of apartheid. International law does hold that apartheid is intrinsically a form of racial discrimination: the Apartheid Convention defines apartheid as domination by 'one racial group over any other racial group or groups' and the Rome Statute also defines apartheid as involving 'racial groups'.[2] This language could be interpreted to mean that Jews and Palestinians must first be identified as racial groups in order to test for a regime of apartheid. Since neither group is normally called a 'race' today, this could seem to obviate any further inquiry.

The question of race is especially sensitive in this context and requires careful attention. It also raises challenges for a study of international law, because – although race is a topic much described and theorised in the social sciences – until recently international human rights law did not define 'race' or clarify by what criteria groups should be understood as racial groups (or as ethnic or national groups). The United Nations Charter (1945), the Universal Declaration of Human Rights (1948) and ICERD (1965) all prohibit discrimination on the basis of race as well as other identities, but none defines 'race' itself.

ICERD does, however, define *racial discrimination* and stipulates that it embraces several categories of group identities:

> In this Convention, the term 'racial discrimination' shall mean any distinction, exclusion, restriction or preference based on *race, colour, descent, or national or ethnic origin* which has the purpose or effect of nullifying or impairing the recognition, enjoyment or exercise, on an equal footing, of human rights and fundamental freedoms in the political, economic, social, cultural or any other field of public life.[3]

The Apartheid Convention invokes ICERD in its Preamble, so its definition of apartheid as involving '*racial segregation and discrimination*' would therefore seem to allude to this same range of identities.

These social identities – 'race, colour, descent, or national or ethnic origin' – are grouped together because they are all perceived socially as being effectively immutable in a person. This notion of immutability is essential to the patterns of discrimination considered most dangerous: the targeting of people, whatever their age, gender, views or behaviour, on the basis of some perceived essential quality that is understood to have been acquired at birth. Hence ICERD prohibits racial discrimination under any label. This inclusive approach is especially important for group members who experience discrimination under different labels: notably, for example, Jews. In the United States, 'Jewish' is considered an ethnic or religious identity, and not a racial or national identity, while in Israel, 'Jewish' is considered a national identity as well as a religious one. Yet, everywhere, anti-Semitism is correctly considered a form of racism. It would indeed be sophistic and disingenuous to affirm that Jews cannot be subject to racism because they are not called a 'racial group'. ICERD's definition captures this point by indicating that racial discrimination exists wherever relations between the groups reproduce practices of domination and oppression associated with racial discrimination, whether the term 'race' is used or not.

Adopting this more inclusive interpretation of 'race' in a study testing for apartheid is supported further by recalling that meanings (and values) associated with the term 'race' have changed dramatically over the past century, and even since the Apartheid Convention was drafted. Until the late nineteenth century, 'race' was often used loosely for any group that was considered to share a common origin, and thus was often used as a synonym for 'people', 'nation' or what today we would call 'ethnic groups'.[4] In the late nineteenth century, ideas about race were formalised as doctrines about biology and hierarchy, mostly by European scientists whose work complemented European colonial rule and notions of superior civilisation. In this period, formal racial typologies were developed, generating elaborate charts measuring the somatic parameters of 'Caucasoid', 'Mongoloid', 'Negroid' and so forth. After the mid twentieth century and the horrors of the Second World War, both racial nationalism and the racial 'pseudo-sciences' were fatally discredited and ideas shifted again to understand race as a group identity that is socially constructed.

Thus, in the twenty-first century, the term 'race' has fallen out of common use in most settings, except where speaking of racial discrimination. Contemporary theory of race now understands racial discrimination as resulting from social dynamics: usually, where a population is racially defined for the purpose of ensuring its political subordination and economic exploitation.[5] Groups that in earlier eras were called 'races' are now described in terms considered more scientifically and socially 'correct' (and polite), such as 'ethnic group' or 'nationality': thus Serbs, Bosnians and Roma are now called ethnicities or nationalities rather than races.[6]

A change in terminology by itself does not, however, necessarily ameliorate social prejudices and practices of discrimination. A switch in terms from 'race' to 'ethnicity' regarding the same group may only perpetuate discrimination by glossing over enduring racist biases.[7] Consequently, whether groups are functioning socially as 'racial groups' – in the sense of imposing, or being subjected to, systemic racial discrimination – cannot be determined simply by checking whether they are called 'races': it must be determined by observing whether perceptions of immutable qualities are still shaping group relations and hierarchies.

Finally, ethnic and racial typologies are not the same in all parts of the world, a social fact confronted by many individuals when they travel (for example, different definitions of 'black' in South and North America). Hence a group identity like 'Jewish' or 'Palestinian' cannot be affirmed as intrinsically racial or non-racial, in some abstract universal sense, outside the social context in which the identities are socially constructed and perceived. Their construction in the local setting – how they are understood, signalled, valued and practised – is the only relevant reference for considering whether practices of racial discrimination and domination are operating in that setting.

Hence determining whether relations among Jews and Palestinians in the OPT match ICERD's definition of 'racial discrimination' – and therefore the Apartheid Convention's definition of 'racial groups' – cannot be determined simply by checking whether either group is called 'racial' in the local setting. The answer depends on whether these group identities are perceived as immutable and how they function in ways that generate domination, discrimination and segregation.

The next section illustrates these points by considering briefly how racial identities functioned – under various labels, including 'ethnic' – in apartheid South Africa. The subsequent section considers how the challenge of defining groups confronted the International Criminal Tribunals on Rwanda and Yugoslavia. This short comparison then provides a basis for considering whether Jewish and Palestinian identities are operating like racial identities in Israel-Palestine.

### The politics of racial terminology in South Africa

Even in a system as openly racial as apartheid South Africa, labels for group identities were changeable and, for this very reason, were deliberately manipulated. On its face, the regime's system of racial categories was simple and clinical. Shortly after taking power in 1948, the National Party propagated the Population Registration Act 30 (1950), which classified all South Africans as either 'white', 'Coloured' or 'Native'.[8] In 1959, the 'Coloured' group was further divided by law into 'Cape Coloured', 'Cape Malay', 'Griqua', 'Indian', 'Chinese', 'other Asiatic' and 'other Coloured'.[9] The consequences of these classifications were immense, determining the daily life experience and long-term life chances of every individual in the country, so determining (assigning) racial categories was a crucial matter. For purposes of law, purportedly scientific tests were used by white authorities to determine a person's race:

> Fingernails have been examined. Combs have been pulled through people's hair: if the comb is halted by tight curls, the person is more likely to be classified Coloured than white. In July 1983 an abandoned baby, named Lise Venter by hospital staff, was found near Pretoria. To classify her by race, as the Population Registration Act demands, a strand of her hair

was examined by the Pretoria police laboratory: she was then classified Coloured.[10]

Such tests inevitably failed to account for the full spectrum of human variations, however, generating confusion and controversies. Even children of the same parents might be given different classifications: parents classified as black could be told that their children were coloured and must therefore live in a separate group area. Couples of different race groups (who had married before such unions were declared illegal) could find their children assigned indiscriminately to several other groups. A Race Classification Board took the final decision on disputed cases: changes resulted in so-called 'chameleons', whom the State had formally confirmed to have changed racial identity.

Because physical tests were well understood to create confusion, the Population Registration Act also included, in its definitions of racial groups, social perceptions and attitudes, 'acceptance' and 'repute':

> A White person is one who is in appearance obviously white – and *not generally accepted* as Coloured – or who is *generally accepted* as White – and is not obviously Non-White, provided that a person shall not be classified as a White person if one of his natural parents has been classified as a Coloured person or a Bantu ... A Bantu is a person who is, or is *generally accepted* as, a member of any aboriginal race or tribe of Africa.

Thus apartheid was openly and incontestably a racial system. Still, in the 1970s the apartheid government tried to deny this by affirming that the black African population of the country was actually divided into various 'ethnic' groups: Zulu, Xhosa, Venda, Tswana, Sotho, and so forth (each being defined unilaterally by the white government according to linguistic, historical and geographic criteria).[11] The regime's policy of 'Grand Apartheid' held that each ethnic group or 'people' should have its own 'Homeland' where it would obtain independence over time. In practice, 'Grand Apartheid' reserved the best land for the white 'people' and forcibly transferred of millions of black South Africans out of white areas into black 'Homelands' they had never seen, that had been unilaterally delineated by the white government as black 'reserves'. In rhetoric, the regime's philosophy supporting this doctrine of forced separation co-opted the international principle that every people has the right to self-determination:

> In keeping with Afrikaner nationalism's stress on the realisation of *ethnic identity* (volkseie), each of these *'national/ethnic minorities'* was to be given the right to realise its divinely ordained *national* calling in its own 'homeland'. In introducing the Bill, Minister de Wet Nel explained to parliament that this new policy of 'separate freedoms' rested on three principles: 'The first is that God has given a divine task and calling to every *People* [volk] in the world, which dare not be denied or destroyed by anyone. The second is that every *People* in the world of whatever *race* or

colour, just like every individual, has the inherent right to live and develop. Every *People* is entitled to the right of self-preservation. In the third place, it is our deep conviction that the personal and national ideals of every *ethnic group* can best be developed within its own *national* community. Only then will other groups feel they are not being endangered ... This is the philosophical basis of the policy of Apartheid.'[12]

Switching from 'race' to 'ethnic group' served the apartheid regime in two ways. First, it supported the State's defensive claim (made to both domestic white and international audiences) that South Africa did not have a 'black' African majority, because the white population was larger than any one black African 'ethnic' nation (Zulu, Xhosa, Sotho, and so forth). Second, it supported the white government's crucial argument that members of each African ethnic 'nation' could legitimately be excluded from civil and political rights in white-dominated South Africa because they would rightly gain those rights in their own states (black Homelands). Thus, the regime argued, black-ethnic 'nations' would exercise their right to self-determination in their Homelands while the white-ethnic 'nation' would exercise its right to self-determination in the rest of South Africa.[13] That the Homelands were, for the most part, impoverished cantons, with artificial boundaries drawn in archipelagos by the regime to preserve intervening white industry and farmland, was just one inconvenient truth belying this rosy claim.

The African National Congress (ANC) always rejected the language of ethnic-black national self-determination as a mere trick to preserve white supremacy and disenfranchise black African citizens. The ANC and United Democratic Front (the domestic anti-apartheid coalition) insisted that the only true 'national' unit in South Africa was the entire population within South African territory. Hence the Freedom Charter of 1955, which established lasting principles for opposing apartheid that guided most of the anti-apartheid movement for the remainder of the struggle, declared in its opening sentence that 'South Africa belongs to all who live in it, black and white'.

### Interpreting identity: the International Criminal Tribunals

Appreciating that group labels can be both genuinely fluid and manipulated for political purposes helps to explain the difficulties faced by the International Criminal Tribunals for the former Yugoslavia (ICTY) and for Rwanda (ICTR). For both Tribunals, even superficially 'objective' markers like legal classifications on identity (ID)documents – particularly relevant in the case of the Rwandan genocide – were found not to be entirely reliable indications about group membership.

The ICTR, in the seminal *Akayesu* case, attempted to establish meanings for national, ethnical, racial or religious identities, as these are listed in Article 2 of its Statute (which is based on the 1948 Genocide Convention). The Tribunal arrived at the following definitions:

- a *national* group is 'a collection of people who are perceived to share a legal bond based on common citizenship, coupled with reciprocity of rights and duties';[14]
- an *ethnic* group was defined as 'a group whose members share a common language and culture';[15]
- a *religious* group is one whose members 'share the same religion, denomination or mode of worship';[16]
- a *racial* group is one that shares 'hereditary physical traits often identified with a geographical region, irrespective of linguistic, cultural, national or religious factors.'[17]

(Regarding the category of *national* groups, the ICTR drew on an earlier International Court of Justice (ICJ) case that associated nationality with citizenship.[18] In social usage, however, the term 'nationality' may also refer to groups without States, such as nationalities in the former Soviet Union, or identities retained through generations, as, for example, the origins of immigrant populations. ICERD uses 'national origin', which suggests this wider meaning.[19])

Despite this attempt at definitions, the Tribunals recognised that they could not be externally determined by an outside authority with any reliability. Rather, local *perceptions* of group identities were a determinative factor in identifying protected groups. Even where identities were codified in legislation and ID cards,[20] the ICTR Trial Chamber found that what mattered principally was whether perpetrators *perceived* victims – and whether victims *perceived* themselves – as belonging to one of the protected groups. A 2005 ICTY judgment summarised this line of jurisprudence as follows:

> In accordance with the case-law of the Tribunal, a national, ethnical, racial or religious group is identified by using as a criterion the stigmatisation of the group, notably by the perpetrators of the crime, on the basis of its *perceived* national, ethnical, racial or religious characteristics.[21]

The ICTR observed that, for all these identities (national, ethnic, racial and religious), the protected group should be perceived as 'stable and permanent': that is, membership is normally acquired at birth and is continuous, immutable, and not usually challengeable by its members.[22] This immutable quality is thus the common denominator of identities based on race, colour, descent, and national and ethnic origin: that is, the groups cited by ICERD as being targets of racial discrimination.

In conclusion, determining whether any group is a 'racial group' in the sense provided by the Apartheid Convention must begin from four premises. First, changing notions of race after the mid twentieth century have mostly purged the term 'race' from social discourse even where racial discrimination continues in the sense provided by ICERD. Second, the group identities of ICERD – 'race, colour, descent, or national or ethnic origin' – are all understood in international law to be identities normally acquired at birth and retained throughout a person's lifetime. Third, no absolute, measurable, and consistent scientific or legal criteria exist for distinguishing one of these identities from another, as identities are matters of local perception and both perceptions and labels may change (and be manipulated for political purposes). Fourth, because racial, ethnic and other identities emerge and become socially embedded in particular settings, the same categories and labels do not necessarily hold even for the same individual moving among world regions.

Accordingly, the question for this study is not whether Jews and Palestinians are 'races' in the older (discredited) sense of race but whether Jews and Palestinians in the OPT comprise 'racial groups', in their local relations to each other, in the sense of the Apartheid Convention: that is, groups in a relationship of domination and subordination, for which membership is understood to be acquired at birth and thus is perceived by the society as being immutable.

### Race and identity in the OPT

Group identities are in all cases complicated and Jewish and Palestinian identities are no exceptions. The full complexities of Jewish and Palestinian identities, however, need not be explored here. Relevant here is whether they function in ways that underwrite the concern for racial discrimination expressed in ICERD and so carry through the definition of apartheid in the Apartheid Convention: that is, their perceived immutability. This question involves some exploration of their constituent marking features, as perceived by their members and by members of the other group.

*Jewish identity*

Today, Jews are not normally called a 'race'. If the term is arises at all, it is usually to assert that Jews come from 'many races' in the sense of the old colour categories (black, white, Asian, and so forth). Still, relevant here is that this aversion to the term 'race' is relatively recent. Like many groups we now call 'ethnic' or 'national', Jews often were called a 'race' until the mid twentieth century, even by Jewish and Zionist thinkers, reflecting contemporary currents of racial-nationalist thought. For example, Max Nordau commonly used the term 'race' for Jews in speaking of Jewish interests in Palestine.[23] The founder of Revisionist Zionism, Vladimir Jabotinsky, wrote passionately for decades about the Jewish 'race' and how the 'spiritual mechanism' associated with race authorized the creation of a Jewish state.[24] The Memorandum of Association of the Jewish National Fund (JNF) in Article 2(c) cites one objective of the JNF as being to 'benefit, directly or indirectly, those of Jewish race or descendency'. Only after the Second World War did 'race' fall into disrepute generally – after the whole idea was so appallingly discredited by its deployment in Nazi doctrine to authorise Aryan supremacy and the mass murder of Jews and other so-called 'degenerative races', such as Slavs and Gypsies.

In the twenty-first century, 'race' is therefore usually scrupulously avoided as a term for Jews. Nonetheless, as discussed earlier, a change in label, by itself, is not definitive of whether group relations still involve 'racial discrimination' according to the definition provided by ICERD. Testing for practices of racial discrimination in Israel-Palestine must consider whether the relevant identities are perceived as immutable, such that they inspire the exclusion, domination and discrimination characteristic of racism. As observed by the ICTR and ICTY, it also requires considering the identities' internal and external constructions.

Regarding internal perceptions among Jews, 'who is a Jew' is an age-old and even Talmudic question that remains highly contested in Israel (as elsewhere), particularly around questions of conversion.[25] 'Jewish' is certainly considered a religious identity in the sense that Judaism is a religious faith and anyone can convert to Judaism if willing and able to follow the required procedures. On this basis, opponents of Zionist thought often insist that Jewishness is not a national identity but simply a religious one. Yet religious criteria are inadequate to defining 'Jewish', in several ways.

First, Halakhah law[26] as well as social norms in Jewish communities provide that Jewish identity is conveyed from mother to child: hence those who have a Jewish mother are considered Jewish, irrespective of their actual religious practices and beliefs. This is partly why Jews have long been subjected to anti-Semitic attack, extending to pogroms and genocide: because Jewish identity is seated notionally in bodies and bloodlines as well as faith.[27] This importance of descent to Jewish identity is codified in Israel's Law of Return:

> For the purposes of this Law, 'Jew' means a person who was born of a Jewish mother or has become converted to Judaism and who is not a member of another religion.[28]

Second, 'Jewish' is not a religious identity for those people who acquired Jewish identity at birth but do not practice or believe in the Jewish religion. People who are secular or atheist, for example, may still see themselves, and be seen by their communities, as Jewish on the basis of their Jewish descent.[29]

Third, religion is not the core concept that informs the Zionist movement's conceptualisation of 'Jewish' as a *national* identity: that is, as a *people* or *nation* which holds the right to self-determination in Palestine.[30] This foundational Zionist doctrine rests on the premise that Jews today share an ancestry dating back to antiquity, as inscribed in the Bible. For example, Israel's Declaration of Independence states this idea plainly by affirming that Jews today trace their lineal ancestry to an earlier national life in the geography of Palestine and so have an inalienable right to 'return' there:[31]

> ERETZ-ISRAEL [(Hebrew) – the Land of Israel] was the birthplace of the Jewish people. Here their spiritual, religious and political identity was shaped. Here they first attained to statehood, created cultural values of national and universal significance and gave to the world the eternal Book of Books.

After being forcibly exiled from their land, the people kept faith with it throughout their Dispersion and never ceased to pray and hope for their return to it and for the restoration in it of their political freedom.

Impelled by this historic and traditional attachment, Jews strove in every successive generation to re-establish themselves in their ancient homeland. In recent decades they returned in their masses ...

These references to 'every successive generation' and 'attained to statehood' equate Jewish identity with a national origin – that is, one of the group identities that ICERD affirms as potentially subject to racial discrimination. By implication, Zionist doctrine holds that people who do not descend from this Jewish-national origin have no similar right to a national life today in Israel. This ethno-nationalist dimension of Jewish identity is reinforced in Israeli law that establishes Israel as a 'Jewish State', as discussed next.

*Jewish national identity: Israel as a Jewish state*

Israeli Basic Law establishes Israel as the State of the Jewish people. Basic Law: Knesset[32] describes Israel as 'the state of the Jewish people' while Basic Law: Human Dignity and Liberty[33] and Basic Law: Freedom of Occupation[34] both specify concerns with 'the values of the State of Israel as a Jewish and democratic state'. The 1952 World Zionist Organisation–Jewish Agency (Status) Law,[35] whose importance is discussed below, also specifies that Israel is the State of the Jewish people:

1. The State of Israel regards itself as the creation of the entire Jewish people, and its gates are open, in accordance with its laws, to every Jew wishing to immigrate to it.

That these provisions are not merely symbolic formulas but establish a juridical basis for systematic racial discrimination is clarified by how they intersect with other Israeli laws. Especially, Basic Law: Israel Lands[36] provides that real property held by the State of Israel, Israel's Development Authority and the JNF must be held in perpetuity for the exclusive benefit of the Jewish people. Within the 1949 Armistice borders of Israel, about 93 per cent of land falls into this category and cannot be leased even by non-Jewish Israeli citizens.[37] Relevant here is that the same law applies to any 'State' land in the OPT, administered by the Israel Lands Authority (ILA), which is also charged with administering it for the benefit of the Jewish people. Article 1 of the State Property Law of 1951[38] provides that land becomes State land in any area 'in which the law of the State of Israel applies'. As all Jewish settlements in the OPT are ostensibly built on State land (although this is only partly true, as discussed later) and large areas of the West Bank have been declared State lands and closed to Palestinian use, this legal formula places much of the West Bank under the authority of an Israeli State institution that is legally bound to administer it for the exclusive benefit of the Jewish people.

Similar discrimination is authorised by the 1952 Status Law, which confirms the Jewish Agency and World Zionist Organisation (hereafter JA-WZO) as the 'authorised agencies' of the state to administer Jewish national affairs in Israel and in the OPT.[39] The authority of these conjoined institutions is detailed in a Covenant that provides for a Co-ordinating Board – composed half of government and half of JA members – which is granted broad authority to serve the Jewish people, including:

> The organising of immigration abroad and the transfer of immigrants and their property to Israel; co-operation in the absorption of immigrants in Israel; youth immigration; agricultural settlement in Israel; the acquisition and amelioration of land in Israel by the institutions of the Zionist Organisation, the Keren Kayemeth Leisrael [Jewish National Fund] and the Keren Hayesod [United Jewish Appeal]; participation in the establishment and the expansion of development enterprises in Israel; the encouragement of private capital investments in Israel; assistance to cultural enterprises and institutions of higher learning in Israel; the mobilisation of resources for financing these activities; the co-ordination of the activities in Israel of Jewish institutions and organisations acting within the limits of these functions by means of public funds.[40]

A principal task of the JA-WZO, as expressed in the Status Law, is to work actively to build and maintain a Jewish majority in Israel:

> 5. The mission of gathering in the exiles, which is the central task of the State of Israel and the Zionist Movement in our days, requires constant efforts by the Jewish people in the Diaspora; the State of Israel, therefore, expects the cooperation of all Jews, as individuals and groups, in building up the State and assisting the immigration to it of the masses of the people, and regards the unity of all sections of Jewry as necessary for this purpose.[41]

This imperative was reaffirmed in 2004 by the WZO's operational platform, formulated as 'the Jerusalem Programme', which reads in part:

> Zionism, the national liberation movement of the Jewish people, brought about the establishment of the State of Israel, and views a Jewish, Zionist, democratic and secure State of Israel to be the expression of the common responsibility of the Jewish people for its continuity and future. The foundations of Zionism are:
> The unity of the Jewish people, its bond to its historic homeland Eretz Yisrael, and the centrality of the State of Israel and Jerusalem, its capital, in the life of the nation;
> Aliyah to Israel from all countries and the effective integration of all immigrants into Israeli Society;
> Strengthening Israel as a Jewish, Zionist and democratic state and shaping it as an exemplary society with a unique moral and spiritual character,

marked by mutual respect for the multi-faceted Jewish people, rooted in the vision of the prophets, striving for peace and contributing to the betterment of the world;

Ensuring the future and the distinctiveness of the Jewish people by furthering Jewish, Hebrew and Zionist education, fostering spiritual and cultural values and teaching Hebrew as the national language;

Nurturing mutual Jewish responsibility, defending the rights of Jews as individuals and as a nation, representing the national Zionist interests of the Jewish people, and struggling against all manifestations of anti-Semitism;

Settling the country as an expression of practical Zionism.

Relevant to this study of Israeli practices in the OPT is that, in 1978, the head of the JA-WZO Settlement Department, Matityahu Drobles,[42] declared that the entire West Bank (including East Jerusalem) is an integral part of the Land of Israel and proposed a 'Master Plan' for settling Jews in the territory to consolidate this status.[43] Thus the JA-WZO extended into the OPT its mandate to serve Jewish-national interests, according to the terms of the Covenant. Legal restrictions on the JA-WZO (concerned mostly with fundraising abroad) require that the JA operates only inside Israel and the WZO in the OPT, but these geographic ambits actually facilitate a strategic partnership between the two agencies in completing the fusion of the OPT into Israel: for example, by jointly building Jewish-only towns that straddle the Green Line and the elaborate highway system that seamlessly integrates cities and towns inside Israel with Jewish-only settlements in the OPT.[44]

The Status Law is linked to a second body of Israeli law and jurisprudence that distinguishes between citizenship (in Hebrew, *ezrahut*) and nationality (*le'um*). Other states have made this distinction: for example, in the former Soviet Union, Soviet citizens were also divided by nationalities although all nationalities had juridically equal standing. In Israel, by contrast, only one nationality has standing or rights and only one is associated with the legitimacy and duties of the state. According to Israel's Supreme Court, Israel is indeed not the State of the 'Israeli nation' but of the 'Jewish nation'.[45] Collective rights are reserved to Jewish nationality. For instance, the 1950 Law of Return[46] serves the 'in-gathering' mission cited above by allowing any Jew to immigrate to Israel and, through the Citizenship Law, to gain immediate citizenship. No other national group has a comparable right or any other collective right under Israeli law.

This legal formulation and privileging of Jewish nationality shapes Israeli policy in the OPT in several ways. First, it has contributed to determining the demography of the OPT. About 1.8 million of the Palestinians now living in the OPT are refugees who fled or were expelled from homes inside Israel in 1948, yet are not allowed to return to Israel and obtain Israeli citizenship because they are not Jews. Second, it has contributed to the construction of Jewish settlements in the OPT. As noted above, because Israel is the State of the Jewish people, its agencies – the ILA and the JA-WZO – must administer 'State' lands and property in the OPT in the exclusive interests of the Jewish people. As clarified later, these services and protections are accorded to Jewish residents in the OPT on grounds of their Jewish identity (as members of the 'Jewish people'), irrespective of whether they are Israeli citizens. Residents in the same territory who are not Jews are excluded from this special ambit of privileges. Because Israeli military policy is to protect and facilitate Jewish-national institutions in privileging Jewish residents of the OPT in this way, military occupation has the purpose and effect of dominating the Palestinian population on the basis of 'national origin'.

Thus, Israeli law constructs Jewish identity in ways that fit the concerns of ICERD and the Apartheid Convention. Under Israeli law, 'Jewish' is an identity based on descent and national origin, such that the Jewish people holds the right to self-determination and sovereignty in historic Palestine. Israeli law does not recognise any other national identity under the State's authority as having comparable rights or any group rights. Israeli law does not explicitly construct Palestinians as a distinct racial group. But by formulating Jewish identity and rights as being based on a shared ancestry tracing to a national life in antiquity, Israeli law and doctrine implicitly constructs all other groups – including Palestinian Arabs – as lacking any comparable right to a national life in Palestine by virtue of their different ancestry. This formulation fits the concerns of ICERD by according different rights to groups on the basis of identities that are understood to be acquired at birth and are experienced as mostly immutable for group members. Hence it constitutes a policy of racial discrimination according to international law. Whether this discrimination constitutes apartheid, according to the definition in the Apartheid Convention, is considered in Part II.

*Palestinian identity under the terms of ICERD*

'Palestinian' is experienced by Palestinians primarily as a national identity, associated with present residence or family origins in the territory of Mandate Palestine. During the British Mandate, 'Palestinian' was a citizenship and many residents held Palestine passports, although Palestine was not then an independent State.[47] After 1948, hundreds of thousands became stateless and today millions of Palestinians remain stateless, while millions more have obtained the citizenship of third States. Palestinian national identity is thus associated with *national origin* (rather than *nationality* in the sense of citizenship).

Like 'Jewish', therefore, Palestinian identity is inter-generational. Today Palestinian Arabs, wherever they reside,[48] draw strongly on ideas of family origins and the collective (frustrated) need and desire for a full national life in Palestine. By proposing indigeneity in Palestine as the core quality of Palestinian identity, Palestinian nationalism directly challenges the Zionist claim of *terra nullius* in Palestine and rejects claims of a superior Jewish indigeneity and right to self-determination in Palestine.

In Palestinian nationalist discourse as well as social norms, Palestinian identity has always been nested within (and in a dialectic with) the regional identity 'Arab'. The Charter of the Palestine Liberation Organisation (PLO), composed in 1968, affirms the importance of Arab identity in Article 1:

> Palestine is the homeland of the Arab Palestinian people; it is an indivisible part of the Arab homeland, and the Palestinian people are an integral part of the Arab nation.

The PLO's 1988 Declaration of Independence reiterated this formula, invoking pan-Arab nationalism and solidarity:

> The State of Palestine is an Arab state, an integral and indivisible part of the Arab nation, at one with that nation in heritage and civilisation, with it also in its aspiration for liberation, progress, democracy and unity. The State of Palestine affirms its obligation to abide by the Charter of the League of Arab States, whereby the coordination of the Arab states with each other shall be strengthened.[49]

In this conception, the Palestinian nation is still part of the larger pan-Arab nation, but it is the Palestinian people that holds the right to self-determination.

Ethnicity (characteristic customs such as language, dress and cuisine) is not a consistent factor in Palestinian identity. Within the territory which formed Mandate Palestine, Palestinian identity is indeed ethnic in the sense of being distinguished by local customs and the Arabic language.[50] Millions of Palestinians living elsewhere do not necessarily share these customs, however, though they may celebrate them symbolically as part of Palestinian nationalist expression.

Religion is not a consistent marker of Palestinian identity, either, due to the population's multi-sectarian composition.[51] Religious pluralism is also formalised, for political purposes, in the PLO Charter, which affirms an inclusive and non-discriminatory view:

> Article 16: The liberation of Palestine, from a spiritual point of view, will provide the Holy Land with an atmosphere of safety and tranquillity, which in turn will safeguard the country's religious sanctuaries and guarantee freedom of worship and of visit to all, without discrimination of race, colour, language, or religion. Accordingly, the people of Palestine look to all spiritual forces in the world for support.

Hence not only Muslims and Christians but also Jews (and other believers and nonbelievers) may be considered Palestinian if their family origins trace to Palestine. The PLO Charter limits Jewish membership only by specifying that those Jews 'who had normally resided in Palestine until the beginning of the Zionist invasion' are considered Palestinian, a distinction related to the mass Jewish immigration organised by the Zionist movement, which is viewed as illegitimate ethnic engineering. Despite this inclusive approach, 'Palestinian' has largely obtained a religious quality as 'non-Jewish' because

Israeli policy is to appropriate Jewishness exclusively for the Zionist project of Jewish nation-building and to exclude Palestinians *qua* non-Jews from Israeli citizenship, civil rights and privileges accorded to Jews, as explored later.

Thus Jewish and Palestinian identities, as they operate in the OPT in relation to each other, fit the concerns of ICERD regarding racial discrimination and so function as 'racial groups' for the purpose of the definition of apartheid. 'Jewish' and 'Palestinian' are group identities that are understood to be acquired at birth, in which membership is seen as continuous, immutable and not usually challengeable. Further, 'Jewish' functions in Israel-Palestine as a group identity in which ideas about descent, nation, religion, and ethnicity combine to support doctrines, promoted by the State and embedded in Israeli law, which hold that lineal Jewish descent from antiquity justifies extending special rights and privileges to Jews in historic Palestine and denying the rights of non-Jewish Palestinians in the same territory.

*Inadmissibility of discrimination based on citizenship*

It may be argued that Israel cannot be held responsible for apartheid because the State's differential treatment of Jewish and Palestinians residents in the same territory arises not from any notions of immutable identities but only from the Palestinians' not being Israeli citizens. As discussed in Chapter 2, Israel's arguments for legitimate discrimination in the OPT on the basis of citizenship is unsupportable in light of international humanitarian law. The question remains, however, of whether Israel could still affirm that its policies toward the Palestinians as non-citizens at least fall outside the ambit of ICERD and the Apartheid Convention.

Such an argument would be tautological, for one obvious reason: Israel has excluded Palestinians in the OPT from Israeli citizenship precisely and solely because Palestinians are (by definition, as noted earlier) not Jewish. As discussed earlier, Israeli law holds that Israel is the state of the Jewish people: 'in-gathering' of Jews is a central mission of Israeli State institutions and the State actively promotes *aliyah* or the naturalisation of Jews from other parts of the world as Israeli citizens. Hence it is a fair assumption that the Palestinians, born in territory under the State's exclusive control, would have been granted Israeli citizenship from the outset if they were Jewish (and if they wanted it). The heart of the Israeli-Palestinian conflict has indeed always centred on this problem: that Israel's exclusion of the Palestinians, as non-Jews, has resulted in the Palestinians in the OPT having no citizenship.

This practice of limiting citizenship on the basis of racial discrimination (in ICERD's sense) violates international human rights law. The Committee on the Elimination of Racial Discrimination (CERD) has expressed its concern precisely with the case of long-term residents who are denied citizenship on the grounds of their race, ethnicity or descent group, as noted earlier. Regarding 'access to citizenship', CERD recommends that States:

> [r]ecognise that deprivation of citizenship on the basis of race, colour, descent, or national or ethnic origin is a breach of States parties' obligations to ensure non-discriminatory enjoyment of the right to nationality; ...[52]

Deprivation of citizenship to serve racial domination is indeed one of the 'inhuman acts' cited by the Apartheid Convention (concerning the 'right to a nationality').[53]

Finally, the definition of apartheid in the Apartheid Convention refers to the crime of apartheid in '*southern* Africa' (a region), not South Africa (the country). This broader term reflects the fact that South Africa had, at the time, extended its apartheid practices into neighbouring South West Africa (now Namibia), which was occupied but not officially annexed to South Africa and whose population – black and white – did not hold South African citizenship. Through the 1960s, United Nations (UN) bodies condemned South Africa for its doctrine of apartheid in South West Africa[54] and so in 1973 the Apartheid Convention was adopted with language referring to 'southern Africa' to include this territory. Hence UN condemnation of South Africa for apartheid practices outside its sovereign territory – and in respect to non-citizens – is a legal precedent for applying the Apartheid Convention to Israel's practices to non-citizens in the OPT, where Israel similarly exercises jurisdiction but not formal sovereignty in ruling over non-citizens.

### Domination as the purpose of policy

Both the Apartheid Convention and the Rome Statute define 'acts of apartheid' as acts committed for the purpose of establishing and maintaining *domination* by one racial group over another. It could therefore be argued that Israeli practices do not constitute apartheid because they are not intended to maintain Jewish domination over Palestinians in the OPT – comparable, for instance, to long-term white dominion over blacks in South Africa for labour purposes. In this argument, Israeli practices are only temporary measures, imposed on Israel to keep order until a peace agreement removes the need for such control. In other words, domination is not the 'purpose' or goal of Israeli policy but only a defensive and temporary onus.

Irrespective of whether it is temporary, domination remains prohibited by the international legal definition of apartheid. The Apartheid Convention does not specify, and is not concerned with, any long-term vision regarding a policy of domination and oppression. Rather, it is concerned with inhuman acts committed for the purpose of establishing or maintaining a system of domination and oppression by one racial group over another, whatever their claimed goal. Doctrine in South Africa regarding 'Grand Apartheid' illustrates this point. After the 1960s, as discussed earlier, the apartheid regime in South Africa sought to deflect international criticism by establishing black Homelands and forcibly transferring South Africa's black African population into them. In these Homeland territories, the State proposed, black 'nations' would become self-governing and ultimately independent. Thus even the white government of apartheid South Africa could argue that domination was not a goal in itself but a defensive measure (to preserve white ways of life) and a means toward a mutually beneficial end in which all would enjoy peaceful coexistence.

## APPLICATION OF THE APARTHEID CONVENTION OUTSIDE SOUTHERN AFRICA

The Apartheid Convention defines the 'crime of apartheid' as 'similar policies and practices of racial segregation and discrimination as practiced in southern Africa'. This wording clearly indicates that the Apartheid Convention can be applicable outside southern Africa. Indeed, the prevailing scholarly view is that, while the Apartheid Convention was drafted with southern Africa in mind, it was meant to be universal in character and not confined to the practice of apartheid as seen in southern Africa.[55] During its drafting, State representatives acknowledged that its terms could apply beyond the geographical limits of southern Africa.[56] In the words of the Cypriot delegate: 'When drafting and adopting such an international convention, it must be remembered that it would become part of the body of international law and might last beyond the time when *apartheid* was being practiced in South Africa.'[57] That the drafters intended that it supply a self-standing and universal human rights instrument is further confirmed in Article 1:

> The States Parties to the present Convention declare that apartheid is a crime against humanity and that inhuman acts resulting from the policies and practices of apartheid *and similar* policies and practices of racial segregation and discrimination, as defined in Article 2 of the Convention, are crimes violating the principles of international law, in particular the purposes and principles of the Charter of the United Nations, and constituting a serious threat to international peace and security.[58]

The language of the Apartheid Convention could also be interpreted to indicate that practices elsewhere must conform to the precise and unique template provided by the southern African context in order to be considered apartheid. This interpretation is clearly incorrect. For one thing, any human rights abuses and crimes against humanity – including apartheid – will inevitably present unique features, reflecting local histories and social particularities. Limiting the Apartheid Convention's application to precise congruence with practices in apartheid South Africa would therefore effectively exclude any other case from qualifying as a 'crime of apartheid'. For another, acts in potential violation of international law are correctly measured against the provisions of the legal instruments drafted to address them; other instances of such violations are illustrative, not definitive. This interpretation is supported by CERD, which held in 1995 that the reference to 'apartheid' in Article 3 of ICERD 'may have been directed exclusively to South Africa, but the article as adopted prohibits all forms of racial segregation in all countries'.[59] Clark also contends that 'the [Apartheid] Convention is drafted in such a way as not to apply solely to the South African case, although South Africa is mentioned as an example'.[60]

Some comparative reference to apartheid South Africa proved useful to this study, however, as it helped to indicate what the international community sought to prohibit in adopting the Apartheid Convention and illuminated other practices that could fall within the ambit of the Apartheid Convention. In the course of the study, some differences were found to distinguish the two cases: for instance, apartheid in South Africa entailed the legislation of racial micro-differences in ways not seen in Israeli discourse and the adjudication of group identities was accomplished differently. Other features, such as laws that secure privileged access to land by one group to the exclusion of the other, are strikingly similar, as explained in Part II.

## APARTHEID IN SOUTH AFRICA: LEGISLATIVE FOUNDATIONS

Although often traced to the victory of the right-wing Nationalist Party in 1948,[61] the system of laws that comprised South Africa's apartheid regime was not invented whole cloth. It drew from almost 300 years of settler-colonial conflicts, dispossession and oppression, during which black Africans progressively lost their sovereignty, rights, livelihoods, and even the acknowledgement of their human dignity.[62] Key laws underpinning later apartheid legislation included the Natives Land Act (No. 27) of 1913, which made it illegal for blacks to purchase or lease land from whites except in 'reserves' and thus restricted black occupancy to less than 8 per cent of South Africa's land.[63] In the 1960s, these reserves were converted into Bantustans (Bantu Homelands).[64]

The Natives (Urban Areas) Act of 1923 laid the foundations for residential segregation in urban areas. The Act divided South Africa into 'prescribed' (urban) and 'non-prescribed' (rural) areas, and strictly controlled the movement of black males between the two. Each local authority was made responsible for the blacks in its area and 'Native Advisory Boards' were set up to regulate the inflow of black workers and to order the removal of 'surplus' blacks (those not employed). As a result, towns became almost exclusively white. Only domestic workers were allowed to live in towns, and only as tenants (usually in staff quarters), as they were not allowed to own real property.[65]

After 1948, the Afrikaner leadership of the National Party formally established South Africa as the State of the white population exclusively, and a cluster of new laws prohibited black citizens from having any voice in its governance. Laws enforcing so-called 'petty apartheid' were discussed earlier; 'Grand Apartheid' imposed a plan to confine black 'self-government' within isolated 'Homelands' and hold the rest of the country as the exclusive preserve of white South Africans. The term 'apartheid' – Afrikaans for 'separateness', sometimes called 'separate development' – was therefore a system that went beyond mere segregation. As Mokgethi Motlhabi points out:

> Although the word 'apartheid' means (race) separation, it is often distinguished by Afrikaner writers from segregation, which has always been the norm of race relations in South Africa and was guaranteed by a pass system for Africans, first introduced by the British in 1809. For the Afrikaner segregation, as opposed to apartheid, did not go far enough.

It still offered Black people some hope, according to them, that through education and adequate assimilation of Western civilization they could become equals of whites and finally have a share in the government of the country. Apartheid not only did away with such 'false hopes', but went further to 'retribalize' black people by emphasizing their ethnic differences, separating them residentially on this basis. As a result of this policy, most of the Africans would be resettled in their supposed homelands, visiting 'white South Africa' only as 'migrant' workers.[66]

After coming to power in 1948, the National Party rapidly introduced a series of laws that would to implement its vision of a white South Africa serviced by black migrant workers.[67] The three legislative foundations underpinning the apartheid system were the Population Registration Act 30 of 1950, the Group Areas Act 41 of 1950, and the Pass Laws, which included several acts. Although other legislation would follow (discussed below), these statutes formed the bedrock of the apartheid state. The Population Registration Act of 1950 established that all South Africans must be categorised on the basis of race and carry at all times a card that stipulated their racial group. The Group Areas Act of 1950 partitioned the country into different geographic areas allocated to each racial group. The Pass Laws then restricted people to their assigned area by restricting or prohibiting their entering any area not assigned to their group. Resistance to this system was ruthlessly suppressed.

So-called 'petty apartheid' was the strict segregation of these groups in public facilities and space, such as South Africa's beaches. The Reservation of Separate Amenities Act 49 of 1953 required that separate buildings, services and conveniences be provided for and used exclusively by different racial groups.[68] By the end of the 1950s, the use of all public facilities – railway stations, post offices, park benches, public toilets, beaches and so forth – was strictly controlled according to the race of the person wishing to use them. Signs indicated which seat, entrance, cubicle, or stretch of beach was reserved for a particular racial group. (The system forced peculiar special arrangements and sometimes controversies: for example, passionate debates about whether black nursemaids should be allowed on a 'whites only' beach if they were tending white children.)

Dan O'Meara paints the following portrait of apartheid South Africa's legal climate during the 1960s:

> This was perhaps the bleakest period in South Africa's dismal history. The relentless, paranoid witch hunt for perceived enemies, the morally-blind and fanatical implementation of the smallest details of apartheid, the Mother Grundy censorship, and the imposition of fundamentalist Calvinist values on the broader society, all conspired to reinforce the most mean-spirited, petty-minded and ignorant parochial philistinism in public and intellectual life. These were years when Black Beauty was banned as subversive literature; when 'swimming on Sundays' was condemned as a moral outrage; when prominent theologians could seriously claim that the devastating

drought of 1966 was God's punishment for the fact that white women had adopted the miniskirt; when the whole society thrilled to salacious (and frequent) newspaper reports of the prosecution under the Immorality Act of pro-apartheid Dutch Reformed Church clerics, and thousands of other white males, who had slept with black women.[69]

As this description suggests, apartheid legislation became too vast and complicated to discuss comprehensively here,[70] but highlights can suggest its breadth. Examples of the following laws will be discussed in Part II where relevant.

- The Suppression of Communism Act of 1950 banned the South African Communist Party (SACP) as well as any other party that the government chose to label as 'communist'. It made membership in the SACP punishable by up to ten years' imprisonment.
- The Riotous Assemblies Act of 1956 prohibited disorderly gatherings.
- The Unlawful Organisations Act of 1960 outlawed organisations that were deemed threatening to the government.
- The Sabotage Act was passed 1962, the General Law Amendment Act in 1966, the Terrorism Act in 1967 and the Internal Security Act in 1976.
- The Bantu Authorities Act of 1951 created separate government structures for blacks. It was the first piece of legislation established to support the Government's plan of separate development in the Bantustans.
- The Prevention of Illegal Squatting Act of 1951 allowed the government to demolish black shack-land slums.
- The Native Building Workers Act and Native Services Levy of 1951 forced white employers to pay for the construction of housing for black workers recognised as legal residents in 'white' cities.
- The Reservation of Separate Amenities Act of 1953 prohibited people of different races from using the same public amenities, such as restaurants, public swimming pools and restrooms .
- The Bantu Education Act of 1953 crafted a separate and inferior didactic scheme for African students under the aegis of the Department of 'Bantu' Education.
- The Bantu Urban Areas Act of 1954 curtailed black migration to cities.
- The Mines and Work Act of 1956 formalised racial discrimination in employment.
- The Promotion of Black Self-Government Act of 1958 entrenched the National Party's policy of separate development. It set up separate territorial governments in the 'Homelands', designated lands for black people where they could have a vote. The map of South Africa thus had a white centre with a cluster of black states along its borders.
- The Bantu Investment Corporation Act of 1959 set up a mechanism to transfer capital to the Homelands in order to create employment there.

- The Extension of University Education Act of 1959 created separate and ultimately inferior universities for blacks, coloureds and Indians. Under this act, existing universities were not permitted to enrol new black students.
- The Physical Planning and Utilisation of Resources Act of 1967 allowed the government to stop industrial development that employed black labour in 'white' areas and redirect such development to homeland border areas.
- The Black Homeland Citizenship Act of 1970 changed the status of the inhabitants of the black Homelands so that they were no longer citizens of South Africa.
- The Afrikaans Medium Decree of 1974 required the use of Afrikaans and English on a 50:50 basis in high schools outside the Homelands.

The regime's progressive clamp-down on civil liberties, harsh enforcement and punishments, and conditions of humiliation, extreme poverty and sometimes starvation in the black townships and Homelands swiftly inspired modes of resistance. In response to the first spate of apartheid legislation, the Defiance Campaign of 1952 resulted in the arrest of thousands of protesting South Africans and the banning of many of their leaders.[71] Sporadic violence and protests continued throughout the 1950s, culminating in the Sharpeville massacre of 1960 when police shot dead 69 people who were protesting against the Pass Laws. A state of emergency was declared and the Unlawful Organisations Act was passed, outlawing the African National Congress (ANC) and the Pan-African Congress (PAC). In terms of this Act, those found guilty of furthering the aims of either of these two organisations could be convicted and sentenced to up to ten years' imprisonment. Both the ANC and the PAC went underground and took up arms against the apartheid government.

The Black Consciousness movement, led by Steve Biko, emerged in the late 1960s and contributed to the Soweto uprising which began on 16 June 1976. This famous uprising, which started as a protest by schoolchildren against the compulsory use of Afrikaans as a medium of instruction in African schools, triggered retaliatory State repression that soon engulfed the entire country in a wave of violent anti-apartheid protests. Hundreds of protesters were killed and imprisoned, and many others fled into exile. Violence and unrest continued throughout the 1980s, during which the apartheid regime declared successive states of emergency and ultimately adopted a 'total strategy' to resist what it called a 'total onslaught' from anti-apartheid forces. During this period, extrajudicial killings, torture, arbitrary detention and other abuses by the regime became commonplace.

Finally, facing ungovernable mass protests and a failing national economy impacted also by an international boycott, in 1990 the last white nationalist President of South Africa, W.A. de Klerk, announced the unbanning of the anti-apartheid political movements and the release of their leaders, including Nelson Mandela. The apartheid regime ended formally with the passing of South Africa's Interim Constitution of 1993, which paved the way for the country's first democratic election and the inauguration of Nelson Mandela as South Africa's first black president on 10 May 1994. South Africa's current constitution, a liberal and progressive document, was passed in 1996 and went into effect in February 1997. Healing the deep social wounds inflicted by apartheid was a longer and continuing process, sought partly through the hearings by the Truth and Reconciliation Commission, whose 1998 report provides the principal citations on South African practices for this study.

## PART II: REVIEW OF ISRAELI PRACTICES IN THE OPT

### INTRODUCTION

This chapter now reviews Israel's practices in the OPT to confirm whether they correspond to the 'inhuman acts' listed in Article 2 of the Apartheid Convention. In Chapter 1, we noted that this list of acts was intended by the Convention's drafters to be illustrative, not all-inclusive or exclusive: if practised for the purpose of racial domination, acts not listed here may nonetheless be relevant to a finding of apartheid, while only some or conceivably none of these specific acts may be evident. Still, this list offers an uncontroversial framework, within the ambit of international law, for checking whether Israel's practices are consistent with the definition of apartheid as codified in the Convention (and the Rome Statute).

Each practice listed by the Apartheid Convention is addressed here in three parts: (1) the legal meaning and significance of the provision; (2) a short overview of relevant practices in apartheid South Africa, for illustrative and comparative purposes; and (3) a discussion of relevant Israeli practices in the OPT. As commentary on the Apartheid Convention is scant, discussion of legal meaning is drawn principally from international human rights and humanitarian law. Review of apartheid practices and policies in South Africa draws principally from the 1998 report of South Africa's Truth and Reconciliation Commission (TRC), which provides a concise and authoritative assessment. Consideration of Israeli practices and policies, and their impact on Palestinians, draws from reports and findings of the UN and other international organisations, jurisprudence of international and domestic courts including the Supreme Court of Israel, works by scholars of international law, and reports and documentation by Palestinian and Israeli human rights organisations.

### ARTICLE 2(a)(i) – DENIAL OF RIGHT TO LIFE BY MURDER OF MEMBERS OF A RACIAL GROUP

#### Interpretation

The Apartheid Convention's formulation of the provision regarding 'denial of right to life' is drawn from Article 2 of the Genocide Convention, although the latter Convention speaks of 'killing', rather than 'murder'. This distinction is significant because 'killing' can include taking life as sanctioned by law, such as the death penalty. In specifying the category of 'murder', the Apartheid Convention expresses a narrower concern with State-sanctioned extra-judicial killings. Such killing falls under the prohibition of racial discrimination in Article 5(b) of ICERD, regarding the enjoyment of 'the right to security of person and protection by the State against violence or bodily harm, whether inflicted by government officials or by any individual group or institution'. As defined by Article 7(2)(h) of the Rome Statute, the crime against humanity of murder amounts to an 'inhumane act' of apartheid when perpetrated in the context of an institutionalised regime of systematic oppression and domination by one racial group over another.

### Practices in apartheid South Africa

The TRC determined that 'denial of right to life by murder' was a key tool for the apartheid regime of South Africa, used to eliminate the regime's more influential opponents and frighten the rest into submission. Judicial killings were myriad: between 1960 and 1994, over 2,500 people were hanged in South Africa[72] (of whom 95 per cent were black and only one was white[73]) and, during 'the Christmas rush of 1988', 28 people were hanged in one week.[74] All of the condemned were sentenced by white (male) judges. To the extent that taking of life was sanctioned by South African law, and carried out in accordance with due process standards, it would not amount to 'murder' prohibited in this section. Even judicial killings, however, frequently violated due process.

Beyond capital punishment, the TRC concluded that the apartheid regime sanctioned the murder of its opponents.[75] This practice included the shooting of demonstrators (famously, at Sekhukhune, Pondoland, Sharpeville and Soweto) as well as assassinations. The State Security Council (SSC) – which sat atop the National Security Management System – initially targeted members of groups designated as 'terrorist' operating outside South Africa, but eventually it also targeted their supporters and hosts in cross-border raids that cost thousands of lives. In the 1980s, SSC agents began to target the regime's opponents within South Africa.[76]

While secrecy has made reliable statistical data difficult to obtain and the true scale of these extrajudicial killings hard to determine, some indication can be obtained from the amnesty applications before the TRC, which included 114 applications for the killing of 889 people.[77] These applications were categorised by the TRC as (a) abductions followed by killing (deaths in detention, suicides, accidents and natural causes); (b) assassinations of persons considered to have a high political profile both inside and outside the country; (c) assassinations of individual MK (Umkhonto we Sizwe – 'Spear of the Nation') and Azanian People's Liberation Army (APLA) personnel both inside and outside the country, and (d) cross-border raids.[78]

The murder of people in detention is well documented (Steve Biko's death is perhaps the most publicised).[79] The TRC identified a pattern of targeted killings of political opponents and resistance forces in which the regime's opponents were abducted, interrogated, tortured and killed. An additional twist was that the bodies of those who, under torture, gave information about the resistance and were then killed in detention were often not returned to their families, which resulted in the dual punishment of families in not knowing what had happened to their loved ones while being associated with the stigma of betraying the resistance.[80]

The TRC Report observed that the state resorted to targeted extrajudicial killings because unexplained deaths were, by law, followed by an inquest which required access to the body of the deceased for examination of the cause of death.[81] While such inquests usually relied on the word of the police alone, with very little circumspect interrogation, the inquest allowed the victim's families to appoint counsel to cross-examine police and other witnesses.[82] In order to suppress evidence and maintain political control, the court system effectively condoned and tolerated extrajudicial killings, 'which [led] to a culture of impunity throughout the security forces'.[83] The creation of the Civil Co-operation Bureau and Vlakplaas were measures reflecting a policy of planned elimination of resistance by whatever means.[84]

### Israeli practices in the OPT

Since the occupation began in 1967, thousands of Palestinians in the OPT have been killed by the Israeli military forces. Over the 24 years from the first *intifada* in December 1987 until May 2011, such deaths totalled more than 7,000.[85]

One form of these killings is a pattern of excessive use of force against civilian demonstrators protesting Israeli practices in the OPT.[86] Also analogous to practices in apartheid South Africa is Israel's extrajudicial, summary or arbitrary execution[87] of Palestinians opposing Israel's regime of occupation. Israeli authorities have routinely designated the targets of extrajudicial executions as 'terrorists' and contend that these killings are necessary due to difficulties in arresting suspects. Witnesses to such killings, however, have described them as often constituting summary executions of Palestinians, already under the control of Israeli agents, who were then killed or died due to denial of essential medical treatment.[88]

In the early 1990s, the Israeli army and the Border Police established undercover military units in which Israeli soldiers were disguised as Arab civilians (known in Hebrew as *Mista'arvim*) in order to infiltrate Palestinian areas. Their official mission was to capture 'wanted' Palestinians but in practice they assassinated many 'wanted' Palestinians[89] even when evidence suggests that the targeted person could have been arrested.[90] These units operated in conjunction with the General Security Services (GSS, or Israel Security Agency, ISA), and made use of State intelligence.[91] Israel has traditionally denied that these undercover units were assassination squads[92] but later policy shifts discredit this claim, especially following the outbreak of the second *intifada* in September 2000[93] when the army was given 'a broader license to liquidate Palestinian terrorists' and 'act against known terrorists even if they are not on the verge of committing a major attack'.[94] Targets for killing have included militants and political leaders belonging to Palestinian political parties and factions. Killings have been carried out by sniper fire, missiles fired and bombs dropped from combat aircrafts, ground-to-ground missiles, tank fire and explosive devices planted in cars and public telephone booths.

In 2001, then Attorney-General Elyakim Rubinstein argued that such 'targeted killings' (a term he prefers to 'liquidation') are legal because they are conducted according to Israeli military law and orders. Military orders, he implied, in themselves constitute sufficient due process and so make targeted killings consistent with international law.[95] Since military orders to kill Palestinians are made unilaterally by military authorities, in a process kept secret, this claim cannot be credited. Nor are such killings open to meaningful review. Until 2011, the Israeli Military Advocate General's office opened investigations into the killings of Palestinians in the OPT only in exceptional cases.[96] In April 2011, when the legal centre Adalah petitioned the Supreme Court on this matter, the Israeli military announced a policy change that investigations will take place in all such cases. As the rule is made provisional on prevailing 'security circumstances', however, its implementation remains subject to military fiat.[97]

Targeted killings have been carried out under circumstances that sometimes suggest both disproportionality and a failure to discriminate, resulting in hundreds of deaths of innocent bystanders. One such case was the 'targeted killing' of Salah Mustafa Muhammad Shehadeh, suspected leader of the Izz ad-Din al-Qassem Brigade, the military wing of Hamas. On 22 July 2002, the Israeli army targeted the building in which Shehadeh was staying, using a one-ton bomb dropped by an F-16 plane in a densely populated neighbourhood of Gaza City. Fifteen people were killed, including Shehadeh's assistant, wife and nine children, while 150 others were injured.[98] A special Israeli investigatory commission later held Israeli authorities blameless for the deaths of 13 civilians that it admitted were 'uninvolved'.[99]

At the beginning of the second *intifada*, the Israeli Supreme Court first refused to consider the legality of the policy, stating in response to a petition that, 'the choice of means of war employed by respondents ... is not among the subjects in which this court will see fit to intervene'.[100] In January 2002, however, the Court accepted to hear such a challenge.[101] In its December 2006 judgment, the Court dismissed the petition, ruling that it cannot be determined that 'targeted killings' are always legal or always illegal: 'All depends upon the question of whether the standards of customary international law regarding international armed conflict allow that preventative strike or not.'[102] The Court's decision hinged on the definition of civilians and combatants under international humanitarian law and how 'taking direct part in hostilities' is construed:

> [T]he 'direct' character of the part taken should not be narrowed merely to the person committing the physical act of attack; those who have sent him, as well, take 'a direct part'. The same goes for the person who decided

upon the act and the person who planned it. It is not to be said about them that they are taking an indirect part in the hostilities.[103]

Thus the Court's judgment shifted the judicial focus from the assassination policy to the individual culpability of its targets.[104] This interpretation corresponds with the position of the Israeli military and political establishment that all Palestinians involved in militant resistance to the Israeli occupation are 'terrorists' and legitimate targets for targeted killings, including non-militant members of the Palestinian political and spiritual leadership.[105] Sheikh Ahmad Yassin and Abd el-Aziz Rantissi are among the more prominent political and spiritual leaders of Hamas extrajudicially executed by Israel in recent years.[106]

In conclusion, as in apartheid South Africa, extrajudicial killing is sustained and defended by Israeli authorities as an appropriate tool to repress Palestinian resistance and the practice is formally sanctioned by the executive and judicial branches of the State. As it is a policy designed to ensure the continuing domination of a Jewish nation-state over Palestinians under Israel's control, this policy therefore matches the 'inhuman act' listed in the Apartheid Convention regarding the 'denial of right to life by murder'.

### ARTICLE 2(a)(ii) – DENIAL OF RIGHT TO LIFE AND LIBERTY OF PERSON BY SUBJECTION TO TORTURE OR TO CRUEL, INHUMAN OR DEGRADING TREATMENT OR PUNISHMENT

#### Interpretation

The prohibition on the use of torture or cruel, inhuman or degrading treatment is absolute under international law: it is outlawed even during times of war.[107] Article 5 of the Universal Declaration of Human Rights states that '[n]o one shall be subjected to torture or to cruel, inhuman or degrading treatment or punishment'. Similar or identical phrasing can be found in Article 7 of the International Covenant on Civil and Political Rights (ICCPR), Article 3 of the European Convention for the Protection of Human Rights and Fundamental Freedoms, and other regional human rights instruments. While not making explicit reference to torture, Article 5(b) of ICERD prohibits racial discrimination in the enjoyment of 'the right to security of person and protection by the State against violence or bodily harm, whether inflicted by government officials or by any individual group or institution'. The UN Convention against Torture and Other Cruel, Inhuman or Degrading Treatment or Punishment (CAT) has been ratified by 144 States.

Legal academics and practitioners generally agree that the prohibition on torture is both absolute and non-derogable. As Lord Bingham of the House of Lords stated, '[t]here can be few issues on which international legal opinion is more clear than on the condemnation of torture. Offenders have been recognised as the "common enemies of mankind".'[108] Like the crime of apartheid, violation of the prohibition on torture and cruel, inhuman or degrading treatment is an *international crime*.[109] Thus the International

Criminal Court could – if the Rome Statute's jurisdictional provisions are satisfied – exercise criminal jurisdiction over individuals responsible for torture committed as a crime against humanity (if practised on a widespread or systematic basis). Some have suggested that the prohibition on torture is part of customary international law and a *jus cogens* norm.[110] It has been posited that States can exercise universal jurisdiction over such violations.[111] (At the same time, recent events at a global level – most notably the 'war on terror' – have brought these rogue practices back into the limelight and courts have had to grapple with alleged violations of what was hitherto widely considered a settled area of human rights law.[112])

The language of the Apartheid Convention regarding torture thus reflects a well-established prohibition, but shifts the focus from individuals to groups by expressing a concern for the practice as connected to a policy of racial oppression. Under the Rome Statute, as well, torture amounts to apartheid where 'committed in the context of an institutionalized regime of systematic oppression and domination by one racial group over any other racial group or groups and committed with the intention of maintaining that regime'.[113]

### Practices in apartheid South Africa

Torture and cruel, inhuman or degrading treatment of detainees were the main grievances reported to the TRC. The TRC estimated that as many as 20,000 detainees were tortured in detention in the Eastern Cape alone, while nationally, the number was more than a hundred thousand.[114]

Torture with police impunity was found to be the cornerstone of the detention system, as 'extracting information, statements and confessions, often regardless of whether true or not' allowed the state 'to secure a successful prosecution and neutralisation of yet another opponent of the apartheid system'.[115] Torture in detention sometimes led to death.[116] Beatings were the most frequently mentioned violation, but electric shocks were also common, as well as caning, 'spare' diet (slow starvation), leg irons, solitary confinement and even allegations of poisoning.[117] Most torture was inflicted before trial, during interrogation, but some of those jailed after sentencing were also mistreated.[118] As a consequence of torture, some detainees returned home blind and/or deaf, some mentally ill.

As the most frequently reported perpetrator was the security police,[119] the TRC concluded that it was the official policy of the Department of Prisons to inflict a variety of cruel, degrading and inhuman forms of punishment on prisoners. Thus torture and other abuses in the prisons were integral to the apartheid regime's system of domination.[120]

### Israeli practices in the OPT

Torture and other forms of ill-treatment are widespread during the arrest and interrogation of Palestinians by the Israeli military forces and Border Police.[121] Particularly harsh interrogation methods are used by the GSS to obtain information and confessions. In one study of detainees held between July 2005 and January 2006, 49 per cent of the Palestinians detained for interrogation by the GSS reported being beaten during the stages preceding interrogation, 33 per cent being held in painful bindings, 34 per cent being subjected to curses and humiliation, 23 per cent being denied basic needs, and 67 per cent reported being exposed to at least one of the above abuses.[122] During interrogation by the GSS, 68 per cent of Palestinian prisoners reported being held in isolation during all or most of the interrogation period, 88 per cent being held in solitary confinement and experiencing sensory deprivation during all or most of the interrogation period, 45 per cent being deprived of sleep, 73 per cent being given poor-quality food, 96 per cent being cuffed for protracted periods in the painful *shabah* position (in which the detainee's hands and feet are tightly bound to a chair or low stool), 29 per cent being subjected to a naked body search, and 73 per cent to insults and other humiliations.[123]

Conditions of confinement in Israeli prisons also constitute ill-treatment that can amount to torture, including cramped and unhygienic living spaces and medical neglect. Israeli law permits the imposition of separate, harsher conditions of confinement on 'security' detainees as compared to ordinary criminal detainees simply because they are alleged to have committed offences defined as security offences.[124] These discriminatory conditions violate the fundamental rights of Palestinian detainees.

The absolute prohibition on torture in international law has not been incorporated into Israeli criminal law,[125] but in 1999 the Israeli Supreme Court held certain methods of interrogation to be illegal. In the same decision, however, the Court allowed the use of pressure and 'discomfort' for the purpose of extracting information from detainees.[126] The Court further indicated that agents of the General Security Services (GSS, or ISA), if they claimed to be using torture on so-called 'ticking bombs'[127] could avoid prosecution on the basis of the 'necessity defence' set forth in Article 34K of Israel's Penal Law.[128] The Court also failed to define precisely the circumstances in which the 'ticking bomb' defence is applicable, leaving scope for a broad interpretation by the GSS and a concomitant continuation of torture and other cruel, inhuman or degrading treatment or punishment.[129] Thus, the Supreme Court left a legal ambiguity regarding torture that allowed for its continued use in the case of 'security' prisoners and detainees, the overwhelming majority of whom are Palestinians. (According to statistics obtained from the Israel Prison Service in January 2009, of 8,200 'security prisoners' only 14 were Jewish.[130])

Following the Supreme Court's 1999 ruling and the outbreak of the second *intifada* in 2000, Israel's continuing practices of physical and psychological torture have drawn concern by the UN Committee Against Torture in 2001 and 2009,[131] the UN Human Rights Committee in 2003 and 2010,[132] and the UN Special Rapporteur on the Promotion and Protection of Human Rights and Fundamental Freedoms while Countering Terrorism in November 2007.[133] In 2003, the Public Committee Against Torture in Israel (PCATI) affirmed that torture in Israel was still being 'carried out in an orderly and institutional fashion'.[134] On 2 December 2008, Israeli human rights organisations filed a contempt-of-court motion with the Supreme Court against the State of Israel for its policy of granting GSS investigators prior permission to practise torture in violation of the Court's 1999 decision.[135] In July 2009, the Supreme Court rejected the motion (ruling that the contempt-of-court procedure is not the appropriate one for clarifying claims of violation of court decisions whose nature is 'declarative').[136]

By contrast, the handful of Israeli Jewish prisoners who are classified as 'security' prisoners have been permitted to exercise numerous rights, including conjugal visits. For example, prisoner Yigal Amir, who was convicted in 1996 of murdering Prime Minister Yitzhak Rabin for ideological reasons, has since fathered a son in prison and has been allowed open visits with his family and phone calls. Similarly, Jewish-Israeli prisoner Ami Popper, who was convicted in 1990 of murdering seven Palestinian labourers and wounding eleven others, was married in prison in 1993 and fathered his first child in prison in 1995. He has since fathered another two children. He has also been granted leave to take furloughs from prison. No Palestinian security prisoner has been awarded such privileges.[137]

As documented by the PCATI, some Palestinian detainees have been subjected to a form of psychological torture by the GSS: the arrest and exploitation of innocent family members of the detainees under interrogation, in order to pressure prisoners into a confession or to obtain information.[138] In some cases the GSS has informed prisoners, either falsely or accurately, that their relatives are also being tortured, for the same purpose.

No criminal investigation has been opened and no prosecutions have been brought against alleged Israeli perpetrators of torture and ill-treatment. This may be true partly because, until 2011, the inspector who investigated complaints of torture and ill-treatment against GSS interrogators was an employee of the GSS and therefore, in practice, the GSS was a self-regulating body. According to data provided in Israel's Fourth Periodic Report on the implementation of the CAT, in 2002–05, the GSS inspector initiated some 386 'examinations', of which only four resulted in disciplinary measures and not one in prosecution.[139] In this regard, the UN Special Rapporteur raised his concerns 'about the ability of the inspector, as an employee of the Israel Security Agency, to act truly independently from the Agency and thus vigorously investigate allegations of ill-treatment or torture'.[140]

In September 2010, the PCATI wrote to Attorney-General Yehuda Weinstein on behalf of six other human rights NGOs (non-governmental organisations), requesting a change in policy that would require the opening of criminal investigations in complaints arousing suspicions of torture or ill-treatment. The Ministry of Justice declared in November 2011 that the mechanism for investigation will be transferred to the Ministry of Justice and will answer to the Ministry's executive director.[141] No information has been forthcoming from the authorities regarding the substance of this change, however.

The impunity that was effectively afforded by the Supreme Court's 1999 decision (discussed earlier) was further consolidated in the General Security Service Law (2002), which specifies that a GSS employee 'shall *not* bear criminal or civil responsibility for any act or omission performed in good faith and reasonably by him within the scope and in performance of his function'.[142] The lack of an effective mechanism to enforce CAT and Israel's failure to ratify the Optional Protocol to CAT mandating independent visits to prisons have also contributed to a culture of impunity. Torture is also facilitated by the recently amended Criminal Procedure (Interrogation of Suspects) Law (Amendment No. 4) 2008, which exempts the GSS and the police from making audio and video documentation of their interrogations of suspects in security offences (section 7). The same law supports the policy of restricting the access of prisoners and detainees to legal counsel, often with the acquiescence of other state authorities and the courts.[143]

Thus Israeli State institutions provide legal and procedural protection to torturers. As noted, the Supreme Court remains reluctant to enforce international standards prohibiting torture and ill-treatment. The State Prosecutor's Office perfunctorily rejects complaints of torture and the Attorney-General unquestioningly accepts the 'ticking bomb' and 'necessity defence' claims presented by the GSS. The result is that the policy of State-sanctioned torture against Palestinians continues unabated.

## ARTICLE 2(a)(iii) – DENIAL OF RIGHT TO LIBERTY OF PERSON BY ARBITRARY ARREST AND ILLEGAL IMPRISONMENT OF MEMBERS OF A RACIAL GROUP

### Interpretation

The prohibition on arbitrary arrest is a pillar of international human rights law. The ICCPR's Human Rights Committee holds that detention is arbitrary if it continues beyond the period for which a State can provide appropriate justification.[144] Otherwise, the deprivation of liberty permitted by law must not be 'manifestly *unproportional*, unjust or *unpredictable*, and [that] the specific manner in which an arrest is made must not be *discriminatory* and must be able to be deemed *appropriate* and *proportional* in view of the circumstances of the case'.[145]

Thus Article 9 of the Universal Declaration of Human Rights (UDHR) declares that, 'No one shall be subjected to arbitrary arrest, detention or exile.' Article 9 of the ICCPR reiterates this prohibition and states further that 'no one shall be deprived of his liberty except on such grounds and in accordance with such procedures as are established by law'. The UN Human Rights Committee holds that administrative detention is unlawful where it amounts to arbitrary detention, or where it violates basic due process rights if information of the reasons for detention is not given, or if adequate judicial review of the detention is not available.[146] Permitted derogations, it holds, must not violate the fundamental protections provided by the Covenant on Human Rights.[147] Article 78 of the Fourth Geneva Convention does permit an Occupying Power to use internment, but only 'for imperative reasons of security'.

Under international human rights and humanitarian law, an administrative detainee should be informed promptly of the reasons for his or her detention.[148] Article 9 of the ICCPR enshrines the rights of detainees to seek a judicial review to determine the lawfulness of their detention[149] and of those arrested or detained to be informed of the reasons for arrest and detention, while implicitly prohibiting indefinite detention.

In its language, it is unusual that the Apartheid Convention cites 'illegal' (rather than 'arbitrary') measures, as international human rights law typically uses 'arbitrary' regarding both arrest and imprisonment. The term 'illegal' indeed begs the question, 'illegal under what system of law?'[150] Had the Apartheid Convention referred to arbitrary (rather than illegal) detention, it would have more clearly invoked international standards regarding this concern. It is unclear why the drafters of the Convention did not do this, but the probable reason is that it was simply a careless oversight.[151] Absent an explanation, inferring that the intent of the provision was to accord with international standards keeps this provision in line with the overall aim of the Apartheid Convention. Indeed, the Rome Statute specifies that 'inhumane acts' constituting the crime of apartheid include 'imprisonment or other severe deprivation of physical liberty in violation of fundamental rules of international law'.[152] Thus this provision of the Apartheid Convention can be construed as the deprivation of liberty by arbitrary arrest and detention in violation of standards as established in international law. The use of the term 'illegal' does bring the right of judicial review into the equation, such as contained in Article 8 of the UDHR and other human rights instruments. In the *Barayagwiza* case, the ICTR confirmed the established nature of the right to judicial review in respect of the lawfulness of detention.[153]

One manifestation of such arbitrary detention is administrative detention or internment, which entails the imprisonment of individuals without charge or trial, by administrative rather than judicial procedure. As a concept it is intended to be an exceptional emergency measure, preventive rather than punitive in disposition, but has historically been used to imprison opponents of repressive regimes.[154]

## Practices in apartheid South Africa

In apartheid South Africa, detention of political activists was a primary means of repression.[155] With the introduction of detention without trial in the 1960s, it became one of the main tools of control under apartheid.[156] In the 1980s, detention was used also as 'a preventive measure (as in 1986, where it affected whole communities), or as a deliberate form of intimidation'.[157] The TRC has estimated that some 80,000 South Africans were detained without trial between 1960 and 1990, including about 10,000 women and about 15,000 children under the age of 18. Up to 80 per cent of these detainees were eventually released without charge and barely 4 per cent were ever convicted of any crime.[158] In addition to constituting a human rights violation in itself, 'detention without trial allowed for the abuse of those held in custody'.[159]

The first of the security laws introduced by the National Party was the Suppression of Communism Act of 1950. This Act was extremely broad in its scope, being aimed not only at the suppression of Communism as a narrowly defined political ideology, but also at the suppression of any doctrine 'which aims at bringing about any political, industrial, social or economic change within the Union by the promotion of disturbances or disorder, by unlawful acts or omissions or by means which include the promotion of disturbance or disorder, or such acts or omissions or threats'.[160] This scope embraced any doctrine of anti-racism that threatened white supremacy in South African governance.

After many amendments and extensions, the Suppression of Communism Act was replaced by the Internal Security Act 79 of 1976,[161] which was also amended and extended as the struggle against apartheid intensified. This latter Act provided for preventative detention for periods of twelve months. These periods of detention could be successive and indefinite. The Act gave discretion to the Minister of Justice to detain any person on the basis of 'security' or 'public order', without defining the parameters of those terms. The subjective nature of this vested discretion enabled the Minister, without due process or justification, to declare that someone should be detained, without the existence of objective factors to warrant such detention. It enabled the Minister to label someone as a threat to public order, whether or not any verifiable factors existed as to whether they indeed constituted such a threat. The effect of this discretion was to render the application of the law capricious and unpredictable. Criticism of such discretion is that it should never be widely construed. Contemporary principles of administrative and constitutional law preclude the arbitrary exercise of discretion, without due consideration. In fact modern constitutionalism suggests that the concept of an unfettered discretion, such as that afforded the Minister under the Internal Security Act, is anathema to the principle of legality.[162]

The apartheid regime also made frequent use of detention without trial in order to silence its opponents. In terms of the Criminal Procedure Act of 1965, potential state witnesses in political trials could be detained without trial for up to 180 days. An even more draconian provision was put into effect by the Terrorism Act 83 of 1967, which allowed for indefinite detention without trial of those suspected of being 'terrorists'. Detainees could be held until they had replied 'satisfactorily' to all questions put to them under interrogation. The Terrorism Act placed the onus on the accused to prove his innocence, rather than on the prosecution to prove his guilt. The Act provided for a minimum sentence of five years upon conviction, and courts of law were prohibited from pronouncing upon the validity of any detention order, or ordering the release of any particular detainee, while such detainee was still being interrogated or awaiting charges to be brought against him.[163] Under the 1976 Internal Security Amendment Act in South Africa, the Minister of Justice was 'given a completely subjective discretion to detain a person'[164] when satisfied that the person may endanger the 'security of the State' or the 'maintenance of public order', terms which were not defined anywhere in the Act.

The apartheid regime also made use of banning and banishment to silence its opponents. Many organisations and individuals were affected. Individuals who were banned might be ordered to resign from political organisations, prohibited from attending gatherings, confined to certain magisterial districts, or subjected to house arrest.[165] Banishment orders were used to isolate political opponents in remote rural areas in order to stifle their opposition to the apartheid system. Motlhabi points out that certain banning orders were drafted effectively to banish the person concerned.[166]

Israeli practices in the OPT

Since June 1967, Israel has arrested and imprisoned Palestinians in the OPT on a massive scale. In one count, at least 650,000 Palestinians, constituting around 20 per cent of the total Palestinian population of the OPT and close to 40 per cent of the male population, have been imprisoned at some time by the Occupying Power.[167] From the beginning of the second *intifada* in September 2000 and February 2007, approximately 45,000 Palestinians were imprisoned.[168] In June 2011, the number of Palestinians being held in Israeli prisons totalled 5,554, of whom 229 were in administrative detention (without charge or trial).[169] Mass imprisonment has also severely impacted the Palestinian community and families of prisoners in the OPT.[170]

Israel has argued that arrests and detentions of Palestinians are guided solely by security concerns, citing the risk of terrorist and other militant attack on its own population, but practices indicate a policy to target political crimes. Since 2007, elected members of the Palestinian Legislative Council (PLC) have been and continue to be administratively detained (in June 2011, 17 PLC members were reported to be in prison). Israel's use of administrative detention against human rights defenders has prompted the UN Special Representative on Human Rights Defenders to express concern that, in the OPT, 'administrative detention is being used as a means to deter defenders from carrying out their human rights activities'.[171] As arrest and imprisonment are often accompanied by torture and abuses used to extract confessions and gain information about resistance activities (as discussed in the previous section), it is reasonably concluded that a primary purpose of the detention policy is to suppress resistance to the occupation and cement Israel's domination over the Palestinian population in the OPT.[172]

Special Israeli law regarding 'security' detainees effectively facilitates the practice of torture in detention (discussed in the previous section). For example, to give Israeli authorities greater powers to handle Palestinians from Gaza after Israel's unilateral 'disengagement', in 2006 the Criminal Procedure (Detainees Suspected of Security Offences) Law was enacted to allow 'security' detainees to be detained for 96 hours without any judicial oversight (in ordinary criminal cases, suspects may be detained for only 24 or 48 hours); have their detention extended in their absence; not to be told of the court's decision to lengthen their arrest; and be denied access to legal counsel for a period of 21 days.[173] In February 2010, the Supreme Court struck down Article 5 of this law, holding that security detainees must be present at the hearing where their detentions were extended.[174] However, a subsequent amendment to the law in December 2010[175] attempted to bypass this decision by allowing the courts to extend a security suspect's detention for up to 20 days at a time (instead of 15 days) and to hold extension-of-detention hearings in his/her absence.[176] Thus the law removes a number of essential procedural safeguards from detainees, placing them at a greater risk of torture and ill-treatment.

*Administrative detention in the OPT*

Within the criminal justice system, Israel has effectively created a distinct track for Palestinian detainees that operates in parallel with, but separately from, the 'ordinary' criminal track. This is especially notable in Israel's widespread use of 'administrative detention' against political opponents of the occupation. This special category is accordingly examined here in greater detail.

Israeli military forces in the OPT have autonomous executive authority to issue administrative detention orders. Israel bases such authority on the British Mandate Government of Palestine's Defence (Emergency) Regulations of 1945,[177] which empowered a military area commander to detain any person if he considered it was 'necessary or expedient to make the order for securing the public safety ... the maintenance of public order or the suppression of mutiny, rebellion or riot'. The commander was not obliged to limit the duration of such a detention or prescribe rules of evidence. After Israel's creation in 1948, these same Regulations were used to institute administrative detention primarily of Palestinians living inside Israel until the passing of the Emergency Powers Law (Detention) of 1979. After 1967, administrative detention was effected in the OPT on the same basis.

In 1970, Israel enacted its own laws relating to administrative detention. Military Order No. 378 stipulated that

> [the Israeli] military commander, or anybody to whom he delegates his authority in his capacity, may issue an order determining that an individual be detained in whatever place of detention specified by the order.[178]

Military Order No. 378 has been amended a number of times, most significantly in 1988 by Military Order No. 1229,[179] which permits military commanders to order Palestinians detained for up to six months without charge or trial and renew and extend these detentions indefinitely.[180] A person administratively detained is supposed to be brought before the Military Court of Administrative Detention within 96 hours. In this *in camera* review, the military judge may confirm, set aside or shorten the administrative detention order.

Israeli authorities have claimed that they use the policy of administrative detention as a special preventative measure: that is, only against 'those whose activities are considered hostile and constitute a continuous threat to security and public safety'.[181] In practice, administrative detention has been both common and a way to avoid due process. By 1970, 1,131 Palestinians in the OPT were incarcerated under administrative detention orders and the practice remained common through the decade.[182] In response to strong international pressure, in 1980 Israel began to phase out the practice and the last administrative detainee of that period was released in 1982. On 4 August 1985, however, the practice was reinstated and an estimated 316 Palestinians were administratively detained by Israel between August 1985 and 9 December 1987.[183] After the outbreak of the first *intifada*, Military Order No. 1229 (issued in March 1988) granted any Israeli military commander the authority to administratively detain an individual for up to six months if he has 'reasonable grounds to presume that the security of the area or public security require the detention'. The numbers of Palestinian detainees subsequently soared: of over 50,000 Palestinians arrested between December 1987 and December 1989, more than 10,000 were under administrative detention.[184] Thus, what was originally codified as an exceptional measure was being used as a common standard of detention.

After the outbreak of the second *intifada* in 2000, the Israeli military authorities once again increased their use of administrative detention, including for non-violent political offences. From September 2000 to September 2002, cases involving the administrative detention of Palestinians increased from less than 100 to 1,860.[185] Between 2004 and 2006, a total of 8,150 administrative detention orders were issued by Israeli military commanders in the OPT.[186] By June 2011, 229 Palestinians were being held in administrative detention, including eight elected members of the PLC[187] and six children.[188] Some administrative detainees have been interned for continuous periods of up to six years.

Another relevant law is the Internment of Unlawful Combatants Law (2008), which provides for the indefinite administrative detention of 'foreign' (that is, non-Israeli) citizens. The law effectively creates a third category of person, 'unlawful combatants' (contrary to the distinction in international humanitarian law between combatants and civilians). Under this law, a person suspected of being an 'unlawful combatant' may be held for up to 14 days without judicial review and, if the detention order is approved by a court, administratively detained for indefinite periods or until 'hostilities against Israel have come to an end'. Judicial review of the detention is mandated only once every six months. The Supreme Court upheld the original law, enacted in 2002, on 11 June 2008.[189] On 28 July 2008, the Knesset amended the law to include harsher provisions such as extending the period in which the detainee is denied access to legal counsel from seven days to up to 21 days.

Under Article 87 of amended Military Order No. 378, Palestinians under administrative detention orders can be detained for months, if not years, without ever being informed about the reasons or length of their detention. Almost all information presented to the court is classified and the review judge reserves the right not to disclose this evidence or even whether evidence exists.

*Incompatibility of Israel's practice with international law*

As discussed earlier, international humanitarian law allows administrative detention in very limited circumstances. It is untenable to argue, however, that permitted derogations extend to allowing thousands of Palestinians to be detained without charge, trial or the right to have their imprisonment reviewed by an impartial body.[190] It is especially untenable that administrative detention in the OPT can be based on secret evidence, to which the detainee and counsel are denied access.

Noting the arbitrary nature of imprisonment under Military Order 1229, the UN Special Rapporteur on the promotion and protection of human rights and fundamental freedoms while countering terrorism has observed,

> The terms 'security of the area' and 'public security' are not defined, their interpretation being left to military commanders, and thus lack the level of precision required by the principle of legality.[191]

Israeli authorities have argued that Israel's policy of administrative detention is not arbitrary, partly because it is subject to judicial oversight. Nevertheless, review of related procedures finds them severely inadequate. For example, under Military Order No. 1229 of 1988, detainees can appeal their detention only to an advisory board that is authorised only to make non-binding recommendations. Military Order No. 1229 also cancelled the previous mandatory three-month review of administrative detention orders by a military judge.[192] In some circumstances, review procedures of any description have been completely suspended by Israeli military orders, such as during Israel's large-scale incursions in West Bank cities in 2002.[193]

Palestinian administrative detainees can submit appeals against their detention order before an appeal judge in an Israeli military court, where a process similar to the initial review hearing takes place. However, Israeli military judges make extremely limited use of their powers, generally deferring to the military commander and upholding the detention orders. This is also true of appeals against administrative detention orders in Israel's Supreme Court. In both instances, the appeal decision can be based on confidential material or 'secret evidence' not provided to the detainee or his lawyer. This places the detainee's counsel in the impossible position of trying to prove to the judge that the order in question is not required for security reasons, without having access to any details of the evidence on which the administrative order is based.

(Ironically, that Israel's detention policy is arbitrary and violates international standards was supported before 1948 by Zionist movement leaders, many of whom would later become prominent members of the Israeli Knesset, government and judiciary. Before the creation of the State of Israel, some were themselves administratively detained under the 1945 Defence (Emergency) Regulations and at the time voiced strong opposition to this practice by the British authorities.[194])

### Israel's discriminatory use of administrative detention

Israel's discriminatory use of administrative detention as a measure against Palestinians is indicated by the relatively rare use of this practice against Jewish-Israeli settlers. Only nine Israeli settlers in the OPT have been administratively detained over the course of the occupation.[195] Major differences in the practice as it is applied to the two groups further indicate a discriminatory policy. First, while Palestinians are typically issued six-month administrative detention orders (often renewed for years), Israeli settlers have more commonly been ordered to 40 or 60 days of detention.[196] Second, Israeli regional military commanders throughout the OPT may administratively detain Palestinians at their own discretion, but orders to detain Israeli settlers must be signed by the Minister of Defence.[197]

Third, discrimination is indicated by differential access of Jews and Palestinians to the courts. Judicial review of administrative detention of Palestinians is done by a military judge; for settlers, by a civil district court inside Israel. For Palestinians, the military court has 96 hours following the administrative order before it must conduct a review;[198] for Israeli settlers, the equivalent period (being governed by standard Israeli criminal detention procedure) is 24 hours. For Palestinians, since 1988 the law has provided for no automatic periodic reviews of administrative detention orders; for Israeli settlers interned for six months, the order is reviewed by the District Court after three months. Finally, under Article 9(5) of the ICCPR, '[a]nyone who has been the victim of unlawful arrest or detention shall have an enforceable right to compensation'. Yet, after 38 years of occupation, during which tens of thousands of Palestinians were arbitrarily denied their liberty by being placed in administrative detention, no Palestinian has received such compensation. In 2005, Jewish-Israeli settler Noam Federman became the first victim of administrative detention to be awarded damages on the grounds of unlawful imprisonment.[199]

To conclude, Israel's policies of arrest and administrative detention operate on such a mass scale and in violation of international standards as to manifest as part of a policy of domination and control over the Palestinian population. As in apartheid South Africa, administrative detention is justified on security grounds but has frequently been used to silence opponents and suppress dissent. Indeed, a clear parallel to this policy is the 1976 Internal Security Amendment Act in South Africa, discussed earlier. Discriminatory legal practices regarding the arrest and detention of Jewish settlers and Palestinians in the same territory connect these policies to a larger system that accords superior rights and ensures domination by one group over the other. Thus Israel's practices to deny Palestinians the right to liberty are consistent with the 'inhuman act' stipulated by the Apartheid Convention to comprise a crime of apartheid when associated with the purpose of sustaining a system of domination and oppression by one racial group over another.

## ARTICLE 2(b) – IMPOSITION ON A RACIAL GROUP OF LIVING CONDITIONS CALCULATED TO CAUSE ITS PHYSICAL DESTRUCTION IN WHOLE OR IN PART

Here the Apartheid Convention borrows language from Article 2 of the Convention on the Prevention and Punishment of the Crime of Genocide (hereafter 'Genocide Convention'). In this convention, genocide is defined as any of five acts 'committed with intent to destroy, in whole or in part, a national, ethnical, racial or religious group,' including '(c) imposition on the group of living conditions calculated to cause its physical destruction in whole or in part'. The Apartheid Convention notes in its chapeau that, having been codified this way, genocide is already a crime under international law. The question is when such practices also constitute the crime of apartheid. On this point, the principle of *intent* remains essential: to be culpable of this 'inhuman act', practices must be taken with the conscious intention of destroying a group physically, through the deaths of its members.[200]

Confirming such intent can be problematic, however, when an absence of official statements regarding intent is juxtaposed against mass death that, to any reasonably impartial observer, would seem an inevitable outcome of State policies. For example, in apartheid South Africa, forced transfer of millions of black South Africans had devastating effects when wretched living conditions in the Homelands resulted in wide-scale suffering and deaths through malnutrition, disease, and higher infant and child mortality. Yet the South African TRC found that the South African government did not sustain an intentional policy to destroy blacks as a group. Indeed, ensuring that most black Africans survived as a population, to provide essential cheap labour for white-owned industries and businesses, was a central mission of apartheid. The ruinous impact of forced transfer on black South Africans (such as women and children confined to unviable Homelands) thus could be interpreted as resulting more from wilful blindness and racist bias than a deliberate policy to cause human suffering and death.

Certainly, under the regime of military occupation imposed on the OPT since 1967, Palestinians have experienced thousands of killings by the Israeli military (as described earlier)[201] as well as generally higher mortality rates due to rising poverty and malnutrition and inadequate medical care. Israel's 'siege' or draconian closure of the Gaza Strip since 2006 has especially created conditions inimical to human life through resulting shortages of potable water, electricity and basic nutrition, and inaccessibility of essential medicines and medical care. The Independent Fact Finding Committee on Gaza indeed found that, in 'Operation Cast Lead' in January 2009, Israel's actions satisfied the *actus reus* of the Genocide Convention.[202]

Nonetheless, this study does not find sufficient evidence to conclude that Israel has pursued policies and practices intended to impose on the Palestinian people 'living conditions calculated to cause its physical destruction in whole or in part'. The Committee on Gaza also recalled the ICJ's finding that a specific intent to destroy a group 'could not be inferred from the siege of a city, deprivation of food and fuel, or from the obstruction of medical and humanitarian assistance'.[203] Israel's policies concerning Palestinians in the OPT do suggest a policy of collective punishment and acts that arguably constitute war crimes and crimes against humanity. They may also indicate a policy to fragment the Palestinian people, through forced partition and emigration, so that it ceases to exist as a physical community. Even in the aggregate, however, these policies do not indicate an intention to cause the physical destruction of the Palestinian people as a whole group of human beings.

## ARTICLE 2(c) – ANY LEGISLATIVE MEASURES AND OTHER MEASURES CALCULATED TO PREVENT A RACIAL GROUP OR GROUPS FROM PARTICIPATION IN THE POLITICAL, SOCIAL, ECONOMIC AND CULTURAL LIFE OF THE COUNTRY AND THE DELIBERATE CREATION OF CONDITIONS PREVENTING THE FULL DEVELOPMENT OF SUCH A GROUP OR GROUPS, IN PARTICULAR BY DENYING TO MEMBERS OF A RACIAL GROUP OR GROUPS BASIC HUMAN RIGHTS AND FREEDOMS, ...

This provision holds that measures to restrict fundamental rights and freedoms constitute the crime of apartheid if they are calculated to prevent a group's full development and participation in 'the political, social, economic and cultural life of the country'. Here the approach of the Apartheid Convention is reinforced by a similar list of rights in Article 5 of ICERD, which associates their impairment, if made on the basis of group identities such as race and national origin, with racial discrimination. All these rights must therefore be guaranteed by States parties to ICERD within their jurisdiction without discrimination.

As discussed earlier, the list of measures in Article 2(c) is illustrative and inclusive rather than comprehensive and exclusive: other practices might be considered here, if relevant to preventing 'participation' and 'full development', while not all practices need be practised to constitute a regime of apartheid. To avoid controversy, this study nonetheless reviews all these measures and not others, breaking them down into component provisions as appropriate and slightly reordering them for purposes of discussion:

- Denial of the right to freedom of movement;
- Denial of the right to freedom of residence;
- Denial of the right to leave and to return to one's country;
- Denial of the right to a nationality;
- Denial of the right to work;
- Denial of the right to form recognised trade unions;
- Denial of the right to education;
- Denial of the right to freedom of opinion and expression;
- Denial of the right to freedom of peaceful assembly and association.

While these prohibited acts involve violations of civil and political rights in themselves and regarding individuals, Article 2(c) is concerned with their impact on a group's social and cultural development and its political and economic development. Thus examining Israel's policies in terms of Article 2(c) requires considering a range of social indicators to determine their impact. As this approach can become reductionist in looking at discrete social factors, this study also considers that their aggregate impact may have a cumulative effect on a group. A final subsection therefore provides a snapshot of how Israeli policies in these areas combine to shape social conditions in the Gaza Strip.

Article 2(c)(1) – Denial of the right to freedom of movement

*Interpretation*

The right to freedom of movement is guaranteed by numerous human rights treaties, most notably in Article 12 of the ICCPR. Flowing from the guarantee contained in ICERD that everyone should enjoy the right to freedom of movement without racial discrimination,[204] the Apartheid Convention condemns any legislative and other measures calculated to deny members of a racial group the right to freedom of movement.

In international law, the right to freedom of movement has 'internal' aspects, which include the right to move freely and to choose one's place of residence within the borders of the country, and 'external' aspects, which include the right to leave one's country and to return to it.[205] The next sections deal with these 'internal' and 'external' rights in turn.

*Practices in apartheid South Africa*

Denial of the rights to freedom of movement and residence was a cornerstone of apartheid policy in South Africa. The Natives Laws Amendment Act of 1952 and the Natives (Urban Areas) Amendment Act of 1955 established the legal mechanisms to restrict the right of access by Africans to 'white areas'. In order to qualify to live in a white area, a black applicant had to qualify under Section 10 of the infamous Bantu (Urban Areas) Consolidation Act. Documentary proof had to be provided by the applicant of uninterrupted residence in the area for at least 15 years, or that the applicant had worked for a white employer for an uninterrupted period of at least ten years.

No black person could leave a rural for an urban area without a permit from the local authorities. Those who fled from impoverished Homelands to white cities without a permit were regarded as 'illegal' and were liable to arrest, imprisonment, fines and deportation. The main mechanism of control was the 'dompas' or pass book, which every African over the age of 16 was required to carry at all times, in terms of the Natives (Abolition of Passes and Co-ordination of Documents) Act 67 of 1952. A pass included a photograph, details of place of origin, employment record, tax payments, and encounters with the police. It was a criminal offence to be unable to produce a pass when required to do so by the police. On arrival in an urban area a permit to seek work had to be obtained within 72 hours. Dan O'Meara points out that

> Until the formal abandonment of influx control in 1986, literally hundreds of thousands of Africans were convicted every year for not having a reference book in their possession. When coupled with the establishment of labour bureaux throughout the country, this enabled the state to begin to control and channel the flow of black labour as required in the various sectors of the economy.[206]

The physical and psychological wounds which the Pass Laws inflicted on black South Africans are incalculable:

> Subjected to forced removals from the 'black spots', endless pass raids, the mind-numbing racist bureaucracy in the labour bureaux, Africans were constantly reminded who was *baas* [boss] in the land of their forefathers. And as Verwoerd pressed ahead with his planned 'self government' for the 'ethnic homelands', black South Africa was given the news that it was soon to be deprived of even this third-rate citizenship. The baas decreed that as 'temporary sojourners' in a whites-only country, blacks were no longer even considered to be South Africans. They would be given 'separate freedoms' in places many had never seen.[207]

South African courts became clogged with the burdens of enforcing this system:

> The courts are daily jammed with offenders. In 1978, 273,000 arrests were made for pass law offences (50,000 more than in 1977), an average of 750 a day. The magistrates work a production line of punishment: a fine here, imprisonment there; 'endorsement out'; 'remanded for identification'; two minutes, rarely more, for a case ... No one knows how many 'illegals' are in the cities; in Soweto alone they may be half a million. What is known is that they are the workers who will take any job that is offered for pay well below the recognised rate, just to keep body and soul together, to send a postal order to the family in the homelands, to buy school books and clothes and a better chance for the children.[208]

*Israeli practices in the OPT*

The Palestinian population in the OPT is subject to sweeping collective restrictions on its movement, through a combination of physical obstacles and administrative impediments imposed by Israeli occupation authorities. According to the UN Office for the Coordination of Humanitarian Affairs (OCHA), 'there are some 70 [Palestinian] villages and communities, with a combined population of nearly 200,000, compelled to use detours that are between two to five times longer than the direct route to the closest city'.[209] The adverse impact of these restrictions on Palestinian social, cultural, economic and political life is vast. By contrast, Jewish Israelis are free to move without constraint, between settlements in the OPT and between Israel and OPT settlements,[210] on roads reserved for their exclusive use. They may not enter certain Palestinian towns and cities in the OPT without permission from the Israeli military authorities, but as roads to settlements are designed to bypass these areas this constraint does not impede their socio-economic, cultural and political life.

*Visible infrastructure: checkpoints, the Wall and separate roads.* According to OCHA, in June 2011 Israel was imposing 522 restrictions to physical movement within the West Bank,[211] including checkpoints, roadblocks, trenches, earth mounds, road gates, and other physical barriers. A monthly average of 490 'flying' checkpoints (established temporarily and without warning) were further controlling and disrupting Palestinian movement.[212] Most of these checkpoints and barriers to movement are positioned so as seriously to hinder Palestinian movement within the West Bank, rather than between the West Bank and Israel. Palestinians must present the necessary ID card or documentation required by the Occupying Powers to cross a given checkpoint from one part of the West Bank to another. More than simply scattered structures of concrete, steel and earth, the barriers to movement erected by Israel in the OPT enforce the growing territorial fragmentation of the OPT, isolating Palestinians from their land and each other while securing Israel's settlement enterprise and ensuring complete segregation between the two groups. In addition to restricting movement physically, the checkpoints constitute a psychological barrier to movement by imposing humiliating and dehumanising procedures.

The Wall ('security barrier') constitutes the most significant individual barrier to Palestinian movement, aside from its de facto impact on negotiations toward future borders. The ICJ has already held that 'the construction of the wall and its associated regime impede the liberty of movement of the inhabitants of the Occupied Palestinian Territory, with the exception of Israeli citizens and those assimilated thereto'.[213] In June 2011, the Wall was 62 per cent completed and construction was ongoing.[214]

In creating a kind of 'road apartheid', this segregated highway system goes beyond apartheid practices in South Africa, as the UN Special Rapporteur on the OPT has pointed out.[215]

The notion of a separate road system was first conceived by the Israeli occupying authorities during the surge in settlement activity in the late 1970s. The Israeli *Settlement Master Plan for 1983–1986* discussed the need for special roads to service planned settlements and 'bypass the Arab population centres'.[216] Road Plan No. 50 served to shift the existing north–south backbone of the West Bank's road system to a more east–west centred approach in order to integrate it into the Israeli road system for the benefit of Jewish-Israeli settlers.[217] Four hundred kilometres of such roads were built by 1993.[218] Under the Oslo Accords, an expanded maze of bypass roads then effected the geopolitical division of the West Bank in order to accommodate the free movement of settlers throughout the West Bank without having to pass through areas administered by the Palestinian Authority (PA). At this time, plans for a further 650 kilometres of roads were developed to consolidate this bypass network.[219] Israel demonstrated its commitment to implement such plans by spending US$600 million on bypass roads in 1995 alone.[220] Thus the segregated road system became a reality and continues to be expanded and consolidated.

On some public roads built for settler use, Palestinian travel is prohibited, without exception.[221] Palestinian vehicles are not merely prevented from travelling on these roads, but are also barred from crossing them in order to access other roads upon which they are permitted to travel. In such cases, passengers have to get out of their vehicles, cross the road by foot, and find further transportation on the far side.[222] On a second category of roads, Palestinians must obtain special permits to travel on them. Palestinians who live in villages that can be accessed only by such roads are allowed permits while Palestinian commercial vehicles and public transportation may similarly be permitted to use such roads.[223]

A separate and overlapping system of roads has been created for Palestinian use in the West Bank, requiring a system of bridges, tunnels and interchanges where roads for settlers and roads for Palestinians meet in order maintain strict segregation. One example of such segregation is Israeli policy regarding Road 443, the only main road in the southern district of Ramallah which dates back to the British Mandate. Ironically, parts of Road 443 – on which Palestinian travel is now banned – were constructed on land expropriated in the 1980s from Palestinians. (This expropriation was upheld at the time by the Supreme Court[224] on the basis that the road was intended primarily for the benefit of the local Palestinian population – the same population which is today prohibited from using the road.) Until 2000, it was the main thoroughfare for 160,000 local residents, connecting area villages to the city of Ramallah. Since then, the Israeli military has prohibited both pedestrian and vehicular Palestinian travel on the road[225] and reserved its use exclusively for Israelis, principally Israeli settlers commuting to and from Jerusalem. Permanent physical obstacles have been placed at the exit points of the six Palestinian villages situated adjacent to the road. With Palestinian access to Road 443 blocked, a new, separate 'Fabric of Life' road was opened in December 2008 by the Israeli authorities, to connect Beit Ur al-Fauqa (one of the Palestinian villages closed off from Road 443) to Ramallah, cutting through Palestinian agricultural land in the process.[226]

On 5 March 2008, Israel's Supreme Court issued a one-paragraph interim decision[227] approving the prohibition of Palestinian travel on Road 443. The decision (described as 'judicial hypocrisy' by Professor David Kretzmer[228]) effectively approved the segregation of roads in the West Bank according to national origin. In December 2009, responding to a petition by the Association for Civil Rights in Israel (ACRI), the Supreme Court issued another ruling finding the closure illegal and ordering that the road be opened to Palestinian use by May 2010. ACRI has reported, however, that implementation of this ruling by the Israel Defence Forces (IDF) has been made with such adjustments as to have negligible effect.[229]

Another recent case of segregation is the new road system east of Jerusalem, which will divert Palestinian traffic around the E1 area and the Ma'ale Adumim settlement bloc and render Road 1 an Israeli-only road.[230] The precedent of Road 443, however, demonstrates that even where roads are built in apparent attempts to provide some sort of recompense for violations of Palestinian freedom of movement, these roads may not always remain to the 'benefit' of the local population.

Thus the segregated road system carves the West Bank up into cantons and turns Palestinian cities into controlled and encircled enclaves with no space to expand. This effect is indeed a stated policy of the Israeli authorities, who have indicated their intention to use the bypass road system as a tool to 'reduce the uncontrolled spread of Arab settlement'.[231] The effect has been ruinous on Palestinians' social, economic, political and cultural life.

*The permit regime.* Accompanying Israel's physical infrastructure of segregation within the OPT is a complementary invisible system of administrative restrictions and military orders that further impedes and controls Palestinian movement. The myriad of ways this system operates can be treated here only briefly.

The permit regime that Israel imposes on Palestinians replicates many of the limitations imposed by South Africa's Pass Laws. Since the 1990s, individual Palestinian entry into Israel (within the Green Line), to Jewish settlement blocs in the OPT, and to East Jerusalem from other parts of the OPT has been conditional on acquiring a personal entry permit. In addition, since 2002, Palestinians in some parts of the OPT have been precluded even from accessing certain other Palestinian areas without Israeli-issued permits.

Movement permits are also required for, *inter alia*, Palestinian passenger and commercial vehicles to enter areas such as the 'Seam Zone', the Jordan Valley and the Nablus district, and to leave areas under Israeli military siege. Humanitarian permits are needed for those who want to leave certain areas in order to receive medical care. Permits are also required for Palestinian movement between the West Bank and the Gaza Strip, although these permits have become virtually impossible to obtain.[232]

Requests for permits in general are very frequently denied, with the Israeli authorities placing burdensome obligations on applicants to prove that they pose no security risks and detailed explanations for why they need to go from one place to another inside the West Bank. The granting of a permit is treated as a favour which Israel's District Coordination Office may grant to individual Palestinians in exceptional circumstances, rather than as an administrative formality.

Palestinians now require special permits to enter the areas in the 'Seam Zone' (land between the Wall and the Green Line, discussed in the next section) and the Jordan Valley, which are integral parts of the West Bank according to international law. The Jordan Valley accounts for over 25 per cent of the West Bank and contains some of its most fertile agricultural areas, but, since the early days of the occupation, Israel has designated most of the Jordan Valley as a closed area and anyone wishing to enter it must obtain a permit.[233] In the early planning stages regarding the route of the Wall, the Israeli government considered building an 'eastern Wall' to separate the West Bank highlands from the Jordan Valley.[234] This eastern Wall would have enclosed the Palestinian West Bank entirely within a physical barrier passable only through gates guarded by Israeli security forces. Although the plan for the second Wall was suspended, it has been supplanted by physical barriers that have the same effect: in 2011, OCHA found that the Jordan Valley has been sealed off with 30 kilometres of trenches and earthworks, and entry by residents was confined to three checkpoints.[235] Starting in 2005, entry was restricted to those with official documentation proving residence in the Jordan Valley. Entry remains at the discretion of the occupying forces and private West Bank-registered vehicles (that is, Palestinian vehicles) remain prohibited from entering the area.[236] In 2006, such restrictions were found by B'Tselem to constitute particularly harsh and aggravated impediments to Palestinian movement.[237] No such restrictions are placed on Israeli settlers, who, as noted, use separate roads to travel freely between settlements throughout the West Bank (including the Seam Zone and the Jordan Valley) and between the West Bank settlements and Israel.

*Case study of an apartheid policy: the Seam Zone.* Israel's segregation policies are particularly clear in their application within West Bank land caught between the Wall and the Green Line, which Israel terms the 'Seam Zone'. In October 2003, the West Bank's military commander declared the Seam Zone to be a closed military zone that civilians are not allowed to enter without a permit.[238] By June 2011, 6,500 Palestinians were living in this area,[239] all of whom are covered by the terms of closure and must have permits even to live in their own homes in the Seam Zone. If this permit regime is extended to all land embraced by the Wall when it is completed along its full planned route, OCHA estimates that around 22,000 Palestinians in nine rural communities will be trapped – by physical and administrative barriers – inside the Seam Zone.[240]

The same military declaration in October 2003 stated that this restriction does not apply to 'Israeli' persons. 'Israeli' was here defined as a 'citizen of the State of Israel, a resident of the State of Israel ... *and those entitled to immigrate to Israel by virtue of the Law of Return ...*' As Israel's Law of Return applies only to Jews, the last provision meant that people who may not be citizens or even legal residents of Israel are exempt from the restriction solely on grounds of their group identity.

The Major-General also signed, on the day of the declaration, a general permit exempting three 'types of persons': tourists, who may enter and stay in the Seam Zone 'for any reason'; Palestinians holding permits to work in Israel; and Palestinians holding permits to work in Israeli settlements, who may enter the Zone only for purposes of work and during work hours.[241] Later, the Head of the Civil Administration subsequently provided for intricate bureaucratic mechanisms allowing Palestinians to apply for entry permits to the Seam Zone.[242] Fifteen different forms were issued for Palestinians wishing to apply for entry into the Zone,[243] including separate forms for:

- Palestinian residents of the Zone;
- farmers whose lands are in the Zone;
- professionals of various vocations,

- workers in aid organisations who by virtue of their duties are required to enter the Zone;
- business-owners in the Zone;
- workers in the Zone, and
- Palestinians who wish to visit friends and relatives.

Permits granted to Palestinians are usually limited to certain hours or seasons: for example, owners of olive orchards may enter only during the olive harvest season, on (incorrect) grounds that they do not need to tend to the orchards between harvests.

A distinct procedure is required for entering the Zone with a vehicle, again with different forms: for example, a 'permanent resident application for passage with vehicle' form; a 'permanent resident application for admittance of a new vehicle into the Seam Zone' form; and a 'holder of personal permit application to enter with vehicle' form.[244] Passage is further prohibited into the Seam Zone, even for a Palestinian holding a permit, other than by specified gates. Of the 67 gates which line the northernmost 200 kilometres of the Wall, only 19 are open to Palestinians for use all the year round on a daily basis, while a further 19 are open seasonally or for one or two days weekly, and 29 are never open to Palestinians.[245]

In effect, the Seam Zone's permit regime created four classes of people in Israeli law:

1. Palestinians who work in Israel or in Jewish settlements, who are granted a general permit allowing them to enter or pass through the Seam Zone for work purposes.
2. All other Palestinians, including those who live in the Seam Zone, who are prohibited from entering or staying in the Zone (including in their own homes) without a permit.
3. Jews of any nationality or residence, to whom the prohibition to enter and stay in the Zone does not apply.
4. Tourists with leave to stay in Israel, who are granted a general and automatic permit that exempts them from applying for an entry permit to enter the Seam Zone.

In November 2003, the Israeli human rights organisation HaMoked petitioned the Supreme Court to order the cessation of the construction of the Wall where it deviated from the Green Line[246] and further requested a Court order to cancel the declarations and decrees that compose the Seam Zone permit regime.[247] On January 2004, ACRI also petitioned the Supreme Court to rule on the legality of the permit regime.[248] In April 2011, the Court rejected the petitions,[249] but while they were pending, several policy adjustments were made. The first was to unify the status of 'Israelis' and permanent Palestinian residents of the Seam Zone with that of tourists: that is, instead of exempting Israelis, a general permit would be granted, exempting them from the need to apply for a permit for entry to the Seam Zone. Palestinian residents of the

Zone no longer had to apply actively for special permits but were granted a general permit.[250] In addition, the general permit no longer included those entitled to enter Israel according to the Law of Return (that is, Jews who are not citizens of Israel). Although proclaimed by the Supreme Court, at the time of this writing this change has not been publicly announced and remains unknown in the West Bank: signs at the Separation Wall's crossings still include in the definition of 'Israelis' those entitled to Israeli citizenship according to the Law of Return.

Eventually, the Head of the Civil Administration signed directives providing that Palestinian residents of the Zone are entitled to a 'permanent resident of the Seam Zone certificate', which shall allow them to pass through the gates.[251] Now, in place of applying for a permit, the Palestinian residents of the Seam Zone were required to apply for a 'resident certificate'. For that purpose, two new forms were issued: 'Application for a Permanent Resident of the Seam Zone Certificate Form' and 'Application for the Granting of a New Resident of the Seam Zone Form'.

All these and other amendments[252] did not change the principle: for Palestinians, the Seam Zone is a closed area, except for those who can prove that 'they have any business there' and receive a permit to live or work there. In 2009, OCHA found that only 18 per cent of Palestinian landowners or workers who farmed land in the closed zone in the northern West Bank before the construction of the Wall receive permits to access the area.[253] Notably, 90 per cent of rejected permits are not denied on grounds of security but failure to prove 'connection to the land'.[254] For Israelis and tourists, the Seam Zone is an open and free area; they require no certificate or document issued by the military authorities or the Civil Administration and can enter the Zone 'for any reason'.

*Access to Jerusalem and the closure of the Gaza Strip.*  Although Israel's annexation of East Jerusalem has been deemed illegal (as discussed in Chapter 2), Israel continues to treat East Jerusalem as part of the sovereign territory of the State of Israel. Access to the city for Palestinian residents anywhere in the OPT outside East Jerusalem has, since 1991, been limited to those who can obtain personal entry permits similar to those required for Palestinians to enter Israel. The city is now surrounded by checkpoints, isolated from the rest of the OPT.[255]

These restrictions are aggravated by the continued construction of Israeli settlements in East Jerusalem, in defiance of international law and in an attempt to alter the demographic balance of the city. The Wall, which weaves in and out of Palestinian villages, towns and neighbourhoods, blocks even access by Palestinians with Jerusalem residence ID cards to the city. Only five kilometres of the 168-kilometre section of the Wall within the Jerusalem Governorate actually follows the Green Line.[256]

The population in the Gaza Strip also faces severe restrictions on movement into and out of the territory. Despite the unilateral Israeli withdrawal of settlers and permanent military posts in 2005, Israel still controls the Gaza

Strip's airspace, territorial sea and land borders. Following the election of Hamas and the capturing of an Israeli soldier in the Gaza Strip in 2006, and more particularly since Hamas' complete takeover of the Gaza Strip in June 2007, a near blanket closure has been imposed on the territory's borders by Israel. Thousands of Palestinians have been stranded in Egypt for lengthy periods, while thousands more have been prevented from leaving the Gaza Strip, including students with scholarships to study abroad and patients with life-threatening conditions requiring urgent medical treatment unavailable in the Gaza Strip.

In conclusion, the systematic restrictions on Palestinian movement described in this section cannot be justified on reasonable security grounds and are unjustifiably sweeping in their application. They reflect a racially discriminatory premise that *all* Palestinians are potential security threats and their freedoms should therefore be curtailed on the basis of their identity as Palestinians. Moreover, Jewish-Israeli settlers living in the OPT remain relatively unaffected, indicating a system of racial discrimination. The World Bank – which has estimated that over 50 per cent of the West Bank is now off-limits to Palestinians – has noted that it is 'difficult to reconcile the Israeli use of movement and access restrictions for security purposes [with] their use to expand and protect settlement activity and the relatively unhindered movement of settlers and other Israelis in and out of the West Bank'.[257] In 2007, CERD expressed its deep concern over the 'severe restrictions on the freedom of movement in the Occupied Palestinian Territories, targeting a particular national or ethnic group'.[258]

As Israel's restrictions on Palestinian movement clearly obstruct Palestinians' participation in the political, social, economic and cultural life of the OPT and impede their full development as a group, these practices fit the category of 'inhuman acts' in the Apartheid Convention.

### Denial of the right to freedom of residence

#### Interpretation

The freedom to choose one's residence is protected in Article 12 of the ICCPR. Everyone who is lawfully present within a territory under the jurisdiction of a State party to the ICCPR must enjoy the 'freedom to choose his residence'. ICERD also holds that the right to choose one's residence must be free from racial discrimination according (Article 5(d)(i)). The UN Human Rights Committee has observed that 'the right to reside in a place of one's choice within the territory includes protection against all forms of forced internal displacement. It also precludes preventing the entry or stay of persons in a defined part of the territory.'[259] The Apartheid Convention condemns, in Article 2(c), any legislative and other measures calculated to deny members of a racial group the right to freedom of residence.

#### Practices in apartheid South Africa

Throughout the twentieth century, restrictions on residence and property ownership divided the national territory of South Africa into racial zones, policed by checkpoints, random document checks and raids on homes. Freedom of movement and residence was therefore severely inhibited and strictly controlled on the basis of race. Issuing a passport, essential to the exercise of the right to leave the country, was a matter of government discretion and was routinely denied to opponents of the regime.[260]

The State designated places of residence for all racial groups, such that coloured, Indian and black South Africans all had their own areas.[261] As white urban areas required black labour, black townships were located within commuting distance of white businesses and homes. Those not permitted to reside and work in townships (by virtue of Section 10 of the Blacks (Urban Areas) Consolidation Act)[262] were relocated to the 'Homelands' and any travel outside of the Homelands was limited by travel restrictions and the Pass Laws.

The human toll of these restrictions was captured by one contemporary source observing about the office of the sympathetic liberal white women's association, 'Black Sash':[263]

> Here, every day, [Black Sash staff] are confronted with thirty years of Nationalist government. Here, every day, they witness the toll on family life the system takes, the misery of the contract worker who seeks to have near him the children who are growing up without him; the incomprehension of the wife who asks only to live with the man she legally married; the tears of the young man, a boy really, who does not understand why, since he cannot find work, he is classified as 'idle' and must now leave his parents and be sent to a homeland he has never seen … Here the language is of '10(1)(a) and (b) and (c)', of affidavits to prove employment, of letters to prove residence, of witnesses to prove birth, of certificates to prove existence. The labelled files in the Johannesburg office tell the story of the rows of patient black South Africans who wait: 'Workman's Compensation', 'Name Change', 'Employer's Abuse', 'Pensions', 'Administration Board', 'Farm Labour', 'Bribery and Corruption', 'Work Permit', 'Endorsed Out'…[264]

*Israeli practices in the OPT*

Israel imposes draconian limitations regarding Palestinian freedom of residence that fall into several categories of practices. First and most obvious is the division of the OPT into cantons based entirely on ethnicity: only Jews are allowed to live in the settlements, while Palestinian residence is confined to assigned areas. As described in later sections, ethnic zoning has extended to dividing the groups into 'separate reserves and ghettos', the inhuman act specified in Article 2(d) of the Apartheid Convention. This practice is accordingly addressed in this study under that section.

A second practice is to deny Palestinians their right to reside in the OPT, which is done in several ways. Three months after its occupation of the West Bank, including East Jerusalem, and the Gaza Strip in June of 1967, Israel conducted a census of the Palestinian population in these areas. New military orders were then passed making the possession of an Israeli-issued

ID card a condition for permanent residency in the OPT.[265] These new orders supplemented the military orders passed in the immediate aftermath of the Six-Day War which declared the OPT closed military zones, making entry and exit subject to the permission of the regional military commander. As a result of these orders, an estimated 325,000 Palestinians[266] who had fled the fighting or who were outside what became the OPT at the time of the armistice were excluded from returning, causing severe disruption to their family lives. Palestinians can also lose their residency rights if they leave the OPT for work or study for more than three years: an estimated 130,000 Palestinians had their residency rights revoked between 1967 and 1994.[267]

Palestinians in East Jerusalem hold permanent residency but the status is not entirely secure. In the 1967 war, Israel conquered East Jerusalem and, with an additional 64 square kilometres of surrounding West Bank land, defined this larger area as the expanded Jerusalem municipality. Israel then conducted a census of this expanded municipality that became the basis for granting permanent residency in the city. The population of East Jerusalem until June 1967 was 75,000 and the total population, including the annexed outlying areas, was 130,000,[268] but the number of Palestinian residents of expanded East Jerusalem who received permanent residency status was 66,000, only 25 per cent of the population of the 'united city'.[269] More than 60,000 residents of Jerusalem who were not present in East Jerusalem during the census (for example, those studying or travelling abroad) lost their right to reside in East Jerusalem and could regain that right only by applying to the Israeli Ministry of the Interior for family unification.[270]

Since 1967 and 2007, about 253,000 Palestinians held Jerusalem permanent-residency ID cards.[271] Residency can also be revoked at the discretion of the Israeli Minister of the Interior,[272] but the bases for these decisions are unpublished, unclear, and change frequently.[273] In practice, Israel has taken several measures that suggest a deliberate policy to reduce the number of Palestinians residing in East Jerusalem. Central among these is a measure adopted by the Israeli Ministry of Interior in 1995 regarding a 'centre of life' test for permanent residency in Jerusalem. According to this policy, the Minister will revoke the permanent residency of a Palestinian if his or her 'centre of life' is no longer in East Jerusalem. An absence of seven years or the procurement of residency or citizenship in another country is taken as proof that the resident's centre of life has changed.[274] The burden to prove that East Jerusalem is their 'centre of life' is on the Palestinian residents and the requirements include providing property tax bills, electricity and telephone bills, work certificates, and children's school certificates for the past two to seven years.[275] Residing in a foreign country for a period greater than three years for purposes other than education is further grounds for revocation.[276] On the basis of these standards, between 1996 and 1999, the Minister of the Interior revoked the permanent-residency rights of hundreds of Palestinians in what some Israeli human rights organisations have dubbed a 'quiet deportation'.[277] Total figures for East Jerusalem, from 1967 to 2006, suggest that the Ministry of the Interior revoked the permanent residency status of 8,269 Palestinians.[278]

*Family unification.* Several human rights instruments affirm that the family is the 'natural and fundamental group unit of society' and requires and deserves protection.[279] While the right to family unification is not expressly stated in international treaties, there is universal consensus that the right to a shared family life is entitled to protection from the state.[280] Despite giving States broad discretion on issues related to the entry of aliens into the state, the European Court of Human Rights recognises the right to family life and that protecting this right may require the imposition of positive duties on the state.[281] When the foreigner is married to a citizen/national or a resident of the State then the State cannot arbitrarily interfere with their right to maintain a family life together.[282] Article 27 of the Fourth Geneva Convention states that: 'Protected persons are entitled, in all circumstances, to respect for their persons, their honour, their family rights, their religious convictions and practices, and their manners and customs.' Israel recognises such norms as applicable to its actions.[283]

Shortly after the census, the Israeli authorities instituted a 'family unification' process that was to allow Palestinians registered in the census to apply for the return of family members who, as a result of the military orders, had lost their residency in the OPT. From 1967 through 2000, Israel implemented a rigid 'family unification' policy in the OPT. This policy was neither transparent nor accessible, involved lengthy and expensive bureaucratic procedures and was then repeatedly changed to match perceived political or policy imperatives. In 2000, the outbreak of the second *intifada* was used as a pretext for Israel to cease operating even this flawed 'family unification' process.

In the five years following the Six-Day War, only first-degree relatives who became refugees following the war, excluding males aged 16–60, were allowed to return. Of some 140,000 requests for family unification, only 45,000–50,000 people were approved.[284] From 1973 onwards, when even more stringent criteria were imposed, until 1983, when the policy was re-evaluated and further restricted, approximately 1,000 applications were approved per year, while some 150,000 remained pending. The increased restrictions reduced successful applications from 1984 onwards to a few hundred a year. The reason given for the change in the process was that 'over the years, the type of requests for family unification changed significantly, and deviated from the original objectives of the said policy, dealing instead with families that had been created after the war'.[285] The 1990s saw quotas set of a few thousand applicants per year through decisions of the Israeli Supreme Court and then the 1995 Israeli-Palestinian Interim Agreement. In the OPT in 2000, Israeli froze the family unification process entirely. In 2007, more than 120,000 applications for family unification in the West Bank, excluding East Jerusalem, and the Gaza Strip were still pending.[286]

Israel's intention to exercise demographic control over all of the territory is further illustrated by its policies relating to child registration. Between 1967 and 1987, children under 16 who were born in the OPT or born abroad to a parent who is a resident of the OPT were allowed to be officially registered as residents.[287] However, this policy was changed in 1987 through an order issued by the military commander and children over the age of five were denied registration.[288] In 1995, the interim peace agreement authorised the Palestinian Authority to register children without Israel's approval as long as one of the child's parents was registered. Nevertheless, between December 2002 and September 2005, Israel refused to recognise the registration of children whose ages were between five and 16 who were born abroad.[289] In September 2005, Israel again decided to accept the registration of children under the age of 16, but those who had already turned 16 continued to encounter difficulties, although they had applied for registration prior to turning 16.[290]

Due to the significant obstacles to achieving family unification and the lengthy procedures involved, many families were forced to rely upon repeatedly obtaining short-term visitor permits to stay temporarily in the OPT with their families. These permits were subject to a capricious bureaucracy similar to, or sometimes as part of, the family unification process. However, the grant of these permits was also frozen in 2000. In effect, Palestinians living in the OPT and wishing to form a family where one spouse is not resident of the OPT must forgo the unity of their family or forgo living in their homeland.

A policy that deliberately aims to stifle the formation and unity of Palestinian families within the OPT through the systematic denial of the rights to freedom of residence and to return to their country therefore clearly contributes to preventing the full development of Palestinians as a group. Israel's policies in the OPT, far from providing families with the protection and assistance required by international human rights law, in fact prevent specific families from living together and hinder or prevent unification of Palestinian families.

A second concern is the difficulty faced by East Jerusalem residents who marry a Palestinian spouse from the OPT and wish to live with their spouses in East Jerusalem. Such people must apply to the Israeli Ministry of Interior for 'family unification'.[291] Between June 1967 and May 2002, the Ministry of the Interior granted family unification and allowed such couples to live in East Jerusalem, albeit after many years of foot-dragging and bureaucratic delays. Between 1993 and 2002, an estimated 100,000–140,000 residents of the OPT gained status to reside in East Jerusalem and Israel as a result of the family unification process.[292]

In May 2002, the Israeli government issued Decision No. 1813, which froze the processing of all family unification applications by citizens or residents of Israel and East Jerusalem involving Palestinian spouses from the OPT.[293] Various statements by government officials made it clear that the freeze was due to the government's fear that Palestinians were achieving a 'creeping right of return' through the family unification process.[294] The freeze had grave effects, as Palestinian residents of Israel whose spouses were from the OPT had either to leave Israel, in order to live with their spouses, or to live in Israel with a spouse who did not have legal status. Unlike some Palestinians who have Israeli citizenship, East Jerusalem residents who decide to move to the

OPT risk losing their permanent-residency status because their 'centre of life' is no longer in Jerusalem.[295]

In July 2003, the Knesset amended existing legislation, the Citizenship and Entry into Israel Law, by passing a temporary order that extended the government's 2002 freeze on 'family unification' applications involving Palestinian spouses from the OPT. The new law exclusively targeted Palestinian residents of the OPT, leaving the general policy for residency and citizenship status for all other foreign spouses unchanged, including Israeli settlers living in the OPT. Immediately thereafter, in August 2003, Adalah filed a petition to the Supreme Court challenging the constitutionality of the law. In the petition, Adalah argued that the 'law constitutes one of the most extreme measures in a series of governmental actions aimed at undermining the rights of Palestinian citizens of Israel, as well as Palestinians from the OPT'.[296] Before the Court, Israel justified Government Decision No. 1813 and the subsequent law by arguing argued that Palestinians who had been granted status in Israel through family unification were increasingly involved in assisting 'terror' organisations. Israel referred to 23 individuals (out of thousands of status-receivers) allegedly involved in 'terror', but did not provide details of these cases to the court. Moreover, even if reliable, this figure constitutes a relatively tiny number of people, and the Government Decision, and the law upon which it is based, are disproportionate. In May 2006, the Supreme Court rejected the petition in a split 6:5 decision, which effectively approved the law.[297]

By contrast, CERD in its 2007 Concluding Observations on Israel found that 'such restriction targeting a particular national or ethnic group in general is not compatible with the Convention, in particular the obligation of the State party to guarantee to everyone equality before the law (Articles 1, 2 and 5)'. CERD thus recommended that Israel 'revoke the Citizenship and Entry into Israel Law (Temporary Order), and reconsider its policy with a view to facilitating family reunification on a non-discriminatory basis'.[298]

Instead, in March 2007 the Knesset passed an amendment to the law (which maintains the ban on family unification where one spouse is a Palestinian from the OPT) by extending the ban to family unification where one spouse is a resident or citizen of Syria, Lebanon, Iran or Iraq – States all defined by Israeli law as 'enemy States' – and/or an individual defined by the Israeli security forces as residing in an area where activity is occurring that is liable to endanger Israeli security. A Supreme Court petition filed in May 2007 challenging this new law is currently pending.[299]

In this petition, Adalah argued that the law constitutes racial discrimination as it bars certain individuals from family unification solely on the basis of their nationality.[300] It also prevents Palestinian citizens of Israel from having contact with their families, with members of the Arab nation or with the Palestinian people, in violation of international law.[301]

Tens of thousands of Palestinian families have been affected by the ban on family unification since 2002.[302] In 2004, it was estimated that the ban affected between 16,000 and 24,000 families.[303] As did the apartheid regime in South Africa, Israel justifies these measures under the pretext of 'security'.

Contrary to such claims, they are in fact part of an overall regime aimed at preserving demographic superiority of one racial group over the other in certain areas. Separating and discriminating against Palestinian citizens of Israel and Palestinian residents of East Jerusalem in such a systematic fashion, using mechanisms that are institutionalised by law and explicitly privilege Israeli Jews over Palestinians, results in the oppression and domination of the former over the latter.

An interpretation that Israel's ban on family reunification serves the purpose of establishing and maintaining racial domination in the OPT is supported by the fact that no such restrictions are placed on Jewish families wishing to reside in the OPT. On the contrary, Israel's efforts to restrict the ability of Palestinians to unify and form families in the OPT have been paralleled by concerted efforts to transfer Israeli individuals and families into the OPT. This illegal transfer has been achieved primarily through massive government investment in settlement infrastructure and the provision of numerous incentives to encourage Jewish individuals and families to move to the unlawful settlements. Thus, Israel's policy regarding family unification contravenes international human rights law, in that it is clearly discriminatory and, in forming part of an overall system which dominates and subjugates members of the Palestinian population, it amounts to an inhuman act of apartheid.[304]

### Denial of the right to leave and to return to one's country

*Interpretation*

The right to leave and return to one's country was legally recognised as early as 1215, in the English Magna Carta, which provided that '[i]t shall be lawful to any person, for the future, to go out our Kingdom, and to return, safely and securely, by land or by water'. The right of an individual to return to his country is guaranteed in the ICCPR (Article 12(4)), and the Universal Declaration of Human Rights (Article 13(2)), which is reflective of customary international law.[305] The Apartheid Convention prohibits the denial of the right of members of a racial group to leave and return to their country as part of a system of domination and oppression against that group, thus drawing on Article 5(d)(ii) of ICERD, which prohibits racial discrimination in the application of those rights.

The right to return to one's 'own country' applies even if the territory in question is disputed or has changed hands. The law of nationality, a subset of the larger 'law of nations', stipulates that in case of State succession, the newly emerging successor State must allow habitual residents of a territory undergoing change in status or sovereignty to exercise their right to return to their own homes or places of origin, regardless of where they may have been on the actual date of succession.[306] The right of return applies not only to those individuals directly expelled and their immediate families, but also to their descendants who have 'maintained close and enduring connections' with the area.[307]

### Practices in apartheid South Africa

The right of black South Africans to leave and return to their country was limited in several ways. The policy that affected millions of black people was the Homelands policy, which unilaterally redefined the 'state' to which black South Africans belonged by partitioning sections of South Africa into titular ethnic nation-states. Discussed in greater detail regarding Article 2(d), the Bantu Homeland Citizenship Act sought permanently to divest black South Africans of their citizenship and eliminate any juridical claim to a right of return to 'white' areas of South Africa.[308] Millions of black South Africans were forcibly transferred into the Homelands and a cluster of laws restricting freedom of movement, expressed ultimately as visa requirements, then prohibited them from returning to white areas, which were now another 'country'. Access to white South Africa was controlled by the South African Government's Minister of Bantu Administration and Development.

Another policy of the apartheid regime was to deny its opponents a passport, which is essential to exercising the right to leave and return to the country. Legislation permitted people who were denied a passport to apply for an 'exit permit', but exit on this basis essentially led to permanent expulsion and statelessness.

### Israeli practices in the OPT

The Palestinian 'refugee problem' – the predicament faced by millions of Palestinian refugees who are not permitted to return to their country – is a hallmark of the Israeli-Palestinian conflict. By June 2010, 4.8 million people were registered with the UN Relief and Works Agency (UNRWA) as 'Palestine refugees'. Of these, 1.9 million live in the West Bank and Gaza Strip.[309] The remaining 2.9 million remain displaced in the surrounding countries of Lebanon, Syria and Jordan.[310]

The refugee problem dates to the 1947–48 war, when some 750,000 Palestinians became refugees as a consequence of the fighting.[311] Israel's later invasion and occupation of East Jerusalem, the West Bank and the Gaza Strip in June 1967 resulted in some 550,000 Palestinians being displaced, the majority of whom fled or were expelled to Jordan.[312]

Under human rights law and General Assembly resolutions, these refugees, as well as their descendants, have the right to return to their former places of habitual residence. General Assembly Resolution 194 of 1948 stipulated that Palestinian refugees should be permitted 'to return to their homes' at the 'earliest practicable date',

> and that compensation should be paid for the property of those choosing not to return and for loss of or damage to property which, under principles of international law or in equity, should be made good by the Governments or authorities responsible.[313]

Israel has not complied with these stipulations. Palestinians expelled in 1948 have not been allowed to return to their homes, regain their property or compensation, or obtain residency or citizenship in Israel.

Palestinian refugees are excluded by Article 3 of Israel's 1952 Citizenship Law from eligibility for Israeli citizenship on grounds that they were not 'in Israel, or in an area which became Israeli territory after the establishment of the State, from the day of the establishment of the State [May 1948] to the day of the coming into force of this Law [April 1952 ]'.[314] Only by maintaining continuous residence in Israel from 1948 to 1952 were Palestinians living inside Israel eligible to acquire Israeli citizenship and thus remain in the country.[315]

The great majority of those Palestinians who fled what are now the OPT in the 1967 war have also been prevented by Israel from returning to their homes,[316] in contravention of Security Council Resolution 237.[317] Of Palestinian refugees registered with UNRWA and living in surrounding states, 650,000 originally resided in land now in the OPT. An estimated 90,000 Palestinian residents of the West Bank, including East Jerusalem, were abroad at the time of the 1967 war and were thus not registered in the census conducted thereafter by Israel.[318] The Israeli authorities refused to consider Palestinians not registered in the census as legal residents of the OPT and employed administrative measures to prevent them from returning.[319] CERD has repeatedly expressed concern on this and called on Israel to 'to assure equality in the right to return to one's country'.[320]

Racial discrimination regarding this right is demonstrated in Israel's policy actively to encourage Jewish immigration to Israel and, since 1967, to Israeli settlements in the OPT. As discussed in Part I of this chapter, the 1950 Law of Return allows any Jewish person to immigrate and the 1952 Citizenship Law grants such people Israeli citizenship. Thus Jews need not meet the restrictive criteria (proof of continuous residence from 1948 to 1952) imposed on any Palestinian wishing to return. (Even the US State Department has noted that the 1950 Law of Return and the 1952 Citizenship Law are explicitly discriminatory, concluding that they 'confer an advantage on Jews in matters of immigration and citizenship'.[321]) Moreover, again as discussed in Part I, the State of Israel has authorised the JA-WZO to act as its 'authorised agencies' to promote Jewish immigration to Israel from anywhere in the world. This privileged treatment of Jewish immigration signifies that Israel's State policy is explicitly to secure different rights and privileges to Jews and Palestinians in 'returning' to the country with the goal of ensuring Jewish demographic dominance of the country.

### Denial of the right to a nationality

*Interpretation*

Although still a relatively fluid concept in international law, nationality (citizenship) can be understood as 'the political and legal bond that links a person to a given State and binds him to it with ties of loyalty and fidelity, entitling him to diplomatic protection from that State'.[322] Nationality is thus a prerequisite for the exercise of political rights and bears strongly on the individual's legal capacity. A State's power to confer and regulate nationality is therefore circumscribed by obligations to ensure the full protection of human rights.[323]

The right to nationality, in this sense, is affirmed in the American Declaration of the Rights of Man (Article 19), the UDHR (Article 15), the Convention on the Reduction of Statelessness (Articles 1 and 10), the ICCPR (Article 24(3)), the American Convention on Human Rights (Article 20), the Convention on the Rights of the Child (Article 7) and the European Convention on Nationality (Article 4). Protection from racial discrimination in the exercise of one's right to nationality is ensured by Article 5(d)(iii) of ICERD. Since the Second World War, 'denationalisation' or the unilateral revocation of an individual's citizenship by the State has been illegitimate.[324] If practised on the base of race, sex, language or religion, denationalisation could be considered to contravene a peremptory norm of international law.[325]

As international humanitarian law is concerned with the rights of people who are not nationals of the Occupying Power, it could be assumed that an Occupying Power has no role or responsibility regarding the nationality (citizenship) of protected persons, except to refrain from imposing its own citizenship on them. Nonetheless, practices of an Occupying Power can impede the exercise of the right to nationality, as shown later, and if such practices are found to serve a policy of domination on the basis of race, descent, ethnic or national origin, then they would constitute an act of apartheid.[326]

A word on terminology is due here: the terms 'nationality' and 'citizenship' are often used interchangeably (and loosely) by politicians and lawyers to indicate a legal connection between individual and State.[327] 'Nationality' is essentially a term of international law and denotes that there is a legal connection between the individual and state for external purposes. 'Citizenship' is a term of constitutional law and is best used to describe the status of individuals internally, particularly regarding civil and political rights to which they are entitled.[328] Normally, an individual's citizenship and nationality are the same: for example, to refer to 'French' or 'Chinese' nationality – as inscribed on a passport – signifies 'French' or 'Chinese' citizenship (unless 'nationality' is used more loosely in the sense of 'national origin', as discussed earlier.

However, as discussed in Part I of this chapter, Israeli law distinguishes between citizenship and nationality in constructing Israel as the state of the Jewish nation and not an 'Israeli nation'. Israeli citizenship may be held by anyone who qualifies under the Citizenship Law and some 1.3 million Palestinians today hold Israeli citizenship. Jewish *nationals* – that is, members of the Jewish people or nation whose interests are served through parastatal institutions such as the Jewish National Fund and the Jewish Agency – then enjoy special privileges under Israeli Basic Law and other laws like the Law of Return. These special privileges include exclusive access by Jewish nationals to most of the state's territory; other national groups holding Israeli citizenship lack comparable privileges. Given the importance of this distinction between citizenship and 'nationality' in Israeli law – relevant here as it is channelled into the OPT to provide Jewish and Palestinian civilians with different rights and privileges – the terms 'nationality' and 'citizenship' will both be used in this discussion as appropriate.

*Practices in apartheid South Africa*

Part of the 'Grand Apartheid' strategy of the apartheid regime in South Africa to ensure permanent racial separation was to deprive black South Africans of their South African citizenship. In this policy, black African citizens were forcibly relocated to the so-called Homelands if they were not already living there, where they were to be given the citizenship of those Homelands and stripped of their South African citizenship when those Homelands were declared independent.[329] As Dr Mulder, the Minister of Bantu Administration and Development, told South Africa's Parliament on 7 February 1978:

> [I]f our policy is taken to its full logical conclusion as far as the black people are concerned, there will be not one black man with South African citizenship ... [E]very black man in South Africa will eventually be accommodated in some independent new state in this honourable way and there will no longer be a moral obligation on this Parliament to accommodate these people politically.[330]

'Denationalisation', as it was termed in apartheid South Africa, required first establishing governments in the Homelands and ultimately declaring them 'independent'. As discussed elsewhere, the Bantu Authorities Act (No. 68) of 1951 provided for establishing separate black authorities on tribal, territorial, and regional bases. In 1959, the Promotion of Bantu Self-Government Act provided for creating eight national units for African self-government supposedly reflective of African ethnic groupings (Xhosa, Zulu, Ndebele, Swazi, Basotho, Batswana, Bapedi, Venda and Tsonga). Under the Promotion of Bantu Self-Government Act (No. 46) of 1959, each ethnic group had a Commissioner-General who was tasked to develop a homeland that would, in name, ultimately be allowed to govern itself independently without white intervention. In 1970, the Bantu Homelands Citizens Act then compelled all black people to become a citizen of the Homeland that responded to their ethnic group, regardless of whether they had ever lived there or not. Their South African citizenship was then removed when the Homeland was declared 'independent'. The Bantu Homelands Citizens Act was designed to ensure that no black person would eventually qualify for South African citizenship and the right to work or live in South Africa.

In 1972, Zululand and Bophuthatswana were granted self-governing status, while Transkei, which had been self-governing since 1963, was given more autonomy as the model Homeland. Transkei was declared 'independent' in 1976; Bophuthatswana followed in 1977, Venda in 1979, and Ciskei in 1981. Black Africans holding these new citizenships became aliens in South Africa and could only occupy their own homes in the urban areas by special permission of the Minister.[331]

*Israeli practices in the OPT*

This study finds that Israel denies Palestinians living in the OPT the right to nationality, in the sense of citizenship, in two ways. The first is by prohibiting

Palestinian refugees who are now living in the OPT from holding citizenship in Israel, the state that formed in the territory of their birth. Under the British Mandate, Palestinian Arabs held 'Palestinian' citizenship, as did Jews living in Palestine.[332] This citizenship was effectively extinguished with the dissolution of the Mandate and the formation of Israel in part of Mandate Palestine. As the war of 1947–48 entailed a mass refugee flow of Palestinian Arabs from territory that became the modern State of Israel into what are today the OPT (as well as surrounding states), Palestinian refugees now living in the OPT have the right of return and the right to citizenship in Israel as the successor State in that part of Mandate Palestine where they were formerly habitual residents.[333] Yet, as noted earlier, Palestinian refugees from what became the internationally recognised territory of modern Israel are not permitted to return to their homes or obtain citizenship in Israel. Thus Israel's policy toward refugees violates the principle that habitual residents of a territory that becomes a new State are entitled to acquire citizenship in the successor State.[334] Israel's intention to discriminate on the basis of race in this regard is expressed by the Law of Return (1950) and the Citizenship Law (1952),[335] which facilitate the acquisition of Israeli citizenship by Jewish immigrants but deny the right of return and citizenship to Palestinian refugees.

Second, Israel has so far denied the Palestinian people living in the OPT the right to citizenship by sustaining the occupation and refusing to withdraw to allow an independent Palestinian State to be established. Thus most Palestinians in the OPT have been rendered stateless (although some have acquired the citizenship of a third State).

As this study was being conducted, peace negotiations were still ostensibly aimed toward a two-State solution that would create a Palestinian State in the OPT and provide Palestinians now resident in the OPT with citizenship in that State. If it is created, however, South Africa's practice of denationalising black citizens by forcibly relocating them to black Homelands suggests a qualification: that Israel would not thus be absolved of its obligation to allow Palestinians who fled homes inside Israel and are now living in the OPT (and abroad) to return to Israel and obtain citizenship in Israel, the successor State governing the territory of their original residence. Otherwise, Israel could be found further to violate the Palestinians' right to nationality.

Finally, regarding citizenship, we may again recall Roberts' observation, noted in Chapter 2, that a prolonged occupation can

> have the effect of leaving a whole population in legal and political limbo: neither entitled to citizenship in the occupying state, nor able to exercise any other political rights except of the most rudimentary character. If there is any risk at all that the law on occupations might prove, paradoxically, the basis for a kind of discrimination that might bear comparison with apartheid, the causes of that risk need to be identified and possible solutions explored.[336]

### Denial of the right to work

*Interpretation*

As affirmed in the International Covenant on Economic, Social and Cultural Rights (ICESCR) (Article 6), everyone has the right to gain their living by work freely chosen or accepted. A state is required to safeguard this right by providing the necessary tools to achieve steady economic, social and cultural development and full and productive employment. ICERD affirms that '[t]he rights to work, to free choice of employment, to just and favourable conditions of work, to protection against unemployment, to equal pay for equal work, to just and favourable remuneration' shall be enjoyed free from racial discrimination (Article 5(e)(i)). The Apartheid Convention condemns any legislative measures and other measures calculated to deny members of a racial group the right to work.

*Practices in apartheid South Africa*

In apartheid South Africa, the right to work was restricted through two general methods. First, individuals were restricted to certain kinds of work on the basis of their race, enforced through the Job Reservation Act (1963) and other measures that restricted skilled and higher-paid jobs to whites. Second, Pass Laws made it impracticable for blacks to apply for work in white areas other than at jobs specifically authorised for them, such as domestic work.[337] Third, the Pass Laws afforded job opportunities to workers classified as resident in the Bantustans or townships while precluding those same workers from accepting particular employment by virtue of their race.

South African workers could be broadly categorised as those who were permitted, under Section 10 of the Blacks (Urban Areas) Consolidation Act,[338] to live and work in towns without special permission to do so, and those who fell outside that category. The so-called 'Section 10' workers were those who had been born in a particular urban area or had worked there continuously for 15 years or had worked for a white employer for over ten years. This system created an effective 'urban citizenship' requirement beyond that of national citizenship, and successfully restricted employment opportunities. Workers would be cautious about leaving a particular urban area for fear of losing their Section 10 status, creating an insidious dependence: because workers preferred a lower-paying job where they had Section 10 status to the uncertainty of moving outside the designated urban area in search of employment elsewhere, white employers had wider options for their exploitation.

*Israeli practices in the OPT*

*Labour and the economy in the OPT.*   In 2010, the unemployment rate in all the OPT was 16.5 per cent, contrasting with 6.4 per cent in Israel.[339] Prior to Israel's military attacks on the Gaza Strip in December 2008–January 2009, the UN reported that unemployment in Gaza had reached 49.1 per cent.[340] In the immediate aftermath of the attacks, which saw widespread destruction of factories, offices and shops, the Palestinian Central Bureau of Statistics estimated a jump in the unemployment rate to more than 60 per cent.[341]

Palestinian labour has seen massive structural changes since the occupation began, becoming highly dependent on the Israeli economy as well as foreign aid. Before the Six-Day War, agriculture in the West Bank and Gaza accounted for 37 per cent of gross domestic product (GDP) while industry and construction accounted for 13 per cent.[342] After 1967, jobs inside Israel became increasingly important to Palestinian labourers in the OPT and Palestinian labour became especially important to Israel's construction industry both within Israel and in the OPT. Israel initially encouraged Palestinian labourers from the OPT to work in Israel and opened the market in the OPT to Israeli imports and the Israeli market to OPT exports. These measures exposed the local Palestinian economy to market forces that resulted in high differences in wage and price levels between Israel and the OPT. Israel also limited trade from the OPT with Jordan and restricted public investment in the OPT, other than investment serving Jewish settlements.[343] With the first *intifada* in 1987, however, Israel shut down access by Palestinian labourers to jobs inside Israel's Green Line. Punitive restrictions (such as closing the checkpoints to Palestinian workers) and employing foreign workers instead of Palestinians resulted in a major loss of jobs and reduced wages.

After the Oslo Accords were signed in the early 1990s, the Palestinian economy entered a period of rapid growth and by 1999 real GDP had grown to US$4,512 million.[344] In 2000, however, after the beginning of the second *intifada*, Israel instituted a strict closure policy and GDP fell to US$3,557 million.[345] The economy in the OPT recovered briefly in 2003 but remained severely affected by Israeli restrictions on exports and movement. In 2003, 47 per cent of Palestinians lived below the poverty line and as many as 600,000 Palestinians could not afford basic needs such as food, clothing and shelter.[346] The GDP of the OPT fell 6.6 per cent between 2005 and 2007, from US$4,443 million[347] to US$3,901 million.[348] With expenditures of less than US$1.50 a day per person, the population as a whole became vulnerable to economic shocks.[349]

Following the restrictions on Palestinian workers, Israel has sought out cheap foreign migrant labour from countries in Asia and Eastern Europe as replacements.[350] Palestinian unemployment rates, which had run about 10 per cent before 2000, soared to 25 per cent by 2003.[351] In 2011 the number of people living in deep poverty rose to 1.3 million.[352] In 2011, a survey of Gaza, conducted by UNRWA, found that the number of Palestine refugees in 'abject poverty' – that is, completely unable to secure access to food and purchase even the most basic items, such as soap, school stationery and safe drinking water – has tripled since the tightening of Israel's blockade in June 2007.[353]

Palestinian agricultural workers have also been affected by physical damage to Palestinian land, resources and property by Israeli military forces. For example, from June 2006 to May 2007, the Israeli army destroyed around 12,900 dunums of cultivated land, 332 greenhouses, and uprooted around 2,775 fruit trees in the West Bank alone.[354] The right to work for Palestinians in the OPT has thus been impacted upon greatly by restrictions on labour imposed by Israel's occupation and by damage on the Palestinian economy as a whole. Highlighted here are three factors affecting work opportunities: restrictions on Palestinian worker mobility; Palestinian labour flow into East Jerusalem and Israel; and the imports and exports of goods.[355]

*Impact of movement restrictions on Palestinian labour.* As a result of the second *intifada* and a spike in Israeli security measures, the number of physical obstacles to Palestinian movement within the West Bank increased from 376 in August 2005 to 522 in July 2011.[356] Coupled with many other restrictions (including the Wall, restrictions on access to the Seam Zone, and difficulties for Palestinians to obtain permits, as discussed earlier), farmers are increasingly prevented from accessing their farmland. The effects are devastating since agriculture, fishing and forestry account for 15.1 per cent of the Palestinian workforce.[357] In 2007, 30 out of 57 communities surveyed by the UN in the West Bank did not have direct, regular access to their land:

> Restrictive gate openings and permit allocations are already having a negative impact on agricultural practices and on rural livelihoods. Many farmers cultivate their land infrequently or not at all, or have changed to lower maintenance and lower yield crops. The longer term consequences for these communities are uncertain, as they lose contact with the land on which they depend both for their present livelihood and for their future survival ... [In the closed area between the Wall and the Green Line] some 70 percent of the almond trees have now died because of lack of regular maintenance. In the past, the land in the closed area produced about 10 tons of almonds. The fresh almonds were worth 5 NIS per kilo and were a valuable asset to the village.[358]

Over 50 per cent of land in the West Bank is inaccessible to Palestinians due to settlements, roadblocks and other 'closed' areas.[359] Many of the main roads are limited to cars with Israeli licence plates, forcing Palestinians to take long, circuitous routes through multiple checkpoints to travel to neighbouring areas. The impact of these delays on labour is graphic:

> Unsurprisingly, these restrictions make the movement of people and goods more expensive, inefficient and unpredictable and therefore have a particularly chilling effect on economic activity. Beyond the personal hardship, an economy cannot run effectively if there is significant uncertainty about the ability of workers to reach their jobs, of goods reaching their markets, and of entrepreneurs being present to manage their place of business.[360]

Israel has also suppressed the Gaza fishing industry by restricting how far from the coast the fishermen can fish. In the 1990s, they were allowed to travel twelve nautical miles off shore and were hauling in around 3,000 tons of fish a year; by 2008, they were hauling in less than 500 tons a year.[361] The Oslo Accords provided that Gaza fishermen could travel 20 nautical miles from the coast but this has not been enforced. Gaza fishermen are prevented from accessing some 85 per cent of the maritime areas they were entitled to access under this agreement.[362] As a result, nearly 90 per cent of the fishermen are now considered either poor (with a monthly income of between US$100 and US$190) or very poor (earning less than US$100 per month), which constitutes a sharp increase from 2008 when 50 per cent of fishermen fell into these categories.[363] With agricultural exports greatly reduced by Israeli restrictions, the impact has been severe. In 2007, a senior UN official warned that 'The Gaza Strip will soon become entirely dependent on foreign aid and face "disastrous consequences" if Gaza remains sealed off.'[364]

None of the above restrictions on movement and the transportation of goods apply to Israeli Jewish settlers living in the West Bank, who have free access to all goods and uninhibited freedom of movement between the West Bank and Israel related to their work, trade, and social networks. By contrast, Palestinians who formerly comprised a significant part of the workforce can no longer seek employment in East Jerusalem or Israel.

*Restrictions on access to jobs in East Jerusalem and Israel.* In the year 2000, 146,000 Palestinians were employed in Israel.[365] By 2007, this number had decreased to 66,806, a third of whom had a Jerusalem ID card or a foreign passport.[366] In 2005, a daily average of approximately 44,800 Palestinians worked in Israel.[367] These workers were earning around US$405 million a year (around 7 per cent of gross domestic income).[368] After the elections to the PLC in 2006, at which time Hamas obtained a majority of seats, labour flows dropped to 25,000–30,000 per day.[369] Even prior to the election, the Israeli government adopted a policy to aim to diminish the number of permit-holding Palestinian workers to zero by 2008.[370]

By 2007, 90.7 per cent of the Palestinian labour force worked inside the OPT.[371] The median monthly wage for Palestinians inside the OPT was much lower, at NIS (New Israeli Shekels) 1,696.2 in the West Bank and NIS 1435.8 in Gaza, compared to the average monthly wage of Palestinians inside Israel, which stood at NIS 2677.6.[372] In contrast, the average monthly salary for Israelis employed in Israel was NIS 8,237.[373]

The UN Committee on Economic, Social and Cultural Rights expressed concern about the restriction of labour into Israel in its concluding observations of 2003:

19. The Committee continues to be gravely concerned about the deplorable living conditions of the Palestinians in the occupied territories, who – as a result of the continuing occupation and subsequent measures of closures, extended curfews, roadblocks and security checkpoints – suffer from impingement of their enjoyment of economic, social and cultural rights enshrined in the Covenant, in particular access to work, land, water, health care, education and food.

20. The Committee also expresses concern about the rate of unemployment in the occupied territories, which is over 50 per cent as a result of the closures which have prevented Palestinians from working in Israel.
22. The Committee is concerned about the fact that it is extremely difficult for Palestinians living in the occupied territories and working in Israel to join Israeli trade unions or to establish their own trade unions in Israel
...
36. The Committee further recommends that the State party ensure that workers living in the occupied territories are permitted to continue to work in Israel.[374]

Within the OPT, the Palestinian workers most affected by Israel's closure policy is the sector of the labour force working in East Jerusalem but living elsewhere in the West Bank. An integral part of the West Bank, East Jerusalem was for decades its economic centre. With the tightening of restrictions after the outbreak of the second *intifada* and the subsequent construction of the Wall, Palestinians living elsewhere in the West Bank need permits to work in East Jerusalem, which in practice are very difficult to obtain. Certain sectors have been particularly impacted by the restrictions from working in East Jerusalem: many teachers in Palestinian schools in Jerusalem can no longer teach and many doctors and nurses working in hospitals in Jerusalem have been forced to leave their positions. According to UN estimates, 95 per cent of Palestinians from elsewhere in the West Bank and 77 per cent from East Jerusalem itself had difficulties reaching their workplace in 2007,[375] while 51.2 per cent of East Jerusalem households with West Bank ID cards reported the main earner being forced to change their place of work in 2011 due to the Wall.[376]

*Restriction of imports and exports.* Unemployment is also fostered by Israel's draconian restrictions on imports and exports of primary products. Agriculture, fishing and forestry currently generate around 25 per cent of all Palestinian exports and this sector is directly affected by difficulties in export and the restrictions on free movement of goods.[377] In 2004, the World Bank examined the effects of such restrictions of trade: 'Closures are a key factor behind today's economic crisis in the West Bank. They have fragmented Palestinian economic space, raised the cost of doing business and eliminated the predictability needed to conduct business.'[378]

In 2005, imports and exports totalled almost US$3.4 billion, accounting for 83 per cent of Palestinian GDP.[379] In Gaza, measures taken in 2010 to ease access into and out of the area have had little effect and imports are still only 45 per cent of pre-2007 levels.[380] In the rest of the OPT, Palestinians still have no access to external markets through their own airports or sea ports, while no Palestinian development or investment can take place in Area C, which represents 60 per cent of the West Bank's territory.

The Wall has had a particularly adverse impact on the traditionally strong trade links between the West Bank and East Jerusalem.[381] Traders' maintenance of a regular delivery schedule is impossible; goods are damaged during inspection and waiting periods. As a result, many external buyers have ceased their contracts with Palestinians because of the unreliability of delivery schedules.[382] The Palestinian trade deficit deteriorated from 57 per cent of GDP in 2008 to 59 per cent in 2009, with a continued dependence on Israel as a source of import and an outlet for exports. Israeli closure policies and the losses of the local production to imports, notably from Israel, have been found to account for over half of the Palestinian trade deficit.[383] As noted by the United Nations Conference on Trade and Development (UNCTAD), '[p]art, but not all, of the trade between the OPT and Israel could be mutually beneficial but its involuntary and unequal nature has rendered Palestinian economic development subservient to Israeli economic and political imperatives, often masked under "security requirements"'.[384] The impact of these restrictions on the Palestinian population is most evident in the spike in unemployment and the lack of future work opportunities for younger Palestinian generations. Many businesses that rely on the movement of goods have been bankrupted on account of increased costs and inefficiency due to unpredictable delivery schedules, resulting in major job losses.

Thus the right to work has been hindered in multiple ways, resulting in cresting unemployment. Due to travel restrictions, Palestinians are unable to reach jobs; due to restrictions on trade, they are unable to work or to sustain industries that employ the Palestinian population. As a result of Israel's policies, both the West Bank and the Gaza Strip have become increasingly dependent on foreign aid. Israeli restrictions on the Palestinian right to work serve to prevent full participation in the economic life of the OPT and to hinder Palestinian development.

### Denial of the right to form recognised trade unions

*Interpretation*

Article 8 of ICESCR provides that:

> The States Parties ... undertake to ensure (a) The right of everyone to form trade unions and join the trade union of his choice, subject only to the rules of the organization concerned, for the promotion and protection of his economic and social interests ... The right of trade unions to establish national federations or confederations and the right of the latter to form or join international trade-union organizations; (c) The right of trade unions to function freely subject to no limitations other than those prescribed by law and which are necessary in a democratic society in the interests of national security or public order or for the protection of the rights and freedoms of others; (d) The right to strike, provided that it is exercised in conformity with the laws of the particular country.

Furthering the protection from racial discrimination in one's exercise of 'the right to form and join trade unions' enshrined in Article 5(e)(ii) of ICERD, the

Apartheid Convention establishes denial of 'the right to form recognized trade unions' as an act of apartheid where committed in the context of a system of domination and systematic oppression by one racial group over another.

*Practices in apartheid South Africa*

During apartheid, black South African trade unions were denied official standing by the government. The Industrial Conciliation Act defined a 'trade union' as being made up of 'any number of employees in any particular undertaking, industry, trade or occupation',[385] but 'employee' was characterised as 'any person (other than a native) employed'.[386] Hence black African trade unions were excluded from the Act's domain.[387] In addition, black Africans were prohibited from representing workers and so the appointment of black Africans as union officers was forbidden.[388]

The South African Trade Union Council (later the Trade Union Council of South Africa, TUCSA) was formed to represent registered trade unions in opposition to the State's interference in the operation of private unions. African unions were not recognised by the State at this time and, until 1962, were not permitted to join TUCSA. The leadership of TUCSA was closely affiliated with government, thereby ensuring disposition from the state in favour of white labour unionists and against black unions. In concert the Industrial Conciliation Act of 1956 and the Native Labour (Settlement of Disputes) Act of 1953 denied any African the right to participate in collective bargaining.[389]

Black African unions nevertheless existed. The South African Congress of Trade Unions (SACTU), formed in the 1950s, became the leader of the anti-apartheid struggle in the labour movement.[390] Union leaders were accordingly often arrested and harassed for political campaigning. In 1977, the apartheid government realised that it had to exert greater control over African trade unions and initiated the Wiehahn Commission which recommended legalising black unions to control native labour activists. Black unions were recognised in 1979 – a measure that some, in hindsight, consider the beginning of the end of apartheid. The Afrikaner Trade Institute, which represented Afrikaner commercial interests, was forced to negotiate with black labour leaders for the first time in 1980.

The 1979 reforms encouraged black labour unions to register in the hope of eventual legitimisation and recognition of black labour unions. While the freedom to organise was now allowed, in practice this was not always so in the workplace, where employers sought any means to eradicate unionisation amongst members. Where workers were identified as union members, they were often faced with summary dismissal (and could not obtain the protection that collective bargaining and fair labour practices would demand). Dismissals occurred on a large scale where workers were seen to have organised in the workplace. While this practice undermined the trade unions, it propelled them to increasing militancy and action.

The eventual enactment of the Labour Relations Act 51 of 1982 removed the oversight of the Minister of Manpower in labour disputes and vested that authority solely in the industrial court. Workers were then able to enforce fair labour practices to a greater extent than before, with labour unions using the courts of law to enforce their rights. This mobilisation through the courts, along with frequent strike action, destabilised the regime's ability to rely on the subservience of union workers, and was likely one of the causes of its impending downfall. Nevertheless, black unions could not achieve all their most pressing goals and were prevented from conducting themselves professionally until the apartheid regime fell in 1993.

*Israeli practices in the OPT*

Palestinian trade unions existed during the British mandate of Palestine, but primarily represented industrial labourers and only one in seven Palestinian workers was unionised.[391] After 1948, trade unions flourished in the West Bank under Jordanian administration until King Hussein curbed political reforms in 1957, resulting in a fall in the number of unions. The largest labour body during this period was the General Federation of Unions (GFU) with headquarters in Amman, and later in Nablus. The GFU evolved into the Palestinian General Federation of Trade Unions (PGFTU), and its headquarters are still in Nablus.

After the 1967 Six-Day War and initiation of Israel's occupation of the OPT, Israel's rapid economic growth increased the demand for cheap labour. The newly occupied Palestinian territories proved valuable for Israel because they contained 'a large pool of unskilled, cheap labour with no political rights'.[392] To take full advantage of these workers, Israel refused to recognise Palestinian trade unions and attempted to close them down: union leaders were arrested, abused, exiled, jailed, harassed, and deported. Israeli forces raided union centres, destroyed union files and documents, and closed down union offices. Union leaders and representatives were prevented from meeting. As a result, Palestinian unions were greatly weakened and had no leverage over Israeli employers.

The Israeli government also attempted to prevent workers in the OPT from organising new unions. For example, the Union of Construction and General Workers in the small village of Ya'abad in the West Bank had only 150 members, but Israeli troops raided its offices twice in the 1970s, destroying archives, posters and publications, and the union's leaders were detained and imprisoned several times without charge. In the Gaza Strip, unionisation was banned by the military commander. Under pressure from the International Labour Organisation (ILO), Israel agreed to lift the ban on unionisation in 1979, but 'insisted that unions could not hold elections or extend their membership to the handful of aging men who had been members before 1967'.[393] When the Builders and Carpenters Union decided to hold elections in violation of Israeli military orders, many of its members were harassed and beaten.[394]

The Histadrut, Israel's national trade union, was founded in Palestine in 1920 as a Jewish trade union to promote Jewish workers' rights and employment as well as settlement of Jewish immigrants. Before and after the creation of Israel, the Histadrut acquired a number of industrial conglomerates and Israel's largest bank, Bank HaPoalim, and was for a time the largest employer in the country. Thus the Histadrut has played an important role in the building of the Jewish state and functions effectively as a parastatal institution. Nonetheless, Palestinian workers in the OPT are obliged to register with the Histadrut if they are working in Israeli economic sectors. Dues of 11 per cent are deducted from their wages for the national insurance tax and 1 per cent as membership dues to the Histadrut, but they do not receive the benefits associated with membership: for example, 'unemployment compensation, old age pension, disability benefits, a monthly child allowance, and vocational training'.[395] Rather, the Histadrut has cooperated with the Israeli army to tighten control over the Palestinians in the OPT.[396]

The Israeli government has placed no such restrictions on Israeli unions and unions established by Jewish settlers in the West Bank and Gaza Strip. Histadrut strikes are never confronted violently; Jewish union members are never targeted by the Israeli police or military because of their affiliation with specific trade unions.

With the signing of the Oslo Accords in the 1990s, Palestinian trade unions gained more freedom to function in areas that fell under PA control. The 1994 Paris Protocol on Economic Relations[397] called upon Israel to 'respect any agreement between ... a trade union representing Palestinian workers in Israel and ... an organization representing employers in Israel'.[398] Palestinian unionists interpreted this article of the protocol to mean that the Israeli government would allow them to function in Israel: minimally, to allow their lawyers to represent union members in Israeli courts. Hence they lobbied the PLC to pass laws that benefited workers and labourers and initiated training courses and hired litigators to take factory owners and employers to court over violations of labour rights.

However, the Israeli government and Histadrut refused to allow Palestinian lawyers to represent Palestinian workers in Israeli courts on grounds that it infringed Israeli sovereignty. Nor did Israel recognise Palestinian trade unions, although about 116,000 Palestinians from the OPT (approximately 20 per cent of the OPT Palestinian labour force) worked in Israel between 1993 and 2000.[399] Union leaders were still harassed and trade unions were systematically targeted by raids and closures. In 1994, the PGFTU and the Histadrut began normalisation, but problems quickly arose when the Histadrut refused to discuss recompensing Palestinian workers for the 1 per cent of their wages that the Histadrut took as dues.[400] In 1995, they agreed that the PGFTU would receive half of the 1 per cent dues that Palestinian workers paid to the Histadrut, but in practice the Histadrut often delayed the monthly payments, further increasing tension and bitterness between the unions.

Unable to reach its workers in Israel, the PGFTU agreed for the Histadrut to provide four Palestinian lawyers with Israeli citizenship to represent Palestinian workers in Israeli courts. The Histadrut employs the lawyers, decides what cases they are allowed to pursue and controls their access to the national labour court, even though the Histadrut itself is a major employer and, as mentioned previously, participated in the exploitation of Palestinian labourers before Oslo. The Histadrut's de facto control over the conditions in which the PGFTU can take legal action strips the latter's negotiating power and violates its right to defend workers from abuses.[401]

Finally, Palestinian trade unions are prohibited from functioning in Israeli settlements, leaving workers vulnerable. For example, in October 2007, at the Lieberman factory in Mishor Adomim industrial park in the West Bank, Palestinian workers were informed of a Israeli Supreme Court ruling that required Israeli companies operating in the OPT and employing Palestinian labourers to follow Israeli labour laws.[402] Palestinian labourers at the Lieberman factory accordingly requested their employer to comply with Israeli standards that provide safer working conditions. He refused their request and they resorted to striking. They also went to the PGFTU's centre in Jericho and asked for advice so that they would not break any laws during their strike. The PGFTU, in turn, supplied them with lawyers who explained their legal rights and informed the Histadrut. On 14 November 2007, after two days of striking, Israeli police arrived at the Lieberman factory and evicted the Palestinian workers from the industrial park.[403]

The PGFTU was unable to take action in that case as it is overwhelmed by hundreds of cases of clear and severe violations by Israeli employers of labour rights. These include Palestinian workers being forced to wear distinctive uniforms and yellow arm bands to distinguish them from Israeli workers, not being allowed to eat in the same place as Israeli workers, even dying on the job. According to representatives of the PGFTU:

> But we are restricted. We can't get to job sites to monitor working conditions. In most cases we cannot meet with the lawyers hired by the Histadrut, and in many cases the labourers whose rights have been violated cannot get to the lawyers either. The lawyers assigned to us are not very knowledgeable about the Palestinian workers' situation in the OPT, and many of them are not very experienced. The Histadrut does not allow us to get more lawyers. We may succeed in a limited amount of cases, but the vast majority never even reaches the court. Our hands are tied.[404]

Legal action is also very expensive, especially since only Israeli lawyers can represent Palestinians. The vast majority of Palestinian workers, and most small unions, cannot afford continually to hire lawyers to attempt to take their employers to court, especially as the chances of a Palestinian winning a case in an Israeli court are slim.[405]

Thus Israel's policy is to suppress Palestinian trade unions. The consequence of this policy is effectively to obstruct Palestinian economic development and impede the full participation of Palestinians in the political, social, economic and cultural life of the country.

## Denial of the right to education

*Interpretation*

The right to education, as outlined in the UDHR and detailed in ICESCR, requires a state to provide free compulsory primary education, generally available and accessible secondary education and, based on capacity, equally accessible higher education. The Apartheid Convention condemns any measures calculated to deny members of a racial group the right to education. This echoes ICERD, which prohibits racial discrimination with regard to '[t]he right to education and training' (Article 5(e)(v)). Minimally, under international law, States must not act in any way that negatively impacts the right to education, particularly through discriminatory practices.

*Practices in apartheid South Africa*

In apartheid South Africa, the Bantu Education Act, Act No. 47 of 1953 established a Black Education Department in the Department of Native Affairs, which would compile a curriculum that suited the 'nature and requirements of the black people'. The author of the legislation, Dr Hendrik Verwoerd (then Minister of Native Affairs, later Prime Minister), stated that its aim was to prevent Africans receiving an education that would lead them to aspire to positions they would not in any event be allowed to hold in South African society. As he infamously phrased it: 'The Natives will be taught from childhood to realise that equality with Europeans is not for them. There is no place for the Bantu child above the level of certain forms of labour.'

Apartheid policy was thus to ensure that Africans received an education that would confine them to working under whites in all sectors. The curriculum provided to black children omitted fundamental subjects – such as mathematics and science – that provided essential skills for further qualification.[406] The syllabuses taught histories replete with racial segregationist philosophies, such as the superiority of white European civilisation and the backwardness and inherent inferiority of African 'tribes'.[407] In 1959, the Extension of University Education Act 45 ended admission of black students to white universities and created separate tertiary institutions for whites, coloureds, blacks and Asians.

The result was systematic and deliberate under-education of millions of black South Africans. The policy was so successful in its goals that eventually it began to impede the economic growth of the country, as the need for skilled workers outstripped supply.

*Israeli practices in the OPT*

Israel has no explicit policy to develop school curricula and access to education on the basis of ethnicity, race, or nationality comparable to the system imposed by South Africa's Bantu Education Act. In practice, Israel does not need such a law because mixed schools do not exist in the OPT. Palestinian children are not allowed to attend Jewish schools in the settlements, as a consequence of the comprehensive territorial compartmentalisation of the territories on the basis of identity.

Israeli policy has been to allow Palestinians in the OPT to establish their own curricula, schools and universities. Currently, 2,415 primary and secondary schools and 22 universities and technical schools, run by the PA, Hamas, private institutions and Islamic and Christian organisations, serve Palestinians in the West Bank and Gaza.[408] Enrolment is exceptionally high, comparable to a country like Iceland, which is ranked first in the Human Development Index, and Palestinians had a secondary education enrolment rate of 88 per cent in 2005:[409]

> In spite of the harsh conditions in which schools have had to operate, impressive achievements have been made during the past five years. The education system has experienced massive expansion and attained equitable access, reaching a level of development that by most accounts is comparable with middle-income countries. Enrolment in basic education is universal, and the enrolment rate for secondary education is above 80 percent. These figures put the West Bank & Gaza in the lead in the MENA region. Equally important is the high enrolment rate in tertiary education – above 40 percent for the 18–24 age group – which is high when compared with middle-income countries. The fact that for the first time Palestinian children participated in international tests and scored above the average for MENA countries is another major accomplishment. To the PA's credit, access to basic and secondary education is highly equitable with respect to gender, location, refugee status, and household income.[410]

Nevertheless, this study finds that Israel's policies amount to racial discrimination by actively interfering with the exercise of Palestinians' right to education. These measures have the combined result of preventing Palestinian economic and intellectual development, in turn facilitating the continuation of Israel's system of domination and control over the population of the OPT.

*School closures and attacks.* Since the second *intifada* began in September 2000, Palestinian schools and universities have come under military attack. According to the Palestinian Ministry of Education and Higher Education, around 300 schools and eight universities have been shelled, shot at or raided by the Israeli army between 2000 and 2005.[411] In the Gaza Strip, 73 educational institutions were partially or totally destroyed between 2000 and 2004.[412]

These attacks have cost the lives of students as well as permanent disability. This study found many examples, even if taking short sample periods: for example:

- In March 2003, a twelve-year old girl was hit in the head by a bullet outside Khan Yunis while sitting at her desk, which left her blind.[413]
- On 1 June 2004, two ten-year-old boys in UNRWA's Al-Umariye Elementary Boys' School in Rafah were hit by a bullet and ricochets from a Israeli tank.[414]

- On 7 September 2004, a ten-year-old girl sitting at her desk in UNRWA's Elementary C Girls' School in Khan Yunis camp was struck in the head by an Israeli bullet and died.[415]
- On 3 October 2004, the Israeli army broke down the walls of three schools in the Gaza Strip in the Jabaliyah refugee camp, while children were still in class, and took over to use them as firing positions for tanks.[416]
- On 15 October 2004, the army shot and killed a child sitting in the classroom of a UN-flagged school.[417]
- On 12 December 2004, the Israeli army opened fire on a school, wounding seven children under the age of nine.[418]
- A month later, on 31 January 2005, the army again opened fire on an elementary school in Rafah, this time killing an eleven-year-old and injuring another child in the schoolyard.[419]
- In 2006, the Israeli army disrupted classes in 18 schools in Jenin, Tulkarem, Nablus and Jericho through raids, attacks and arrests. It also raided the Polytechnic University in Hebron and a girls' school in the village of Anata in the district of Jerusalem.[420]
- In 'Operation Cast Lead', '164 students and 12 teachers from [Palestinian government] schools were killed and a further 454 students and 5 teachers were injured. A total of 86 children and 3 teachers who attend UNRWA schools were killed, and a further 402 students and 14 teachers were injured.'[421]
- In June 2006, an F-16 fighter plane bombed the Islamic University in Gaza,[422] and in 'Operation Cast Lead' six university buildings were destroyed and 16 damaged.[423] According to the Palestinian Ministry of Higher Education the cost of damages to university properties due to Israeli military attacks amounted to US$7,888,133 from 2000 to 2008.[424]

Between 1988 and 1992, the Israeli military closed Birzeit University in the West Bank – along with all other Palestinian educational institutions, including schools and kindergartens – multiple times. The Palestinian community continued to pursue its education by holding classes in homes, offices, churches, mosques and community centres, but the Israeli army often raided these classes and arrested students and teachers attending.[425] For most of 2003, Hebron University and the Palestine Polytechnic University were closed down by Israeli military order, suspending the education of more than 6,000 students for over six months. Between 2003 and May 2008, 349 Birzeit University students and around 80 students from An-Najah National University in Nablus were arrested on political grounds, often without been given access to their lawyers or any visitors.[426] In November 2004, four students from Gaza who were studying at Birzeit University were arrested and, although no charges were brought against them, they were nevertheless prevented from returning to university to continue their studies.[427]

In April 2008 alone, 14 Hebron-area schools and orphanages, serving approximately 7,000 Palestinian children and orphans, were threatened with closure by the Israeli army after multiple raids. In July 2008, the Islamic School for Girls in Nablus was shut down after being raided and ransacked based on accusations of an affiliation with Hamas.[428]

Since September 2000, Israel has arrested and detained almost 6,000 children. In 2007 alone, 700 children were arrested without being provided with any form of education while in prison.[429] The alleged offenses for which they are imprisoned span from throwing stones at protests over the Separation Wall, to being affiliated with Hamas and inciting protests. Until 2011, Israeli Military Order No. 132 designated Palestinians as adults at the age of 16, and Palestinian children incarcerated in Israeli prisons are provided with education only until age 15. The majority of Palestinian children incarcerated in Israeli prisons and detention centres, however, have no access to classes or educational materials.[430] By contrast, Israeli juvenile prisoners until the age of 18 are given the opportunity to continue their education in Hebrew following the Israeli curriculum in prison, while only a few Palestinian juvenile prisoners are given this opportunity.

All of these measures are justified by the Israeli authorities on grounds of security, yet in practice constitute a collective measure impeding access of Palestinians as a group to education. A discriminatory policy of favouring Jewish students in the same territory is evidenced by Israel's establishment and maintenance of separate schools in Jewish settlements that serve Jews exclusively that are not subjected to military violence and are supported by government subsidies.

*Restrictions on movement.* The restriction of mobility of Palestinian students is the main obstacle to their exercising their right of education. In 2002, the UN Committee on the Rights of the Child (CRC) highlighted this problem:

52. The Committee is concerned about the serious deterioration of access to education of children in the occupied Palestinian territories as a result of the measures imposed by the Israeli Defence Forces, including road closures, curfews and mobility restrictions, and the destruction of school infrastructure.
53. The Committee recommends that the State party guarantee that every Palestinian child has access to education, in accordance with the Convention. As a first step, the State party should ensure that restrictions on mobility are lifted throughout the occupied Palestinian territories during school hours.[431]

This recommendation did not lead to improvements, however, and since 2002 the situation has worsened dramatically. The Qalandiya checkpoint, for example, delays students by about one to two hours daily, and at most universities around 60 per cent of the students have to cross at least one checkpoint to reach the university.[432] A survey at Birzeit University showed that

91 per cent of students have missed classes because of delays at checkpoints.[433] Since the beginning of 2006, thousands of Palestinians with foreign passports have been denied entry to study and teach in the OPT, and as a result 50 per cent of these staff members at Birzeit University can no longer teach there.[434] Since 2004, Palestinians from Gaza have been banned from studying in the West Bank: consequently, the number of students from Gaza studying at Birzeit University fell from 350 in 2000 to 35 in 2005, to zero in 2008.[435] In 2003, 120 students from Jenin were registered: in 2005, none were registered.[436]

Al-Quds University in Abu Dis was also issued with a military order in 2003 commanding an eight-metre-high concrete wall to be built through the campus, confiscating one-third of the campus. Although an international campaign was launched and the position of the wall was moved, it still cuts through the path of 36 per cent of the university's students and prevents about 15,740 students from reaching other schools.[437]

The Wall has also resulted in a shortage of teachers in East Jerusalem, as many live in the West Bank and are unable to obtain permits to enter the city. In July 2007, the English department of the Arab American University of Jenin was nearly closed due to the difficulties in attracting native English-speaking teachers, after having lost staff members to Israeli restrictions on the entry of Palestinians holding foreign passports to the OPT.[438]

Israeli curfews have created another obstacle to education by preventing students from attending classes. In 2006, for example, the Israeli army imposed a curfew in Hebron, thereby preventing students from accessing two schools.[439] In March 2008, curfews also prevented students in the West Bank towns of Azzun, Al-Funduq and Haja from attending their classes.[440]

Israel's policies have especially damaged education in the Gaza Strip, where more than half the population is under the age of 18 and the embargo and unrepaired damage from 'Operation Cast Lead' have generated crippling shortages of every kind. At least 280 schools and kindergartens were damaged in Israel's 2008 attack, including 18 facilities that were totally destroyed (eight governmental schools, two private schools and eight kindergartens). In 2010, OCHA found that a total of 441,452 students were being served by 640 schools, including 383 government schools, 221 UNRWA schools and 36 private schools.[441] But the great majority – 88 per cent of UNRWA schools and 82 per cent of government schools – were operating on a shift system due to overcrowding; in one area, 4,000 students were crowded into just two schools. OCHA found that about '1,200 secondary students in governmental schools in north Gaza ... were currently at risk of not having a local school to attend.' OCHA traced the problem to partly recurrent electricity power cuts and Israel's restrictions on fuel imports. Schools also suffered from shortages of 'paper, text books, computers, and educational kits' resulting from the embargo. In combination, these problems were having a grave impact. 'In the first semester of the 2007–2008 school year, for example, only 20% of 16,000 sixth graders in Gaza passed standardized exams in Math, science, English and Arabic.'[442]

*Prevention of Palestinian students from studying abroad.* In June 2007, Israel denied exit permits to approximately 2,000 primary and secondary school pupils and 722 university students from Gaza, preventing the continuation of their studies abroad. Of the 1,100 students wishing to attend universities abroad, only 480 were granted permission by Israel. In May 2008, the visas of seven winners of US Fulbright scholarships were revoked and they were consequently not allowed to leave Gaza, even after a major international campaign was launched on their behalf.[443] This near-complete travel ban constitutes a form of collective punishment imposed by Israel on all residents of Gaza and amounts to a systematic form of oppression.

*Discrimination in East Jerusalem.* In East Jerusalem, public education is provided by Israel. Barriers to Palestinian education have been created by the Separation Wall, however, which cuts through the city. As a result, many children and teachers who live on its eastern side and attend schools in East Jerusalem have to walk long distances to reach checkpoints through which they must pass in order to cross to the other side. Hundreds of teachers have faced difficulties in obtaining permits to cross the checkpoints. The same difficulty applies to students and teachers travelling in the opposite direction: the majority of the students living in East Jerusalem who attend schools and universities elsewhere in the West Bank (that is, the other side of the Wall) have trouble attending and many have been forced to drop out as a result.

The Jerusalem Education Authority (JEA) of the Jerusalem Municipality, together with the Ministry of Education, is responsible for providing free education to the 79,000 eligible Palestinian Arab school students in East Jerusalem. However, only 39,400 students are actually attending public schools. The remaining students are forced to attend private or unofficial schools because of a lack of classroom facilities provided by the Israeli authorities.[444] Six per cent of Palestinian children are not enrolled in school at all.[445] The percentage of students that enter high school but drop out stands at around 50 per cent, compared to a figure of 7.4 per cent of Jewish students in Jerusalem.[446] Unequal funding can be seen in every aspect of the public school education: in West Jerusalem, for example, there is one computer for every ten students, while in East Jerusalem there is one computer for every 26 students.[447] Thus, in this one area, almost three times as many resources are being spent on Jewish Israeli children in Jerusalem as compared with Palestinian children.

In 2006, for example, only NIS 113 million or 29 per cent of the annual JEA budget was allocated to education in East Jerusalem, though 35 per cent of school-aged children in Jerusalem are living in East Jerusalem.[448] A study in 2005 found a shortage of more than 1,500 classrooms in East Jerusalem, such that Palestinian students were being taught in overcrowded, ill-suited and makeshift rooms, including bathrooms and kitchens that had been converted into classrooms.[449] A study in 2010 found that, although the government had promised to remedy the situation, classroom construction totalled only

52 per cent of what had been promised and Palestinian students faced the same conditions.[450]

The issue of severe classroom shortages in East Jerusalem was brought before the Supreme Court in 2000.[451] On 15 February 2001, the Ministry of Education and the Jerusalem Municipality committed before the court to build 245 classrooms in Arab schools in East Jerusalem over a four-year period. By 2010, however, the shortage of schoolrooms had risen to over 1,000, while of those that existed (1,398) over half were substandard. As a consequence of inadequate facilities, close to 5,000 Palestinian children were not attending school at all.[452] The Ministry of Education has argued that one cause of the shortage in classrooms is the refusal of Arab residents of East Jerusalem to sell their land, but this claim is contradicted by the State's concomitant policy to confiscate approximately 35 per cent of the land in East Jerusalem for constructing Jewish settlements.[453]

The Compulsory Education Law covers all three- and four-year-olds in Israel. The law was initially not enforced with regard to children under the age of five, however, because of budgetary shortages. In 1999 an amendment was passed requiring that Israel implement free pre-school education in stages over a period of ten years. In West Jerusalem the law was implemented in numerous neighbourhoods, whereas in East Jerusalem it was only implemented in one neighbourhood, Beit Safafa. As a result, 90 per cent of three- and four-year-old Palestinian children in East Jerusalem are not receiving any pre-school education.[454]

That the outcome of all of these discriminatory policies can only be a dire and ominous impact on the future of the Palestinian population is inescapable. In February 2010, former Israeli Deputy Attorney-General Yehudit Karp wrote a warning memo to Attorney-General Yehuda Weinstein:

> The consequences for the education system in East Jerusalem are disastrous. In the present school year, thousands of Arab students in East Jerusalem of compulsory education age are denied access to free public education … The destructive effects of the said neglect on the population of Jerusalem cannot be overstated, and it is doubtful that the damage can be undone.[455]

In conclusion, this study finds that Israel's policies are severely impeding the right to education in the OPT. Israel denies Palestinians the right to education not through open bans but through indirect yet draconian measures: in the West Bank, through obstacles to movement, closures of schools, and military attacks on schools and students; in East Jerusalem, through substandard funding and facilities; in Gaza, through the embargo and military assaults that have destroyed school facilities. Yet in East Jerusalem and the West Bank, where Jewish Israelis and Palestinians coexist, the Jewish Israeli population enjoys very different conditions: for example, in Jerusalem, 41 times more Jewish students qualify for a matriculation certificate than their Palestinian counterparts.[456] Therefore, Israel's policy regarding education is found to be discriminatory on the basis of group membership and so to fit the definition of an inhuman act of apartheid.

### Denial of the right to freedom of opinion and expression

*Interpretation*

The right to freedom of opinion and expression is affirmed in the UDHR and the ICCPR. Protection from racial discrimination in exercising freedom of opinion and expression is ensured by of ICERD (Article 5(d)(viii)) and in the Apartheid Convention's condemnation of measures calculated to deny members of a racial group the right to freedom of opinion and expression.

The right to freedom of expression straddles numerous aspects of a functioning liberal democracy, enveloping the rights to freedom of speech, the press and academic research and publication. It includes 'the freedom to seek, receive and impart information of ideas of all kinds, regardless of frontiers'[457] and thus is pivotal to freedoms of choice, religion, conscience, association, protest and political identification. Nonetheless, the right to freedom of expression is not absolute.

Propaganda for war, as prohibited by Article 20(1) of the ICCPR, and the Declaration on Friendly Relations 1970,[458] obliges states to refrain from and prohibit all forms of propaganda for wars of aggression.[459] The *ad hoc* tribunals have given significant attention to the impact of propaganda and incitement in the commission of war crimes, crimes against humanity, and genocide in the Former Yugoslavia and Rwanda. In the *Nahimana* decision, the ICTR focused in particular on how the media linked to the Rwandan government acted in violation of the right to freedom of expression, noting that 'the expression charged as incitement to violence was situated, in fact and at the time by its speakers, not as a threat to national security but rather in defence of national security, aligning itself with state power rather than in opposition to it'.[460] ICTY is currently hearing a case against the former Serbian Prime Minister Vojislav Seselj who is accused in the indictment of participation in 'war propaganda' through incitement to hatred, to violence including aiding and abetting the killing of civilians.[461]

The ICCPR (Article 19(3)(b)) considers that the restriction of freedom of information may be limited "[f]or the protection of national security or of public order (*ordre publique*), or of public health or morals.' In both apartheid South Africa and Israel, this restriction has been used liberally, but these provisions are meant to defend the right to freedom of expression: they are aimed at ensuring that expression does not violate other rights and that all can engage in a market place of ideas.[462]

The ICCPR further prohibits 'Any advocacy of national, racial or religious hatred that constitutes incitement to discrimination, hostility or violence shall be prohibited by law' (Article 20(2)). In its commentary on the ICCPR, the Human Rights Committee further affirmed that a state of emergency may not be invoked 'in advocacy of national, racial or religious hatred that would constitute incitement to discrimination, hostility or violence'.[463]

*Practices in apartheid South Africa*

The apartheid regime, by controlling and restricting the right to exercise freedom of expression, was capable of permeating a climate of fear and anxiety into every aspect of social, political, cultural and intellectual life in South African civil society. The list of banned items included any object that carried an ANC symbol, including lighters, buttons and T-shirts. These legislative restrictions created a mechanism for comprehensive social control designed to suppress creation of a 'black consciousness', thus sustaining the entire apartheid regime.

The banning of films, books or other 'controversial' materials was used to systemise the wider process of eradicating from public consciousness any dissenting political, social and economic opinions. The first legislative measure introduced to institutionalise censorship was the Publications and Entertainments Act of 1963, which granted the Ministry of the Interior the power to ban 'undesirable' material for a multitude of reasons, including obscenity, moral harmfulness, blasphemy, and harming relations among sections of the population. Under this statute, approximately 8,768 publications were prohibited.[464] This law was repealed and replaced by the Publications Act of 1974, under which 8,898 publications were banned between 1975 and 1982.[465]

*Israeli practices in the OPT*

Israel limits freedom of expression in the OPT through several measures: direct censorship; restrictions on freedom of movement by journalists; wilful intimidation and harassment of journalists; and closure and destruction of Palestinian media outlets.

*Censorship.* Israel limits Palestinian freedom of expression primarily through direct censorship: in the OPT and regarding Israeli media published about the OPT. Israeli censorship laws remain based upon the 1945 mandatory British Defence (Emergency) Regulations,[466] which allow '[t]he censor [to] prohibit the importation or exportation or the printing of any publication which the importation, exportation, printing or publishing of which, in his opinion, would be or likely to become prejudicial for the defence of Palestine or to the public safety or to public order' (Article 88(1)).

In 1948, the Press Ordinance – a signed censorship agreement between the Israeli government, the army and newspaper editors and press owners – determined a codified practice of self-censorship to ensure that there would be no breaches of 'State security'. This agreement created a system for submitting any materials that could involve 'national security' to the military censor for approval prior to publication.[467] The Editors Committee, an informal forum comprised by the editors and owners of the main Israeli media, met regularly with the Prime Minister, Cabinet members and senior officials to decide policy and practices.[468] After Israel's occupation of East Jerusalem in 1967, East Jerusalem was subjected to the same censorship system.

Although the role of the military censor for the Hebrew- and English-speaking media has diminished since the 1948 agreement, restrictions on freedom of expression for the Palestinian media in Israel and occupied East Jerusalem remain. Article 97 of the Defence (Emergency) Regulations grants the censor the power to review materials before publication. Arabic newspapers in Israel and East Jerusalem have historically had this power more readily enforced against them. These outlets must submit two copies of every news article, regardless of its topic, to the Israeli Government Press Building in Beit Argon the day before publication. Hebrew- and English-language newspapers are required only to submit articles about 'military security' matters.

In the rest of the West Bank and the Gaza Strip, military censorship is further guided by multiple military orders and many restrictive provisions of the Defence (Emergency) Regulations. Military Order No. 50[469] forbids the import and distribution of newspapers into the West Bank without obtaining an Israeli military-approved permit. Publishing in the West Bank is restricted by Military Order No. 101,[470] which forbids anyone 'to distribute or publish a political article and pictures with political connotations'. Thus Israel's limitations 'cover most methods of expressing or communicating ideas, giving Israeli military censors restrictive control over all publications which they consider to have any political meaning'.[471]

In 1989, Israel's Supreme Court determined that censorship should only be exercised when it is certain that the publication of the item in question would harm public safety.[472] With the outbreak of the second *intifada* in 2000, however, Israeli courts began issuing media bans with increasing frequency, granting restrictions of coverage of certain cases upon the petition of the prosecutors or security forces.[473]

The Israeli press is complicit in self-censorship both regarding the topics and slant of articles and in language used for reporting on events. For example, the Nakdi Report[474] (a paper drafted by the Israeli broadcasting authority first set down in 1972) stipulated that Israeli media should not use terms like 'East Jerusalem' and should refer to the occupied territory of the West Bank as 'Judea and Samaria'.

*Restrictions on freedom of movement.* Israel limits freedom of expression further by restricting the movements of journalists. Journalists operating in the OPT face two kinds of obstacles: administrative controls regarding the dissemination of press cards, and the pervasive system of checkpoints operated by the Israeli military within the OPT. Israel's different treatment of journalists working in Israel or the OPT is captured in the annual *Press Freedom Index* compiled by Reporters Sans Frontières.[475]

The Israeli Government Press Office (GPO), which operates as an arm of the Prime Minister's office, is responsible for journalist accreditation in both Israel and the OPT. To obtain a press card, all foreign journalists must sign a document 'whereby they undertake to abide by the rules of the Military Censor which are designed to safeguard [State] security'.[476] Hence they cannot publish any article that the military censor considers detrimental to Israel's security without jeopardising their press pass. Since 2005, entry by journalists into the Gaza Strip has been additionally conditional on a special permit: entering the Strip without this permit is a criminal offence and cause for revoking a journalist's press card.[477] GPO press cards are renewed annually.

| Year | No. of countries ranked | Rank for Israel within Israeli territory | Rank for Israel in the OPT |
|---|---|---|---|
| 2003 | 166 | 44 | 146 |
| 2004 | 167 | 36 | 115 |
| 2005 | 167 | 47 | not specified |
| 2006 | 168 | 50 | 135 |
| 2007 | 169 | 44 | 103 |
| 2008 | 173 | 46 | 149 |
| 2009 | 175 | 93 | 150 |
| 2010 | 178 | 86 | 150 |

By law, residents of the OPT are not given a press card unless they are determined by the GPO, after consulting with military occupation authorities, not to be a security threat to the State of Israel.[478] In 2001, the GPO refused to renew press accreditation to Palestinian journalists on grounds that all of them posed a security threat. Following a court case brought by the Reuters news agency and Al-Jazeera satellite television network, the Supreme Court ruled in 2004 that the 2001 GPO decision was discriminatory and therefore unconstitutional.[479] Despite this, the Supreme Court later acceded to the government request to allow the suspension of press cards for selected individuals at the request of the GSS.

The denial of press cards to Palestinian journalists, an obstacle generally not faced by Israeli journalists, restricts their ability to move not solely between Israel and the OPT but also to cross the complex intra-territory checkpoints and *ad hoc* roadblocks in the OPT.

In addition to restrictions on journalists, Israel restricts freedom of expression by Palestinian political and human rights activists through travel bans that prevent them from leaving the OPT to testify, share documentation and express their opinions at conferences and meetings abroad.[480]

*Intimidation, harassment, and targeting of media installations and journalists.* Article 52(2) of Additional Protocol I to the Geneva Conventions states that radio and TV installations may be regarded as legitimate targets only if they are used for military purposes and directly contribute to the war effort. Determining the 'military purpose' of media installations may be politicised, however, where criticism of occupation itself is considered a military threat. However, Israeli policy allows targeting of media installations.

For example, on 19 January 2002, Israeli troops blew up the Voice of Palestine Radio and Television station offices and studios in Ramallah, accusing it of transmitting provocative material. On 12 December 2007, three media outlets, including the Nablus-based TV station Al-Afaq, were forced to stop broadcasting after Israeli troops seized transmission equipment. Closure orders, destruction and damage of property and confiscation of materials result not only in the closing down or obstruction of the media outlet in question but also in the intimidation of other outlets and organisations that are critical of Israel, fostering greater self-censorship.

Violent attacks, harassment, and arbitrary arrest and detention of journalists obstruct the pursuit of information and ideas while intimidating and deterring reporting. Harassment of media personnel in the OPT ranges from the confiscation of journalistic material to the arbitrary arrest and detention of Palestinian journalists. The case of Mohammed Omer is illustrative. Mr Omer, a journalist from the Gaza Strip, was stopped by Israeli border authorities when crossing back into the OPT from Jordan on 26 June 2009, after receiving the Martha Gellhorn Prize for Journalism at a ceremony in London. He was detained without being given a reason and subjected to cruel, inhuman and degrading treatment by Israeli security authorities, beaten to the point of unconsciousness and hospitalised with several broken ribs.[481] The UN Special Rapporteur on the OPT notes that this incident, which he finds to be a violation of the right to freedom of expression, 'cannot be discounted as an accident or an anomaly involving undisciplined Israeli security personnel', but is rather 'part of a broader pattern of Israeli punitive interference with independent journalistic reporting on the occupation'.[482]

In Israeli military operations in the OPT, the killing of journalists constitutes a more serious violation of the law. Some press organisations have interpreted the Israeli military's targeting of press personnel as deliberate, where journalists are killed in isolated settings while wearing clothing and helmets clearly identified as 'Press' or 'TV'. In one case, Fadel Shana, a Palestinian cameraman working for Reuters, was killed by Israeli forces in the Gaza Strip while wearing a blue flak jacket marked with the word 'PRESS', as commonly worn by journalists and standing by his car, which also carried large 'PRESS' and 'TV' markings, in a large exposed area.[483] Such incidents have led Reporters Sans Frontières to list the Israeli military among its 'Predators of Press Freedom'.[484]

The net impact of Israeli measures curtailing Palestinian freedom of expression and opinion is to foster a culture of intimidation and to curtail the ability of Palestinians to express themselves and their opinions freely. In apartheid South Africa, such restrictions were understood as a necessary corollary of apartheid, as any system that attempts to engineer comprehensive social control must limit freedom of expression and opinion. As restrictions on freedom of expression also constitute repression of resistance to apartheid, Israel's practices fit both the concerns here, under Article 2(c), and Article 2(f) – 'Persecution of organizations and persons, by depriving them of fundamental rights and freedoms, because they oppose apartheid.'

### Denial of the rights to freedom of peaceful assembly and association

*Interpretation*

The rights to freedom of peaceful assembly and association are enshrined in the UDHR (Article 20) and the ICCPR (Article 21). These rights are qualified only where restrictions are necessary for public safety, the protection of public health or morals, or the protection of the rights and freedoms of others.[485] Such restrictions must not be disproportionate and must entail the least feasible impediment to the exercise of the rights. Otherwise, the rights to peaceful assembly and to associate have long been regarded as the foundation of a democratic society, as De Tocqueville stated:

> The most natural privilege of man, next to the right of acting for himself, is that of combining his exertions with those of his fellow creatures and of acting in common with them. The right of association therefore appears to me almost as inalienable in its nature as the right of personal liberty. No legislator can attack it without impairing the foundations of society.[486]

ICERD requires protection from racial discrimination in the exercise of one's rights to freedom of peaceful assembly and association (Article 5(d)(ix)). This provision informs the reference to the rights to freedom of peaceful assembly and association in the Apartheid Convention.

*Practices in apartheid South Africa*

Many laws in apartheid South Africa targeted free association. The most notable was the 1950 Suppression of Communism Act,[487] which empowered the Minister of Justice to prohibit a particular assembly or any specified person from being present in a particular area for a specified period.[488] Those who violated the Minister of Justice's prohibitions were subject to harsh penalties. No warrant was required for the authorities to enter premises suspected of harbouring illegal gatherings. To generalise this Act, the apartheid government then passed the 1960 Unlawful Organisation Act,[489] which allowed the Governor-General to declare any organisation as illegal and thus granted the apartheid government authority to silence it. The 1956 Riotous Assembly Act[490] also empowered the ruling regime to prohibit gatherings in a public space or specific individuals from attending public gatherings.

*Israeli practices in the OPT*

Israel's military legislation does not allow public gatherings of more than ten people unless the government receives notice of the gathering and is given the names of the attendees, thus making it even more restrictive in nature than the legislation in apartheid South Africa. Under Military Order No. 101,[491] '[i]t is forbidden to conduct a protest march or meeting (grouping of ten or more where the subject concerns or is related to politics) without permission from the Military Commander'. Even Palestinian schools and universities have not been immune to this ban. Thousands of Palestinians were detained for organising and participating in public gatherings during the second *intifada*. Live ammunition, tear gas, sound bombs, steel-coated rubber bullets, and physical violence continue to be used against gatherings of Palestinian civilians, particularly at demonstrations against Israel's illegal construction of the Wall in the West Bank.

Further, the Israeli military authorities have adopted a policy of closing down Palestinian organisations that they deem to be security threats. Israel has also declared most Palestinian political parties to be 'terrorist' organisations, and thus, illegal. Hence any organisation connected directly or indirectly to a political party may be subject to closure, destruction, or even military attack. For example, a recent Israeli military order has targeted a residential area, a school, two medical clinics and two orphanages in the West Bank city of Hebron for destruction because some of the donors to the charity that built them are allegedly affiliated to Hamas.[492] In 2007, Israeli authorities shut down dozens of charities and organisations participating in educational, social, cultural and humanitarian activities because of their alleged connections to Hamas. Direct membership of a Palestinian political party designated in Israeli law as a 'terrorist' organisation is a crime that can be punished by detention, house arrest, exile, or a travel ban.

Palestinian organisations and entities in East Jerusalem have been subject to particular repression by the Israeli authorities. In its 2007 *Country Reports on Human Rights Practices,* the US State Department highlighted the closure by Israel of '[p]rominent Palestinian centers in East Jerusalem, such as the Chamber of Commerce and Orient House' as a violation of the Palestinian right to freedom of association.[493] Such closures are based on affiliation of the organisations concerned with the PA, which Israel prohibits from organising events in East Jerusalem. Events and gatherings in March 2009 to mark the celebration of Jerusalem as the 'Capital of Arab Culture 2009' were banned and forcefully dispersed by the Israeli authorities on this basis.[494]

By contrast, Jewish Israelis in the OPT and Israel are allowed full enjoyment of their rights to freedom of association and peaceful assembly. When the law is applied against Israelis, it usually targets 'pro-Palestinian' demonstrators and peace activists or those whom the Occupying Power considers may threaten the 'security' of Israel or its existence as a demographically Jewish State. Discriminatory treatment is suggested further by disparities in Israeli responses to Jewish demonstrations and violence in the OPT. For example, Israeli forces regularly open fire on peaceful Palestinian demonstrations against the Wall,[495] but do not do so in cases of demonstrations by settlers in the West Bank when removing settlement outposts. Nor did they do so against Jewish Israeli rioters during the evacuation of settlements from the Gaza Strip in 2005.

Together, Israel's military legislation in the OPT operates to repress Palestinians' rights to freedom of peaceful assembly and association. Taken together, laws and practice indicate a widespread policy aimed at suppressing political opposition to Israel's occupation and expression of Palestinian cultural identity, in order to preserve Israeli domination in both spheres.

### Case study: impact of combined practices in the Gaza Strip

In Article 2(c), the Apartheid Convention is concerned with a cluster of measures that prevent members of a racial group from participating in the 'political, social, economic and cultural life of the country' and prevent 'the full development of such a group'. This framing concern suggests that an appraisal of Israel's practices under Article 2(c) must not stop with practices as separate categories but must consider their aggregate or holistic impact on a group. A larger portrait of conditions in the Gaza Strip, where these measures are deliberately practised by Israel with particular rigour, will demonstrate that such an aggregate impact has emerged.

*Overview*

The Gaza Strip has experienced a long-term pattern of 'de-development'[496] due to decades of occupation, closures and Israeli military attacks resulting in widespread home demolitions,[497] killings and injuries.[498] Since the victory of the Hamas movement in the 2006 Palestinian legislative elections, and particularly since the Hamas takeover of the Gaza Strip in June 2007, the Israeli government has imposed severe restrictions on the access of goods and services and the movement of people to and from the Gaza Strip.[499] In September 2007, Israel claimed that it was exempted from its legal obligations towards the Palestinians in Gaza as a consequence of 'disengagement'.[500] Israel subsequently declared the Gaza Strip to be a 'hostile entity' and imposed punitive measures on the Palestinian civilian population in order to bring a change in the political regime there.[501] On 27 December 2008, the Israeli military launched a far-reaching military offensive against the Gaza Strip which continued for over three weeks until 18 January 2009. In 'Operation Cast Lead', at least 1,380 Palestinians were killed, of whom 431 were children and 112 women. At least 5,380 people were injured, including 1,872 children and 800 women.[502] The offensive ended with Israel's announcement of a unilateral ceasefire, and the Israeli forces withdrew three days later.

Since then, the Gaza Strip has been completely closed to all but very limited transportation of goods and the few individuals who can obtain special permits. This closure policy, combined with military attacks and especially 'Operation Cast Lead', has had an extremely detrimental impact on the lives and living conditions of Palestinian civilians. It has even been argued that the 'siege' imposed by Israel on the Gaza Strip since 2007 and the conditions that it has created, as discussed below, amounts to 'cruel, inhuman and degrading treatment' and is a violation of the UN CAT.[503]

This section is divided into two parts: first, figures concerning a first phase of the siege, mostly between June 2007 and December 2008; and second, conditions in Gaza immediately following 'Operation Cast Lead'.

*Initial phase of the siege, June 2007–08*

The Palestinian economy had been in decline since the beginning of the second *intifada* in 2000, but Israel's economic restrictions imposed after the 2006 elections caused a severe collapse. Karni is the vital crossing for the movement of foods and goods to and from the Gaza Strip, yet Israel closed this crossing in mid June 2007. Soon thereafter, Palestinian human rights organisations petitioned the Israeli Supreme Court demanding the immediate reopening of the crossing, arguing that the denial of essential provisions to residents of Gaza violates their rights to life, health and to an adequate standard of living, and amounts to collective punishment. The Court stated that it was unconvinced that there was a humanitarian crisis in Gaza and advised the petitioners in October 2007 to withdraw the petition.[504]

Nonetheless, data indicate that the closure of the Karni crossing had heavily impacted the Palestinian economy by 2008:

- In September 2000, some 24,000 Palestinians crossed out of Gaza every day to work in Israel.[505] In 2008, that figure was zero.
- Unemployment was close to 40 per cent in the Gaza Strip in 2007 and was set to rise to 50 per cent in 2008.
- More than 75,000 workers out of approximately 110,000 employed by the private sector were laid off because of the impact of the closures, and the majority of private businesses closed down.
- Nearly 90 per cent of all industrial establishments have shut down since mid June 2007, including the most significant factories at the Karni Industrial Zone.
- Pre-disengagement in June 2005, there were 3,900 factories in Gaza employing 35,000 people; by the end of 2007, there were 195 factories employing only 1,750 workers.[506]
- Nearly all public infrastructure and maintenance projects, private construction and ministerial and municipal projects were halted due to the closure of factories and the lack of building materials.[507]
- In the months before the blockade began in June 2007, around 250 trucks a day entered Gaza through Karni with supplies.[508] In 2008, other crossings like Kerem Shalom only accommodate a maximum of 45 trucks a day. In most cases, this number was barely reached.[509]
- Ninety-five per cent of Gaza's industrial operations are suspended due to the ban on imported raw materials and the block on exports.[510]

As a consequence of these conditions, poverty in Gaza reached unprecedented levels. In 2007, around eight out of ten households, approximately 1.1 million people, were living below the poverty line of NIS 2,300 (US$594) per month, a sharp rise from 63.1 per cent in 2005. Of these, 66.7 per cent of households were living in deep poverty on less than NIS 1,837 (US$474) per month.[511] Eighty per cent of families in Gaza in 2007 relied on food aid, compared to 63 per cent in 2006. Poverty was aggravated by sharp price increases of many items resulting from shortages. In 2007, households were spending approximately 62 per cent of their total income on food compared with 37 per cent in 2004.[512] During the period May–June 2007 alone, prices for wheat flour, baby milk and rice rose 34 per cent, 30 per cent and 20.5 per cent respectively.[513] During the period June–September 2007, the number of households in Gaza earning less than US$1.2 per person per day soared from 55 per cent to 70 per cent.[514]

In October 2007 the Israeli government began limiting the supply of fuel and electricity to Gaza.[515] In November 2007, responding to a petition filed by Adalah and Gisha on behalf of ten Palestinian and Israeli human rights organisations, the Israeli Supreme Court approved the cuts to fuel supplies; by the end of January 2008, the Court also sanctioned reductions in the supply of electricity.[516] The Court accepted the State's claim that it is only bound to safeguard 'a minimal humanitarian standard' in Gaza, a term that does not exist in international humanitarian law.

As a result of fuel and electricity restrictions, hospitals were experiencing power cuts lasting for eight to twelve hours a day, due to a 60–70 per cent shortage reported in the diesel required for hospital power generators.[517] All of the Gaza Strip, except the Rafah district, was facing a daily electricity outage for an average of eight hours.[518] As of April 2008, no fuel was available in Gaza on the open market and power cuts of three hours per day were experienced in almost all of the Gaza Strip.[519] UNRWA stopped its food delivery to 650,000 refugees in Gaza for five days in April 2008 due to a lack of fuel for its trucks.[520] The Coastal Municipalities Water Utility (CMWU) provides drinking water and removes and treats sewage for the Gaza Strip. Without fuel, electricity and proper maintenance, the network cannot function and 30–40 million litres of sewage goes into the sea every day because of a lack of fuel to pump or treat human waste.[521] The CMWU estimates that between 25 per cent and 30 per cent of the population of Gaza did not receive running water in their homes; before the blockade the CMWU was able to distribute water to 100 per cent of its beneficiaries.[522]

Health care has been heavily impacted by the siege. Many specialised and life-saving medical treatments are not available in hospitals in Gaza. Current measures imposed by Israel have prevented a large number of patients with treatment referrals from leaving Gaza for specialised medical care. Excessive delays in obtaining permission to leave the Gaza Strip reduce the patients' possibility of survival.

Rulings delivered by the Israeli Supreme Court in January 2008 involved patients in life-threatening conditions requesting to exit Gaza for medical care. In these cases, the Supreme Court refused to intervene in the State's decision to deny access to health care to nine patients on security grounds.[523] In a previous ruling, delivered on 28 June 2007, the Supreme Court refused to discuss the issue of Israel's legal responsibility towards the Gaza Strip, or the State's position that entry into Israel should be permitted only as a humanitarian gesture. The Court limited the discussion to the 'operative common denominator, i.e., to humanitarian aspects'.[524] The Court did question the 'life/limb' distinction (according to which the State argued that a danger to limb constitutes a danger to the 'quality of life' and does not necessitate access to health care outside of Gaza). However, it did not intervene in this issue, deciding that intervention in such cases could, 'by the stroke of a pen, expose IDF soldiers and civilians at the Crossing to danger'.[525] Following this comment, the Court refused to intervene in the security prohibition of two patients to whom denial of care would entail the loss of a limb.[526]

Medical conditions in the Gaza Strip are changing rapidly, but it is relevant here that Israel's closures had brought the medical system to the brink of collapse even before 27 December 2008 and that Israeli authorities were unresponsive to warnings of a growing humanitarian crisis. Physicians for Human Rights-Israel (PHR-I) reported that, since June 2007, it had collected testimonies from least 30 patients seeking urgent medical help who were denied passage by the GSS.[527] According to GSS policy, patients were being detained at the Erez Crossing and requested to provide information or to act as regular collaborators as a condition for permission to leave the Gaza Strip for medical treatment.[528] The deliberate withholding of medical care for non-medical reasons constitutes a form of torture, PHR-I argues.[529] The Israeli authorities denied carrying out such practices at Erez and dismiss them as Palestinian propaganda.[530] Of patients seeking emergency treatment in hospitals outside Gaza in 2007, 18.5 per cent were refused permits to leave.[531] The proportion of patients given permits to exit Gaza for medical care decreased from 89.3 per cent in January 2007 to 64.3 per cent in December 2007, an unprecedented low.[532] While the overall number of patients requesting a permit to pass through Erez crossing increased after June 2007 due to the Rafah crossing (border with Egypt) closure, the percentage of permits that were denied increased from 7 per cent in January 2006 to 36 per cent in December 2007.[533] During the period October–December 2007, the World Health Organisation (WHO) confirmed the deaths of 20 patients, including five children, among people awaiting visas.[534] The Ministry of Health (MoH) hospitals were working within a declared state of emergency. The Palestinian Health Ministry reported that urgently needed drugs (85 items), medical supplies (52 items) and lab reagents (24 items) were out of stock at MoH facilities.[535]

*Aftermath of 'Operation Cast Lead'*

In the aftermath of 'Operation Cast Lead', the population in the Gaza Strip experienced intensifying difficulties regarding basic supplies and services.[536] For example, during the week of 4–10 March 2009, OCHA found that 50,000 people continued to have no running water; an additional 100,000 received water only every five to six days, primarily in the North Gaza district, eastern areas of Khan Younis and Az Zeitoun area of Gaza City.[537] During the week of 11–17 March 2009, nine truckloads carrying supplies for water projects were allowed into Gaza, but due to restrictions on the entry of other essential materials – including water pipes – the benefit of these supplies is limited.[538]

During the same week, 90 per cent of the Gaza population was experiencing intermittent power cuts as a result of scheduled power cuts.[539] The remaining 10 per cent of Gaza's population remained without electricity, due to damages sustained by the electricity network.[540] During February 2009, the Gaza Power Plant (GPP) was only able to operate at about 80 per cent of its full capacity (65 megawatts out of 80 megawatts), creating a shortage of almost 20 per cent throughout the Gaza Strip.[541] During February 2009, approximately 8.3 million litres of industrial fuel were imported from Israel and used exclusively for the operation of the GPP, an amount that is significantly below the 14 million needed to operate the plant at full capacity.[542] The following week, nearly 50,000 litres of diesel and 30,000 litres of petrol entered Gaza daily via the Gaza–Egypt tunnels.[543] These supplies eased the fuel shortage, but the amount of fuel reaching Gaza remained far below the needs of the population. Overall levels of humanitarian aid allowed into Gaza remained below what was urgently required.[544] Israeli clearance procedures for access into Gaza by international humanitarian agency personnel continued to be very lengthy, greatly hindering their capacity to provide humanitarian aid and services.[545]

During February 2009, 324 permit applications were submitted by patients who required medical treatment abroad, of whom only 183 (56.5 per cent) had their permits granted in a timely manner by the Israeli District Coordination Liaison (DCL) office; 109 (33.6 per cent) had their applications delayed; nine (2.8 per cent) had their application denied, and another 23 (7.1 per cent) were interviewed by the ISA and were still awaiting an exit permit.[546] According to the Palestinian Liaison Officer at Erez, only 258 patients exited during February 2009.[547]

During February 2009, a daily average of 127 truckloads of goods entered the Gaza Strip, a figure that is well below the level of imports in May 2007 (475 truckloads), and the level of imports was insufficient to meet market needs: over 80 per cent of the truckloads carried food stuffs, to the exclusion of other major essential supplies.[548] In the same month, Israeli approval was arbitrarily denied for the import of other goods, including some food items (chickpeas and macaroni), recreational kits, stationery and veterinary drugs.[549] The import of goods from Israel, particularly by humanitarian agencies, remains subject to unclear and often inconsistent criteria at the Israeli-controlled crossings.[550] By the end of 2010, many critically needed items (spare parts, construction materials, and so on) remained restricted for entry, preventing reconstruction and recovery efforts, including spare parts for water and waste-water infrastructures.[551] Spare parts and consumables needed to repair the GPP waited for clearance to enter Gaza for months.[552] Restrictions on imports were still severely hampering reconstruction of houses demolished during 'Operation Cast Lead'.[553]

Access by farmers to their land in the north and east of the Gaza Strip and east along the border with Israel remains limited. Fishermen remain limited to a territory of three nautical miles from the Gaza shoreline,[554] despite an agreement reached under the Oslo Accord for fishing grounds extending to 20 nautical miles west of Gaza that was adhered to until June 2007 with Hamas' takeover of Gaza. In June 2007 the fishing ground was cut to six nautical miles, which was halved to three nautical miles after 'Operation Cast Lead', severely damaging the livelihood of Gaza's 3,000 fishermen and their families.[555] Israel enforces the three-nautical-mile limit by opening fire on Palestinian fishing vessels found in water beyond it.[556]

Erez crossing was opened on 23 days during February 2009, allowing only 1,978 people to exit Gaza, the majority of whom were diplomats and international humanitarian staff (730), and Palestinian patients and their accompaniers (505) with valid permits to cross Erez for medical treatment in Israel and the West Bank;[557] 370 Palestinians carrying permits were allowed to cross Erez to visit their families in Israel, the West Bank and Jordan.[558]

The Rafah crossing was exceptionally opened on 15 days during February 2009 to allow mainly urgent medical cases to enter Egypt and cross back into Gaza; 2,662 Palestinians, including 590 patients, were allowed to enter Egypt and 1,855 others to return back to Gaza during February 2009. The daily average of people who crossed into Egypt (95) and who entered Gaza (66) constitutes just 31 per cent and 23 per cent of the parallel figures for May 2007, at 310 and 292 respectively.

As a consequence of these conditions, by the end of 2010 unemployment in the Gaza Strip was 37.4 per cent, among the highest in the world. Food insecurity affected 52 per cent of the population and 69 per cent in rural areas. The number of truckloads allowed to enter Gaza remained only 35 per cent of numbers before the closure. The construction industry had been revived to some extent by loosened restrictions on importation of building materials, but most materials were still coming through the tunnels, job creation was very small, and OCHA found that the impact on food insecurity was minimal.[559] Economic desperation drove thousands of people to work in prohibited areas, such as agricultural land along the border fence or the tunnels to Egypt and banned agricultural land along the border fence. But tunnel work remained very hazardous: in 2010, 43 people died in construction accidents in the tunnels (including five children) and 88 were injured. As Israeli forces continued to shoot civilians who came too close to the fence, in 2010 'at least 15 Palestinian civilians, including four children, were killed in the access restricted areas on the land and at sea, and another 169 civilians, including 45 children, were injured'.[560]

These few figures can only suggest some of the conditions in the Gaza Strip that continue to be documented by UN and other observers. The concern here is whether Israel's policies, which have created these conditions, are 'calculated to prevent [the Palestinians] from participation in the political, social, economic and cultural life of the country' and reflect a deliberate attempt to create conditions that will prevent their 'full development' as a group. The raw data, in combination with Israeli political statements, make an incontestable case for concluding that Israel's policies are designed to have precisely this effect.

## ARTICLE 2(d) – MEASURES DESIGNED TO DIVIDE THE POPULATION ALONG RACIAL LINES BY THE CREATION OF SEPARATE RESERVES AND GHETTOS FOR THE MEMBERS OF A RACIAL GROUP OR GROUPS, THE PROHIBITION OF MIXED MARRIAGES AMONG MEMBERS OF VARIOUS RACIAL GROUPS, THE EXPROPRIATION OF LANDED PROPERTY BELONGING TO A RACIAL GROUP OR GROUPS OR TO MEMBERS THEREOF

### Creation of separate reserves and ghettos

*Interpretation*

Reference to 'reserves' or to 'ghettos' is not found elsewhere in international law and there is little national or international jurisprudence clarifying the meaning of these phrases. In general use, the term 'reserves', when speaking of separate treatment of racial groups or peoples, applies generally to areas of land set aside for their exclusive use. Reserves may be used to confine people, 'protect' them, or provide them with limited autonomy, as in the reservation system for Native Americans in the United States. The special relevance of the term here, therefore, is specific to South Africa: the 1913 Land Act established that black land ownership would be confined to certain areas of the country that were called black 'Reserves' and the term remained in use when the Apartheid Convention was drafted. Although the term 'Homelands' was then current, the text of the Apartheid Convention as adopted by the UN General Assembly in 1973 omitted any explicit reference to the Homelands (most likely with the intention of denying them any semblance of recognition or legitimacy), referring instead to the 'creation of separate reserves and ghettos'.

The term 'ghetto' is associated with urban districts characterised by geographic isolation and discrimination[561] and is used regarding, for example, Roma communities in Europe.[562] Although urban ghettos may be formed through voluntary choices by people, reflecting the propensity of ethnic groups and especially immigrant groups to cluster together for mutual support, the term today is commonly associated with vulnerability, poverty, discrimination and marginality relative to a dominant society. In Europe, for many centuries Jews were confined by law to residence to ghettos, which often became cradles of Jewish culture. The most notorious ghetto in modern history was the Jewish Ghetto in Warsaw, to which Jews were transferred and imprisoned during the Second World War in order to facilitate the execution of the Holocaust.

For the purposes of the Apartheid Convention, reference to 'reserves and ghettos' are taken here as referring respectively to rural and urban enclaves to which residence by a racial group is restricted. Article 2 confirms that it is an inhuman act constituent of apartheid to confine a racial group to reserves and ghettos in order to exclude the group from the life of the country.

*Practices in apartheid South Africa*

Division of the population in South Africa was orchestrated through legislation that categorised the entire population by racial type and allowed each group the right to live only in its assigned geographic zones. In rural areas, this system became the Homelands policy; in urban areas, it generated black townships, such as Soweto, that functioned as labour reservoirs for white cities.

The use of reserves to exclude blacks from the life of South Africa traces to the Glen Grey Act of 1874 and the Bantu Land Act of 1913,[563] which established the principle of geographic segregation on the basis of race, and the Native Trust and Land Act of 1936 which further legislated this principle.[564] Under the National Party, these earlier laws provided the basis for the first major step toward 'Grand Apartheid', the Group Areas Act 41 of 1950. This Act divided South Africa into separate areas, each reserved exclusively for the use of a particular racial group, while ensuring that the white group maintained control over the most economically productive areas of the country.[565] The Prevention of Illegal Squatting Act of 1952 ensured that the separation policy would succeed by empowering the Minister of

Native Affairs to remove blacks from public or privately owned land and establish resettlement camps to house these displaced people. The Natives Laws Amendment Act of 1952 also narrowed the category of blacks who had the right of permanent residence in towns to those who had been born in a town and had lived there continuously for not less than 15 years, or who had been employed there continuously for the same period of time, or who had worked continuously for a white employer for at least ten years.

Implemented from 1954, these Acts authorised the State to uproot black citizens from their homes of generations. Millions of black people were eventually forcibly ejected from 'white' land, often dumped unceremoniously to 'adapt or die' in remote and primitive 'resettlement' areas. The policy also resulted in the wholesale destruction of urban communities like Sophiatown (Johannesburg), District Six (Cape Town), Cato Manor and South End in Port Elizabeth, with consequences of immense suffering and huge losses of property and income. With the enactment of the Natives (Prohibition of Interdicts) Act, Act No. 64 of 1956, those forcefully removed could not appeal to the courts against their removals. The generally appalling conditions in these dumping grounds regularly produced terrible poverty, disease and high rates of infant and child mortality. The intense human suffering in places such as Dimbaza, Limehill, Soetwater and hundreds of other locations provoked international outrage and led to charges of genocide against the National Party government.[566]

The notion of self-governing black Homelands did not come to fruition until the 1960s and 1970s[567] when they were seen as an escape route for the regime. South Africa's white government was finding that the policies of forced removal – and other overt practices of racial segregation and discrimination – were attracting widespread international criticism and condemnation, particularly from the UN.[568] In a 1961 Parliamentary debate, South Africa's Prime Minister, Dr Verwoed[569] admitted that the Homelands were

> a form of fragmentation which we would not have liked if we were able to avoid it. In light of the pressure being exerted on South Africa there is, however, no doubt that eventually this will have to be done, thereby buying for the white man his freedom and the right to retain domination in what is his country ... If the Whites could have continued to rule over everybody, with no danger to themselves, they would certainly have chosen to do so. However, we have to bear in mind the new views in regard to human rights ... the power of the world and world opinion and our desire to preserve ourselves.[570]

The ideology underpinning the creation of the Bantu Homelands in South Africa – as well as those which would be subsequently established in Namibia – was most clearly expressed in a 1954 government report written by an eleven-man commission chaired by Professor F.R. Tomlinson.[571] The Tomlinson Report, which took almost five years to complete, concluded that separate development of the European and Bantu communities should be striven for, as the only direction in which racial conflict may possibly be eliminated, and racial harmony possibly be maintained. The only obvious way out of the dilemma lies in the sustained development of the Bantu Areas on a large scale.[572]

'Grand Apartheid' thus reflected, most fundamentally, a strategy by the National Party to escape the political conundrums for white people resulting from South Africa's majority-black demography. It was evident to the Tomlinson Commission that, were they to give in to international pressure and form a multiracial society with equal rights for all in a single State, whites would lose control of national politics and ultimately, it was feared, their European cultural lifestyles:

> At whatever speed, and in whatever manner the evolutionary process of integration and equalisation between European and Bantu might take place, there can be no doubt as to the ultimate outcome in the political sphere, namely that the control of political power will pass into the hands of the Bantu.
>
> It is possible that European paramountcy might be maintained for some time, by manipulation of the franchise qualifications; but without a doubt the government of the country will eventually be exercised by those elected by the majority of voters. Theoretically, it is possible that the non-Europeans who then constitute the majority of voters, might prefer to have the country ruled by Europeans. Such a supposition appears highly doubtful, and certainly improbable. But, even if such were to be the case, the rulers of a democratic country would have to carry out the will of the majority of the people, which means to say, that the European orientation of our legislation and government will eventually disappear.[573]

Hence the Tomlinson Commission warned that, if all South Africans were represented in a unified parliamentary democracy, power would pass into the hands of the blacks. Because blacks were not considered capable of maintaining a 'European' democracy, to sustain South Africa as a democracy required excluding blacks from political rights and representation. Yet excluding blacks from equal rights as citizens would undermine and ultimately destroy the 'European' democracy (which only whites could maintain) because it would require measures that were profoundly undemocratic and illiberal. Thus to preserve democracy for white people, some solution had to be found.

The Homelands were the National Party's answer to this dilemma, as well as a way to stave off criticism of its racial policies by the outside world. Apartheid architects like Henrik Vervoerd (first as Education Minister and later as Prime Minister) argued that South Africa was a State with many nationalities, instead of one nation, and that separate development of each nation was mandated, as only disaster could result from multiracialism, multinationalism and multiculturalism.[574] In 1959, the South African Parliament passed the Promotion of Bantu Self-Government Act which introduced 'national' divisions in the country for particular ethnic groups and which would form the basis for the Homeland system.[575] The Preamble provided:

> Whereas the Bantu peoples of the Union of South Africa do not constitute a homogenous people, but form separate national units on the basis of language and culture; and whereas it is desirable for the welfare and progress of said peoples to afford recognition to the various national units and to provide for their gradual development within their own areas to self-governing units on the basis of Bantu systems of government ...[576]

The Act established a number of white Commissioners-General to act as agents of the Central Government in the Homelands, and set up eight Bantu authorities.[577] It also completed the process of removing African's civil rights in South Africa with the elimination of the (white) native representatives from the National Assembly.[578]

Thus the Homelands were designed to remove the demographic threat to racial democracy by tapping into the UN principle that every people has the right to self-determination. 'Grand Apartheid' prescribed that whites would exercise this right in the great majority of the country's territory, including in all major towns and cities and 90 per cent of its arable land. Black South Africans would do so in ten 'independent' Homelands invented and demarcated by the South African government: Transkei, Bophuthatswana, Ciskei, Lebowa, Venda, Gazankulu, Qwaqwa, KaNgwane, KwaNdebele, and KwaZulu.[579] In 1963, Transkei became the first Homeland to be granted 'self-government' status, although this was primarily a publicity exercise to show to the ICJ that South Africa was sincere about granting the blacks self-determination.[580] The other Homelands would not be granted 'self-governing' status until the mid 1970s. In 1976, Transkei was granted 'independence' although the UN General Assembly had already called upon its members to refuse recognition to Transkei or to any other Homeland.[581] Three other Homelands were declared independent: Bophuthatswana (1977), Venda (1979) and Ciskei (1981).

The reality of 'Grand Apartheid' was that black South Africans (80 per cent of the country's population) were to be confined to a mere 12–13 per cent of the area of South Africa, whilst the whites (20 percent) would rule over the remaining 88 percent of the land.[582] Moreover, the fact that the Homelands were spread around South Africa in a fragmented horseshoe comprising 81 large and 200 smaller blocks of land led many to argue that they could never form independent and viable sovereign states.

International rejection of the Bantustan system was categorical, on several grounds: that black South Africans' right to self-determination included a right to territorial integrity over the entirety of South Africa; that black South Africans lacked 'the legal capacity to give the consent necessary to any divestiture envisaged by the Bantustan policy';[583] and because the implementation of the Bantustan policy was reliant on dividing the population along racial lines to be forcibly transferred from their homes into the Bantustans. In 1971, the UN General Assembly denounced the policy 'artificially to divide the African people into "nations" according to their tribal origins' and justify 'the establishment of non-contiguous Bantu homelands (Bantustans) on that basis', and condemned 'the establishment of Bantu homelands (Bantustans) and the forcible removal of the African people of South Africa and Namibia to those areas as a violation of their inalienable rights, contrary to the principle of self-determination and prejudicial to territorial integrity of the countries and the unity of their peoples'.[584]

Two days after the granting of 'independence' to Transkei, the UN General Assembly adopted Resolution 31/6A (1976) by 130 votes to none. This resolution condemned 'the establishment of Bantustans as designed to consolidate the inhuman policies of apartheid, to destroy the territorial integrity of the country, to perpetuate white minority domination and to dispossess the African people of South Africa of their inalienable rights'. It further rejected Transkei's independence as 'invalid', and called upon all governments 'to deny any form of recognition to the so-called independent Transkei'. This call for non-recognition of the Transkei would be endorsed by the UN Security Council in Resolutions 402 (1976) and 407 (1977).[585] Similar resolutions and denunciations were passed by the UN calling on all States not to recognise the 'independence' of Bophuthatswana in 1977, Venda in 1979 and Ciskei in 1981.[586]

South Africa also attempted to establish Bantustans in Namibia (formerly South West Africa), which it had administered under League of Nations mandate after the First World War and refused to relinquish after the Second World War. In 1964, the Odendaal Commission[587] recommended that 40.07 per cent of the territory be allocated for non-white Homelands,[588] while allocating to the whites control of 43.22 per cent of the land where nevertheless the majority of the population was black.[589] In 1968, the South African government passed the Development of the Self-Government for Native Nations in South-West Africa Act. Black territories were divided into ten blocks: Basterland, Bushmanland, Damaraland, East Caprivi, Hereroland, Kaokoland, Kavangoland, Namaland, Ovamboland and Tswanaland. (Only East Caprivi, Hereroland and Kavangoland were granted self-rule.[590]) The policy was opposed by the South West Africa People's Organisation (SWAPO) and the Democratic Development Co-operative Party (DEMCOP), which demanded independence for the whole of Namibia.[591]

International rejection of the Bantustan strategy in Namibia was equally strong. The UN General Assembly terminated the Mandate of South Africa over Namibia in 1966.[592] In 1968, the UN General Assembly denounced the black 'self-government' plans as designed to 'destroy the national unity and territorial integrity of Namibia'.[593] The UN Security Council described the establishment of Bantustans in Namibia as 'contrary to the provisions of the United Nations Charter' and condemned the Native Nations Act as 'a violation of the relevant resolutions of the General Assembly'.[594] In 1976, the UN Security Council declared that, 'in order that the people of Namibia may be enabled freely to determine their own future, it is imperative that free elections under the supervision and control of the United Nations be held for the whole of Namibia as one political entity'.[595] In paragraph 11(c) of that resolution, the Security Council called on the South African government to abolish the application in Namibia of 'all racially discriminatory Bantustans and homelands'.[596] Due to international opposition, no Bantustan in Namibia became an 'independent' state. In 1990, Namibia was admitted to the UN as an independent State, its territorial integrity intact.[597]

*Israeli practices in the OPT*

As in South Africa, Israel's division of the civilian population in the OPT is orchestrated through legislation that categorises the entire population by its identity and allows each group the right to live only in its assigned geographic zones. The principal expression of this policy is the creation of Jewish-only settlements within contiguous areas of land reserved for Jewish use, effectively confining Palestinians to cantons delineated by Jewish areas. That the settlements are illegal under international law was clarified in Chapter 1. Here our concern is with how they function to divide the two groups on the basis of their identities.

Formal plans to divide the West Bank into Jewish and Palestinian zones trace to at least 1978, when the parastatal Jewish Agency, responsible for developing and managing Jewish-national assets in Israel,[598] formally declared that the West Bank was a permanent part of 'Eretz-Israel' (the Land of Israel) and presented a 'Master Plan' for inserting Jewish settlements into the region in order to secure permanent Jewish-Israeli control over its geography.[599] Known as the Drobles Plan, it proposed as a premise that 'a strip of settlements at strategic sites enhances both internal and external security alike, as well as making concrete and realizing our right to Eretz-Israel'. The Plan then detailed how these settlements should be placed 'not only *around* the settlements of the minorities [Palestinians], but also *in between* them' and developed to encourage 'dispersion of the [Jewish] population from the densely populated urban strip of the coastal plain eastward to the presently empty areas of J&S [Judea and Samaria]'.[600] Subsequently, the JA developed other master plans for particular settlement blocs, like Rehan, Ariel and Gush Etzion, in which smaller settlements were established around larger ones to consolidate blocs of land. The language of these plans was explicitly to 'Judaise' the land: that is, increase the Jewish proportion of its population and ensure a strategic geographic dispersal of Jewish settlement.

By the late 1990s, the grid of Jewish settlement had reached its present geographic configuration and had consolidated an integrated system of territory for exclusively Jewish use. Settlement blocs are connected to each other and to Israel through contiguous belts of land, closed zones and highways that have the cumulative effect of carving Palestinian zones into a series of disarticulated enclaves connected by smaller separate roads, from which passage is controlled by checkpoints staffed by the Israeli military and private Israeli security forces, as dealt with in detail earlier in this chapter.

OCHA published an exhaustive study of the settlement grid in 2007.[601] Through GIS (Geographic Information System) mapping, the study determined that almost 40 per cent of the West Bank is now taken up by Israeli infrastructure, in which settlements, linked by a major highway system to Israel, have geographically fragmented Palestinian communities. Palestinian access to the West Bank road network is restricted by a closure regime consisting of approximately 85 checkpoints, 460 roadblocks and a permit system for Palestinian vehicles, noting that:

> Each Palestinian enclave is geographically separated from the other by some form of Israeli infrastructure including settlements, outposts, military areas, nature reserves and the Barrier. However, the Israeli road network is the key delineator in marking the boundaries of the enclaves. The road network functions to provide corridors for travel from Israel, and between settlements in the West Bank, and barriers for Palestinian movement.[602]

The operation of this system to divide territory into 'reserves and ghettos' is illustrated by the case of Nablus.[603] A city with a population of 130,000 and the regional hub for some 350,000 Palestinians, Nablus is encircled by 14 Israeli settlements and 26 outposts connected to each other by roads used primarily by settlers that stretch around the city and across Nablus governorate. These roads are in turn linked to ten checkpoints, including seven that encircle the city and through which all Palestinians going in and out of Nablus must cross. According to OCHA, in April 2007, only 10 per cent of Nablus buses (22 out of 220) and 7 per cent of Nablus taxis (150 out of 2,250) had permits to access and use the checkpoints around Nablus city. Only 50 private Palestinian cars were permitted to use the checkpoints while more than 70 obstacles installed by the Israeli army block the road junctions and physically prevent Palestinian traffic from reaching the roads used primarily by settlers.[604] The city of Nablus thus constitutes a Palestinian reserve, in the sense noted above: a physical area enclosed for the purpose of dividing the population along racial lines.

Conversely, Israeli settlements in the West Bank are also areas physically enclosed for the purpose of dividing the population along racial lines. Settlements and their surrounding lands constitute contiguous areas, designated for Jewish Israeli use and banned to Palestinian entry and use, which geographically delineate the enclaves for the Palestinian group, to the detriment of the Palestinian population.

## Prohibition of mixed marriages

### Practices in apartheid South Africa

In apartheid South Africa, the Prohibition of Mixed Marriages Act 55 of 1949 prohibited marriages between white people and people of other races. The Immorality Amendment Act of 1950 further prohibited adultery, attempted adultery or related 'immoral acts' (extramarital sex) between white and black people and strictly forbade 'unlawful carnal intercourse' as well as 'any immoral or indecent act' between a white person and a member of any other racial group.[605] Those found guilty of 'unlawful carnal intercourse' or 'any immoral or indecent act' could be sentenced to imprisonment for up to seven years with hard labour and up to ten lashes where the male was under 50 years of age.[606] In some cases, even a kiss between people of different races could lead to a conviction in terms of the Act.[607] In order to apprehend persons ostensibly engaged in unlawful carnal intercourse across the racial divide, the South African Police were driven to bizarre measures:

> Special Force Order O25A/69 detailed the use of binoculars, tape recorders, cameras and two-way radios to trap offenders. It also spelled out how bed sheets should be felt for warmth and examined for stains. Police were also reported to have examined the private parts of couples and taken people to district surgeons for examination.[608]

Writing in 1981, David Harrison estimated that the last 30 years had seen over 10,000 convictions under the Immorality Act.[609] He observed that 'prosecution has trailed in its wake social disgrace, family break-up and many cases of suicide'.[610]

*Israeli practices in the OPT*

Israel does not formally prohibit mixed marriages among members of various racial groups either within Israel or in the OPT. Mixed marriages are discouraged in practice, however, by the absence of civil marriage. In Israel, the Family Courts Law of 1995 provides that religious courts – Rabbinical courts for Jews and separate courts for Muslim, Christian and Druze[611] – have exclusive jurisdiction in the matters of marriage and divorce.[612] This arrangement creates insuperable obstacles for couples from different religious groups (or without religious affiliation) who wish to marry, forcing them to leave the country and marry abroad. While these marriages are legally recognised in Israel and can be registered with the Ministry of the Interior, the Rabbinate does not recognise marriages when one of the partners is not Jewish. This symbiotic relationship between State law and Rabbinical authority regarding mixed marriage obviates an outright ban on inter-marriage by Jews, as inter-faith marriages in Israel will fail to gain the legal rights accorded to spouses – and, not least, equate with severing significant relationships with the Jewish community.[613]

As outlined in Chapter 3, Israeli law applies to Israeli settlers in the OPT, and thus impedes 'mixed' marriage between an Israeli and a Palestinian in the OPT, in three ways. First, as noted, such a marriage can only take place outside of Israeli jurisdiction. Second, even if allowed to register the marriage with the Israeli Ministry of the Interior, the couple cannot legally live together in Israel or East Jerusalem, as the Citizenship and Entry into Israel Law of 2003 precludes the Palestinian spouse from having any status that would allow them to live in Israel or East Jerusalem for the purposes of family unification.

Third, the couple will face daunting practical and legal obstacles to living together in the OPT, because the Jewish Israeli spouse is de jure barred from entering or living in Area A of the West Bank or the Gaza Strip while the Palestinian spouse is de facto barred from living in a Jewish Israeli settlement. The latter is due to the restrictions on access and residence on Palestinians (by virtue of the permit system in the West Bank) and the rules of the various settlement councils, Jewish agencies and religious institutions that operate the settlements, which restrict residence in them to Jews only.

The effect of these obstacles is that mixed marriages between Jews and other religious sects in the OPT, while not directly and formally prohibited, are rendered almost impossible in practice. In this light, the absence of a formal law to ban mixed marriages is less significant, as a cluster of other juridical measures ensures the same effect.

### Expropriation of landed property

*Interpretation*

Under Article 23(g) of the Hague Regulations, the Occupying Power is forbidden from destroying or seizing enemy property except for the 'necessities of war'. The Hague Regulations place an additional duty on the Occupying Power to administer public buildings and lands 'in accordance with the rules of usufruct' (Article 55). To show a breach of the prohibition against land expropriation in Article 2(d) of the Apartheid Convention, however, it is not enough to establish a practice of land expropriation *per se*: the practice must be established as designed to 'divide the population along racial lines' and to serve 'purposes of establishing and maintaining domination by one racial group of persons over any other racial group of persons'.

*Practices in apartheid South Africa*

In South Africa, deprivation of property ultimately disenfranchised the black population and ensured servitude and was further designed to divide the population along racial lines. The 1913 Land Act disenfranchised in perpetuity those blacks who were able to own property by limiting, and in some instances obliterating, their rights of land ownership except in designated 'black' areas (about 8 per cent of the country). Re-designation of urban areas along racial lines was effected through forced removal of blacks from their properties by state expropriation and their relocation to black townships. The effect of expropriation was to leave certain urban areas either derelict or as sites for white buildings.[614] Black people were allowed the right to acquire land only in designated areas, separate from the settled white areas, and ultimately only in the Bantustans. The comment by Stanford in 1892 rang true during the apartheid regime: 'the labour question is bound up with the land question. The man who has no land and no trade must work for some one else who has.'[615]

*Israeli practices in the OPT*

Israeli land practices in the OPT rest on a complex system. Under Article 43 of the Hague Regulations,[616] Israel must respect 'unless absolutely prevented, the laws in force in the country'. Israel has done so, but selectively, retaining vestiges of Jordanian and Ottoman laws where these contribute to restricting Palestinian property development and expanding Jewish settlements. Israel has also relied on the argument of 'military necessity' regarding 'enemy property' as well as 'State' lands and even private property.

Upon assuming authority over the OPT, Israel upheld the Jordanian system of land law (except in East Jerusalem),[617] although it had rejected Jordan's claim to be the rightful sovereign of the territory between 1948 and 1967.[618] Jordanian law was infused with earlier Ottoman law regarding land: ultimate title rested in the Sultan (or State), but private and collective land rights were derived through usufruct, as codified partly by tax laws.[619] Formal land registration was indeed avoided by many smaller cultivators because it incurred additional Ottoman taxes, and was seen as advantageous only with the advent of British and then Jordanian rule. By the time the OPT was occupied in 1967, only around one-third of land was registered. Israel then reinterpreted untitled lands as 'State' lands in a different sense: as land to which individual users had no registered title and therefore no legal claim.

Yet through reforms to extant land law, combined with military orders,[620] Israel has ensured de facto and de jure possession of the majority of Palestinian lands. Such actions do not constitute 'requisition'[621] or 'expropriation' as allowed in the Hague Regulations, but rather *appropriation*, or unlawful expropriation, of Palestinian lands resulting in the annexation-by-proxy of the OPT through Israeli settlers.[622] The Israeli government's reliance on the argument of 'military necessity', coupled with its active support of settlements, highlights a blurring between public and private interests in land. Use of land, whether termed 'expropriation' or 'appropriation', is only permitted in international humanitarian law when overriding military needs dictate. These needs are inherently public in nature and reflect the transfer of administration from enemy hands to those of the occupiers; private actors are not part of the equation. Yet Israel has consistently drawn on such public sphere arguments to facilitate the discriminatory transfer of land to private individuals, namely Israeli settlers.

At the commencement of the occupation in 1967, the Israeli government immediately froze all pending cases[623] and implemented new requirements for land registration.[624] Public inspection of land registers was forbidden and any land transaction required permission from the newly endowed registrar of lands.[625] Jewish purchase of Palestinian lands was later facilitated through Military Order Nos 811 and 847, which extended the Jordanian laws' irrevocable power of attorney from five to 15 years.[626] Only Israelis were empowered to validate signatures through this process, which avoided informing the land registry and thus public knowledge about the sale of land.[627] Local Palestinian courts had no jurisdiction over unregistered West Bank lands.[628]

Since 2002, large areas of 'State' land and Palestinian private land have been seized and/or destroyed for Israel's construction of the Wall.[629] Although these measures were termed 'temporary',[630] the ICJ has recognised that the substantial alteration of landed property produces facts on the ground possessing long-term legal significance.[631] Seizures of private property are illegal and this illegality is increased when such lands are handed over to Israeli settlers, whose presence in the OPT is in breach of Article 49, as discussed earlier.[632]

The discriminatory purpose of Israel's land and settlement policies in the West Bank was clarified in 1978 by Matityahu Drobles, then Head of the WZO Department for Rural Settlement, in his 'Master Plan for the Development of Settlement in Judea and Samaria 1979–1983'. Drobles emphasised that the purpose of the Master Plan was demographic engineering in the interest of annexing the West Bank permanently to Israel:

> The civilian presence of Jewish communities is vital for the security of the state ... There must not be the slightest doubt regarding our intention to hold the areas of Judea and Samaria for ever ... The best and most effective way to remove any shred of doubt regarding our intention to hold Judea and Samaria forever is a rapid settlement drive in these areas.[633]

The Drobles Plan laid out a pragmatic programme of land appropriation:

> State and uncultivated land should be seized immediately for the purpose of settlement in the areas located among and around the population centres with the aim of preventing as much as possible the establishment of another Arab state in these territories. It will be difficult for the [Arab] minority to form a regional connection and political unity when split by Jewish colonies ... in light of the current negotiations on the future of the West Bank, we are entitled to compete with time, as in this period everything will be decided on the basis of the facts that we create in these Territories.[634]

Aside from requirements for proving and maintaining title under Jordanian law, a number of different 'legal' mechanisms were also introduced with the occupation to seize Palestinian lands in support of this settlement drive. One was the 1950 Absentee Property Law which, in conjunction with Military Order No. 58,[635] characterises an absentee as anyone outside of the territory during the 1967 conflict. Such lands could be seized by the Custodian (acting as part of the Lands Administration in West Jerusalem), who is then permitted to transfer such properties to the Development Authority, which included members of the JNF.[636] This mechanism is essentially immune from review thanks to Article 5 of the Order, which states that:

> Any transaction carried out in good faith between the custodian of absentee property and any other person concerning property which the custodian believed when he entered into the transaction to be absentee property, will not void and will continue to be valid even if it is subsequently proved that the property was not at the time absentee property.[637]

This provision effectively allows an Israeli acting in 'good faith' to override all existing Palestinian claims to land: for example, Israel seized 430,000 dunums, along with 11,000 buildings, under this provision in the first few years of the occupation, facilitating their later categorisation as 'State' land.[638] Thus, the declaration of 'absentee' lands was an important first step in establishing settlements across the West Bank.

In the first decade or so of the occupation, settlements were also built extensively on Palestinian private lands sealed for 'security' reasons or expropriated for 'military purposes'.[639] In this early stage, settlements were often erected on military bases. Until 1979, the Israeli Supreme Court accepted military arguments for this practice on grounds of 'security', although a clear pattern was emerging between military lands and their later use by (Jewish) civilians. A petition brought by Palestinian landowners in 1979 sought to challenge such definitions and was ultimately successful in its object of distinguishing settlement ownership from 'military necessity'. In the *Elon Moreh* case, the Supreme Court held that:

- The army could not offer *post facto* justifications for land seizures when they were in fact initiated by a pro-settler political group (Gush Emunim, or Bloc of the Faithful).
- Security grounds offered by the army needed to be specific and consistent with national security objectives.
- Ideological and/or political motivations for the establishment of settlements was distinct from security reasons.
- Permanent settlements could not be established on lands temporarily 'requisitioned' for military purposes as per the Hague Regulations.[640]

In this judgment, the Supreme Court affirmed the application of the Hague Regulations along with its ban on the appropriation of private lands. Effectively, this ruling prevented future military seizures of private land for settler use unless an overriding security need could be proved.[641]

The Israeli government at the time responded to the Supreme Court by respecting its ruling, but simultaneously sought new methods of land acquisition. An exhaustive land survey was accelerated immediately after the decision, to provide the Occupying Power with specific data about land holdings, to determine which lands were privately or publicly owned.[642] Public lands would be the source for most future settlements.[643] As mentioned above, Israel retained the Jordanian system of tenure yet altered this significantly through military orders. One example was Military Order No. 59, which authorises a designated authority to seize 'enemy' property for State land.[644] This Order enabled the Israeli government to declare 13 per cent of the West Bank as 'State' land, parts of which were used for settlement construction.[645] Ambiguities and complexities over the definition of 'State' lands – lands that were unregistered or collectively owned – enabled Israel to declare a further 26 per cent of the West Bank as 'State' land.[646] Although this interpretation of 'State' lands eliminated the usufruct ensured by Ottoman law and custom, the appeal mechanisms devised for West Bank lands ensured that such decisions vis-à-vis 'public' lands were usually impossible to review.[647] Palestinians had no standing to sue in Israeli municipal courts over 'public' lands.[648]

Furthermore, although the Supreme Court had accepted to review private land requisitions, it has refused to hear matters over ownership status.[649] Thus, for Palestinians whose private land holdings has been categorised as 'public',[650] the only recourse is to military-appointed administrative tribunals tasked to advise the military commander. The burden of proof in such cases rested on Palestinian owners, who were required to show indisputable title through formal Jordanian title deeds[651] in costly and complicated proceedings conducted mostly in Hebrew. Given the military tribunals' strict requirements about modes of land use, these formalities proved too onerous for many landowners, who then saw their 'State' lands turned over to settlement construction.

In contrast to rapid growth in Jewish settlements, development in Palestinian zones has been stifled. Zoning and municipality laws for Palestinians are a combination of Jordanian laws and military orders[652] and municipal boundaries in the OPT were frozen in 1967 despite rapid natural population growth.[653] Lands outside such zones are typically classified as agricultural lands or nature reserves and any construction on such lands is severely restricted.[654] Under the Oslo Accords, Palestinian construction was only possible in Areas A and B, about 40 per cent of the West Bank.[655]

The picture in Jerusalem is much the same: between 1967 and 1995, an estimated 64,867 housing units were built in the Municipality, only 8,890 of which were for Palestinians.[656] In addition, despite the pressures of an expanding population, no new Palestinian communities have been established since 1967 in the area.[657] Where buildings have been constructed without the required permits, thousands of them have been destroyed in a concerted policy to stem development and punish Palestinian landowners through legal, administrative mechanisms. Particularly during periods of heightened unrest, house demolitions are common on 'security' grounds or as collective punishment where a link, often tenuous, is made between the building and an attack. Since 2002, the Israeli authorities have also used the absence of valid permits to destroy many properties during the construction of the Separation Wall.

This systematic transfer of land from Palestinians to settlers is racially discriminatory in intent and effect because all settlers in the OPT, although usually referenced as 'Israeli', are Jewish. An exclusively Jewish demography in the settlements is secured partly through internal rules developed by the settlement movements and partly through their planning by Jewish-national institutions, whose bylaws and 'Covenant' require that their funds and services benefit only Jews, yet which operate as 'authorised agencies' of the State (as discussed earlier).[658] The body that approves settlement construction, the Joint Settlement Committee – jointly composed by the Jewish Agency and World Zionist Organisation – is comprised of an equal number of relevant Israeli ministers and executive members of the WZO. The Ministry of Agriculture funds the WZO's Settlement Division and, until 1993, it was assisted by staff members from the JA's Settlement Department.[659] A discrete legal sphere for Jewish settlers in the OPT is then secured through the dual legal system, as described in Chapter 3.

## ARTICLE 2(e) – EXPLOITATION OF THE LABOUR OF THE MEMBERS OF A RACIAL GROUP

### Interpretation

Almost all international human rights instruments prohibit slavery, servitude and forced labour.[660] The ILO Convention Concerning Forced Labour (1930) defines 'forced or compulsory labour' as 'all work or service which is extracted from any person under the menace of any penalty and for which the said person has not offered himself voluntarily'.[661] Exploitation is a broader term that can embrace conditions of extreme worker vulnerability, in which people are under-compensated for their work yet have no effective means of redressing poor wages or conditions.

### Practices in apartheid South Africa

The apartheid economy relied on the exploitation of black African and coloured labour. A complex of apartheid laws ensured that white-owned industries, businesses had access to effectively unlimited sources of artificially cheap labour and that white workers faced no competition from black workers. The result was a 'daunting legal complex' establishing far-reaching controls over Bantu, coloured and Indian employment, housing, access to land and citizenship rights.[662] For example, the Bantu Laws Amendment Act of 1970 reserved white-collar and skilled manual labour exclusively to white people and confined employment opportunities of blacks to the lowest wage sectors.[663] The Pass Laws confined black people's residence to segregated townships (or the Homelands/Bantustans) while securing their availability as low-wage workers to white-owned industries.[664] To prevent migrant black workers from establishing viable communities outside their designated group area, men working in the mines were forced to live in segregated all-male communities far from their families, who remained in the Bantustans or the townships.[665] Women remained with their children in Homelands or in townships where the only source of wage labour was domestic service in white areas.[666]

All black labourers working outside the Black Homelands were designated as migrants. Migrant labourers were not in a position to bargain within the workplace and lacked any trade union representation. One high official in the apartheid government described the migrant labour system as integral to the economic structure of apartheid: 'This is, in fact, the entire basis of our policy as far as the white economy is concerned.'[667] The Public Safety Act 3 of 1953 and later the Internal Security Act 74 of 1982 effectively prohibited gatherings among workers that could foment dissent or political organising by trade unions. In 1968, Prime Minister B.J. Vorster said plainly, 'We need *them* to work for *us*, but the fact that they work for us can never entitle them to claim political rights. Not now, nor in the future ... under any circumstances.'[668]

Not until South African workers mobilised effectively through underground associations was workers' representation somewhat enabled through enactment of the Labour Relations Act 51 of 1982. This Act offered workers some rights regarding disputes over dismissals but did not relieve the fundamental inequalities that structured the labour sector. In the 1980s, union-organised mass strikes and demonstrations would ultimately contribute heavily to bringing down the apartheid regime.

### Israeli practices in the OPT

Israel has no legal system of allotting particular jobs to different racial group. Otherwise, control of Palestinian labour has been integral to Israeli occupation policy, in two general phases: first, as a policy to exploit Palestinian labour; later, as a policy to exclude it.

As discussed earlier, after 1967 and until the first *intifada* in 1987, Israeli policy was to suppress Palestinian industry that competed with Israeli industry, partly by restricting exports, denying building permits and business licences, and other measures that increased Palestinian dependency on manual labour inside Israel, such as agricultural work. Through the mid 1980s, over 100,000 Palestinian workers from the OPT crossed daily into Israel. This 'migrant' labour system mirrored some of the labour dynamics associated with South Africa's Group Areas Act, and the Palestinian workforce experienced much of the vulnerability and restrictions that black South African workers experienced under apartheid:

- low and insecure wages;
- lack of union representation;
- often substandard working conditions;
- employment confined to the lowest-wage jobs (called 'black' labour in Israel);
- prohibitions on living in the areas of their employment inside Israel;
- forced by Pass Laws to return nightly to the OPT (or stay over illegally inside Israel).

Since Palestinian workers were subjected to these restrictive conditions solely because they are not Jewish, the system constituted a form of labour exploitation on the basis of race (recalling again the meaning of 'race' under international law, as discussed at the beginning of this chapter).

The first *intifada* raised security obstacles to this system and the flow of cross-border labour was cut to negligible numbers. Concomitantly, the prominent role of black trade unions in forcing the fall of apartheid in South Africa in 1989–90 graphically demonstrated the political risks of mixing populations in a racially divided society. Israeli obstacles to Palestinian employment inside Israel, originally erected as temporary security measures, were accordingly made permanent. Since 1993, the number of Palestinians from the OPT (excluding East Jerusalem) working in Israel has dropped to a few thousand (Israel sponsored the immigration of other ethnic groups to replace Palestinian workers in 'black' job sectors such as domestic service). For some years after 1993, during closures Palestinian workers could still evade checkpoints and get over or around barriers to pass illegally into Israel. With the construction of the Wall as a continuous barrier around the West Bank, however, the number of workers able to enter Israel during closures has dropped to nearly zero. Since the election of Hamas in January 2006, access by Palestinians in the Gaza Strip to work inside Israel has also dropped to insignificant numbers and now is effectively zero.

As this loss of income has had severe economic effects on the Palestinian economy in both territories, it is a source of great concern to Palestinians and to the PA. Rather than exploiting Palestinian labour for its low wages and vulnerability, Israel has appeared to exploit that very dependency by using access to jobs in Israel as a bargaining chip in negotiations with the PA.[669] Within the OPT, cheap Palestinian labour remains valuable to Israel regarding construction work on the settlements.

## ARTICLE 2(f) – PERSECUTION OF ORGANISATIONS AND PERSONS, BY DEPRIVING THEM OF FUNDAMENTAL RIGHTS AND FREEDOMS, BECAUSE THEY OPPOSE APARTHEID

### Interpretation

Article 2(f) raises difficulties for analysing Israeli practices in two ways. First, the provision could be read as tautological: almost all the practices discussed in earlier sections of this chapter can be interpreted as measures to persecute people who 'oppose apartheid', but only if a regime of apartheid has been identified as such, a legal fact that is established partly by identifying such practices. This seemingly circular logic is resolved here by assuming that the core of the definition resides in the opening paragraph of Article 2, such that specific 'inhuman acts' are only indicative or illustrative of a deliberate system of racial domination. Thus Article 2(f) can be tested by submitting to a second examination all the practices already reviewed, to see if their larger purpose is to defend the system itself from criticism and dissent.

Second, because apartheid is a system of domination run by and fused with State institutions, it is not entirely specious to argue that opposition to apartheid equates with sedition. This raises a quandary because, while international law has held that all resistance to colonialism and apartheid consistent with international law is legitimate, any State would view armed struggle directed at its institutions as seditious. Denouncing the anti-apartheid movement as illegitimate on grounds of sedition was indeed a common ploy of the apartheid government in South Africa and might be expected of any apartheid government. As an argument, this position is clearly legally untenable: a State loses its legitimacy when it adopts apartheid as a mode of governance and therefore its legal standing to affirm and defend its own survival. Nonetheless, the legal and moral ground regarding sedition may sometimes be more murky – illustrated, for example, in controversies about the legitimacy of armed struggle. Whether Palestinian armed struggle is a legitimate form of opposition to a regime of apartheid – at least, where such struggle does not involve terrorism – is a highly sensitive political argument and possibly an important question here.

This study did not broach this thorny question, however, in testing for this category of inhuman acts. The approach here is deliberately conservative in focusing on State policies that target peaceful political dissent by depriving people of fundamental rights and freedoms.

### Practices in apartheid South Africa

The TRC found that 'in the period 1960–94, virtually all opposition to apartheid was labelled "communist" in its (overwhelmingly negative) "Cold War" sense'. The so-called 'total onslaught' of Soviet-led world communism was supposedly directed toward overthrowing the South African government, not eliminating apartheid.[670] Extra-parliamentary, and particularly black, opposition was treated as illegitimate on this basis, and individuals associated with such opposition were effectively criminalised.[671]

The apartheid government's efforts to suppress resistance to apartheid extended to a broad counter-insurgency strategy, sometimes called the 'total strategy'. The TRC found that this approach reshaped the regime's entire approach to the resistance movement:

> Thus counter-insurgency thinking was turned not only on a foreign but on a domestic civilian population. Increasingly, gross violations [of human rights] were attributed to those responsible for public order policing, among them the riot police and later the [South African Defence Force] ... This trend intensified from the mid-1980s, as the rationale of counter-revolutionary warfare took hold within dominant quarters of the security establishment.[672]

State repression of opposition to apartheid included arrests and torture as well as more sweeping measures to silence and punish dissent. In the early 1960s, the government banned the ANC and PAC, which were forced underground. In following decades, the apartheid government targeted both armed and nonviolent opposition to apartheid. The armed struggle was suppressed through broad definitions of outlawed conduct, including 'communism,' which was defined widely enough to include any doctrine or ideology considered undesirable by the state. 'Listed persons' could not be quoted in the media. The *Government Gazette* detailed weekly inventories of publications (national and international) that were banned under the Publications Control Act for their political content.

National leaders and activists of the ANC were also targeted for extrajudicial persecution by the State police, through harassment, beatings and killings: for example, beating some leaders to death (such as Black Consciousness leader Steve Biko), maiming others in letter bombs (such as lawyer Albie Sachs) or eliminating prominent activists by assassination (such as Communist Party and Umkhonto wa Sizwe leader Chris Hani). Such measures eliminated or terrorised many prominent anti-apartheid activists.

### Israeli practices in the OPT

In the OPT, security for the State of Israel is conflated with the security of State institutions that fund, enforce and implement the system of domination over Palestinians. As described at length in earlier sections, the State of Israel is directly responsible for all policies and practices in the OPT that violate the rights of the Palestinian population under international law. These policies and practices are defended by Israeli State spokespeople as necessary to preserving Israel as a Jewish State. Consequently, all Palestinian resistance to Israel's occupation, or to any specific policy associated with it, is seen and treated as part of a comprehensive threat (subsumed under the umbrella term 'terrorism') to Israel's security as a Jewish State. As did the apartheid regime in South Africa, in facing the perceived 'total onslaught' against apartheid, Israel's response to this threat has been to criminalise peaceful protest as well as armed struggle and actual acts of terrorism.[673]

As noted in earlier discussions of Article 2(a) and (c), Palestinian political leaders and activists are subject to arrest and arbitrary detention because of their political views and membership of political parties. By the end of March 2009, 45 members of the PLC – over one-third of the democratically elected Parliament – were imprisoned in Israeli jails. The majority were convicted only of membership of political parties designated as illegal by Israel; eight were administratively detained without charge or trial.

As discussed earlier regarding Article 2(c), practices relevant to 2(f) include denying rights to freedom of expression and opinion, peaceful assembly and association, including the targeting and closure of charitable, educational and cultural organisations suspected of association with banned political parties; arrests and restrictions imposed on human rights activists; and widespread arrests and excessive use of force against Palestinian individuals and civil society organisations demonstrating against the Wall and the discriminatory administration of land, water and infrastructure in the OPT. From all these practices, it can be concluded that Israel is engaged in persecuting Palestinians who oppose the larger system of forced segregation and domination on the basis of race – that is, apartheid.

Since its formation in 2009, Benjamin Netanyahu's coalition government has also pursued legislative measures that would entrench discriminatory measures against the Palestinian citizens of Israel.[674] As these measures are concerned with protecting the institutions and policies that underpin Israel's constitution as a Jewish State (that privileges Jewish nationals), such measures are relevant to the regime of domination over the Palestinians, including in the OPT. Notably, the 2011 Law Preventing Harm to the State of Israel by Means of Boycott legislation makes it a civil wrong to call for a boycott against the State of Israel.[675] This applies to boycotts imposed on actors due to their association with the State of Israel, one of its institutions, or an area under its control,[676] including the OPT, thus encompassing boycotts of items produced in illegal Israeli settlements in the West Bank. The legislation is a clear attack on non-violent resistance to Israeli domination over Palestinians.

CONCLUSION

The analysis in this chapter aimed to answer two legal questions: (1) whether the terms of the definition of apartheid in the Apartheid Convention, regarding racial discrimination and domination, apply to Israel's practices regarding Palestinians in the OPT; and (2) whether Israel's practices in the OPT fit the list of 'inhuman acts' listed in the Convention and considered to signify a breach of the prohibition of apartheid. On the basis of the evidence presented, this study concludes that Israel has introduced a system of apartheid in the OPT,[677] in violation of a peremptory norm of international law.

Whether groups involved in a conflict are racial groups, in terms of international law, is fundamental to determining whether a governing system has assumed the legal aspect of apartheid. Since neither Jews nor Palestinians are normally called 'races' today, this question required probing the meaning of 'race' and 'racial discrimination' in international law. Several legal sources taken together – the broad definition of 'racial discrimination' in ICERD, jurisprudence of the *ad hoc* international criminal tribunals on the interpretation of 'racial group', and mutual perceptions and self-perceptions of Jewish identity and Palestinian identity – indicate that the term 'race' is legally inclusive of Jewish and Palestinian group identities as, in the local setting, they are perceived as being immutable. Thus Israeli Jews and Palestinian Arabs should be considered 'racial groups' for the purposes of the Convention's definition of apartheid.

The purpose of domination is also fundamental to the Convention's definition of apartheid. Israel's status as a 'Jewish State' is inscribed in its Basic Law, and it has developed legal and institutional mechanisms by which the State ensures its enduring Jewish 'character'. These mechanisms are channelled through numerous legal and policy instruments into the OPT to convey privileges to Jewish settlers and systematically disadvantage Palestinians. This domination is associated principally with transferring control over land in the OPT to exclusively Jewish use, altering the demographic character of the territory and conveying superior rights, freedoms and access to resources to Jewish settlers. This discriminatory treatment cannot be explained or excused on grounds of citizenship because certain provisions in Israeli civil and military law provide that Jews present in the OPT who are not citizens of Israel also enjoy privileges conferred on Jewish Israeli citizens in the OPT. Thus Israel's policies are found to reflect the larger purpose of maintaining domination by Israeli Jews over Palestinian non-Jews in the same territory, and so fit the Convention's definition of apartheid.

The 'inhuman acts' described in Article 2 of the Apartheid Convention are intended by the drafters as illustrative, not as exhaustive or exclusive. A positive finding of apartheid need not establish that all practices cited in

Article 2 are present, or that precisely those listed practices are present, but rather that 'policies and practices of racial segregation and discrimination' form a comprehensive system that has not only the effect but the purpose of maintaining racial domination by one racial group over the other. Summarising this report's discussion of the relevant practices with Article 2 of the Apartheid Convention as the guiding framework, the report has found the following:

- Article 2(a) regarding denial of the right to life and liberty of person is satisfied by Israeli measures serving to repress Palestinian dissent against the occupation and its system of domination. Israel's policies and practices include murder, in the form of targeted extrajudicial killings; torture and other cruel, inhuman or degrading treatment or punishment of detainees; a military court system that falls far short of international standards for fair trial; and arbitrary arrest and detention of Palestinians, including administrative detention imposed without charge or trial and lacking adequate judicial review. Palestinians are subject to different legal systems and different courts, which apply different standards of evidence and procedure that result in harsher penalties than those applied to Jewish Israelis.
- Article 2(b) regarding 'the deliberate imposition on a racial group or groups of living conditions calculated to cause its or their physical destruction in whole or in part' is not satisfied, as Israel's policies and practices in the OPT are not found to have the intent of causing the physical destruction of the Palestinian people. Policies of collective punishment that entail grave consequences for life and health – such as closures imposed on the Gaza Strip that limit or block Palestinian access to essential health care and medicine, fuel, and adequate nutrition, and Israeli military attacks that inflict high civilian casualties – are serious violations of international humanitarian and human rights law but do not meet the threshold required by this provision, which reflects the language of the Genocide Convention.
- Article 2(c) regarding measures calculated to prevent a racial group from participation in the political, social, economic and cultural life of the country and to prevent the full development of a group through the denial of basic human rights and freedoms is satisfied on a number of counts:
    - Restrictions on Palestinians' right to freedom of movement are endemic, including Israel's control of the OPT border crossings, extensive impediments to travel and access raised by the Wall, the matrix of checkpoints and separate roads within the West Bank, and the obstructive and all-encompassing permit and ID card systems.
    - Palestinian freedom of residence is severely curtailed by systematic administrative restrictions on both residency and building in East Jerusalem, by discriminatory legislation that operates to prevent Palestinian spouses from living together on the basis of which part

of the OPT they originate from, and by the strictures of the permit and ID systems.
- Palestinians are systematically denied enjoyment of their right to leave and return to their country. Palestinian refugees now living in the OPT (approximately 1.8 million people) are not allowed to return to their homes, while Palestinian refugees outside Israel and the OPT (approximately 4.5 million) are not allowed to return to either territory. Similarly, hundreds of thousands of Palestinians displaced from the West Bank and Gaza Strip in 1967 have been prevented from returning to the OPT. Many Palestinian residents of the OPT must obtain Israeli permission to leave the territory (which is often denied), political activists and human rights defenders are often subject to arbitrary and undefined 'travel bans', while many Palestinians who travelled abroad for business or personal reasons have had their residence IDs revoked and been prohibited from returning.
- Palestinians are denied their right to a nationality in two ways. Israel denies Palestinian refugees now living in the OPT who fled homes inside the Green Line the right to return, reside and obtain citizenship in the successor State (Israel) now governing the land of their birth. Israel also effectively denies Palestinians their right to a nationality by obstructing the exercise of the Palestinian right to self-determination and preventing the formation of an independent Palestinian State in the West Bank (including East Jerusalem) and the Gaza Strip.
- Palestinians are restricted in their right to work through Israeli policies that severely curtail Palestinian agriculture and industry in the OPT, restrict exports and imports, and obstruct internal movement by Palestinians, including by impairing their access to their own agricultural land and travel for employment and business. Although formerly significant, Palestinian access to work inside Israel has been curtailed in recent years by prevailing closure policies and is now negligible. Palestinian unemployment in the OPT as a whole has reached almost 50 per cent.
- Palestinian trade unions exist but are not recognised by the Israeli government or by the Histadrut (the largest Israeli trade union) and cannot effectively represent Palestinians working for Israeli employers and businesses. Palestinian unions are also prohibited from functioning in Israeli settlements. Although they are required to pay dues, the interests and concerns of Palestinian workers are not represented by the Histadrut, and Palestinians have no voice in Histadrut policies.
- Palestinians' right to education is not impacted directly by Israeli policy, as Israel does not operate the school system in the OPT, but is severely impeded by military rule. Israeli military actions have included extensive school closures, direct attacks on schools, severe

restrictions on movement, and arrests and detention of teachers and students. Israel's denial of exit permits, particularly for Palestinians from the Gaza Strip, has prevented thousands of students from continuing their education abroad. Discrimination in relation to education is striking in East Jerusalem, and is further indicated by a parallel Jewish Israeli school system in illegal settlements throughout the West Bank, supported by the Israeli government.

- Palestinians are denied the right to freedom of opinion and expression through censorship laws enforced by the military authorities and endorsed by the Supreme Court. Palestinian newspapers must have a military permit and publications must be pre-approved by the military censor. Since 2001, the Israeli GPO has drastically limited Palestinian press accreditation. Journalists are regularly restricted from entering the Gaza Strip and Palestinian journalists suffer from patterns of harassment, detention, confiscation of materials, and even killing.
- Palestinians' right to freedom of peaceful assembly and association is impeded through military orders that ban public gatherings of ten or more persons without a permit from the Israeli military commander. Non-violent demonstrations are regularly suppressed by the Israeli army with live ammunition, tear gas and arrests. Most Palestinian political parties have been declared illegal and institutions associated with those parties, such as charities and cultural organisations, are regularly subjected to closure and attack.
- Taken together, the violations in this section systematically prevent the Palestinians from participating in the political, economic, social and cultural life of their country. This is starkly demonstrated by the cumulative effects of Israel's ongoing siege of the Gaza Strip.

- Article 2(d), relating to division of the population along racial lines, is satisfied in the following ways:
  - Israeli policies have divided the OPT into a series of reserves into which Palestinians are effectively confined. Israel has forcibly segregated the population of the West Bank by creating zones for exclusively Jewish use, to which Palestinian entry is prohibited without a permit, and by banning Israeli travel into Palestinian zones. The Wall and its infrastructure of gates and permanent checkpoints suggest Israel's intention to reify this segregation as a system of permanent cantons, in which residence and entrance or exit will be determined by racial identities. A deliberate State policy of racial discrimination is indicated further by the role of Israeli government ministries, as well as the WZO and other Jewish-national institutions operating in partnership as authorised agencies of the State, in planning, funding and implementing construction of the West Bank settlements and their infrastructure for exclusively Jewish use.

- Israeli law does not formally prohibit mixed marriages between Jews and Palestinians, but the proscription of civil marriage in Israeli law and the authority of religious courts in matters of marriage and divorce, coupled with restrictions on where Jews and Palestinians can live in the OPT, present major practical obstacles to any potential mixed marriage.
- Israel has extensively appropriated Palestinian land in the OPT for exclusively Jewish use. Private Palestinian land comprises about 30 per cent of the land unlawfully appropriated for Jewish settlement in the West Bank. Presently, approximately 40 per cent of the West Bank is completely closed to Palestinian use, with significant restrictions on access to much of the rest of it.

- Article 2(e) relating to exploitation of labour is today not significantly satisfied, as Israel has raised barriers to Palestinian employment inside Israel since the 1990s and Palestinian labour is now used extensively only in the construction and services sectors of Jewish Israeli settlements in the OPT. Otherwise, exploitation of labour has been replaced by practices that fall under Article 2(c) regarding the denial of the right to work. Arrest, imprisonment, travel bans and the targeting of Palestinian parliamentarians, national political leaders and human rights defenders, as well as the closing down of related organisations by Israel, represent persecution for opposition to the system of Israeli domination in the OPT, within the meaning of Article 2(f).

Thus Israel is found to be implementing and sustaining policies 'for the purpose of establishing and maintaining domination' over Palestinians in the OPT and to suppress opposition to those policies.

Finally, we found in this study that some common features emerged, forming patterns within the complex of policies and practices being imposed by Israel. The comparative analyses of South African apartheid practices threaded throughout this chapter are there to illuminate, rather than define, the meaning of apartheid, and there are certainly differences between apartheid as it was applied in South Africa and Israel's policies and practices in the OPT. Still, we found that the two systems shared some dominant features.

The key legislative foundations underpinning the South African apartheid regime – especially, the troika of the Population Registration Act, Group Areas Act, and Pass Laws[678] – laid the foundations for apartheid. The first of these laws provided the first pillar: it allowed the regime to categorise the entire population of the country along racial lines, which then enabled the government to impose a pervasive system of racial discrimination and prevent non-white South Africans from enjoying basic human rights and freedoms. The second pillar (called 'Grand Apartheid' by its South African architects) was to segregate people on the basis of their ascribed identities into assigned geographic areas and restrict passage by members of any group into areas allocated to other groups, in order to limit contact between groups that might ultimately compromise white supremacy. The third pillar was the matrix of draconian 'security' laws and policies that was employed to suppress any opposition to apartheid: administrative detention, torture, censorship, banning, extrajudicial killing and other violations of fundamental human and civil rights.

The analysis in this chapter demonstrates that Israel's practices in the OPT can be defined by the same three 'pillars' of apartheid. The first pillar derives from how Jewish identity is codified in Israeli law, with the effect and purpose of extending preferential status and privileges to Jewish settlers in the OPT on the basis of their Jewish identity and accord Palestinians an inferior status. The review of Israel's practices under Article 2(c) of the Apartheid Convention provides abundant evidence of such discrimination in realms such as freedom of movement and residence and the right to leave and return to one's country. The 2003 Citizenship and Entry into Israel Law banning family unification, the application of Israeli civil law to Jewish settlers in the OPT who are not Israeli citizens on grounds of their Jewish identity, and the denial of the Palestinian right to nationality through the 1950 Law of Return and 1952 Citizenship Law are particularly egregious examples of legislation that confers preferential benefits to Jews and adversely impacts people identified as Palestinian Arabs. The inferior status of Palestinians is further highlighted through the harsher laws and different courts and court procedures for Palestinians in the OPT.

The second pillar is Israel's 'Grand Apartheid' policy to segregate the Jewish and Palestinian populations into different geographic areas. This strategy is evidenced by the State's policy to shrink the territorial space available to Palestinians; hermetically close and isolate the Gaza Strip from the rest of the OPT; sever East Jerusalem from the rest of the West Bank; and carve the West Bank into an intricate and well-serviced network of connected settlements for Jewish-Israelis and an archipelago of besieged and non-contiguous enclaves for Palestinians. That these measures are intended to segregate the population along racial lines is clear from how the visible barriers are coupled to permit and ID systems, comparable to South Africa's Pass Laws. In combination, this system ensures that Palestinians remain confined to the reserves designated for them while Israeli Jews are prohibited from entering those reserves but enjoy freedom of movement throughout the rest of the OPT. Much as the same restrictions functioned in apartheid South Africa, this policy has the effect of crushing Palestinian socio-economic life, securing Palestinian vulnerability to Israeli economic dominance, and enforcing the rigid segregation of Palestinian and Jewish populations in the territory.

The third pillar of Israel's apartheid system in the OPT is expressed by its 'security' laws and policies. Extrajudicial killing, torture and cruel, inhuman or degrading treatment and arbitrary arrest and imprisonment of Palestinians – all mirroring practices in South Africa and listed as 'inhuman acts' in the Apartheid Convention – are all practised by Israel and justified, as they were in apartheid South Africa, on the pretext of security. These policies are State-sanctioned, frequently formally approved by the Israeli judicial system, and supported by an oppressive code of military laws and a system of improperly constituted military courts. This study finds that Israel's invocation of 'security' to validate sweeping restrictions on Palestinian freedom of opinion, expression, assembly, association and movement cannot be credited. Rather, these restrictions indicate a deliberate policy to suppress dissent and maintain domination over Palestinians as a group.

Thus Israel, claiming to act for the 'Jewish people' as a group, employs a cluster of methods to dominate Palestinians as a group and systematically oppress them: that is, subject the Palestinian population of the OPT to a regime of apartheid. The grave legal consequences of this conclusion – for Israel, for the Palestinians, for third States, and for international organisations – are addressed in the next chapter.

# 5
# Conclusion – Legal Implications

SUMMARY FINDINGS

Both colonialism and apartheid are prohibited by international law. This study has found that Israel has violated, and continues to violate, both prohibitions in the occupied Palestinian territories. If the conclusions drawn here are confirmed by an authoritative body – for example, by the International Court of Justice (ICJ) through an advisory opinion – then the legal consequences for Israel, the Palestinians and third-party states would be far-reaching.

A careful review of Israel's practices in light of the prohibition on colonialism has found that Israel is implementing colonial practices by denying the Palestinians their right to self-determination – that is, their right freely to determine their political status and pursue their own economic, social and cultural development. The territorial integrity of the occupied Palestinian territories, a central concern of the Declaration on Colonialism, is being violated through Israel's claim to have annexed East Jerusalem permanently and through Jewish settlements that partition the West Bank into cantons, suggesting a policy of permanent fragmentation and annexation. The separation between Israel's economy and infrastructure and that of the occupied Palestinian territories has been obliterated by Israel's extension of its own legal system into the Occupied Palestinian Territories (OPT) and by the customs union and other measures that have fused the two economies. Israel has also violated the Palestinians' right to permanent sovereignty over their natural resources, through the State's discriminatory appropriation of land and water resources. All these policies are unlawful and, taken together, indicate a deliberate policy by Israel to colonise and annex the OPT.

Israel has also introduced a system of apartheid in the OPT. International law defines apartheid not as isolated acts but as a *system*, designed to establish and maintain the domination of one racial group over another. Further, the precedent of international condemnation of South Africa's practices in South West Africa (Namibia) demonstrates that a State may breach the prohibition of apartheid in territory that lies beyond its borders but under its jurisdiction. In the OPT, which are under Israel's jurisdiction, Israeli state policy has constructed Jewish and Palestinian identities in ways that function effectively as racial identities in the sense provided by the International Convention on the Elimination of All Forms of Racial Discrimination (ICERD), the Apartheid Convention, and the International Criminal Tribunals for Rwanda (ICTR) and the Former Yugoslavia (ICTY). Israel's domestic laws and institutions are then channelled into the OPT to convey special rights and privileges to Jewish settlers while denying fundamental rights and freedoms to Palestinians.

Domination over Palestinians is associated principally with transferring control over land in the OPT to exclusively Jewish use; forcibly dividing the population of the territory into discrete Jewish and Palestinian enclaves; restricting movement between these zones on discriminatory grounds; and disadvantaging Palestinians in all areas of economic, social and political life. This discriminatory treatment cannot be justified or excused on grounds of citizenship: it is implemented on the basis of identities that are perceived in the local setting as immutable. Consequently, this study finds that the Israel's system of ensuring domination by Jews over Palestinians constitutes a breach of the prohibition of apartheid.

Israel's breaching the international legal prohibitions of apartheid and colonialism in the OPT would render the occupation itself is illegal on these grounds. This does not preclude assessments that Israel's occupation may also be unlawful on other grounds. The Palestinian territories remain occupied: Israel's duty to comply with international humanitarian law remains undiminished, and States parties to the Fourth Geneva Convention are obliged to ensure that Israel fulfils that duty.[1] A finding of colonialism and apartheid does impose new duties and responsibilities on the entire international community, however, because ensuring that a State desists from policies of colonialism and apartheid is an obligation *erga omnes*. What legal consequences of this finding arise for other States and competent intergovernmental organisations?

Confronting South Africa's illegal occupation of Namibia, the United Nations (UN) General Assembly found that South Africa was 'under obligation to withdraw its administration from Namibia immediately and thus put an end to its occupation of the Territory'.[2] Finding that Israel is breaching the international legal prohibition on apartheid and colonialism suggests that similar legal consequences may result.

## CRIMINAL RESPONSIBILITY OF INDIVIDUALS AND STATES

As was stated at the outset, this study does not consider whether certain individuals might bear criminal responsibility for acts of apartheid and colonialism. Nor does it consider possible criminality or liabilities that private non-State actors – such as Israeli corporations – might bear as a consequence of their involvement in colonialism or apartheid. Rather, this study has focused on the question of State responsibility. The International Law Commission (ILC) has provided for State criminal responsibility in its 2001 Draft Articles of State Responsibility,[3] giving examples of 'colonial domination' and apartheid. The ILC ultimately dropped the notion of State criminal responsibility from its Articles, due to opposition to the inclusion of this concept by some States,[4] opting instead for a special regime regulating serious violations of peremptory norms without involving State criminal responsibility.[5] Nevertheless, excising State criminal responsibility from the Articles was not intended to indicate, as a matter of law, that this category of crimes does not exist.[6] After this substitution had been made, Japan commented that 'the text ... is still haunted by the ghost of "international crime"'. Indeed, serious breaches of peremptory norms and the discarded notion of 'State crimes' arguably refer to the same thing. (Eric Wyler, for example, has termed them 'the twin brothers of horror'.[7])

The ILC stipulated in the 2001 Articles that States are responsible for the actions of its official organs or any others who acted under the direction, instigation or control of those organs. This general rule embraces the conduct of the State of Israel, whose ministries and authorised agencies are principally responsible for imposing regimes of apartheid and colonialism in the OPT. Under the UN Charter and numerous human rights treaties, all member States are obliged to promote 'universal respect for, and observance of human rights and fundamental freedoms for all without distinction as to race, sex, language or religion'.[8] But the legal consequences arising from an internationally wrongful act are not uniform: Israel bears the greatest responsibility for remedying the illegal situation it has created.

Among the more obvious responsibilities that Israel bears as the violating State are reparations. The UN has paid particular attention to the issue of reparations, through work by a series of Special Rapporteurs[9] that developed into the Basic Principles and Guidelines on the Right to a Remedy and Reparation for Victims of Gross Violations of International Human Rights Law and Serious Violations of International Humanitarian Law, adopted by the UN General Assembly on 16 December 2005.[10] According to the Basic Principles, where a State has violated internationally recognised human rights, it is responsible for making just and adequate reparation to all persons within its jurisdiction.[11] Reparation should respond to the needs and wishes of the victims, be proportionate to the gravity of the violation and the resulting harm, and include restitution, compensation, rehabilitation, satisfaction and guarantees of non-repetition of the offence. Collective reparations are due to groups of victims and special measures should be taken to afford opportunities for self-development and advancement to groups which, as a result of human rights violations, have been denied such opportunities.[12]

## RESPONSIBILITY OF THIRD-PARTY STATES

The prohibitions concerning colonialism and apartheid are peremptory norms; all States have a legitimate interest that they be observed and legal obligations if they are breached. When the ILC dropped the notion of State criminal responsibility from its 2001 Articles, it still accepted that violations of peremptory norms were of particular concern to the international community as a whole.[13] Hence Article 40 of the ILC's 2001 Articles provides:

1. This Chapter applies to the international responsibility which is entailed by a serious breach by a State of an obligation arising under a peremptory norm of general international law.
2. A breach of such an obligation is serious if it involves a gross or systematic failure by the responsible State to fulfil the obligation.

The consequences of a serious breach are multilateral and imposed on all States, not just for States directly injured by the internationally wrongful act of another State,[14] as Article 41 spells out:

1. States shall cooperate to bring to an end through lawful means any serious breach within the meaning of Article 40.
2. No State shall recognise as lawful a situation created by a serious breach within the meaning of Article 40, nor render aid or assistance in maintaining that situation ...

Although these two articles have not been fully developed, academic research has supported their customary status,[15] the ICJ's ruling in the *Wall* advisory opinion echoes their terms[16] and both have been affirmed by domestic supreme courts.[17] For example, the German Federal Constitutional Court referred implicitly to Article 40 in a 2004 decision, stating:

Article 40 (2) of the International Law Commission articles on the responsibility of States contains the definition of a serious violation of ius cogens and obliges the community of States to cooperate in order to terminate the violation using the means of international law. In addition, a duty is imposed on States not to recognize a situation created in violation of ius cogens.[18]

The particular concern in these articles is with legal consequences arising from systematic and gross violations of international law, as the ILC observed:

To be regarded as systematic, a violation would have to be carried out in an organised and deliberate way. In contrast, the term 'gross' refers to the intensity of the violation or its effects; it denotes violations of a flagrant nature, amounting to a direct and outright assault on the values protected by the rule. The terms are not of course mutually exclusive; serious breaches will usually be both systematic and gross. Factors which may establish the seriousness of a violation would include the intent to violate the norm; the scope and number of individual violations, and the gravity of their consequences for the victims.[19]

By its nature and definition in the Apartheid Convention, apartheid is a 'systematic failure' to observe an international obligation, within the terms of Article 40(2). It does not lie in isolated acts of racial discrimination, but is constituted by a systematic programme undertaken by one racial group to dominate and oppress any other. Sustained over decades, and implemented through comprehensive and systematic practices, it is also a gross violation.

As this report has demonstrated, Israel's colonial practices in breach of Palestinian self-determination are equally as systematic. Its settlements policy is not a series of isolated acts but a concerted enterprise, implemented by consolidating settlements into contiguous blocs connected by a highway network and segregated from Palestinian zones by the Wall. Coupled with Israel's discriminatory appropriation of land and water, which violates the principle of permanent sovereignty over natural resources, Israel has effected the integration of the Palestinian economy and infrastructure into that of Israel and so targeted Palestinian self-determination in 'an organised and deliberate way'. Thus Israel's practices meet the threshold set by the ILC for the application of Article 40.

The consequences for third States that arise from these breaches are clear: they must cooperate to bring these violations to an end, and must not recognise as lawful the situation created by these violations, or render aid or assistance in maintaining that situation. This last consequence is also dictated by Article 16 of the ILC's Articles, which provides that:

> A State which aids or assists another State in the commission of an internationally wrongful act by the latter is internationally responsible for doing so if: (a) that State does so with knowledge of the circumstances of the internationally wrongful act; and (b) the act would be internationally wrongful if committed by that State.

Faced with a serious breach of peremptory norms – in this case, Israel's introduction of apartheid and colonial regimes within the OPT – Article 41 imposes two broad and distinct obligations on all States, 'whether or not they are individually affected by the serious breach':[20] namely, the duty to *cooperate* and the duty to *abstain*.

The duty to *cooperate* is a 'positive duty': that is, a duty to act, by cooperating to end serious breaches of a peremptory norm, such as the prohibition of apartheid.[21] The ILC considered that such cooperation would normally be taken within the framework of international organisations, but did not specify just what measures might be required. Presumably, the choice of appropriate measures would depend on the particular situation. In any case, measures must be lawful and constitute 'a joint and coordinated effort by all States to counteract the effects of these breaches'.[22]

The duty of *abstention* includes two elements. First, States must not recognise as lawful any situations created by serious breaches of peremptory norms. This obligation has been explicitly associated by the ILC with an 'attempted acquisition of sovereignty over territory through the denial of the right of self-determination'.[23] In relation to Israel's colonial practices in the occupied Palestinian territories, this principle mandates minimally that all States refuse to recognise Israel's purported annexation of East Jerusalem or any areas of the West Bank on which settlements have been constructed, including 'seam' areas between the Green (Armistice) Line and the Wall. States should also refrain from locating their embassies in Jerusalem, lest this be interpreted as recognition of Israel's claim to have annexed East Jerusalem,[24] and ensure that the application of treaty relationships with Israel are not extended to the OPT.[25] The duty of non-recognition also clearly requires that States deny Israel title to the natural resources of the OPT.

The second element is the duty not to render aid or assistance in maintaining a serious breach of peremptory norms. This obligation is a logical extension of the duty of non-recognition, but extends to any actions that support the breach: for example, international trade with a State practising apartheid.[26] In relation to South Africa's illegal presence in Namibia, the International Court of Justice ruled that States had a duty 'to abstain from entering into economic and other forms of relationship or dealings with South Africa on behalf of or concerning Namibia which may entrench its authority over the territory'.[27] A more elaborated account of this duty argued that it prohibited:

> [A]ll economic, industrial or financial assistance, in the form of gifts, loans, credit, advances or guarantees, or in any other form. This prohibition is not confined to States. It naturally extends to institutions in which States have voting rights, such as the International Bank for Reconstruction and Development, the International Development Association and the International Finance Corporation.[28]

In the economic realm, the duty of abstention requires all States not to support the economic viability of Israel's colonial and apartheid projects in the OPT. For example, the obligation not to recognise Israel's unlawful title over Palestinians' natural resources suggests that trade in these resources should not be conducted, either in primary or processed form. This general duty extends to international and regional organisations whose activities are determined or controlled by their member States, such as the European Union. Should a State fail these duties to abstain, then it can become complicit in Israel's internationally wrongful act.

Thus the law is clear. Faced with Israel's breach of the prohibitions of colonialism and apartheid, all States must cooperate to bring Israel's apartheid and colonial practices to an end and must not aid or support Israel in maintaining them. If a State fails to fulfil these twin duties, axiomatically it commits an internationally wrongful act, becoming complicit in the commission of apartheid and colonialism.

## RESPONSIBILITY OF INTERNATIONAL ORGANISATIONS

The peremptory prohibitions on apartheid and colonialism bind not only States but also, by extension, the intergovernmental organisations to which they belong. but international organisations themselves can be considered capable of committing internationally wrongful acts that constitute serious breaches of peremptory norms of international law: for example, by failing to act to prevent genocide.[29] Gaja's conclusion reflects established international doctrine. For example, in an early phase of the ICTY, Judge *ad hoc* Lauterpacht ruled that the UN Security Council could not lawfully adopt a resolution which breached a peremptory norm and, if it did so, that act would be 'void and legally ineffective'.[30]

In the *Wall* advisory opinion, the ICJ specifically recalled that, according to resolutions of the General Assembly:

> Every State has the duty to promote, through joint and separate action, realization of the principle of equal rights and self-determination of peoples, in accordance with the provisions of the Charter, and to render assistance to the United Nations in carrying out the responsibilities entrusted to it by the Charter regarding the implementation of the principle.[31]

The Court also underlined that the General Assembly should encourage efforts aimed at reaching a negotiated solution to the Israel–Palestine conflict which would lead to the creation of a Palestinian State,[32] and that both General Assembly and the Security Council should consider what further action was required to bring an end to the illegal situation resulting from the construction of the Wall.[33]

Failure by the United Nations to combat apartheid when it is in a position to do so is therefore no different from a failure to prevent genocide. In both cases, the UN would be failing to act to discharge peremptory obligations which are incumbent on all its member States, as well as on itself. While the duty of States to cooperate to bring an end to serious breaches of peremptory norms of international law does not necessarily imply that such cooperation should take place within the UN,[34] this is a duty which the principal political organs of the UN should also discharge, as the ICJ indicated.[35] As both norms prohibiting apartheid and colonialism have peremptory status, a failure to act to end such regimes amounts to a serious breach of international law by the UN and therefore engages its responsibility to do so.

Similarly, Quartet members may have responsibilities over and above those arising for other States. It is significant in this regard that the UN is the principal global political organisation and is also a member of the Quartet and that the European Union is a member of the Quartet. Other regional organisations, even if not part of the Quartet, would in any event have to consider their response to Israel's apartheid and colonial practices within the rubric of their own competence and responsibility to promote human rights.[36]

Thus the consequences and responsibilities attaching to States and intergovernmental organisations overlap regarding apartheid and colonialism. Possibly, States might best discharge some of their obligations through an organisation to which they belong. However, as demonstrated above, the failure of an organisation to act does not exonerate each member State of its responsibility to do so: they cannot evade their international obligations by hiding behind the independent personality of an international organisation of which they are members.[37]

## CONCLUSION

Under international law, Israel carries the primary responsibility for ending its gross violations of the prohibitions on apartheid and colonialism. A realistic appraisal of politics and power relations surrounding the conflict, including Israel's own domestic politics, supports a conclusion that Israel will not act responsibly to do this without international action that changes the international context in which its government perceives and responds to the State's best interests. Thus a finding that Israel is practicing these unlawful regimes on the Palestinian population brings focus on the responsibility of the international community to fulfil its obligations to cooperate and abstain. All States have legal obligations in relation to the internationally wrongful acts committed by Israel in the OPT and so are legally bound to pursue the following policies:

- not to recognise as lawful the illegal situation created by Israel's practices of colonialism and apartheid in the OPT;
- not to render aid or assistance in maintaining that illegal situation;
- to cooperate with a view to bringing the illegal situation to an end;
- not to be complicit in Israel's internationally wrongful acts by failing to fulfil the above obligations.

Facing the possibility of being held to such serious actions and grave responsibilities, concerned States may wish to call on the UN General Assembly to request the ICJ urgently to render an advisory opinion on the following questions: Do the policies and practices of Israel within the Occupied Palestinian Territories violate the norms prohibiting apartheid and colonialism? If so, what are the legal consequences arising from Israel's policies and practices? If the ICJ concurs with the findings here, then the Israeli-Palestinian conflict will then formally be understood to have obtained a new legal character and the international community will face legal duties that cannot be evaded or lightly set aside.

# Notes

## CHAPTER 1

1. A/HRC/4/17, 29 January 2007, 3, emphasis added.
2. *International status of South West Africa* advisory opinion, 11 July 1950; *Voting procedure on questions relating to reports and petitions concerning the territory of South West Africa* advisory opinion, 7 June 1955; *Admissibility of hearings of petitioners by the Committee on South West Africa* advisory opinion, 1 July 1956; *Legal consequences for States of the continued presence of South Africa in Namibia (South West Africa) notwithstanding Security Council Resolution 276 (1970)* advisory opinion, 21 June 1971. The Court had to formulate its own definition of apartheid because the International Convention on the Suppression and Punishment of the Crime of Apartheid had not yet been finalised.
3. *Legal consequences for States of the continued presence of South Africa in Namibia (South West Africa) notwithstanding Security Council Resolution 276 (1970)* advisory opinion, at para. 131.
4. Ibid., at para. 133.
5. *Legality of the construction of a wall in the occupied Palestinian territory* advisory opinion (hereafter, '*Wall* advisory opinion'), ICJ Rep, 2004, at 136. All documents of the International Court of Justice and the Permanent Court of International Justice cited in this study are available online at www.icj-cij.org.
6. Orna Ben-Naftali, Aeyal M. Gross and Keren Michaeli, 'Illegal occupation: framing the Occupied Palestinian Territory' (2005) 23 *Berkeley Journal of International Law* 551, at 552.
7. Although this study is concerned with the legality of Israel's practices in the OPT, the obligation of an Occupying Power to withdraw from occupied territory is not dependent on a finding of illegality. The UN Security Council has called on Occupying Powers to withdraw from the OPT without declaring their presence illegal: for example, regarding Israel's occupation of the OPT (Security Council Resolution 242 of 22 November 1967 and Security Council Resolution 338 of 22 October 1973), Iraq's occupation of Kuwait (Security Council Resolution 660 of 2 August 1990) and Indonesia's occupation of East Timor (Security Council Resolution 384 of 22 December 1975).
8. For a discussion of the *mens rea* required under the Rome Statute of the International Criminal Court in order that an accused may be convicted of the crime of apartheid see, for example, R.S. Lee (ed.), *The International Criminal Court: Elements of Crimes and Rules of Procedure and Evidence* (Ardsley, NY: Transnational Publishers, 2001), at 105–106. It should be recalled that Israel is not a party to the Statute of the International Criminal Court, and that its practice is therefore only illustrative of the need for *mens rea* in the commission of the crime of apartheid.
9. 1969 Vienna Convention on the Law of Treaties, Article 53.
10. 2001 International Law Commission, Articles on the Responsibility of States for Internationally Wrongful Acts, Article 40: 'This Chapter applies to the international responsibility which is entailed by a serious breach by a State of an obligation arising under a peremptory norm of international law. A breach of such an obligation is serious if it involves a gross or systematic failure by the responsible State to fulfil the obligation.'
11. The 2001 Articles were approved, without vote, by the General Assembly in Resolution 56/83 (12 December 2001), following the recommendation of the International Law Commission that the General Assembly take note of the Articles and subsequently decide whether to convene a diplomatic conference with a view to conclude a convention on State responsibility: see International Law Commission, *Report on the work of its Fifty-Third*

session, UN Doc. A/56/10 (2001), at 38–41 and 42, paras 61–67 and 72–73; and also James Crawford, *The International Law Commission's Articles on State Responsibility: Introduction, Text and Commentaries* (Cambridge: Cambridge University Press, 2002), at 58–60. In 2004, the General Assembly reconsidered this matter, and decided to defer its decision: see J. Crawford and S. Olleson, 'The continuing debate on a UN Convention on State Responsibility' (2005) 54 *International and Comparative Law Quarterly* 959. The General Assembly has since adopted Resolution 62/61 (8 January 2008), UN Doc.A/RES/62/61, in which it, once again, commended the Articles to the attention of States 'without prejudice to the question of their future adoption or other appropriate action' (operative para. 1), and included on the provisional agenda of its sixty-fifth session consideration of whether a convention should be adopted, or other appropriate action be taken, on the basis of the Articles (operative para. 4). See also D. Caron, 'The ILC Articles on State responsibility: the paradoxical relationship between form and authority' (2002) 96 *American Journal of International Law* 857.
12. See Articles 30, 31, 34 and 41 of the International Law Commission's *Articles on the Responsibility of States for Internationally Wrongful Acts*: for commentary, see C. Tams, 'Do serious breaches give rise to any specific obligations of the responsible State?' (2002) 13 *European Journal of International Law* 1161.
13. See *Prosecutor v. Naletilic and Martinovic*, available at: www.un.org/icty/naletilic/trialc/judgement/nal-tj030331-e.pdf, at 73, para. 215. The customary nature of the Hague Regulations was declared by the International Criminal Tribunal at Nuremberg in the *Trial of German Major War Criminals*, Cmd. 6964 (1946) 65. The customary status of the Regulations has since been affirmed by various other courts: see, for example, *In re Krupp* (US Military Tribunal at Nuremberg), 15 *Annual Digest of Public International Law Cases* 620, at 622 (the *Annual Digest* was subsequently retitled *International Law Reports*, which is now the title applied to the series as a whole); *R. v. Finta* (Canadian High Court of Justice), 82 *International Law Reports* 425, at 439; *Affo v. IDF Commander in the West Bank* (Israel Supreme Court), 83 *International Law Reports* 122, at 163; *Polyukhovich v. Commonwealth of Australia* (Australian High Court), 91 *International Law Reports* 1, at 123. See also T. Meron, *Human Rights and Humanitarian Norms as Customary Law* (Oxford: Clarendon Press, 1989), at 38–40.
14. The full title of the 1907 Hague Convention is 'The Hague Convention IV respecting the Laws and Customs of War on Land'.
15. In the *Beth El* case (1978): see *Ayyub v. Minister of Defence* (1978) 33(2) PD 113. An English summary is available in 9 *Israel Yearbook of Human Rights* (1979) 337, and full English translation (as *Oyyeb v. Minister of Defence*) in 2 *Palestine Yearbook of International Law* 134 (1985) where this issue is discussed at 140–142.
16. See Security Council Resolution 237 of 14 June 1967; Security Council Resolution 271 of 15 September 1969; and Security Council Resolution 446 of 22 March 1979. For General Assembly Resolutions, see, for example, General Assembly Resolution 56/60 of 10 December 2001 and General Assembly Resolution 58/97 of 9 December 2003. See also Conference of the High Contracting Parties to the Fourth Geneva Convention: Declaration (5 December 2001), available at: http://domino.un.org/UNISPAL.NSF/fd80 7e46661e3689852570d00069e918/8fc4f064b9be5bad85256c1400722951!OpenDocument.
17. *Prosecutor v. Naletilic and Martinovic*, Case No. IT–98–34–T (2003), at 73, para. 214, available at: www.un.org/icty/naletilic/trialc/judgement/nal-tj030(2003), and www.un.org/icty/naletilic/trialc/judgement/nal-tj030331-e.pdf.
18. See A. McNair and A.D. Watts, *The Legal Effects of War* (Cambridge: Cambridge University Press, 1966), at 377–378; and G. Schwarzenberger, *International Law as Applied by International Courts and Tribunals. Vol. II: The Law of Armed Conflict* (London: Stevens & Sons, 1968), at 324.
19. L. Oppenheim, *International Law: A Treatise. Vol. II: Disputes, War and Neutrality* (London: Longman, 1952), 7th edn by H. Lauterpacht, at 434: see also *Re Lepore*, 13 *Annual Digest of Public International Law Cases* 354 (Supreme Military Tribunal,

Italy: 1946), at 355; *Disability pension case*, 90 *International Law Reports* 400 (Federal Social Court, F.R. Germany: 1985), at 403; and G. von Glahn, *The Occupation of Enemy Territory: A Commentary on the Law and Practice of Belligerent Occupation* (Minneapolis: University of Minnesota Press, 1957), at 28–29. See also below on the notion of effective control of occupied territory.
20. J. Pictet (ed.), *Commentary to Geneva Convention IV Relative to the Protection of Civilian Persons in Time of War* (Geneva: ICRC, 1958), at 59–60. See also G. Mettraux, *International Crimes and the* ad hoc *Tribunals* (Oxford: Oxford University Press, 2005), at 64–71; and International Criminal Tribunal for the former Yugoslavia *Prosecutor* v. *Naletilic and Martinovic*, at 74–75, paras 219–221, available at: www.un.org/icty/naletilic/trialc/judgement/nal-tj030331-e.pdf.
21. Trial of Wilhelm List and others (the *Hostages* trial), VIII *Law Reports of Trials of War Criminals* 34 (1949), at 55–56. As Benvenisti notes, however, although an occupant has the legal duty to establish an administration in territory it occupies, today this 'is the rare exception rather than the rule': see Eyal Benvenisti, *The International Law of Occupation* (Princeton: Princeton University Press, 1993), at 4–5: also UK Ministry of Defence, *The Manual of the Law of Armed Conflict* (Oxford: Oxford University Press, 2005), at 276, para. 11(3)(1); *Prosecutor* v. *Tadić*, Case No. IT-94-1-T (trial judgment 7 May 1997), at 204–205, para. 584, available at: www.un.org/icty/tadic/trialc2/judgement/tad-tsj70507JT2-e.pdf; and *Prosecutor v Blaškić*, Case No. IT-95-14-T (trial judgment 3 March 2000), at 51, para. 149, available at: www.un.org/icty/blaskic/trialc1/judgement/bla-tj000303e.pdf. Thus, in the *Armed activities on the territory of the Congo* case, Judge Kooijmans noted in his separate opinion: 'Occupants feel more and more inclined to make use of arrangements where authority is said to be exercised by transitional governments or rebel movements or where the occupant simply refrains from establishing an administrative system': *Armed activities on the territory of the Congo* case (*Democratic Republic of the Congo v. Uganda*), ICJ Rep, 2005, 168, separate opinion of Judge Kooijmans, 306, at 317, para. 41.
22. Ibid.
23. Ibid.
24. The Fourth Geneva Convention is supplementary to Section II and III of the 1907 Hague Regulations. *Wall* advisory opinion, ICJ Rep, 2004, at 172, para. 89. Section III concerns 'military authority of the territory of the hostile state' and is largely concerned with provisions aimed at preserving the institutions and structure of the State.
25. Article 49(6) states, 'The Occupying Power shall not deport or transfer parts of its own civilian population into the territory it occupies.'
26. The ICRC commentary to the Fourth Geneva Convention observes that the extension of protection to public property and to goods owned collectively reinforces the rules already stipulated in the Hague Regulations, Articles 46 and 56, according to which private property and that of municipalities and of institutions dedicated to charity, religion or education, the arts and sciences, must be respected; see Pictet, *Commentary to Geneva Convention IV*, commentary to Article 53, at 301.
27. The authoritative commentary on the Fourth Geneva Convention by the ICRC notes that: 'So far as the local population is concerned, the freedom of movement of civilians of enemy nationality may certainly be restricted, or even temporarily suppressed, if circumstances so require. That right is not, therefore, included among the other absolute rights laid down in the Convention, but that in no way means that it is suspended in a general manner. Quite the contrary: the regulations concerning occupation and those concerning civilian aliens in the territory of a Party to the conflict are based on the idea of personal freedom of civilians remaining in general unimpaired. The right is therefore a relative one which the Party to the conflict or the Occupying Power may restrict or even suspend within the limits laid down by the Convention.' Pictet, *Commentary to Geneva Convention IV*, Commentary to Article 27, at 201–202.
28. Israel's Supreme Court acting as the High Court of Justice has also recognised this, although in equivocal terms. See HCJ 7957/04 *Mara'abe* v. *Prime Minister of Israel*,

21 June 2005, translated from the original Hebrew in (2006) 45 *International Legal Materials* 202, at 215, para. 27 ('... we shall assume – without deciding the matter – that the international conventions on human rights apply in the area').
29. See F. Hampson and I. Salama, 'Working paper on the relationship between human rights law and international humanitarian law' (E/CN.4/Sub.2/2005/14 of 21 June 2005), at 17, paras 69–70. For the United States' position, see also Human Rights Committee, *Consideration of reports submitted under Article 40 of the Covenant. Concluding observations: United States of America*, CCPR/C/USA/CO/3/Rev.1 (18 December 2006) at 2–3, para. 10, and US Department of Defense, *Working Group Report on detainee interrogations in the global war on terrorism: assessment of legal, historical, policy and operational considerations* (6 March 2003) at 6, available at, www.ccr-ny.org/v2/reports/docs/PentagonReportMarch.pdf. For a statement of the Israeli position see, for example, Human Rights Committee, *Summary record of the 1675th meeting* (CCPR/C/SR.1675 of 21 July 1998), statement of Mr. Schoffmann (Israel), para. 23.
30. Human Rights Committee, *Summary record*, statement of Mr. Schoffmann (Israel), para. 23.
31. For contemporary commentary see, for instance, G.I.A.D. Draper, 'The relationship between the human rights regime and the law of armed conflicts' (1971) 1 *Israel Yearbook on Human Rights* 191, and G. von Glahn, 'The protection of human rights in time of armed conflicts' (1971) 1 *Israel Yearbook on Human Rights* 208.
32. Security Council Resolution 237 (14 June 1967).
33. General Assembly Resolution 2675 (XXV) of 9 December 1970, 'Basic principles for the protection of civilian populations in armed conflicts', operative para. 1.
34. Common Article 3 to the four Geneva Conventions of 1949 and 1977 Additional Protocol II attest to this point: see Jean-Marie Henckaerts and Louise Doswald-Beck, *Customary International Humanitarian Law*, 2 vols (Cambridge: Cambridge University Press, 2005). For commentaries on the use of human rights law in this study, see F. Hampson, 'Other areas of customary law in relation to the Study', in Elizabeth Wilmshurst and Susan Breau (eds), *Perspectives on the ICRC Study on Customary International Humanitarian Law* (Cambridge: Cambridge University Press, 2007), at 58 et seq; and also H. Krieger, 'A conflict of norms: the relationship between humanitarian law and human rights law in the ICRC customary law study' (2006) 11 *Journal of Conflict and Security Law* 265. See also Noam Lubell, 'Challenges in applying human rights law to armed conflict' (2005) 860 *International Review of the Red Cross* 737, at 747.
35. For a partial enumeration of *lacunae* in the legal régime of occupation, see von Glahn, 'The protection of human rights in time of armed conflicts' 208, at 212–213.
36. See, for instance, H.S. Burgos, 'The application of international humanitarian law as compared to human rights law in situations qualified as internal armed conflict, internal disturbances and tensions, or public emergency, with special reference to war crimes and political crimes', in F. Kalshoven and Y. Sandoz (eds), *Implementation of International Humanitarian Law* (Dordrecht: Martinus Nijhoff, 1989), at 1; C.M. Cerna, 'Human rights in armed conflict: implementation of international humanitarian norms by regional intergovernmental human rights bodies', in Kalshoven and Sandoz, *Implementation of International Humanitarian Law*, at 31; Y. Dinstein, 'Human rights in armed conflict: international humanitarian law', in T. Meron (ed.), *Human Rights in International Law: Legal and Policy Issues*, Vol. II (Oxford: Clarendon Press, 1984), at 345; L. Doswald-Beck and S. Vite, 'International humanitarian law and human rights law' (1993) 293 *International Review of the Red Cross* 94; A. Eide, 'The laws of war and human rights – divergences and convergences', in C. Swinarski (ed.), *Studies and Essays on International Humanitarian Law and Red Cross Principles in Honour of Jean Pictet* (The Hague: ICRC, 1984), at 675; F. Hampson, 'Human rights and humanitarian law in internal conflicts', in A. Meyer (ed.), *Armed Conflict and the New Law* (London: British Institute of International and Comparative Law, 1989), at 55; P.H. Kooijmans, 'In the shadowland between civil war and civil strife: some reflections on the standard-setting process', in A. Delissen and G. Tanja (eds), *Humanitarian Law of Armed Conflict:*

*Challenges Ahead. Essays in Honour of Frits Kalshoven* (Dordrecht: Martinus Nijhoff, 1991), at 225; T. Meron, *Human Rights in Internal Strife: Their International Protection* (Cambridge: Grotius, 1987); A.H. Robertson, 'Humanitarian law and human rights', in Swinarski, *Studies and Essays on International Humanitarian Law*, at 793; and D. Schindler, 'Human rights and humanitarian law: interrelationship of the laws' (1982) 31 *American University Law Review* 935.

37. *Legality of the threat or use of nuclear weapons* advisory opinion, ICJ Rep, 1996 (1), 226, at 240, para.25. The earlier ruling by the European Court of Human Rights which addressed aspects of the applicability of human rights norms in an international armed conflict, delivered in *Loizidou* v. *Turkey, preliminary objections judgment* (23 March 1995), Series A, No. 310, at 23–24, paras 62–64, is more restricted than that of the International Court in the *Nuclear weapons* advisory opinion. In *Loizidou*, the European Court addressed only the extraterritorial applicability of the European Convention on Human Rights where a State party exercises effective control over foreign territory. It ruled (at 24, para. 62): 'Bearing in mind the object and purpose of the Convention, the responsibilities of a Contracting Party may also arise when as a consequence of military action – whether lawful or unlawful – it exercises effective control of an area outside its national territory. The obligation to secure, in such an area, the rights and freedoms set forth in the Convention derives from the fact of such control whether it be exercised directly, through its armed forces, or through a subordinate local administration.'

38. It could also be seen as counter-intuitive, as international humanitarian law, the law regulating armed conflict, is a much older branch of international law than the protection of human rights. Robertson, however, observed that this apparent anomaly disappears when the issue is considered analytically. Human rights are the basic rights of everyone in all places at all times, whereas humanitarian law ascribes rights to specific categories of persons, in essence those who fall within the categories of protected persons enumerated in the 1949 Geneva Conventions, in the specific circumstances of an armed conflict. Accordingly, human rights provisions constitute the norms of general application and only in exceptional circumstances do the norms of international humanitarian law apply. See Robertson, 'Humanitarian law and human rights', at 797–798: see also R. Wilde, 'Triggering State obligations extraterritorially: the spatial test in certain human rights treaties' (2007) 40 *Israel Law Review* 503, but compare M.J. Dennis, 'Application of human rights treaties extraterritorially in times of armed conflict and military occupation' (2005) 99 *American Journal of International Law* 119, and his 'Non-application of civil and political rights treaties extraterritorially during times of international armed conflict', (2007) 40 *Israel Law Review* 453.

39. *Legal consequences of the construction of a wall in the occupied Palestinian territory*, ICJ Rep, 2004, 136, at 178, para.106.

40. See *Wall* advisory opinion, ICJ Rep, 2004, at 177–181, paras 102–113. Israel ratified both International Covenants and the Children's Convention on 3 October 1991: see ICJ Rep, 2004, at 177, para. 103.

41. The ICJ based this finding on a principle confirmed by the *travaux préparatoires* (preparatory working papers) of Article 2.1 of the Covenant on Human Rights. See, for example, Human Rights Committee, *Consideration of Reports submitted by States parties under Article 40 of the Covenant. Concluding observations: Israel*, CCPR/C/79/Add.93 (18 August 1998), para. 10. For a contrary interpretation of the *travaux préparatoires*, see Dennis, 'Application of human rights treaties', at 123–124 and 122–127 generally, and his 'Non-application of civil and political rights', at 474–477.

42. Respectively, *Wall* advisory opinion, ICJ Rep, 2004, at 179–180, paras 109–111, and 180–181, para.112: compare Dennis, 'Application of human rights treaties', at 127–128.

43. *Armed activities on the territory of the Congo* case (*Democratic Republic of the Congo v. Uganda*), paras 216 and 178.

44. *Wall* advisory opinion, ICJ Rep, 2004, at 172, para. 89.

45. *Congo* case, para. 217.

46. *Loizidou* v. *Turkey* (App no 15318/89 of 18 December 1996), 36 *International Legal Materials* (1997) 440 at 453, para. 52.
47. Hampson and Salama have considered whether Israel is entitled to rely on the principle of persistent objection to claim that the applicability of international humanitarian law precludes that of human rights law in armed conflict. They doubt whether Israel can rely on this principle because Israel's objection does not appear to be sufficiently consistent: Israel has neither made reservations to this effect nor objected to general comments by the Committee that have dealt with the applicability of human rights law in time of armed conflict: see Hampson and Salama, 'Working paper on the relationship between human rights law and international humanitarian law', at 17, para. 70; see also Hampson, 'Other areas of customary law', at 68–72. One may also wonder whether a claim based on persistent objection can be structural as opposed to substantive. Roberts has argued that, in any case, one must be cautious in applying human rights law to situations of belligerent occupation: see Adam Roberts, 'Transformative military occupation: applying the laws of war and human rights' (2006) 100 *American Journal of International Law* 580 at 599–600. For the opposite view, see Hans-Peter Gasser, 'Protection of the civilian population', in Dieter Fleck (ed.), *The Handbook of Humanitarian Law in Armed Conflicts* (Oxford: Oxford University Press, 1995), at 209 at at 255, para. 547(4).
48. See, for example, Articles 72 and 75 (c) of *Protocol Additional to the Geneva Conventions of 12 August 1949, and Relating to the Protection of Victims of International Armed Conflicts* (Protocol I), (1977), entered into force 7 December 1978, 1125 UNTS 3.
49. Ratified by Israel on 9 March 1950.
50. Ratified by Israel on 3 January 1979.
51. Ratified by Israel on 3 October 1991.
52. Ratified by Israel on 3 October 1991.
53. Ratified by Israel on 3 October 1991.
54. As noted by Berman, 'Many contemporary disputes involving assertions of self-determination pose exceptionally "hard cases": unusual competing claims of arguably non-European peoples (Palestine), areas where the indigenous people constitutes an electoral minority (New Caledonia), etc.'. Nathanial Berman, 'Sovereignty in abeyance: self-determination and international law' (1988–1989) 7 *Wisconsin International Law Journal* 51, at 59.

    On contemporary discussion of 'colonialism' in the present day, see, for example, Nadav Carmel-Katz, 'Colonialism to racism' (1981) 10 *Journal of Palestine Studies* 4, at 170–178; see John Strawson, 'Reflections on Edward Said and the legal narratives of Palestine: Israeli settlements and Palestinian self-determination' (2001–2002) 20 *Penn State International Law Review* 363; Geremy Forman and Alexandre Kedar, 'Colonialism, colonization, and land law in Mandate Palestine: the Zor al-Zarqa and Barrat Qisarya land disputes in historical perspective' (2003) 4 *Theoretical Inquiries* 491; Robert Home, 'Colonial and postcolonial land law in Israel/Palestine' (2003) 13 *Social & Legal Studies* 3, at 291; Ralph Wilde, 'The post-colonial use of international territorial administration and Issues of legitimacy' (2005) 99 *Proceedings of the American Society of International Law* 38.
55. Leonard Barnes offers another explanation of simple distance: since '[f]ormulations of human rights naturally tend to reflect the major frustrations of those who made them', the architects of international law are at a far remove from the oppressed of a colony, of territories where 'economic subordination entails political disability; where political disability may bring with it severe restrictions upon civil liberty and an exceptional widening of the legal meaning of "sedition" (such restrictions being at their most severe when the metropolitan authorities regard the native culture as backward or inferior); and where official anxiety about sedition and allied offences lead to judicial and police practices which in the metropolitan country would be regarded as unusually harsh'. See 'The rights of dependent peoples' in *Human Rights: Comments and Interpretations* (UNESCO, Paris, 25 July 1948) UNESCO/PHS/3 (rev.) 253.
56. See Strawson, 'Reflections on Edward Said', at 376.

57. See J.T. Gathii, 'Imperialism, Colonialism and International Law' (2007) 54 *Buffalo Law Review* 1013, at 1014.
58. J.A. Andrews, 'The concept of statehood and the acquisition of territory in the nineteenth century' (1978) 94 *Law Quarterly Review* 408, at 410. *Terra nullius* refers to territory devoid of government and under no sovereignty: see John Dugard, *International Law: A South African Perspective* (Cape Town: Juta & Co. 2001), at 119–120.
59. 'One can speak of colonization when there is, and by the very fact that there is, *occupation with domination*; when there is, and by the very fact that there is, emigration with legislation.' R. Maunier, *Sociologue coloniale (I), Introduction a l'etude du contact des races* (Paris: Domat-Montchrestien, 1932), at 37, quoted in M. Rodinson, *Israel: A Colonial-Settler State?* (New York: Monad Press, 1973), at 92: emphasis in Rodinson.
60. Under Article 1(2) of the UN Charter, self-determination is characterised in the English text as a 'principle' and not a right. This is also the case with the Chinese, Spanish, and Russian texts. In the French text, the term is *droit d'auto-détermination*. According to Article 111 of the UN Charter all five texts are authentic. Article 33(3) of the Vienna Convention on the Law of Treaties 1969 provides that the terms of the treaty are presumed to have the same meaning in each authentic text. It is therefore arguable that the texts must be reconciled if possible, to achieve a meaning that makes sense in each authentic text. In 1945, self-determination was not a binding legal right but a general principle. It was only later within the context of the human rights movement and decolonisation that self-determination was recognised as a right under customary international law. See R. Falk, 'Self-determination under international law: the coherence of doctrine versus the incoherence of experience', in W. Danspeckgruber (ed.), *The Self-Determination of Peoples: Community, Nation and State in an Interdependent World* (Boulder, CO: Lynne Rienner, 2002), at 31–66, 41.
61. *East Timor* case (*Portugal* v. *Australia*), ICJ Rep, 1995, 90, at 102, para. 29.
62. *Wall* advisory opinion, ICJ Rep, 2004, at 171–172, para. 88; see also 199, paras 155–156.
63. By virtue of General Assembly Resolution 2625 (XXV) (24 October 1970). In the *Nicaragua* case, the International Court ruled that resolution 2625 expressed rules of customary international law – see *Military and paramilitary activities in and against Nicaragua case: merits judgment* (*Nicaragua* v. *United States*), ICJ Rep, 1986, 14 at 99–100, para. 188, see also *Wall* advisory opinion, ICJ Rep, 2004, at 171, para. 87.
64. International Law Commission, Report of the work of its 53rd session, UN Doc. A/56/10, Commentary to Article 40 of its 2001 Articles on Responsibility of States for Internationally Wrongful Acts, ibid. 282, at 284, para. 5, available at: http://www.un.org/law/ilc/reports/2001/english/chp4.pdf.; and also Crawford, *The International Law Commission's Articles on State Responsibility*, at 246–247. Doctrine affirms that there is a conceptual connection between the two categories of obligations *erga omnes* and *jus cogens* norms, but does not conclusively affirm their coincidence. See, for instance, A. de Hoogh, *Obligations Erga Omnes and International Crimes* (The Hague: Kluwer, 1996), at 53–56, 91; and M. Ragazzi, *The Concept of International Obligations Erga Omnes* (Oxford: Clarendon Press, 1997), Chapter 3, at 182 and 190. See also I. Scobbie, 'Unchart(er)ed waters?: consequences of the advisory opinion on the Legal consequences of the construction of a wall in the Occupied Palestinian Territory for the responsibility of the UN for Palestine' (2005) 16 *European Journal of International Law* 941, at 949–952. De Hoogh underlines that obligations *erga omnes* are essentially connected with the remedies available to all States following a breach of international law, whereas the notion of *jus cogens* norms places emphasis on their substantive content. See de Hoogh, *Obligations Erga Omnes*, at 53; compare Ragazzi, *Concept Of International Obligations Erga Omnes*, at 203 et seq.
65. President Woodrow Wilson's articulation of self-determination in his Fourteen Points speech before the United States Congress was in response to the Bolsheviks' pronouncement in support of self-determination. See Derek Heater, *National Self-Determination: Woodrow Wilson and His Legacy* (London: Macmillan, 1994), at 36–37.
66. Although the final text of Article 22 of the League of Nations Covenant did not use the term 'self-determination', it was included in earlier drafts: see, for example, President

Wilson's Third Draft presented to the Paris Peace Conference on 20 January 1919, in D.H. Miller, *The Drafting of the Covenant, Volume Two* (London: G.P. Putnam's Sons, 1928), at 103 ('... in the future government of these peoples and territories the rule of self-determination, or consent of the governed to their form of government, shall be fairly and reasonably applied, and all policies of administration or economic development be based primarily upon the well-considered interests of the people themselves').

67. See Article 22, Covenant of the League of Nations (1920) 1 *League of Nations Official Journal* 9.
68. *Namibia* advisory opinion, ICJ Rep, 1971, 16, at 31, para. 53; reaffirmed in *Wall* advisory opinion, ICJ Rep, 2004, at 171–172, para. 88.
69. *Namibia* advisory opinion, ICJ Rep, 1971, at 31–32, paras 52–53.
70. This formulation was employed in operative para. 2 of General Assembly Resolution 1514 (XV) (15 December 1960), the *Declaration on the granting of independence to colonial countries and peoples*, which consolidated the references to self-determination contained in Articles 1(2) and 55 of the United Nations Charter. For an overview of this principle, and its development, see K. Doehring, 'Self-determination', in B. Simma (ed.), *The Charter of the United Nations: A Commentary* (Oxford: Oxford University Press, 2002, 2nd edn), at 47 et seq.
71. The Declaration on principles of international law concerning friendly relations and co-operation among States in accordance with the Charter of the United Nations, contained in General Assembly Resolution 2625 (XXV) of 24 October 1970, is recognised as an authoritative interpretation of the fundamental legal principles contained in the UN Charter.
72. C. Drew, 'The East Timor story: international law on trial' (2001) 12 *European Journal of International Law* 651 at 663, paragraph break suppressed and notes omitted. For a similar affirmation of the substantive core content of self-determination, see A. Orakhelashvili, 'The impact of peremptory norms on the interpretation and application of United Nations Security Council resolutions' (2005) 16 *European Journal of International Law* 59, at 64.
73. Drew, 'East Timor story', at 663.
74. *East Timor* case (*Portugal* v. *Australia*), ICJ Rep, 1995, at 90.
75. On the territorial integrity of self-determination units, albeit within the context of decolonisation, see, for example, A. Cassese, *Self-Determination of Peoples: A Legal Reappraisal* (Cambridge: Cambridge University Press, 1995), at 72 and 78–79.
76. Benvenisti, *International Law of Occupation*, at 183. See also A. Roberts, 'The end of occupation: Iraq 2004' (2005) 54 *International and Comparative Law Quarterly* 27, at 28–29; and M. Sassòli, *Article 43 of the Hague Regulations and peace operations in the twenty-first century*, 14, available at: www.ihlresearch.org/ihl/pdfs/sassoli.pdf. In the separate opinion he appended to the *Wall* advisory opinion, Judge Koroma expressed this point more bluntly: 'Under the régime of occupation, the division or partition of an occupied territory by the occupying Power is illegal'. ICJ Rep, 2004, 204, at 205, para. 4.
77. 'A territory that constitutes the basis of the right of a people themselves to dispose cannot change in juridical status except by an act of self-determination by that people': *East Timor* Pleadings, Portuguese Memorial (18 November 1991), at 195, para. 7.01, emphasis in quotation suppressed. See also *Wall* advisory opinion Pleadings, League of Arab States Written Statement, at 62, para. 8.2, and 76, para. 8.28.
78. This point accords with the inter-temporal rule (a structural principle of international law sometimes expressed in the Latin maxim *tempus regit factum*). See, for instance, Judge Huber in the *Island of Palmas* case (United States/Netherlands, 1928), 2 *Reports of International Arbitral Awards* (1927–1928) 829, at 845; also 4 *Annual Digest of Public International Law Cases* 3, at 4; and 22 *American Journal of International Law* (1928) 867 at 883; *South West Africa: second phase* cases (*Ethiopia* v. *South Africa*; *Liberia* v. *South Africa*), ICJ Rep, 1966, 6, dissenting opinion of Judge Tanaka, 250, at 293–294; *Namibia* advisory opinion, ICJ Rep, 1971, 31–32, paras 52–53; *Western Sahara* advisory opinion, ICJ Rep, 1975, 12, separate opinion of Judge de Castro, 127, at 168–171;

and *Aegean Sea continental shelf* case, ICJ Rep, 1978, 3, at 29–32, paras 71–76. For commentary see T. Georgopoulos, 'Le droit intertemporel et les dispositions conventionnelles évolutives: quelle thérapie contre la vieillesse des traités?' (2004) 108 *Revue générale de droit international public* 123; R. Higgins, 'Some observations on the inter-temporal rule in international law', in J. Makarczyk (ed.), *Theory of International Law at the Threshold of the 21st Century: Essays in Honour of Krzysztof Skubuszewski* (The Hague: Kluwer, 1996), at 173; R.Y. Jennings and A.D. Watts, *Oppenheim's International Law* (London: Longman, 1992, 9th edn), at 1281, section 633(11); H. Lauterpacht, *The Function of Law in the International Community* (Oxford: Clarendon Press, 1933), at 283–25; and S. Rosenne, *Developments in the Law of Treaties* (Cambridge: Cambridge University Press, 1989), at 76–80.

79. See note 64 above.
80. See General Assembly Resolution 1514 (XV), 14 December 1960.
81. This Resolution was adopted unopposed by all the colonial powers, which chose to abstain rather than vote against it: see Umozurike Oji Umozurike, *Self-Determination in International Law* (Connecticut: Archon Books, 1972), at 73.
82. See G.I. Tunkin, *Droit International Public: Problèmes Théoriques* (Paris: A. Pédone, 1965), at 101. See also Christos Theodoropoulos, *Colonialism and General International Law: The Contemporary Theory of National Sovereignty and Self-Determination* (New Horizon, 1989).
83. Frank Abdullah, 'The Right to Decolonization', in Mohammed Bedjaoui (ed.), *International Law: Achievements and Prospects* (Dordrecht: Martinus Nijhoff Publishing, in association with UNESCO, Paris, 1991), at 1209.
84. Emphasis added.
85. See James Crawford, 'The Right of Self-Determination in International Law: Its Development and Future', in Philip Alston (ed.), *People's Rights* (Oxford: Oxford University Press, 2001), at 14.
86. Majorie M. Whiteman, 5 *Digest of International Law* (Washington, DC: Department of State Publication, 1965), at 82, emphasis added, parenthesis in original. The use of the term 'foreign territories' in the passage just quoted is significant because it can be applied to territories that are not a part of the metropolitan State for the purposes of a State's municipal law, to territories which are geographically separate, and to those which are contiguous to it but do not belong to it.
87. Legal consequences for States of the continued presence of South Africa in Namibia (South West Africa), notwithstanding Security Council Resolution 276 (1970) advisory opinion, ICJ Rep, 1971, at 31, para. 52.
88. On definitions of colonialism, see Ronald J. Hovarth, 'A definition of colonialism' (1972) 13 *Current Anthropology* 45, at 46–47; Robert E. Gorelick, 'Apartheid and colonialism' (1986) 19 *Comparative and International Law Journal of Southern Africa* 70, at 71.
89. Pictet, *Commentary to Geneva Convention IV*, at 283, emphasis added.
90. Foreign Ministry of Israel, 'Israeli settlements and International law', available at: www.mfa.gov.il/mfa/peace%20process/guide%20to%20the%20peace%20process/israeli%20settlements%20and%20international%20law.
91. See, for example, Caroline Elkins and Susan Pedersen, *Settler Colonialism in the Twentieth Century: Projects, Practices, Legacies* (Routledge, 2005) and Annie Combes, *Rethinking Settler Colonialism: History and Memory in Australia, New Zealand, Canada, and South Africa* (Manchester University Press, 2006).
92. Literature on the 'frontier' logic of expansion includes M. Legassick, 'The frontier tradition in South African historiography', in S. Marks and A. Atmore (eds), *Economy and Society in Pre-Industrial South Africa* (London: Longman, 1980).
93. The United States Supreme Court, explaining the juridical redefinition of Native Americans (often called 'Indian nations') from foreign powers to domestic entities subject to the plenary powers of the US Congress, applied the innovative term, 'domestic dependent nations': see judgment by Chief Justice Marshall in *Cherokee Nation v. Georgia* (30 US (5 Pet.)) 1 (1831).

94. This reflects the so-called 'Belgian thesis' which would have extended the concept of non-self-governing territories to include disenfranchised indigenous peoples living within the borders of independent states, especially if the race, language and culture of these peoples differed from those of the dominant population. See J.L. Kunz, 'Chapter XI of the United Nations Charter in action' (1954) 48 *American Journal of International Law* 109, at 109; and Patrick Thornberry, 'Self-determination, minorities, human rights: a review of international instruments' (1989) 38 *International and Comparative Law Quarterly* 874. The rights of such peoples were eventually codified in the International Labour Organisation's Convention (No. 169) concerning Indigenous and Tribal Peoples in Independent Countries (adopted on 7 June 1989, entered into force on 5 September 1991), which recognises that groups living in such states still experience enduring conditions of alienation, marginalisation, and discrimination. That their dilemma results from colonisation is built into the definition in Article 1(b): 'Peoples in independent countries who are regarded as indigenous on account of their descent from the populations which inhabited the country, or a geographical region to which the country belongs, at the time of conquest or colonisation or the establishment of present State boundaries and who, irrespective of their legal status, retain some or all of their own social, economic, cultural and political institutions.'
95. The definition of a non-self-governing territory as being 'geographically separate' and 'ethnically and/or culturally' distinct from the metropolitan power has been referred to by scholars as the 'salt-water theory' of colonialism: see Rupert Emerson, 'Colonialism' (1969) 4 *Journal of Contemporary History* 3 (defining colonialism as the imposition of white rule on alien peoples inhabiting lands separated by salt water from the imperial centre); and H.K. Weeseling, *Imperialism and Colonialism: Essays on the History of European Expansion* (London: Greenwood Press, 1997), preface, at ix–x. The salt-water theory is principally a political doctrine rather than a legal concept and is a highly problematic term in international law, the result of a political bargain: see Lee C. Bucheit, *Secession: The Legitimacy of Self-Determination* (New Haven: Yale University Press, 1978), at 18 (describing the theory as a valiant, misguided and unconvincing attempt to limit the scope of self-determination by reading into the principle an arbitrary limitation). See also Michla Pomerance, *Self-Determination in Law and Practice: The New Doctrine of the United Nations* (The Hague: Martinus Nijhoff, 1982), at 15. After the adoption of the Declaration on the Granting of Independence to Colonial Countries and Peoples, the United States representative called the Soviet Union and its satellites 'the largest colonial empire which has ever existed in history': see Whiteman, 5 *Digest of International Law*, at 82.
96. The Bandung final communiqué, upon which the Declaration on Colonialism is based, does not stipulate the colonialism only applies to territories separated from the colonial powers by salt water: see section D(1)(a–d) of the Final Communiqué of the Asian-African Conference, Bandung, 24 April 1955.
97. UN General Assembly Resolution 2649 (XXV), 30 November 1970.
98. Alain Pellet, 'The destruction of Troy will not take place', in Emma Playfair (ed.), *International Law and the Administration of Occupied Territories* (Oxford: Clarendon Press, 1992), at 183.
99. See Article 1(4) of the 1977 Protocol Additional to the Geneva Conventions of 12 August 1949, and relating to the Protection of Victims of International Armed Conflicts (Protocol I); also Ben-Naftali, Gross and Michaeli, 'Illegal Occupation', at 551–614.
100. UN Security Council Resolution 276 of 30 January 1970.
101. UN Declaration of Principles of International Law concerning Friendly Relations and Co-operation among States in accordance with the Charter of the United Nations, General Assembly Resolution 2625 of 24 October 1970.
102. Declaration of Principles of International Law concerning Friendly Relations.
103. International Conventions on the Elimination of All Forms of Racial Discrimination (1965), entered into force 4 January 1969, 660 UNTS195.
104. Emphasis added.

105. UN Doc. A/C.3//SR.1313, cited in David Keane, *Caste-based Discrimination in International Human Rights Law* (Aldershot: Ashgate, 2007), at 190.
106. Convention on the Suppression and Punishment of the Crime of Apartheid (1973), entered into force 18 July 1976 (1015 UNTS 243). The Apartheid Convention is thus intended to complement the requirements of Article 3 of ICERD, as its chapeau suggests in referring to Article 3.
107. See Articles 4 and 5 of the Declaration.
108. See Article 2 of the Declaration.
109. Charter of the United Nations, entered into force 24 October 1945 (59 Stat. 1031, T.S. 993), 3 Bevans 1153.
110. Universal Declaration of Human Rights (1948), GA res. 217A (III), UN Doc. A/810, at 71.
111. Convention on the Elimination of Discrimination Against Women (1979), entered into force 3 September 1981 (1249 UNTS 13), Preamble.
112. Website of the United Nations Treaty Collection, available at: http://treaties.un.org/Pages/ViewDetails.aspx?src=TREATY&id=319&chapter=4&lang=en.
113. Ibid.
114. Resolution 2202 (XXI) of 16 December 1966, *The policies of apartheid of Government of the Republic of South Africa*, para. 1.
115. *Proclamation of Teheran, Final Act of the International Conference on Human Rights, Teheran on 13 May 1968* (UN Doc. A/CONF.32/41), at 3 (1968), para. 7. See also the Convention on the Non-Applicability of Statutory Limitations to War Crimes and Crimes against Humanity (1968), Article 1, which considers crimes against humanity to include 'inhuman acts resulting from the policy of apartheid'.
116. Article 85(4)(c), Protocol Additional to the Geneva Conventions of 12 August 1949, and Relating to the Protection of Victims of International Armed Conflicts (Protocol I), (1977), entered into force 7 December 1978, 1125 UNTS 3.
117. Article 7(1)(j), Rome Statute of the International Criminal Court (1998), UN Doc. A/CONF.183/9, entered into force 1 July 2002, 2187 UNTS 90.
118. Website of the United Nations Treaty Collection, available at: http://treaties.un.org/Pages/ViewDetails.aspx?src=UNTSONLINE&tabid=2&id=325&chapter=4&lang=en#Participants.
119. Myres S. McDougal, Harold D. Lasswell and Lung-chu Chen, *Human Rights and World Public Order* (New Haven/London: Yale University Press, 1980), at 545.
120. Website of the International Committee of the Red Cross, available at: www.icrc.org/IHL.nsf/(SPF)/party_main_treaties/$File/IHL_and_other_related_Treaties.pdf.
121. Website of the International Criminal Court, available at: www.icc-cpi.int/about.html.
122. See Antonio Cassese, *International Criminal Law* (Oxford: Oxford University Press, 2008), at 25.
123. On the conceptual connection between obligations *erga omnes* and *jus cogens*, see note 64 above. Regarding *erga omnes* obligations, the International Court of Justice has observed that: '… an essential distinction should be drawn between the obligations of a State towards the international community as a whole, and those arising vis-à-vis another State in the field of diplomatic protection. By their very nature the former are the concern of all States. In view of the importance of the rights concerned, all States can be held to have a legal interest in their protection; they are obligations *erga omnes*.' *Case Concerning the Barcelona Traction, Light and Power Company, Limited second phase, final judgment* (*Belgium v. Spain*), ICJ Rep, 1970, 3, at 32, paras 33–34.
124. Ibid.
125. See, for example, *United States (Third) Restatement of the Foreign Relations Law* (1986), section 702, note 11.
126. See *Draft articles on Responsibility of States for Internationally Wrongful Acts, with commentaries, 2001, Yearbook of the International Law Commission* (2001) Vol. II, part two, at 112–113.
127. Ibid., at 112.

128. Article 96 provides: '1. The General Assembly or the Security Council may request the International Court of Justice to give an advisory opinion on any legal question; 2. Other organs of the United Nations and specialized agencies, which may at any time be so authorized by the General Assembly, may also request advisory opinions of the Court on legal questions arising within the scope of their activities.'
129. Lauterpacht, a distinguished judge of the International Court, observed that 'the fact of the absence of formally binding force does not exhaust the actual significance of an advisory opinion'. H. Lauterpacht, 'The Security Council and the jurisdiction of the International Court of Justice', in E. Lauterpacht (ed.), *International Law: Being the Collected Papers of Hersch Lauterpacht. Vol. V: Disputes, War and Neutrality* (Cambridge: Cambridge University Press, 2004), at 224–228. Thirlway, a former Principal Legal Secretary of the Court, stressed that, while an advisory opinion is advisory rather than determinative, a State found by the International Court to have a particular obligation under international law 'would be in a weak position if it seeks to argue that the considered opinion of the Court does not represent a correct view of the law: H.W.A. Thirlway, 'The International Court of Justice', in M. Evans (ed.), *International Law* (Oxford: Oxford University Press, 2006), at 582–583: see also S. Rosenne, *The Law and Practice of the International Court, 1920–1996* (The Hague: Martinus Nijhoff, 1997), at 1754–1759. Similarly, Judge Gros of the International Court has observed that 'when the Court gives an advisory opinion on a question of law it states the law', and while 'it is possible for the body which sought the opinion not to follow it in its action ... that body is aware that no position adopted contrary to the Court's pronouncement will have any effectiveness whatsoever in the legal sphere'. *Western Sahara* advisory opinion, ICJ Rep, 1975, 12, declaration of Judge Gros, 69, at 73, para. 6: see also E. Hambro, 'The authority of the advisory opinions of the International Court of Justice' (1954) 3 *International and Comparative Law Quarterly* 2, at 17 and 5; and André Gros, 'Concerning the advisory role of the International Court of Justice', in W. Friedmann, L. Henkin and O. Lissitzyn (eds), *Transnational Law in a Changing Society: Essays in Honour of Philip C. Jessup* (New York: Columbia University Press, 1972), at 315. See further, the opinion expressed by Blaine Sloane, a former director of the UN General Legal Division, in 'Advisory Jurisdiction of the International Court of Justice' (1950) 38 *California Law Review* 830, at 855. This view was echoed in the *Wall* advisory opinion itself, as Judge Koroma stated in his separate opinion: 'The Court's findings are based on the authoritative rules of international law and are of an *erga omnes* character ... [as] States are bound by those rules and have an interest in their observance, all States are subject to these findings.' *Wall* advisory opinion, separate opinion of Judge Koroma, ICJ Rep, 2004, 204, at 205–206, para. 8. In her separate opinion in *Wall*, Judge Higgins further held (after citing a passage from the *Namibia* advisory opinion regarding a Security Council Resolution condemning South Africa's illegal presence in that country) that '[a] binding determination made by a competent organ of the United Nations to the effect that a situation is illegal cannot remain without consequence'.
130. *International status of South West Africa* advisory opinion, ICJ Rep, 1950, 128.
131. *Admissibility of hearings of petitioners by the Committee on South West Africa* advisory opinion, ICJ Rep, 1956, 23, separate opinion of Judge Lauterpacht, 35, at 46–47.
132. See UN General Assembly Resolution ES–10/15, 2 August 2004, operative para. 2.
133. Important aspects of the *Wall* advisory opinion were later reaffirmed by the ICJ in its contentious *Armed activities on the territory of the Congo* judgment: in particular, the relationship between human rights and humanitarian law and the extraterritorial applicability of international human rights instruments. See *Democratic Republic of the Congo v. Uganda*, ICJ Rep, 2005, 168: the Court's discussion of belligerent occupation is found at 227–231, paras 167–180, especially para. 172. Without referring expressly to the *Wall* advisory opinion, the Court reaffirmed the applicability of human rights and international humanitarian law to occupied territory (at 231, paras 178–180), and expressly relied on its rulings in the *Wall* advisory opinion on the interrelationship between human rights and humanitarian law and on the extraterritorial applicability of international human rights instruments (at 242–243, para. 216).

## Chapter 2

1. As the ICJ has confirmed, '[A]n international instrument has to be interpreted and applied within the framework of the entire legal system prevailing at the time of the interpretation': *Legal Consequences for States of the Continued Presence of South Africa in Namibia (South West Africa) notwithstanding Security Council Resolution 276 (1970)*, ICJ advisory opinion of 21 June 1971, ICJ Reports, 1971, 16, at 31, para. 53. All documents of the International Court of Justice cited in this report are available at: www.icj-cij.org.
2. Statement dated 5 August 1937 by Mr. Ormsby-Gore, the Colonial Secretary, at the League of Nations, Permanent Mandates Commission, Minutes of the Thirty-Second (Extraordinary) Session devoted to Palestine, held at Geneva from 30 July to 18 August 1937, including the Report of the Commission to the Council, Official No. C.330.M.222 1937. VI, at 87, emphasis added.
3. Emphasis added.
4. See Annex III to UN Doc. A/43/827 (18 November 1988), Letter dated 18 November 1988 from the Permanent Representative of Jordan to the United Nations addressed to the Secretary-General.
5. UN Doc. A/RES/43/177 (15 December 1988), operative para. 2.
6. The 'Palestinian Interim Self-Government Authority' has served as a government of the Palestinian sector in the OPT under the Oslo Accords since 1993. Terms for the PA were established in Article 1 of the Declaration of Principles on Interim Self-Government Arrangements, signed by the PLO and the Government of Israeli on 13 September 1993.
7. Letter submitted by the Minister of Justice of the Palestinian National Authority to the Registrar of the International Criminal Court, *Declaration Recognizing the Jurisdiction of the International Criminal Court*, 22 January 2009. Article 12(3) of the Statute of the ICC refers to declarations made by States which are not parties to the Statute. In April 2009, the Office of the Prosecutor stated that it was considering whether this declaration meets the requirements of Article 12(3), but by July 2011 had still not issued its opinion.
8. *Legal consequences of the construction of a wall in the occupied Palestinian territory*, ICJ advisory opinion of 9 July 2004, ICJ Rep, 2004, 136 at 201, para.162, emphasis added.
9. See, for instance, F.A. Boyle, 'Creation of the State of Palestine' (1990) 1 *European Journal of International Law* 301; J. Crawford, 'The creation of the State of Palestine: too much too soon?' (1990) 1 *European Journal of International Law* 307; J. Crawford, *The Creation of States in International Law* (Oxford: Clarendon Press, 2006, 2nd edn), 435–442 and R.E. Lapidoth and N.K. Calvo-Goller, 'Les éléments constitutives de l'État et la déclaration du Conseil National Palestinien du 15 novembre 1988' (1992) 96 *Revue générale du droit international public* 777.
10. For a collection of documents on the Palestine question in international law that bear *inter alia* on self-determination, see M. Cherif Bassiouni (ed.), *Documents on the Arab-Israeli Conflict* (New York: Transnational Publishers, 2005).
11. *Wall* advisory opinion, ICJ Rep, 2004, 136, at 182–183, para. 118. This was a unanimous ruling by the Court. Although one judge found that the Court should have exercised its discretion and refused to accede to the request for an advisory opinion, and thus dissented from the Court's formal conclusions, he nonetheless expressly affirmed that the Palestinian people possesses the right to self-determination: see Declaration of Judge Buergenthal, ICJ Rep, 2004, 240, at 241, para. 4.
12. The Mandate entered into force in 1923.
13. On the Balfour Declaration see, for example, J. Schneer, *The Balfour Declaration: The Origins of the Arab-Israeli Conflict* (London: Bloomsbury, 2010).
14. Mandate for Palestine, Article 4.
15. Ibid., Article 22.
16. The Council of the League of Nation, Palestine Mandate, 24 July 1922.
17. In 1911, the Zionist Congress denounced accusations that it intended to establish an independent Jewish state as being inspired by 'gross ignorance, or actuated by malice'. In 1918–19, President of the Zionist Organisation Sokolov affirmed that 'The Jewish

State was never part of the Zionist Programme': cited in Neville Barbour, 'The White Paper of 1939', in *Nisi Dominus: A Survey of the Palestine Controversy*, reproduced as Document no. 47 in Walid Khalidi (ed.), *From Haven to Conquest: Readings in Zionism and the Palestine Problem Until 1948* (Washington, DC: Institute for Palestine Studies, 1971), at 472.
18. Ibid.
19. Palestine: Statement of Policy, Presented by the Secretary of State for the Colonies to Parliament by Command of His Majesty, (1 May 1939), Cmd. 6019; Report of the Anglo-American Committee of Enquiry regarding the problems of European Jewry and Palestine, Miscellaneous No. 8 (1946), Lausanne, 20 April, 1946 (London: HMSO, Cmd. 6808), emphasis added; also Draft Trusteeship Agreement for Palestine, UN Doc. A/C.1/277, 20 April 1948. For a description of the context of the White Paper, see Barbour, 'The White Paper of 1939'.
20. Barbour, 'The White Paper of 1939', at 473.
21. See Report of Sub-Committee II of the Ad Hoc Committee on Palestine, UN Doc. A/AC.14/32 (11 November 1947).
22. Palestine Royal Commission Report, July 1937, Cmd. 5479.
23. General Assembly Resolution 181 (II), 29 November 1947. The Arab states opposed the Partition Plan and demanded independence in a single unitary state. One of their objections, among others, was that they did not think that a Palestinian state in the area allocated to it in the Plan would be viable. See the Official Records of the Second Session of the General Assembly, Ad Hoc Committee on the Palestinian Question, 25 September–25 November 1947, UN Doc. A/AC. 14/32 and Add. 1, 11 November 1947. See also I. Scobbie and S. Hibbin, *The Israel-Palestine Conflict in International Law:Territorial Issues* (New York: US/Middle East Project, 2009) 33–57, available at: www.soas.ac.uk/lawpeacemideast/publications/file60534.pdf.
24. The 1948 war led to a fundamental change in the demographic composition of Palestine. See Janet L. Abu-Lughod, 'The Demographic Transformation of Palestine', in Ibrahim Abu Lughod (ed.), *The Transformation of Palestine: Essays on the Origin and Development of the Arab-Israeli Conflict* (Evanston: Northwestern University Press, 1987, 2nd edn), at 139–163. The literature on the 1948 war is vast: for example, see Walid Khalidi, *Why did the Palestinians Leave? An Examination of the Zionist Version of the Exodus of 1948* (London: Arab Information Centre, 1963); Benny Morris, *The Birth of the Palestinian Refugee Problem, 1947–1949* (Cambridge: Cambridge University Press, 1987); Eugene L. Rogan and Avi Shlaim (eds), *The War for Palestine: Rewriting the History of 1948* (Cambridge: Cambridge University Press, 2007, 2nd edn).
25. Article 21 was added at the fourth meeting of the Palestinian National Congress in 1968, and read in full: 'The Arab Palestinian people, expressing themselves by the armed Palestinian revolution, reject all solutions which are substitutes for the total liberation of Palestine.'
26. General Assembly Resolution 2535 (XXIV), 10 December 1969, *United Nations Relief and Works Agency for Palestine Refugees in the Near East*, Part B, operative para. 1.
27. See UN General Assembly Resolution 2649 (XXV), 30 November 1970.
28. Ibid., operative para. 5.
29. General Assembly Resolution 2672 (XXV), 8 December 1970, *United Nations Relief and Works Agency for Palestine Refugees in the Near East*, Part C, operative para. 1.
30. General Assembly Resolution A/3070 (XXVIII), 30 November 1973: the relevant language reads, '*reaffirms* the legitimacy of the peoples' struggle for liberation from colonial and foreign domination and alien subjugation by all available means, including armed struggle'.
31. General Assembly Resolution 3376 (XXV), 10 November 1975.
32. Ibid.
33. Ibid, operative para. 3.
34. See, for example, General Assembly Resolution 33/24 of 29 November 1978, and General Assembly Resolution 36/9 of 28 October 1981.

35. See the statement by Lord Balfour to the League of Nations, 16 September 1922, regarding Article 25 of the Mandate for Palestine in 3 *League of Nations Official Journal*, November 1922, 1188–1189; also the memorandum by Lord Balfour to the Council of the League of Nations revoking specific articles pertaining to the Jewish national home from the Mandate for Transjordan in 3 *League of Nations Official Journal*, November (1922), at 1390–1391.
36. Incremental steps included the 20 February 1928 Agreement between the United Kingdom and Transjordan respecting the Administration of the Latter (128 BFSP 273 and UKTS No7, 1930) and the 22 March 1946 Treaty of Alliance between the United Kingdom and Transjordan (146 BFSP 461 and UKTS No32, 1946). On the separation of Palestine and Transjordan, see Crawford, *Creation of States*, at 423–424.
37. *Jawdat Badawi Sha'ban v. Commissioner for Migration and Statistics* (1945) (Supreme Court of Palestine sitting as the High Court of Justice, 14 December 1945), 12 *Law Reports of Palestine* 551, at 553.
38. The principle of *uti possidetis iuris* is associated with the decolonisation process, and thus the exercise of the right of self-determination. The ICJ has explained that '(23) ... The essence of the principle lies in its primary aim of securing respect for the territorial boundaries at the moment when independence is achieved. Such territorial boundaries might be no more than delimitations between different administrative divisions or colonies all subject to the same sovereign. In that case, the application of the principle of *uti possidetis* resulted in administrative boundaries being transformed into international frontiers in the full sense of the term ... (24) The territorial boundaries which have to be respected may also derive from international frontiers which previously divided a colony of one State from a colony of another, or indeed a colonial territory from the territory of an independent State, or one which was under protectorate, but had retained its international personality. There is no doubt that the obligation to respect pre-existing international frontiers in the event of a State succession derives from a general rule of international law, whether or not the rule is expressed in the formula *uti possidetis*.' *Case concerning the frontier dispute (Burkina-Faso/Mali)*, ICJ Rep, 1986, 554, at 556, paras 23–24; see generally 565–567, paras 20–25. This judgment was delivered by a Chamber of the International Court, comprising Judges Bedjaoui, Lachs and Ruda, with Judges *ad hoc* Luchaire and Abi-Saab. Under Article 27 of the Statute of the International Court, a judgment given by a Chamber of the Court 'shall be considered as rendered by the Court'. The operation of *uti possidetis* may also be seen in both the granting of independence to Jordan by the 22 March 1946 Treaty of Alliance between the United Kingdom and Transjordan, and the delineation of its boundary with Israel in Article 3 of the 1994 Israel-Jordan Peace Treaty. 6 *United Nations Treaty Series* 74 (subsequently replaced by the 15 March 1948 Treaty of Alliance between the United Kingdom and Transjordan, 77 United Nations Treaty Series 994).
39. Crawford, *Creation of States*, at 424.
40. Legal consequences of the construction of the construction of a wall advisory opinion, ICJ Rep, 2004, at 165, para. 70.
41. See, for example, the arguments advanced by Julius Stone, *Israel and Palestine: Assault on the Law of Nations* (Baltimore, MD: Johns Hopkins University Press, 1981). In a speech before the UN General Assembly on 2 December 1980, Yehuda Z. Blum, Israel's Permanent Representative to the United Nations, said that the claims of the Palestinians to establish a state in the West Bank and Gaza Strip were unfounded. He said that the Palestinians had already achieved self-determination in their own state, namely Jordan. See General Assembly Official Records, XXXVth session, Plenary Meetings, 77th meeting, 1318, paras 108–113.
42. R. Sabel, *The ICJ Opinion on the Separation Barrier: Designating the Entire West Bank as 'Palestinian Territory'* (Jerusalem: Jerusalem Center for Public Affairs, October 2005), available at: www.jcpa.org/JCPA/Templates/ShowPage.asp?DBID=1&LNGID=1&TMID=111&FID=254&PID=0&IID=893.

43. See Foreign Relations of the United States, 1964–68: Vol. XIX, Arab-Israeli crisis and war, 1967 (Washington, DC: US Government Printing Office, 2004) [hereinafter XIX FRUS 1964–68], Doc. 506, Telegram from the Department of State to the Embassy in Israel, 30 November 1967, 998; and Doc. 501, Telegram from the Mission to the United Nations to the Department of State, 4 November 1967, 981, at 982–983.
44. See XIX FRUS 1964–68, Doc. 448, Memorandum of conversation, 24 October 1967, 944, at 946; Doc. 491, Telegram from the Mission to the United Nations to the Department of State, 26 October 1967, 953, at 955; and Doc. 494, Memorandum from the President's Special Counsel (McPherson) to President Johnston, 31 October 1967, 961. Gerson notes that Israel did not contest the lawfulness of Jordan's control over the West Bank, as shown by its calls for a peace treaty which contained border modifications: see A. Gerson, *Israel, the West Bank and International Law* (London: Cass, 1978), at 80. In contrast, Blum claims that the 'non-prejudice clause' in the 1949 Israel-Jordan Armistice Agreement froze the parties' rights and claims to the territory of the West Bank. As long as this remained in force, no unilateral act could alter the rights of either party and Jordan's purported annexation of the West Bank therefore lacked any legal effect: see Y.Z. Blum, 'The missing reversioner: reflections on the status of Judea and Samaria' (1968) 3 *Israel Law Review* 279 at 288. The Israel-Jordan Armistice Agreement terminated, at the latest, with the outbreak of the Six-Day War in 1967: see R. Sabel, 'The International Court of Justice's decision on the separation barrier and the green line' (2005) 38 *Israel Law Review* 316, at 324.
45. For a dossier of the relevant documents, see M. Whiteman (ed.), 2 *Digest of International Law* (Washington, DC: Department of State, 1963), at 1163–1168.
46. For the United Kingdom's statement of recognition, see 474 HC Deb (5th Ser) cols. 1137–1139 (27 April 1950), reproduced in Whiteman, 2 *Digest of International Law*, 1167–1168. A scanned copy of the statement is available at: http://upload.wikimedia.org/wikipedia/en/9/91/UKrecognizesIsraelJordan.pdf.
47. This was announced by King Hussein in his 31 July 1988 *Address to the Nation*, reproduced at www.kinghussein.gov.jo/88_july31.html and (1988) 27 *International Legal Materials* 1637. See also 'Jordan: Statement Concerning Disengagement from the West Bank and Palestinian Self-Determination', Address by His Majesty King Hussein to the Nation, 31 July 1988 (1988) 27 *International Legal Materials* 1637, at 1637–1645.
48. Treaty of Peace between the Hashemite Kingdom of Jordan and the State of Israel, 26 October 1994, 2042 United Nations Treaty Series 35325, reproduced as UN Doc. A/50/73 and S/1995/83 (27 January 1995); and also United Nations Treaty Series, reproduced at: www.kinghussein.gov.jo/peacetreaty.html, and (1995) 34 *International Legal Materials* 43.
49. See the 1993 Declaration of Principles on Interim Self-Government Arrangements, Article 4; and the 1995 Israeli-Palestinian Interim Agreement on the West Bank and the Gaza Strip, Article 11(1). For commentary, see R. Shehadeh, *From Occupation to Interim Accords: Israel and the Palestinian Territories* (London: Kluwer, 1997), at 35–37. The question of Jerusalem is reserved for the permanent status negotiations: see the Agreed Minutes to the Declaration of Principles on Interim Self-Government Arrangements, Understanding in Relation to Article 4; and 1995 Interim Agreement, Articles 17(1) and XXXI.31(5).
50. *Ajuri v. IDF Commander*, HCJ 7015/02, 3 September 2002 (2002) *Israel Law Review* 1, opinion of President Barak, at 17–18, para. 22. Lein noted, *inter alia*, that Israel incorporated the Interim Agreement in its entirety into its military legislation in both the West Bank and Gaza Strip, and that this legislation has not been revoked: see Y. Lein, *One Big Prison: Freedom of Movement to and from the Gaza Strip on the Eve of the Disengagement Plan* (Jerusalem: B'Tselem/HaMoked, 2005), at 20–21, available at: www.hamoked.org.il/items/12800_eng.pdf.
51. See Article 5 of the Israel-Palestine Liberation Organisation: Wye River Memorandum, 23 October 1998 (1998) 37 *International Legal Materials* 1251 at 1255; and Article 8(10), Israel-Palestine Liberation Organisation: The Sharm El-Sheikh Memorandum, 4 September 1999, 38 *International Legal Materials* 1465, at 1468.

52. See, for example, *Wall* advisory opinion Pleadings, Palestine Written Statement, at 239, para. 548, and at 240, para. 549.
53. *Wall* advisory opinion, ICJ Rep, 2004, at 182–183, para. 118.
54. General Assembly Resolution 62/146 (18 December 2007).
55. Security Council Resolution 1860 (8 January 2009).
56. Judea and Samaria are names associated historically with Jewish kingdoms or regions that were located in what is now the southern and northern West Bank respectively.
57. Sabel, *ICJ Opinion on the Separation Barrier*.
58. Article 35 of Israeli Military Proclamation No. 3, June 1967, stated that Israeli military courts in the occupied territory 'must apply the provisions of the [Fourth] Geneva Convention … In case of conflict between this Order and the said Convention, the Convention shall prevail.' This was noted by the International Court in the *Wall* advisory opinion in the formulation of its conclusion that the Fourth Geneva Convention applies in the occupied territories: see ICJ Rep, 2004, at 173–174, para. 93.
59. See Blum, 'Missing reversioner', 279; M. Shamgar, 'The observance of international law in the administered territories' (1971) 1 *Israel Yearbook on Human Rights* 262 at 263–266; Gerson, *Israel, the West Bank, and International Law* at 76–82; and G. Gorenberg, *The Accidental Empire: Israel and the Birth of the Settlements, 1967–1977* (New York: Times Books, 2006), at 101.
60. Article 2(4) provides: 'All Members shall refrain in their international relations from the threat or use of force against the territorial integrity or political independence of any State, or in any other manner inconsistent with the Purposes of the United Nations.' Only Egypt was a member of the United Nations at that time: Israel was admitted to UN membership on 11 May 1949 and Jordan was admitted on 14 December 1955.
61. Blum, 'Missing reversioner', at 288 and 292–293; also Gerson, *Israel, the West Bank, and International Law*, at 78–79 (although Gerson believes that Jordan may have been more than a belligerent occupant in the West Bank, suggesting the category 'trustee-occupant'); and Shamgar, 'Observance of international law in the administered territories', at 265–266.
62. Blum, 'Missing reversioner', at 294. See also Y.Z. Blum, *Secure Boundaries and Middle East Peace in the Light of International Law and Practice* (Jerusalem: Hebrew University, 1971), at 90–91; Gerson, *Israel, the West Bank, and International Law*, at 80–81; E. Rostow, 'Palestinian self-determination: possible futures for the unallocated territories of the Palestine Mandate' (1978–79) 5 *Yale Studies in World Public Order* 147 at 160–161; and S.M. Schwebel, 'What weight to conquest?' (1970) 64 *American Journal of International Law* 64, republished in S.M. Schwebel, *Justice in International Law* (Cambridge: Grotius/Cambridge University Press, 1994), at 521, and in M. Shaw (ed.), *Title to Territory* (Aldershot: Ashgate, 2005), at 393. Compare R.Y. Jennings and A.D. Watts, *Oppenheim's International Law, Vol. I: Peace* (London: Longman, 1992, 9th edn), at 704 n.8; and R.A. Falk and B.H. Weston, 'The relevance of international law to Palestinian rights in the West Bank and Gaza: in legal defence of the intifada' (1991) 32 *Harvard International Law Journal* 129, at 138–144. In particular, Israel claimed that because the OPT did not constitute territories of a High Contracting Party to the Fourth Geneva Convention, the situation did not fall within the terms of Article 2 of the Convention which provides, in part: 'the present Convention shall apply to all cases of declared war or of any other armed conflict which may arise between two or more of the High Contracting Parties … The Convention shall also apply to all cases of partial or total occupation of the territory of a High Contracting Party, even if the said occupation meets with no armed resistance.'
63. Blum, 'Missing reversioner', at 293–294.
64. See Gorenberg, *Accidental Empire*, at 101–102. Gorenberg provides a fragmented account of Meron's opinion (at 99–102). A scan of the original Hebrew text of this opinion is available on Gorenberg's website at: http://southjerusalem.com/settlement-and-occupation-historical-documents/, and a complete English translation on that of the Sir Joseph Hotung Programme in Law, Human Rights and Peace Building in the Middle East

(School of Oriental and African Studies, London) at: www.soas.ac.uk/lawpeacemideast/resources/48485.pdf. See also discussion in Eyal Benvenisti, *The International Law of Occupation* (Princeton: Princeton University Press, 1993), at 109–110.
65. Even the sole dissenting judge, Judge Buergenthal, expressly concurred on this point: see Declaration of Judge Buergenthal, ICJ Rep, 2004, at 240, para. 2.
66. *Wall* advisory opinion, ICJ Rep, 2004, at 173–177, paras 90–101.
67. Gerson, *Israel, the West Bank, and International Law*, at 80. Israel also recognised that Egypt had some interest in Gaza by virtue of Article 2 of the Egypt-Israel Treaty of Peace, 26 March 1979, 1136 United Nations Treaty Series 17813 (registered by Egypt) and 1138 United Nations Treaty Series [UNTS] 17855 (treaty and annexes, registered by Israel) and UNTS 17856 (agreed minutes, registered by Israel); also reproduced in (1979) 18 *International Legal Materials* 362. Article 2 provides: 'The permanent boundary between Egypt and Israel is the recognized international boundary between Egypt and the former mandated territory of Palestine … without prejudice to the issue of the status of the Gaza Strip. The Parties recognize this boundary as inviolable. Each will respect the territorial integrity of the other, including their territorial waters and airspace.'
68. Amendment 11 to the Law and Administrative Ordinance of 1948, passed by the Knesset on 27 June 1967.
69. Israel: Basic Law: Jerusalem, Capital of Israel. Passed by the Knesset on the 17th Av, 5740 (30 July 1980) and published in *Sefer Ha-Chukkim* No. 980 of the 23rd Av, 5740 (5 August, 1980), at 186; the Bill and an Explanatory Note were published in *Hatza'ot Chok* No. 1464 of 5740, at 287; and the official English translation in 21 Laws of the State of Israel 75, and also M. Medzini (ed.), *Israel's Foreign Relations: Selected Documents, 1947–1974*, Vol. I (Jerusalem: Ministry for Foreign Affairs, 1976), at 245.
70. After overthrowing the constitutional monarchy in 1848 and passing a new Constitution in November of that year, the colony of Algeria was declared to be an integral part of the metropolitan territory of France.
71. See Al-Haq, *40 Years after the Unlawful Annexation of East Jerusalem: Consolidation of the Illegal Situation Continues Through the Construction of the Jerusalem Light Rail* (28 June 2007), available at: www.alhaq.org/etemplate.php?id=326.
72. See Security Council Resolution 298 (25 September 1971), quoted in *Wall* advisory opinion, ICJ Rep, 2004, at 166, para. 75.
73. The Preamble to Security Council Resolution 267 (3 July 1969) on the status of the Old City of Jerusalem reaffirms 'the established principle that acquisition of territory by military conquest is inadmissible'.
74. International Law Commission (ILC), 'Draft Articles on the Law of Treaties, with Commentaries', *ILC Yearbook 1966*, Vol. II, at 247. See also *Case concerning military and paramilitary activities in and against Nicaragua: merits judgment* (*Nicaragua* v. *United States of America*), ICJ Rep, 1986, at 100–101, para. 190. For a detailed exposition of the emergence and consolidation of the illegality of territorial acquisition through the use of force, see I. Brownlie, *International Law and the Use of Force by States* (Oxford: Clarendon Press, 1963), at 217; S. Korman, *The Right Of Conquest: The Acquisition of Territory by Force in International Law and Practice* (Oxford: Clarendon Press, 1996); and with specific reference to the June 1967 hostilities, see I. Sagay, 'International law relating to occupied territory: can territory be acquired by military conquest under modern international law?' (1972) 28 *Revue Egyptienne de Droit International*, at 56–64.
75. Especially, the Declaration on the Granting of Independence to Colonial Countries and Peoples and the Declaration on Principles of International Law concerning Friendly Relations and Co-operation among States.
76. J. Pictet (ed.), *Commentary to Geneva Convention IV Relative to the Protection of Civilian Persons in Time of War* (Geneva: ICRC, 1958), at 275.
77. UN Security Council Resolutions 252 (21 May 1968) and 267 (3 July 1969). See also UN Security Council Resolution 298 (25 September 1971) ('all legislative and administrative actions taken by Israel to change the status of the City of Jerusalem, including expropriation of land and properties, transfer of populations and legislation aimed at the incorporation

of the occupied section, are totally invalid and cannot change that status'); UN Security Council Resolution 476 (30 June 1980); UN Security Council Resolution 478 (20 August 1980). Notably, these denunciations of Israel's attempts to alter the status of East Jerusalem were mirrored by the language of UN resolutions rejecting South Africa's endeavours to grant independence to certain Bantustan territories as similarly 'invalid': see, for example, UN General Assembly Resolution 31/6A (1976).
78. Shehadeh, *From Occupation to Interim Accords*, at 15; O. Dajani, 'Stalled between seasons: the international legal status of Palestine during the Interim Period' (1997–98) 26 *Denver Journal of International Law and Policy* 27, at 65–69: also the Declaration of Principles, Article 8, Public Order and Safety; Annex 2, Agreement Minutes to the Declaration of Principles on Interim Self-Government; Interim Agreement, Chapter 2, Article 12(1) and Chapter 3, Article 17(1–2).
79. Interim Agreement, Chapter 3, Article 17(3).
80. The Oslo Accords comprise The Declaration of Principles on Interim Self-Government Arrangements, September 1993 (1993) 32 *International Legal Materials* 1525; the Gaza-Jericho Agreement, May 1994 (1994) 33 *International Legal Materials* 622; The Interim Agreement on the West Bank and the Gaza Strip, September 1995 (1995) 36 *International Legal Materials* 551; Protocol on Redeployment in Hebron, January 1997 (1997) 36 *International Legal Materials* 650; Wye River Memorandum, October 1998 (1998) 37 *International Legal Materials* 1251, and the Sharm el-Sheikh Memorandum, September 1999 (1999) 38 *International Legal Materials* 1465. The latter two documents were focused on securing the compliance of the parties to implement prior agreements. These accords were preceded by Letters of Mutual Recognition in 1993. These agreements are sometimes termed collectively the 'Oslo Accords', 'Oslo' or 'the Oslo process'.
81. Declaration of Principles, Article 8, Public Order and Safety; Annex 2, Agreement Minutes to the Declaration of Principles on Interim Self-Government; Interim Agreement, Chapter 2, Article 12(1) and Chapter 3, Article 17(1–2).
82. Interim Agreements, Chapter 2, Article 13, para. 2; However, movement of Palestinian policemen in certain areas of Area B required approval and coordination by Israel: see Chapter 2, Article 8(4–5).
83. Interim Agreements, Chapter 2, Article 12(1).
84. The proportions of the West Bank cited above as constituting Areas A, B and C respectively derive from the 1995 *Interim Agreement on the West Bank and the Gaza Strip*. Those boundaries were to be gradually redrawn but have been frozen since the 1999 *Sharm el-Sheikh Memorandum on Implementation Timeline of Outstanding Commitments of Agreements Signed and the Resumption of Permanent Status Negotiations* at 17 per cent, 24 per cent and 59 per cent respectively.
85. Interim Agreement, Chapter 2, Article 11, Land, para. 3. In addition, a special formulation for control was crafted for Hebron, dividing it into areas categorised as 'H–1' and 'H–2', due to the presence of Jewish settlers in the heart of the Palestinian populated Old City of Hebron. The PA was to exercise all civil powers and responsibility over the Palestinian population in both sectors; however, in H–2, the location of the concentration of settlers, Israel would retain responsibility for public order and security. See the Protocol Concerning the Redeployment in Hebron (1997). Like Hebron, a different formulation was used in the Gaza Strip, although it was effectively divided under areas of Palestinian authority and areas of Israeli authority, comprising Israeli settlements and military areas. See Article 5, Gaza-Jericho Agreement (1994). As in the West Bank, control of airspace and borders remained effectively under Israeli control, although the Palestinian Authority was allowed to establish a nominal presence at the crossing with Egypt.
86. Article 5(1–3), Gaza-Jericho Agreement (1994).
87. Interim Agreement, Annex 3, Article 4(4).
88. See J. Singer, 'Aspects of foreign relations under the Israeli-Palestinian Agreements on interim self-government arrangements for the West Bank and Gaza' (1994) 26 *Israel Law Review* 268, at 269–273.

89. E. Benvenisti, 'The status of the Palestinian Authority', in E. Cotran and C. Mallat (eds), *The Arab-Israeli Accords: Legal Perspectives* (London: CIMEL/Kluwer, 1996), at 53: see also Benvenisti's 'Responsibility for the protection of human rights under the Interim Israeli-Palestinian Agreements' (1994) 28 *Israel Law Review* 297. Benvenisti's analysis is based on the terms of the 1994 Cairo Agreement on the Gaza Strip and Jericho Area. His main argument is equally applicable to the situation established under the Interim Agreement, which superseded the Gaza-Jericho Agreement: see Article 31(2) of the Interim Agreement.
90. Benvenisti, 'Status of the Palestinian Authority', at 56–57, emphasis in original; see at 53–57 generally; also Benvenisti, 'Responsibility for the protection of human rights', at 307–309.
91. Y. Dinstein, 'The international legal status of the West Bank and the Gaza Strip – 1998' (1998) 28 *Israel Yearbook on Human Rights* 37, at 45.
92. Interim Agreement, Article 17(1); Interim Agreement, Chapter 2, Article 11(2).
93. Interim Agreement, Annex 3, Appendix 1, Article 28(4).
94. Ibid., Article 28 (10).
95. Ibid., Article 22(4)(b).
96. Ibid., Article 15(5)(b)(2).
97. Ibid., Article 40.
98. Ibid., Article 36(b)(6) and (c)(2).
99. Ibid., Article 25(4–7).
100. Ibid., Article 15(5)(b)(2).
101. See, for example, the stipulations of Article 40 of Appendix 1 of Annex 3, Protocol Concerning Civil Affairs of the Interim Agreement on 'Water and Sewage' and the Joint Water Committee, or Article 22(4)(b) thereof on the Professional Joint Committee to deal with land issues.
102. This provision stipulated that draft legislation must be submitted to Israel for review and could be abrogated by Israel if it were deemed to amend or abrogate existing military orders, which would exceed the jurisdiction of the Council, or were otherwise inconsistent with the Declaration of Principles or the Interim Agreement: see Interim Agreement, Chapter 3, Article 18(4–5).
103. Shehadeh, *From Occupation to Interim Accords*, at 157.
104. Interim Agreement, Annex 3, Article 22(3).
105. Ibid., Article 40(5).
106. Article 1(2) of the Interim Agreement provides: 'Pending the inauguration of the Council, the powers and responsibilities transferred to the Council shall be exercised by the Palestinian Authority established in accordance with the Gaza-Jericho Agreement, which shall also have all the rights, liabilities and obligations to be assumed by the Council in this regard. Accordingly, the term "Council" throughout this Agreement shall, pending the inauguration of the Council, be construed as meaning the Palestinian Authority.' Chapter 1, Article 1 on the 'Transfer of Authority', specifies: 'Israel shall transfer powers and responsibilities as specified in this Agreement from the Israeli military government and its Civil Administration to the Council in accordance with this Agreement. Israel shall continue to exercise powers and responsibilities not so transferred.' On the status and powers of the Palestinian National Authority under the Interim Agreement, see Dajani, 'Stalled between seasons', at 60–74.
107. Dajani, 'Stalled between seasons' at 69; see also Crawford, *Creation of States*, at 443–444. Dajani provides a detailed analysis of the provisions of the Interim Agreement regulating the competence and jurisdiction of the Palestinian National Authority in Areas A and B (61–69) and estimates that the residual area of Area C covered 35–40 per cent of Gaza and 70 per cent of the West Bank (63). Under the terms of the Agreement, this included all settlements, any areas that Israel considered to be of strategic importance, and unpopulated areas, over which Israel was to retain territorial jurisdiction while the Palestinian National Authority assumed limited functional and personal jurisdiction over

Palestinians only: see Dajani, 'Stalled between seasons' at 69; see also Crawford, *Creation of States*, at 443–444.
108. Dajani, 'Stalled between seasons', at 64.
109. J. Singer, 'The Declaration of Principles on Interim Self-Government Arrangements: some legal aspects' (1994) 1 *Justice* 4 at 6, available at: www.intjewishlawyers.org/html/justice.asp.
110. C. Bruderlein, *Legal aspects of Israel's disengagement plan under international humanitarian law*, at 6, available at: www.ihlresearch.org/opt/pdfs/briefing3466.pdf.
111. Crawford aptly describes it as 'an interim local government body with restricted powers': see Crawford, *Creation of States*, 444: see also Dajani, 'Stalled between seasons', at 67; and Pictet, *Commentary to Geneva Convention IV*, at 62–63 and 272–276. As Dajani observes, there is a presumption against the creation of a new State on a territory under belligerent occupation: see his 'Stalled between seasons', at 77–78. These are generally seen as puppet States which lack independence. Dajani argues that separation between the PLO and PA preserves Palestinian negotiators' independence from Israel, and thus avoids the application of this presumption (at 90–91). See also Crawford, *Creation of States*, at 78–83 and 156–157; and K. Marek, *Identity and Continuity of States in Public International Law* (Geneva: Droz, 1968, 2nd edn), at 110–120.
112. Pictet, *Commentary to Geneva Convention IV*, at 69 and 274–275.
113. Ibid., at 69–70.
114. Ibid., at 275
115. Ibid., at 76.
116. Ibid., at 75.
117. Article 47, emphasis added.
118. In the Madrid talks, launched in 1991, and subsequently in the Oslo talks, the PLO was considered to be the legitimate representative of the Palestinian people. The Palestinian negotiation team, devoid of members of the PLO because they were barred from participating by Israel and the US, took its direction from the PLO leadership based in Tunis. See, for example, Shehadeh, *From Occupation to Interim Accords*, at 120; and Hanan Ashrawi, *This Side of Peace: A Personal Account* (New York: Touchstone, 1995), at 116, 147 and 199.
119. Although the PLO did not formally accede to the Conventions, Switzerland considered its unilateral undertaking to be valid: see *Wall* advisory opinion, ICJ Rep, 2004, at 173, para. 91.
120. Dajani, 'Stalled between seasons', at 71, maintains that the PLO does not have legal authority over decisions of the PA that relate to local governance of Palestinians in the OPT. While that is true, the PLO negotiated the framework for the creation of the PA and its powers. He also notes that while the PA has responsibility for municipal affairs within the OPT, it lacks the legal competence to make decisions regarding the ultimate status of the Palestinians within the OPT which, under the Oslo Accords, was to be addressed in the permanent status negotiations.
121. Had the Accords provided for the Palestinian Authority to assume negotiations with Israel as the authorities of the occupied territories, then those agreements would clearly fall within the scope of the Convention: see Dajani, 'Stalled between seasons', at 69–74, for a discussion of the relationship between the PA and PLO during the 1990s.
122. Pictet, *Commentary to Geneva Convention IV*, at 75.
123. See Article 1, 'Aim of Negotiations' and Article 5, 'Transitional Period and Permanent Status Negotiations', Declaration of Principles. Provisions related to permanent status agreement are very few, namely listing the issues to be addressed during permanent status talks, the timing of the talks and the caveat that arrangements reached during the interim period will not impact final status: see Article 1 and Article 5(2)–(4) of the Declaration of Principles. The Declaration of Principles and the subsequent agreements recognise these phases. It states that 'the two parties agree that the outcome of permanent status negotiations should not be prejudiced or pre-empted by agreements reached for the interim period'. See Article 5(4), Declaration of Principles.

NOTES to pp. 41–46  251

124. See 'A performance-based roadmap to a permanent two-state solution to the Israeli-Palestinian conflict' annexed to a letter dated 7 May 2003 from the Secretary-General addressed to the President of the Security Council, UN Doc. S/2003/529, 7 May 2003. For Israel's 14 reservations, see 'Israel's Response to the Road Map, 25 May, 2003', available at: www.knesset.gov.il/process/docs/roadmap_response_eng.htm. In light of the temporal stipulation – a final and comprehensive settlement of the Israel-Palestinian conflict in 2005 – as mentioned in the Roadmap, the Quartet (the EU, the UN, Russia and the US) launched the Annapolis process on 27 November 2007 to restart the moribund peace negotiations. On 16 December 2008, the Security Council declared its support for the negotiations initiated at Annapolis and 'its commitment to the irreversibility of the bilateral negotiations'. See Security Council Resolution 1850 (16 December 2008).
125. 'Performance-based roadmap', UN Doc. S/2003/529, 7 May 2003, emphasis added.
126. *Wall* advisory opinion, ICJ Rep, 2004, at 201, para. 162.
127. See 'The Cabinet Resolution Regarding the Disengagement Plan: Addendum A – Revised Disengagement Plan – Main Principles' and 'Addendum B – Format of the Preparatory Work for the Revised Disengagement Plan' (6 June 2004), available at: www.mfa.gov.il/MFA/Peace+Process/Reference+Documents/Revised+Disengagement+Plan+6-June-2004.htm.
128. Revised Disengagement Plan, Section 1 (*Political and Security Implications*), Principle Three. This passage went on to specify: 'On the other hand, it is clear that in the West Bank, there are areas which will be part of the State of Israel, including major Israeli population centers, cities, towns and villages, security areas and other places of special interest to Israel.' In his separate opinion appended to the *Wall* advisory opinion, Judge Elaraby stated that the Disengagement Plan's claim that parts of the West Bank would become 'part of the State of Israel' was relevant in assessing the legality of the wall, as this demonstrated a clear intent to annex those areas in breach of international law. See the separate opinion of Judge Elaraby, ICJ Rep, 2004, 246, at 253–254, para. 2.5.
129. Revised Disengagement Plan, Section 2.A (*Main Elements: The Process*), Article 3(1), *The Gaza Strip*.
130. IDF, *Declaration regarding end of military rule in Gaza Strip* (12 September 2005), available at: www.mfa.gov.il/MFA/Government/Communiques/2005/Exit+of+IDF+Forces+from+the+Gaza+Strip+completed+12-Sep-2005.htm.
131. IDF, *Declaration regarding end of military rule in Gaza Strip*. This decree annulled the 6 June 1967 proclamation that originally instituted military rule.
132. *Jaber al Bassouini Ahmed et al v. Prime Minister and Minister of Defense*, HCJ 9132/07, delivered 30 January 2008, opinion of President Beinisch, para. 12, available at: www.adalah.org/eng/gaza%20report.html. For commentary, see Y. Shany, 'The law applicable to non-occupied Gaza', paper delivered at the 'Complementing IHL: exploring the need for additional norms to govern contemporary conflict situations' conference (Jerusalem, 1–3 June 2008), available at: http://law.huji.ac.il/upload/Shany_The_Law_Applicable_to_gaza.pdf.
133. For instance, Y. Shany, 'Faraway, so close: the legal status of Gaza after Israel's disengagement' (2006) 8 *Yearbook of International Humanitarian Law* 369, and Shany's 'Binary law meets complex reality: the occupation of Gaza debate' (2008) 41 *Israel Law Review* 68. See also Bruderlein, *Legal aspects of Israel's disengagement plan*; E. Benvenisti, 'The law on the unilateral termination of occupation', in A. Zimmermann and T. Giegerich (eds), *Veröffentlichungen des Walther-Schücking-Instituts für Internationales Recht an der Universität Kiel* 371(2009); A. Bockel, 'Le retrait israelien de Gaza et ses consequences sur le droit international' (2005) 51 *Annuaire francais de droit international* 16; M.S. Kaliser, 'A modern day exodus: international human rights law and international humanitarian law implications of Israel's withdrawal from the Gaza Strip' (2007) 17 *Indiana International and Comparative Law Review* 187; M. Mari, 'The Israeli disengagement from the Gaza Strip: an end of the occupation?'(2005) 8 *Yearbook of International Humanitarian Law* 356; and I. Scobbie, 'An intimate disengagement: Israel's withdrawal from Gaza, the law of occupation and of self-determination' (2004–2005)

11 *Yearbook of Islamic and Middle Eastern Law* 3, reprinted in V. Kattan (ed.), *The Palestine Question in International Law* (London: British Institute of International and Comparative Law, 2008), at 637. The most recent comprehensive analysis of Gaza's status under the laws of occupation, robustly refuting Shany's position, can be found in Shane Darcy and John Reynolds, 'An enduring occupation: the status of the Gaza Strip from the perspective of international humanitarian law' (2010) 15:2 *Journal of Conflict and Security Law* 211.
134. Bruderlein, *Legal aspects of Israel's disengagement plan*, at 9.
135. *Namibia* advisory opinion, ICJ Rep, 1971, 16, at 31, para. 53.
136. A 'lightly edited version' of this report has been published as G. Aronson, 'Issues arising from the implementation of Israel's disengagement from the Gaza Strip' (2005) 34 *Journal of Palestine Studies* 49.
137. Available at: http://electronicintifada.net/bytopic/historicaldocuments/264.shtml; and also www.mfa.gov.il/MFA/Peace+Process/Reference+Documents/Disengagement+Plan+-+General+Outline.htm.
138. Aronson, 'Issues arising from the implementation of Israel's disengagement', at 51–53. See also Darcy and Reynolds, 'An Enduring Occupation'; Gisha–Legal Center for Freedom of Movement, *Disengaged Occupiers: The Legal Status of Gaza* (Tel Aviv: Gisha, 2007); and Scobbie, 'An intimate disengagement'. See also S. Roy, 'Praying with their eyes closed: reflections on the disengagement from Gaza' (2005) 34 *Journal of Palestine Studies* 64, at 70.
139. For an account of the basic principles of the Israel-Egypt 'military arrangement' on the deployment of Egyptian border guards on the Egyptian side of the corridor, see the Israeli Cabinet Communiqué of 28 August 2005, available at: www.mfa.gov.il/MFA/Government/Communiques/2005/Cabinet+Communique+28-Aug-2005.htm.
140. Sub-section 1.1 of Section 3 ('Security Situation following the Relocation') provides: 'The State of Israel will guard and monitor the external land perimeter of the Gaza Strip, will continue to maintain exclusive authority in Gaza air space, and will continue to exercise security activity in the sea off the coast of the Gaza Strip.'
141. Shany, 'Faraway, so close', at 373. For more detail, see Gisha–Legal Center for Freedom of Movement, *Disengaged Occupiers*, Chapter 3.
142. See Aronson, 'Issues arising from the implementation of Israel's disengagement', at 51.
143. Aronson, 'Issues arising from the implementation of Israel's disengagement', at 51–53. See also Gisha–Legal Center for Freedom of Movement, *Disengaged occupiers*, and Scobbie, 'An intimate disengagement'.
144. Gisha–Legal Center for Freedom of Movement, *Disengaged occupiers*, at 54–55.
145. The instruments dealing with the Rafah crossing include: the Israel-PA Agreement on Movement and Access, annexed Agreed Principles for Rafah Crossing (15 November 2005) and Agreed Arrangement on the European Union Border Assistance Mission at the Rafah Crossing Point on the Gaza-Egyptian Border (23 November 2005, concluded at the invitation of Israel and the Palestinian Authority): available at: www.nad-plo.org/listing.php?view=palisraeli_roadagree; and at: www.mfa.gov.il/MFA/Peace+Process/Reference+Documents/Agreed+documents+on+movement+and+access+from+and+to+Gaza+15-Nov-2005.htm. See also the EU Council press release 15011/05 (Presse 322) which gives an account of the mission of the Border Assistance Mission, available at: http://register.consilium.eu.int/pdf/en/05/st15/st15011.en05.pdf.
146. See Bruderlein, *Legal aspects of Israel's disengagement plan*; Shany, 'Faraway, so close'; and *Jaber al Bassouini Ahmed et al v. Prime Minister and Minister of Defense*, HCJ 9132/07, opinion of President Beinisch, para. 12.
147. Von Glahn raises the hypothesis of an occupation being created through control of a territory's airspace: 'Since international law does not contain a rule prescribing the military arm through which an effective belligerent occupation is to be exercised, it might be theoretically possible to maintain necessary control through the occupant's air force alone.' Nevertheless he comments that the practical problems which would arise in this type of occupation 'would seem to rule out such an experiment'. See G. von Glahn, *The*

*Occupation of Enemy Territory: A Commentary on the Law and Practice of Belligerent Occupation* (Minneapolis: University of Minnesota Press, 1957), at 28–29.
148. A. Roberts, 'The end of occupation: Iraq 2004' (2005) 54 *International and Comparative Law Quarterly* 27, at 28.
149. Von Glahn, *Occupation of Enemy Territory*, at 257.
150. L. Oppenheim, *International Law: A Treatise, Vol. II: Disputes, War and Neutrality* (London: Longman, 1952, 7th edn by H. Lauterpacht), at 436. See also W. Heintschel von Heinegg, 'Factors in war to peace transitions' (2003–04) 27 *Harvard Journal of Law and Public Policy* 843 at 845: 'The end of an occupation is a question of fact. It will be brought about by any loss of authority over the territory in question.'
151. Oppenheim, *International Law, Vol. II*, at 618.
152. See Security Council Resolution 1546 (8 June 2004), reproduced (2004) 43 *International Legal Materials* 1459; and also A. Carcano, 'End of occupation in 2004? The status of the multinational force in Iraq after the transfer of sovereignty to the interim Iraqi government' (2006) 11 *Journal of Conflict and Security Law* 41; C. McCarthy, 'The paradox of the international law of military operations: sovereignty and the reformation of Iraq' (2005) 10 *Journal of Conflict and Security Law* 43; and Roberts, 'End of occupation', n.155. For critical accounts of the conduct of the occupation of Iraq, see E. Afsha, 'Limits and limitations of power: the continued relevance of occupation law' (2006) 7 *German Law Journal* 563, available at: www.germanlawjournal.com; and G.H. Fox, 'The occupation of Iraq' (2005) 36 *Georgetown Journal of International Law* 195.
153. On the same day, 18 October 1907, that the Hague Peace Conference adopted its various conventions, it also promulgated Declaration XIV prohibiting the Discharge of Projectiles and Explosives from Balloons. This prohibited 'the discharge of projectiles and explosives from balloons or by other new methods of a similar nature'. Although technically still in force, this Declaration has few parties and has been rendered obsolete by subsequent practice.
154. Quoted in D. Li, 'The Gaza Strip as laboratory: notes in the wake of disengagement' (2006) 35 *Journal of Palestine Studies* 38, at 48.
155. See Benvenisti, 'Unilateral termination', especially text to n.10, and text following n.17.
156. See Bruderlein, *Legal aspects of Israel's disengagement plan*, at 9 n.14. *Tsemel v. Minister of Defence*, HCJ 102/82, 37(3) Piskei Din 365; also cited employing a more extended quotation in Lein, *One Big Prison*, at 73–74, available at: www.hamoked.org.il/items/12800_eng.pdf. *Tsemel* is summarised in (1983) 13 *Israel Yearbook on Human Rights* 360: see 362–363 in particular.
157. See Trial of Wilhelm List and others (the Hostages trial), VIII *Law Reports of Trials of War Criminals* 34 (1949), at 55–56; quotation at 56.
158. *Prosecutor v. Naletilic and Martinovic, Case No.IT-98-34-T* (trial judgment, 31 March 2003), available at: www.un.org/icty/naletilic/trialc/judgement/nal-tj030331-e.pdf, 74, para. 217. In support of this ruling, the Trial Chamber cited as authority the United Kingdom's *Manual of Military Law of War on Land*, Part III, paras 502 and 506 (1958); the United States' *The Law of Land Warfare: Field Manual No. 27–10*, Chapter 6, para. 356 (1956); and the New Zealand Defence Force's *Interim Law of Armed Conflict Manual*, paras 1302(2), 1302(3) and 1302(5) (1992).
159. Benvenisti, 'Unilateral termination', text to n.33.
160. General Assembly Resolution 2625.
161. *Wall* advisory opinion, ICJ Rep (2004), at 185, para. 125; at 185–187, paras 125–126.
162. Final Record of the Diplomatic Conference of Geneva of 1949, Vol. II A, at 815.
163. See, for example, A. Imseis, 'Critical reflections on the international humanitarian law aspects of the ICJ advisory opinion on the Wall' (2005) 99 *American Journal of International Law*, at 105–109.
164. *Public Committee against Torture in Israel and Palestinian Society for the Protection of Human Rights and the Environment v. (i) the Government of Israel, (ii) the Prime Minister of Israel, (iii) the Minister of Defence, (iv) the Israel Defense Forces, (v) the Chief of the General Staff of the Israel Defense Forces, (vi) Shurat HaDin – Israel Law Center*

*et al*, judgment of 13 December 2006 (the *Targeted Killings* case). An official English translation of this judgment is available on the Israel Supreme Court's website at: http://elyon1.court.gov.il/files_eng/02/690/007/A34/02007690.a34.pdf.
165. *Targeted Killings* case, opinion of President Emeritus Barak, para. 16.
166. Ibid., para. 18.
167. Ibid., para. 21.
168. Ibid., para. 21.
169. See Declaration of Principles, Article 4; and Interim Agreement, Article 11(1); for commentary, see Shehadeh, *From Occupation to Interim Accords*, at 35–37.
170. *Ajuri v. IDF Commander*, HCJ 7015/02 (3 September 2002), [2002] *Isr LR* 1, opinion of President Barak, at 17–18, para. 22. See also Lein, *One Big Prison*, at 20–21, who notes, *inter alia*, that Israel incorporated the Interim Agreement in its entirety into its military legislation in both the West Bank and Gaza, and that this legislation has not been revoked.
171. See Pictet, *Commentary to Geneva Convention IV*, at 62–63; for the *travaux*, see *Final Record of the Diplomatic Conference of Geneva of 1949* (Berne: Federal Political Department, 1949), Vol. II A, at 623–625, 775–776 and 815–816, and Vol. II B, at 386–388. See also above (pp. 41–45) on agreements made under Article 47 of the Fourth Geneva Convention, but compare Dinstein, 'International legal status of the West Bank and the Gaza Strip'.
172. Pictet, *Commentary to Geneva Convention IV*, at 63.
173. *Wall* advisory opinion, ICJ Rep, 2004, at 200, para. 159. Even if self-determination is regarded only as an obligation *erga omnes*, as opposed to a *jus cogens* norm, then its breach entails a duty of non-recognition for third States.
174. Settlements are defined here as organised communities of Israeli civilians established on land in the OPT with the approval, protection and direct or indirect support of the Israeli government. Apart from a few exceptions in East Jerusalem, residence in these communities is open only to persons of Jewish descent, defined as people entitled to Israeli citizenship or residency under Israel's Law of Return. As this study was being concluded, Israel had established 149 settlements in the West Bank, including East Jerusalem, which together held close to half a million Jewish residents. This number excluded approximately 100 settlement 'illegal outposts', which are established without the formal authorisation of the government of Israel.
175. For the avoidance of any doubt, even according to the highly controversial ruling of the ICJ in the *Wall* advisory opinion, about the cessation of the applicability of the Fourth Geneva Convention after the general close of military operations, Article 49(6) survives the one-year time limit on application of certain provisions in the Convention in occupied territory laid down in Article 6(3): see Imseis, 'Critical reflections', at 106.
176. Pictet, *Commentary to Geneva Convention IV*, at 276.
177. Article 8(2)(b)(viii) of the Rome Statute of the International Criminal Court. On the difference between Article 49(6) of the Fourth Geneva Convention and Article 8(2)(b)(viii) of the Rome Statute, see D. Kretzmer, 'Agora: ICJ advisory opinion on Construction of a Wall in the Occupied Palestinian Territory: the advisory opinion: the light treatment of international humanitarian Law' 99 *American Journal of International Law* 88 at 91. Kretzmer considers that broadening Article 49(6) in the Rome Statute by adding the words 'directly or indirectly' indicates that not all measures taken to bring about a transfer are included in Article 49(6) itself; see also the ICJ's *Wall* advisory opinion, para. 135.
178. Between 1967 and 1979, Israel established altogether 133 settlements in the occupied territories, including 79 in the West Bank and seven in the Gaza Strip: see the report of the Security Council Commission established under Resolution 446 (1979), available at: http://domino.un.org/UNISPAL.NSF/2f86ce183126001f85256cef0073ccce/9785bb5ef4 4772dd85256436006c9c85!OpenDocument.
179. Israel's 1952 Status Law confirms the Jewish Agency and World Zionist Organisation as the 'authorised agencies' of the state to administer Jewish national affairs in Israel and in the OPT: see further discussion in Chapter 4. The Status Law was amended in 1975

180. to restructure this relationship: see World Zionist Organisation–Jewish Agency for Israel (Status) (Amendment) Law, 5736–1975.
180. Extract of the Drobles Plan, from Matitiyahu Drobles, *The Settlement in Judea and Samaria – Strategy, Policy and Program* (in Hebrew) (Jerusalem: World Zionist Organisation, September 1980), at 3; quoted in B'Tselem, *Land Grab: Israel's Settlement Policy in the West Bank* (May 2002), at 14.
181. Quoted in Al-Haq, 'Discrimination is real: discriminatory Israeli policies in Israel, the occupied Tterritories and occupied East Jerusalem', Draft Paper presented to the World Conference Against Racism, Durban, South Africa, 28 August–7 September 2001, at 21. The Drobles Plan went through several versions after its composition in 1978. See also C. Jackson, 'Israeli West Bank Settlements, the Reagan Administration's policy towards the Middle East and international law' (1987) 79 *American Society of International Law Proceedings* 217, at 226.
182. See Al-Haq, *The Israeli Settlements from the Perspective of International Law* (Ramallah: Al-Haq, 2000), also available at: www.alhaq.org/pdfs/The%20Israeli%20Settlements%20from%20the%20Perspective%20of%20International%20Law.pdf. See also B'Tselem, *Israeli Settlement in the Occupied Territories as a Violation of Human Rights: Legal and Conceptual Aspects* (March 1997), available at: www.btselem.org/Download/199703_Settlements_Eng.rtf.
183. See D. Kretzmer, *The Occupation of Justice: The Supreme Court of Israel and the Occupied Territories* (Albany, NY: SUNY Press, 2002); also Gorenberg, *Accidental Empire*.
184. Israel Ministry of Foreign Affairs, 'Israeli Settlements and International Law' (May 2001), available at: http://tinyurl.com/2jlgb3.
185. See *Wall* advisory opinion, para. 120.
186. Ibid.
187. See, for example, Resolution 465 (1980) in which the Security Council 'Determines that all measures taken by Israel to change the physical character, demographic composition, institutional structure or status of the Palestinian and other Arab territories occupied since 1967, including Jerusalem, or any part thereof, have no legal validity and that Israel's policy and practices of settling parts of its population and new immigrants in those territories constitute a flagrant violation of the Fourth Geneva Convention relative to the Protection of Civilian Persons in Time of War and also constitute a serious obstruction to achieving a comprehensive, just and lasting peace in the Middle East': see also Security Council Resolutions 446, 452 and 471.
188. General Assembly Resolution 62/108 of 10 January 2008 is one of dozens of resolutions to this effect.
189. See *Declaration of the High Contracting Parties to the Fourth Geneva Convention*, 5 December 2001. The High Contracting Parties are those States which have ratified and are bound by the Geneva Conventions.
190. Jean-Marie Henckaerts and Louise Doswald-Beck, *Customary International Humanitarian Law, Volume I: Rules* (Cambridge: Cambridge University Press, 2005), at 457.
191. See, for example, Kretzmer, 'Light treatment of international humanitarian law', at 89.
192. Security Council Resolution 465 (1 March 1980), operative para. 5.
193. Ibid., operative para. 6.
194. Ibid., operative para. 7.
195. A scan of the original Hebrew text of this opinion is available at: http://southjerusalem.com/settlement-and-occupation-historical-documents/, and a complete English translation is on the website of the Sir Joseph Hotung Programme in Law, Human Rights and Peace Building in the Middle East (School of Oriental and African Studies, London) at: www.soas.ac.uk/lawpeacemideast/resources/48485.pdf.
196. See United States: Letter of the State Department Legal Adviser Concerning the Legality of Israeli Settlements in the Occupied Territories, 21 April 1978, in 17 *International Legal Materials* (1978) 777, at 779.

197. See the 1993 Declaration of Principles on Interim Self-Government Arrangements, Article 4; and the 1995 Israeli-Palestinian Interim Agreement on the West Bank and the Gaza Strip, Article 11(1)(5).
198. See, for example, Security Council Resolution 446 (22 March 1979); Security Council Resolution 452, (20 July 1979); and Security Council Resolution 471, (5 June 1980).
199. See operative para. 9 of the Venice European Council Declaration (13 June 1980), available at: www.ec.europa.eu/external_relations/mepp/docs/venice_declaration_1980_en.pdf.
200. See *Mara'abe et al v. The Prime Minister of Israel et al*, HCJ 7957/04, para. 18.
201. See Articles 30–31 of the Vienna Convention on the Laws of Treaties (1969), 1155 UNTS 331.
202. See Articles 43, 48, 49, 55 of the Hague Regulations and para. 88 of the *Wall* advisory opinion. See also Benvenisti, *International Law of Occupation*, at 6, and O. Ben-Naftali, A.M. Gross and K. Michaeli, 'Illegal occupation: framing the occupied Palestinian territory' (2005) 23 *Berkeley Journal of International Law* 551, at 21–36; A. Roberts, 'What is a military occupation?' (1984) 55 *British Yearbook of International Law* 249, at 293–295; A. Wilson, 'The laws of war in occupied territories' (1933) 18 *Transactions Grotius Society* 17, at 38.
203. See *Hess v. Commander of the IDF Forces in the West Bank*, HCJ 10356/02, 58 (3) PD 443. For an extensive overview of this trend, see Kretzmer, *Occupation of Justice*.
204. The *lex specialis* norms of international humanitarian law hold that the rights of protected persons cannot generally be restricted, and that any exceptional restriction may only be in accordance with the limitation clauses in the relevant provisions: see Ben-Naftali et al, 'Illegal occupation', at 596, and Kretzmer, *Occupation of Justice*. Compare with Articles 13–26 of the Fourth Geneva Convention which apply humanitarian norms to every individual happens to be in the occupied territory. For comprehensive discussion on the *lex specialis* doctrine applied by the ICJ, see O. Ben-Naftali and Y. Shany, 'Living in denial: the application of human rights in the Occupied Territories' (2003–04) 37 *Israel Law Review*, at 17–118. For general discussion of the interplay between international humanitarian and human rights law, see F. Hampson and I. Salama, 'Working paper on the relationship between human rights law and international humanitarian law', *UN Sub-Commission on the Promotion and Protection of Human Rights*, E/CN.4/Sub.2/2005/14, 21 June 2005.
205. *Mara'abe*, para. 28, emphasis added.
206. See H. Krieger, 'A conflict of norms: the relationship between humanitarian law and human rights law in the ICRC Customary Law Study' (2006) 11(2) *Journal of Conflict and Security Law*, 265–291, at 284.
207. Ibid., para. 25.
208. See R. Lapidot, 'Public international law', in *Forty Years of Israeli Law* (Jerusalem: Harry Sacher Institute for Legislative Research and Comparative Law, 1990), at 807.
209. For discussion of the Supreme Court's jurisdiction to examine the legality of the Israeli army in the OPT, see Kretzmer, *Occupation of Justice*, Chapter 1, 'Jurisdiction, Justiciability and Substantive Norms', at 19–29.
210. See *Bargil v. Government of Israel*, HCJ 4481/91, 47 (4) PD 210, 216.
211. See, for example, *Ayyub v. Minister of Defense*, HCJ 606/78, (1978) 33 (2) PD 113.
212. See Kretzmer, *Occupation of Justice*, at 44.
213. *Abu Helou and others v. Government of Israel*, HCJ 302/72, (1972) 27(2) PD 169.
214. Ibid., at 181, unofficial translation.
215. *Ayyub v. Minister of Defense*, HCJ 606/78, (1978) 33 (2) PD 113 (*Beit El* case).
216. See the *Beit El* case. The court has also rejected the argument that the establishment of a civilian settlement cannot be regarded as temporary use of the land, accepting the governments' statement that the settlement will exist only as long as the army holds the land, subject to international negotiations which will determine the fate of the settlements. This decision must be considered in its immediate political context: see pp. 116–117 of the judgment.
217. The *Beit El* case, at 117 (unofficial translation).
218. Benvenisti, *International Law of Occupation*, at 3.

219. *Dweikat v. Israel*, HCJ 390/79, 34(1) PD1 (hereafter the *Elon Moreh* case).
220. *Elon Moreh* case, at 17. For analysis of the atmosphere enabled the court to give this decision, see Kretzmer, *Occupation of Justice*, at 88–89.
221. This decision was surprisingly especially because in the *Matityahu* case decision (*Amira v. Minister of Defence* case 34 (1) PD 90), issued in 1979, the court dismissed a petition in which an affidavit given by a General Reserves to support the petition refuted the security arguments for the settlement. The Court found the affidavit unconvincing. The court also dismissed the argument that the requisition order was invalid since the decision to make the order had been made by the Cabinet committee on security rather than the military authorities.
222. *Elon Moreh* case, at 22 (unofficial translation).
223. See B'Tselem, *Land Grab* (Jerusalem: B'Tselem, 2002).
224. This was possible due to the fact that no comprehensive registration of land ownership existed for the West Bank or Gaza in 1967. See Kretzmer, *Occupation of Justice*, at 90 and references there.
225. See Kretzmer, *Occupation of Justice*, at 90 and references there to *Master Plan for the Development of Settlements in Judea and Samaria, 1979–1983*, prepared by Matityahu Drobles; also Al-Haq, *The Israeli Settlements*, at 41. For more details on the content of the Drobles Plan, see *Israeli Settlements in Gaza and the West Bank (Including Jerusalem) Their Nature and Purpose, Prepared for, and under the guidance of the Committee on the Exercise of the Inalienable Rights of the Palestinian People*, 31/12/1982 available at: http://domino.un.org/UNISPAL.NSF/c25aba03f1e079db85256cf40073bfe6/b795b2d7f e86da4885256b5a00666d70!OpenDocument.
226. *Al-Naazer v. Commander of Judea and Samaria* (1981) 36 (1) PD 701.
227. See criticism on this presumption in A. Cassese, 'Powers and duties of an occupant in relation to land and natural resources', in E. Playfair (ed.), *International Law and the Administration of Occupied Territories* (Oxford: Clarendon Press, 1992), at 437–438.
228. *Ayreib v. Appeals Committee*, HCJ 277/84, 40(2) PD 57, at 69.
229. Kretzmer, *Occupation of Justice*, at 93.
230. Ibid., at 94.
231. Ibid., at 70–71.
232. *Tabeeb v. Minister of Defense*, HCJ, 202/81, PD.36(2), 622.
233. *Jami'at Ascan Al-Moa'limin al-Mahdudat al-Masauliyeh, Communal Society Registered at the Judea and Samaria Area Headquarters v. The Commander of IDF Forces in the Judea and Samaria Area*, HCJ 393/82, 37(4) PD 785.
234. This interchange connects the highways linking Tel Aviv, Jerusalem and Ma'ale Adumim (a large Jewish-Israeli urban settlement in the West Bank between Jerusalem and Jericho).
235. See *Jami'at Ascan*, 794.
236. *Jami'at Ascan*, para. 36 (unofficial translation).
237. See *Ottoman debt* arbitration (1925) 3 *Annual Digest of Public International Law Cases* 472 (1925–26); and Benvenisti, *International Law of Occupation*, at 3–6; G.H. Hackworth, *Digest of International Law* (Washington, DC: Department of State, 1940), at 145–146; A. McNair and A.D. Watts, *The Legal Effects of War* (Cambridge: Cambridge University Press, 1966, 4th edn), at 363–369; Oppenheim, *International Law, Vol. II*, at 436–438; G. Schwarzenberger, *International Law as Applied by International Courts and Tribunals, Vol. II: The Law of Armed Conflict* (London: Stevens, 1968), at 166–173; and UK Ministry of Defence, *The Manual of the Law of Armed Conflict* (Oxford: Oxford University Press, 2004), at 278–279, paras 11(9)–11(11).
238. An overview of the consolidation of the Hague Regulations into customary international law was given by Acting President Shamgar of the Israel Supreme Court in *Bassil Abu Aita et al v. The Regional Commander of Judea and Samaria and Staff Officer in charge of matters of customs and excise*, HCJ 69/81 (5 April 1983), 37(2) PD 197, at 251–252, para. 19(b) (original Hebrew text), 7 *Selected Judgments of the Supreme Court of Israel* 1 (1983–87) 46–47, para. 19(b) (English translation), 63–64, para. 19(d) (English translation available at: http://elyon1.court.gov.il/files_eng/81/690/000/z01/81000690.

z01.pdf). Hereinafter, this case will be cited as *Abu Aita*. Extracts from Shamgar's opinion in *Abu Aita* are provided at 13 *Israel Yearbook on Human Rights* (1983) 348.

239. Israel's Supreme Court fulfils two broad functions. As the Supreme Court it serves as a court of appeal from the decisions of lower courts, and as the High Court of Justice it acts as a court of first and last instance in petitions for the review of governmental actions, including actions taken in the occupied Tterritories: see Benvenisti, *International Law of Occupation*, at 118–123; Y. Dotan, 'Judicial rhetoric, government lawyers, and human rights: the case of the Israeli High Court of Justice during the intifada' (1999) 33 *Law and Society Review* 319, at 322–324; and Kretzmer, *Occupation of Justice*, at 10–11. The principal judgments of the Supreme Court relevant to prolonged occupation include *Christian Society for the Holy Places* v. *Minister of Defence et al*, HC 337/71, 2 *Israel Yearbook on Human Rights* 354 (1972), and 52 *International Law Reports* 512; *Electric Corporation for Jerusalem District Ltd* v. *Minister of Defence et al*, HC 256/72, 5 *Israel Yearbook on Human Rights* 381 (1975) [hereinafter *Electricity Company No. 1*]; *Jerusalem District Electricity Co Ltd* v. *Minister of Energy and Infrastructure and Commander of the Judea and Samaria Region*, HC 351/80, 11 *Israel Yearbook on Human Rights* 354 (1981) [hereinafter *Electricity Company No. 2*]; *Jami'at Ascan Al-Moa`limin* v. *IDF Commander in Judea and Samaria* (1982) 37(4) PD 785, discussed *in extenso* in Kretzmer, *Occupation of Justice*, at 69–71 and partially reported in translation as '*A Cooperative Society Lawfully Registered in the Judea and Samaria Region* v. *Commander of IDF Forces in the Judea and Samaria Region et al*, HC 393/82' (1984) 14 *Israel Yearbook on Human Rights* 301; *Abu Aita*; *Dwadin et al* v. *Commander of the IDF Forces in the West Bank*, HC 4154/91, 25 *Israel Yearbook on Human Rights* (1985) 333; *Economic Corporation for Jerusalem Ltd* v. *Commander of IDF Forces in the Judea and Samaria Region et al*, HC 5808/93, 30 *Israel Yearbook on Human Rights* 322 (2000); and *Na-ale: An Association for the Settlement of employees of the Israeli Aircraft Industry in Samaria* v. *the Supreme Planning Committee of the Judea and Samaria Area, the Sub-Committee for Mining and Quarrying et al*, HC 9717/03, *International Law in Domestic Courts* database, ILDC 70 (IL 2004), also summarised as *Na'ale* v. *Planning Council for the Judea and Samaria Region et al*, 37 *Israel Yearbook on Human Rights* (2007), at 332.

240. See Benvenisti, *International Law of Occupation*, at 144–148; Cassese, 'Powers and duties of an occupant', at 426–427; Y. Dinstein, 'The international law of occupation and human rights' (1978) 8 *Israel Yearbook on Human Rights* 104, at 112–114, and Dinstein's 'Legislation under Article 43 of the Hague Regulations: belligerent occupation and peacebuilding' (2004) 8 *Harvard Program on Humanitarian Policy and Conflict Research, Occasional Paper No. 1*, available at: www.hpcr.org/pdfs/OccasionalPaper1.pdf; R. Falk, 'Some legal reflections on prolonged Israeli occupation of Gaza and the West Bank '(1989) 2 *Journal of Refugee Studies* 40; G. von Glahn, 'Taxation under belligerent occupation', in Playfair, *International Law and the Administration of Occupied Territories*, at 349; C. Greenwood, 'The administration of occupied territory in international law', in Playfair, *International Law and the Administration of Occupied Territories*, at 263; A. Roberts, 'Prolonged military occupation: the Israeli-occupied territories since 1967'(1990) 84 *American Journal of International Law* 44; E. Schwenk, 'Legislative power of the military occupant under Article 43, Hague Regulations' (1944–45) 54 *Yale Law Journal* 393, at 401; and M. Sassoli, 'Legislation and maintenance of public order and civil life by occupying powers' (2005) 16 *European Journal of International Law* 661, at 679–680.

241. Roberts, 'Prolonged military occupation', at 47.
242. Ibid., at 51.
243. See, for example, O. Ben-Naftali, '"A la recherche du temps perdu": rethinking Article 6 of the Fourth Geneva Convention in the light of the Legal Consequences of the Construction of a Wall in the Occupied Palestinian Territory advisory opinion' (2005) 38 *Israel Law Review* 211, at 215 and 218; Ben-Naftali et al, 'Illegal occupation', at 596; Benvenisti, *International Law of Occupation*, at 144; D.A. Graber, *The Development of the Law of Belligerent Occupation 1863–1914: A Historical Survey* (New York: Columbia University Press, 1949), at 290–291; and Roberts, 'Prolonged military occupation', at 47.

244. Graber, *Development of the Law of Belligerent Occupation*, at 290–291.
245. Roberts, 'Prolonged military occupation', at 52.
246. See, for example, Benvenisti, *International Law of Occupation*, at 147–148; Dinstein, 'The international law of occupation and human rights', at 112, and 'Legislation under Article 43 of the Hague Regulations', at 8; Roberts, 'Prolonged military occupation', at 52; Sassoli, 'Legislation and maintenance of public order', at 679; and Schwenk, 'Legislative power under Article 43', at 401.
247. Dinstein, 'The international law of occupation and human rights', at 113.
248. Benvenisti, *International Law of Occupation*, at 147.
249. On the interpretation of Article 43, see Dinstein, 'Legislation under Article 43 of the Hague Regulations'; von Glahn, *Occupation of Enemy Territory*, Chapter 8, and also his 'Taxation under belligerent occupation', at 347–350; Greenwood, 'Administration of occupied territory in international law'; E. Playfair, 'Playing on principle? Israel's justification for its administrative acts in the occupied West Bank', in Playfair, *International Law and the Administration of Occupied Territories*, at 207–215; Kretzmer, *Occupation of Justice*, Chapter 4; M. Qupty, 'The application of international law in the Occupied Territories as reflected in the judgments of the High Court of Justice in Israel', in Playfair, *International Law and the Administration of Occupied Territories*, at 92–98; Schwarzenberger, *International Law as Applied by International Courts and Tribunals, Vol. II*, at 191–207; Schwenk, 'Legislative Power under Article 43'; Sassoli, 'Legislation and maintenance of public order'; and J. Stone, *Legal Controls of International Conflict* (Sydney: Maitland, 1959, rev. edn), at 698–699.
250. This is the standard English translation of the authoritative French text. The French text reads: 'L'autorité du pouvoir légal ayant passé de fait entre les mains de l'occupant, celui-ci prendra toutes les mesures qui dépendent de lui en vue de rétablir et d'assurer, autant qu'il est possible, l'ordre et la vie publics en respectant, sauf empêchement absolu, les lois en vigueur dans le pays.' It is, however, accepted that to render the key phrase 'l'ordre et la vie publics' as 'public order and safety' is unsatisfactory. Following Schwenk, this phrase is better translated as 'public order and civil life' to import the idea that 'la vie publique' should be conceived broadly to refer to 'the whole social, commercial and economic life of the country'. See Schwenk, 'Legislative Power under Article 43', at 393 n.1 and 398; and also Greenwood, 'Administration of occupied territory in international law', at 246; and Sassoli, 'Legislation and maintenance of public order', at 663–664. Otherwise, see on these points see Benvenisti, *International Law of Occupation*, at 7; Dinstein, 'Legislation under Article 43 of the Hague Regulations', at 2; von Glahn, 'Taxation under belligerent occupation', at 348; Greenwood, 'Administration of occupied territory in international law', at 246; Playfair, 'Playing on principle?', at 207; Sassoli, 'Legislation and maintenance of public order', at 663–664; Schwarzenberger, *International Law as Applied by International Courts and Tribunals, Vol. II*, at 180; and Schwenk, 'Legislative Power under Article 43', at 393 n.1 and 398. This misinterpretation was noted in the pivotal first case dealing with the implications of prolonged occupation decided by Israel's Supreme Court, *Christian Society for the Holy Places* v. *Minister of Defence and others*: see 52 *International Law Reports* 512, opinion of Deputy President Sussman, at 513–514. This passage does not appear in the summary of the case provided at 2 *Israel Yearbook on Human Rights* (1972) 354.
251. Article 64 of the Fourth Geneva Convention has been described as 'a more precise and detailed [expression of] the terms of Article 43 of the Hague Regulations': see Pictet, *Commentary to Geneva Convention IV*, at 335.
252. Pictet, *Commentary to Geneva Convention IV*, at 337.
253. For commentaries on Article 64, see Ben-Naftali et al, 'Illegal occupation', at 594; Benvenisti, *International Law of Occupation*, at 100–105; Dinstein, 'Legislation under Article 43 of the Hague Regulations', at 5–8; Pictet, *Commentary to Geneva Convention IV*, at 334–336; Sassoli, 'Legislation and maintenance of public order', at 669–670; and Schwarzenberger, *International Law as Applied by International Courts and Tribunals, Vol. II*, at 193–195. See also T. Ferraro, 'Enforcement of occupation law in domestic

courts: issues and opportunities' (2008) 41 *Israel Law Review* 331.There is a presumption against measures adopted by the occupant having extra-territorial effect. In 1970, an Israeli military court sitting in Ramallah ruled that Article 64 only conferred extraterritorial legislative competence on the occupant in relation to 'classical' security offences, namely, those offences whose prevention was 'necessary in order to preserve the physical security of the Occupying Power and its forces': see *Military Prosecutor v. Akrash Nazimi Bakir*, 48 *International Law Reports* 478, at 483–484 (n.d.).

254. Greenwood, 'Administration of occupied territory in international law', at 247. Interpretations of these articles have differed. For example, Schwarzenberger has claimed that by adopting this enumeration 'the Conference of 1949 took it for granted that it had not extended the traditional scope of occupation legislation': see his *International Law as Applied by International Courts and Tribunals, Vol. II*, at 194. Others argue that Article 64(2) attenuates the restrictions on the occupant's legislative competence imposed by Article 43 of the Hague Regulations: see, for example, Ben-Naftali et al, 'Illegal occupation', at 594; Benvenisti, *International Law of Occupation*, at 100–105; and Sassoli, 'Legislation and maintenance of public order', at 670.

255. Von Glahn, *Occupation of Enemy Territory*, at 99.

256. Playfair, 'Playing on principle?', at 207; see also Sassoli, 'Legislation and maintenance of public order', at 673–674; and Schwenk, 'Legislative Power under Article 43', at 399–400.

257. Schwenk, 'Legislative Power under Article 43', at 399.

258. Sassoli, 'Legislation and maintenance of public order', at 673; and Dinstein, 'Legislation under Article 43 of the Hague Regulations', at 4, and 'Occupation and human rights', at 112; E.H. Feilchenfeld, *The International Economic Law of Belligerent Occupation* (Washington, DC: Carnegie Endowment for International Peace, 1942), at 89; Kretzmer, *Occupation of Justice*, at 63; and Schwarzenberger, *International Law as Applied by International Courts and Tribunals, Vol. II*, at 193.

259. Dinstein, 'Legislation under Article 43 of the Hague Regulations', at 8.

260. Benvenisti, *International Law of Occupation*, at 147: see also Dinstein, 'Legislation under Article 43 of the Hague Regulations', at 9–10; and also '*In re Krupp and others* (United States Military Tribunal at Nuremberg, 30 June 1948)', 15 *International Law Reports* 620, at 623: 'The occupying power is forbidden from imposing any new concept of law upon the occupied territory unless such provision is justified by the requirements of public order and safety.'

261. Dinstein, 'Legislation under Article 43 of the Hague Regulations', at 9–10, and also 'Occupation and human rights', at 112: see also *Christian Society for the Holy Places, Minister of Defence and others*, 52 *International Law Reports* 512, dissenting opinion of Cohn J, 518, at 520; and T. Meron, 'Applicability of multilateral conventions to occupied territories' (1978) 72 *American Journal of International Law* 542, at 548–550.

262. *Abu Aita*, opinion of Acting President Shamgar, 314–315/98–99/135–136, para. 50(e): see also 13 *Israel Yearbook on Human Rights* (1983) 348, at 357: but compare *Economic Corporation for Jerusalem Ltd v. Commander of IDF Forces in the Judea and Samaria Region et al* (2000) 30 *Israel Yearbook on Human Rights* 322, at 324.

263. Pictet, *Commentary to Geneva Convention IV*, 336; see also Roberts, 'Prolonged military occupation', at 94; and Sassoli, 'Legislation and maintenance of public order', at 677.

264. Meron, 'Applicability of multilateral conventions', at 550.

265. Dinstein, 'Legislation under Article 43 of the Hague Regulations', at 6; Kretzmer, *Occupation of Justice*, at 60: see also Sassoli, 'Legislation and maintenance of public order', at 674 and 676–677.

266. The Supreme Court's interpretation of Article 43 has been criticised on the ground that it attenuates unduly the restrictions placed on legislative competence, substituting administrative convenience for the criterion of necessity: see, for example, Kretzmer, *Occupation of Justice*, at 57–72; Playfair, 'Playing on principle?', at 211 et seq; Qupty, 'Judgments', at 91–97; and Sassoli, 'Legislation and maintenance of public order', at 674: 'The practice of Israeli courts concerning legislation in the Israeli occupied territories is ... very permissive.' On the other hand, Cassese sees some merit in the approach

adopted by the Supreme Court: see his 'Powers and duties of an occupant', at 423–427: see also Singer, 'Aspects of foreign relations under the Israeli-Palestinian Agreements', at 275–277. Singer's exegesis of Article 43 ignores the point that only factual authority, but not sovereignty, passes to the occupant.

267. See von Glahn, 'Taxation under belligerent occupation', at 345–346.
268. See, for example, *A Cooperative Society Lawfully Registered in the Judea and Samaria Region* v. *Commander of IDF Forces in the Judea and Samaria Region et al* (1984) 14 *Israel Yearbook on Human Rights* 301, at 307–308, and as *Jami'at Ascan*, Kretzmer, *Occupation of Justice*, at 70; *Dwadin et al* v. *Commander of IDF Forces in the West Bank* (1985) 25 *Israel Yearbook on Human Rights* 333 at 334; *Economic Corporation for Jerusalem Ltd* v. *Commander of IDF Forces in the Judea and Samaria Region et al* (2000) 30 *Israel Yearbook on Human Rights* 322, at 324; and *Na'ale* v. *The Supreme Planning Committee of the Judea and Samaria Area et al* (IL 2004) ILDC 70 para. 6 and 37 (2007) *Israel Yearbook on Human Rights* 332, at 333.
269. *Abu Aita*, opinion of Acting President Shamgar, 313/97/133–134, para. 50(e): see also 309/94–95/128–129, para. 50(c).
270. Shamgar was relying on Graber: see Graber, *Development of the Law of Belligerent Occupation*, at 290–291.
271. *Abu Aita*, opinion of Acting President Shamgar, 273/65–66/89, para. 25(g).
272. *Abu Aita*, opinion of Acting President Shamgar, 268/61/83, para. 24(c).
273. *In re Krauch and others (IG Farben trial)*, (US Military Tribunal at Nuremberg, 29 July 1948) (1994) 15 *International Law Reports* 668, at 677.
274. For commentary on Article 55, see I. Scobbie, 'Natural resources and belligerent occupation: mutation through permanent sovereignty', in S. Bowen (ed.), *Human Rights, Self-Determination and Political Change in the Occupied Palestinian Territories* (The Hague: Kluwer, 1997), at 232–234 and 238–242, for an account of Israel's exploitation of hydrocarbon resources in occupied Sinai and the Gulf of Suez.
275. *Na'ale* v. *The Supreme Planning Committee of the Judea and Samaria Area et al*, quotation at 333.
276. Benvenisti, *International Law of Occupation*, at 144–145.
277. *In re Krauch and others (I.G. Farben) trial* (US Military Tribunal at Nuremberg, 29 July 1948), 15 *International Law Reports* 668, at 677.
278. See, for example, Cassese, 'Powers and duties of an occupant', at 419–420; von Glahn, 'Taxation under belligerent occupation', at 345–347, 373; and Greenwood, 'Administration of occupied territory in international law', at 263.
279. See Military Proclamation No. 2, *Concerning Regulation and Authority of the Judiciary (the West Bank Area)* (7 June 1967), equivalent Military Proclamation for the Gaza Strip and Northern Sinai.
280. See the decisions of the High Court of Justice in the *Christian Society for Holy Places* and *Abu Aita* cases.
281. Exceptions deal principally with family law and succession and are applied on a personal basis depending on the individual's formal/nominal religious affiliation. The Ottoman Mejelle and also the 'Constitution of the Mandate' – the King's Order-In-Council – applied the laws of personal status (among which are the laws of marriage and divorce, child adoption, faith conversion and inheritance) in a personal manner to the members of the different denominations, so that the religious law of each member applied to him. This arrangement is therefore an arrangement of personal application of the law, rather than territorial application.
282. Military Order No. 892, *Order Concerning Administration of Regional Councils (Settlements)* (1 March 1981).
283. Military Order No. 783, *Order Concerning Administration of Regional Councils (Judea and Samaria)* (25 March 1979).
284. Section 140(B) of the Local Councils Regulations grants the holders of Israeli statutory powers to act also within the boundaries of the local councils in the West Bank and in accordance with Israeli law. The Appendices to the Regulations include a list of Israeli

laws to be applied as aforesaid in the following fields: welfare laws, family laws, statistics laws, education laws, heath laws, labour laws, agricultural laws, apartment buildings laws, environmental laws, consumer, industry and trade laws, communications law.

285. Amnon Rubinstein and Barak Medinah, *The Constitutional Law of the State of Israel* (5th edn, 1996), at 1181 (Hebrew).
286. *Educational Enterprises v. Roth Yosef, Supervisor of Jewish Settlements in the Civilian Administration*, HCJ 10104/04 SAL (unpublished; judgment dated 14 April 2006).
287. Rubinstein and Medinah, *Constitutional Law of the State of Israel*, at 1182.
288. Benvenisti, *International Law of Occupation*, at 135.
289. The Extension of Power of Emergency Regulations Law (Judea and Samaria and the Gaza Strip – Adjudication of Offences and Legal Aid), 1977 [last amendment: August 6, 2003], LSI 1977, at 48.
290. Ibid., section 2.
291. The Law of Return (5710–1950) provides that Jewish immigrants and Jews in other categories qualify for an *oleh* immigration visa, such that other laws and rules can cite this law to grant special rights and privileges preferentially to Jews or to Jews exclusively. A substantive amendment in 1970 allowed *oleh* status to be extended to various family relations of Jews immigrating to Israel, including non-Jewish relatives, but the proportion of non-Jews affected by this change remains small.
292. Rubinstein and Medinah, *Constitutional Law of the State of Israel*, at 1182 n.39.
293. See Sections 51A and 78 of the Decree Respecting Security Directives (No. 378).
294. The Criminal Procedure Law (Enforcement Powers – Arrests), 1996, provides in Section 29(a) that an arrest by a police officer stands for only 24 hours. Section 298 of the Penal Law, 1977, provides a maximum sentence of 20 years of incarceration for the manslaughter offence.
295. *The Regional Council of Gaza Coast et al v. The State of Israel et al*, HCJ 1661/05 (9 June 2005) 59(2) *Israel Law Review* 481.
296. Amnon Rubinstein, 'The Changing Status of the Held Territories' (1986) 11 *Eyunei Mishpat* 439, translation from Hebrew.
297. The Basic Law of Israel comprises Israel's constitutional law: see Rubinstein and Medinah, *Constitutional Law of the State of Israel*, and CA 6821/93, *United Bank Mizrachi v. Migdal*, 49(4) PD 221.
298. See the *Gaza Coast* case, para. 80 and the *Mara'abe* case, para. 21.
299. See the *United Bank Mizrachi v. Migdal* case.
300. *Adalah v. The Minister of Defense*, HCJ 8276/05 (judgment dated 12 December 2006, translation by Adalah).
301. It should be noted that in the *Gaza Coast* case, the court did not address Article 11 at all.
302. Justice Gronis dissented from this opinion: see paras 2–3 of his opinion.
303. See *Adalah et al v. Minister of Interior et al*, HCJ 7052/03, (judgment of 14 May 2006), available at: http://elyon1.court.gov.il/files_eng/03/520/070/a47/03070520.a47.htm.
304. Aharon Barak, *Shofet be-Hevra Demoqratit* [*A Judge in a Democratic Society*] (University of Haifa Press, Keter, Nevo, 2004), at 147.
305. *Hess* case, para. 14, at 460.
306. Ibid., para. 19, at 465.
307. Ibid., para. 14, at 461.
308. The *Hess* decision was prior to the *Gaza Coast* decision, so it cannot be considered as setting new ruling on the issue of the applicability of the Basic Law to Palestinians in the OPT.
309. *Bethlehem Municipality v. State of Israel*, HCJ 1890/03, 3 February 2005, available in English at: http://elyon1.court.gov.il/files_eng/03/900/018/N24/03018900.n24.pdf.
310. Unlike *Hess*, this decision came after the *Gaza Coast* case; however, the court did not address the applicability of Basic Law to the Palestinians, as they would be applicable through the administrative law doctrine.
311. *Mara'abe*, para. 20.

312. *Hess* case, at 460–461.
313. See Aeyal M. Gross, 'The construction of a wall between The Hague and Jerusalem: the eenforcement and limits of humanitarian law and the structure of occupation' (2006) 26 *Leiden Journal of International Law*, at 393–440.
314. Ibid,. at 33: also generally Kretzmer, *Occupation of Justice*, and Ben-Naftali et al, 'Illegal occupation'.
315. See *Jami'at Ascan*.
316. *The Association for Civil Rights in Israel et al v. Minister of Defence et al*, HCJ 2150/07.
317. Military Proclamation No. 2, *Concerning Regulation and Authority of the Judiciary* (7 June 1967).
318. Military Order No. 38, *Order Concerning Alcoholic Beverages* (4 July 1967).
319. See, *inter alia*, Military Order No. 92, *Order Concerning Jurisdiction Over Water Regulations* (15 August 1967).
320. See, for example, Military Order No. 474, *Order Concerning Amending the Law for the Preservation of Trees and Plants* (26 July 1972); Military Order No. 1039, *Order Concerning Control over the Planting of Fruit Trees* (5 January 1983), Military Order No. 1147, *Order Concerning Supervision over Fruit Trees and Vegetables* (30 July 1985).
321. According to the Association for Civil Rights in Israel, 'In the same territorial area and under the same administration live two populations who are subject to two separate and contrasting legal systems and infrastructure. One population has full civil rights while the other is deprived of those rights ... The settlers' lives, although they live in an area under military rule, are in almost every respect the same as those of Israeli citizens living in Israel.' Association for Civil Rights in Israel, *The State of Human Rights in Israel and the Occupied Territories, 2008 Report* (Jerusalem: ACRI, 2008), at 17.
322. Military Order No. 378, *Order Concerning Security Provisions* (20 April 1970).
323. Military Order No. 1229, *Order Concerning Administrative Detention (Provisional Regulations)* (17 March 1988). Due to numbering inconsistencies among Israeli military orders, Military Order No. 1229 is alternatively referred to as Military Order No. 1226, depending on whether it was issued individually or in a bound volume by the Israeli authorities.
324. Military Order No. 378, Article 78C(c)(1).
325. Military Order No. 378, Articles 78C(c)(2), 78D (b)(3), and 78D(b)(4).
326. Military Order No. 1500, Order Concerning Detention in Time of Combat (Temporary Order) (April 2002).
327. Military Order No. 151, *Order Concerning Closed Areas (Jordan Valley)* (1 November 1967).
328. Military Order No. 146, *Order Concerning Closed Areas* (23 October 1967).
329. See John Reynolds, *Where Villages Stood: Israel's Continuing Violations of International Law in Occupied Latroun, 1967–2007* (Ramallah: Al-Haq, 2007), at 39 and 87.
330. See, for example, Criminal Procedure (Enforcement Powers – Detention) (Non-Resident Detainees Suspected of Security Offence) (Temporary Provision) Bill 5765–2005.
331. Lisa Hajjar, *Courting Conflict: The Israeli Military Court System in the West Bank and Gaza* (Berkeley: University of California Press, 2005), at 2.
332. Pictet, *Commentary to Geneva Convention IV*, at 340.
333. Ibid.
334. Article 71 of the Fourth Geneva Convention states: 'Accused persons who are prosecuted by the Occupying Power shall be promptly informed, in writing, in a language which they understand, of the particulars of the charges preferred against them.' Article 14(3) of the International Covenant on Civil and Political Rights similarly entitles an individual accused of a crime to be 'informed promptly and in detail in a language which he understands of the nature and cause of the charge against him'.
335. For a detailed technical analysis of the incompatibility with international legal standards of numerous individual aspects of the Israeli military court system, see generally Yesh Din, *Backyard Proceedings: The Implementation of Due Process Rights in the Military Courts in the Occupied Territories* (Tel Aviv: Yesh Din, 2007).

336. Paul Hunt, *Justice? The Military Court System in the Israeli-Occupied Territories* (Ramallah: Al-Haq, 1987), at 3–4 and 34–38.
337. Figures from the Palestinian Ministry of Prisoners and Ex-Detainees, quoted in Al-Haq, *Waiting for Justice* (Ramallah: Al-Haq, 2005), at 258.
338. Yesh Din, *Backyard Proceedings*, at 19.
339. Ibid., at 10.
340. Ibid., at 119.
341. Hajjar, *Courting Conflict*, at 3; also Yesh Din, *Backyard Proceedings*, at 120.
342. Yesh Din, *Backyard Proceedings*, at 61.
343. Kathleen Cavanaugh, 'The Israeli Military Court System in the West Bank and Gaza' (2007) 12 *Journal of Conflict and Security Law* 197.
344. Military Order No. 130, *Order Concerning Interpretations* (27 September 1967).
345. Cavanaugh, 'The Israeli Military Court System'.
346. Yesh Din, *Backyard Proceedings*, at 9 and 36.
347. Israeli army members accused of offences are processed and may be tried through military judicial proceedings in military courts, under the Military Justice Law 5715–1955. On this, Cavanaugh notes that 'the experience of the IDF in the military justice system shifts the narrative from questions related to fair trial, which accompanies the discourse of Palestinians in the Court system, to one of impunity': Cavanaugh, 'The Israeli Military Court System'.
348. While Israeli civil law applies to Jewish-Israelis being prosecuted in civil courts, the military courts enforce Israeli military legislation against Palestinians, as well as sometimes the 1945 Defence (Emergency) Regulations (despite the fact that these regulations were repealed by the British upon termination of the Mandate), and the pre-existing criminal law which applied in the territory before occupation (that is, Jordanian criminal law in the case of the West Bank).
349. With different criminal procedures applying in Israel and the OPT, the Israeli Supreme Court has even rejected arguments that the substantial Israeli domestic law of criminal procedure should apply to suspects arrested in the West Bank under military orders who are detained in Israel: see *Abed Al-Rachman Al Hamed* v. *General Security Services*, HCJ 1622/96.
350. Although not applicable in the legal system applying inside Israel, the death penalty is applicable under military laws governing the OPT: see Military Order No. 378, *Order Concerning Security Provisions*, Article 51(a).
351. In contrast with basic human rights principles as well as Israeli criminal law, the military courts sentence Palestinians according to their age at the time of sentencing, as opposed to their age at the time the alleged offence was committed.
352. Hunt, *Justice?*, at 7.
353. ICERD, Article 1(2).
354. The duty to apply a treaty in good faith is codified in Article 2(6) of the Vienna Convention of the Law of Treaties. Article 2(6), which is a codification of pre-existing custom, provides: 'Every treaty in force is binding upon the parties to it and must be performed by them in good faith.' On the doctrines of good faith and the related matter of abuse of right (*abus de droit*) see, for example, B. Cheng, *General Principles of Law as Applied by International Courts and Tribunals* (London: Stevens, 1953), at 106–160; H. Lauterpacht, *The Function of Law in the International Community* (Oxford: Clarendon Press, 1933), at 286–306; V. Paul, 'The abuse of rights and bona fides in international law' (1977) 28 *Österreichische Zeitschrift für Öffentliches Recht und Völkerrecht* 107; G. Schwarzenberger, 'The fundamental principles of international law' (1956) 87 *Recueil des cours*, at 290–326; G. Taylor, 'The content of the rule against the abuse of rights in international law' (1972–73) 46 *British Yearbook of International Law* 323; H. Thirlway, 'The law and procedure of the International Court of Justice 1960–1989 Part One' (1989) 60 *British Yearbook of International Law* 4, at 7–49; and G. White, 'The principle of good faith', in V. Lowe V and C. Warbrick (eds), *The United Nations and the Principles of International Law: Essays in Memory of Michael Akehurst* (London: Routledge, 1994).

355. Committee on the Elimination of Racial Discrimination, *General Comment No. 30: Discrimination Against Non-Citizens*, 1 October 2004, para. 2.
356. Ibid., para. 5.
357. David Keane, *Caste-based Discrimination in International Human Rights Law* (Aldershot: Ashgate, 2007), at 183.
358. In the alternative, it may be argued that this approach is mandated by Article 31(3)(c) of the Vienna Convention on the Law of Treaties which requires treaties to be interpreted in good faith, taking into account 'any relevant rules of international law'. On this, see C. McLachlan, 'The principle of systemic integration and Article 31(3) of the Vienna Convention' (2005) 54 *International and Comparative Law Quarterly* 279.
359. Hans-Peter Gasser, 'Protection of the civilian population', in Dieter Fleck (ed.), *The Handbook of Humanitarian Law in Armed Conflicts* (Oxford: Oxford University Press, 1995), at 255, para. 547(4).
360. The illegality of settlements, and thus of the presence of settlers, was a unanimous finding of the International Court in the *Wall* advisory opinion: see the opinion of the Court, ICJ Rep, 2004, at 183, para. 120, and the Declaration of Judge Buergenthal, at 244, para. 9.
361. 'A State or person acts in bad faith where it abuses its rights – by pursuing an improper purpose, taking an account of an irrelevant factor, or acting unreasonably – and does so knowing that it is abusing its rights': Taylor, *Abuse of rights*, at 333.

## Chapter 3

1. Declaration on the Granting of Independence to Colonial Countries and Peoples, adopted by General Assembly Resolution 1514 (XV) of 14 December 1960. The International Court of Justice, in *Legal consequences for States of the continued presence of South Africa in Namibia (South West Africa) notwithstanding Security Council resolution 276 (1970)*, ICJ Rep, 1971, 16, ruled that the Declaration was an important stage in the development of the law relating to non-self-governing territories: at 31, para. 52.
2. The trusteeship system, as established in the United Nations Charter, contradicts this injunction. Article 76(a) of the United Nations Charter cites the objective of the trusteeship system as being 'to promote the political, economic, social, and educational advancement of the inhabitants of the trust territories, and their progressive development towards self-government or independence as may be appropriate to the particular circumstances of each territory and its peoples and the freely expressed wishes of the peoples concerned, and as may be provided by the terms of each trusteeship agreement'.
3. C. Drew, 'The East Timor story: international law on trial' (2001), 12 *European Journal of International Law* 65. For a similar affirmation of the substantive core content of self-determination, see A. Orakhelashvili, 'The impact of peremptory norms on the interpretation and application of United Nations Security Council resolutions' (2005), 16 *European Journal of International Law* 59 at 64.
4. J. Pictet (ed.), *Commentary to Geneva Convention IV Relative to the Protection of Civilian Persons in Time of War* (ICRC: Geneva: 1958): 'Commentary to Article 49' at 283, emphasis added.
5. In all citations in this section, emphasis is added.
6. UN OCHA, 'The Humanitarian Impact on Palestinians of Israeli Settlements and Other Infrastructure in the West Bank' (July 2007) at 40.
7. Cited in Uri Blau, 'Secret Israeli database reveals full extent of Israeli settlement,' *Ha'aretz* (1 February 2009), available at: www.haaretz.com/hasen/spages/1060043.html.
8. Under the 1995 Israeli-Palestinian *Interim Agreement on the West Bank and the Gaza Strip (Oslo II)*, Area A (assigned to full Palestinian civil and security control) accounted for 2 per cent of the territory of the West Bank. Area B, in which the Palestinian Authority assumed civil responsibilities and Israel held security control) accounted for 26 per cent and Area C (in which Israel had both civil and security control) for 72 per cent. Those boundaries were gradually to be redrawn, but have been frozen since the 1999 *Sharm*

    *el-Sheikh Memorandum on Implementation Timeline of Outstanding Commitments of Agreements Signed and the Resumption of Permanent Status Negotiations* at 17 per cent, 24 per cent and 59 per cent respectively.
9. B'Tselem, *Land Grab: Israel's Settlement Policy in the West Bank* (Jerusalem: B'Tselem, 2002), at 85–90.
10. See, for example, Amnesty International, *Unlawful Homes for Israeli Settlers, Demolitions for Palestinians*, Amnesty (31 March 2008), available at: www.amnesty.org/en/news-and-updates/feature-stories/unlawful-homes-israeli-settlers-demolitions-palestinians-20080331; and *Palestinian Homes Demolished without Warning* (11 March 2008), available at: www.amnesty.org/en/news-and-updates/news/palestinian-homes-demolished-without-warning-20080311. See also B'Tselem reports on Israeli's policy of home demolitions: available at: www.btselem.org/english/publications/Index.asp?TF=06.
11. Israeli Ministry of Agriculture and Settlement Division of the World Zionist Organisation, *Master Plan for Settlement of Samaria and Judea, Plan for Development of the Area for 1983–1986* (Jerusalem, 1983), at 27 (Hebrew), cited in B'Tselem, *Forbidden Roads: Israel's Discriminatory Road Regime in the West Bank* (Jerusalem: B'Tselem, 2004), at 6.
12. Al-Haq, 'Law in the service of man, Israeli proposed road plan for the West Bank: a question for the International Court of Justice?' (30 November 1984), available at: http://domino.un.org/UNISPAL.nsf/c25aba03f1e079db85256cf40073bfe6/8ad0157015a6c53885256982005703ab!OpenDocument.
13. See Al-Haq, *The Israeli Proposed Road Plan for the West Bank: A Question for the International Court of Justice?* (Ramallah: Al-Haq, 1984).
14. Al-Haq, 'Discrimination is real: discriminatory Israeli policies in Israel, the occupied territories and occupied East Jerusalem', Draft Paper presented to the World Conference Against Racism, Durban, South Africa (28 August–7 September 2001), at 24.
15. Samira Shah, 'On the road to apartheid: the bypass road network in the West Bank' (1997–1998) 29 *Columbia Human Rights Law Review* 221, 222.
16. Foundation for Middle East Peace, *Report on Israeli Settlement in the Occupied Territories* (May 1996), at 3.
17. B'Tselem, *Statistics: Restrictions on Movement*, available at: www.btselem.org/English/Freedom_of_Movement/Statistics.asp.
18. See Robert Home, 'An "irreversible conquest"? Colonial and Postcolonial Land law in Israel/Palestine' (2003) 12(3) *Social and Legal Studies* 292.
19. Marco Sassoli, 'Legislation and maintenance of public order and civil life by occupying powers' (2005) 16 *European Journal of International Law* 661.
20. Alain Pellet, 'The destruction of Troy will not take place', in Emma Playfair (ed.), *International Law and the Administration of Occupied Territories* (Oxford, Clarendon Press, 1992), at 201.
21. Emphasis added. The original and binding language of the Convention was French, in which language the text of Article 43 reads: 'L'autorité du pouvoir légal ayant passé de fait entre les mains de l'occupant, celui-ci prendra toutes les mesures qui dépendent de lui en vue de rétablir et d'assurer, autant qu'il est possible, l'ordre et la vie publics en respectant, sauf empêchement absolu, les lois en vigueur dans le pays'. In the English-language version, 'public order and safety' was a mistranslation of the French 'l'ordre et la vie publics' which, when correctly translated, refers to 'public order and life', implying a broader obligation not to interfere with a country's existing institutions. See Edmund Schwenk, 'Legislative power of the military occupant under Article 43, Hague Regulations' (1945) 54 *Yale Law Journal* 393 n.1.
22. Jean Pictet, *Commentary on the Geneva Conventions of 12 August 1949, Vol. 4* (ICRC, Geneva, 1952), at 336.
23. Military Order No. 38, *Order Concerning Alcoholic Beverages* (4 July 1967).
24. See, *inter alia*, Military Order No. 92, *Order Concerning Jurisdiction Over Water Regulations* (15 August 1967).
25. See, for example, Military Order No. 474, *Order Concerning Amending the Law for the Preservation of Trees and Plants* (26 July 1972); Military Order No. 1039, *Order*

*Concerning Control over the Planting of Fruit Trees* (5 January 1983), and Military Order No. 1147, *Order Concerning Supervision over Fruit Trees and Vegetables* (30 July 1985).

26. Israeli Ministry of Foreign Affairs, *The Disengagement Plan – General Outline* (18 April 2004), Article 1(vi); *Revised Disengagement Plan* (6 June 2004), Article 1(vi).
27. Criminal Procedure (Enforcement Powers – Detention) (Detainees Suspected of Security Offences) (Temporary Provision) Law 5765–2006. The original bill provided that it should apply solely to non-residents of the State of Israel.
28. For more on the colonial nature of the territorial annexation of East Jerusalem, see below, pp. 85, 102 and 105.
29. On capitulations, see Edwin Pears, 'Turkish capitulations and the status of British and other foreign subjects residing in Turkey' (1905) 21 *Law Quarterly Review* at 408–425; Lucius Ellsworth Thayer, 'The capitulations of the Ottoman Empire and the question of their abrogation as it affects the United States' (1923) 17 *American Journal of International Law* at 207–233; Norman Bentwich, 'The abrogation of the Turkish capitulations' (1923) 5 *Journal of Comparative Legislation and International Law*, at 182–188; and Norman Bentwich, 'End of the capitulatory system' (1933) 14 *British Yearbook of International Law*, at 89–100.
30. See *Christian Society for Holy Places* v *Minister of Defence et al*, HC 337/71, 2 *Israel Yearbook on Human Rights* 354 (1972) and 52 *International Law Reports* 512. In this case, the Court was asked to adjudicate on military activity in the OPT and gave a ruling on the merits without raising the question of jurisdiction. This expansion of the Court's territorial jurisdiction has remained in effect since then.
31. Michael Sfard, 'The human rights lawyer's existential dilemma' (2005) 38 *Israel Law Review* 154.
32. Pictet, *Commentary on the Geneva Conventions of 12 August 1949*, at 340.
33. See, for example, Kathleen Cavanaugh, 'The Israeli military court system in the West Bank and Gaza' (2007) 12 *Journal of Conflict and Security Law* 197; Yesh Din, *Backyard Proceedings: The Implementation of Due Process Rights in the Military Courts in the Occupied Territories* (Tel Aviv: Yesh Din, 2007); Lisa Hajjar, *Courting Conflict: The Israeli Military Court System in the West Bank and Gaza* (Berkeley: University of California Press, 2005); Al-Haq and Gaza Centre for Rights and Law, *Justice? The Military Court System in the Israeli-Occupied Territories* (Ramallah: Al-Haq, 1987). In his 2007 mission report on Israel and the OPT, the UN Special Rapporteur on the promotion and protection of human rights and fundamental freedoms while countering terrorism, Martin Scheinin, reported that Israel's military courts 'have an appearance of a potential lack of independence and impartiality, which on its own brings into question the fairness of trials': see *Report of the Special Rapporteur on the promotion and protection of human rights and fundamental freedoms while countering terrorism, Martin Scheinin, Addendum: Mission to Israel, including visit to the Occupied Palestinian Territory*, UN Doc. A/HRC/6/17/Add.4, 16 November 2007, para. 29.
34. Palestinian lawyers appearing in the military courts consistently have difficulties meeting with their clients because prisoners are normally detained in prison facilities inside Israel rather than in the OPT. Other problems include a lack of adequate facilities for taking confidential instructions; availability of court documents only in Hebrew; and provision only of incomplete prosecution material. See Yesh Din, *Backyard Proceedings*, at 100–125. In practice, lawyers commonly take instructions from their clients minutes before the hearing in the military court. Plea bargains are entered into to avoid the likelihood of harsher sentences even without access to any evidence.
35. Article 9 of Military Order No. 378 stipulates that the Israeli law of evidence applies to proceedings in the military courts and therefore provides for the presumption of innocence. Practice, however, suggests a presumption of guilt: acquittals were obtained in just 0.29 per cent of cases in the military courts in 2006. See Yesh Din, *Backyard Proceedings*, at 59.
36. Full evidentiary trials entailing adequate examination and cross-examination of witnesses were conducted in just 1.42 per cent of cases concluded in the military courts in 2006. See Yesh Din, *Backyard Proceedings*, at 119.

37. Indictments containing the charges against a defendant are given to his/her lawyer only on the day of the hearing to determine whether the accused remains in detention until the end of the proceedings. See Yesh Din, *Backyard Proceedings*, at 92–99.
38. See Military Order No. 783, *Order Concerning Administration of Regional Councils* (25 March 1979), and Military Order No. 892, *Order Concerning Administration of Regional Councils (Settlements)* (1 March 1981). It has been noted that the powers and responsibilities of the local councils established under Military Order No. 892, for example, 'are identical to the powers and responsibilities of ordinary Israeli municipalities, since the Order is a copy of the Israeli Municipal Ordinances (with some alterations)'. See Meron Benvenisti, *Israeli Rule in the West Bank: Legal and Administrative Aspects* (Jerusalem: West Bank Data Base Project, 1983), at 9.
39. Article 147 of the Election Law, consolidated version (1969), grants settlers the right to vote, while Article 6 denies the same right to Israeli citizens residing outside the 'geographic boundaries' of Israel, thus implying that the OPT are considered to be inside those boundaries.
40. *Amendment and Extension of the Validity of the Emergency Regulations (Judea and Samaria, the Gaza Strip, Sinai and South Sinai – Jurisdiction and Legal Assistance)*, 5744–1984, Section 6.B(b). It should also be noted that, in *Regional Council Gaza Beach v. The Knesset*, HCJ 1661/05, para. 78–80, the High Court of Justice affirmed the applicability of the Israeli Basic Law to Jewish settlers in the OPT. The same law empowers the Minister of Justice to add other laws and regulations to this list, with the approval of the Knesset's Constitution, Law and Justice Committee.
41. Development Towns and Areas Law, 5748–1988, Section 3(E).
42. Sassoli, 'Legislation and maintenance of public order'.
43. Myres McDougal and Florentino Feliciano, *Law and Minimum World Public Order* (New Haven, CT: Yale University Press, 1961), at 767.
44. Article 47 of the Fourth Geneva Convention provides further that the occupied population shall not be deprived of any of the benefits of the Convention by any change introduced into the institutions or government of an occupied territory.
45. Sassoli, 'Legislation and Maintenance of public order'.
46. See *Teacher's Housing Cooperative Society v. The Military Commander of the Judea and Samaria Region*, HCJ 393/82.
47. Military Proclamation No. 2, *Concerning Regulation of Authority and the Judiciary* (7 June 1967).
48. Military Order No. 947, *Order Concerning Establishment of a Civil Administration* (8 November 1981).
49. Jonathan Kuttab and Raja Shehadeh, *Civilian Administration in the West Bank: Analysis of Israeli Military Government Order No. 947* (Ramallah: Al-Haq, 1982), at 14.
50. Notably, not long before the Civil Administration was created, an official Ministry of Defence spokesperson announced that this new administration would be under the direct control of the Minister for Defence: see J. Singer, 'The establishment of a civilian administration in the areas administered by Israel' (1982) 12 *Israeli Yearbook on Human Rights* 278.
51. A. Roberts, 'Prolonged military occupation: the Israeli-occupied territories since 1967' (1990) 84:1 *American Journal of International Law* 44, at 98.
52. M. Rishmawi, 'Administrative detention in international law: the case of the Israeli-occupied West Bank and Gaza' (1989) 5 *Palestine Yearbook of International Law*, at 267.
53. See, for example, Military Order No. 80, *Order Concerning Extension of Period of Service of the Local Administrative Authorities* (2 August 1967).
54. See histories of this period in M. Tessler, *A History of the Israeli-Palestinian Conflict* (Bloomington: Indiana University Press, 1994), at 548–549.
55. Article VII, *Declaration of Principles on Interim Self-Government Arrangements (Oslo I)*, 1993.
56. Article I, *Interim Agreement on the West Bank and the Gaza Strip (Oslo II)*, 1995.

57. Article IX, *Declaration of Principles on Interim Self-Government Arrangements (Oslo I)*, 1993.
58. Military Order No. 101, *Order Concerning Prohibition of Incitement and Hostile Propaganda* (27 August 1967).
59. Article XVIII, *Interim Agreement on the West Bank and the Gaza Strip (Oslo II)*, 1995.
60. This figure was established as of 20 May 2008 by the human rights organisation Addameer, which monitors the numbers and conditions of Palestinian prisoners. In 2011, numbers of parliamentarians in prison were fluctuating.
61. Kuttab and Shehadeh, *Civilian Administration in the West Bank*, at 10.
62. For evidence of Israel's objectives in formulating the idea of Palestinian autonomy as an interim arrangement, see Aryeh Shalev, *The Autonomy – Problems and Possible Solutions*, Paper No. 8, Centre for Strategic Studies (Tel Aviv: Tel Aviv University, January 1980), at 55, summarised in Raja Shehadeh, *From Occupation to Interim Accords* (The Hague: Brill, 1997), at 15.
63. General Assembly Resolution 2625 (XXV) (24 October 1970), *Declaration on principles of international law concerning friendly relations and co-operation among States in accordance with the Charter of the United Nations*, expressly provides that, under the UN Charter, the territory of a non-self-governing territory has 'a status separate and distinct from the territory of the State administering it'.
64. Pictet, *Commentary to Geneva Convention IV*, 273, para. 2.
65. Ibid.
66. UK Ministry of Defence, *The Manual of the Law of Armed Conflict* (Oxford: Oxford University Press, 2004), 284 para. 11.25; see Articles 47–49, 51–52, 55–56 of the 1907 Hague Regulations.
67. C. Greenwood, 'The administration of occupied territory', in Emma Playfair (ed.), *International Law and the Administration of Occupied Territories* (Oxford: Clarendon Press, 1992), at 241. While other authorities, such as Schwenk and Dinstein, view Article 43 as providing the Occupying Power with greater leeway to amend legislation in force, all agree that the law cannot be amended for the purpose of benefiting the Occupying Power: see Yoram Dinstein, *Legislation under Article 43 of the Hague Regulations: Belligerent Occupation and Peacebuilding*, Occasional Paper Series, Program on Humanitarian Policy and Conflict Research (Fall 2004), available at: www.hpcr.org/pdfs/OccasionalPaper1.pdf; and Schwenk, 'Legislative power of the military occupant'.
68. Greenwood, 'Administration of occupied territory', at 260 and 265. Although the obligation to create a separate administrative regime persists, Judge Kooijmans has observed that many Occupying Powers have not created a formal administration; see Separate Opinion of Kooijmans, *Armed Activities on the Territory of the Congo* case (*Democratic Republic of the Congo v. Uganda*) ICJ Rep, 2005, 306 at 316–317, paras 40–41.
69. See Iain Scobbie, 'Natural resources and belligerent occupation: mutation through permanent sovereignty', in S. Bowen (ed.), *Human Rights, Self-Determination and Political Change in the Occupied Palestinian Territories* (The Hague: Kluwer, 1997), at 233–234.
70. Gerhard von Glahn, *The Occupation of Enemy Territory: A Commentary on the Law and Practice of Belligerent Occupation* (Minneapolis: University of Minnesota Press, 1957), at 176–178.
71. Ibid.
72. Article 46 of the 1907 Hague Regulations provides for this prohibition; the provision regarding private property falls under the category of *munitions de guerre* by virtue of Article 53.
73. Von Glahn, *Occupation of Enemy Territory*, at 186.
74. *In re Krupp* (US Military Tribunal, Nuremberg, 30 June 1948), 15 *International Law Report*, at 620 at 622, see 622–625 generally: see also *Trial of the Major War Criminals (In re Goering and others)*, International Military Tribunal, Nuremberg (1 October 1946), 13 *International Law Reports* 203 at 214–216; *In re Flick*, US Military Tribunal, Nuremberg,

(22 December 1947), 14 *International Law Reports* 266, at 271; *In re Krauch (IG Farben trial)*, US Military Tribunal, Nuremberg (29 July 1948) 15 *International Law Reports* 668, at 672–678; and *N.V. De Bataafsche Petroleum Maatschappij and others v. The War Damage Commission, (Singapore Oil Stocks Case)*, 23 *International Law Reports* 810.
75. See Articles 52 and 53 of the 1907 Hague Regulations.
76. See, for example, E. Cummings, 'Oil resources in occupied Arab territories under the law of belligerent occupation' (1974), 9 *Journal of International Law and Economics* 533 at 574–78; US Department of State, 'The laws of war: legal regulation of use of force', in 1979 *Digest of United States Practice in International Law*, at 920–922; and E. Feilchenfeld, *The International Economic Law of Belligerent Occupation* (Washington, DC: Rumford Press, 1942), at 34–36.
77. Cummings, 'Oil resources in occupied Arab territories', 155, citing I. Vasarhelyi, *Restitution in International Law* (1964); and Greenwood, 'Administration of occupied territory', at 251.
78. *In re Krupp*, 154 *International Law Reports*, at 622–623. The laws of usufruct permit the occupier to continue the reasonable exploitation of already-operating oil wells, but do not permit the development and exploitation of new oil fields: see US Department of State *Memorandum of Law on Israel's Right to Develop New Oil Fields in Sinai and the Gulf of Suez of 1 October 1976*, 16 ILM 733 (1977) 734; and Scobbie, 'Natural resources and belligerent occupation', at 239–240.
79. Eyal Benvenisti, *The International Law of Occupation* (Princeton, NJ: Princeton University Press, 1993), at 144.
80. Geoffrey Aronson, *Israel, Palestinians and the Intifada* (London: Kegan Paul International and Institute for Palestine Studies, 1990), 14–19, 24–28; also Sarah Roy, *The Gaza Strip: The Political Economy of De-Development* (Washington, DC: Institute for Palestine Studies, 1995), at 147–150.
81. Roy, *The Gaza Strip*, at 147.
82. B'Tselem, *Land Grab*, at 73–76.
83. Ibid., at 77–84.
84. The Knesset adopted a *Law for extending the validity of emergency regulations (Judea and Samaria and the Gaza Strip – Jurisdiction in crimes and legal aid)* 2002 on 26 June 2002 and subsequently extended it until 30 June 2012. This law was published in the Israeli 'Law Book' No. 1853 Page No. 458 on 27 June 2002.
85. Military Order No. 103 of 1967.
86. See David Kretzmer, *The Occupation of Justice: The Supreme Court of Israel and the Occupied Territories* (New York: SUNY, 2002), at 58–59.
87. *Christian Society for the Holy Places v. Minister of Defence and others*, 52 International Law Reports 512, opinion of Deputy President Sussman at 515: see also *A Cooperative Society Lawfully Registered in the Judea and Samaria Region v. Commander of the IDF Forces in the Judea and Samaria Region et al* (1984) 14 Israel Yearbook on Human Rights 301, opinion of Justice Barak at 304, and as *Jami'at Ascan*; Kretzmer, *Occupation of Justice*, 69: 'The military commander may not consider the national, economic or social interests of his own country, unless they have implications for his security interest or the interests of the local population.'
88. *Electricity Corporation for Jerusalem District Ltd v. Minister of Defence et al*, as discussed in Kretzmer, *Occupation of Justice*, 65. This aspect of the judgment is not noted in the summary contained in 5 *Israel Yearbook on Human Rights* (1975) 381. Settlers are not protected persons for the purposes of the Fourth Geneva Convention because they are nationals of the Occupying Power: see Article 4.
89. *Economic Corporation for Jerusalem Ltd v. Commander of the IDF Forces in the Judea and Samaria Region et al* (2000) 30 *Israel Yearbook on Human Rights* 322 at 324. This feature is even more marked in proceedings that pit the interests of the indigenous population against those of settlers, such as cases involving the confiscation of privately owned land in order to ensure the security of Jewish worshippers within the West Bank:

see, for example, *Hass v. IDF Commander in the West Bank* (the *Machpela Cave* case), HCJ 10356/02, 4 March 2004 (2004) *Israel Law Reports* 53 (this case joined with HCJ 10497/02, *Hebron Municipality v. IDF Commander in Judaea and Samaria*); *Bethlehem Municipality v the State of Israel (Rachel's Tomb* case), HCJ 1890/03 (3 February 2005), available at: http://elyon1.court.gov.il/files_eng/03/900/018/n24/03018900.n24.pdf. See also those cases dealing with the route of the barrier wall in the West Bank: for example, *Beit Sourik Village Council v. Government of Israel and Commander of the IDF Forces in the West Bank*, HCJ 2056/04, 30 June 2004, 43 ILM 1099 (2004) and *Mara'abe and others v. The Prime Minister of Israel and others*, HCJ 7857/, 15 September 2005, 45 ILM 202 (2006). These judgments are available in English on the website of the Israeli Supreme Court, at: http://elyon1.court.gov.il/eng/home/index.html.

90. See *A Cooperative Society Lawfully Registered in the Judea and Samaria region v. Commander of the IDF Forces in the Judea and Samaria Region et al* (1984) 14 *Israel Yearbook on Human Rights* 301, and as *Jami'at Ascan*; Kretzmer, *Occupation of Justice*, 69–70; compare *Tabib et al v. (a) Minister of Defence and (b) Military Governor of Tulkarem* (1983) 13 *Israel Yearbook on Human Rights* 364.
91. See *Electricity Corporation for Jerusalem District, Ltd v. Minister of Defence et al* (1975) 5 *Israel Yearbook on Human Rights* 381; and compare *Jerusalem District Electricity Co Ltd v. Minister of Energy and Infrastructure and Commander of the Judea and Samaria Region* (1981) 11 *Israel Yearbook on Human Rights* 354. See also *Jaber al Bassiouni Ahmed et al v. The Prime Minister and Minister of Defence*, HC 9132/07, 30 January 2008, unofficial English translation available at: www.adalah.org/eng/gaza%20report.html.
92. *Dweikat v. Government of Israel* (1979) 9 *Israel Yearbook on Human Rights* 345 at 350.
93. *Jerusalem District Electricity Co Ltd*, at 357.
94. *A Cooperative Society*, at 308–309.
95. Kretzmer, *Occupation of Justice*, at 68.
96. *A Cooperative Society*, at 310.
97. Ibid., at 313.
98. Kretzmer, *Occupation of Justice*, at 70, note omitted.
99. *Bassil Abu Aita et al v. The Regional Commander of Judea and Samaria and Staff Officer in charge of matters of customs and excise*, HC 69/81 (5 April 1983), 37(2) PD 197 (original Hebrew text), 7 *Selected Judgments of the Supreme Court of Israel* 1 (1983–87): English translation available at: http://elyon1.court.gov.il/files_eng/81/690/000/z01/81000690.z01.pdf. Extracts from Shamgar's opinion in *Abu Aita* are provided at (1983) 13 *Israel Yearbook on Human Rights* 348.
100. Feilchenfeld, *International Economic Law of Belligerent Occupation*, at 83.
101. *In re Krupp* (US Military Tribunal at Nuremberg, 30 June 1948), 15 *International Law Reports* 620 at 622–623: compare *In re Krauch and others (IG Farben trial)* (US Military Tribunal at Nuremberg, 29 July 1948), 15 *International Law Reports* 668, at 674.
102. *Customs regime between Germany and Austria (Protocol of March 19th, 1931)* advisory opinion, PCIJ, Ser. A/B, No. 41 (1931).
103. *Austro-German customs union* advisory opinion, PCIJ, Ser. A/B, No. 41 (1931) 45.
104. *Abu Aita*, 223/23/31, para. 7.
105. *Abu Aita*, 321/104/143, para. 52(c).
106. *Abu Aita*, 222/22/29, para. 7.
107. *Abu Aita*, 272–273/64–65/88, para. 25(e).
108. *Abu Aita*, 314/98/135, para. 50(e).
109. *Abu Aita*, 314–315/98–99/135–136, para. 50(e).
110. Kretzmer, *Occupation of Justice*, at 64.
111. *Abu Aita*, 317/101/138, para. 51.
112. *Abu Aita*, 321/105/143–144, para. 52(c).
113. Benvenisti, *International Law of Occupation*, at 143.
114. HC 9132/07, delivered 30 January 2008, available at: www.adalah.org/eng/gaza%20report.html.

115. N. Schrijver, *Sovereignty over Natural Resources: Balancing Rights and Duties* (Cambridge: Cambridge University Press, 1997), at 260.
116. See General Assembly Resolution 1803 (XVI) (14 December 1962), *Declaration of Permanent Sovereignty over Natural Resources*; General Assembly Resolution 3201 (S.VI) (1 May 1974), *Declaration on the Establishment of a New International Economic Order*; and General Assembly Resolution 3281 (XXIX) (12 December 1974), *Charter of Economic Rights and Duties of States*. Similarly, General Assembly Resolution 3295 (XXIX) (13 December 1974), Part IV, operative para. 8, and General Assembly Resolution 57/132 (25 February 2003), *Economic and other activities which affect the interests of the peoples of the Non-Self-Governing Territories*, both affirmed the right of permanent sovereignty over natural resources of non-self-governing territories, while the Preamble of the United Nations Council for Namibia's *Decree No. 1 for the Protection of Natural Resources of Namibia*, adopted 27 September 174, noted that its aim was to secure 'for the people of Namibia adequate protection of the natural wealth and resources of the Territory which is rightfully theirs'. Permanent sovereignty over natural resources is also expressly identified as an aspect of the right of self-determination in Article 1(2) of the International Covenant on Civil and Political Rights (1976) and Article 1(2) of the International Covenant on Economic, Social and Cultural Rights (1976). See also Drew, 'The East Timor Story', at 663–664; Orakhelashvili, 'Impact of peremptory norms', at 52–53; and Schrijver, *Sovereignty over Natural Resources*, Chapter 5.
117. Schrijver, *Sovereignty over Natural Resources*. The ICJ recently affirmed the customary nature of this principle in the *Case concerning armed activities on the territory of the Congo (Democratic Republic of the Congo v. Uganda)*, ICJ Rep, 2005, 168, at 251–252, para. 244.
118. Ibid., at 264–278.
119. Affirmed General Assembly Resolution 48/46 (10 December 1992) and General Assembly Resolution 49/40 (9 December 1994).
120. See, for example, A. Hardberger, 'Life, liberty, and the pursuit of water: evaluating water as a human right and the duties and obligations it creates' (2005) 4 *Northwestern Journal of International Human Rights* 331 at 332–333, 337–338, 340 and 345; and J. Scanlon, A. Cassar and N. Nemes, *Water as a Human Right?* IUCN Environmental Policy and Law Paper No. 51 (Cambridge, 2004), at 12.
121. In contrast, Article 14(2)(h) of the 1979 Convention on the Elimination of All Forms of Discrimination against Women requires States parties to take all appropriate measures to eliminate discrimination against women in rural areas and to ensure them the right to adequate living conditions, particularly in relation to housing, sanitation, electricity and water supply, transport and communications. Article 24(2)(c) of the 1989 Convention on the Rights of the Child includes, in its enumeration of the elements of the child's right to health, the duty of States parties 'to combat disease and malnutrition, including within the framework of primary health care, through, inter alia, the application of readily available technology and through the provision of adequate nutritious foods and clean drinking-water, taking into consideration the dangers and risks of environmental pollution'.
122. See UN Economic and Social Council, Commission on Human Rights, *Economic, social and cultural rights: relationship between the enjoyment of economic, social and cultural rights and the promotion of the realization of the right to drinking water supply and sanitation. Final report of the Special Rapporteur, El Hadji Guissé*, E/CN.4/Sub.2/2004/20 (14 July 2004), at 8–10, paras 23–24 and 29; Hardberger, 'Life, liberty, and the pursuit of water', 331 at 337–338 and 345; S.C. McCaffrey, 'A human right to water: domestic and international implications' (1992) 5 *Georgia International Environmental Law Review* 1, at 1 and 10–12; M.A. Salman and Siobhan McInerney-Lankford, *The Human Right to Water: Legal and Policy Dimensions* (Washington, DC: World Bank, 2004), 56–60; and Scanlon et al, *Water as a Human Right?*, at 4–5 and 18–20.
123. General Comment No. 15, *The right to water (Articles 11 and 12 of the International Covenant on Economic, Social and Cultural Rights)*, E/C.12/2002/11 (20 January 2003).

For an account of the Committee's role and competence to issue General Comments, see Salman and McInerney-Lankford, *The Human Right to Water*, at 33–53.
124. Ibid., para. 3, notes omitted.
125. Ibid., at 8, para. 17, and in greater detail, at 12–13, para. 37.
126. Ibid., at 13, para. 40.
127. Ibid., at 9–11, paras 20–29.
128. Ibid., at 9, para. 21, emphasis in original.
129. Ibid., para. 23.
130. Ibid., at 11–12, para. 32.
131. These are codified in the 1966 Helsinki Rules on the Uses of Waters of International Rivers and the 1997 UN Convention on the Law of Non-Navigational Uses of International Watercourses. In *Case concerning the Gabcikovo-Nagymoros project*, the ICJ assumed that the doctrine of reasonable and equitable share formed part of customary international law: see *Case concerning the Gabcikovo-Nagymoros project (Hungary/Slovakia)*, ICJ Rep, 1997, 7, at 56, para. 85. Although this judgment was delivered before the 1997 UN Watercourses Convention entered into force, the Court cited it with approval in its finding that Hungary had been deprived 'of its right to an equitable and reasonable share of the natural resources of the Danube'.
132. Available at: http://untreaty.un.org/ilc/texts/instruments/english/draft%20articles/8_3_1994_resolution.pdf.
133. Available at: http://daccessdds.un.org/doc/UNDOC/LTD/G08/615/84/PDF/G0861584.pdf?OpenElement. For commentary on these draft Articles, see International Law Commission, *Fifth report on shared natural resources: transboundary aquifers*, UN Doc. A/CN.4/591 (21 February 2008), available at: http://daccessdds.un.org/doc/UNDOC/GEN/N08/249/11/PDF/N0824911.pdf?OpenElement.
134. See International Law Commission, *Shared natural resources: comments and observations by Governments on the draft articles on the law of transboundary aquifers*, UN Doc. A/CN.4/595 (26 March 2008) 24, para.103, available at: http://daccessdds.un.org/doc/UNDOC/GEN/N08/284/80/PDF/N0828480.pdf?OpenElement.
135. An assessment as to the constitution of 'fairly and reasonably' is to be based on a number of criteria, such as the social and economic needs of the watercourse States concerned, the population dependent on the watercourse in each watercourse State and the effects of the use or uses of the watercourses in one watercourse State on other watercourse States. For a full enumeration of these criteria, see Article 6, UN Convention on the Law of Non-Navigational Uses of International Watercourses.
136. Birgit Schlutter, 'Water rights in the West Bank and in Gaza' (2005), 18 *Leiden Journal of International Law* 3, at 621–644, 622.
137. The Mountain Aquifer is itself divided into three sub-aquifers, each of which contains a recharge area and a storage area. The Western Aquifer is by far the most significant in terms of the amount of water supplied. The majority of its recharge area is situated in the West Bank, while the majority of its storage area is located inside Israel. The water of the Northern Aquifer and Eastern Aquifer is located almost entirely in the West Bank. The division of the water of the Mountain Aquifer system between Israel, the settlements and Palestinians will be examined below.
138. See, for example, Oxfam, *Assessment Report Gaza, September 2006* (16 October 2006), available at: www.reliefweb.int/rw/RWFiles2006.nsf/FilesByRWDocUnidFilename/AMMF-6VCH9B-oxfam-opt-30sep.pdf/$File/oxfam-opt-30sep.pdf.
139. Military Order No. 92, *Order Concerning Jurisdiction over Water Regulations* (15 August 1967), and Military Order No. 158, *Order Concerning Amendment to Supervision over Water Law* (19 November 1967), as cited in Centre for Housing Rights and Evictions (COHRE) and BADIL, Resource Centre for Palestinian Residency and Refugee Rights, *Ruling Palestine: A History of the Legally Sanctioned Jewish-Israeli Seizure of Land and Housing in Palestine*, (May 2005), at 91, available at: www.cohre.org/store/attachments/COHRE%20Ruling%20Palestine%20Report.pdf.

140. *Report of the Secretary-General prepared in pursuance of General Assembly decision 39/442*, A/40/381, E/1985/105 (17 June 1985).
141. See Military Order No. 484 *Concerning Water Works Authority (Bethlehem, Beit Jala and Beit Sahour)* (15 September 1972), establishing a water authority and specifying its functions and jurisdiction. This order was subsequently amended and then superseded by Military Order No. 1376, *Order Concerning the Water and Sewage Authority (Bethlehem, Beit Jala and Beit Sahour)* (24 July 1991), which also made projects and functions of this authority subject to the Israeli authority in charge and granted him authority to assume control if he felt it was not meeting its responsibilities: cited in COHRE and BADIL, *Ruling Palestine*, at 91.
142. COHRE, *Hostage to Politics: the Impact of Sanctions and the Blockade on the human Right to Water and Sanitation in Gaza* (23 January 2008), 5, available at: www.cohre.org/store/attachments/COHRE%20Report%20-%20Hostage%20to%20Politics.pdf.
143. COHRE and BADIL, *Ruling Palestine*, at 91.
144. UN General Assembly, *Report of the Special Committee to Investigate Israeli Practices Affecting the Human Rights of the Palestinian People and Other Arabs of the Occupied Territories*, UN Doc. A/61/500/Add.1, 8 June 2007, section 29.
145. Palestinian Hydrology Group, *Water for Life, Continued Israeli Assault on Palestinian Water, Sanitation and Hygiene During the Intifada* (Ramallah: PHG, 2006), at 13. The remainder is supplied by the statutory Palestinian Water Authority, by water departments of Palestinian municipalities and village councils and by independent public bodies such as the Jerusalem Water Undertaking.
146. Ibid.
147. See UN General Assembly, *Report of the Special Committee to Investigate Israeli Practices Affecting the Human Rights of the Palestinian People and Other Arabs of the Occupied Territories*, UN Doc. A/61/500/Add.1, 8 June 2007, section 30.
148. Catherine Bertini, 'Personal Humanitarian Envoy of the UN Secretary-General', *OPT Mission Report* (August 2002), at section 45.
149. Ibid.
150. See *The Israeli-Palestinian Interim Agreement on the West Bank and the Gaza Strip* (Oslo II), 1995, Annex III, Protocol Concerning Civil Affairs, Article 40. One of the primary ways through which the Israeli authorities maintain control of Palestinian water resources is by virtue of their effective veto in the Joint Water Committee. See, for example, Clemens Messerschmid, 'Hegemony and counter-hegemony over shared aquifers: the Palestinian experience', presented at the Third International Workshop on Hydro-Hegemony, London School of Economics (May 2007).
151. Jan Selby, 'Dressing up domination as cooperation: the case of Israeli-Palestinian water relations' (2003), 29 *Review of International Studies* 121, at 131. See also Schlutter, 'Water rights in the West Bank and in Gaza', at 621–644.
152. Figures derived from Israel and the PLO Interim Agreement, Annex III, Appendix 1, Schedule 10.
153. Selby, 'Dressing up domination as cooperation', at 132.
154. See B'Tselem, *Thirsty for a Solution: Resolving the Water Crisis in the West Bank in the Occupied Territories and its Resolution in the Final-Status Agreement* (Jerusalem: B'Tselem, 2000), at 30, based on the Israeli-Palestinian Interim Agreement on the West Bank and the Gaza Strip (Oslo II), 1995, Annex III, Schedule 10, *Data Concerning Aquifers*.
155. Israel and the PLO, Interim Agreement on the West Bank and Gaza Strip (Washington, DC, 28 September 1995), Annex III, Appendix 1, Article 40(13,14).
156. Israel and the PLO Interim Agreement, Annex III, Appendix 1, Schedule 8(1.b, as cited in Selby, 'Dressing up domination as cooperation', at 15.
157. Selby, 'Dressing up domination as cooperation', at 135.
158. Ibid., 137.
159. Mark Zeitoun, *Power and Water in the Middle East: The Hidden Politics of the Palestinian-Israeli Water Conflict* (London: I.B. Tauris, 2008), at 51–52.

160. Ibid.; also B'Tselem, *Thirsty for a Solution*, at 42: available at: www.btselem.org/Download/200007_Thirsty_for_a_Solution_Eng.doc.
161. COHRE, *Hostage to Politics*, at 91.
162. Amnesty International, *Unlawful Homes for Israeli Settlers*, at 76.
163. Ibid., at 2.
164. COHRE, *Hostage to Politics*, at 10.
165. Ibid., at 4; also OCHA, *Special Focus, The closure of the Gaza Strip: The economic and Humanitarian Consequences*, available at: www.ochaopt.org/documents/Gaza_Special_Focus_December_2007.pdf.
166. See UN Committee on the Exercise of the Inalienable Rights of the Palestinian People, *Water Resources of the Occupied Palestinian Territory* (New York: United Nations, 1992), Table 6: Estimates of the total and per capita annual water consumption in the occupied Palestinian territory and Israel, mid 1980s.
167. B'Tselem, *Thirsty for a Solution*, 2006. Figure is exclusive of the East Jerusalem area of the West Bank.
168. Ibid., 54. The World Health Organisation's recommended minimum quantity for basic consumption is 100 litres: see ibid., at 57.
169. Ibid., at 56.
170. See Foundation for Middle East Peace, *The Socio-Economic Impact of Settlements on Land, Water, and the Palestinian Economy* (July 1998).
171. Note by the Secretary-General, *Economic and social repercussions of the Israeli occupation on the living conditions of the Palestinian people in the occupied Palestinian territory, including Jerusalem, and of the Arab population in the occupied Syrian Golan*, A/61/67, E/2006/13 (3 May 2006), at 12–13, para. 47. This statistic is drawn from a B'Tselem report which notes that these settlements had an approximate population of 5,000, compared to a Palestinian population of 2 million: see B'Tselem, *Land Grab*, 95. See also Note by the Secretary-General, *Economic and social repercussions of the Israeli occupation on the living conditions of the Palestinian people in the occupied Palestinian territory, including Jerusalem, and of the Arab population in the occupied Syrian Golan*, A/62/75, E/2007/13 (3 May 2007) at 12, paras 40–41; Note by the Secretary-General, *Report of the Special Committee to investigate Israeli practices affecting the human rights of the Palestinian people and other Arabs of the Occupied Territories*, A/61/500/Add.1 (8 June 2007) at 10, paras 29–30; Office for the Coordination of Humanitarian Affairs, *The humanitarian impact on Palestinians of Israeli settlements and other infrastructure in the West Bank* (July 2007), at 114, available at: www.ochaopt.org/documents/TheHumanitarianImpactOfIsraeliInfrastructureTheWestBank_full.pdf; World Bank, *Two years after London: restarting Palestinian economic recovery* (24 September 2007), at 22–23, para. 64, available at: http://siteresources.worldbank.org/INTWESTBANKGAZA/Resources/AHLCMainReportfinalSept18&cover.pdf; and B'Tselem, *Thirsty for a Solution*, especially Chapters 3–5.
172. COHRE, *Hostage to Politics*, at 5–6.
173. Palestine Monitor, *Fact Sheet: Water*, available at: http://palestinemonitor.org/spip/spip.php?article14.
174. UN Economic and Social Council, *Economic and social repercussions of the Israeli occupation on the living conditions of the Palestinian people in the occupied Palestinian territory, including Jerusalem, and of the Arab population of in the occupied Syrian Golan*, UN Doc. A/62/75-E/2007/13 (3 May 2007), section 40.
175. See David Arsenault and Jamie Green, 'The effects of the separation barrier on the viability of a future Palestinian state', in Israel/Palestine Centre for Research and Information, *Second Israeli-Palestine International Conference on Water for Life in the Middle East* (Atalya, Turkey, 10–14 October 2004), available at: www.ipcri.org/watconf/papers/daniel.pdf.
176. The most explicit statement on culture as an individual right is expressed in Article 15(1) of the International Covenant on Economic, Social and Cultural Rights (1966). The Convention 169 Concerning Indigenous and Tribal Peoples in Independent

176. Countries addresses cultural rights as collective rights by codifying a package of cultural rights associated with culturally distinct peoples living in post-colonial and other independent States.
177. The Hague Regulations, Articles 27 and 56. Much of the 1954 Convention on the Protection of Cultural Property in the Event of Armed Conflict is now regarded as customary law: see J.M. Henckaerts and L. Doswald-Back, *Customary International Humanitarian Law, Volume 1: Rules* (Cambridge: Cambridge University Press, 2005), at 127–135.
178. Howard M. Hensal, 'The protection of cultural objects during armed conflicts', in Howard M. Hensal (ed.), *The Law of Armed Conflict: Constraints on the Contemporary Use of Military Force* (Aldershot: Ashgate, 2007), at 39–104, 83.
179. A most prominent case over archaeology concerns Israel's excavations at the Haram al-Sharif/Temple Mount in Jerusalem. Palestinians and Israelis have accused each other of removing and/or damaging precious relics: see Reynolds, 'In Jerusalem Archaeology is Politics', BBC News (9 February 2007).
180. See, for example, Military Order No. 25, *Order Concerning Transactions in Property, and Related Laws* (18 June 1967).
181. Raja Shehadeh, *The Law of the Land: Settlements and Land Issues under Israeli Military Occupation* (Jerusalem: PASSIA, 1993), at 86.
182. For an example of this, see ibid., at 87.
183. Meron Benvenisti, *Sacred Landscape: The Buried History of the Holy Land since 1948* (University of California Press, 2000), Chapter 3.
184. On the situation inside Israel in particular, see Y. Suleiman, *A War of Words: Language and Conflict in the Middle East* (Cambridge: Cambridge University Press, 2004), Chapter 5.
185. Military Order No. 50, *Order Concerning the Bringing and Distribution of Newspapers in the West Bank* (11 June 1967).
186. Military Order No. 107, *Order Concerning the Use of School Books* (26 August 1967).
187. At one point, Israel controlled the admission and tenure of all primary, secondary and tertiary pupils and instructors, under Military Order No. 854, *Order Concerning the Law of Education no.16 for the Year 1964* (Amendment) (Judea and Samaria) (854) of 1980. Although control over the education system was transferred to the PA in 1994, the military orders discussed are still in force and can be used by the Occupying Power at any time.
188. For example, in occupied Jerusalem alone, 80 associations of a political, cultural, media, social or economic nature have been closed on the grounds of 'public safety': see *Human Rights Bulletin for Jerusalem*, Vol. 2(1) (February 2008), 4. In relation to the closure, destruction of property and appropriation of charities and orphanages in Hebron on the basis of alleged links to Hamas, see Al-Haq, 'Defence for Children International et al', 24 April 2008, *NGO Statement on Closure of Islamic Charities in Hebron*, available at: www.dci-pal.org/english/display.cfm?DocId=740&CategoryId=1; also 'Thousands protest in Hebron against charity closures', *Ha'Aretz* (27 March 2008), available at: www.haaretz.com/hasen/spages/969278.html.
189. Revised Disengagement Plan, Section 1 (*Political and Security Implications*), Principle Three, emphasis added.
190. Pictet, *Commentary to Geneva Convention IV*, at 283.
191. *A Cooperative Society Lawfully Registered in the Judea and Samaria region v. Commander of the IDF Forces in the Judea and Samaria Region et al* (1984) 14 *Israel Yearbook on Human Rights* 301, at 310.
192. Kretzmer, *Occupation of Justice*, at 70.
193. Feilchenfeld, *The International Economic Law of Belligerent Occupation*, at 83.
194. Benvenisti, *International Law of Occupation*, at 144.
195. *Abu Aita*, 317/101/138, para. 51.
196. Ibid., para. 51.

## Chapter 4

1. The Convention on the Suppression and Punishment of the Crime of Apartheid (1973), entered into force 18 July 1976, 1015 UNTS 243.
2. *Elements of Crimes*, ICC–ASP/1/3 (part II–B), entered into force 9 September 2002, Article 7(1)(j), Element 4.
3. Article 1(1), emphasis added.
4. For example, Argentine nationalist Jose Ingenieros reflected this general usage when he wrote in 1915 that, 'to say nation, is to say race; national unity is not equivalent to political unity, but to spiritual and social unity, to national unity': 'La formación de una raza argentina' (1915) 11 *Revista de Filsofía*, at 146.
5. See especially Michael Omi and Howard Winant, *Racial Formation in the United States: From the 1960s to the 1990s* (New York: Routledge, 1994); also the collected studies in Paul Spickard (ed.), *Race and Nation: Ethnic Systems in the Modern World* (New York and London: Routledge, 2005). Notable exceptions to economistic models for racial formation include areas of Oceania, where colonial notions of race have largely survived and continue to shape social thought about human identity and all dimensions of social life.
6. Recognition that race was a concept in flux inspired UNESCO to solicit essays in 1950, 1951, 1965 and 1967, issued in 1969 as *Four Statements on the Race Question* (COM.69/II.27/A), available at: http://unesdoc.unesco.org/images/0012/001229/122962eo.pdf. See David Keane, *Caste-based Discrimination in International Law* (Aldershot: Ashgate, 2007), at 162–168. On evolving concepts of race and ethnicity, see also Omi and Winant, *Racial Formation in the United States*; Kenan Malik, *The Meaning of Race: Race, History, and Culture in Western Society* (New York University Press, 1996); and works by Anthony D. Smith, especially his classic, *The Ethnic Origin of Nations* (Oxford: Blackwell, 1986).
7. An example is the late-twentieth-century switch by dominant Ladino societies to using the term 'ethnic' for indigenous peoples in Latin America, while systemic practices of racial discrimination against those peoples proceed unchecked: see Virginia Tilley, 'Mestizaje and the "Ethnicization" of Race in Latin America', in Spickard, *Race and Nation*.
8. The term 'Native' was later changed to 'Bantu' and later still to 'black'.
9. Proclamation 46 of 1959.
10. Roger Omond, *The Apartheid Handbook* (Harmondsworth: Penguin Books, 1986, 2nd edn), at 26.
11. See further discussion of this policy in section on Article 2(d).
12. Dan O'Meara, *Forty Lost Years: The Apartheid State and the Politics of the National Party 1948–1994* (Randburg: Ravan Press, 1996), at 73.
13. See discussion and description in *Truth and Reconciliation Commission Report* (hereafter 'TRC Report'), Vol. 2, Chapter 5, available at: www.stanford.edu/class/history48q/Documents/. See also discussion of Article 2(d) in this chapter.
14. *Prosecutor v. Jean-Paul Akayesu*, Case No. ICTR-96-4-T, Judgment (TC), 2 September 1998, Akayesu Trial Judgment, para. 511.
15. Ibid., para. 512.
16. Ibid., para. 514.
17. Ibid., para. 513.
18. The ICTR cited the *Nottebohm case: second phase judgment* (*Liechtenstein v. Guatemala*) 1955, ICJ Reps, 4.
19. The United States Census, for example, groups 'race' and 'national origin' as one category and specifies that these are self-identifications rather than externally determined: *2000 Census of Population and Housing: Profiles of General Demographic Characteristics* (May 2001), available at: www.census.gov/prod/cen2000/dp1/2kh00.pdf.
20. *Prosecutor v. Rutaganda*, paras 400–401. See also the objective approach followed by the ICTR Trial Chamber in *Prosecutor v. Akayesu*, at para. 702.

21. *Prosecutor* v. *Vidoje Blagojevic and Dragan Jokic*, Case No. IT-02-60-T, Trial Judgement (TC), 17 January 2005, para. 667, emphasis added. The ICTR Trial Chamber made clear the importance of perception, of self or other, in *Prosecutor* v. *Rutaganda*: see para. 56.
22. *Prosecutor* v. *Jean-Paul Akayesu*, , at para. 511.
23. See also Max Nordau, Address to the First Zionist Congress, 29 August 1897, available at: www.mideastweb.org/nordau1897.htm.
24. See, for example, Vladimir Jabotinsky, 'A Lecture on Jewish History' (1933), cited in David Goldberg, *To the Promised Land: A History of Zionist Thought* (London, New York, Victoria, Toronto and Aukland: Penguin, 1996), at 181.
25. Most debates about conversion are between the Jewish religious movements and are pursued through the religious courts and other channels, but see, for example, *Tais Rodriguez-Tushbeim* v. *Minister of Interior and Director of the Population Register, Ministry of Interior* (HCJ 2597/99), and *Tamara Makrina and others* v. *Minister of Interior and Director of the Population Register, Ministry of Interior* (HCJ 2859/99), decided 31 March 2005.
26. See Tractate Kiddushin 68b. Talmudic debates were not greatly concerned with the question of Jewish identity but the terms for conversion were of serious concern.
27. The Nuremberg Laws of Nazi Germany, for example, defined a 'Jew' as anyone descended from three Jewish grandparents or from two Jewish grandparents if that person was also active in a Jewish religious community.
28. Law of Return (Amendment No. 2) 5730–1970.
29. Arguments within Jewish communities about what behaviour is requisite to being Jewish sometimes reference who is 'really Jewish': see, for example, Noah Efron, *Real Jews: Secular versus Ultra-Orthodox: The Struggle for Jewish Identity in Israel* (New York: Basic Books, 2003).
30. Literature on Jewish nationalist (Zionist) discourse is very wide, reflecting its many currents: major architects include Theodor Herzl (*The Jewish State*, first published in Vienna in 1896), Vladimir Jabotinsky, Alan Ginsberg (Ahad Ha'am), David Ben-Gurion, Yehuda Magness, Martin Buber, and many other political leaders and philosophers.
31. See Israel's Declaration of the Establishment of the State of Israel, 14 May 1948, available at: www.mfa.gov.il/MFA/Peace+Process/Guide+to+the+Peace+Process/Declaration+of+E stablishment+of+State+of+Israel.htm.
32. Passed by the Knesset on 12 Adar Bet, 5752 (17 March 1992) and published in Sefer Ha-Chukkim No. 1391 of the 20 Adar Bet, 5752 (25 March 1992); the Bill and an Explanatory Note were published in *Hatza'ot Chok* No. 2086 of 5752, at 60.
33. Passed by the Knesset on 12 Adar 5752 (17 March 1992) and amended on 21 Adar, 5754 (9 March 1994). Amended law published in *Sefer Ha-Chukkim* No. 1454 of the 27 Adar 5754 (10 March 1994), at 90; the Bill and an Explanatory Note were published in *Hatza'ot Chok* No. 2250 of 5754, at 289.
34. Passed by the Knesset on 22 Shevat, 5718 (12 February 1958) and published in *Sefer Ha-Chukkim* No. 244 of 30 Shevat, 5718 (20 February 1958), at 69; the Bill was published in *Hatza'ot Chok* No. 180 of 5714, at 18.
35. 7 Israel Laws 3 (1952).
36. Passed by the Knesset on 24th Tammuz, 5720 (19 July 1960) and published in *Sefer Ha-Chukkim* No. 312 of the 5 Av, 5720 (29 July,1960), at 56; the Bill and an Explanatory Note were published in *Hatza'ot Chok* No. 413 of 5720, at 34.
37. Israel Land Administration, 'General Information: Background', available at: www.mmi.gov.il/Envelope/indexeng.asp?page=/static/eng/f_general.html.
38. State Property Law (5711–1951), passed by the Knesset on 30 Shevat, 5711 (6 February 1951) and published in *Sefer Ha-Chukkim* No. 68 of 9 Adar Alef, 5711 (15 February 1951); the Bill and an Explanatory Note were published in *Hatza'ot Chok* No. 54 of 2 Cheshvan, 5711 (13 October 1930), at 12.
39. The Status Law was amended in 1975 to restructure this relationship: see World Zionist Organisation–Jewish Agency for Israel (Status) (Amendment) Law, 5736–1975.

40. Covenant Between the Government of Israel and The Zionist Executive called also the Executive of the Jewish Agency, signed 26 July 1954.
41. World Zionist Organisation—Jewish Agency (Status) Law, 5713–1952.
42. As the JA and WZO operate in tandem, particularly in the Settlement Department which shares one office, the distinction between them is largely meaningless. Hence Drobles may be listed as head of one or the other.
43. WZO Department for Rural Settlement, *Master Plan for the Development of Settlement in Judea & Samaria 1979–1983* (October 1978), available as UN Doc. S./13582 Annex (22 October 1979).
44. For details on one such collaboration by the JA and WZO in developing Jewish settlements that straddle the Green Line, see a description of the Master Plan for the Rehan bloc in Virginia Tilley, *The One-State Solution* (Ann Arbor: University of Michigan Press, 2005), at 37–42.
45. *George Rafael Tamarin v. State of Israel*, 20 January 1972, in *Decisions of the Supreme Court of Israel* (Jerusalem: Supreme Court, 1972), Vol. 25, pt 1, at 197 (in Hebrew). See also Roselle Tekiner, 'On the Inequality of Israeli Citizens', *Without Prejudice*, Vol. 1, No. 1 (1988), at 9–48.
46. Law of Return 5710–1950, 10 March 1970.
47. See, for example, Mutaz Qafisheh, 'A Legal Examination of Palestinian Nationality under the British Rule', unpublished doctoral thesis (No. 745), University of Geneva, Institut Universitaire de Hautes Etudes Internationales (Geneva, 2007).
48. The Palestinian population totals some 9–10 million people, of whom about 3.9 million live in the OPT, about 1.3 million live in Israel, and about 1.8 million live as refugees in Jordan, Syria and Lebanon.
49. Palestinian Declaration of Independence, Algiers, 15 November 1988: reproduced in Yehuda Lukacs, *The Israeli-Palestinian Conflict: A Documentary Record 1967–1990* (Cambridge: Cambridge University Press, 1992).
50. On Palestinian national identity, see especially Rashid Khalidi, *Palestinian Identity: The Construction of Modern National Consciousness* (New York: Columbia University Press, 1997).
51. A survey in 1944 found that about 8 per cent of the population of Palestine was Christian, although other sources put the proportion higher: see Table I: 'Population of Palestine by Religions', in *A Survey of Palestine: Prepared in December 1945 and January 1946 for the Information of the Anglo-American Committee of Inquiry*, Vol. I, at 141; reprinted by the Institute for Palestine Studies (Washington, DC, 1991).
52. Committee on the Elimination of Racial Discrimination, General Recommendation XXX, 'Discrimination against Non-Citizens' (2004), Article 14.
53. Ibid.
54. For example, General Assembly Resolution 2074 (XX) of 17 December 1965 and General Assembly Resolution 2145 (XXI) Question of South West Africa (1966).
55. See, for example, Ilias Bantekas and Susan Nash, *International Criminal Law* (London: Cavendish, 2003, 2nd edn), at 121–122.
56. See the statement by Mr Wiggins (United States of America), UN General Assembly, Official Records, 28th Session, 1973, 3rd and 4th Committees, 2003rd meeting, 22 October 1973, Agenda Item 53, Draft Convention on the Suppression and Punishment of the Crime of *Apartheid (continued)* (A/9003 and Corr. 1, chaps XXIII, sect. A.2, A/9095 and Add. 1), at 142, para. 36 ('Article I would be open to very broad interpretations going beyond both the intentions of its drafters and the geographical limits of southern Africa'). See also the statement by Mr Petherbridge (Australia) at 143, para. 4 ('the concept of apartheid was being widened to such an extent that it could be applicable to areas other than South Africa'). The additional words 'as practised in southern Africa' inserted into Article 2 was first suggested by Mrs Warzazi (Morocco) at the 2005th meeting, 24 October 1973, at 150, para. 12.
57. See the statement by Mr Papademas (Cyprus), ibid., at 142–143, para. 39.
58. Emphasis added.

59. Committee on the Elimination of Racial Discrimination, *General Recommendation No. 19: Racial Segregation and Apartheid (Art. 3)*, para. 1, 18 August 1995.
60. Roger S. Clark, 'Apartheid', in M. Cherif Bassiouni, *International Criminal Law*, Vol. I (The Hague: Kluwer, 1999), 643 at 643–644.
61. The National Party came to power in 1948 under the leadership of Dr D.F. Malan. In 1954, Malan was succeeded as leader of the National Party by J.G. Strijdom, who was replaced by Dr H.F. Verwoerd in 1958. These three Afrikaner nationalist leaders are generally regarded as the principal architects of apartheid.
62. TRC Report, Vol. 1, Chapter 2, para. 6.
63. The Cape was the only province excluded from the Act, as a result of the existing black franchise rights that were enshrined in the South Africa Act.
64. The Native Land Act was repealed by the Abolition of Racially Based Land Measures Act (No. 108) of 1991.
65. The 1923 Act was superseded by the Native (Urban Areas) Consolidation Act No. 25 of 1945, which was repealed by the Abolition of Influx Control Act No. 68 of 1986.
66. Mokgethi Motlhabi, *The Theory and Practice of Black Resistance to Apartheid: A Social-Ethical Analysis* (Johannesburg: Skotaville Publishers, 1984), at xvii.
67. Described by Brian Bunting as 'South Africa's Nuremberg Laws': see his *The Rise of the South African Reich* (Harmondsworth: Penguin, 1964).
68. Omond, *The Apartheid Handbook*, at 53.
69. O'Meara, *Forty Lost Years*, at 110.
70. TRC Report, Vol. 1, Chapter 2, paras 22–24.
71. Omond, *The Apartheid Handbook*, at 16.
72. TRC Report, Vol. 2, Chapter 3, para. 21.
73. Ibid., para. 27.
74. Testimony of Paula McBride, before TRC: see TRC Report, Vol. 4, Chapter 2, para. 49.
75. TRC Report, Vol. 1, Chapter 2, para. 80.
76. Ibid., para. 79.
77. Ibid., Vol. 6, Section 3, Chapter 1, para. 51.
78. Ibid., Section 5, Chapter 2, at 629.
79. Ibid., Vols 3 and 4.
80. Ibid., Vol. 6, Section 5, Chapter 2, at 624.
81. Ibid., Vol. 2, Chapter 3, at 205–215.
82. Ibid., Vol. 6, Section 5, Chapter 2, at 627.
83. Ibid., Section 3, Chapter 6, Part 2, at 509. The Report identifies phrases used in security documents and Parliamentary speeches which implied killing with impunity of resistance members.
84. TRC Report, Vol. 6, Section 5, Chapter 2, at 628.
85. For statistics on fatalities see B'Tselem, placing the number of Palestinians in the OPT killed by Israeli forces during the first *intifada* at 1,376, and between 29 September 2000 and 31 May 2011 at 6,379: available at: www.btselem.org/english/Statistics/Index.asp. According to B'Tselem, the number of Israelis killed by Palestinians in the OPT from 29 September 2000 to 31 May 2011 is 252 civilians and 252 security force personnel. See also the Palestinian Centre for Human Rights-Gaza (PCHR), 'Statistics related to Al Aqsa Intifada: 29 September, 2000–5 January, 2010', available at: www.pchrgaza.org/alaqsaintifada.html.
86. Palestinian demonstrations against the Wall in the West Bank, for example, are consistently met with excessive and disproportionate use of force by Israeli forces. The village of Ni'lin is one case in point. See, for example, Al-Haq, *Right to Life of Palestinian Children Disregarded in Ni'lin as Israel's Policy of Wilful Killing of Civilians Continues* (7 August 2008), available at: www.alhaq.org/template.php?id=387.
87. 'Extrajudicial', 'summary' and 'arbitrary executions' are legal terms used to describe killings which have taken place in circumstances which contravene international law. See Special Rapporteur of the Commission on Human Rights on Extrajudicial, Summary or Arbitrary Executions, available at: www.stanford.edu/class/history48q/Documents/.

88. For details of four separate incidents of such extrajudicial and summary executions in the same area in a short period of time, see Al-Haq, *Intervention to Diplomatic Representatives Regarding the Extrajudicial Executions of Palestinians in the Jenin Area* (9 May 2007), available at: www.alhaq.org/etemplate.php?id=312.
89. See B'Tselem, *Activity of the Undercover Units in the Occupied Territories* (May 1992), available at: www.btselem.org/Download/199205_Undercover_Units_Eng.doc; also Middle East Watch, *A License to Kill: Israeli Undercover Operations Against 'Wanted' and Masked Palestinians* (New York, Washington, Los Angeles, London: Human Rights Watch, 1993).
90. Ibid., at 11–12.
91. Ibid.
92. Ibid., at 90.
93. For historical background for the outbreak of the second *intifada*, see Baruch Kimmerling, *Politicide – Ariel Sharon's War Against the Palestinians* (London and New York: Verso, 2003), at 129–138.
94. Amos Harel and Aluf Benn, 'Kitchen cabinet okays expansion of liquidation list', *Ha'aretz*, 4 July 2001.
95. See Gideon Alon, 'Rubinstein backs IDF's policy of "targeted killings"', *Ha'aretz*, 2 December 2001 (Hebrew): 'The Attorney General added "The hits are carried out according to detailed orders, published by the military prosecutor's office, and in accordance with international law, Rubinstein said."'
96. Human Rights Watch, *Promoting Impunity – The Israeli Military's Failure to Investigate Wrongdoing* (June 2005), available at: www.hrw.org/reports/2005/06/21/promoting-impunity. See also HC 9594/03, *B'Tselem, et al. v. The Military Judge Advocate General et al* (still pending), in which B'Tselem and the Association for Civil Rights in Israel (ACRI) demanded the initiation of criminal investigations in all cases of Israeli soldiers killing Palestinian civilians not involved in hostilities. See also Hala Khoury-Bisharat, 'Israel and the cultural of impunity', *Adalah Newsletter*, Vol. 37 (June 2007), available at: www.adalah.org/newsletter/eng/jun07/ar1.pdf. Attorney-General Rubinstein has also held that the term 'liquidations' damages Israel's image and that it is preferable to use the phrase 'targeted killings': see Alon, 'Rubinstein backs IDF's policy'.
97. See B'Tselem, 'Change in military investigation policy welcome, but it must not be contingent on the security situation', 6 April 2011, available at: www.btselem.org/press-release/6-april-11-change-military-investigation-policy-welcome-it-must-not-be-contingent-secu.
98. See also *Matar v. Dichter*, a federal class action lawsuit brought by the Centre for Constitutional Rights (CCR) and the Palestinian Centre for Human Rights-Gaza against the former Director of Israel's GSS, Avi Dichter, charging Dichter with war crimes, extrajudicial killing and other gross human rights violations for his participation in the aerial bombing of a Gaza residential neighbourhood. The suit charges that Dichter provided the necessary intelligence and gave final approval to drop a one-ton bomb on an apartment building in the middle of the night, which killed 15 persons and injured over 150 others. Legal documents available at: http://ccrjustice.org/ourcases/current-cases/matar-v.-dichter.
99. Ido Rosenzweig and Yuval Shany, *Special Investigatory Commission Publishes Report on Targeted Killing of Shehadeh [27/2/2011]* (Israel Democracy Institute), available at: www.idi.org.il/sites/english/ResearchAndPrograms/NationalSecurityandDemocracy/Terrorism_and_Democracy/Newsletters/Pages/27th%20Newsletter/1/1.aspx.
100. HC 5872/01, *MK Mohamad Barakeh v. Prime Minister Ariel Sharon*, PD 46 (3), 1, dismissed 29 January 2001.
101. The petition was filed to the Supreme Court on 24 January 2002 by PCATI and LAW. See HC 769/02, *The Public Committee against Torture in Israel v. The Government of Israel*, available at: http://elyon1.court.gov.il/files_eng/02/690/007/A34/02007690.a34.pdf.
102. Para. 60 of the judgment.

103. Para. 37 of the judgment. For a different position, see Expert Opinion by Antonio Cassese, 'On Whether Israel's Targeted Killings of Palestinian Terrorists is Consonant with International Humanitarian Law', available at: www.stoptorture.org.il. Some scholars have opined that this part of the Court's decision is adequately supported in the existing literature: see, for example, William J. Fenrick, 'The *Targeted Killings* judgment and the scope of direct participation in hostilities' (2007) 4 *Journal of International Criminal Justice* 2, at 332–338.
104. Ben Naftali, 'A judgment in the shadow of international criminal law' (2007) 5 *Journal of International Criminal Justice* 322.
105. The Israeli leadership and army do not distinguish between Palestinian attacks on soldiers and settlements and Palestinian attacks on civilians. The Israeli Chief of Staff has declared that all members of Hamas are legitimate targets for assassinations. See Amos Harael, 'The IDF presents moral arguments for assassinations', *Haaretz*, 5 September 2003 (Hebrew), available at: www.haaretz.co.il/hasite/pages/ShArt.jhtml?itemNo=337186.
106. See BBC News, 'Israel's "targeted killings"', 17 April 2004, available at: http://news.bbc.co.uk/1/hi/world/middle_east/3556809.stm.
107. All four Geneva Conventions prohibit the use of torture. See also Article 2(2) of the UN Convention Against Torture.
108. *A (FC) and others (FC) (Appellants) v. Secretary of State for the Home Department (Respondent)* [2004] UKHL 56, at 255.
109. Robert Cryer, Hakan Friman, Darryl Robinson and Elizabeth Wilmshurst, *An Introduction to International Criminal Law and Procedure* (Cambridge: Cambridge University Press, 2010), at 295.
110. In *Delalic*, the ICTY (Trial Chamber II) stated that the definition of Torture contained in the UN CAT was 'representative of customary international law': *The Prosecutor* v. *Zejnil Delalic, Zdravko Mucic (a/k/a/ "Pavo"), Hazim Delic, Esad Landzo (a/k/a "Zenga")* Case No. IT-96-21-T, 16 November 1998, para. 459.
111. Ibid.
112. See further *A (FC) v. Secretary of State for the Home Department* (2005) UKHL 71, *Public Committee Against Torture in Israel* v. *Government of Israel*, Supreme Court of Israel, 1999 HC 5100/94, and US Department of Justice, Memorandum from Jay Bybee, Assistant Attorney-General, to Alberto Gonzales, Counsel to the President, 1 August 1 2002.
113. See Article 7(1)(f).
114. Report, Vol. 4, Chapter 7, para. 14. See entire volume for figures from other provinces.
115. Max Coleman (ed.), *Crime Against Humanity: Analysing the Repression of the Apartheid State* (London: Human Rights Committee of South Africa, 1998), Part A(3): 'The Detention Weapon', available at: www.sahistory.org.za/pages/library-resources/online%20books/crime-humanity/detention%20weapon.htm.
116. TRC Report, Vol. 4 Chapter 7, para. 13; see Appendix to Chapter 7, 'Death in Detention'.
117. Ibid., para. 67.
118. Ibid., Vol. 3, Chapter 2, para. 15.
119. Ibid., Vol. 2, Chapter 7, para. 28.
120. Ibid., Vol. 4, Chapter 7, para. 1, and Coleman, *Crime Against Humanity*, at 36–38.
121. See, for example, PCATI, *No Defense: Soldier Violence against Palestinian Detainees* (June 2008), available at: www.stoptorture.org.il/files/No_Defense_Eng.pdf.
122. B'Tselem, Centre for the Defence of the Individual, *Absolute Prohibition: The Torture and Ill-treatment of Palestinian Detainees* (July 2007), at 38, available at: www.btselem.org/Download/200705_Utterly_Forbidden_eng.pdf.
123. Ibid., at 63.
124. Regulation 22 of the Criminal Procedure (Enforcement Powers – Detentions) Law (Enforcement Powers – Detention) (Conditions of Detention) – 1997. On the basis of this regulation, security detainees are also not entitled to a daily walk in the open air or to use the telephone, even to call their attorney. Criminal detainees, by contrast, are permitted a daily hour-long walk in the open air and are allowed to make a daily telephone call to

their attorneys, as well as daily calls to their family and friends. Criminal detainees are provided with a bed, while security detainees are provided a thin mattress and blankets; criminal detainees, but not security detainees, are provided newspapers, books, TVs, radios, a razor and mirror, an electric kettle, a wall light, a fan and a heater. Some of the discriminatory conditions are hygiene-related: for example, the cells of security detainees do not contain a basin, and while criminal detainees' cells must be sanitised and disinfected annually and provided with detergents, this is not the case for security detainees.

125. UN Committee Against Torture, concluding observations, May 2009, para. 13: available at: www2.ohchr.org/english/bodies/cat/docs/cobs/CAT.C.ISR.CO.4.pdf. Israel ratified the International Convention Against Torture and Other Cruel, Inhuman or Degrading Treatment or Punishment on 3 October 1991. It has placed two reservations to the Convention: '1. In accordance with Article 28 of the Convention, the State of Israel hereby declares that it does not recognise the competence of the Committee provided for in Article 20; 2. In accordance with paragraph 2 of article 30, the State of Israel hereby declares that it does not consider itself bound by paragraph 1 of that article.' Israel has not signed the Optional Protocol to the Convention.

126. HC 5100/94, *The Public Committee Against Torture in Israel v. The Government of Israel*, 53(4) PD 817.

127. The term 'ticking bomb' is used to describe individuals who present an immediate physical threat to the security of the State of Israel or who hold information about such a threat, and refers to the race against time to prevent the threat from materialising. Proponents of the use of torture to extract information from 'ticking bombs' justify their stance on the potentially great loss of life that could result from such a threat. See, generally, PCATI, *Ticking Bombs: Testimonies of Torture Victims in Israel* (May 2007), available at: www.stoptorture.org.il/files/140[1].pdf. See also Jeremy Waldron, 'Torture and positive law: jurisprudence for the White House' (October 2005) 105:6 *Columbia Law Review* 5, at 1714, and David Luban, 'Liberalism, torture and the ticking bomb' (October 2005) 91 *Virginia Law Review*, at 1140. However, Israel regularly perpetrates torture in situations that do not comply with the problematic 'ticking bomb' scenario. See, for example, PCATI, *Ticking Bombs*, at 10–11. The report submitted by the Special Rapporteur on the Promotion and Protection of Human Rights and Fundamental Freedoms while Countering Terrorism, Martin Scheinin, to the UN Human Rights Council on 28 November 2007, Addendum (A/HRC/6/17/Add.1) stated that 'The Special Rapporteur was shocked by the unconvincing and vague illustrations by the ISA of when such "ticking bomb" scenarios may be applicable. He was troubled by the process by which individual interrogators would seek approval from the Director of the ISA for the application of special interrogation techniques, potentially rendering this as a policy rather than a case-by-case, ex post facto, defence in respect of wrongful conduct.' Available at: http://domino.un.org/unispal.nsf/eed216406b50bf6485256ce1007 2f637/5f8dd0dc16603dd5852573aa0056d736!OpenDocument.

128. Article 34K of the Penal Law, entitled 'Necessity', stipulates that, 'A person will not bear criminal liability for committing an act that was immediately necessary for the purpose of saving the life, liberty, body or property, either of himself or his fellow person, from a real danger of serious harm, due to the conditions prevalent at the time the act was committed, there being no alternative means for avoiding the harm.' The UN Committee Against Torture in its concluding observations on Israel in 2009 recommended that Israel remove the 'necessity defense' as a possible justification for the crime of torture (para. 14); available at: www2.ohchr.org/english/bodies/cat/docs/cobs/CAT.C.ISR.CO.4.pdf.

129. See LAW – The Palestinian Society for the Protection of Human Rights and the Environment, The Public Committee Against Torture in Israel (PCATI), and The World Organisation Against Torture (OMCT), *Comments on Issues relating to Palestinian Detainees in the Third Periodic Report of the State of Israel Concerning the Implementation of the International Covenant on Civil and Political Rights* (September 2002), at 13–24; available at: www.stoptorture.org.il/files/comments.pdf. The UN Human Rights Committee stated its concern that 'interrogation techniques incompatible with article 7 of the Covenant are

still reported frequently to be resorted to and the "necessity defence" argument, which is not recognized under the Covenant, is often invoked and retained as a justification for ISA actions in the course of investigations', and recommended that Israel review its recourse to this argument. See *Concluding Observations of the Human Rights Committee: Israel*, 21 August 2003 (CCPR/CO/78/ISR), para. 18, available at: www.unhchr.ch/tbs/doc.nsf/(Symbol)/CCPR.CO.78.ISR.En?Opendocument. See also *Concluding Observations on Israel* from September 2010, para. 11.

130. Letter from the Israel Prison Service to Adalah, dated 29 January 2009; see also http://mrzine.monthlyreview.org/2009/baker150509p.html.
131. *Conclusions and Recommendations of the Committee Against Torture: Israel*, 23 November 2001, CAT/C/XXVII/Concl.5. For the Committee's concluding observations on Israel for May 2009 see: www2.ohchr.org/english/bodies/cat/docs/cobs/CAT.C.ISR.CO.4.pdf.
132. *Concluding Observations of the Human Rights Committee: Israel*, 21 August 2003, CCPR/CO/78/ISR.
133. Report of the Special Rapporteur on the Promotion and Protection of Human Rights and Fundamental Freedoms while Countering Terrorism, Martin Scheinin, Addendum, *Mission to Israel, Including Visit to Occupied Palestinian Territory*, A/HRC/6/17/Add.4, 16 November 2007. Available at: http://domino.un.org/unispal.nsf/c25aba03f1e079db85256cf40073bfe6/7ad9a5183461be7e852573aa0058b5ba!OpenDocument.
134. PCATI, *Back to a Routine of Torture: Torture and Ill-treatment of Palestinian Detainees during Arrest Detention and Interrogation* (September 2001–April 2003), at 12; available at: www.stoptorture.org.il/files/back%20to%20routine.pdf.
135. For more information, see PCATI, *PCATI, ACRI, HaMoked Filed a Contempt of Court Motion to the High Court of Justice* (2 December 2008), available at: www.stoptorture.org.il/en/node/1332.
136. See www.stoptorture.org.il/en/node/1460 and http://elyon1.court.gov.il/files/94/000/051/n15/94051000.n15.htm (decision delivered on 6 July 2009) (Hebrew).
137. See, for example, Prisoners' Petition 609/08, *Walid Daka v. the Israel Prison Service* (Nazareth District Court). This political prisoner – a Palestinian citizen of Israel – is the first Palestinian to seek conjugal rights. In September 2009 the District Court ruled that 'security prisoners' are prohibited from fathering children; in October 2009 Adalah submitted an appeal to the Supreme Court; in June 2010, the Supreme Court recommended that the Israel Prison Service re-examine the possibility of allowing the petitioner to have conjugal rights to father a child.
138. For more information, see PCATI, *Family Matters: Using Family Members to Pressure Detainees* (April 2008), available at: www.stoptorture.org.il/files/Fmily%20Matters%20full%20report%20eng.pdf. On 16 April 2008, PCATI and a number of other Israeli and Palestinian human rights organisations filed a petition to the Supreme Court of Israel to demand that the use of family members as means of exhorting pressure on suspects during interrogations by State authorities be absolutely prohibited. See HC 3533/08, *Maisoun Suweti, et al v. The General Security Services, et al* (case pending).
139. The State of Israel, *4th Periodic Report Concerning the Implementation of the International Convention Against Torture and Other Cruel, Inhuman or Degrading Treatment or Punishment*, October 2006, para. 46 (CAT/C/ISR/4), available at: www2.ohchr.org/english/bodies/cat/docs/CAT.C.ISR.4.doc.
140. Report of the UN Special Rapporteur, Martin Scheinin.
141. Tomar Zarchin, 'Israel's Justice Ministry to probe claims of Shin Bet torture and abuse', *Ha'aretz* (18 November 2011), available at: www.haaretz.com/print-edition/news/israel-s-justice-ministry-to-probe-claims-of-shin-bet-torture-and-abuse-1.325282.
142. Emphasis added. An official translation of the law into English is available at: www.justice.gov.il/NR/rdonlyres/C7E5F996-458F-4910-B343-776C5A9495F8/0/GeneralSecurityServicesLawedited.doc.
143. In 2010, Adalah filed a petition in 2010 against the GSS exemption from audio/video recording: see www.adalah.org/eng/pressreleases/pr.php?file=21_12_10_1.

144. *Baban* v. *Australia*, Communication No. 1014/2001, Views adopted August 6, 2003, UN Doc. CCPR/C/78/D/1014/2001.
145. Manfred Nowak, *UN Covenant on Civil and Political Rights, CCPR Commentary* (Arlington: N.P. Engel, 1993), at 173.
146. See UN Human Rights Committee, *General Comment 8: Article 9*, UN Doc. HRI/GEN/1/Rev.1 at 8 (1994), para. 4
147. UN Human Rights Committee, *General Comment No. 29*, CCPR/C/21/Rev.1/Add.11 (31 August 2001), para. 16: 'Safeguards related to derogation, as embodied in article 4 of the Covenant, are based on the principles of legality and the rule of law inherent in the Covenant as a whole ... In order to protect non-derogable rights, the right to take proceedings before a court to enable the court to decide without delay on the lawfulness of detention, must not be diminished by a State party's decision to derogate from the Covenant.'
148. See ICCPR Article 9(2), Additional Protocol I, Article 75 (3); see also Jean-Marie Henckaerts and Louis Doswald-Beck, *Customary International Law – Volume I: Rules* (Cambridge: Cambridge University Press, 2005), at 344.
149. The right to review has recently been affirmed by the US Supreme Court in relation to internees in Guantanamo Bay. Internees being held as 'enemy combatants' were held to be entitled to habeas corpus review. See *Boumediene, et al v. Bush, President of the United States, et al*, 553 US 723 (2008).
150. For example, the most egregious arbitrary arrests and detention in South Africa came pursuant to the Pass Laws, which although inherently discriminatory, were legitimate under the prevailing domestic legal system. The same is true for Palestinians arbitrarily arrested and detained for being in a certain area without the required permit, or for constituting a 'security threat' without any evidence being openly presented against them, measures which are taken in the OPT in accordance with relevant Israeli military legislation and thus, according to Israel, are not 'illegal'.
151. This interpretation is supported by the absence of any specific reference to the wording of this particular provision in the *travaux préparatoires*: UN General Assembly, Official Records, 28th Session (1973), Third Committee, Agenda Item 53, at 138–170.
152. See Article7(1)(e). The Apartheid Convention refers to 'inhuman acts', but the Rome Statute refers to '*inhumane* acts'.
153. *Prosecutor v. Barayagwiza*, Case No. ICTR–97–19. Appeals Chamber, Decision (3 November 1999), para. 88.
154. Administrative detention has its origins in the measures adopted by the British authorities during the Boer Wars in South Africa at the end of the nineteenth century. The use of internment was a prominent feature of British oppression in Northern Ireland, where 1,874 Republicans were detained without charge or trial between 1971 and 1975. During the same period, 107 Loyalists were detained under the policy of internment. Statistics from CAIN Archive, *Conflict and Politics in Northern Ireland (1968 to the Present)*, available at: http://cain.ulst.ac.uk.
155. TRC Report, Vol. 2, Chapter 7, para. 28.
156. Ibid., Vol. 4, Chapter 7, para. 22.
157. Ibid., para. 13.
158. Coleman, *Crime Against Humanity*, at 55; TRC Report, Vol. 2, Chapter 3, para. 91.
159. TRC Report, Vol. 6, at 619.
160. The Suppression of Communism Act, No. 44 of 1950 (originally introduced as the Unlawful Organisations Bill), approved on 26 June, entry into force on 17 July 1950.
161. Amending the Suppression of Communism Act 44 of 1950.
162. Cora Hoexter, *Administrative Law in South Africa* (Cape Town: Juta, 2007), at 45–46.
163. Motlhabi, *Theory and Practice of Black Resistance to Apartheid*, at 28–31.
164. John Dugard, *Human Rights and the South African Legal Order* (Princeton, NJ: Princeton University Press, 1978), at 122.
165. Motlhabi, *Theory and Practice of Black Resistance to Apartheid*, at 32–33.
166. Ibid., at 33.

167. Addameer, Prisoners' Support and Human Rights Association, Political Detention, available at: www.addameer.org/detention/background.html.
168. The Palestinian Central Bureau of Statistics, *Press Release on the Occasion of Palestinian Prisoners Day* (14 April 2007), available at: www.pcbs.pna.org/Portals/_pcbs/PressRelease/e-Prisoners_Day2007.pdf.
169. Addameer, *Monthly Detention Report, June 2011*, available at: http://addameer.info/?p=2209.
170. See, for example, testimonies gathered by HaMoked and B'Tselem, in B'Tselem, *Absolute Prohibition*.
171. Report submitted by the Special Representative of the Secretary-General on the Situation of Human Rights Defenders, Hina Jilani, *Addendum: Mission to Israel and the Occupied Palestinian Territory*, E/CN.4/2006/95/Add.3 (10 March 2006), para. 36.
172. See, for example, Lisa Hajjar, 'International humanitarian law and "wars on terror": a comparative analysis of Israeli and American doctrines and policies', *Journal of Palestine Studies*, Vol. XXXVI, No. 1 (Autumn 2006), at 21–42.
173. See HC 2028/08, *The Public Committee Against Torture in Israel, et al v. The Minister of Justice, et al*.
174. The Supreme Court struck down Article 5 of the Criminal Procedure (Detainees Suspected of Security Offences) (Temporary Order) Law (2006): see www.adalah.org/eng/pressreleases/pr.php?file=23_02_10.
175. The Criminal Procedure Law (Suspects of Security Offenses) (Temporary Order) (Amendment No. 2) (2010), enacted on 20 December 2010.
176. See HC 2028/08, *The Public Committee Against Torture in Israel, et al v. The Minister of Justice, et al* (petition withdrawn 24 March 2009).
177. Israel has used these regulations even though they were formally repealed by the British immediately prior to the termination of the mandate by the Palestine (Revocations) Order-in-Council, 1948, and the Jordanian Constitution overturned them in the West Bank in May 1948. The Defence (Emergency) Regulations were thus not 'the laws in force in the country' at the time Israel occupied the West Bank and Gaza Strip, as required under Article 43 of the Hague Regulations to be valid. Israel therefore has been applying these laws illegally in the OPT.
178. Military Order No. 378 (Order Concerning Security Provisions), Article 87.
179. Military Order No. 1229 relates to the West Bank, its equivalent being Military Order No. 941 in the Gaza Strip. Due to numbering inconsistencies among Israeli military orders, Military Order No. 1229 is alternatively referred to as Military Order No. 1226, depending on whether it was issued individually or in a bound volume by the Israeli authorities. Military legislation and military courts are no longer used by Israel in the Gaza Strip since the 2005 'disengagement', although arrests and detention of Palestinians from Gaza continue to be carried out under civil criminal legislation.
180. Between 1989 and 1991, the maximum length of single administrative detention orders was increased to twelve months under Military Order No. 1281.
181. From a public letter issued on 9 June 1989 by the Director of Human Rights and International Relations Department at the Israeli Ministry of Justice: cited in Al-Haq, *A Nation Under Siege* (Ramallah: Al-Haq, 1990), at 286.
182. Emma Playfair, *Administrative Detention in the Occupied West Bank* (Ramallah: Al-Haq, 1986), at 4.
183. Al-Haq, *Punishing A Nation* (Ramallah: Al-Haq, 1988), at 148.
184. Al-Haq, *A Nation Under Siege*, at 285.
185. Unpublished statistics from Al-Haq database.
186. Yesh Din, *Backyard Proceedings: The Implementation of Due Process Rights in the Military Courts in the Occupied Territories* (Tel Aviv: Yesh Din, 2007), at 54. This figure comprises 'initial' administrative detention orders plus extension orders.
187. Statistics from Addameer, 31 March 2009.
188. Addameer, *Monthly Detention Report, June 2011*.

189. See Crim. App. 6659/06, *A. v. The State of Israel*, available in English at: http://elyon1.court.gov.il/files_eng/06/590/066/n04/06066590.n04.pdf.
190. Among the violations identified in Article 147 of the Fourth Geneva Convention as grave breaches is wilfully depriving a protected person of the rights of fair and regular trial.
191. Report of the UN Special Rapporteur, Martin Scheinin, section 25.
192. The original stipulations of Military Order No. 378 had been liberalised to a certain extent by Military Order Nos 815 and 876 of 1980, which granted the right to 'judicial review' before a military judge within 96 hours of issuance of a detention order and made detention orders subject to periodic review by a judge at least once every three months.
193. This requirement was reimposed in 1999 but subsequently revoked again during the second *intifada*. Military Order No. 1506 effectively precluded any right of review for Palestinians that had been administratively detained during these incursions.
194. Knesset Records, Vol. 9 (12 May 1951), at 1807: quoted in B'Tselem, *Detained Without Trial: Administrative Detention in the Occupied Territories Since the Beginning of the Intifada* (Jerusalem: B'Tselem,1992), at 24.
195. B'Tselem, *Statistics on Administrative Detention*, available at: www.btselem.org/english/Administrative_Detention/Statistics.asp.
196. See, for example, Amnesty International, *Administrative Detention Cannot Replace Proper Administration of Justice* (11 August 2005), AI Index: MDE 15/045/2005, regarding the detention of alleged Kach activists Ephraim Hershkowitz and Gilad Shochat.
197. For example, then Minister of Defence, Shaul Mofaz, ordered the arrest of Neria Ofen, a resident of Yitzhar settlement in the West Bank in relation to attacks against Palestinians in the run-up to the 2005 'disengagement'. See Chris McGreal, 'Sharon delays Gaza withdrawal', *Guardian*, 10 May 2005.
198. Amendment No. 43 to Military Order No. 378. In practice this period of detention without judicial review may be even longer if an administrative detention order is signed against a Palestinian after he/she been initially detained under criminal detention procedures, allowing a further 96 hours on top of the initial detention period.
199. 'Federman awarded damages for false imprisonment', *Jerusalem Post*, 11 October 2005. No damages have been awarded to date.
200. Two forms of intent are required to establish the crime of genocide arising from the act of 'deliberately inflicting conditions of life likely to bring about physical destruction': the intention to inflict harm through the said conditions of life; and the special intention to destroy the relevant group in part or in whole. See G. Verdirame, 'The Genocide Definition in the jurisprudence of the *ad hoc* tribunals' (2000) 49 *International and Comparative Law Quarterly*, at 578–598; see also William Schabas, *Genocide in International Law* (Cambridge: Cambridge University Press, 2000).
201. See the discussion above, pp. 131–133.
202. Independent Fact-Finding Committee on Gaza, Report to the League of Arab States, *No Safe Place* (30 April 2009), at 135, para. 551, citing *Genocide (Bosnia v. Serbia)*, ICJ Reports 118 (327–8), available at: www.arableagueonline.org/las/picture_gallery/reportfullFINAL.pd.
203. Ibid., at 129, para. 521.
204. Article 5(d)(i).
205. See Dugard, *Human Rights*, at 136; see also Article 13 of the UDHR; Article 12 of the ICCPR; Article 12 of the African Charter on Human and Peoples' Rights.
206. O'Meara, *Forty Lost Years*, at 70.
207. Dugard, *Human Rights*, at 111.
208. David Harrison, *The White Tribe of Africa* (Johannesburg: Macmillan South Africa, 1981), at 252.
209. OCHA, *West Bank Movement and Access Update* (August 2011), at 3; available at: www.ochaopt.org/documents/ocha_opt_movement_and_access_report_august_2011_english.pdf.
210. In theory Palestinian citizens of Israel enjoy much, if not all, of the same freedom of movement as Israeli settlers and other Jewish citizens of Israel travelling in the OPT, but

in practice Palestinian citizens of Israel experience difficulties, due to racial profiling at checkpoints, for example.
211. OCHA, *Movement and Access Report* (April 2009–March 2010), available at: www.ochaopt.org/documents/ocha_opt_movement_and_access_report_august_2011_english.pdf .
212. Ibid., at 5.
213. Legal consequences of the construction of a wall in the occupied Palestinian territory, advisory opinion, ICJ Rep, 2004, para. 134.
214. OCHA, *West Bank Movement and Access Update* (August 2011), at 2, available at: www.ochaopt.org/documents/ocha_opt_movement_and_access_report_august_2011_english.pdf.
215. Report of the Special Rapporteur on the Situation of Human Rights in the Palestinian Territories Occupied since 1967, John Dugard, 21 January 2008, UN Doc. A/HRC/7/17, para. 30.
216. Israeli Ministry of Agriculture and WZO Settlement Division, *Master Plan for Settlement of Samaria and Judea, Plan for Development of the Area for 1983–1986* (Jerusalem, 1983), at 27 (in Hebrew), cited in B'Tselem, *Forbidden Roads: Israel's Discriminatory Road Regime in the West Bank* (Jerusalem: B'Tselem, 2004), at 6.
217. See Al-Haq, *The Israeli Proposed Road Plan for the West Bank: A Question for the International Court of Justice?* (Ramallah: Al-Haq, 1984).
218. Al-Haq, 'Discrimination is real: discriminatory Israeli policies in Israel, the occupied territories and occupied East Jerusalem', Draft Paper presented to the World Conference Against Racism, Durban, South Africa (28 August–7 September 2001), at 24.
219. Samira Shah, 'On the road to apartheid: the bypass road network in the West Bank' (1997–98) 29 *Columbia Human Rights Law Review* 221, at 222.
220. Foundation for Middle East Peace, *Report on Israeli Settlement in the Occupied Territories* (May 1996), at 3. FMEP Reports are available at: www.fmep.org/reports/archive.
221. Implementation by the occupying forces of the prohibition and restrictions described in this section is effected through the prohibition and restriction of the movement of vehicles belonging to Palestinian residents of the West Bank (excluding East Jerusalem), distinguishable from the vehicles of Israelis and Israeli settlers by the colour of their registration plates, as required under Israeli Military Order No. 1251 of 18 August 1988.
222. B'Tselem, *Ground to a Halt: Denial of Palestinians' Freedom of Movement in the West Bank* (Jerusalem: B'Tselem, August 2007), at 20.
223. B'Tselem, *Forbidden Roads*, at 16–17.
224. *Jami'at Ascan v. Commander of the IDF in Judea and Samaria*, HCJ 393/82, 37(4) PD 785.
225. This prohibition has been absolute, applying even in cases of emergency where urgent medical treatment is required. Vehicles delivering goods from Israel or other parts of the West Bank to Palestinian villages in the area are similarly not permitted to use the road any more.
226. OCHA, *Humanitarian Monitor: Occupied Palestinian Territory*, No. 32 (December 2008), at 7.
227. *The Association for Civil Rights in Israel et al v. Minister of Defence et al* [HCJ] 2150/07.
228. Ethan Bronner, 'Palestinians fear two-tiered road system', *New York Times*, 28 March 2008.
229. Association of Civil Rights in Israel (ACRI), *The Illusion of Rule of Law on Route 443* (25 May 2010), available at: www.acri.org.il/en/?p=725.
230. See Al-Haq, *Open Letter to Quartet Members: Israel's Recent Land Confiscations East of Occupied Jerusalem* (1 November 2007), available at: www.alhaq.org/etemplate.php?id=337.
231. See Israeli Ministry of Agriculture and WZO Settlement Division, *Master Plan For Settlement of Samaria and Judea, Plan for Development of the Area for 1983–1986* (Jerusalem, 1983), at 27 (in Hebrew), cited in B'Tselem, *Forbidden Roads*, at 6.

232. For further details on the permit system see, for example, B'Tselem, *Ground to a Halt*, at 24–27.
233. Military Order No. 151 of 1 November 1967.
234. See Al-Haq, *The Wall in the West Bank: State of Implementation of the International Court of Justice Advisory Opinion* (November 2006), at 5; available at: http://tinyurl.com/alhaq-wall.
235. OCHA, *West Bank Movement and Access Update* (August 2011), at 22.
236. B'Tselem, *Dispossession and Exploitation – Israel's Policy in the Jordan Valley* (May 2011), at 42–43; available at: www.btselem.org/.../201105_dispossession_and_exploitation_eng.pdf.
237. B'Tselem, 'Israel has de facto annexed the Jordan Valley' (13 February 2006), available at: www.btselem.org/.../20060213_annexation_of_the_jordan_valley.
238. Declaration Concerning the Closing of a Zone No. 2/03/S (the Seam Zone), 2 October 2 2003. This area does not include East Jerusalem, almost all of which lies between the Wall and the Green Line, Palestinian territory already annexed by Israel, engulfing another 250,000 Palestinian residents.
239. Data are from OCHA, *West Bank Movement and Access Update* (August 2011), at 29. Statistics have varied: in 2007, B'Tselem held that 17 Palestinian communities, in which 27,520 Palestinians reside, had been enclosed within the Seam Zone: see B'Tselem, 'Separation Barrier, Statistics', available at: www.btselem.org/english/Separation_Barrier/Statistics.asp.
240. OCHA, *West Bank Movement and Access Update* (August 2011).
241. General Permit to Enter and Stay in the Seam Zone (Judea and Samaria), 2003, signed on 2 October 2 2003 by Major General Moshe Kaplinsky.
242. The Major General authorised the Head of the Civil Administration of the West Bank to determine rules for Palestinian entry into the Seam Zone: Declaration Concerning the Closing of a Zone No. 2/03/S, section 4.
243. Directives Concerning a Permit for Permanent Resident of the Seam Zone (Judea and Samaria), 2003; Directives Concerning Permits of Entry to the Seam Zone and Stay therein (Judea and Samaria), 2003, both signed on 7 October 2003 by the Head of the Civil Administration, Brigadier-General Ilan Paz.
244. Directives Concerning Passageways in the Seam Zone (Judea and Samaria), 2003, signed on 7 October 2003 by the Head of the Civil Administration, Brigadier-General Ilan Paz.
245. Ibid.
246. CJ 9961/03 *HaMoked – Centre for the Protection of the Individual v. The State of Israel et al* (still pending). The petitioner contributed to discussion in this section.
247. Court order No. 5 requested by the petitioner was: '[Cancellation of] the Declaration Concerning the Closing of a Zone No. 2/03/S (the Seam Zone), 2003 (hereinafter: 'the Declaration') and ... the Orders regarding Security Directives installed by its virtue concerning entry permits to the Seam Zone'.
248. *The Association for Civil Rights in Israel v. The Commander of IDF Forces in Judea and Samaria et al* (pending), HCJ 639/04.
249. ACRI, *High Court Endorsed Systematic Discrimination* (6 April 2011), available at: www.acri.org.il/en/?p=1920.
250. Declaration Concerning the Closing of a Zone No. 2/03/S (the Seam Zone) (Judea and Samaria) (Amendment No. 1), 2004; General Permit for Entry to the Seam Zone and Stay Therein (Judea and Samaria) (Amendment No. 1), 2004. Both were signed on 27 May 2004 by Major General Moshe Kaplinsky.
251. Directives Concerning Passageways in the Seam Zone (Judea and Samaria), (Amendment No. 1), 2004; Directives Concerning a Permanent Resident of the Seam Zone Certificate (Judea and Samaria), 2004. Both were signed by Brigadier-General Ilan Paz on 3 June 2004.
252. Declaration Concerning the Closing of a Zone No. 2/03/S (the Seam Zone) (Judea and Samaria) (Amendment No. 2), 2005; signed on 13 December 2005 by the Commander of IDF Forces in the West Bank, Major General Yair Naveh. Directives Concerning Permits

to Enter the Seam Zone and Stay Therein (Amendment No. 1) (Judea and Samaria), 2005; signed by the Head of the Civil Administration, Brigadier-General Kamil Abu-Rukkun on 13 December 2005. Directives Concerning Passageways in the Seam Zone (Amendment No. 2) (Judea and Samaria), 2005; signed on 13 December 2005 by the Head of the Civil Administration, Brigadier-General Kamil Abu-Rukkun. Declaration Concerning the Closing of a Zone No. 2/03/S (the Seam Zone) (Judea and Samaria) (Extension of Effect and Amendment of Boundaries), 2005; signed on 27 December 2005 by the Commander of IDF Forces in the West Bank, Major General Yair Naveh, applying the permit regime to the Fence section in phase B (from the village of Sallem going east to Tirat Zvi).

253. OCHA Special Focus, *The Barrier Gate and Permit Regime Four Years On: The Humanitarian Impact in the Northern West Bank* (November 2007), at 3; available at: www.ochaopt.org/documents/OCHA_SpecialFocus_BarrierGates_2007_11.pdf.
254. OCHA, *West Bank Movement and Access Update* (August 2011), at 27.
255. See, for example, Al-Haq, *Building Walls, Breaking Communities: The Impact of the Annexation Wall on East Jerusalem Palestinians* (Ramallah: Al-Haq, 2005). See also B'Tselem, *Ground to a Halt*, at 63.
256. OCHA, *The Humanitarian Impact of the West Bank Barrier on Palestinian Communities: East Jerusalem*, Update No. 7 (June 2007), at 14; available at: www.ochaopt.org/documents/Barrier_Report_July_2008.pdf.
257. See World Bank Technical Team, *Movement and Access Restrictions in the West Bank: Uncertainty and Inefficiency in the Palestinian Economy* (May 2007), at 2; available at: http://siteresources.worldbank.org/INTWESTBANKGAZA/Resources/RafahCorridor-March07.pdf.
258. CERD, *Concluding observations of the Committee on the Elimination of Racial Discrimination: Israel* (March 2007), UN Doc. ICERD/C/ISR/CO/13, section 34, emphasis added.
259. United Nations Human Rights Committee, *General Comment No. 27*, CCPR/C/21/Rev.1/Add.9 (2 November 1999), para. 7.
260. Reflecting this history, section 20 of the South African Constitution (1996) guarantees freedom of movement to every person who is lawfully in the national territory. The right to freely choose a place of residence in the national territory – in many human rights instruments, closely associated with the freedom of movement – is covered in section 19.
261. Evidence of this was especially marked in the mining industry where black mine-workers were required, until the late 1980s, to reside in mine compounds while white workers were free to choose where they lived.
262. Blacks (Urban Areas) Consolidation Act, Act No. 25 of 1945.
263. The 'Black Sash' was founded in 1955 to protest against the removal of coloured people from the common voters' roll.
264. Harrison, *The White Tribe of Africa*, at 254.
265. Al-Haq, *Occasional Paper No. 8: The Right to Unite* (Ramallah: Al-Haq, 1990), at 3.
266. Ibid.
267. Harriet Sherwood, 'Israel stripped 140,000 Palestinians of their residency rights', *Guardian*, 11 May 2011.
268. Memorandum concerning the measures taken by Israel with respect to the City of Jerusalem, Submitted by Ruhi Al-Khatib, 26 August 1967, printed in the *Journal of Palestine Studies* 145, Vol. 37, No. 1 (autumn 2007), at 95. Ruhi Al-Khatib was the elected Mayor of Jerusalem from 1951 until he was dismissed by the Israeli authorities in 1967.
269. Israel Central Bureau of Statistics, Press Release, 14 May 2007, 084/2007, at 2; available at: www.cbs.gov.il/hodaot2007n/11_07_084b.doc; Ir Amim website at: www.ir-amim.org.il/; Maya Coshen, Jerusalem Institute of Israel Studies, *Statistical Yearbook of Jerusalem, 2005*, available at: www. jiis.org.il/imageBank/File/shnaton_2006/shnaton_C1005_2005.pdf.
270. Ruhi Al-Khatib, Memorandum, in *Journal of Palestine Studies* 145.

271. OCHA, *Humanitarian Impact of the West Bank Barrier on Palestinian Communities*, at 10.
272. Entry into Israel Law of 1952, section 11(a).
273. O. Feller, *The Ministry: Violations of Human Rights by the Ministry of Interior's Population Registrar* (ACRI, 2004), at 9–10 (Hebrew), available at: www.acri.org.il/portal.aspx?id=15.
274. HC 282/88, *Mabrook Awwad v. Yitzhak Shamir and The Minister of Interior*; Administrative Appeal to the Supreme Court 5829/05, *Dari et al v. The Ministry of Interior*; see also Feller, *The Ministry: Violations*, at 9; Entry to Israel Regulations No. 11(a) and (c) of 1973.
275. Jerusalem Centre for Social and Economic Rights (Fact Sheets, Residency Rights), available at: www.jcser.org/english/index.html.
276. World Bank Technical Team, *Movement and Access Restrictions in the West Bank*, at 11.
277. B'Tselem and HaMoked, *The Quiet Deportation: Revocation of Residency of East Jerusalem Palestinians* (April 1997), available at: www.btselem.org/Download/199704_Quiet_Deportation_Eng.doc.
278. B'Tselem statistics (August 2008), available at: http://www.btselem.org/english/Jerusalem/Revocation_Statistics.asp. B'Tselem cites the following sources for its statistics: Ministry of the Interior (figures until 1994 are taken from the letter of the attorney Moriah Bakshi, of the legal department of the Ministry of the Interior, to attorney Mahliel Blass, of the Attorney-General's Office, in HCJ 7316/75. The figures for 1995–98 were provided to B"selem by the Ministry of the Interior on 13 February 2000. Figures for 2003 and 2004 were provided to the Jerusalem Centre for Social and Economic Rights by the Department for Strategic Planning of the Interior Ministry in letters from 16 June and 5 August 2004. B'Tselem did not cite its sources for the 2005 and 2006 figures.
279. Relevant instruments include of the UDHR (Article 16(3)), the ICESCR (Article 10(1)), the ICCPR (Article 2(3) and Article 17); and the International Convention on the Protection of the Rights of All Migrant Workers and Members of their Families.
280. L. Abu Mukh, *Family Unification of Palestinians in the Occupied Territories: Laws, Regulations and Facts* (May 2007), at 1; available at: http://cadmus.iue.it/dspace/bitstream/1814/7990/1/CARIM-RR_2007_05.pdf.
281. Ibid., at 23.
282. Ibid., at 1.
283. David Kretzmer, *The Occupation of Justice: The Supreme Court of Israel and the Occupied Territories* (Albany: SUNY Press, 2002), at 31.
284. Ibid., at 4.
285. A. Ashkar, *Perpetual Limbo: Israel's Freeze on Unification of Palestinian Families in the Occupied Territories* (Jerusalem: B'Tselem and HaMoked, 2006), at 9, quoting the Response of the State Attorney's Office of 18 November 1992, Section 6 in HCJ 4494/91, *Sarhan et al. v. Commander of IDF Forces in Judea and Samaria et al.*
286. B'Tselem, *Human Rights in the Occupied Territories, 2007 Annual Report* (December 2007), at 37, available at: www.btselem.org/sites/default/files2/publication/200712_annual_report_eng.pdf.
287. Abu Mukh, *Family Unification*, at 6.
288. Order No. 297, 5729–1969, section 11(a) (amended by Order No. 1208 of 13 September 1987) as cited in Abu Mukh, *Family Unification*, at 7.
289. Ashkar, *Perpetual Limbo*, at 26; Abu Mukh, *Family Unification*, at 9.
290. Ashkar, *Perpetual Limbo*, at 26.
291. B'Tselem and HaMoked, *Forbidden Families: Family Unification and Child Registration in East Jerusalem* (January 2004), p. 26; available at: www.btselem.org/Download/200401_Forbidden_Families_Eng.doc.
292. Ibid., at 15.
293. Ibid., at 9.
294. Ibid., at 18.
295. Regulation 11(c) of the Entry to Israel Regulation – 1974.

296. See Adalah, 'The Nationality and Entry into Israel Law', *Special Report: Ban on Family Reunification* (20 December 2008), available at www.adalah.org/eng/famunif.php.
297. *Adalah, et al, v. The Minister of Interior, et al* (decision delivered 14 May 2006), HC 7052/03.
298. UN Committee on the Elimination of Racial Discrimination, Concluding Observations: Israel (March 2007), UN Doc. CERD/C/ISR/CO/13, at para. 20.
299. *Adalah v. The Minister of Interior, et al* (case pending), HC 830/07.
300. Ibid., at 15.
301. Ibid., at 25.
302. See, for example, HC 4608/02, *Abu Assad, et al v. The Prime Minister of Israel, et al*, available at: www.adalah.org/eng/famunif.php#2002_petition; and Ashkar, *Perpetual Limbo*.
303. OCHA, *Humanitarian Impact of the West Bank Barrier on Palestinian Communities*, at 4 and 23.
304. See also A. Schocken, 'Citizenship law makes Israel an apartheid state', *Ha'aretz*, 29 June 2008.
305. Article 13(2) of the UDHR states: 'Everyone has the right to leave any country, including his own, and return to his country'; Article 12(4) of the ICCPR states: 'No one shall be arbitrarily deprived of the right to enter his own country'; Article 5(d)(ii) of ICERD protects 'the right (of everyone) to leave any country, including one's own, and to return to one's country'.
306. See the International Law Commission's *Articles on Nationality of Natural Persons in Relation to the Succession of States*, which reflected customary international law in 1948.
307. UN Human Rights Committee, *General Comment No. 27* (1999), para. 21.
308. TRC Report, Vol. 2, Chapter 5, para. 23.
309. UNRWA for Palestine Refugees in the Near East, figures as of 30 June 2010, available at www.unrwa.org/userfiles/2011031065331.pdf .
310. Ibid.
311. Benny Morris, *Righteous Victims* (New York: Vintage Books, 2001), at 252. The figure of 750,000 is used as this is the most commonly figure cited for Palestinian Arab displacement in 1948 in the prevailing literature. Statistics for refugee figures have been as high as 935,573 according to UNRWA registrations, to as low as 530,000 according to some Israeli sources. The British Foreign Office estimated the total number of refugees to be 810,000 in February 1949 and then issued a revised estimate of 600,000. The UNCCP Technical Office gave a figure of 760,000. The US government estimated a total refugee population of 875,000 as of 1953. For further information see BADIL, *Survey of Palestinian Refugees and Internally Displaced Persons 2002* (Bethlehem: BADIL Resource Centre, 2003), at 25, note to Table 1.1.
312. See Report of the Commissioner-General of UNRWA, Official Records of the General Assembly, 22nd session, Supplement No. 13, 1 July 1966–30 June 1967, UN doc. A/6713. See also *Survey of Palestinian Refugees*.
313. General Assembly Resolution 194 (III), 11 December 1948, para. 11.
314. Nationality (Citizenship) Law 5712–1952, LSI, Vol. XI, at 50.
315. See Victor Kattan, 'The nationality of denationalized Palestinians' (2005) 74 *Nordic Journal of International Law* 67–102, at 85–87.
316. Only 14,000 were allowed back in to the West Bank by September 1967, when the census was conducted. After that, 'only a trickle of "special cases" were allowed back, perhaps 3,000 in all'. See Morris, *Righteous Victims*, at 329.
317. UN Security Council Resolution 237 of 14 June 1967.
318. See BADIL, *Occasional Bulletin No. 18* (July 2004), at 3, available at: www.badil.org/Publications/Bulletins/Bulletin-18.htm.
319. Ibid.
320. See, for example, *Concluding Observations of the Committee on the Elimination of Racial Discrimination: Israel*, 70th session, 19 February–9 March 2007, UN Doc. CERD/C/ISR/CO/13 (March 2007), para. 18.

321. US Department of State, *1983 Country Reports on Human Rights Practices*, at 1286. It is also evident that '[a]part from its implications for immigration, the Law of Return is used in legislation in import duties in a fashion that discriminates between Jew and Arab'. See John Quigley, 'Apartheid outside Africa: the case of Israel' (1991–92) 2 *Indiana International & Comparative Law Review* 221, at 230.
322. See Proposed Amendment to the Naturalization Provisions of the Political Constitution of Costa Rica, Advisory Opinion OC-4/84, Inter-American Court of Human Rights, 19 January 1984, in Elihu Lauterpacht and C.J. Greenwood (eds), *International Law Reports* (Cambridge: Grotius Publications, 1989), at 295, para. 35.
323. Ibid., at 294.
324. See Paul Abel, 'Denationalization' (1942) 5 *Modern Law Review*, at 57–68, examining the Nazi denationalisation decrees of 1941 in the context of contemporary international law.
325. Paul Weis, *Nationality and Statelessness in International Law* (The Netherlands: Alphen aan den Rijn, 1979), at 125; see also V. Panhuys, *The Role of Nationality in International Law* (Leiden: Sijthoff, 1959), at 163.
326. Geneva Convention relative to the Protection of Civilian Persons in Time of War, Article 4.
327. John Dugard, *International Law: A South African Perspective* (Cape Town: Juta, 2000), at 208.
328. Weis, *Nationality and Statelessness*, at 4–5.
329. See John Dugard, 'South Africa's independent Homelands: an exercise in denationalization' (1980) 10 *Denver Journal of International Law and Policy*, at 11–36.
330. 72 House of Assembly Debates, col. 579, 7 February 1978, quoted in Dugard, 'South Africa's independent Homelands', at 16.
331. TRC Report Vol. 2, para. 40.
332. During the British Mandate of Palestine (1922–48), no distinction was made in the Palestine Citizenship Order in Council regarding the acquisition of citizenship on grounds of race or religion (*Official Gazette*, 16 September 1925, at 459). The exception was the preference granted to Jews by Article 7 of the Mandate, which provided that there would be provisions framed in the law 'so as to facilitate the acquisition of Palestinian citizenship by Jews who take up their permanent residence in Palestine'.
333. The cause of this refugee flow has been examined through close review of related documentary evidence and oral accounts by Israeli historian Benny Morris and Ilan Pappé to indicate that it resulted from a deliberate programme of ethnic cleansing by Zionist and Israeli forces under the command of Ben-Gurion. Different interpretations and claims about this history are beyond the scope of the present study as they do not affect the rights of return for Palestinian refugees or non-discrimination regarding citizenship provided by international law.
334. The Treaty of Neuilly (1919), the Rumanian Minorities Treaty (1919), the Treaty of Versailles (1919), the Treaty of St Germaine (1919), the Treaty of Trianon (1920), the Treaty of Sèvres (1920), and the Treaty of Lausanne (1923), all support the view that nationality followed the change of sovereignty so that those persons habitually resident in a territory that became a new state or part of a new state would automatically acquire the nationality of that state. See Articles 39 (Serb-Croat-Slovene nationality), 44 (Greek nationality), 51 and 52 (Bulgarian nationality) of the Neuilly Treaty; Articles 36 (Belgian nationality), 84 (Czechoslovakian nationality), 91 (Polish nationality), 105 (nationality of the Free City of Danzig) and 112 (Danish nationality) of the Versailles Treaty; Articles 64–65 (Austrian nationality), 70–71 (Italian nationality) of the St Germaine Treaty; Article 57 (Hungarian nationality) of the Trianon Treaty; Articles 102 (Egyptian nationality), 117 (Cypriot/British nationality); 123 (general), 129 (Palestinian nationality) of the Sèvres Treaty; and Article 30 of the Lausanne Treaty. See both volumes of the *Treaties of Peace 1919–1923* (New York: Carnegie Endowment for International Peace, 1924). Brownlie is of the view that the precedent value of these treaties is considerable due to the uniformity of practice and the importance of the treaties concerned. See Ian Brownlie, *Principles of*

*Public International Law* (Oxford: Oxford University Press 1998), at 657. An attempt to codify the law of nationality in 1929, for the purposes of international law, concluded that nationality followed the change of sovereignty, unless the persons concerned declined the nationality of the successor state. See Article 18 of the Draft Convention on Nationality prepared in anticipation of the First Conference on the Codification of International Law, The Hague, 1930, Research in International Law, Harvard Law School, 1929, in 29 *American Journal of International Law Special Supplement* (1929), at 15. See also the decision by the Tel Aviv District Court in *A.B v. M.B.* 6 April 1951 (1950) 17 *International Law Reports*, at 111.

335. Law of Return 5710–1950; Law of Return (Amendment 5714–1954), Law of Return (Amendment No. 2) 5730–1970, and the Citizenship Law 5712–1952. The Citizenship Law was amended by adding section 3A, which somewhat eased the difficult process of acquiring citizenship. Yet section 3A leaves in force the distinction between the conditions of acquiring citizenship for Jews as compared to non-Jews, even if both candidates for citizenship have a similar history of leaving and re-entering the State.
336. A. Roberts, 'Prolonged military occupation: the Israeli-occupied territories since 1967' (1990) 84:1 *American Journal of International Law* 44, at 52.
337. Michael Savage 'The imposition of Pass Laws on the African population in South Africa 1916–1984', (1986) 85:339 *African Affairs*, at 181–182.
338. Act No. 25 of 1945.
339. CIA *World Factbook 2010*, available at www.telegraph.co.uk/finance/economics/8331631/Middle-East-economies-by-numbers.html.
340. OCHA, *Gaza Humanitarian Situation Report: The Impact of the Blockage on the Gaza Strip: A Human Dignity Crisis* (15 December 2008), available at: www.ochaopt.org/documents/ocha_opt_gaza_situation_report_2008_12_17_english.pdf.
341. See Gil Feiler and Doron Peskin, 'Estimates put Gaza damage at $1.5–2 billion', *Yedioth Aharanot*, 18 January 2009, available at: www.ynetnews.com/articles/0,7340,L-3657045,00.html.
342. Brian Van Arkadie, 'The impact of the Israeli occupation on the economies of the West Bank and Gaza' (1977) 6 *Journal of Palestine Studies* 2, at 104–105.
343. Ibid.
344. World Bank, *West Bank and Gaza: Economic Developments and Prospects* (March 2008), available at: http://web.worldbank.org/WBSITE/EXTERNAL/COUNTRIES/MENAEXT/WESTBANKGAZAEXTN/0,,contentMDK:21694302~menuPK:294370~pagePK:2865066~piPK:2865079~theSitePK:294365,00.html.
345. Ibid.
346. World Bank, *World Bank Report: Palestinian Economy Remains Stagnant after Four Years of Intifada* (November 2004), available at: http://siteresources.worldbank.org/INTWESTBANKGAZA/Resources/wbgaza-4yrassessment.pdf.
347. Palestinian Central Bureau of Statistics.
348. World Bank, *Economic Developments and Prospects*.
349. Ibid.
350. International Federation for Human Rights and Euro-Mediterranean Human Rights Network, Migrant Workers in Israel – A Contemporary Form of Slavery' (June 2003), at 6, available at: www.reliefweb.int/library/documents/2003/fidh-opt-25aug.pdf.
351. Ibid.
352. UNDP (2011), statistics available at www.undp.ps/en/index.html.
353. UNRWA (2011), available at: www.unrwa.org/userfiles/file/publications/gaza/UNRWA%20Gaza%20Poverty%20Survey.pdf.
354. UN Consolidated Appeals Process, *2007 Mid-Year Review*, available at: www.ochaopt.org/?module=displaysection&section_id=137&format=html.
355. World Bank, *West Bank and Gaza: Economic Update and Potential Outlook* (15 March 2006), available at: http://siteresources.worldbank.org/INTWESTBANKGAZA/Resources/WBGEconomicUpdateandPotentialOutlook.pdf.
356. OCHA, *West Bank Movement and Access Update* (June 2011), at 3.

NOTES to pp. 166–172   295

357. Ibid.
358. OCHA, Special Focus, *Three Years Later: The Humanitarian Impact of the Wall since the International Court of Justice Opinion* (9 July 2007), available at: www.un.org/unrwa/access/ICJ4_Special_Focus_July2007.pdf.
359. World Bank Technical Team, *Movement and Access Restrictions in the West Bank: Uncertainty and Inefficiency in the Palestinian Economy* (9 May 2007), available at: http://siteresources.worldbank.org/INTWESTBANKGAZA/Resources/WestBankrestrictions9Mayfinal.pdf.
360. Ibid.
361. Palestinian Centre for Human Rights, *Narratives Under Siege (3): Rafah Fishermens' Syndicate* (7 February 2008), available at: www.pchrgaza.org/Interventions/Narratives%20Under%20Siege%203.pdf.
362. OCHA and UN World Food Programme, Special Focus, *Between a Fence and a Hard Place* (August 2010), at 5; available at: http://www.ochaopt.org/documents/ocha_opt_special_focus_2010_08_19_english.pdf.
363. ICRC, *Gaza Closure: Not Another Year*, News Release (14 June 2010), available at: www.icrc.org/eng/resources/documents/update/palestine-update-140610.htm.
364. Ibrahim Barzak, 'U.N. warns on Gaza economy amid blockade', *USA Today*, 9 August 2007, available at: www.usatoday.com/news/topstories/2007-08-09-3462899240_x.htm.
365. World Bank, *West Bank and Gaza Update* (September 2006), available at: http://siteresources.worldbank.org/INTWESTBANKGAZA/Resources/UpdateSept06Eng.pdf.
366. Ibid.
367. Palestinian Central Bureau of Statistics.
368. World Bank, 'West Bank and Gaza: economic update and potential outlook', *Economic Update and Potential Outlook* (15 March 2006).
369. Ibid.
370. Ibid.
371. Palestinian Central Bureau of Statistics, *Labour Force Survey Report Series* (July–September 2007), available at: www.pcbs.gov.ps/DesktopDefault.aspx?tabID=3355&lang=en.
372. Ibid.
373. Israel Central Bureau of Statistics, July 2007.
374. *Concluding Observations of the Committee on Economic, Social and Cultural Rights: Israel*, UN Doc. E/C.12/1/Add.90 (23 April 2003), para. 19.
375. UNISPAL, *The Separation Wall in Jerusalem: Economic Consequences* (28 February 2007), available at: http://domino.un.org/UNISPAL.NSF/3d14c9e5cdaa296d85256cbf005aa3eb/b4a30a68ce68632a852572ce00515a1a!OpenDocument.
376. OCHA, *Barrier Update* (June 2011), at 16; available at: www.ochaopt.org/documents/ocha_opt_barrier_update_july_2011_english.pdf.
377. Palestine Central Bureau of Statistics.
378. World Bank, *Four Years– Intifada, Closures and Palestinian Economic Crisis: An Assessment* (October 2004), available at: http://siteresources.worldbank.org/INTWEST-BANKGAZA/Resources/wbgaza-4yrassessment.pdf.
379. World Bank, 'West Bank and Gaza: economic update and potential outlook', *Economic Update and Potential Outlook* (15 March 2006).
380. OCHA, *Humanitarian Situation in the Gaza Strip* (July 2011), available at: www.ochaopt.org/documents/ocha_opt_Gaza_Fact_Sheet_July_2011.pdf.
381. IMF, *Macroeconomic and Fiscal Framework for the West Bank and Gaza* (21 September 2010), available at: http://unispal.un.org/UNISPAL.NSF/0/729B065A70854337852577A8006A5CE8.
382. B'Tselem, *Gaza Prison: Freedom of Movement to and from the Gaza Strip on the Eve of the Disengagement Plan* (March 2005), available at: www.btselem.org/Download/200503_Gaza_Prison_English.doc.
383. UNCTAD, *Report on Assistance to the Palestinian People* (Geneva: UNCTAD, July 2007), available at: www.unctad.org/en/docs/tdb54d3_en.pdf.

384. UNCTAD *Report on UNCTAD Assistance to the Palestinian People: Developments in the Economy of the Occupied Palestinian Territory* (Geneva: UNCTAD, 15–28 September 2010), available at: www.unctad.org/en/docs//tdb57d4_en.pdf.
385. Act No. 28 of 1956, 1 (xxxviii).
386. Act No. 28 of 1956, 1 (xi).
387. Elizabeth S. Landis, 'South African apartheid legislation II: extension, enforcement and perpetuation' (1962) 71 *Yale Law Journal* 3, at 437–500.
388. Act No. 28 of 1956, 21(5), added by Act No. 41 of 1959, at 5.
389. Stuart Coupe, 'Divisions of labour: Racist trade unionism in the iron, steel, engineering and metallurgical industries of post-war South Africa' (1995) 21 *Journal of Southern African Studies* 3, at 451–455.
390. M. Sutcliffe and at P. Wellings, 'Worker militancy in South Africa: a sociospatial analysis of trade union activism in the manufacturing sector' (1985) 3 *Environment and Planning D: Society and Space* 3, at 357–379.
391. Nina Sovich, 'Palestinian Trade Unions' (2000) 29 *Journal of Palestine Studies* 4, at 66–79.
392. Joost R. Hiltermann, 'Mass mobilization under occupation: the emerging trade union movement in the West Bank', and 'West Bank, Gaza, Israel: marching toward civil war', *MERIP Reports*, Nos 136/137 (October–December, 1985), at 26–31.
393. Paul Cossali, 'Gaza's trade unions' (1988) 17 *Journal of Palestine Studies* 2, at 194–197.
394. Ibid. One union official was ordered to cancel the election's results; when he refused, his son was kidnapped and assaulted by Israeli soldiers.
395. Dani Ben Simhon, 'Unmaking of the Histadrut', *Challenge*, Vol. 88 (November 2004), available at: www.workersadvicecentre.org/Challenge88-Histadrut.htm.
396. Ibid.
397. Signed by Israel and the PLO as part of the Oslo process, the 1994 Protocol on Economic Relations established a customs union to formalise existing economic relations between Israel and the Palestinians and provide a framework for 'interim period' economic relations between Israel and the PA.
398. Protocol on Economic Relations between the Government of Israel and the PLO, Paris, 29 April 1994.
399. European Institute for Research on Mediterranean and Euro-Arab Cooperation.
400. The Palestinians estimated the sum owed to them at NIS 1.5 billion. The Histadrut agreed to give them NIS 8 million when the final agreement was reached.
401. Sovich, 'Palestinian Trade Unions', at 66–79.
402. See Agence France Presse, 'Israel labour law apply to Palestinian workers', 10 October 2007.
403. *Sawt Al-'Aamel* (The Voice of Labourers), PGFTU journal (January 2008).
404. Interview with Mr Al-Fuqaya, Board of Trustees of PGFTU, 12 August 2008, at PGFTU offices, Ramallah, West Bank.
405. Yoav Dotan, 'Judicial rhetoric, government lawyers, and human rights: the case of the Israeli High Court of Justice during the intifada' (1999) 33:2 *Law & Society Review* 319.
406. Baruch Hirson, *Year of Fire, Year of Ash: The Soweto Revolt: Roots of a Revolution* (London: Kallaway, 1979), and Mokubung O. Nkomo, 'The contradictions of Bantu education' (1981) 5 *Harvard Educational Review*, at 126–38.
407. Harold Wolpe, 'Educational resistance', in John Lonsdale (ed.), *South Africa in Question* (London: James Currey, 1988), at 202, cited in Janice Love and Peter C. Sederberg, 'Black education and the dialectics of transformation in South Africa, 1982–8' (1990) 28 *Journal of Modern African Studies* 2, at 309.
408. Ministry of Education, Statistics about Palestinian General Education, 2007/08; PCBS, Education Statistics; PCBS Press Release on International Literacy Day (8 September 2006).
409. UNDP Human Development Reports, 'Net secondary enrolment rate', *Human Development Index, 2007/2008*, available at: http://HDR_2007/2008_EN_Complete.pdf.

410. *West Bank and Gaza Public Expenditure Review, Vol. 1: From Crisis to Greater Fiscal Independence* (February 2007), available at: www-wds.worldbank.org/external/default/.../382071GZ0v2.txt.
411. Helen Murray, 'Education is freedom', Adalah *Newsletter*, Vol 18 (September 2005).
412. Palestinian Centre for Human Rights-Gaza , 'Press Release 44/2004', *PCHR-Gaza Report* (16 March 2004).
413. UNRWA, 'UNRWA condemns Rafah school shooting', Press Release (June 2004).
414. Ibid.
415. UNRWA, '10-year-old girl hit in UNRWA classroom by Israeli gunfire', Press Release (7 September 2004).
416. UNRWA, 'Gaza field assessment of IDF Operation Days of Penitence' (20 October 2004), available at: http://unispal.un.org/unispal.nsf/1ce874ab1832a53e85 2570bb006dfaf6/34d778171ac57b5d85256f34004ba1b5?OpenDocument.
417. UNRWA, 'Israeli gunfire hits 11-year-old girl sitting at her desk in an UNRWA school', Press Release (12 October 2004).
418. Palestine Centre for Human Rights, 'Seven school children wounded in a school in Khan Younis', Press Release (12 December 2004).
419. UNRWA 'Israeli gunfire hits 11-year-old girl'.
420. Palestinian Monitoring Group, Negotiations Affairs Department, '12 Assaults on Right to Education in Month of May' (June 2006), available at: http://right2edu.birzeit.edu/news/article398.
421. Association of International Development Agencies (AIDA) and OCHA, *The Gaza Blockade: Children and Education Fact Sheet* (28 July 2009), available at: www.ochaopt.org/documents/un_ngo_fact_sheet_blockade_figures_2009_07_28_english.pdf.
422. Birzeit University, *Right to Education Fact Sheet*, Right to Education Campaign (2 June 2008), available at: http://right2edu.birzeit.edu/news/article495.
423. AIDA and OCHA, *The Gaza Blockade*.
424. Palestinian Ministry of Higher Education, *The Effect of the Israeli Occupation on the Palestinian Education* (28 September 2000–1 October 2007), available at: www.mohe.gov.ps/downloads/textdoc/assE.doc.
425. Riham Barghouti and Helen Murray, *The Struggle for Academic Freedom in Palestine* (Birzeit University Right to Education Campaign, September 2005), available at: right2edu.birzeit.edu/downloads/pdfs/AcademicFreedomPaper.pdf.
426. Right to Education Campaign, *Right to Education Factsheet*.
427. Right to Education Campaign, 'Demand the return of Gaza students to Birzeit University' (Birzeit University, 24 February 2005), available at: right2edu.birzeit.edu/news/article263.
428. Right to Education Campaign, 'Institutions raided and shut down in Nablus, including a girls' school' (Birzeit University, 7 July 2008), available at: right2edu.birzeit.edu/news/printer548.
429. Seth Freedman, 'Children are paying the price of injustice', *Guardian*, 17 July 2008, available at: www.dci-pal.org/english/display.cfm?DocId=856&CategoryId=31.
430. Defence for Children International-Palestine Section, 'Israeli Prison Education: Learning the Lessons of Institutionalized Racism' (August 2001).
431. UN Committee on the Rights of the Child, 'Concluding Observations of the Committee on the Rights of the Child: Israel, UN Doc. CRC/C/15/Add.195 (9 October 2002), paras 52–53.
432. Right to Education Campaign, *Right to Education Fact Sheet*.
433. Ibid.
434. Ibid.
435. Ibid.
436. 'The Right to Education Campaign's Submission to the United Nations Human Rights Council's Universal Periodic Review of Israel' (December 2008).
437. Right to Education Campaign, *Right to Education Factsheet*.
438. Ibid.

439. Palestinian Monitoring Group, Negotiations Affairs Department, '12 assaults on right to education in month of May' (June 2006), available at: right2edu.birzeit.edu/news/article398.
440. 'Israeli Forces Killed 22 Palestinian Students Over Last Week,' Palestinian Ministry of Education and Higher Education, Maan News Agency (March 2008).
441. AIDA and OCHA, *The Gaza Blockage*.
442. UN Humanitarian Coordinator and AIDA, *The Gaza Blockade: Children and Education Factsheet* (28 July 2009), cited in OCHA, *Locked In: The Humanitarian Impact of Two Years of Blockade on the Gaza Strip* (August 2009), available at: www.ochaopt.org/documents/Ocha_opt_Gaza_impact_of_two_years_of_blockade_August_2009_english.pdf.
443. Right to Education Campaign, *Right to Education Factsheet*.
444. Ir Amim, *The Scandal Continues: An Assessment of the Arab-Palestinian Educational System in East Jerusalem in the 2007–2008 School Year* (September 2007), available at: www.ir-amim.org.il/Eng/_Uploads/dbsAttachedFiles/EducationReport2007Eng(1).doc.
445. ACRI and Ir Amin, *Failed Grade – The Palestinian Education System in East Jerusalem* (August 2010), available at: www.ir-mim.org.il/Eng/_Uploads/dbsAttachedFiles/FailedGrade.pdf.
446. The annual yearbooks of the Jerusalem Education Administration, population data of the Jerusalem Institute for Israel Studies; Yuval Wargen, 'Education in East Jerusalem', Knesset Research and Information Centre, Jerusalem (16 October 2006).
447. Jonathan Lis, 'Discrimination in Jerusalem: the municipality allocated three times the number of computers to educational institutions in West Jerusalem than it did in East Jerusalem', *Ha'aretz*, 4 April 2005.
448. Ibid.
449. ACRI, *Facts and Figures about East Jerusalem* (June 2008), available at: www.acri.org.il/en/2008/06/.../facts-and-figures-about-east-jerusalem...
450. ACRI, *Failed Grade: The Education System in Easter Jerusalem 2010* (August 2010), available at: www.acri.org.il/pdf/EJeducation2010en.pdf.
451. HC 5125/00, *Shirine Eweida et al v. The Jerusalem Municipality* (unpublished).
452. ACRI, *Failed Grade*.
453. Wargen, 'Education in East Jerusalem'; Ir Amim, *Inadequacies in the Public Education Infrastructure for Palestinians in East Jerusalem: Overview – September 2006* (September 2006), available at: www.ir-amim.org.il/Eng/_Uploads/dbsAttachedFiles/EducationReport2006Eng(1).doc.
454. ACRI, *Facts and Figures about East Jerusalem*.
455. Yehudit Karp to Attorney General Yehuda Weinstein, 8 February 2010.Cited in ACRI, *Failed Grade*, at 12.
456. Shlomo Swirski and Itai Schurtz, *Success Rates in the Matriculation Exam, by Locality: 2004–2005*, Adva Centre (August 2006), available at: www.adva.org/uploaded/rights-short.pdf.
457. Article 19(2), International Covenant on Civil and Political Rights.
458. General Assembly Resolution 2615 (XXV), 24 October 1970, para. 3.
459. See further Michael Kearney, *The Prohibition of Propaganda for War in International Law* (Oxford: Oxford University Press, 2007).
460. *The Prosecutor* v. *Nahimana, Barayagwiza, and Ngeze*, Case no. ICTR–99–52–T, Judgment and Sentence (3 December 2003), para. 1008.
461. *Prosecutor* v. *Vojislav Seselj*, Modified Amended Indictment, Case no. IT–03–67, 15 July 2005.
462. General Comment 11 (Article 20) UN Doc. HRI/GEN/1/Rev.1 at 12 (1994).
463. General Comment No. 29 States of Emergency (Article 4), CCPR/C/21/Rev.1/Add.11 (2001) para. 13(e). See also International Commission of Jurists, *States of Emergency: Their Impact on Human Rights* (Geneva: International Commission of Jurists, 1983), at 440.

464. Gilbert Marcus, *Borders for Books: South Africa under Apartheid* (AIDA Nederland, April 2008); see also 'Jacobsen's Index of Objectionable Material' (2006) housed at Beacon for Freedom of Expression, www.beaconforfreedom.org/about_database/south%20africa.html.
465. Marcus, *Borders for Books*.
466. As noted earlier, these regulations are used by the Israeli authorities in both Israel and the OPT, despite the fact that (as noted earlier) they were repealed by the British authorities prior to the termination of the British Mandate by the Palestine (Revocations) Order-in-Council, 1948, and overturned in the West Bank in May 1948 by the Jordanian Constitution.
467. See Israeli Ministry of Foreign Affairs, www.mfa.gov.il/MFA/Facts%20About%20Israel/Culture/The%20Printed%20Media-%20Israels%20Newspapers.
468. Pnina Lahav, 'The press and national security' (1990) 28 *Israeli Democracy* (winter), at 177–178.
469. Military Order No. 50, *Order Concerning Distribution of Newspapers* (11 July 1967).
470. Military Order No. 101, *Order Concerning Prohibition of Incitement and Hostile Propaganda* (27 August 1967).
471. Virgil Falloon, *Excessive Secrecy, Lack of Guidelines: A Report on Military Censorship in the West Bank* (Ramallah: Al-Haq, Law in the Service of Man, 1985).
472. Abraham Ben-Zvi, 'The limits of Israel's democracy in the shadow of security' (2005) 1 *Taiwan Journal of Democracy* 2, at 8–9.
473. See Yuval Karniel, 'Balancing the protection of civil liberties during wartime: how the Supreme Court shaped Palestinian freedom of expression during the Second Intifada' (2002) 22 *Government Information Quarterly*, at 626–643.
474. The Nakdi Report was published by the Israel Broadcasting Authority in 1995 under the title *Guidelines for Coverage of News and Current Affairs*. It is named for its original author, Nakdimon Rogel.
475. Reporters Sans Frontières/Reporters Without Borders, *Annual Worldwide Press Freedom Index*. Data taken from tables available at: en.rsf.org.
476. GPO, home page: www.pmo.gov.il/PMOEng/PM+Office/Departments/GPO.htm.
477. GPO, Rules Regarding Cards and Certificates for Journalists, Press Technicians and Media Assistants – Temporary Amendments (11 August 2005).
478. GPO, Rules Regarding Cards and Certificates for Journalists, Press Technicians and Media Assistants, para. 3(G).
479. *Saif v. Government Press Office*, [HCJ] 5627/02, 25 April 2004.
480. See *Entrepreneurship and Publishing Promotion Inc. v. The Broadcasting Authority* [HCJ 606/93] v.48 1(2).
481. See, for example, Reuters, 'Gaza reporter: Israeli security officials broke my ribs', *Ha'aretz*, 30 June 2008; Mel Frykberg, 'Israelis assault award winning IPS journalist', Inter Press Service, 28 June 2008.
482. Report of the Special Rapporteur on the Situation of Human Rights in the Palestinian Territories Occupied by Israel since 1967, Professor Richard Falk, UN Doc. A/63/326, 25 September 2008, at paras 19–20.
483. See Al-Haq, *Israeli Military Investigation Sanctions Wilful Killing of Civilians, including Reuters Cameraman, and Demonstrates Complete Disregard for Principle of Precautions in Attack* (20 August 2008), available at: www.alhaq.org/etemplate.php?id=388.
484. See Reporters Sans Frontières, available at: www.rsf.org/article.php3?id_article=26822.
485. See Article 21 of the ICCPR; Article 11(2) of the European Convention on Human Rights; Article 11 of the African Charter on Human and Peoples' Rights.
486. See A. De Tocqueville, 'Democracy in America', cited in G.A. Beaudoin and E. Ratushny (eds), *The Canadian Charter of Rights and Freedoms* (Toronto: Carswell, 1989, 2nd edn), at 235.
487. Act No. 44 of 1950, as amended.
488. Ibid.
489. Act No. 34 of 1960.

490. Act No. 17 of 1956.
491. Military Order No. 101, *Order Concerning Prohibition of Incitement and Hostile Propaganda* (27 August 1967).
492. BADIL, 'Palestinian Civil Society Organizations express grave concern about Israeli closure of Islamic Charitable Society in Hebron' April 24, 2008: available at: www.badil.org/Publications/Press/2008/press460-08.htm.
493. See: www.state.gov/g/drl/rls/hrrpt/2007/100597.htm.
494. See Al-Haq, *A Culture of Repression: Israeli Authorities Ban Palestinian Cultural Festival in East Jerusalem* (21 March 2009), available at: www.alhaq.org/etemplate.php?id=436.
495. The West Bank village of Ni'lin is a case in point. On 29 July 2008, 50 children and 50 elderly citizens from Ni'lin planned to march from the village to the Wall in protest of the annexation of their land. Confronted by an Israeli Border Police vehicle, the crowd dispersed and the organisers led the children and elderly to safety. Ahmad Husam Musa, a ten-year-old child, hid in an olive grove. Field reports indicated that a 'member of the Israeli Border Police saw Ahmad Musa, left the Border Police vehicle, aimed his rifle and fired a live bullet. Shot from a distance of 50 metres, the bullet entered Ahmad Musa's forehead and exited through the back of his skull.' See Al-Haq, *Right to Life of Palestinian Children Disregarded in Ni'lin*.
496. Sara Roy, *The Gaza Strip: The Political Economy of De-Development* (Institute for Palestine Studies, April 2005).
497. Human Rights Watch, *Razing Rafah: Mass Home Demolitions in the Gaza Strip* (October 2004), available at: www.hrw.org/campaigns/gaza/. See also statistics gathered by PCHR-Gaza, available at; www.pchrgaza.org/alaqsaintifada.html.
498. See statistics gathered by PCHR-Gaza, available at: www.pchrgaza.org/alaqsaintifada.html. See also statistics gathered by B'Tselem, available at: www.btselem.org/english/statistics/Casualties.asp; and OCHA's *Humanitarian Monitor* reports, issued periodically and available at: www.ochaopt.org/.
499. The access to and from Gaza of people, goods, fuel and electricity is almost completely dependent on Israel, even after the completion of Israel's 'disengagement'.
500. See Gisha Legal Centre for Freedom of Movement, *Disengaged Occupiers – The Legal Status of Gaza* (January 2007), at 21; available at: www.gisha.org/UserFiles/File/Report%20for%20the%20website.pdf.
501. Israel Ministry of Foreign Affairs, 'Security Cabinet declares Gaza hostile territory', Press Release (19 September 2007), available at: www.mfa.gov.il/MFA/Government/Communiques/2007/Security+Cabinet+declares+Gaza+hostile+territory+19-Sep-2007.htm. See also C. Urquhart, 'Israel declares Gaza Strip hostile territory', *Guardian* (20 September 2007), at 22.
502. See UN Human Rights Council's Combined Special Rapporteur, Human Rights Situation in Palestine and Other Occupied Arab Territories, A/HRC/10/22, 20 March 2009, at 5, and Report of the Special Rapporteur on the Situation of Human Rights in the Palestinian Territories Occupied since 1967, Richard Falk, *Human Rights Situation in Palestine and other Occupied Arab Territories*, 11 February 2009, A/HRC/10/20, at 7.
503. The Committee Against Torture reviewed Israel's compliance with CAT in May 2009: findings were issued in the summary report, *ConcludingObservations of the Committee Against Torture : Israel* (23 June 2009), CAT/C/ISR/CO/4, available at: www.unhcr.org/refworld/docid/4a85632b0.html.
504. HC 5523/07, *Adalah v. The Prime Minister, et al* (petition withdrawn October 2007).
505. World Bank, 'West Bank and Gaza: economic update and potential outlook'.
506. World Bank, *West Bank and Gaza: Economic Developments and Prospects* (March 2008), available at: http://web.worldbank.org/WBSITE/EXTERNAL/COUNTRIES/MENAEXT/WESTBANKGAZAEXTN/0,,contentMDK:21694302~menuPK:294370~pagePK:2865066~piPK:2865079~theSitePK:294365,00.html.
507. Ibid.
508. House of Commons, International Development, *Aid Under Pressure: Support for Development Assistance in a Global Economic Downturn* (hereafter '*Aid Under*

509. *Pressure*'), Report of Session 2008–09, available at: www.publications.parliament.uk/pa/cm200809/cmselect/.../179ii.pdf, at 8.
509. Ibid.
510. World Bank, *Investing in Palestinian Economic Reform and Development* (17 December 2007), available at: http://siteresources.worldbank.org/INTWESTBANKGAZA/Resources/294264-1166525851073/ParisconferencepaperDec17.pdf.
511. OCHA, Special Focus, *The Closure of the Gaza Strip: The Economic and Humanitarian Consequences* (December 2007), at 2. Statistics in this section are from this source unless noted otherwise. Available at: www.ochaopt.org/documents/Gaza_Special_Focus_December_2007.pdf.
512. House of Commons, *Aid Under Pressure*, at 4.
513. World Food Programme, *Food Security and Market Monitoring Report* (9 June 2007), available at: http://unispal.un.org/UNISPAL.NSF/0/85349AC323C04AB385257307004AF6F0.
514. House of Commons, *Aid Under Pressure*, at 7.
515. Sixty-three per cent of Gaza's power supply is provided directly by Israel, paid for by deductions from Palestinian tax revenues, and 28 per cent is produced in Gaza, powered by fuel paid for by the European Commission through the Temporary International Mechanism (TIM). All of Gaza's fuel is imported through Israel (OCHA, *Closure of the Gaza Strip*). Recall that Israel destroyed all six transformers in Gaza's only power plant in June 2006. See B'Tselem, *Act of Vengeance: Israel's Bombing of the Gaza Power Plant and its Effects* (September 2006), available at: www.btselem.org/Download/200609_Act_of_Vengeance_Eng.pdf.
516. HC 9132/07, *Jaber al-Basyouni Ahmed v. The Prime Minister*. Case documents and the Supreme Court's decisions are available on Adalah's website at: www.adalah.org/eng/gaza%20report.html.
517. House of Commons, *Aid Under Pressure*, at 8.
518. WHO West Bank and Gaza, *Health Situation in Gaza* (3 March 2008), available at: www.who.int/entity/hac/crises/international/wbgs/sitreps/opt_31dec2008.pdf.
519. OCHA, *Gaza Strip Fuel Situation Report as of 23 April 2008*, available at: www.ochaopt.org/documents/Gaza_Strip_Fuel_Situation_Report_as_of_23_April_2008.pdf.
520. OCHA, 'ISRAEL–OPT: Food distribution halted, cooking gas running out in Gaza', IRIN Humanitarian News and Analysis (28 April 2008), available at: www.irinnews.org/Report.aspx?ReportId=77959.
521. Ibid., at 10.
522. House of Commons, *Aid Under Pressure*, at 10.
523. HC 11105/07, *PHR-Israel and 15 Patients v. The Commander of the Israeli Military in Gaza, Chief Commander of the Southern District, et al* (unpublished decision), and HC 559/08, *PHR-Israel and 1 Patient v. The Commander of the Israeli Military in Gaza, Chief Commander of the Southern District, et al* (unpublished decision). See also PHR-Israel, *Gaza: No Justice, No Hope for Patients* (2 January 2008), available at: www.phr.org.il/phr/article.asp?articleid=538&catid=55&pcat=45&lang=ENG.
524. See HC 5429/07, *PHR-Israel, et al v. The Minister of Defence*.
525. Ibid.
526. Ibid.
527. See PHR-Israel, *Holding Health to Ransom: GSS Interrogation and Extortion of Palestinian Patients at Erez Crossing* (August 2008), at 6; available at: www.phr.org.il/phr/files/articlefile_1217866249125.pdf.
528. Ibid.
529. 'PHR-Israel believes that the fact that refusal to collaborate leads to prevention of treatment, may constitute a breach of the UN Convention against Torture and Other Cruel, Inhuman or Degrading Treatment or Punishment, as it contributes to physical suffering and may even lead to death, where a person's life could have been saved or his suffering alleviated by receiving treatment.' See PHR-Israel, *Holding Health to Ransom*, at 30.

530. Tim McGirk, 'Israelis blocking medical care in Gaza', *Time Magazine*, 25 March 2008, available at: www.time.com/time/world/article/0,8599,1725422,00.html.
531. WHO West Bank and Gaza, *Access to Healthcare for the Palestinian People* (April 2008), at 36–37, available at: www.emro.who.int/palestine/reports/monitoring/WHO_special_monitoring/access/access%20to%20health%20services%20(April%202008).pdf.
532. Ibid.
533. Ibid.
534. House of Commons, *Aid Under Pressure*, at 11.
535. WHO West Bank and Gaza, *Health Situation in Gaza*.
536. For regular updates on this information see, for example, reports by OCHA, available at: www.ochaopt.org; the Al Mezan Centre for Human Rights, available at: www.mezan.org; and the PCHR, available at: www.pchrgaza.org.
537. OCHA, *Protection of Civilians Weekly Report* (4–10 March 2009), available at: www.ochaopt.org/documents/ocha_opt_protection_of_civilians_weekly_2009_03_10_english.pdf.
538. OCHA, *Protection of Civilians Weekly Report* (11–17 March 2009), available at: www.ochaopt.org/documents/ocha_opt_protection_of_civilians_2009_03_13_english.pdf.
539. Ibid.
540. Ibid.
541. OCHA, *Humanitarian Monitor: Occupied Palestinian Territory*, No. 34 (February 2009), available at: www.ochaopt.org/documents/ocha_opt_humanitarian_monitor_2009_02_01_english.pdf.
542. Ibid.
543. Ibid.
544. OCHA, *Field Update on Gaza from the Humanitarian Coordinator* (10–16 March 2009), available at: www.ochaopt.org/documents/ocha_opt_gaza_humanitarian_situation_report_2009_03_16_english.pdf.
545. OCHA, *Protection of Civilians Weekly Report* (11–17 March 2009).
546. OCHA, *Humanitarian Monitor: Occupied Palestinian Territory*, No. 34.
547. Ibid.
548. Ibid.
549. Ibid.
550. OCHA, *Protection of Civilians Weekly Report* (18–24 March 2009), available at: www.ochaopt.org/documents/ocha_opt_protection_of_civilians_weekly_2009_03_24_english.pdf.
551. OCHA, *Protection of Civilians Weekly Report* (4–10 March 2009), available at: www.ochaopt.org/documents/ocha_opt_protection_of_civilians_weekly_2009_03_10_english.pdf.
552. OCHA, *Humanitarian Monitor: Occupied Palestinian Territory*, No. 34.
553. OCHA, Special Focus, *Easing the Blockade: Assessing the Humanitarian Impact on the Population of the Gaza Strip* (East Jerusalem: OCHA, March 2011).
554. OCHA, *Protection of Civilians Weekly Report* (11–17 March 2009).
555. OCHA, *Protection of Civilians Weekly Report* (18–24 March 2009).
556. Ibid.
557. OCHA, *Humanitarian Monitor: Occupied Palestinian Territory*, No. 34.
558. Ibid.
559. OCHA, *Easing the Blockade*, at 10.
560. Ibid.
561. See, for example, Report of the independent expert on minority issues, Addendum, *Mission to France*, UN Doc. A/HRC/7/23/Add.2 (2008).
562. See, for example, Consideration of Reports, Comments and Information Submitted by States Parties under Article 9 of the Convention (Slovakia), CERD/C/SR.1655 (2004).
563. See James Crawford, *The Creation of States in International Law* (Oxford: Oxford University Press, 2006), at 338.

564. For example, the Bantu Land Act of 1913 restricted African land ownership to the 'native reserves' and the Native Affairs Act of 1920 established separate administrative structures for Africans with the result that 80 per cent of the country (that is, the black African population) was confined to 13 per cent of the land. The Native (Urban Areas) Act of 1913 provided for urban segregation and African influx control and the Native Trust and Land Act of 1936 consolidated the reserves, and forbade the transfer to, or lease of land by, other races within these reserves. Meanwhile, Africans were prohibited from acquiring land elsewhere. See Dugard, *Human Rights*, at 78–79. See also D.L. Carey Miller and Anne Pope, *Land Title in South Africa* (Cape Town: Juta, 2000), at 19–20, and Crawford, *Creation of States*, at 338–339. The term 'Bantu' was the way in which Africans were described by South African law; See Dugard, *Human Rights*, at 61.
565. In 1985, the apartheid government itself estimated that a total of 126,176 families had been forced out of their homes in terms of the Act: Omond, *The Apartheid Handbook*, at 37.
566. O'Meara, *Forty Lost Years*, at 69.
567. See Nigel Worden, *The Making of Modern South Africa: Conquest, Apartheid, Democracy* (Oxford: Blackwell, 2007), at 81–88, and Miller and Pope, *Land Title in South Africa*, at 23.
568. See generally, John Dugard, 'The legal effect of United Nations Resolutions on apartheid', (1963) 83 *South African Law Journal*, at 44.
569. See Barbara Rogers, *Divide and Rule: South Africa's Bantustans* (London: International and Defence Aid Fund, 1976), at 8 (observing that Dr Verwoerd was very concerned about South Africa's image in the world, and the threat of decolonisation in the rest of Africa).
570. 107 House of Assembly Debates, cols. 4191–93, 10 April, 1961, cited in Dugard, *International Law*, at 447.
571. See Summary of the *Report on the Commission for the Socio-Economic Development of the Bantu Areas within the Union of South Africa* (Pretoria: The Government Printer, 1955) (hereafter the 'Tomlinson Commission').
572. Ibid., at 194.
573. Ibid., at 103.
574. See Merle Lipton, 'Independent Bantustans?' (1972) 48 *International Affairs*, at 1–19.
575. Apparently, the name of this Act was changed so as to sound more appealing. There were protests within the National Party that so negative a bill, without some positive compensation, would alienate some domestic opinion and provide foreign critics with ammunition against South Africa: see Gwendolen M. Carter, Thomas Karis and Newell Stultz, *South Africa's Transkei: The Politics of Domestic Colonialism* (London: Heinemann, 1967), at 12–13.
576. Quoted from Crawford, *Creation of States*, at 339.
577. See Rogers, *Divide and Rule*, at 21.
578. Ibid.
579. There were also two other smaller Bantustans called KwaNdebele and KaNgwane.
580. See Carter et al, *South Africa's Transkei*, at 12–13.
581. See General Assembly Resolution 3151G, 14 December 1973, and General Assembly Resolution 3411D, 28 November 1975.
582. Ibid., at 3.
583. Henry J. Richardson, 'Self-determination, international law and the South African Bantustan policy' (1978) 17 *Columbia Journal of Transnational Law* 185, at 217.
584. General Assembly Resolution 2775 of 29 November 1971.
585. For further reading, see Geoffrey E. Norman, 'The Transkei: South Africa's illegitimate child' (1976–77) 12 *New England Law Review*, at 585–646; Donald E. deKieffer and David A. Hartquist, 'Transkei: a legitimate birth' (1977–78) 13 *New England Law Review*, at 428–452, and Geoffrey E. Norman, 'The Transkei revisited' (1977–78) 13 *New England Law Review*, at 792–801. See also Merrie Faye Watkin, 'Transkei: an analysis of the

practice of recognition – political or legal?' (1977) 18 *Harvard International Law Journal*, at 605–627.
586. See John Dugard, *Recognition and the United Nations* (Cambridge: Grotius Publications, 1987), at 98–108.
587. Report of the Commission of Enquiry into South West African Affairs, 1962–63, RP 12 / 1964. For a very useful map of the envisaged ten black 'Homelands' for Namibia by the Odendaal Commission, see Laurent W.C. Kaela, *The Question of Namibia* (Basingstoke: Palgrave Macmillan, 1996), at 80.
588. See John Dugard, *The Southwest Africa/Namibia Dispute: Documents and Scholarly Writings on the Controversy between South Africa and the United Nations (Perspectives on Southern Africa)* (Berkeley: University of California Press, 1973), at 238 (citing UN *Monthly Chronicle*, June 1964, at 33 ff.).
589. Ibid. See also Itsejuwa Sagay, *The Legal Aspects of the Namibia Dispute* (Ile-Ife, Nigeria: University of Ife Press, 1975), at 359. In 1965, the UN General Assembly added its protests to that of the Special Committee of 24. General Assembly Resolution 2074 (XX), 17 December 1965.
590. See Sagay, *Legal Aspects of the Namibia Dispute*, at 363–369 (describing the Homelands of Ovamboland, Kavangoland, Damaraland, Hereroland, the Caprivi Strip, Bushmanland, Rehoboth Gebiet and Namaland).
591. Ibid., at 370. SWAPO and DEMCOP called for a boycott of the elections to the Legislative Council of the Ovambo 'Homeland' held on 1 and 2 August 1973. As a result, only 823 out of 50,000 eligible voters cast their ballots.
592. Ibid. See also General Assembly Resolution 2145 (XXI) of 27 October 1966 (where the General Assembly terminated the Mandate of South West Africa and assumed direct responsibility for the Territory until its independence).
593. General Assembly Resolution 2403 (XXIII) of 16 December 1968.
594. Security Council Resolution 264 of 20 March 1969.
595. Security Council Resolution 385 of 30 January 1976, para. 7.
596. Ibid.
597. Security Council Resolution 652 of 17 April 1990. See further, Cedric Thornberry, *A Nation is Born: The Inside Story of Namibia's Independence* (Winhoek: MacMillan, 2004), in which the author details the negotiations which led to Nambia's transition to independence.
598. The role and authority of the Jewish Agency was confirmed in 1952 by the World Zionist Organisation–Jewish Agency (Status) Law, 5713–1952 and by a 1954 'covenant' that was reaffirmed at the 34th World Zionist Organisation Congress: see 'Covenant Between the Government of Israel and The Zionist Executive called also the Executive of the Jewish Agency', cited in W. Thomas Mallison and Sally V. Mallison, *The Palestine Problem in International Law and World Order* (London: Longman, 1986), at 433.
599. WZO Department for Rural Settlement, *Master Plan for the Development of Settlement in Judea and Samaria 1979–1983*, emphasis in original.
600. Ibid., emphases and acronym in original.
601. OCHA, *The Humanitarian Impact on Palestinians of Israeli Settlements And Other Infrastructure in the West Bank* (July 2007), available at: www.ochaopt.org/documents/TheHumanitarianImpactOfIsraeliInfrastructureTheWestBank_Intro.pdf.
602. Ibid., at 70.
603. See ibid., at 89–93, 'Nablus: a city encircled'.
604. Ibid., at 90.
605. Act No 21 of 1950; amended in 1957 (Act 23): see Omond, *The Apartheid Handbook*, at 30.
606. Ibid., at 32.
607. Ibid., at 33.
608. Ibid.

609. According to Roger Omond, more than 11,500 people were convicted of contravening the Immorality Act between 1950 and 1980, and more than twice that number were charged. See Omond, *The Apartheid Handbook*, at 33.
610. Harrison, *The White Tribe of Africa*, at 172. Roger Omond notes that over the 20-year period prior to the publication of his book in 1986, at least 16 white men had committed suicide by gassing, hanging, shooting, drowning or taking insecticide after being charged under the Immorality Act: Omond, *The Apartheid Handbook*, at 33–34.
611. Palestinian Order in Council (POC)–1922, Article 15(a).
612. Family Courts Law of 1995, section 3(B1).
613. Rabbi and Attorney Kariv, G. (2006, March). 'Religion and State and the Israel Elections', Israel Religious Action Centre (IRAC), available at: http://rac.org/advocacy/irac/; Rabbi and Attorney Kariv, G. (2006, November). 'Civil Marriage Abroad', IRAC; and Meranda, A. (2008, Feb. 13). 'Knesset votes against civil marriage', Jewish World, Ynet, available at: http://www.ynetnews.com/articles/0,7340,L-3506428,00.html.
614. A.J. Christopher ,*The Atlas of Apartheid* (London: Routledge, 1994), at 140.
615. *Cape Native Blue Book*, at 43; cited in H. Corder, *Law and Social Practice in South Africa* (Cape Town: Juta, 1988), at 285.
616. The 'Beit-El-Toubas Case' (1979), *Ayyub et al v. The Minister of Defence* (HCJ 606/78, 610/78), discussed in I. Lustick, 'Israel and the West Bank after Elon Moreh: the mechanics of de facto annexation' (1981) 35 *Middle East Journal* 557.
617. As discussed in Chapter 3, Israel claims to annex East Jerusalem on 28 June 1967 through the Law and Administration Order (No. 1), which states that 'the territory of the Land of Israel described in the appendix is hereby proclaimed territory in which the law, jurisdiction and administration of the state apply'. Quoted in Centre on Housing Rights and Evictions (COHRE) and BADIL Resource Centre for Palestinian Residency and Refugee Rights, *Ruling Palestine: A History of the Legally Sanctioned Jewish-Israeli Seizure of Land and Housing in Palestine* (May 2005), available at: www.badil.org/Publications/Monographs/BADIL-COHRE-Israel%20Land%20Regime.pdf, at 71. By applying Israeli law, the Ministry of Finance seized sizeable portions of East Jerusalem for 'public' purposes before handing these over to private Jewish Israeli developers.
618. Ibid., at 67.
619. Raja Shehadeh, *The Law of the Land: Settlements and Land Issues under Israeli Military Occupation* (Jerusalem: Palestinian Academic Society for the Study of International Affairs, 1993), at 20–24.
620. COHRE and BADIL estimate in their 2005 report that 1500 military orders had been issued by 2002 in relation to regulation of the West Bank and none of these have been revoked. COHRE and BADIL, *Ruling Palestine*, at 80–81.
621. See, for example, Article 52 of the Hague Regulations.
622. 'Requisition' in international humanitarian law implies the lawful taking of private property, which strict limitations and limited temporal scope, for the needs of the occupying army. 'Expropriation', as referred to in the Apartheid Convention, is not generally used in the instruments of international humanitarian law, and is primarily examined in international law through the lens of procedural and substantive protections that international investment treaties provide to foreign investors (primarily against nationalisation). Expropriation entails the taking of private property by a state (or its agent) or the transfer of the power of management or control of a company to the state. It can be either lawful or unlawful. Generally, an expropriation is unlawful when it is discriminatory, not for a public purpose, or not accompanied by just compensation: see Donna Arzt, *The Right to Compensation: Basic Principles Under International Law: Compensation as Part of a Comprehensive Solution to the Palestinian Refugee Problem* (Syracuse, NY: Syracuse University, 1999).
623. 'The land settlement operations were begun by the British in the early 1920s, and were continued by the Jordanian government. In 1967 they were discontinued by Military Order No. 192, and requests by West Bankers to complete these operations, especially

in areas where all the stages except the final registration were completed ... were denied.' Ibid., at 70–71.
624. Military Order No. 291, *Order Concerning Settlement of Disputes over Land and Water* (19 December 1968).
625. Under Military Order No. 25, *Order Concerning Transactions in Property* (18 June 1967). Shehadeh, *Law of the Land*, at 59.
626. Military Order No. 811, *Order Concerning Amendment to Law of Immovable Property* (23 November 1979). This Order was then amended by Military Order No. 847, *Order Concerning Amendment to Law of Immovable Property* (1 June 1980).
627. See B'Tselem, *Land Grab: Israel's Settlement Policy in the West Bank* (Jerusalem: B'Tselem, May 2002), at 63. In the context of occupation, secret land dealings facilitate land alienation from Palestinians to Jews, as such transactions are seen by other Palestinians as a form of collaboration.
628. COHRE and BADIL, *Ruling Palestine*, at 100.
629. Article 46, Hague Regulations.
630. Elin B. Hilwig, *The Barrier in the Occupied Palestinian Territory: Protection of Private Property under International Humanitarian and Human Rights Law* (Nijmegen: Wolf Legal Publishers, 2005), at 41–42.
631. *Legal consequences of the construction of a wall in the Occupied Palestinian Territory*, advisory opinion, ICJ Rep, 2004, 136, at para. 121.
632. Where it can be shown that 'extensive destruction and appropriation of property ... [is] not justified by military necessity and carried out unlawfully and unwantonly', then individuals may be held criminally responsible for such grave breaches of the Fourth Geneva Convention under Article 147.
633. Extract of the Drobles Plan, from Matityahu Drobles, *The Settlement in Judea and Samaria – Strategy, Policy and Program* (in Hebrew) (Jerusalem: WZO, September 1980), at 3; quoted in B'Tselem, *Land Grab*, at 14.
634. Quoted in Al-Haq, 'Discrimination is real', at 21. The Drobles Plan went through several versions after its composition in 1978.
635. Order Concerning Absentee Property (Private Property), 23 July 1967.
636. Shehadeh, *Law of the Land*, at 61–63.
637. Quoted in Al-Haq, 'Discrimination is real', at 22.
638. B'Tselem, *Land Grab*, at 59.
639. Military Order No. 259, *Order Concerning Security Provisions (Closure of Military Training Zones)* (13 June 1968); lands seized from Palestinians have often been handed over to settlers. COHRE & BADIL, *Ruling Palestine*, at 128.
640. Lustick, 'Israel and the West Bank after Elon Moreh', at 561.
641. It is important to note that although this case radically reduced the expropriation of private lands for settlements, the practice has continued to a lesser extent not via 'military necessity' arguments, but based on the Jordanian Law for the Expropriation of Land for Public Purposes. Lustick cites examples whereby such private Palestinian lands 'were used solely for the benefit of Jewish settlements'. In a later HCJ challenge to this method of appropriation, the Court ruled that such land could not be seized when it was intended for the sole benefit of settlers (*Zoo Haderech*, 20 May 1981). Lustick, 'Israel and the West Bank after Elon Moreh', at 572 and 576.
642. Ibid., at 568.
643. However, it is important to note that bypass road construction since 1994 has often occurred on privately held land through the declaration of 'military necessity'. See B'Tselem, *Land Grab*, at 50. As in the case of pre-1979 civilian building projects, these roads have largely been created for the benefit of Israeli settlers and their state-sponsored guards, the Israeli occupying forces. The HCJ has upheld the government's justifications of these roads being essential for security in the *Wafa* case, *Wafa et al v. Minister of Defence et al*, HCJ 2717/96.
644. *Order Regarding Government Property (Judea and Samaria)* (31 July 1967).
645. B'Tselem, *Land Grab*, at 53.

646. Ibid.
647. See generally, Shehadeh, *Law of the Land*, Part 1, at 11–30.
648. Lustick, 'Israel and the West Bank after Elon Moreh', at 568.
649. Ibid.
650. For example, according to a report published in 1950 by the Ad Hoc Committee on the Palestinian Question to the United Nations General Assembly, only 8 per cent of West Bank lands could be considered to be 'public lands'. Lustick, 'Israel and the West Bank after Elon Moreh', at 569.
651. Under the Jordanian Land Settlement Law of 1953.
652. For a general overview about town planning and development, see Anthony Coon, *Town Planning under Military Occupation* (Aldershot: Dartmouth, 1992), Chapter 5.
653. Military Order No. 194. COHRE and BADIL estimate that permits issued only satisfy 10 per cent of the needs of an increasing population. See COHRE and BADIL, *Ruling Palestine*, at 120.
654. See generally Shehadeh, *Law of the Land*, at 84–88. Another way of restricting land use is the classification of land as 'archaeological' through a revision of the Jordanian Antiquities Law. Shehadeh cites examples of lands deemed to have archaeological significance (and hence prohibitions on their development attached) being used later by settlers. Ibid., at 87.
655. COHRE and BADIL, *Ruling Palestine*, at 121.
656. Ibid., at 125.
657. Ibid., at 127.
658. See also Coon, *Town Planning under Military Occupation*, at 172–173.
659. Although the JA had been authorised to develop Jewish-only settlements beyond the Green Line, this role was handed over to the WZO in 1971 when the tax-free status of US donations to the JA faced obstacles. See B'Tselem, *Land Grab*, at 21.
660. Paul Sieghart, *The International Law of Human Rights* (Oxford: Clarendon Press 1983), at 226–229.
661. Convention (No. 29) Concerning Forced Labour, adopted on 28 June 1930 by the General Conference of the International Labour Organisation at its 14th session, entry into force 1 May 1932, Article 2, para. 1.
662. Savage, 'The imposition of Pass Laws', at 182.
663. M. Legassick and D. Innes, 'Capital restructuring and apartheid: a critique of constructive engagement' (1977) 76 *African Affairs*, at 448–449; Wolpe 'South Africa: Class, Race and Occupational Structure', Collected Seminar Paper No. 12, *The Societies of Southern Africa in the 19th and 20th Centuries*, Vol. 2 (Institute of Commonwealth Studies, University of London, 1971), at 103.
664. Owen Crankshaw, 'Changes in the Racial Division of Labour during the Apartheid Era' (1996) 22 *Journal of Southern African Studies* 4, at 634.
665. Ellison Kahn, 'The Pass Laws', in Ellen Hellmann (ed.), *Handbook of Race Relations in South Africa* (Cape Town: Oxford University Press, 1949), at 279–91.
666. C. Simkins, 'The distribution of the African population of South Africa by age, sex and region-type: 1960–1980', SALDRU Working Paper No. 32, South African Labour Development Research Unit, Cape Town (January 1981).
667. The quote is by former nationalist MP and Deputy Minister of Justice, Mines and Planning, G.F. Froneman; cited in Godfrey Mwakikagile, *Africa and the West* (Huntington, NY: Nova Publishers, 2000), at 134.
668. Cited by Christopher Heywood, 'Transformation', in *A History of South African Literature* (Cambridge: Cambridge University Press, 2004), at 156, emphasis added.
669. See B'Tselem, *Restrictions on Movement: The Paris Protocol*, available at: www.btselem.org/English/Freedom_of_Movement/Paris_Protocol.asp.
670. TRC Report, Vol. 2, Chapter 1, paras 108–124.
671. Ibid., at 6.
672. Ibid., at 8, para. 29.

673. Terrorism is defined here as indiscriminately violent acts against a civilian population in order to foster a psychological climate of fear and intimidation.
674. See, for example, Bill to Amend to The 1985 State Budget Law (2009) (the 'Nakba Bill'); Bill on Disclosure Requirements for Recipients of Support from a Foreign Political Entity (2010) (the 'NGO Funding Bill'); Associations (Amutot) Law (Amendment – Exceptions to the Registration and Activity of an Association) (2010) (the 'Universal Jurisdiction Bill'); Boycott Prohibition Bill (2010); Declaration of Allegiance for Citizens Bill; Prohibition of Incitement Bill; Revocation of Citizenship for Individuals Found Guilty of Treason or Terrorism Bill; 'Admissions Committee' Law; Israel Land Administration (ILA) Law (2009); Amendment to the 1943 Land (Acquisition for Public Purposes) Ordinance (2010); Bill to Amend the Basic Law: Human Dignity and Liberty and Limit the Judicial Review Powers of the Supreme Court to Rule on Matters of Citizenship (2009); Amendment No. 8 to the 1952 Civil Wrongs (Liability of the State) Law (2007).
675. Law Preventing Harm to the State of Israel by Means of Boycott 2011, Article 2.
676. Ibid., Article 1.
677. The conclusions of this report draw on the evidence of practice over the course of Israel's occupation of the OPT through April 2009.
678. *Inter alia*, the Native Laws Amendment Act 1952, the Natives (Abolition of Passes and Co-ordination of Documents) Act 1952, the Natives (Urban Areas) Amendment Act 1955, the Bantu (Urban Areas) Consolidation Act.

## Chapter 5

1. See *Wall* advisory opinion, ICJ Rep, 2004, 200, para. 159. The International Committee of the Red Cross claims that all States are now parties to the 1949 Geneva Conventions.
2. Legal Consequences for States of the Continued Presence of South Africa in Namibia (South West Africa) notwithstanding Security Council Resolution 276 (1970), ICJ advisory opinion of 21 June 1971, para. 133.
3. The 2001 Articles were approved, without vote, by the General Assembly in Resolution 56/83 (12 December 2001), UN Doc. A/RES/56/83, operative para. 3 of which provided: '*Takes note* of the articles on the responsibility of States for internationally wrongful acts, presented by the International Law Commission, the text of which is annexed to the present resolution, and commends them to the attention of Governments without prejudice to the question of their future adoption or other appropriate action.' The Articles deal with responsibility in a logical sequence, starting with a definition in Chapter I of the basic principles of responsibility, and moving on (in Chapter II) to define the conditions under which conduct is attributable to the State. Chapter III spells out, in general terms, the conditions under which such conduct amounts to a breach of an international obligation of the State concerned.
4. See James Crawford, *The International Law Commission's Articles on State Responsibility: Introduction, Text and Commentaries* (Cambridge: Cambridge University Press, 2002), at 16–20: the status of draft Article 19(2), regulating crimes of State, had been placed in abeyance in 1998 by the Commission: ibid., 27.
5. See further discussion below on the special regime (represented by Articles 40 and 41 of the 2001 Articles on State Responsibility) for the violation of peremptory norms not involving State criminal responsibility.
6. See ILC, *Report on the work of its Fifty-Second session*, UN Doc. A/55/10 (2000), 59, paras 360–362, available at: http://untreaty.un.org/ilc/reports/2000/repfra.htm; (also II(2) YbILC 59, paras 360–362 (2000)). An extensive literature considers the crimes of States: see, for instance, Georges Abi-Saab, 'The uses of Article 19' (1999) 10 *European Journal of International Law* 339; Ian Brownlie, *International Law and the Use of Force by States* (Oxford: Clarendon Press, 1963), at 150–166, and *System of the Law of Nations: State Responsibility (Part One)* (Oxford: Clarendon Press, 1983), at 32–33; Giorgio Gaja, 'Should all references to international crimes disappear from the ILC draft articles on

State responsibility?' (1999) 10 *European Journal of International Law* 365; Andre de Hoogh, *Obligations erga omnes and International Crimes* (The Hague: Kluwer, 1996); Alain Pellet, 'Can a State commit a crime? Definitely, yes!' (1999) 10 *European Journal of International Law* 425; Shabtai Rosenne, 'State responsibility and international crimes: further reflections on Article 19 of the draft articles on State responsibility' (1997–98) 30 *New York University JILP* 145; Christian Tomuschat, 'International crimes by States: an endangered species?', in Karel Wellens (ed.), *International Law: Theory and Practice. Essays in Honour of Eric Suy* (The Hague: Nijhoff, 1998), at 253; and Joseph Weiler et al (eds), *International Crimes of State* (Berlin: De Gruyter, 1989), Part Two.

7. Eric Wyler, 'From "State crime" to responsibility for serious breaches of obligations under peremptory norms of general international law' (2002) 13 *European Journal of International Law* 1147, at 1159.

8. For example, Article 8 of the Universal Declaration of Human Rights states that, '[e]veryone has the right to an effective remedy by the competent national tribunals for acts violating the fundamental rights granted him by the constitution or by law': General Assembly Resolution 217A (III), Article 2(3)(a) of the International Covenant on Civil and Political Rights. ICERD provides that, 'States Parties shall assure to everyone within their jurisdiction effective protection and remedies ... against any acts of racial discrimination which violate his human rights ... as well as the right to seek from such tribunals just and adequate reparation or satisfaction for any damage suffered as a result of such discrimination.' Article 14 of the UN Convention Against Torture requires each State party to, 'ensure in its legal system that the victim of an act of torture obtains redress and has an enforceable right to fair and adequate compensations, including the means for as full rehabilitation as possible'.

9. Theo Van Boven was appointed Special Rapporteur in 1989 by the UN Sub-Commission on Prevention of Discrimination and Protection of Minorities. The Sub-Commission suggested that international standards needed to be developed and remaining gaps filled to ensure that victims of gross violations in particular would have an enforceable right to restitution, compensation and rehabilitation. Van Boven's study was taken forward by the UN through the appointment of M. Cherif Bassiouni, an expert on reparations. See T. van Boven, *Final Report on the Right to Restitution, Compensation and Rehabilitation for Victims of Gross Violations of Human Rights and Fundamental Freedoms*, UN Doc. No E/CN 4/Sub 2/1993/8 (2 July 1993).

10. General Assembly Resolution A/Res/60/147.

11. See Articles 1–3 of the Basic Principles.

12. Ibid., Articles 15–23.

13. See ILC, Report of the work of its 53rd session, UN Doc.A/56/10, Commentary to Chapter III of its 2001 Articles on Responsibility of States for Internationally Wrongful Acts (henceforth 'ILC Report'), p. 110, available at: http://untreaty.un.org/ilc/reports/2001/2001report.htm; II(2) *Yearbook of the International Law Commission* (henceforth '*Yearbook*') (2001) UN Doc. A/CN.4/SER.A/2001/Add.1 (Part 2), Commentary to Chapter III, 110; and Crawford, *State Responsibility*, Commentary to Chapter III, at 242.

14. As yet, relatively little judicial attention has been paid to Articles 40 and 41. In the Inter-American Court of Human Rights, Judge Cançado Trindade deemed these Articles under-developed: *Myrna Mack Chang* v. *Guatemala*, Inter-American Court of Human Rights (25 November 2003), Ser.C, No.101, [2003] IACHR 4, Opinion of Judge Cançado Trindade, para. 8, available at: www.worldlii.org/int/cases/IACHR/2003/4.html#fn1. In the ICJ's *Wall* advisory opinion, Judge Kooijmans was mystified over the substantive content of the duty not to recognise an illegal act imposed on States by Article 41: *Wall* advisory opinion, ICJ Rep, 2004, 136, separate opinion of Judge Kooijmans, 219, at 231–232, paras 40–45, especially at 232, para. 44.

15. For example, Andrea Gattini convincingly argues that Article 41 is declaratory of existing customary international law: see 'A return ticket to "*communitarianism*", please' (2002) 13 *European Journal of International Law* 1181, at 1185–1195.

16. Paragraph 159 provides that, 'Given the character and the importance of the rights and obligations involved, the Court is of the view that all States are under an obligation not to recognize the illegal situation resulting from the construction of the wall in the Occupied Palestinian Territory, including in and around East Jerusalem. They are also under an obligation not to render aid or assistance in maintaining the situation created by such construction': Simon Olleson, *The Impact of the ILC's Articles on Responsibility of States for Internationally Wrongful Acts* (London: BIICL, 2007), at 237–241; available at: www.biicl.org/files/3107_impactofthearticlesonstate_responsibilitypreliminarydraftfinal.pdf.
17. Article 40 was affirmed by the German Federal Constitutional Court in case No. 2 BvR 955/00 (26 October 2004); see *Responsibility of States for Internationally Wrongful Acts: Comments and Information Received from Governments*, UN Doc. A/62/63 (9 March 2007), statement of Germany, 7, at 15–17, paras 33–38. Article 40 was also affirmed by the United Kingdom House of Lords in *A and others* v. *Secretary of State for the Home Department No.2* [2005] UKHL 71 (8 December 2005), opinion of Lord Bingham of Cornhill, para. 34. Further, in *R (on the application of Al Rawi and others)* v. *Secretary of State for Foreign and Commonwealth Affairs and Secretary of State for the Home Department* [2006] EWHC 972 (Admin) (4 May 2006), the English Divisional Court noted and affirmed a ministerial reliance on Articles 40 and 41; see opinion of Lord Justice Latham, paras 69–70.
18. The case concerned the expropriation of land without compensation in the Soviet Zone of Occupation between 1945 and 1949; see Report of the Secretary-General, *Responsibility of States for Internationally Wrongful Acts: Comments and Information Received from Governments*, UN Doc.A/62/63 (9 March 2007), comments by Germany, 15–16, para. 36; for an account of this case, see 15–17, paras 33–38.
19. ILC Report, *Commentary to Article 40*, UN Doc. A/CN.4/SER.A/2001/Add.1 (Part 2), 113, para. 8; and Crawford, *State Responsibility*, Commentary to Article 40, at 247, para. 8.
20. ILC Report, *Commentary to Article 41*, at 114, para. 3; *Yearbook* (2001), Commentary to Article 41, at 114, para. 3; and Crawford, *State Responsibility*, Commentary to Article 41, at 249, para. 3.
21. ILC Report, *Commentary to Article 41*, at 114, para. 2; *Yearbook* (2001), at 114, para. 2; and Crawford, *State Responsibility*, Commentary to Article 41, at 249, para. 2.
22. ILC Report, *Commentary to Article 41*, para. 3; *Yearbook* (2001), at 114, para. 3; and Crawford, *State Responsibility*, Commentary to Article 41, at 249, para. 3. This non-specific approach appears to follow that adopted by the ICJ in the *Namibia* advisory opinion: see *Namibia* advisory opinion, ICJ Rep, 1971, 55, para.120.
23. ILC Report, *Commentary to Article 41*, 114, para. 5; *Yearbook* (2001), Commentary to Article 41, 114, para. 5; and Crawford, *State Responsibility*, Commentary to Article 41, at 250, para. 5. Indeed, collective non-recognition of this situation is a prerequisite for any collective community response and is the minimum necessary response expected from States: ILC Report, *Commentary to Article 41*, 115, para. 8; *Yearbook* (2001), Commentary to Article 41, at 115, para. 8; and Crawford, *State Responsibility*, Commentary to Article 41, at 251, para. 8.
24. See *Namibia* advisory opinion, ICJ Rep, 1971, 55, para. 123.
25. Ibid., para. 122.
26. ILC Report, *Commentary to Article 41*, at 115, para. 12; *Yearbook* (2001), Commentary to Article 41, 115, para. 12; and Crawford, *State Responsibility*, Commentary to Article 41, at 252, para. 12.
27. See *Namibia* advisory opinion, ICJ Rep, 1971, 55–56, para. 124.
28. *Namibia* advisory opinion, ICJ Rep, 1971, 16, separate opinion of Judge Ammoun, 67 at 94–95, para. 14(7), note omitted.
29. See Giorgio Gaja, *Fifth Report on Responsibility of International Organizations*, UN Doc. A/CN.4/583 (2 May 2007), at 17, para. 55 and A/CN.4/553 (13 May 2005) 4, para. 10; also draft Articles 43 and 44, 19–20: essentially international organisations were assimilated to States in this matter.

30. Case concerning application of the Convention on the Prevention and Punishment of the Crime of Genocide: further requests for the indication of provisional measures, Order of 13 September 1993 (*Bosnia and Herzegovina* v. *Yugoslavia (Serbia and Montenegro)*, ICJ Rep, 1993, 325, separate opinion of Judge *ad hoc* Lauterpacht, 407, at 440–441, paras 100–104.
31. *Wall* advisory opinion, ICJ Rep, 2004, 199, para. 156. The reference is to General Assembly Resolution 2625 (XXV) (24 October 1970), Declaration on Principles of International Law Concerning Friendly Relations and Co-operation among States in Accordance with the Charter of the United Nations.
32. *Wall* advisory opinion, ICJ Rep, 2004, at 201, para. 162.
33. Ibid., at 200, para. 160.
34. ILC Report, *Commentary to Article 41*, at 114, para. 2; *Yearbook* (2001), UN Doc. A/CN.4/SER.A/2001/Add.1 (Part 2), at 114, para. 2; and also Crawford, *State Responsibility*, Commentary to Article 41, at 249, para. 2.
35. See, for example, *Wall* advisory opinion, ICJ Rep, 2004 at 200, paras. 160 and 161 in which the ICJ drew specific attention to 'the urgent necessity for the United Nations as a whole to redouble its efforts to bring the Israeli-Palestinian conflict, which continues to pose a threat to international peace and security, to a speedy conclusion, thereby establishing a just and lasting peace in the region'.
36. For example, the Constitutive Act of the African Union contains no reference to apartheid, but Article 3(h) provides that one of the objectives of the Union is to 'Promote and protect human and peoples' rights in accordance with the African Charter on Human and Peoples' Rights and other relevant human rights instruments'. The Preamble to the African Charter contains a passing reference to apartheid, which it associates with practices including colonialism and Zionism: 'Conscious of their duty to achieve the total liberation of Africa, the peoples of which are still struggling for their dignity and genuine independence, and undertaking to eliminate colonialism, neo-colonialism, apartheid, zionism and to dismantle aggressive foreign military bases and all forms of discrimination, particularly those based on race, ethnic group, colour, sex, language, religion or political opinions.'
37. This question was examined, albeit obliquely, in a case heard by the European Court of Justice, namely *SAT Fluggesellschaft mbH* v. *European Organization for the Safety of Air Navigation (Eurocontrol)*. In his opinion to the Court, Advocate-General Tesauro expressed the view that the fact that Eurocontrol was an international organisation did not insulate it from the Community's competition laws. In justifying his conclusion, Tesauro argued: 'Just as it is not permissible for a Member State to have recourse to its own domestic law in order to limit the scope of Community law, since that would undermine the unity and effectiveness of Community law, so it would not be possible to arrive at a similar result by relying on the obligations arising from an international agreement ... In other words, if national public bodies and Member States themselves, in so far as they carry on an economic activity, are under an obligation to respect the provisions of Article 85 et seq. of the Treaty, they may not escape that obligation by entrusting the activity to an international organization': 101 *International Law Reports* (1994) 17, para. 7. Article 16 has been affirmed as expressing a rule of customary international law by the ICJ and by the German Federal Constitutional Court: 101 *International Law Reports* 9 (1994).

# Index

Abdullah, (King of Jordan), 33
Absentee Property Law (Israel), 207
Adalah, 132, 160, 193, 284 nn137,143
administrative (arbitrary) detention, 2, 41, 73, 76, 128, 137–44, 188, 214, 216, 220, 285 nn154,150, 286 nn180,186, 287 n198
African Charter on Human and Peoples' Rights, 12, 311 n36
African National Congress (ANC), 19, 35, 113, 128, 185, 213
Afrikaans Medium Decree (South Africa), 128
Afrikaners, 19, 112, 125, 173, 280 n61
Alfei Menashe, 71
Algeria, 38, 247 n70
Algiers Declaration, 28
American Convention on Human Rights, 164
American Declaration of the Rights of Man, 164
Amir, Yigal, 136
Anglo-American Committee of Enquiry, 31
Antiquities Law (Jordan), 101, 307 n654
anti-Semitism, 110, 119
apartheid, 1, 2, 3, 4, 5, 21–4, 25, 26, 28, 36, 43, 44, 66, 78 and *passim*
 as crime against humanity, 3–4, 23, 133, 138, 223; defined, in international law, 107–24, 164; 'Grand Apartheid', 112, 123, 125, 165, 197–200, 219–20; in South Africa, 5, 20, 44–5, 111–13, 124, 125–9, 130–1, 134, 138–40, 145, 147–8, 160, 161, 162, 165, 167, 173, 185, 188–9, 197–202, 203–4, 205, 210–11, 212, 213–14, 219–20; international responsibility regarding, 227–8; prohibition of, as *jus cogens* norm and customary law, 4, 13, 22–4, 223; State responsibility regarding, 4, 223–7, 229
 In South West Africa, *see under* Namibia
Apartheid Convention, *see* Convention on the Suppression and Punishment of the Crime of Apartheid
Arafat, Yasir, 28, 32
arbitrary arrest/detention, *see* administrative detention

Ariel, 100, 202
Armistice Agreement (1949), 4, 117, 157, 245 n44
Armistice Line, 35, 66, 97, 100, 102, 119, 151, 152, 153, 154, 168, 169, 217, 279 n44, 289 n238, 307 n659
Aronson Report, 47, 48
Association for Civil Rights in Israel (ACRI), 150, 153, 263 n321, 281 n96
Australia, 20
Austria, 92
Azanian People's Army, 130

Balfour Declaration, 30, 33, 244 n35
Bantu Authorities Act (South Africa), 127, 165
Bantu Education Act (South Africa), 127, 177
Bantu Homelands Citizenship Act (South Africa), 126, 165
Bantu (Urban Areas) Consolidation Act (South Africa), 127, 147
Bantustans, 44, 125, 127, 167, 197–202, 205, 210, 248 n77, 303 n579
Barak, Aharon (Justice), 50–1, 59, 69, 91, 103
Basic Law, Israel, 164, 262 n297
 applied to Jewish settlers in OPT, 67–9, 78, 103, 268 n40; applied to Palestinians in OPT, 68–9, 252 n308, 262 n308; confirming Israel as a Jewish state, 117, 215; Basic Law: Human Dignity and Liberty, 68, 117; Basic Law: Freedom of Occupation, 68, 117; Basic Law: Knesset, 117; Basic Law: Israel Lands, 117
Basic Law, Palestinian, 88
Belgium, 85
belligerent occupation, *see* occupation, belligerent
Benvenisti, Eyal, 40, 49, 50, 56, 89, 104, 232 n21
Bethlehem, 70, 81
Biko, Steven, 128, 130, 213
Black Consciousness Movement, 128, 213
Black Education Department (South Africa), 177

INDEX 313

Black Homelands (South Africa), *see* Bantustans
Black Sash, 156, 290
Bophuthatswana, 165, 200, 201
British Government, *see under* United Kingdom
British Mandate for Palestine, *see under* League of Nations mandate system
Bruderlein, C., 41, 48, 49

Cahan (Justice), 91
Canada, 20
Canada Park, 73
Casesse, Antonio, 50, 260 n266
Cator, Menachem, 100
Cave of the Patriarchs, 60–70
census, 67, 156, 157, 158, 163, 277 n19, 292 n316
Central Bureau of Statistics (Israel), 81
Central Bureau of Statistics (Palestinian), 168
Charter of Economic Rights and Duties of States, 272 n116
Christians, 30, 102, 121, 178, 204, 279 n51
Ciskei, 165, 200, 201
citizenship, 60, 76–7, 84, 107, 122–3, 163–4, 120, 122, 158, 163–5, 215, 293 n333
  and family unification, 160–1, 204, 220; and nationality, 114, 119; provided in Israeli law, 119, 120, 154, 220, 254, 294 n335; in apartheid South Africa, 113, 123, 128, 148, 162, 165, 167, 199, 210; in Mandate Palestine, 120, 293 n332; of Palestinian citizens of Israel, 32, 159, 214, 287 n210; restrictions on Palestinian qualification for, 119, 120, 122, 157, 162–3, 165–6, 217
Citizenship and Entry into Israel Law, 69, 160, 204, 220
Citizenship Law (Israel), 119, 163, 164, 166, 220, 294 n335
Civil Administration (Israeli, in OPT), 86, 87, 99, 152, 154, 249 n106, 268 n50, 289 n242
colonialism, 1, 3, 6, 10, 13, 23, 25, 26, 28, 36, 43, 60, 72, 77, 78, generally Chapter 3, 212, 222
  and duty not to frustrate, 102–4; as annexation, 2, 102–3, 104; as economic integration, 5, 88–94; as legal integration, 5, 62, 64, 82–8; belligerent occupation, comparison to, 2, 18, 21, 86, 223; defined, 6, 17–21, 79–80, 103, 104–5, 235 n54, 238 n88, 239 nn95,96; denial of sovereignty over natural resources, 19, 94–101; international responsibility for, 227–9; prohibition of, in international law, 14–17; state responsibility for, 3–4, 21, 223, 224, 227–9; suppression of culture, 101–2; violation of self-determination, 82, 104, 105–6; violation of territorial integrity, 19, 80–2, 84, 105
  *see also* Declaration on the Granting of Independence to Colonial Countries and Peoples, Self-determination
Committee on the Elimination of Racial Discrimination (CERD), 77, 122, 124, 155, 160, 163
Committee on the Exercise of the Inalienable Rights of the Palestinian People, 33
Convention Against Torture and Other Cruel, Inhuman or Degrading Treatment or Punishment (CAT), 13, 133, 136–7, 191, 282 n110, 301 n529, 300 n503
Convention Concerning Forced Labour (International Labour Organisation), 210
Convention on the Elimination of All Forms of Racial Discrimination (ICERD), 6, 21–2, 23, 76–7, 107, 109–11, 114–15, 116, 117, 120, 122, 124, 130, 133, 146, 147, 155, 161, 164, 167, 172, 177
Convention on the Elimination of Discrimination against Women, 13, 23, 272 n121
Convention on the Prevention and Punishment of the Crime of Genocide, 13, 144–5
Convention on the Reduction of Statelessness, 164
Convention on the Rights of the Child, 12, 13, 164, 272 n121
  Optional Protocol, 12
Convention on the Suppression and Punishment of the Crime of Apartheid, 5, 6, 10, 14, 22–3, 79, 129, 138, 144–5, 146, 156, 167, 173, 177, 184, 189, 190, 197, 205, 215–16, 220, 222, generally Chapter 4; meaning of race in, 107, 109–13
Crawford, James, 34, 250 n111
Criminal Procedure laws (Israel), 83, 137, 140, 262 n294, 267 n27, 282 n124, 286 n174
customs, 5, 90, 92–3, 104, 105, 222, 296 n397
Cyprus, Northern, 12, 17

De Klerk, W.A., 128
Declaration on Colonialism, *see under* Declaration on the Granting of Independence to Colonial Countries and Peoples
Declaration of Permanent Sovereignty over Natural Resources (United Nations), 272 n116
Declaration on Principles of International Law Concerning Friendly Relations and Co-operation among States in Accordance with the Charter of the United Nations (GA Res 2625), 16, 269 n63, 237 n71, 247 n75, 269 n63, 311 n31
Declaration on the Establishment of a New International Economic Order (United Nations), 272 n116
Declaration on the Granting of Independence to Colonial Countries and Peoples (United Nations), 6, 13, 17–21, 80, 82, 94, 105, 222, 239 n96
Declaration on the Rights of Indigenous Peoples (United Nations), 29
Defence (Emergency) Regulations (British), 141, 143, 185, 186, 264 n348, 286 n177
  Extension of Emergency Regulations Law (Israel), 66–7
Democratic Development Cooperative Party (Namibia), 201
Denationalisation, 165
  *see also* citizenship, nationality
Development of Self-Government for Native Nations in South West Africa Act, 201
Development Towns and Areas Law, 84
Dinstein, Yoram, 40, 61, 62, 269 n67
disengagement, *see under* Gaza Strip
Drew, C., 16
Drobles, Matityahu, 119, 207
Drobles Plan, 57, 202, 207, 255 n181, 257 n225
Dugard, John, 1, 2, 14, 25, 106
  *see also* United Nations Special Rapporteurs

E1 Area, 150
East Timor, 16, 230
Egypt, 4, 36, 47, 48, 56, 85, 155, 194, 195, 196, 246 n60, 247 n67, 248 n85, 252 n139, 252 n145
Emergency Powers Law (Israel), 141
ethnicity, 14, 31, 72, 121, 122, 145, 156, 177, 277 n6

defined, 110–15; in Jewish identity, 115; in Palestinian identity, 121; in South Africa, 112–13, 126, 148
European Convention for the Protection of Human Rights and Fundamental Freedoms, 12, 133, 234 n37
European Court of Human Rights, 12, 158, 234 n37, 311 n37
European Economic Community (EEC), 93, 104
European Union, 48, 227, 228
Extension of University Education Act (South Africa), 127, 177

Family Courts Law (Israel), 204
family unification, 69, 157, 158–61, 204, 220
Federal Constitutional Court (Germany), 225
Feilchenfeld, E. H., 92, 104
Fourth Geneva Convention, 19, 25, 26, 37, 38, 39, 41, 44, 80, 223
  administration of justice, 74; applicability to OPT disputed by Israel, 6–8, 36–7, 53–5; application to prolonged occupation, 78; general provisions, 8–9; prohibition of acquisition of territory by force, 60–1, 79; prohibition of colonialism, 80, 103; provisions for end of occupation, 50–1; regarding family unification, 158; regarding legality of settlements, 52–6, 59; regarding occupant's legislative competence, 82, 83; regarding 'special agreements', 41–5; state responsibility for enforcing, 223
  *see also*, Geneva Conventions
France, 38, 247 n70
Freedom Charter (South Africa), 113

Gaja, Giorgio, 227
Galilee, 32
Gaza-Jericho Agreement (of 1994), 40, 248 nn80,85, 249 nn89,106
  *see also*, Gaza Strip, Jericho
Gaza Strip, 4, 5, 14, 32, 35, 55, 56, 64, 67, 68, 69, 72, 74, 145, 156, 168, 190–6, 205, 217, 247 n67, 248 n85, 249 n107
  as integral part of Palestinian self-determination unit, 35, 54; economy and employment in, 168, 169–70, 301 n515; education in, 177–82, 183; governance under Oslo Accords, 39–41, 81; human rights violations in, 132, 140, 151, 158, 162, 172, 174–5, 178, 186, 187–8, 281 n98; international

status as occupied territory, 35, 36, 45–51, 78, 252 n133; Israeli closure (siege) of, 145, 154–5, 170, 171, 191–6, 212, 216, 218, 220; Israel's disengagement from, 50, 67, 74, 82–3, 100, 103, 104, 140, 190, 191, 192, 251 n128, 286 n179, 300 n500; military government in, 85–6; economic integration into Israel, 89; water supply to, 97, 99–100;
see also, 'Operation Cast Lead'
Gaza Strip, Independent Fact Finding Committee on, 145
General Security Services (Israel, GSS), 131, 134, 135, 136, 137, 187, 194, 281 n98, 284 n143
Geneva Conventions, 23, 43, 51, 53, 187, 233 n34, 234 n38, 255 n189, 282 n107, 308 n1
see also Fourth Geneva Convention, Humanitarian law
genocide, 3, 4, 13, 113, 116, 129, 144–5, 184, 198, 227, 228, 287 n200
Genocide Convention, see Convention on the Prevention and Punishment of the Crime of Genocide
Golan Heights, 4, 65, 97
Green Line, see Armistice Line; also Seam Zone
Group Areas Act (South Africa), 126, 197, 211, 219
Gush Etzion, 202

Hamas, 46, 132, 133, 155, 170, 178, 180, 190, 191, 195, 212, 276 n188, 282 n105
HaMoked, 153
Hani, Chris, 214
Hebron, 69, 81, 91, 99, 179, 180, 181, 190, 248 n85, 276 n188
Higher Planning Council (in OPT), 87
Histadrut, 174–6, 217, 296 n400
human rights law, international, 6, 8
defined, 6; in armed conflict and belligerent occupation, 9–14, 25, 77; on apartheid, 107; on arbitrary arrest, 137; on citizenship, 122; on colonialism, 21; on family unification, 159; on genocide, 216; on racial discrimination, 109, 111; on refugees, 162; on torture, 134
see also specific human rights conventions, humanitarian law, self-determination
humanitarian law, international, 3, 4, 5, 6–7, 10, 26, 37, 38, 77, 78, 193, 223

defined, 6; Israeli jurisprudence regarding, 46; on administrative detention, 142; on appropriation of land, 206; on citizenship, 122; on legality of settlements and settlers, 53, 54, 55, 71; on judicial proceedings, 76, 83, 137; on protected persons, 8, 42, 44, 45, 54, 78, 132, 164; on rule of law in OPT, 78, 82; on water, 95, 96, 97; relation to human rights law, 10–13
see also The Hague Regulations, Fourth Geneva Convention, Geneva Conventions
Hussein (King of Jordan), 34, 174, 245 n47

Independent Fact-Finding Committee on Gaza, see Gaza Strip, Independent Fact-finding Committee
Internal Security Act (South Africa), 127, 139, 210
International Committee of the Red Cross/ Red Crescent (ICRC), see Red Cross/ Red Crescent
International Conference on Human Rights, 23
International Court of Justice (ICJ), 1, 2, 222, 228, 242 n1, 244 n38, 313 n37
advisory opinions, 11, 12, 114, 145, 200, 207, 229, 234 n41, 272 n117, 273 n131;
legal authority of advisory opinions, 24; *Legal consequences of the construction of a wall in Occupied Palestinian Territory*, 2, 11, 15, 24, 28, 35, 37, 45, 50, 145, 225, 228, 237 n76, 241 n133, 254 n175, 265 n360, 309 n14, 313 n35; on Israel-Palestine, 2, 7, 51, 53; on Namibia, 2, 15, 18, 24, 227, 310 n22; on self-determination, 15, 18, 242 n11
International Covenant on Civil and Political Rights (ICCPR), 12, 13, 133, 137, 144, 147, 155, 161, 164, 184, 188
International Covenant on Economic, Social and Cultural Rights (ICESCR), 12, 13, 94, 167, 172, 177
International Criminal Court, 14, 22, 23, 28, 230 n8, 242 n7
International Criminal Tribunal for Rwanda (ICTR), 111, 113, 114, 116, 138, 184, 222, 278 n21
International Criminal Tribunal for the Former Yugoslavia (ICTY), 49, 50, 113, 114, 116, 184, 222, 227, 282 n110
International Development Research Centre (Canadian Government), 47

International Law Commission, 4, 15, 24, 96, 223, 224–6, 230 n10, 308 n3
  *see also*, state responsibility
inter-temporal rule, 17, 237 n78
*intifada*
  first, 50, 131, 142, 168, 211, 280 n85;
  second, 72, 131, 132, 135, 140, 142, 158, 168, 169, 171, 178, 186, 189, 191, 281 n93, 287 n193
Islam, 102, 178
Islamic School for Girls (Nablus), 180
Islamic University (Gaza), 179
Israel Security Agency, 131, 135, 136, 195, 283 n127, 284 n129
Interim Agreement on the West Bank and Gaza Strip, *see* Oslo Accords
Israel Defence Forces (IDF), 46, 47, 150, 180, 193, 264 n347
Israel, Government of, 10, 29, 36, 46, 86, 254 n175
Israel, Military Government (of OPT), 35, 41, 59, 63, 85–6, 87; in Gaza Strip, 46; for Jewish settlers, 67–8; international law regarding, 57, 60, 63; Israeli jurisprudence regarding, 46, 57, 59, 60, 63, 92–3
  *see also* military orders, military courts
Israel, State of
  Agriculture Ministry, 209
  Defence Ministry, 72, 81, 86, 268 n50
  Education Ministry, 65, 182, 183
  Foreign Ministry, 19, 34, 36, 37, 41, 54
  Interior Ministry, 157, 159, 291 n278
Izz ad-Din al-Qassem Brigade, 132

Jenin, 81, 179, 181
Jericho, 39, 40, 176, 179, 249 n89
  *see also* Gaza-Jericho Agreement
Jerusalem, 4, 5, 39, 40, 44, 53, 70, 74, 81, 86, 87, 118, 158, 162, 163, 179, 206, 207, 212, 276 n179, 289 n238, 290 n268
  as final status issue, 40, 44, 245 n49; as part of Palestinian self-determination unit, 35, 51, 85, 217, 220; Israeli annexation of, 36–8, 105, 119, 222, 226, 267 n28, 305 n617; Israeli legal administration of, 64, 65, 80, 83, 85, 101, 102, 151, 157, 185–6, 190, 305 n617; Palestinian access, residency or work in, 154, 157, 159–61, 169, 170, 171, 204, 209, 216–17, 254 n174, 276 n188; Palestinian education in, 181–3, 218; population, 81, 157, 254 n174; road grid connecting to, 81, 91, 105, 150, 257 n234; status under international law, 26, 34, 37–8, 53, 78, 85, 102, 226, 247 n77, 255 n187, 310 n16
Jerusalem Program, 118
Jewish Agency, 31, 117, 118, 163, 164, 202, 209, 254 n179, 304 n598
Jewish people, 29–31, 116, 117, 118, 119, 120, 122, 164, 221
Job Reservation Act (South Africa), 167
Joint Water Committee, 99
Jordan, Hashemite Kingdom of, 33, 34, 36, 37, 162, 168, 174, 188, 195, 206, 244 n38, 245 n44, 246 nn60, 61, 297 n48, 305 n623
  *see also*, Transjordan
Jordan option, 34, 35, 244 n41
Jordan River, 33, 34, 97
Jordan Valley, 39, 100, 151, 152
Judaism, 116
Judea and Samaria, 36, 50, 52, 57, 69, 186, 202, 207, 246 n56; *see also* West Bank
*Jus cogens*, *see* peremptory norms

Keane, David, 77
killings, extrajudicial, 128, 130–3, 145, 188, 191, 213, 216, 218, 220, 280 nn83,87, 281 nn96,98
Kiryat Arba, 90
Knesset, 37, 65, 66, 67, 87, 142, 143, 160, 168 n40
Kretzmer, David, 58, 62, 90, 91, 93, 103, 150, 254 n177
KwaZulu (Homeland), 165, 200

labour, 18, 168, 210
  in OPT, 89, 167–71, 174–6, 177, 211–12, 219; in East Jerusalem, 171; in South Africa, 123, 128, 145, 147, 148, 156, 173–4, 177, 197, 205, 210–11
Labour Relations Act (South Africa), 211
Lauterpacht, H. (Justice), 24, 227, 241 n129
Law, Jordanian, 58, 67, 83, 206, 207, 209, 306 n641
Law, Ottoman, 65; regarding land, 206, 208; regarding personal status, 261 n281
Law of Return (Israel), 67, 84, 116, 119, 152, 154, 163, 164, 166, 220, 254 n174, 262 n291, 293 n321
League of Arab States, 27, 121
League of Nations Charter (Covenant), 15, 27
League of Nations mandate system, 15, 17, 29, 18, 30, 88, 236 n66
  Mandate for Palestine (British), 15, 27, 29, 30–3, 34–6, 38, 120, 141, 166, 174,

244 n35, 247 n67, 261 n281, 264 n348, 286 n177, 293 n332, 299 n466; Mandate for South West Africa/Namibia (South Africa), 201, 302 n592
Lebanon, 97, 160, 162, 279 n48
*Lex specialis*, 11, 256 n204

Ma'ale Adumim, 67, 150, 257 n234
Machpela Cave, *see* Cave of the Patriarchs
Magna Carta, 161
Mandate for Palestine (British Mandate), *see under* League of Nations mandate system
Mandela, Nelson, 128, 129
master plans (Israeli, for Jewish settlements in OPT), 52, 81, 119, 149, 202, 207, 279 n44
Matias, Shavit, 48
Meir, Golda (Prime Minister), 30
Mekerot, 91, 97–8
Meron, Theodor, 37, 54, 246 n64
Military Advocate General (Israel), 132
military courts (Israeli), 67, 72, 74–6, 78, 83, 141, 143, 144, 216, 220, 246 n58, 263 n335, 264 nn347,348,351, 267 n33–6, 286 n179
military law (Israel), 26, 67, 74, 75, 76, 78, 132, 215, 220
  *see also* military courts, military orders
military orders (Israeli, in OPT), 72–4, 75, 82–3, 86, 87, 181, 305 n620
  on absentees, 207; on administrative detention, 141, 142, 143, 286 n180, 287 nn192,198; on charities, 190; on children, 180; on demonstrations and peaceful assembly, 189, 218; on education, 276 n187; on land, 70, 101, 206, 305 n623; on Palestinian movement, 151, 288 n221; on military courts, 74; on residency in the OPT, 157, 158; on tariffs and customs duties, 90; on Jewish settler councils, 66, 82, 268 n38; on printing and publication, 102, 186; on extrajudicial killings, 132; on water, 99, 274 n141; Order No.31, 90; Order No.50, 102, 186; Order No.58, 207; Order No.59, 208; Order No.92, 97; Order No.192, 305 n623; Order No.378, 74; Order No.783, 83; Order No.101, 186; Order No.103, 90; Order No.107, 102; Order No.378, 141–2, 267 n35, 287 n192; Order No.811, 206; Order No.847, 206; Order No.892, 83, 268 n38; Order No.1229, 141–3; Order No.1251, 221;

Order No.1281, 286 n180; Order No.1376, 274 n141; Order No.1506, 287 nn192,198
missing reversioner argument, 26, 36–7
Mista'arvim, 131
Motlhabi, Mokgethi , 125, 140
Muslims, 30, 121, 204

Nablus, 81, 151, 174, 179, 180, 187, 203, 297 n428
Namibia, 1, 2, 21, 24, 123, 198, 201–2, 222, 223
  *see also under* International Court of Justice
National Party (South Africa), 111, 125, 126, 127, 138, 197, 198, 199, 280 n61, 303 n575
National Priority Areas (Israeli), 89
nationality, 110, 114, 119–20, 122–3, 146, 160, 161, 163–6, 177, 217, 220, 232 n27, 293 n334
  *see also* citizenship, denationalisation
Native Building Workers Act (South Africa), 127
natives (Abolition of Passes and Co-ordination of Documents) Act (South Africa), 147
Natives Laws Amendment Act (South Africa), 147, 198
Natives (Urban Areas) Amendment Act (South Africa), 125, 147
nature reserves (in OPT), 40, 80, 203, 209
Netanyahu, Benjamin, 214
New Zealand, 20
Nuremberg Laws (Nazi Germany), 278 n27, 280 n67
Nuremberg Tribunal, *see* United States Military Tribunal at Nuremberg

occupation, belligerent, 5, 6, 10, 14, 25, 28, 53, 55, 59, 60, 67, 70, 71, 77, 88, 250 n111, 252 n147
  defined, 7–8; of OPT by Israel, legality of, 2, 3; human rights law applying to, 13, 25, 235 n47, 241 n133; relative to colonialism, 14, 18, 21, 79; as legal condition of OPT, 36–7, 78; legal implications of Oslo Accords for, in OPT, 39–45; legal implications of Israeli withdrawal from Gaza for, 82
  *see also*, occupation, prolonged
occupation, prolonged, 1, 41, 51, 60–4, 84
  equating with colonialism, 21, 86; equating with apartheid, 166; Israeli

jurisprudence regarding, 90, 93, 103, 258 n239, 259 n250
  see also, occupation, belligerent
Odendaal Commission, 201, 305 n587
O'Meara, Dan, 126, 147
Operation Cast Lead, 35, 46, 50, 145, 179, 181, 191, 194, 195
Operation Summer Rain, 50
Oslo Accords, 26, 39, 81, 149, 168, 242 n6, 265 n8
  List of constituent documents, 248 n80; implications of, for international legal status of OPT, 26, 36, 39–45; effect in establishing OPT as territorial unit, 35, 45; provisions of, for governance in OPT, 67, 81, 87, 88, 105, 170, 175, 209, 250 n120; impact of, on water allocation in OPT, 98–100
Ottoman Empire, 27, 83
  see also Law, Ottoman

Pakistan, 34
Palestine, Mandate for, see under League of Nations mandate system
Palestine, State of, 26–8, 43, 121
Palestine Liberation Organisation, 27, 28–9, 32, 35, 85, 121
Palestine National Council, 27, 41, 43
Palestinian Interim Self-Government Authority (PA), 28, 48, 149, 159, 175, 178, 190, 212, 242 n6, 250 nn111,120
  Oslo Accords, status and role under, 36, 39–41, 44–5, 67, 81, 88, 248 n85, 276 n187, 290 n397; allocation of water to, 98; Gaza, role in, 46, 48; Central Bureau of Statistics, 168
  role in Oslo Accords, 39, 40–1, 43–5, 98, 250 nn111,118–21; charter of, 32, 121
Palestinian Legislative Council (PLC), 87, 88, 140, 142, 170, 175, 214
Palestinian people, 14, 20, 25, 32, 77, 82, 101, 102, 104, 121, 145–6, 160, 166, 216
  existence of, 28; historical construction of, 28–32, 121; right to self-determination of, 14, 20, 25, 26–36, 45, 46, 51, 77, 242 n11, 243 n25, 250 n118
Palestinian Water Authority, 98
Pan-African Congress (PAC), 128, 213
Pass Laws (South Africa), 126, 128, 148, 151, 156, 167, 210, 211, 219, 220, 285 n150
Peel Partition Plan, 31
Pellet, Alain, 20

peremptory norms (*jus cogens* rule), 223–4, 226–8, 230 n10
  defined, 4; of acquisition of territory by force, 38, 102; on nationality and denationalisation, 164; on the prohibition of apartheid, 24, 25, 215, 224, 226, 228; on the prohibition of colonialism, 25, 224, 226, 228; on self-determination, 15
Performance-based Roadmap to a Permanent Two-State Solution to the Israeli-Palestinian Conflict, 45, 251 n124
Permanent Court of International Justice, 92
Philadelphi Corridor, 47, 48
police, 90, 235 n55, 262 n294
  Israeli, 131, 134, 137, 175, 176, 300 n495; Palestinian, 248; South African, 112, 128, 131, 134, 147, 204, 213
Popper, Ami, 136
population (count), Jewish settlers, 81, 100, 275; Palestinian, 100, 148, 279 nn48,51, 292 n311; East Jerusalem, 157; Nablus, 203
Population Registration Act (South Africa), 111–12, 126, 219
Portugal, 16
Preventing Harm to the State of Israel by Means of Boycott Law, 214
Prevention of Illegal Squatting Act (South Africa), 127, 197
Procaccia, Ayala (Justice), 69
Proclamation of Tehran, 23
Prohibition of Mixed Marriages Act (South Africa), 203–4
Promotion of Bantu Self-Government Act (South Africa), 127, 165
Public Committee Against Torture in Israel (PCATI), 135, 136, 281 n101, 284 n138

Quartet, 228, 251 n124

Rabin, Yitzhak, 28, 136
race, 9, 12, 18, 21, 23, 29, 52, 77, 146, 164, 224, 277, 239 n94
  and national identity, 277 n4, 277 n7, 277 n19, 293 n332; British Mandate policy regarding, 31; constructions in OPT, 177, 211, 214, 215; defined in international law, 109–15, 277 n6; Jewish identity as, 107, 109, 115–20, 166; Palestinian identity as, 107, 109, 120–2; South African apartheid

doctrine regarding, 111–13, 125–7, 156, 167, 197, 203–4, 303 n564
*see also*, International Convention on the Elimination of All Forms of Racial Discrimination
Race Classification Board (South Africa), 112
Rachel's Tomb, 70
racial discrimination
definition of, 109–11, 114, 117, 215; prohibition of, in international law, 4, 22, 24, 115–16; prohibition of, Israel's obligations, 13; apartheid, legal relation to, 22, 23, 25, 109, 225; in OPT, 116–20, 122; in citizenship, 122; in extrajudicial killing, 130; in full group development and participation, 146; in freedom of movement, 147; in security threats, 155; in residence, 155; in family unification, 160; in right to nationality, 164; in right to work, 167; in trade unions, 172; in education, 177; in freedom of expression, 184; in peaceful assembly, 189; evidenced in OPT settlements, 218
*see also*, apartheid, race
Ramallah, 44, 72, 81, 150, 187, 260
Rantissi, Abd el-Aziz, 133
Red Cross/Red Crescent (International Committee of, ICRC), 8, 37, 38, 51, 53, 232 nn26,27
Refugees, 32, 40, 119, 158, 162–3, 166, 168, 193, 217, 279 n48, 292 n311, 293 n333
Regulations Respecting the Laws and Customs of War on Land, 12
Rehan (settlement bloc), 202, 279 n44
religion, 9, 12, 14, 23, 31, 70, 114, 116, 121, 122, 164, 184, 224, 232 n26, 293 n332, 311 n36
Reservation of Separate Amenities Act (South Africa), 126, 127
Riotous Assemblies Act (South Africa), 127, 189
roadmap, *see* Performance-based Roadmap
roads (in OPT), 58, 59, 72, 81, 91, 102, 148, 149–50, 152, 169, 202, 203, 216, 257 n234, 306 n643
Roberts, Adam, 48, 60, 86, 166, 235 n47
Rome Statute of the International Criminal Court, 14
on apartheid, 22, 23, 107, 109, 123, 129, 130, 138, 285 n152; on transfer of civilians into occupied territory, 52, 254 n177; on torture, 134; regarding *mens rea*, 230 n8

Sabotage Act (South Africa), 127
Sachs, Albie, 213
Scheinin, Martin, 267 n33
*see also under* United Nations Special Rapporteurs
Seam Zone, 73, 100, 151–4, 169, 289 nn238,242
self-determination, 15, 47, 95, 235 n54, 236 nn65,66, 239 n95
as *jus cogens* norm, 15, 254 n173; right to, defined, 15–17, 79, 228, 236 n60, 237 n70, 237 n72; denial of, as indicative of colonialism, 21, 25, 94, 104–5, 222, 225, 226; Jewish people's right to, 116, 120; Palestinian people's right to, 26, 28–33, 44, 46, 77, 121, 242 n10, 242 n11, 244 n41; Palestinian, territorial integrity for, 33–6, 51, 54, 80, 82, 88, 237 n75; doctrine of, in apartheid South Africa, 2, 44, 112, 200, 201; denial by Israel of Palestinian right to, 14, 50, 86, 88, 102, 104, 105–6, 217, 226; involving sovereignty over natural resources, 95, 105, 272 n116; principle of *uti possidetis iuris*, 244 n38
settler colonialism, 19–20
settlers (Jewish, in OPT), 2, 155, 215, 220, 270 n88
detention of, 143–4; freedom of expression, 190; freedom of movement, 170, 287 n210, 288 n221; illegal presence of, in OPT, 9, 14, 20, 77, 265 n360; mixed marriages among, 204; population of, 81; preferential access by, to OPT water and land, 41, 72, 98–100, 101–2, 105, 206–7, 209, 270 n89, 306 nn639,642; separate roads for, 149–50, 152, 203, 306 nn641,643, 307 n654; status of, in international law, 9, 14; status of, in Israeli law, 5, 26, 39, 41, 54–5, 59, 65–72, 74, 76, 78, 83–4, 87, 90, 94, 103, 160, 210, 222, 268 nn39,40; withdrawal of, from Gaza Strip, 154; union membership of, 175
*see also* settlements
settlements (Jewish, in occupied Palestinian territories), 38, 39, 40, 80, 81, 102, 117, 119, 152–3, 154, 156, 176, 205, 212, 215, 218, 219, 220, 222
impact of, on OPT geography, 203, 222, 225; in Jerusalem, 38; Israeli government responsibility for, 39, 81, 84, 87, 89, 98, 100–1, 161, 119, 161, 163, 168, 183, 206; Israeli Supreme Court jurisprudence regarding, 55–60,

69, 71, 90, 208; Jewish Agency involvement in, 202; legal status of, in international law, 9, 52–4, 226; legal status of, in Israeli law, 40, 65–6, 83–4, 86–7, 89–90, 206, 208; preferential land and water allocations to, 4, 98–101, 117, 202, 208; separate roads for, 81, 90, 119, 148–9, 152; special services for, 81, 180; withdrawal from Gaza, 36, 46, 190
  *see also* settlers
settler colonialism, 19–20
Shamgar, Meir (Justice), 63, 83, 92, 93–4, 104, 261 n270
Shany, Yuval, 48, 252 n133
Sharm el-Sheikh Memorandum, 35, 248 n84
Sharpeville, 128, 130
Shehadeh, Raja, 307 n654
Shehadeh, Salah Mustafa Muhammad, 132
Six-Day War (of 1967), 3, 34, 35, 36, 37, 52, 74, 85, 157, 158, 163, 168, 174, 245 n44
South Africa, 5, 19–20, 21, 22, 23, 24, 35, 45; generally Chapter 4; 222, 223, 227
  apartheid in (overview), 125; apartheid laws of (list), 127–8; apartheid, end of, 128–9; apartheid legislative foundations in, 219–21; genocide, 145; illegal arrest and imprisonment in, 138–40; illegal killings in, 130–1; labour exploitation in, 210–11; movement restrictions in, 147–8; nationality laws in (denationalisation), 165; obstacles to leaving and returning, 162; conditions regarding education, 177; freedom of expression, 185; morality laws, 203–4; reserves and ghettos, 197–202; residence, 155; torture, 134; trade unions, 173–4; work, 167; real property, 205; racial doctrines, 111–13; repression of resistance to apartheid, 212, 213–14; restrictions on association, 189
  *see also* Bantustans
South African Communist Party (SACP), 19
South African Defence Force (SADF), 213
South West Africa, *see under* Namibia
South West Africa People's Organisation (SWAPO), 201
sovereignty, 15, 16, 34, 120, 161, 175, 236, 293 n334, 294 n334
  in belligerent occupation, 21, 25, 38, 37, 38, 85, 88, 123; in colonialism, 18, 20, 80, 226; permanent, over natural resources, 16, 21, 79, 80, 94–5, 97,

101, 105, 222, 226, 272 n117; Jordanian, 34; Israeli, in East Jerusalem, 38; Palestinian, 28, 33, 44; Jewish, 120; in South Africa, 125
Soweto, 128, 130, 148, 197
state responsibility (international law), 3–4, 13, 84, 223, 230 n11, 308 n3
  *see also* International Law Commission
Suppression of Communism Act (South Africa), 127, 138–9, 189
Supreme Court of Israel, 5, 83, 129
  on applicability of international law in OPT, 6, 7, 10, 37, 85; on censorship, 186, 187, 218; on extrajudicial killings, 132; on family unification, 158, 160, 284 n137; on freedom of movement, 191; on Gaza Strip, legal status of, 46, 48, 49, 51; on Gaza Strip, access and trade, 193; on Israeli identity, 154; on Israeli legal authority in the OPT, 62; on judicial proceedings in OPT, 140, 142, 143; on Palestinian classroom shortages in Jerusalem, 183; on Palestinian rights and legal status in OPT, 68, 69–71; on permit regime, 153; on prolonged occupation, 60, 62, 64; on relative legal status of Jews and Palestinians in OPT, 71, 78; on roads in OPT, 72, 150; on settler rights and legal status in OPT, 54–9, 67, 69–71; on territorial integrity of OPT, 35, 51; on torture, 135–6, 137, 284 n138; on Wall route, 153
Supreme Court of Palestine, 33
Syria, 97, 160, 162, 279 n48

Terrorism Act (South Africa), 127, 139
territorial integrity, 16, 17, 18–19, 21, 33, 38, 44, 79, 80–2, 105, 200, 201, 202, 222
The Hague Convention, *see* The Hague Regulations
The Hague Regulations (1907), 6–8, 25, 37, 59–62, 71, 82–3, 85, 93, 101, 206, 257 n237, 260 n254, 286 n177; as customary law, 12, 231 n13; on land and property, 41, 205, 208, 232 n26; on natural resources, 97; on prolonged occupation, 60, 63–4, 78, 103, 253 n153
torture, 9, 75, 108, 133–7, 283 n127, 309 n8
  in South Africa, 128, 131, 134, 213; in the OPT, 134–5, 140, 141, 194, 216, 220, 282 n107, 282 n110, 301 n529

INDEX 321

*see also* Convention Against Torture and Other Cruel, Inhuman or Degrading Treatment or Punishment, United Nations Committee Against Torture
trade unions, 172–6
Transjordan, 33, 34, 244 nn35,38
*see also* Jordan
Transkei, 165, 200, 201
trusteeship system (United Nations), 18, 31, 94, 265 n2
Truth and Reconciliation Commission of South Africa (TRC), 3, 129, 130–1, 134, 138, 145, 213

Umkhonto we Sizwe, 130, 214
United Kingdom of Great Britain and Northern Ireland, 23, 34
government of, 30, 31, 33, 125, 143
United Nations Charter, 2, 15, 17, 18–19, 21, 22, 24, 29, 32, 36, 38, 80, 109, 124, 201, 224, 228, 265 n2, 269 n63
United Nations Committee Against Torture, 135
United Nations Committee on Economic, Social and Cultural Rights, 95, 170
United Nations General Assembly, 1, 2, 7, 10, 16, 17, 304 n589, 304 n592, 308 n3
Resolution 181 (1947), 31, 38, 243 n23; Resolution 194 (1948), 292 n313; Resolution 2625 (Declaration on Principles), 16, 269 n63, 237 n71, 247 n75, 269 n63, 311 n31; Resolution 2649, 20; Second Subcommittee on the Question of Palestine, 31
United Nations Human Rights Committee, 12, 135, 137, 155, 184, 283 n129
United Nations Office for the Coordination of Humanitarian Affairs (OCHA), 80, 148, 152, 154, 181, 194, 196, 203
United Nations Relief and Works Agency (UNRWA), 162, 163, 168, 178, 179, 181, 193
United Nations Security Council, 7, 10, 26, 28, 37, 44, 49, 53, 227, 228, 230 n7, 241 n128, 251 n125
actions on Namibia, 2, 21, 201–2, 241 n129; actions on Bantustans, 201–2; Resolution 237 (1967), 163, 231 n16, 233 n32, 292 n317; Resolution 242 (1967), 34, 37, 38; Resolution 252 (1968), 38, 247 n77; Resolution 384 (1975), 230; Resolution 402 (1976), 201; Resolution 407 (1977), 201; Resolution 1397 (2002), 28; Resolution 1515 (2003), 28, 45

United Nations Special Rapporteurs, 224, 309 n9
on the human rights situation in the Occupied Palestinian Territories 1, 4, 14, 25, 149, 188; on the Promotion and Protection of Human Rights and Fundamental Freedoms while Countering Terrorism, 135, 136, 143, 267 n33, 283 n127; on Extrajudicial, Summary or Arbitrary Executions, 280 n87
*see also* Dugard, John, Scheinin, Martin
United Nations Special Representative on Human Rights Defenders, 140
United States Military Tribunal at Nuremberg, 8, 49, 63, 64, 231 n13
Universal Declaration of Human Rights (UDHR), 23, 109, 133, 137, 138, 161, 164, 177, 184, 188, 309 n8
Unlawful Organisations Act (South Africa), 127, 128
*Uti possidetis* rule, 34, 244 n38

value-added tax (VAT), 48, 50, 92, 93, 94
Venda, 165, 200, 201
Venice Declaration, 54
Verwoerd, Hendrik, 148, 177, 280 n61, 303 n569
Vorster, B. J., 210

wall (security barrier), 35, 71, 100–1, 105, 148, 151, 152–4, 169, 171, 180, 181, 182, 189, 190, 206, 209, 212, 214, 216, 218, 226, 228
*see also* Seam Zone
*Wall* advisory opinion (of International Court of Justice), 2, 11, 15, 24, 28
on international responsibility, 225, 227; on military operations, 50; on OPT as territorial basis for self-determination, 35; on Palestinian statehood, 28; on Palestinian self-determination, 34; on Palestinian status as a people, 28
*see also under* International Court of Justice
water, 9, 40, 41, 54, 81, 91, 94, 101, 195
deteriorating supply and quality of, in OPT, 145, 193, 194; discriminatory administration of, in OPT, 97–101, 103, 105, 168, 170, 214, 222, 226, 274 nn141,145,150; right to, in international law, 95–7, 272 n12; sources in OPT, 97, 273 n137
*see also* Mekorot, Palestinian Water Authority

Weinstein, Yehuda (Attorney General), 136, 183
West Bank
  administered under Oslo Accords, 39, 81, 88; as part of Palestinian self-determination unit, 35, 51, 54; barriers to movement in, 149; economic integration into Israel, 89–94; history under Jordanian rule, 34–5, 37; Israeli annexation plans for, 52–3, 119; legal system in, 64–5; territorial fragmentation of, by Israel, 80–2
  *see also* civil administration, military courts, military law, military orders, missing reversioner argument, roads, settlements, settlers, water, wall
White Paper of 1939 (British), 31
World Conference on Human Rights (Vienna Conference), 4
World Zionist Organisation, 52, 117, 118, 119, 163, 207, 209, 218, 254 n179, 279 nn42,44, 307 n659
  *see also* Zionist Organisation
World Zionist Organisation–Jewish Agency (Status) Law, 117, 118, 119, 254 n179, 278 n39, 304 n598
Wye River Memorandum, 35

Yadlin, Amos (Major General), 49
Yassin, Ahmad (Sheikh), 133

Zionism, 30, 31, 32, 35, 115, 116, 117, 118–19, 120, 121, 122, 143, 278 n30, 293 n333, 304 n598, 311 n36
Zionist Congress, 31, 242 n17
Zionist Organisation, 31, 118
  *see also* World Zionist Organisation
Zululand, *see* KwaZulu

Printed in Great Britain
by Amazon